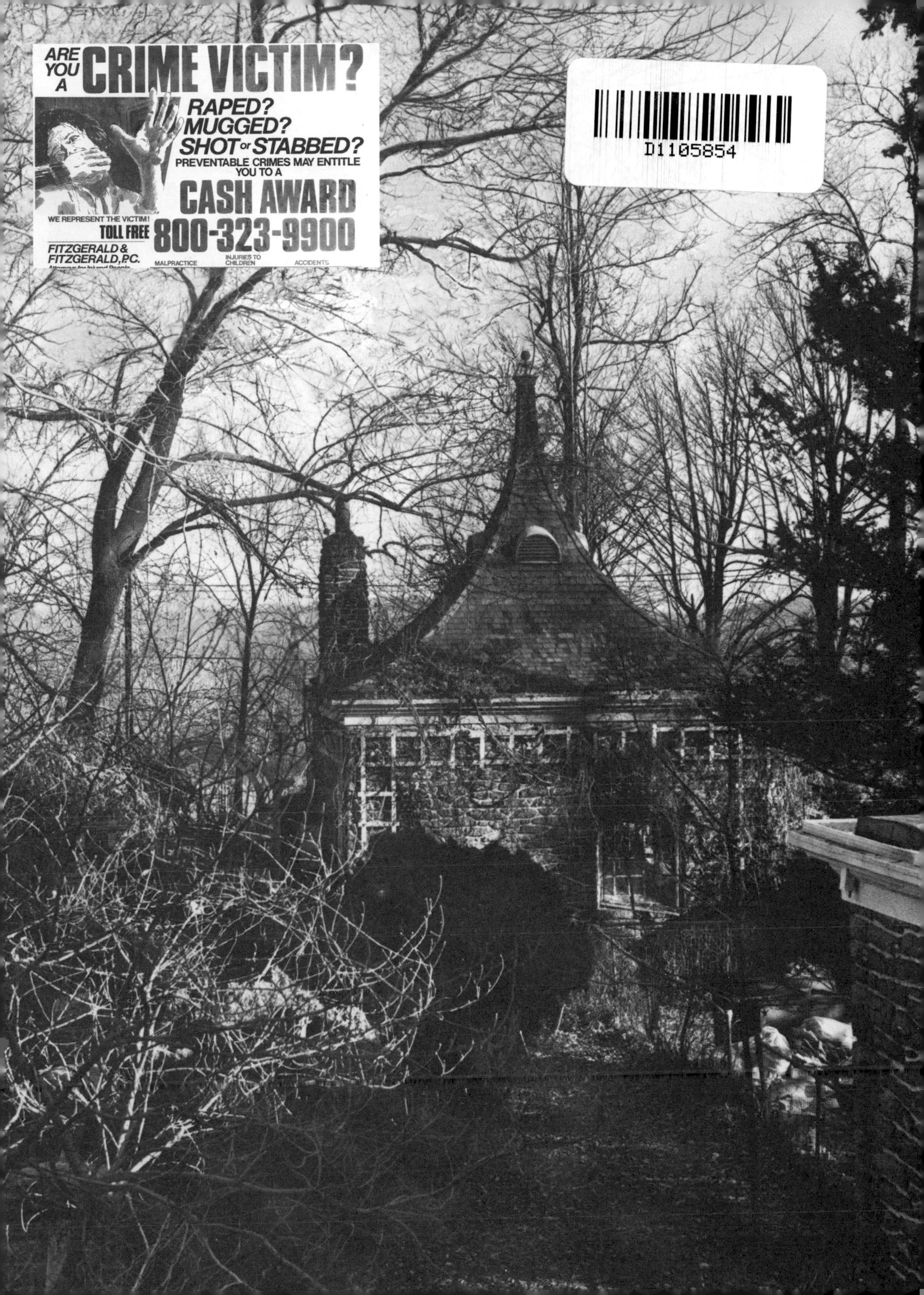
ARE YOU A CRIME VICTIM?
RAPED?
MUGGED?
SHOT or STABBED?
PREVENTABLE CRIMES MAY ENTITLE YOU TO A
CASH AWARD
WE REPRESENT THE VICTIM!
TOLL FREE 800-323-9900
FITZGERALD & FITZGERALD, P.C.
MALPRACTICE
INJURIES TO CHILDREN
ACCIDENTS

CHARTWELL MANOR

GLENN HEAD

Chartwell Manor

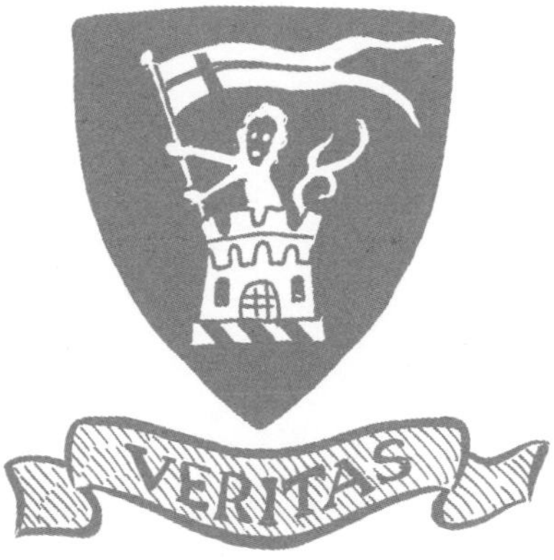
VERITAS

A Comics Memoir by Glenn Head

FANTAGRAPHICS BOOKS SEATTLE, WASHINGTON

For Chartwell kids everywhere.

And to my good friend, Bryan Saradarian.
1958–2013

FANTAGRAPHICS BOOKS INC.
7563 Lake City Way NE
Seattle, Washington, 98115
www.fantagraphics.com
@fantagraphics

Editor and Associate Publisher: Eric Reynolds
Book Design: Justin Allan-Spencer and Glenn Head
Production: Paul Baresh
Publisher: Gary Groth

ISBN 978-1-68396-425-4
Library of Congress Control Number 2020948101

First printing: May 2021
Printed in Thailand

FOREWORD

The book you hold in your hands contains my life story. Not my entire life but a sizable chunk of it. This book tells the story of a childhood boarding school experience, and then delves with even greater detail into the reverberations of that experience in later life.

It is not a recovery memoir. It is a book about scars and how we come to live with them. About how life goes on and we change, even for the better, occasionally. That growth is possible.

My aim in drawing this book was to be as uncompromisingly truthful as possible. There is no attempt to make any of the characters, myself especially, sympathetic. Correspondingly, there was no attempt to make anyone look bad. Simply to depict my life as it happened, and, more importantly, how it felt.

What most interests me is human behavior — especially sexual behavior and its consequences. How it follows us, whether we like it or not. It did with my headmaster, and it did with me.

The two years I did at Chartwell had a profound effect on me. With trauma (this is the only time that word appears in this book!), the aftermath is a motherfucker. That aftermath, more than the boarding school chapter, may be unacceptable to some readers.

If this book is too brutal or upsetting for some, I have to live with that. I grew up with underground comics and found solace in their willingness to expose what society insisted remain hidden. Sometimes they were "too much," but perhaps that's what's required when you're trying to say the unsayable.

No one asks for the childhood they get, and no child ever deserved to go to Chartwell Manor. My experience there had been eating away at me for nearly fifty years. Finally I turned the tables and devoured it.

Here it is.

– Glenn Head

"But I did know that the future was dark ... that was by far the deepest conviction that I carried away."

Such, Such Were the Joys, 1948
— George Orwell

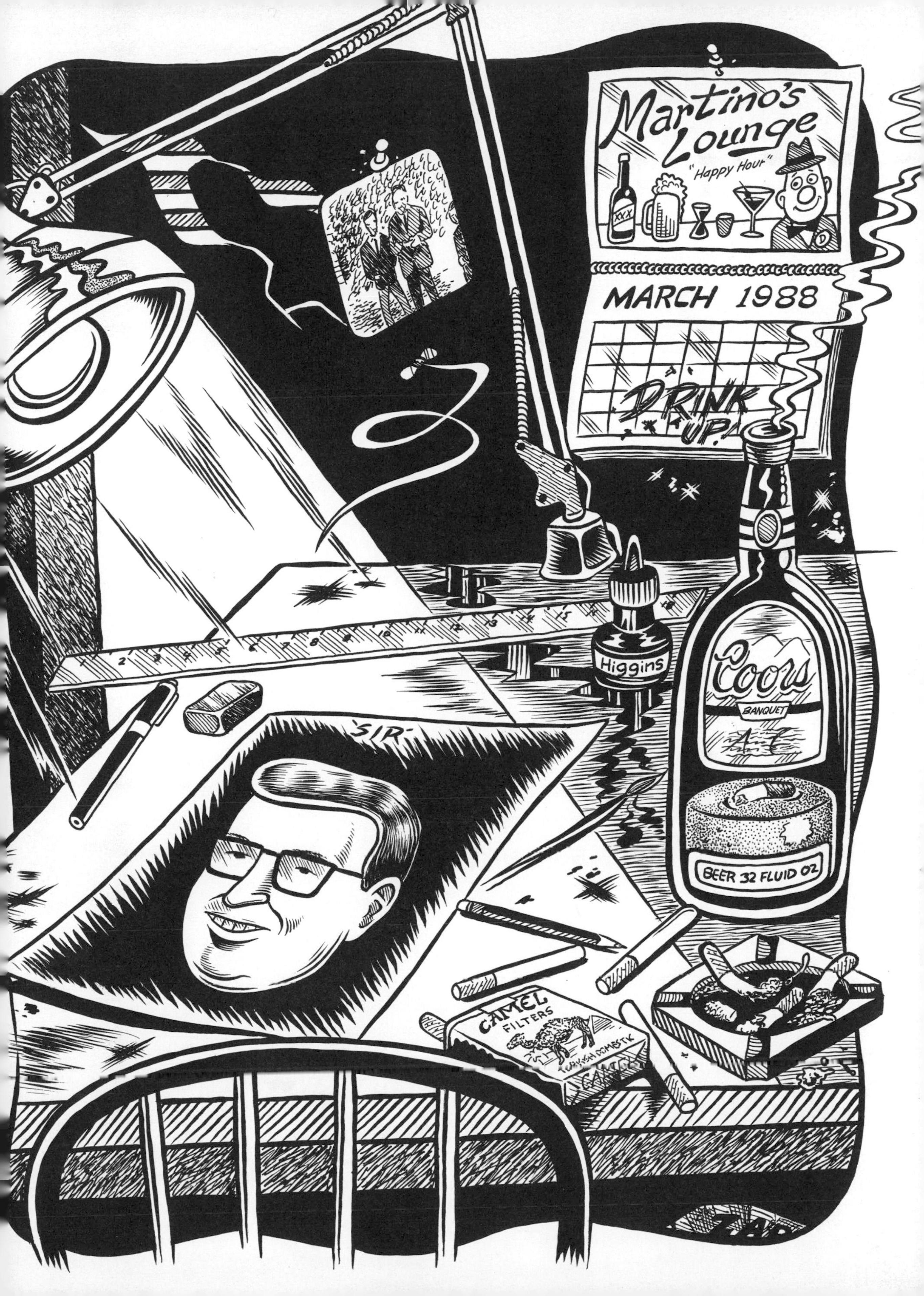

Martino's Lounge
"Happy Hour"
XXX
MARCH 1988
DRINK UP!
Higgins
Coors
BANQUET
BEER 32 FLUID OZ
-SIR-
CAMEL
FILTERS
TURKISH DOMESTIC

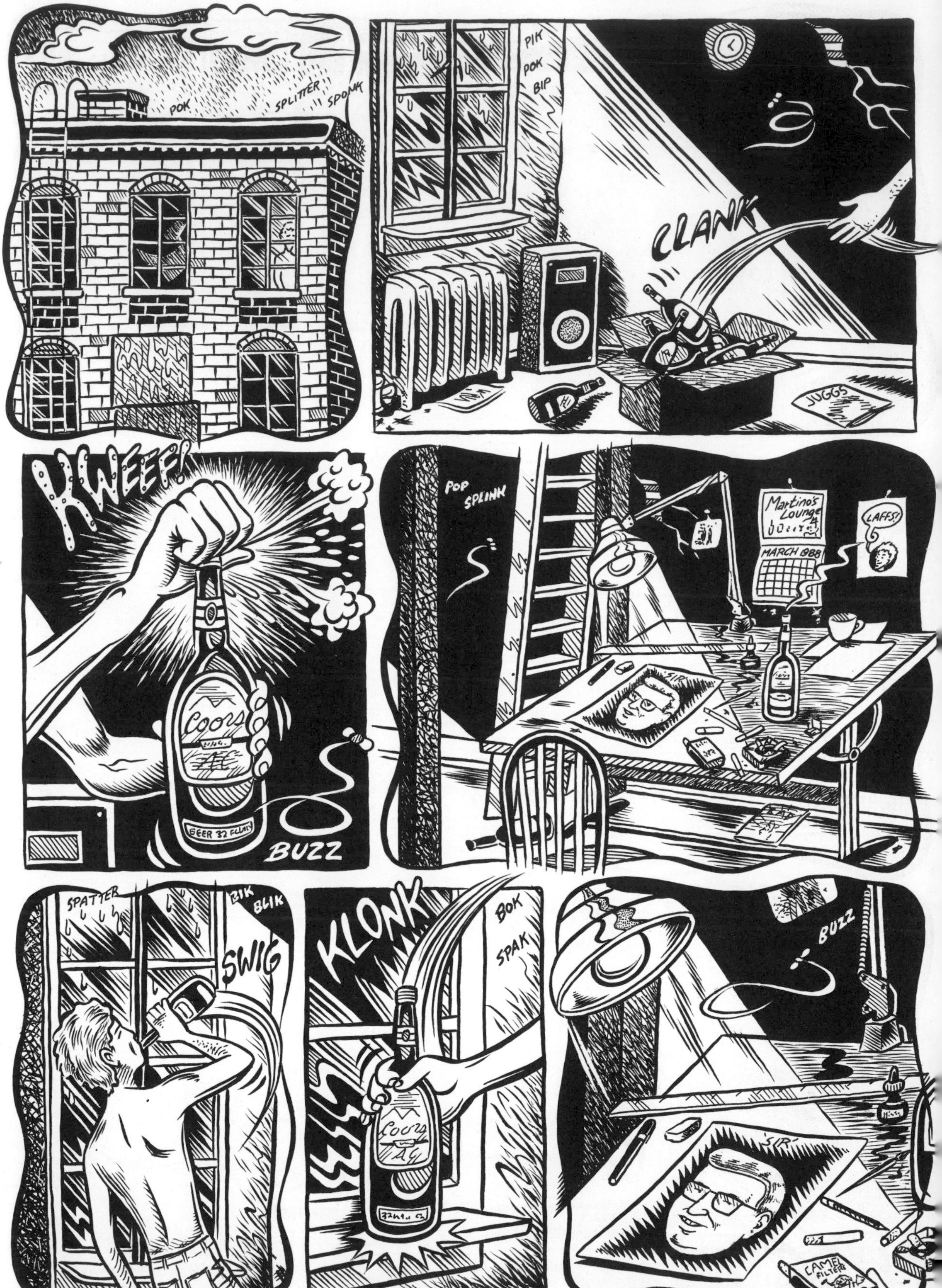
POK
SPLITTER
SPONK
PIK
POK
BIP
CLANK
JUGGS
KWEEF!
Coors
BUZZ
POP
SPLINK
Martino's Lounge
MARCH 1988
LAFFS!
'SIR'
SPATTER
BIK
BLIK
SWIG
KLONK
BOK
SPAK
Coors
BUZZ
'SIR'
CAMEL FILTERS

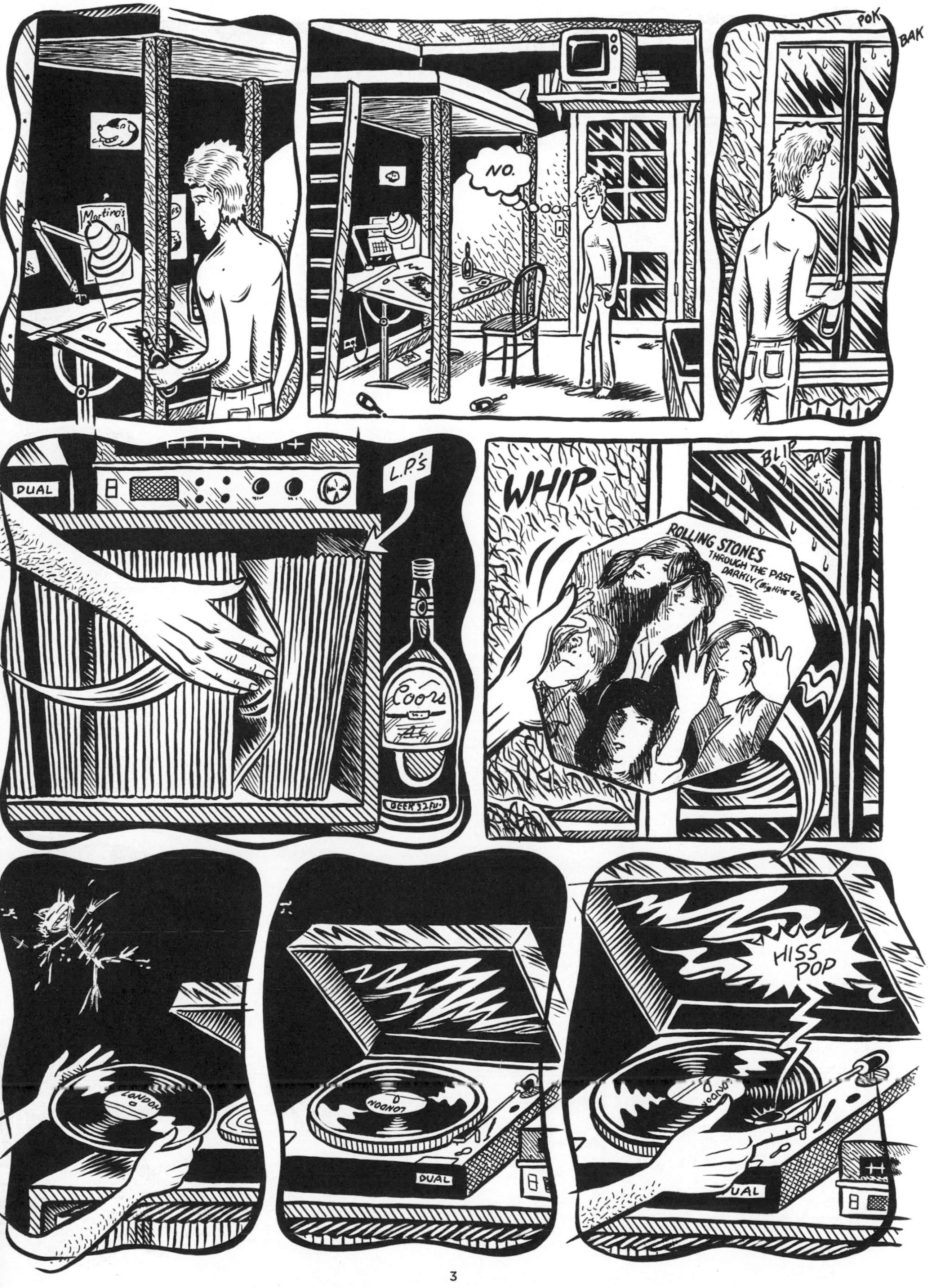

Martino's
NO.
POK
BAK
DUAL
L.P.'s
Coors
BEER 32 FL.
WHIP
BLIP
BAP
ROLLING STONES
THROUGH THE PAST
DARKLY (Big Hits #2)
LONDON
LONDON
DUAL
HISS
POP
DUAL

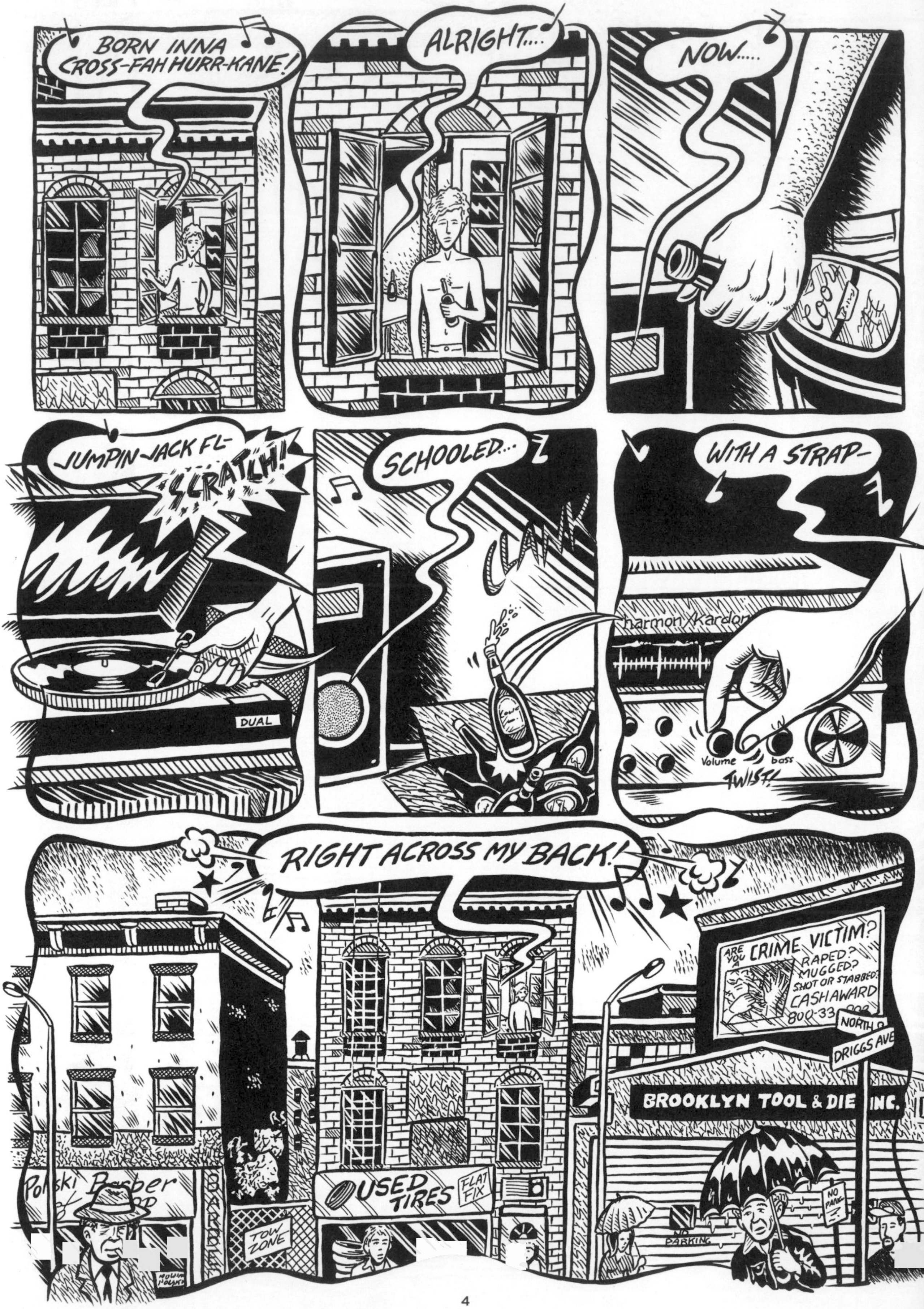
BORN INNA CROSS-FAH HURR-KANE!
ALRIGHT....
NOW.....
JUMPIN-JACK FL-
SCRATCH!
DUAL
SCHOOLED...
CLANK
WITH A STRAP-
harmon/Kardon
Volume
bass
TWIST!
RIGHT ACROSS MY BACK!
ARE YOU A CRIME VICTIM?
RAPED?
MUGGED?
SHOT OR STABBED?
CASH AWARD
DRIGGS AVE
BROOKLYN TOOL & DIE INC.
USED TIRES
FLAT FIX
TOW ZONE
NO PARKING

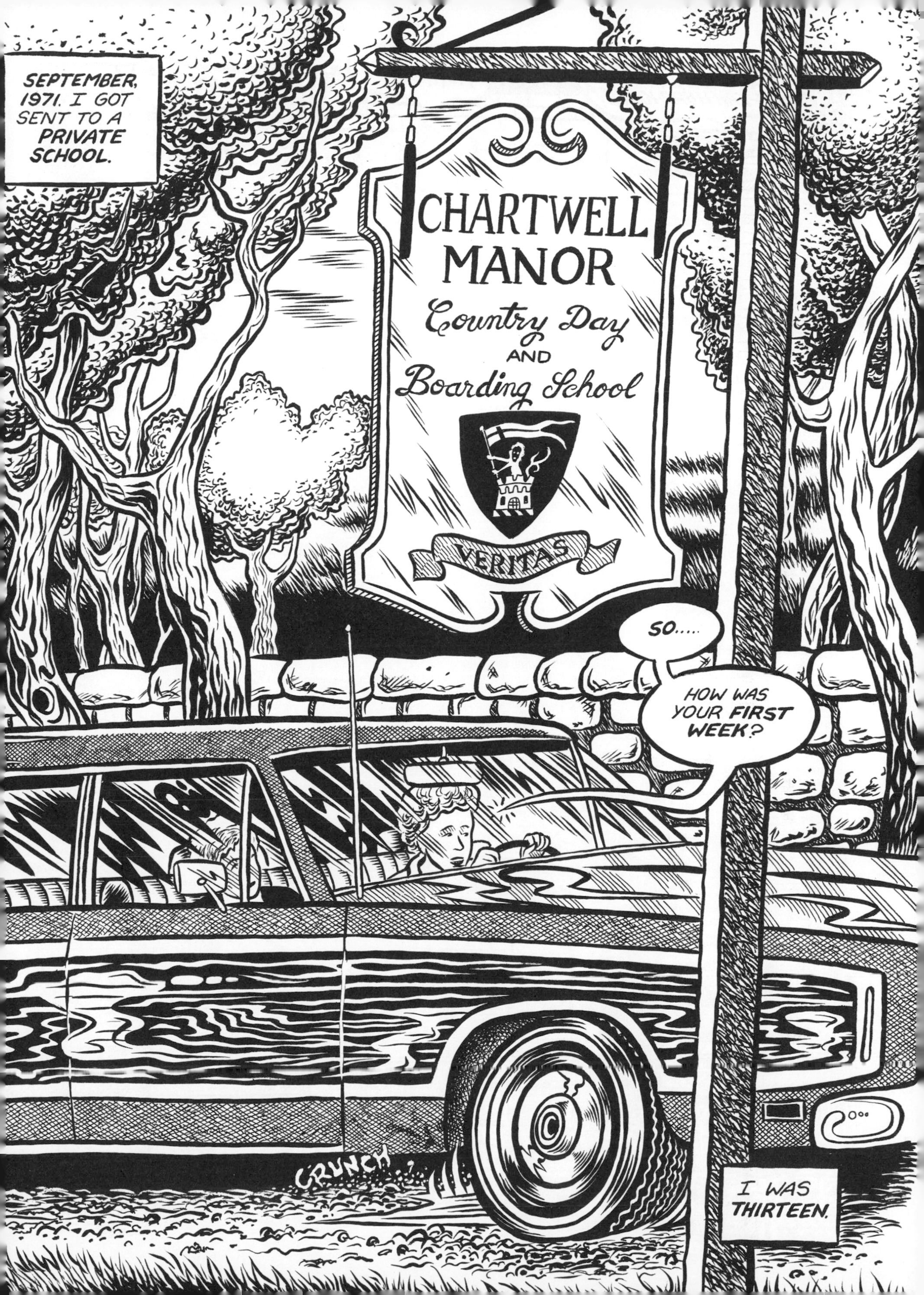
SEPTEMBER, 1971. I GOT SENT TO A PRIVATE SCHOOL.
CHARTWELL MANOR
Country Day
AND
Boarding School
VERITAS
SO.....
HOW WAS YOUR FIRST WEEK?
CRUNCH
I WAS THIRTEEN.

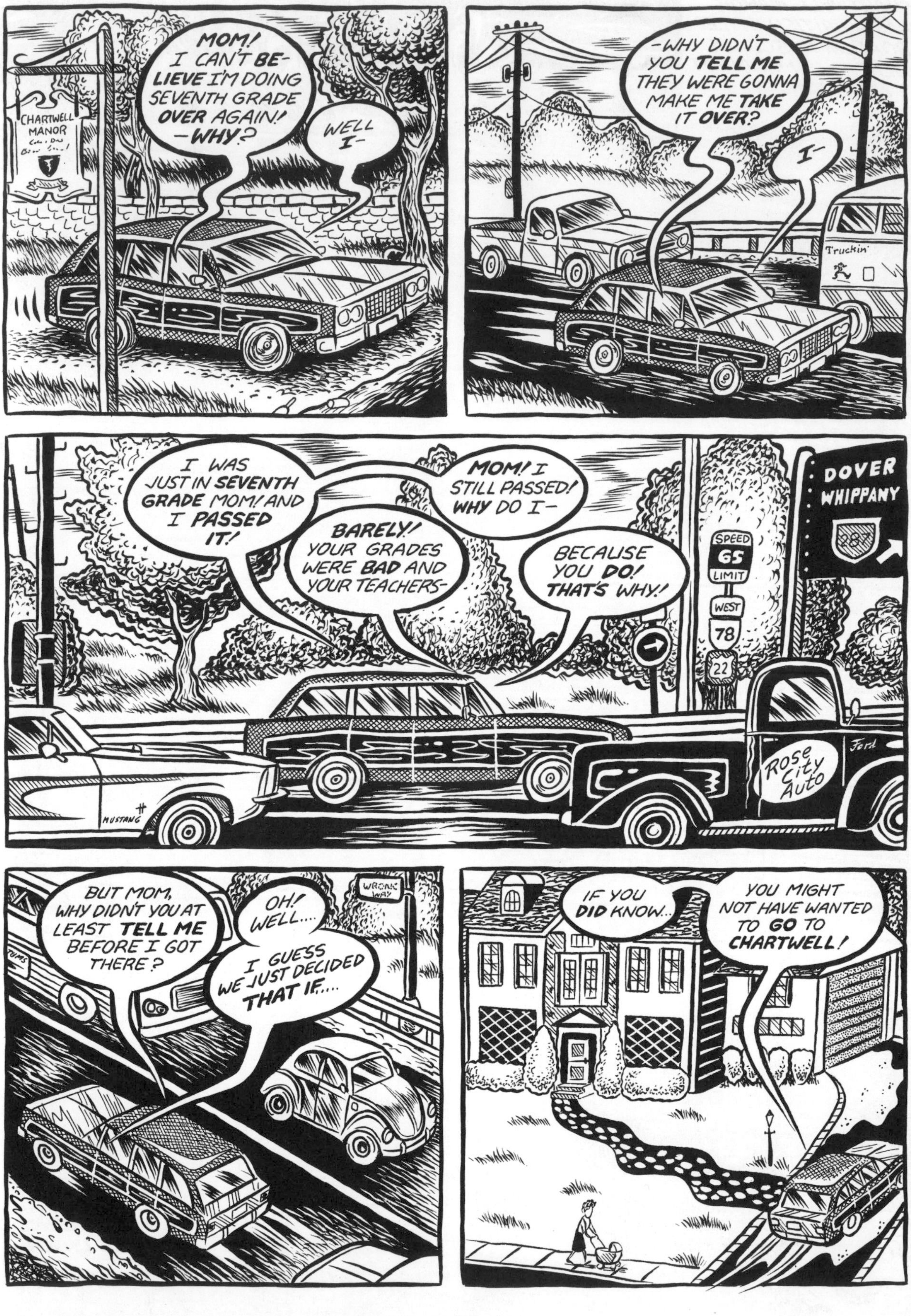
CHARTWELL MANOR
MOM! I CAN'T BE-LIEVE I'M DOING SEVENTH GRADE OVER AGAIN! —WHY?
WELL I-
—WHY DIDN'T YOU TELL ME THEY WERE GONNA MAKE ME TAKE IT OVER?
I-
Truckin'
I WAS JUST IN SEVENTH GRADE MOM! AND I PASSED IT!
BARELY! YOUR GRADES WERE BAD AND YOUR TEACHERS-
MOM! I STILL PASSED! WHY DO I-
BECAUSE YOU DO! THAT'S WHY!
DOVER
WHIPPANY
287
SPEED 65 LIMIT
WEST 78
22
Ford
Rose City Auto
MUSTANG
BUT MOM, WHY DIDN'T YOU AT LEAST TELL ME BEFORE I GOT THERE?
OH! WELL....
I GUESS WE JUST DECIDED THAT IF....
WRONG WAY
IF YOU DID KNOW...
YOU MIGHT NOT HAVE WANTED TO GO TO CHARTWELL!

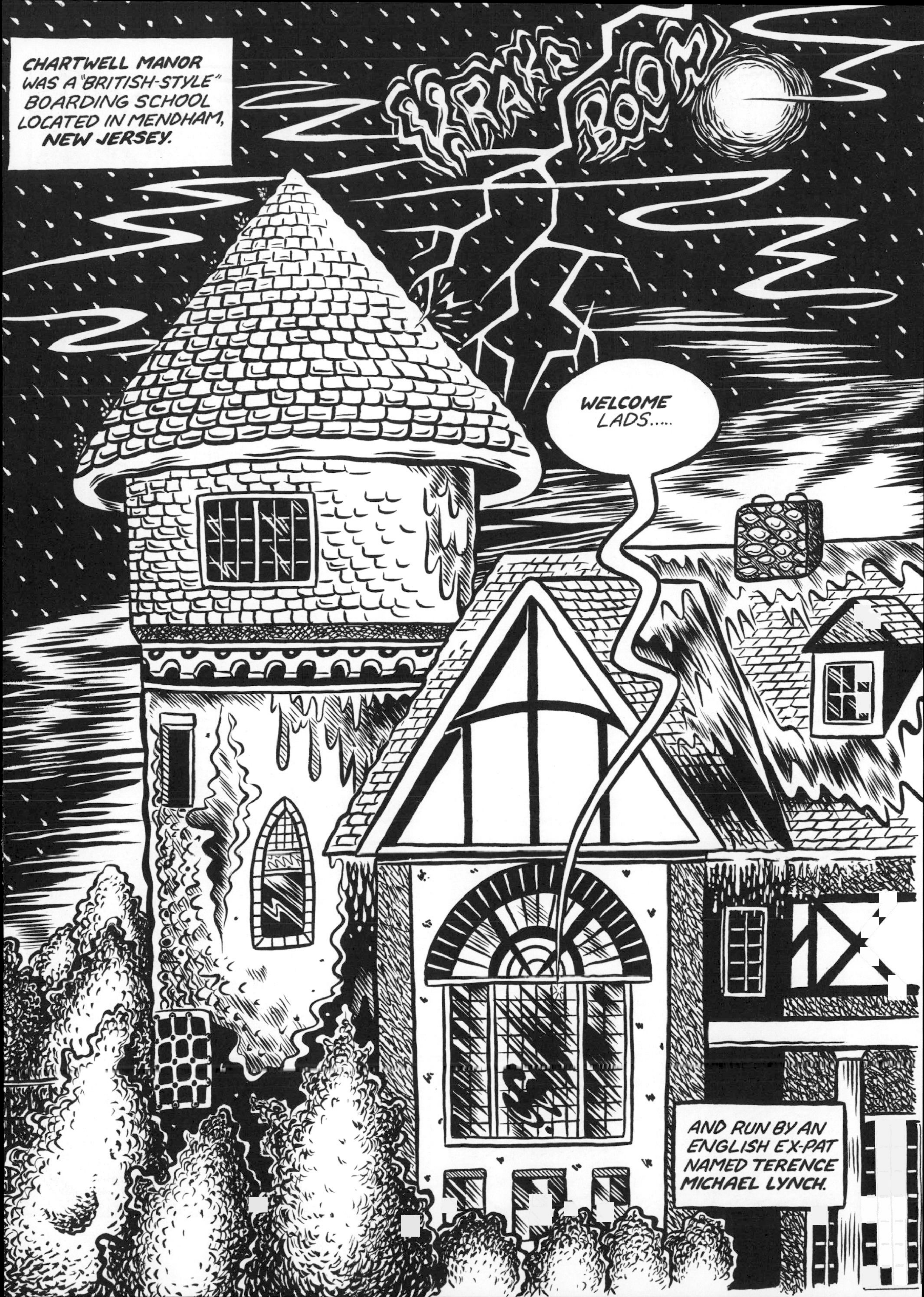
CHARTWELL MANOR WAS A "BRITISH-STYLE" BOARDING SCHOOL LOCATED IN MENDHAM, NEW JERSEY.
KRAKA-BOOM!
WELCOME LADS.....
AND RUN BY AN ENGLISH EX-PAT NAMED TERENCE MICHAEL LYNCH.

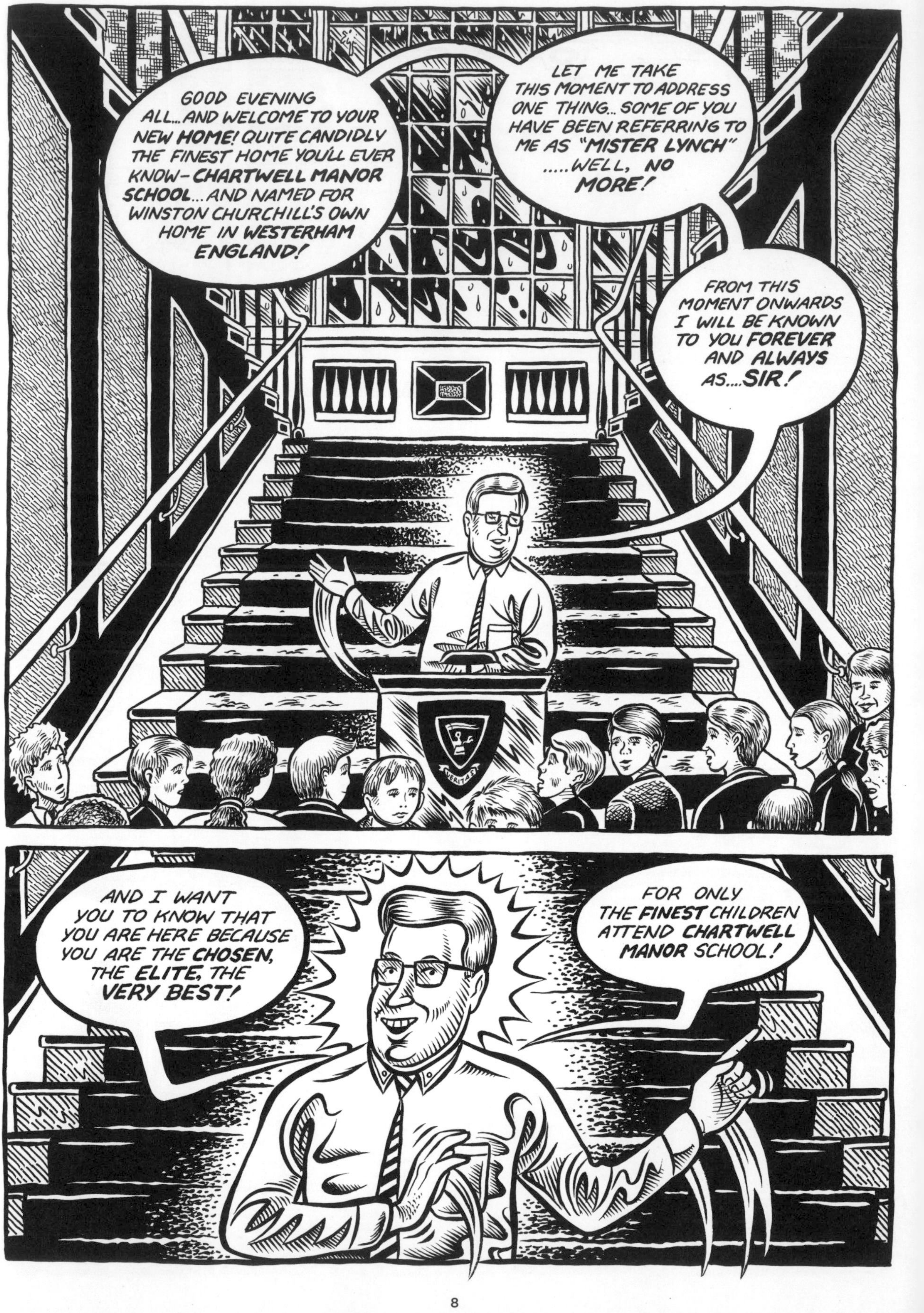
GOOD EVENING ALL... AND WELCOME TO YOUR NEW **HOME**! QUITE CANDIDLY THE FINEST HOME YOU'LL EVER KNOW– **CHARTWELL MANOR SCHOOL**... AND NAMED FOR WINSTON CHURCHILL'S OWN HOME IN **WESTERHAM ENGLAND!**
LET ME TAKE THIS MOMENT TO ADDRESS ONE THING... SOME OF YOU HAVE BEEN REFERRING TO ME AS **"MISTER LYNCH"** .....WELL, **NO MORE!**
FROM THIS MOMENT ONWARDS I WILL BE KNOWN TO YOU **FOREVER** AND **ALWAYS** AS.... **SIR!**
VERITAS
AND I WANT YOU TO KNOW THAT YOU ARE HERE BECAUSE YOU ARE THE **CHOSEN**, THE **ELITE**, THE **VERY BEST!**
FOR ONLY THE **FINEST** CHILDREN ATTEND **CHARTWELL MANOR** SCHOOL!

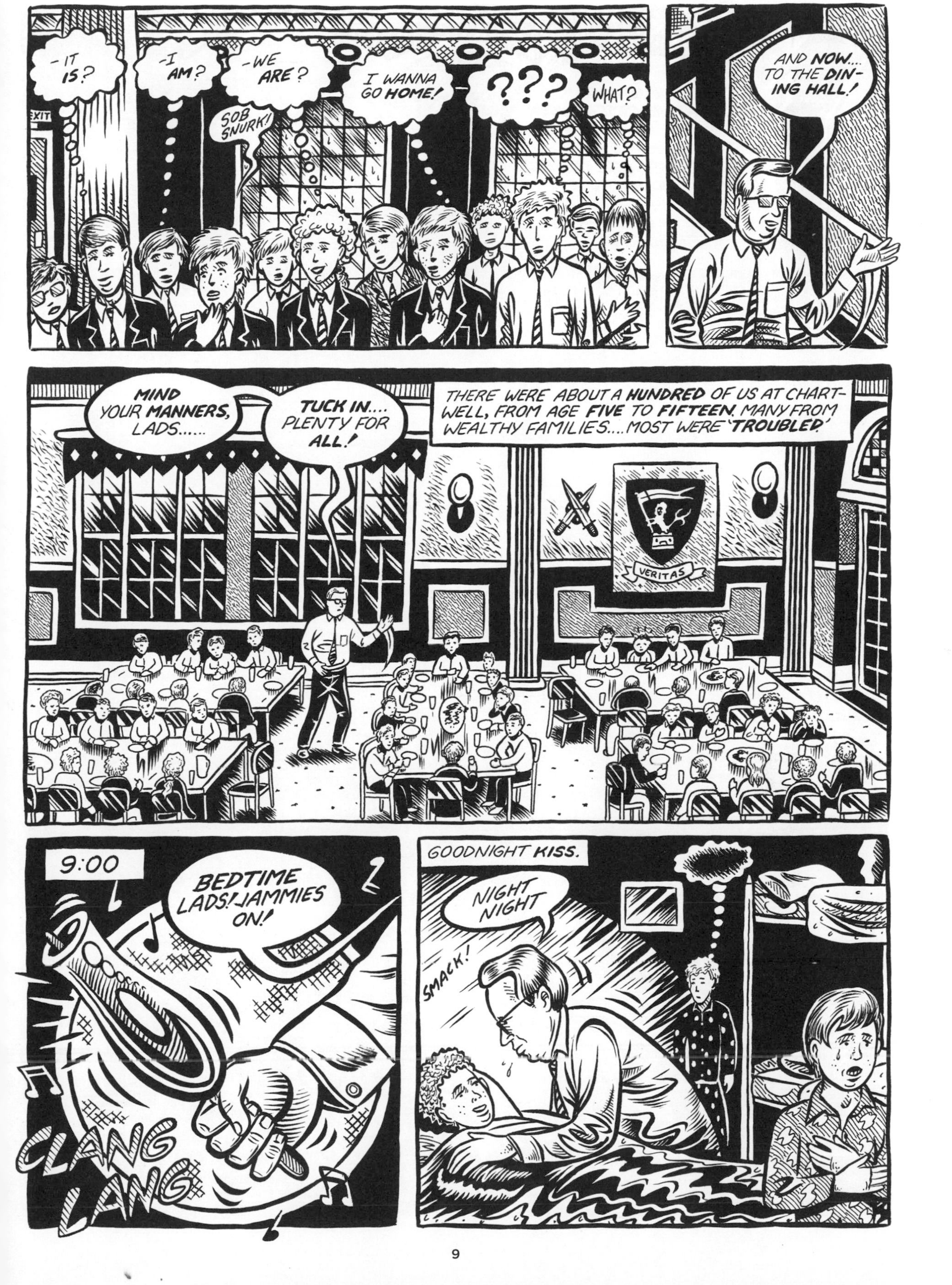
-IT IS?
-I AM?
SOB SNURK!
-WE ARE?
I WANNA GO HOME!
???
WHAT?
AND NOW.... TO THE DINING HALL!
MIND YOUR MANNERS, LADS......
TUCK IN.... PLENTY FOR ALL!
THERE WERE ABOUT A HUNDRED OF US AT CHARTWELL, FROM AGE FIVE TO FIFTEEN. MANY FROM WEALTHY FAMILIES.... MOST WERE 'TROUBLED.'
VERITAS
EXIT
9:00
BEDTIME LADS! JAMMIES ON!
CLANG CLANG
GOODNIGHT KISS.
NIGHT NIGHT
SMACK!

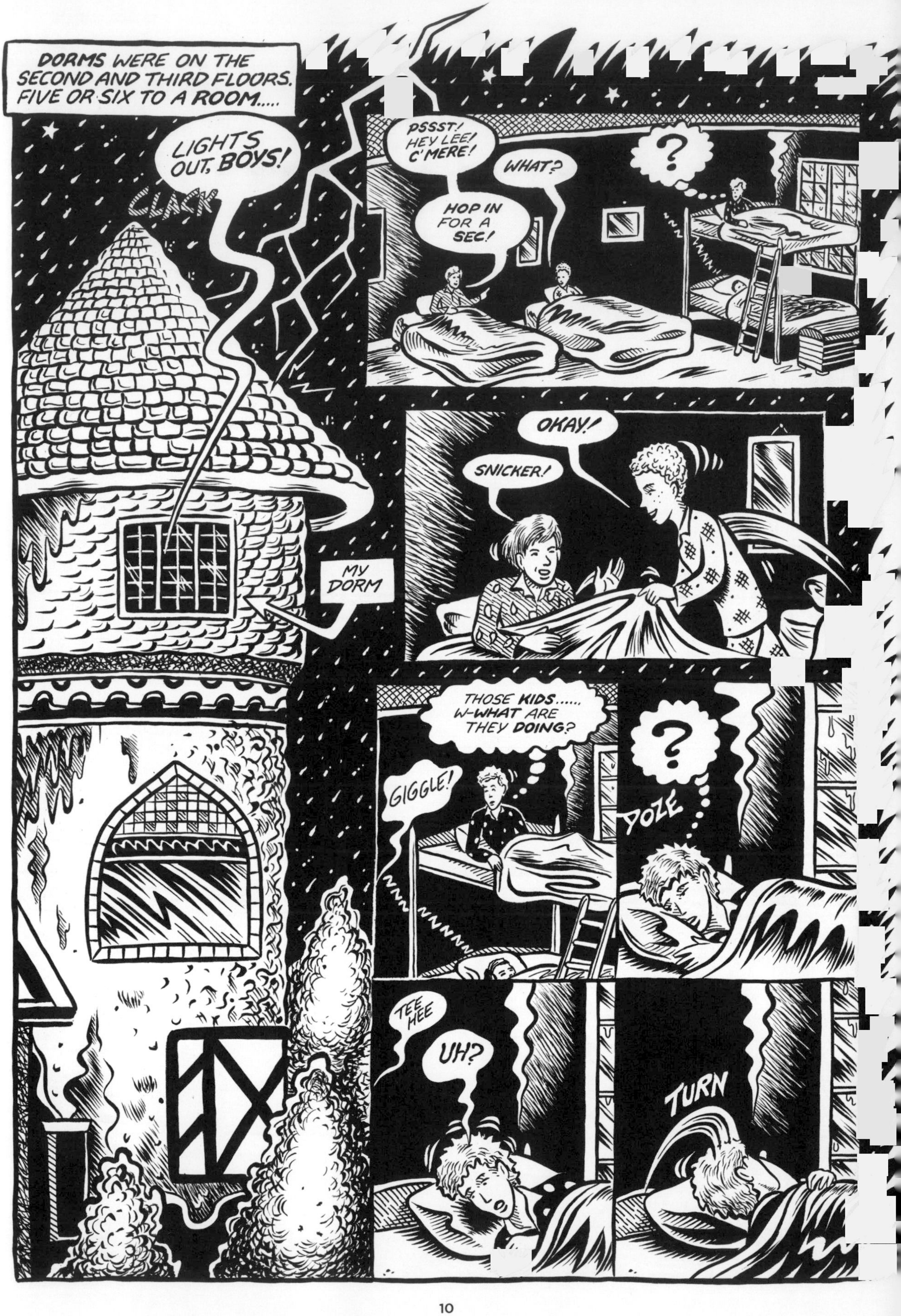

DORMS WERE ON THE SECOND AND THIRD FLOORS. FIVE OR SIX TO A ROOM.....
LIGHTS OUT, BOYS!
CLACK
MY DORM
PSSST! HEY LEE! C'MERE!
WHAT?
HOP IN FOR A SEC!
?
OKAY!
SNICKER!
THOSE KIDS...... W-WHAT ARE THEY DOING?
GIGGLE!
?
DOZE
TEE HEE
UH?
TURN

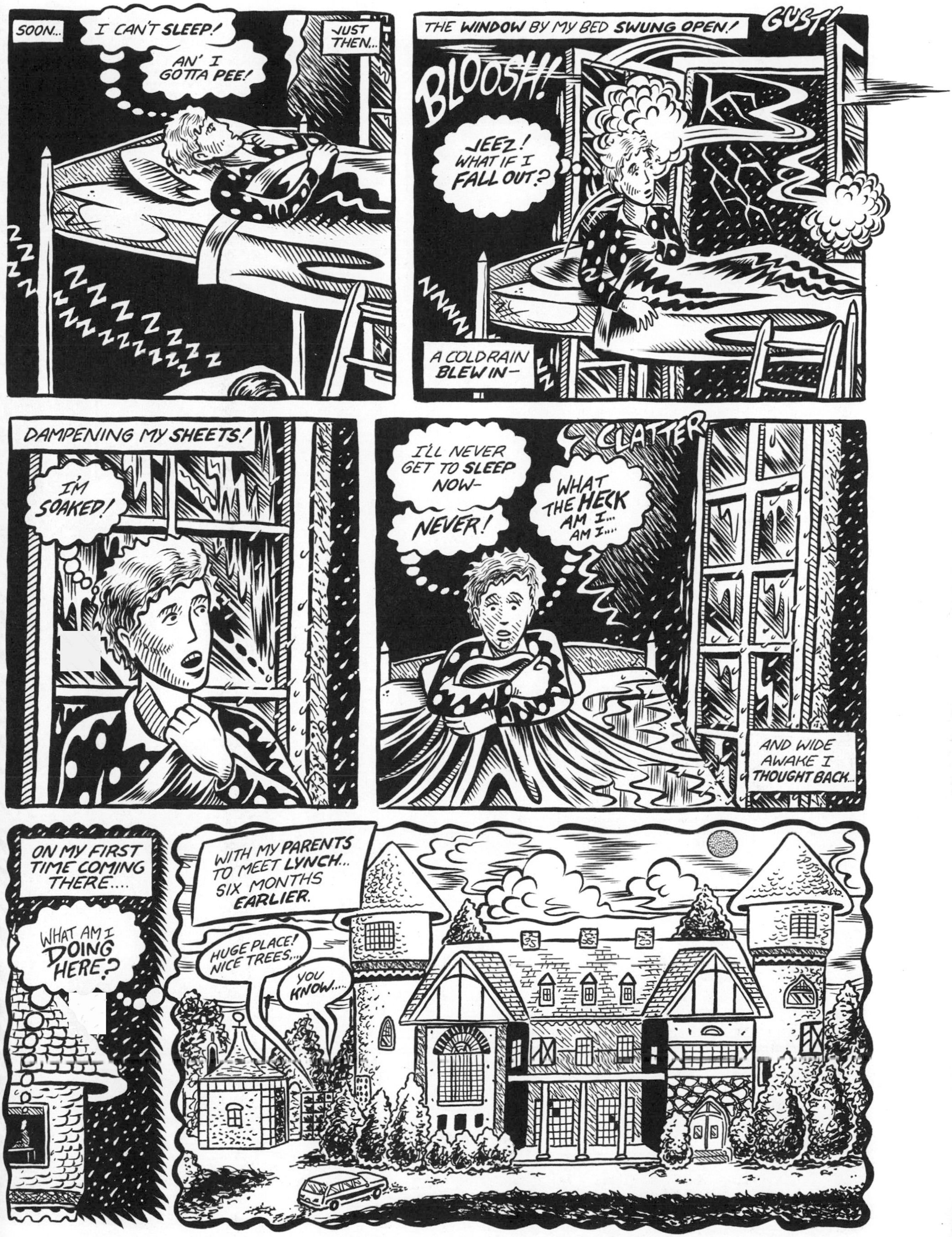
SOON...
I CAN'T SLEEP!
AN' I GOTTA PEE!
JUST THEN...
THE WINDOW BY MY BED SWUNG OPEN!
GUST!
BLOOSH!
JEEZ! WHAT IF I FALL OUT?
A COLD RAIN BLEW IN—
DAMPENING MY SHEETS!
I'M SOAKED!
CLATTER
I'LL NEVER GET TO SLEEP NOW—
NEVER!
WHAT THE HECK AM I... AM I....
AND WIDE AWAKE I THOUGHT BACK...
ON MY FIRST TIME COMING THERE....
WHAT AM I DOING HERE?
WITH MY PARENTS TO MEET LYNCH... SIX MONTHS EARLIER.
HUGE PLACE! NICE TREES....
YOU KNOW.....

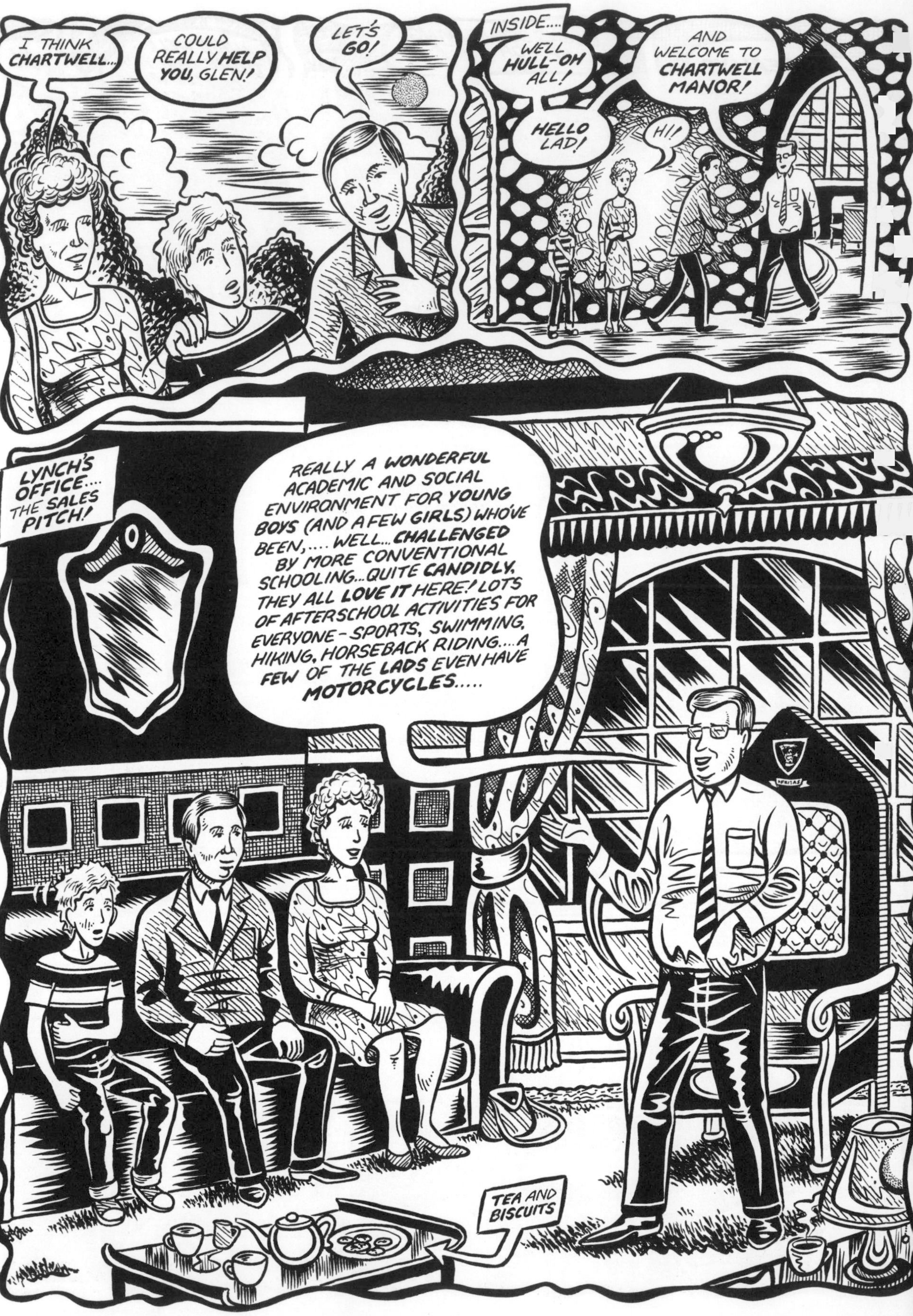
I THINK CHARTWELL...
COULD REALLY HELP YOU, GLEN!
LET'S GO!
INSIDE....
WELL HULL-OH ALL!
HELLO LAD!
HI!
AND WELCOME TO CHARTWELL MANOR!
LYNCH'S OFFICE.... THE SALES PITCH!
REALLY A WONDERFUL ACADEMIC AND SOCIAL ENVIRONMENT FOR YOUNG BOYS (AND A FEW GIRLS) WHO'VE BEEN,.... WELL... CHALLENGED BY MORE CONVENTIONAL SCHOOLING... QUITE CANDIDLY, THEY ALL LOVE IT HERE! LOTS OF AFTERSCHOOL ACTIVITIES FOR EVERYONE - SPORTS, SWIMMING, HIKING, HORSEBACK RIDING.... A FEW OF THE LADS EVEN HAVE MOTORCYCLES.....
TEA AND BISCUITS

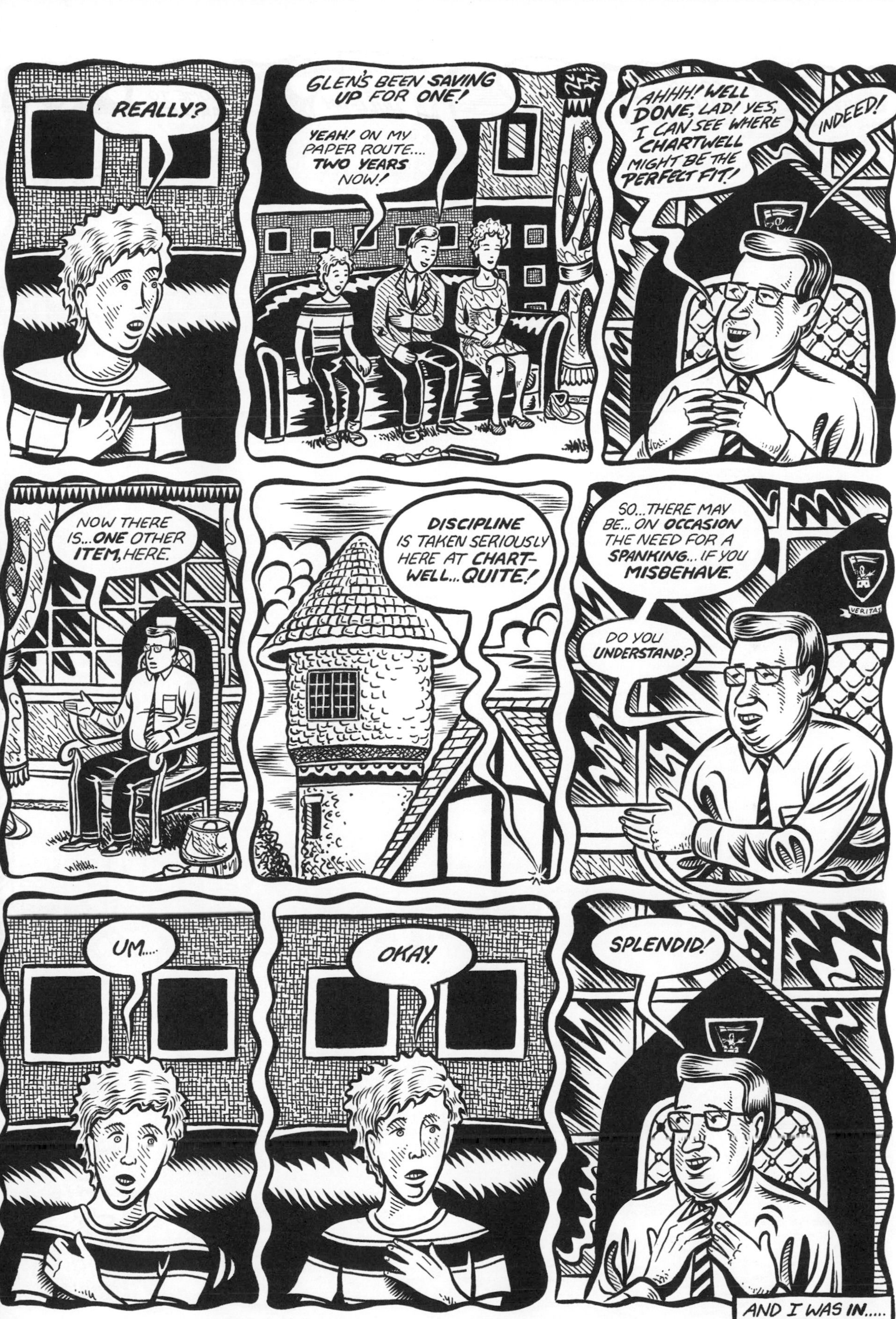
REALLY?
GLEN'S BEEN SAVING UP FOR ONE!
YEAH! ON MY PAPER ROUTE.... TWO YEARS NOW!
AHHH! WELL DONE, LAD! YES, I CAN SEE WHERE CHARTWELL MIGHT BE THE PERFECT FIT!
INDEED!
NOW THERE IS...ONE OTHER ITEM, HERE.
DISCIPLINE IS TAKEN SERIOUSLY HERE AT CHART-WELL...QUITE!
SO...THERE MAY BE...ON OCCASION THE NEED FOR A SPANKING...IF YOU MISBEHAVE.
VERITAS
DO YOU UNDERSTAND?
UM....
OKAY.
SPLENDID!
AND I WAS IN.....

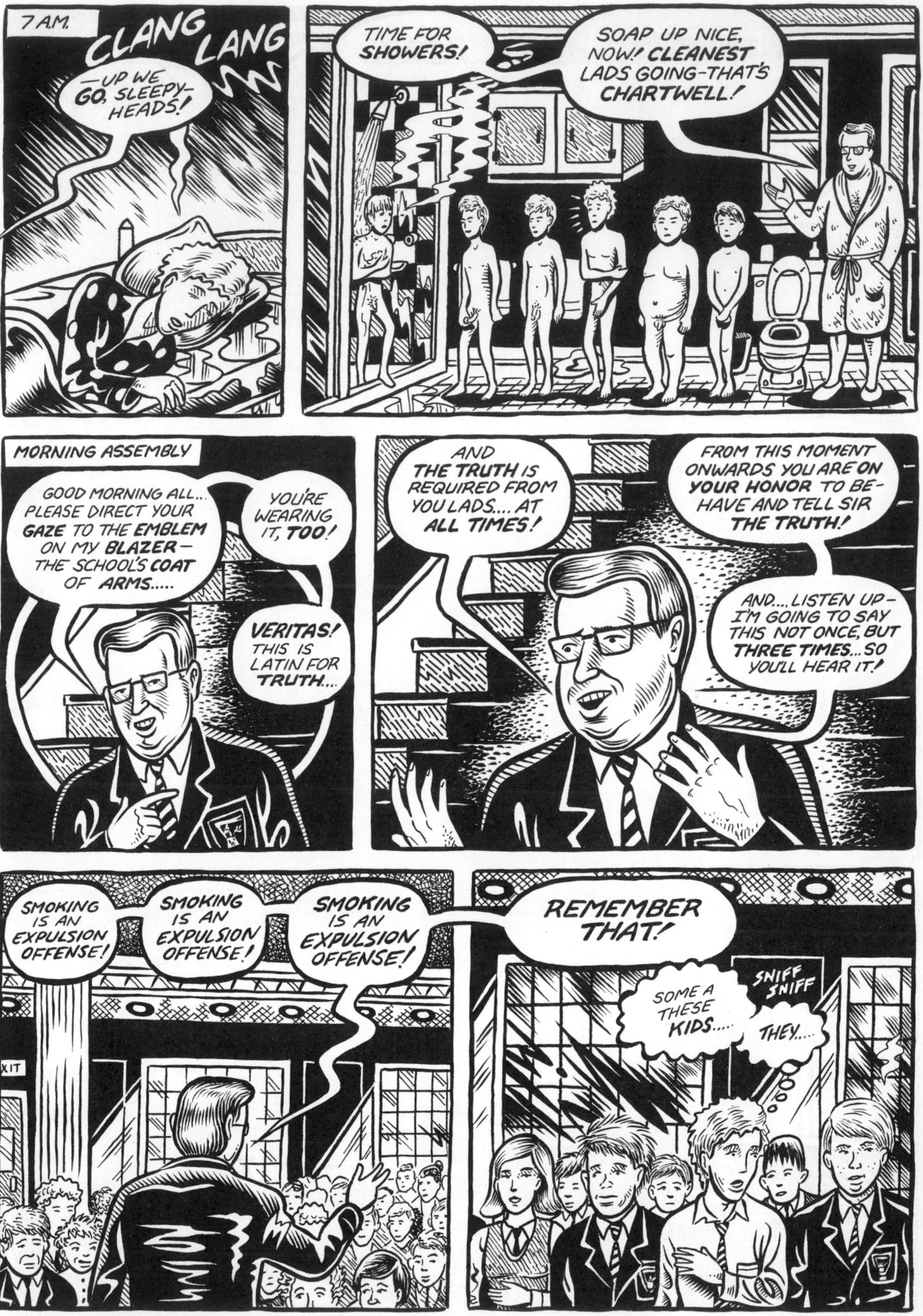
7 A.M.
CLANG LANG
—UP WE GO, SLEEPY-HEADS!
TIME FOR SHOWERS!
SOAP UP NICE, NOW! CLEANEST LADS GOING–THAT'S CHARTWELL!
MORNING ASSEMBLY
GOOD MORNING ALL... PLEASE DIRECT YOUR GAZE TO THE EMBLEM ON MY BLAZER— THE SCHOOL'S COAT OF ARMS.....
YOU'RE WEARING IT, TOO!
VERITAS! THIS IS LATIN FOR TRUTH....
AND THE TRUTH IS REQUIRED FROM YOU LADS.... AT ALL TIMES!
FROM THIS MOMENT ONWARDS YOU ARE ON YOUR HONOR TO BE-HAVE AND TELL SIR THE TRUTH!
AND...., LISTEN UP– I'M GOING TO SAY THIS NOT ONCE, BUT THREE TIMES... SO YOU'LL HEAR IT!
SMOKING IS AN EXPULSION OFFENSE!
SMOKING IS AN EXPULSION OFFENSE!
SMOKING IS AN EXPULSION OFFENSE!
REMEMBER THAT!
SNIFF SNIFF
SOME A THESE KIDS.....
THEY.....

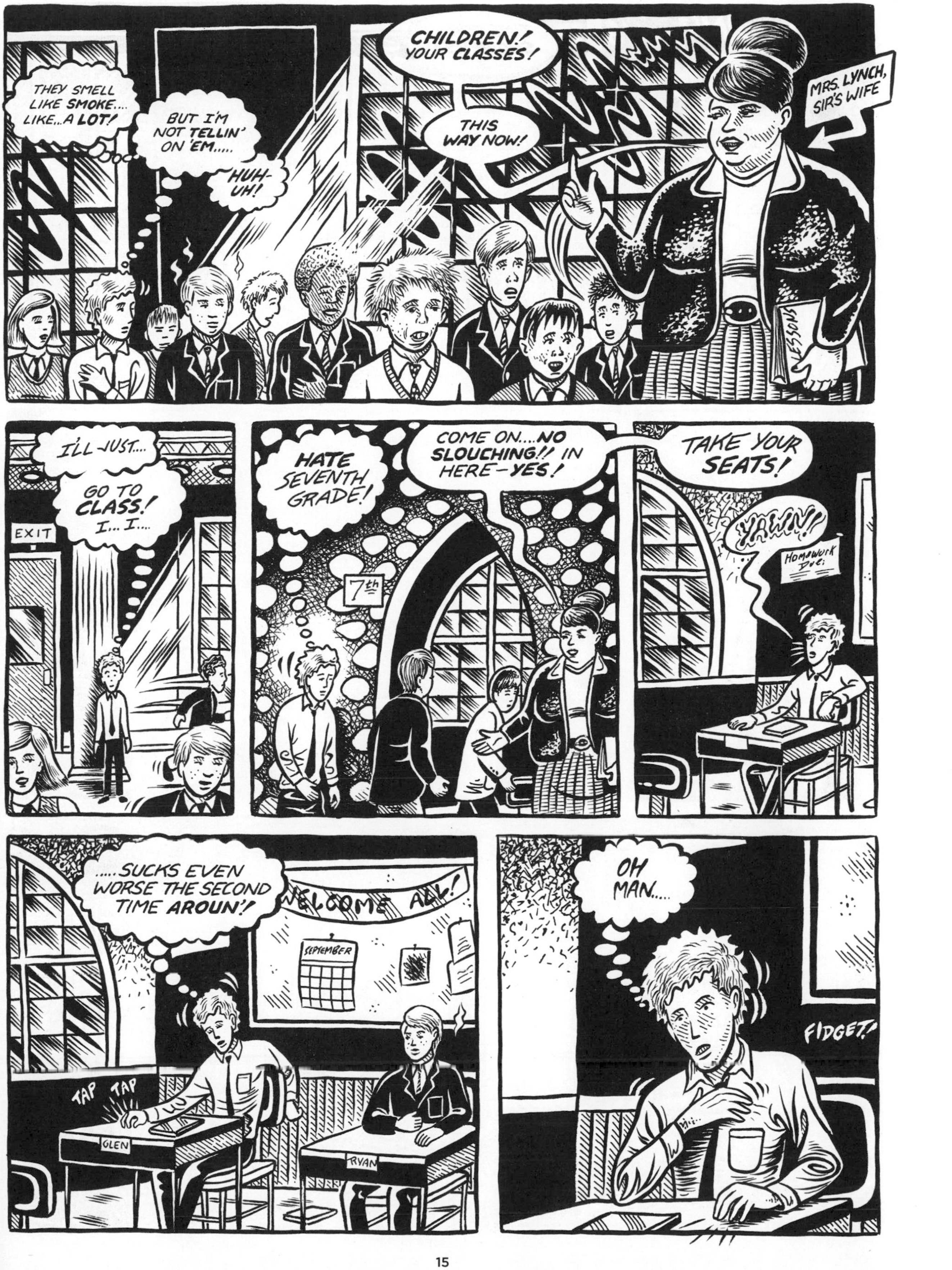
THEY SMELL LIKE SMOKE.... LIKE...A LOT!
BUT I'M NOT TELLIN' ON 'EM.....
HUH-UH!
CHILDREN! YOUR CLASSES!
THIS WAY NOW!
MRS. LYNCH, SIR'S WIFE
LESSONS
I'LL JUST....
GO TO CLASS! I... I....
EXIT
HATE SEVENTH GRADE!
COME ON....NO SLOUCHING!! IN HERE—YES!
7th
TAKE YOUR SEATS!
YAWN!!
HOMEWORK DUE:
.....SUCKS EVEN WORSE THE SECOND TIME AROUN'!
WELCOME ALL!
SEPTEMBER
TAP TAP
GLEN
RYAN
OH MAN.....
FIDGET!

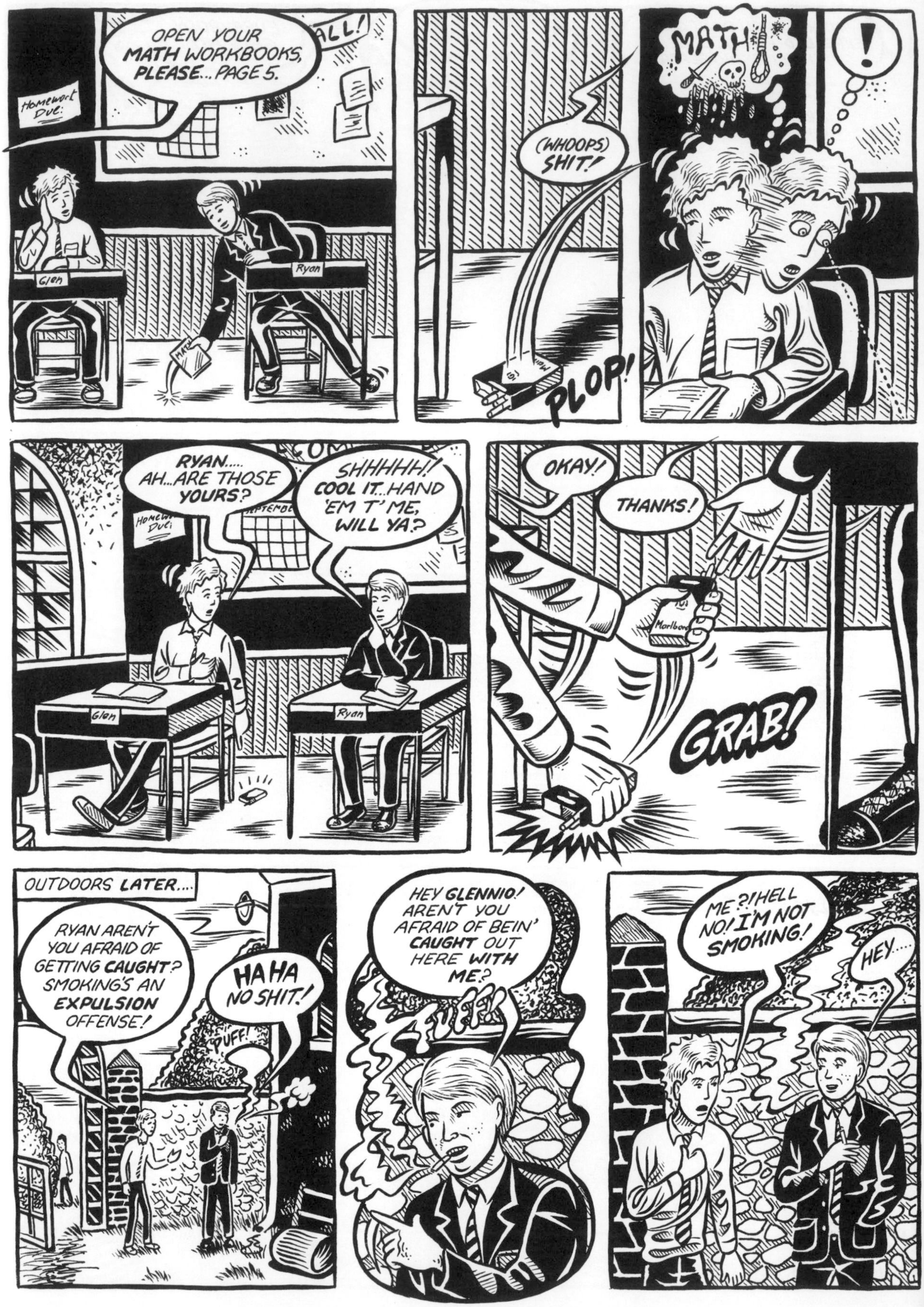

OPEN YOUR MATH WORKBOOKS, PLEASE... PAGE 5.
Homework Due:
Glen
Ryan
(WHOOPS) SHIT!
PLOP!
MATH
!
RYAN..... AH...ARE THOSE YOURS?
SHHHHH! COOL IT...HAND 'EM T' ME, WILL YA?
Glen
Ryan
OKAY!
THANKS!
Marlboro
GRAB!
OUTDOORS LATER....
RYAN AREN'T YOU AFRAID OF GETTING CAUGHT? SMOKING'S AN EXPULSION OFFENSE!
HAHA NO SHIT!
PUFF!
HEY GLENNIO! AREN'T YOU AFRAID OF BEIN' CAUGHT OUT HERE WITH ME?
PUFF!
ME?! HELL NO! I'M NOT SMOKING!
HEY....

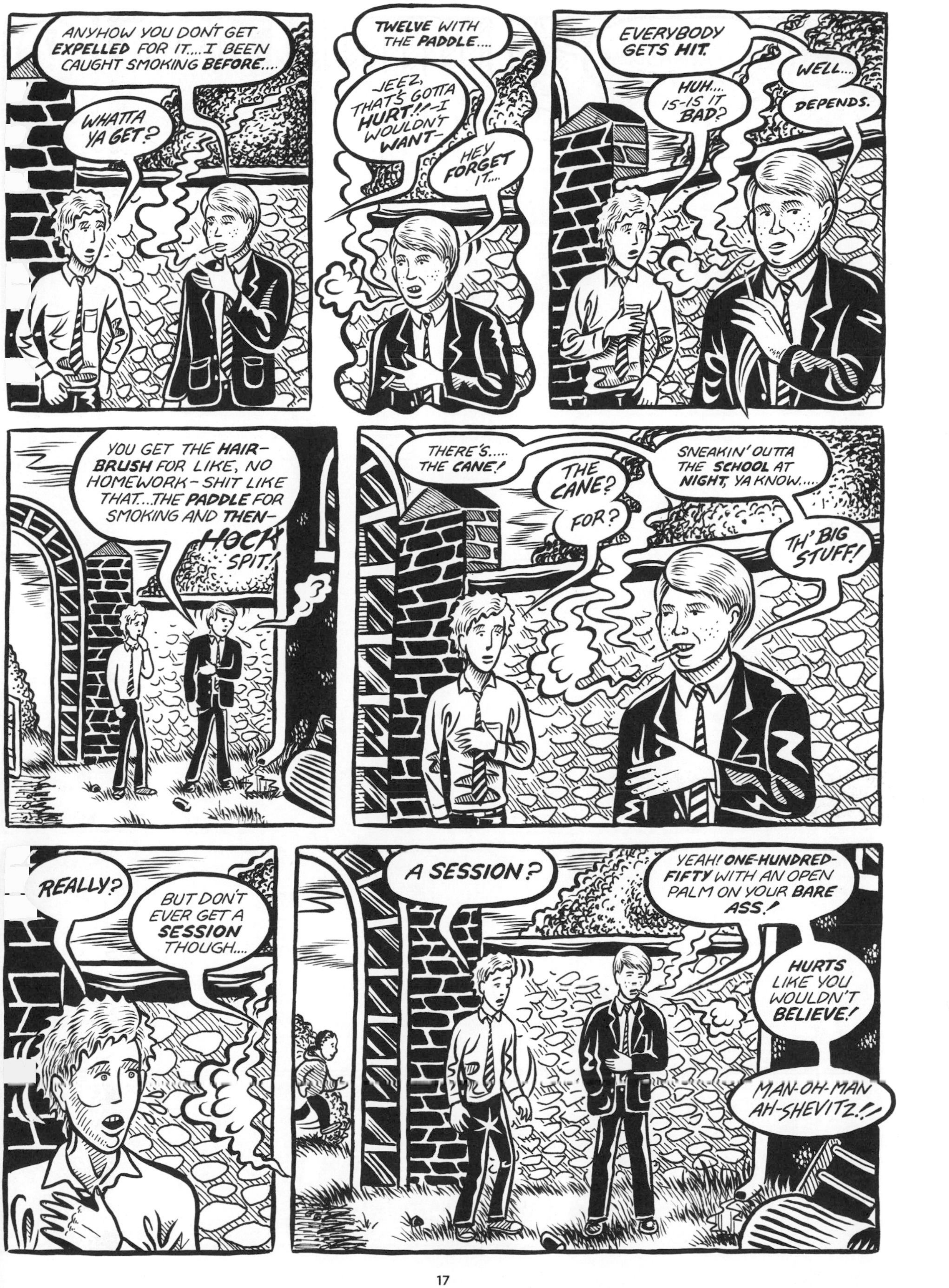
ANYHOW YOU DON'T GET EXPELLED FOR IT.... I BEEN CAUGHT SMOKING BEFORE....
WHATTA YA GET?
TWELVE WITH THE PADDLE....
JEEZ, THAT'S GOTTA HURT!!–I WOULDN'T WANT–
HEY FORGET IT....
EVERYBODY GETS HIT.
HUH.... IS–IS IT BAD?
WELL....
DEPENDS.
YOU GET THE HAIR-BRUSH FOR LIKE, NO HOMEWORK–SHIT LIKE THAT....THE PADDLE FOR SMOKING AND THEN–
HOCK
SPIT!
THERE'S..... THE CANE!
THE CANE?
FOR?
SNEAKIN' OUTTA THE SCHOOL AT NIGHT, YA KNOW.....
TH' BIG STUFF!
REALLY?
BUT DON'T EVER GET A SESSION THOUGH....
A SESSION?
YEAH! ONE-HUNDRED-FIFTY WITH AN OPEN PALM ON YOUR BARE ASS!
HURTS LIKE YOU WOULDN'T BELIEVE!
MAN-OH-MAN AH-SHEVITZ!!

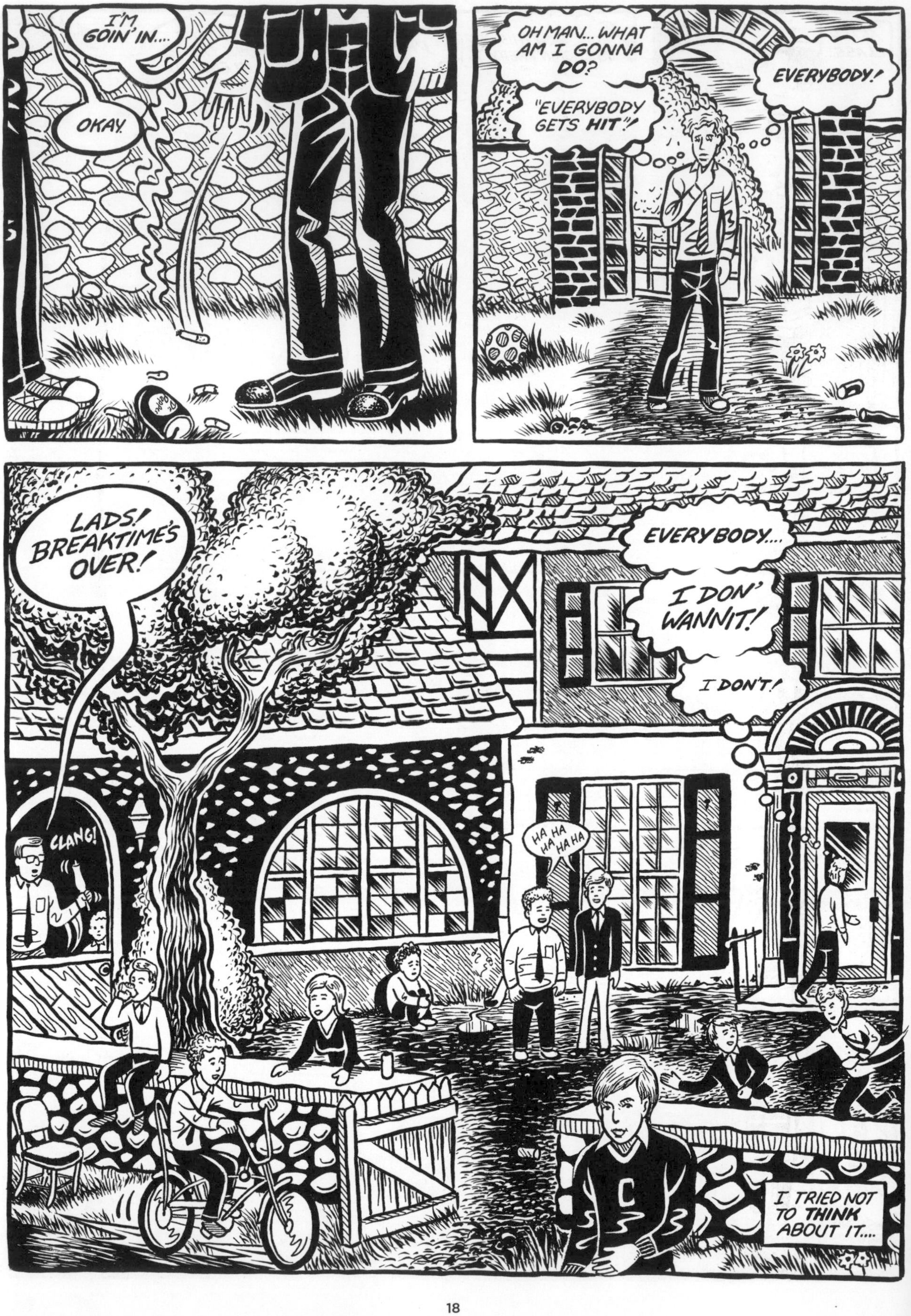
I'M GOIN' IN....
OKAY.
OH MAN... WHAT AM I GONNA DO?
"EVERYBODY GETS HIT"!
EVERYBODY!
LADS! BREAKTIME'S OVER!
EVERYBODY....
I DON' WANNIT!
I DON'T!
CLANG!
HA HA HA HA HA
I TRIED NOT TO THINK ABOUT IT....

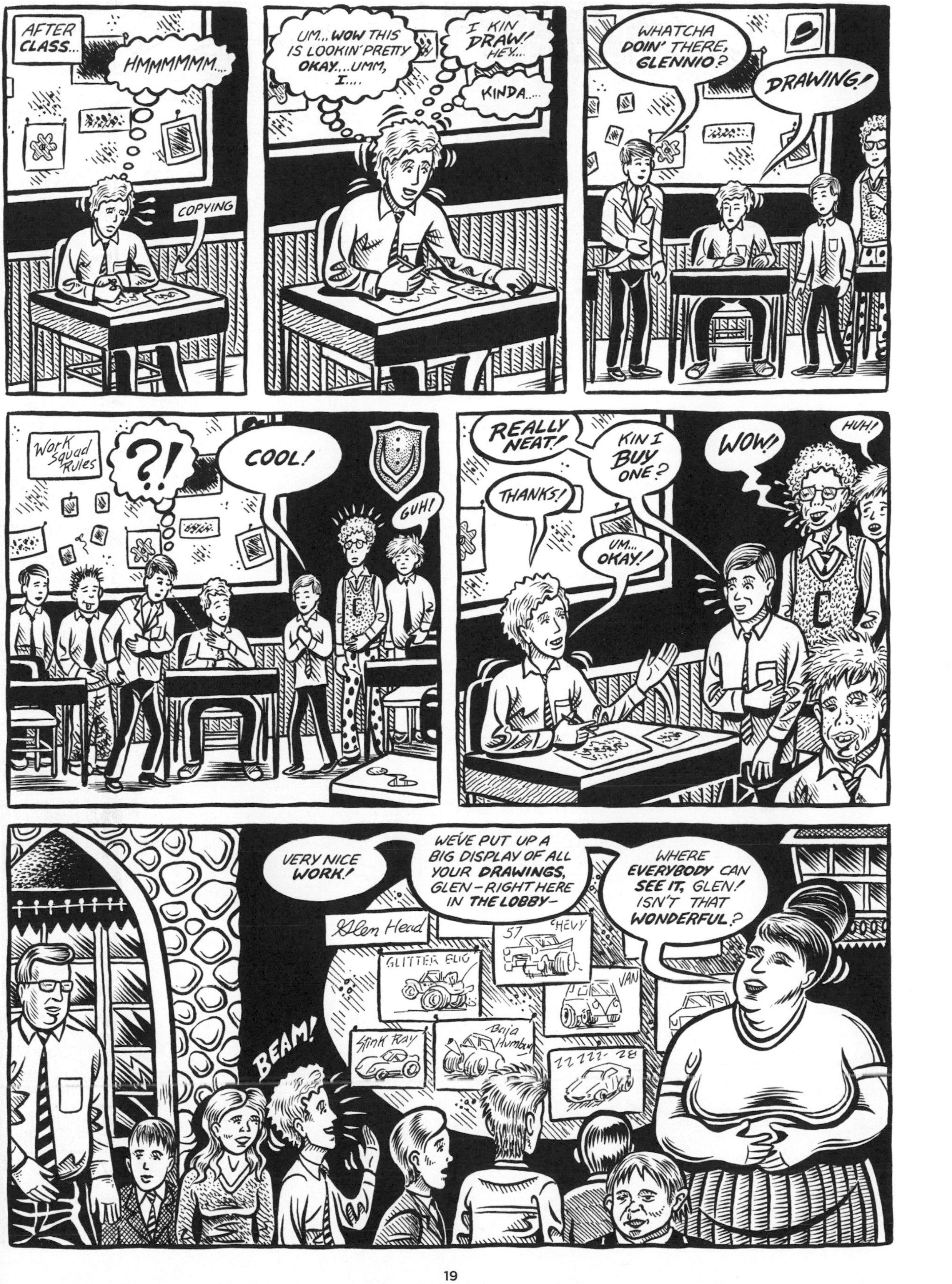
AFTER CLASS...
HMMMMMM...
COPYING
UM... WOW THIS IS LOOKIN' PRETTY OKAY... UMM, I....
I KIN DRAW! HEY...
KINDA.....
WHATCHA DOIN' THERE, GLENNIO?
DRAWING!
Work Squad Rules
?!
COOL!
GUH!
REALLY NEAT!
KIN I BUY ONE?
WOW!
HUH!
THANKS!
UM... OKAY!
VERY NICE WORK!
WE'VE PUT UP A BIG DISPLAY OF ALL YOUR DRAWINGS, GLEN - RIGHT HERE IN THE LOBBY -
WHERE EVERYBODY CAN SEE IT, GLEN! ISN'T THAT WONDERFUL?
Glen Head
57 CHEVY
GLITTER BUG
VAN
Stink Ray
Baja Humbug
ZZZZZ-28
BEAM!

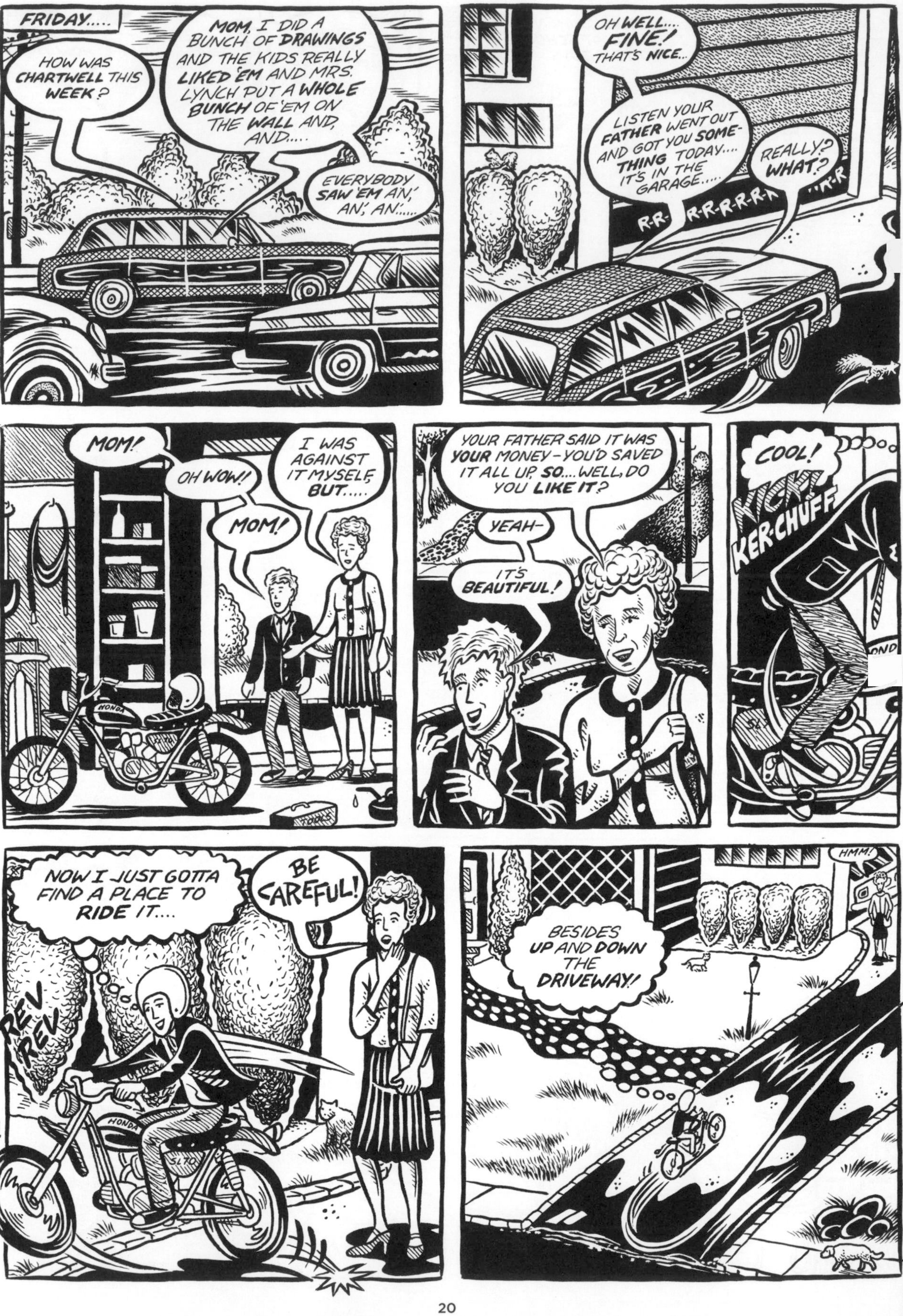

FRIDAY.....
HOW WAS CHARTWELL THIS WEEK?
MOM, I DID A BUNCH OF DRAWINGS AND THE KIDS REALLY LIKED 'EM AND MRS. LYNCH PUT A WHOLE BUNCH OF 'EM ON THE WALL AND, AND.....
EVERYBODY SAW 'EM AN,' AN,' AN'.....
OH WELL.... FINE! THAT'S NICE...
LISTEN YOUR FATHER WENT OUT AND GOT YOU SOME-THING TODAY.... IT'S IN THE GARAGE.....
R-R- R-R-R-R-R-R- 'R-R
REALLY? WHAT?
MOM!
OH WOW!
MOM!
I WAS AGAINST IT MYSELF, BUT.....
HONDA
TOOLS
YOUR FATHER SAID IT WAS YOUR MONEY - YOU'D SAVED IT ALL UP, SO.... WELL, DO YOU LIKE IT?
YEAH-
IT'S BEAUTIFUL!
COOL!
KICK!
KER-CHUFF
NOW I JUST GOTTA FIND A PLACE TO RIDE IT....
BE CAREFUL!
REV REV
POP!
HONDA
SL70
HMM!
BESIDES UP AND DOWN THE DRIVEWAY!

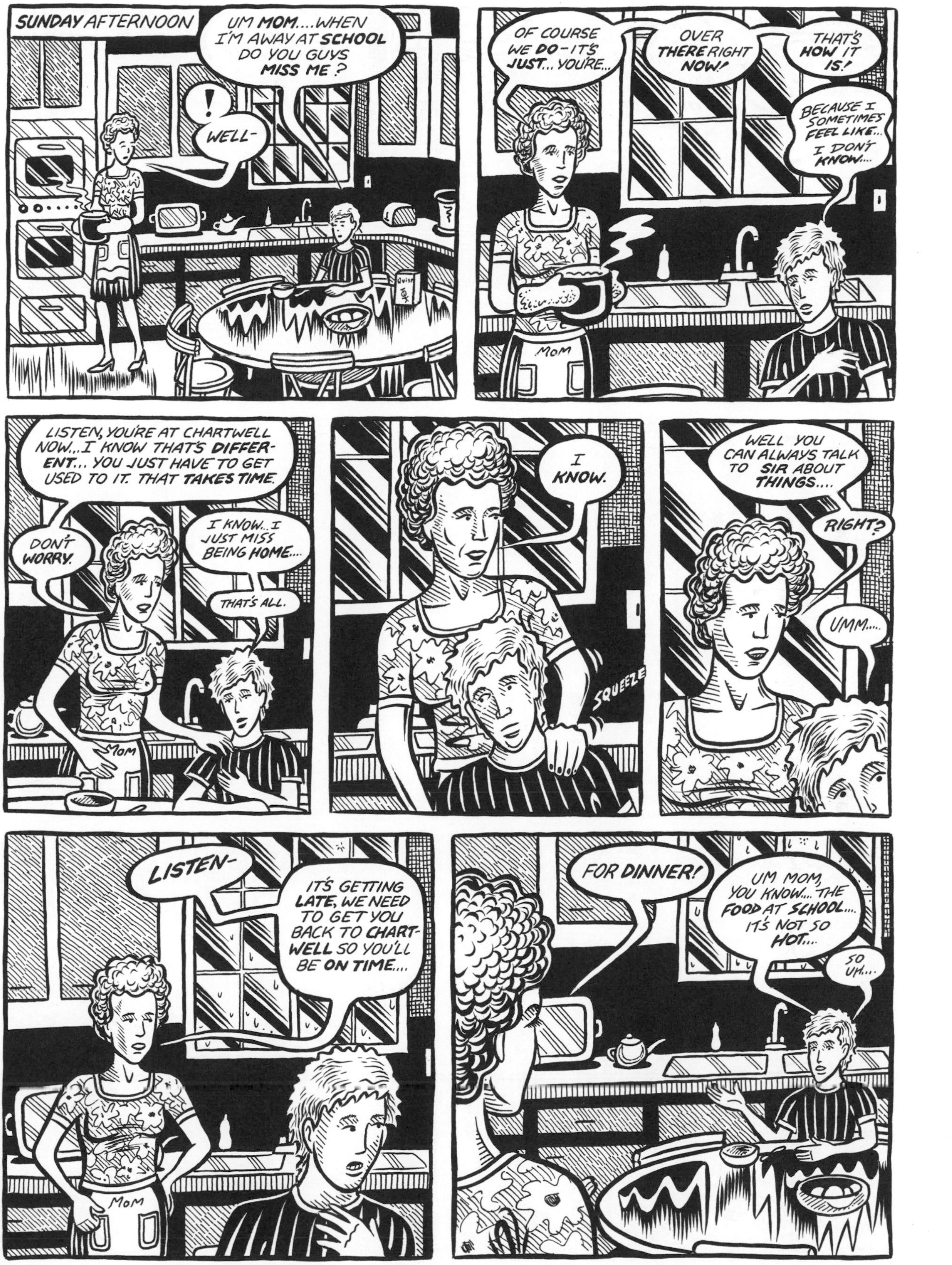

SUNDAY AFTERNOON
UM MOM....WHEN I'M AWAY AT SCHOOL DO YOU GUYS MISS ME?
!
WELL-
OF COURSE WE DO-IT'S JUST... YOU'RE...
OVER THERE RIGHT NOW!
THAT'S HOW IT IS!
BECAUSE I SOMETIMES FEEL LIKE... I DON'T KNOW....
MOM
LISTEN, YOU'RE AT CHARTWELL NOW... I KNOW THAT'S DIFFERENT... YOU JUST HAVE TO GET USED TO IT. THAT TAKES TIME.
DON'T WORRY.
I KNOW...I JUST MISS BEING HOME....
THAT'S ALL.
MOM
I KNOW.
SQUEEZE
WELL YOU CAN ALWAYS TALK TO SIR ABOUT THINGS....
RIGHT?
UMM....
LISTEN-
IT'S GETTING LATE, WE NEED TO GET YOU BACK TO CHARTWELL SO YOU'LL BE ON TIME....
MOM
FOR DINNER!
UM MOM, YOU KNOW... THE FOOD AT SCHOOL.... IT'S NOT SO HOT....
SO UH....

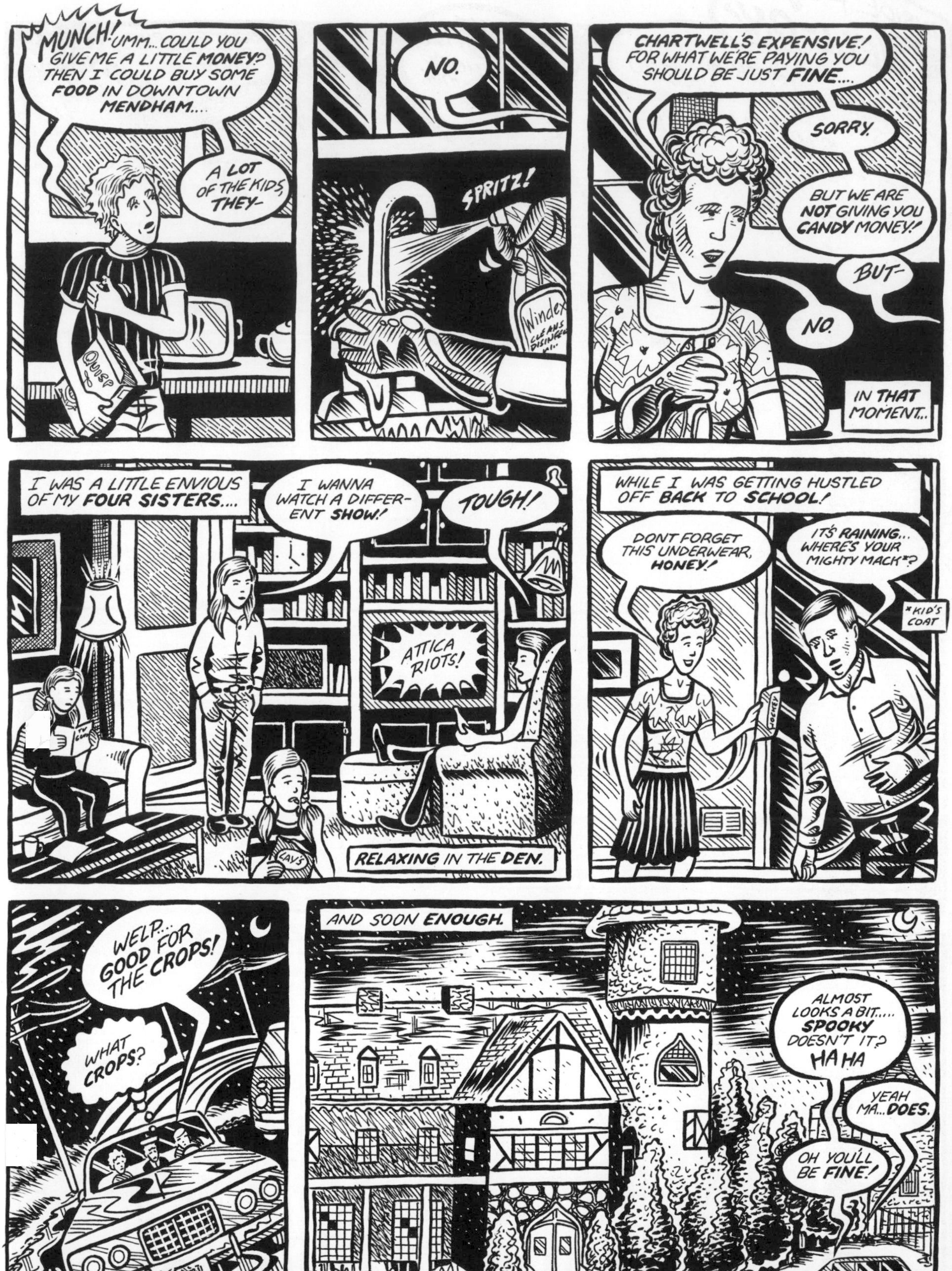
MUNCH!
UMM... COULD YOU GIVE ME A LITTLE MONEY? THEN I COULD BUY SOME FOOD IN DOWNTOWN MENDHAM....
A LOT OF THE KIDS, THEY-
QUISP
NO.
SPRITZ!
Windex
CHARTWELL'S EXPENSIVE! FOR WHAT WE'RE PAYING YOU SHOULD BE JUST FINE....
SORRY.
BUT WE ARE NOT GIVING YOU CANDY MONEY!
BUT-
NO.
IN THAT MOMENT...
I WAS A LITTLE ENVIOUS OF MY FOUR SISTERS....
I WANNA WATCH A DIFFERENT SHOW!
TOUGH!
ATTICA RIOTS!
RELAXING IN THE DEN.
LAY'S
WHILE I WAS GETTING HUSTLED OFF BACK TO SCHOOL!
DONT FORGET THIS UNDERWEAR, HONEY!
IT'S RAINING... WHERE'S YOUR MIGHTY MACK*?
*KID'S COAT
WELP... GOOD FOR THE CROPS!
WHAT CROPS?
AND SOON ENOUGH.
ALMOST LOOKS A BIT..... SPOOKY DOESN'T IT? HA HA
YEAH MA... DOES.
OH YOU'LL BE FINE!

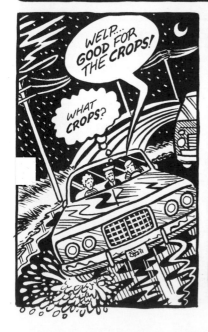

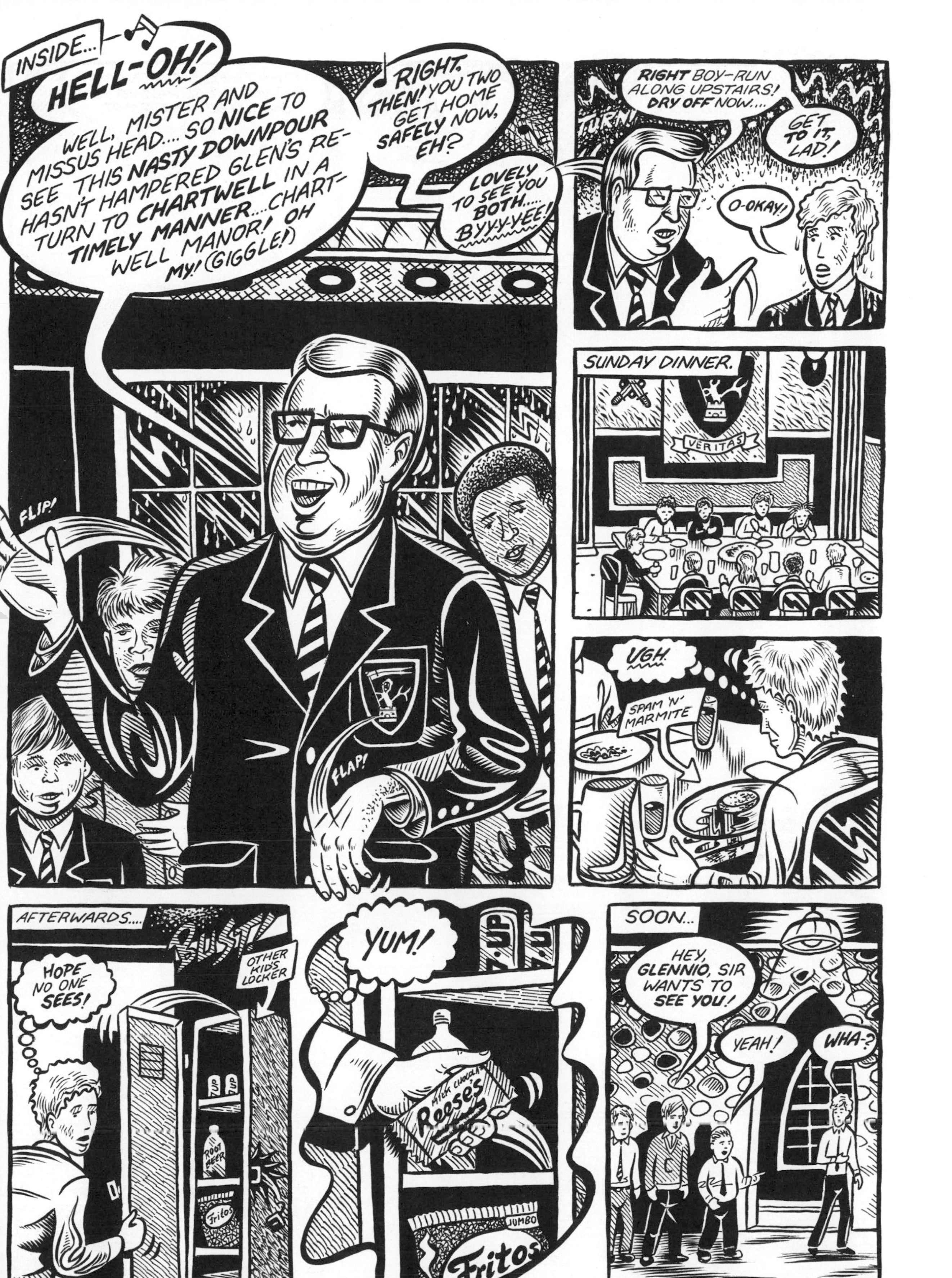
INSIDE...
HELL-OH!
WELL, MISTER AND MISSUS HEAD.... SO NICE TO SEE THIS NASTY DOWNPOUR HASN'T HAMPERED GLEN'S RETURN TO CHARTWELL IN A TIMELY MANNER....CHARTWELL MANOR! OH MY! (GIGGLE!)
RIGHT. THEN! YOU TWO GET HOME SAFELY NOW, EH?
LOVELY TO SEE YOU BOTH..... BYYY-YEE!
FLIP!
FLAP!
RIGHT BOY–RUN ALONG UPSTAIRS! DRY OFF NOW....
GET TO IT, LAD!
O-OKAY!
SUNDAY DINNER.
VERITAS
UGH.
SPAM 'N' MARMITE
AFTERWARDS....
HOPE NO ONE SEES!
OTHER KID'S LOCKER
ROOT BEER
Fritos
YUM!
7-UP
Reese's
JUMBO
Fritos
SOON...
HEY, GLENNIO, SIR WANTS TO SEE YOU!
YEAH!
WHA-?

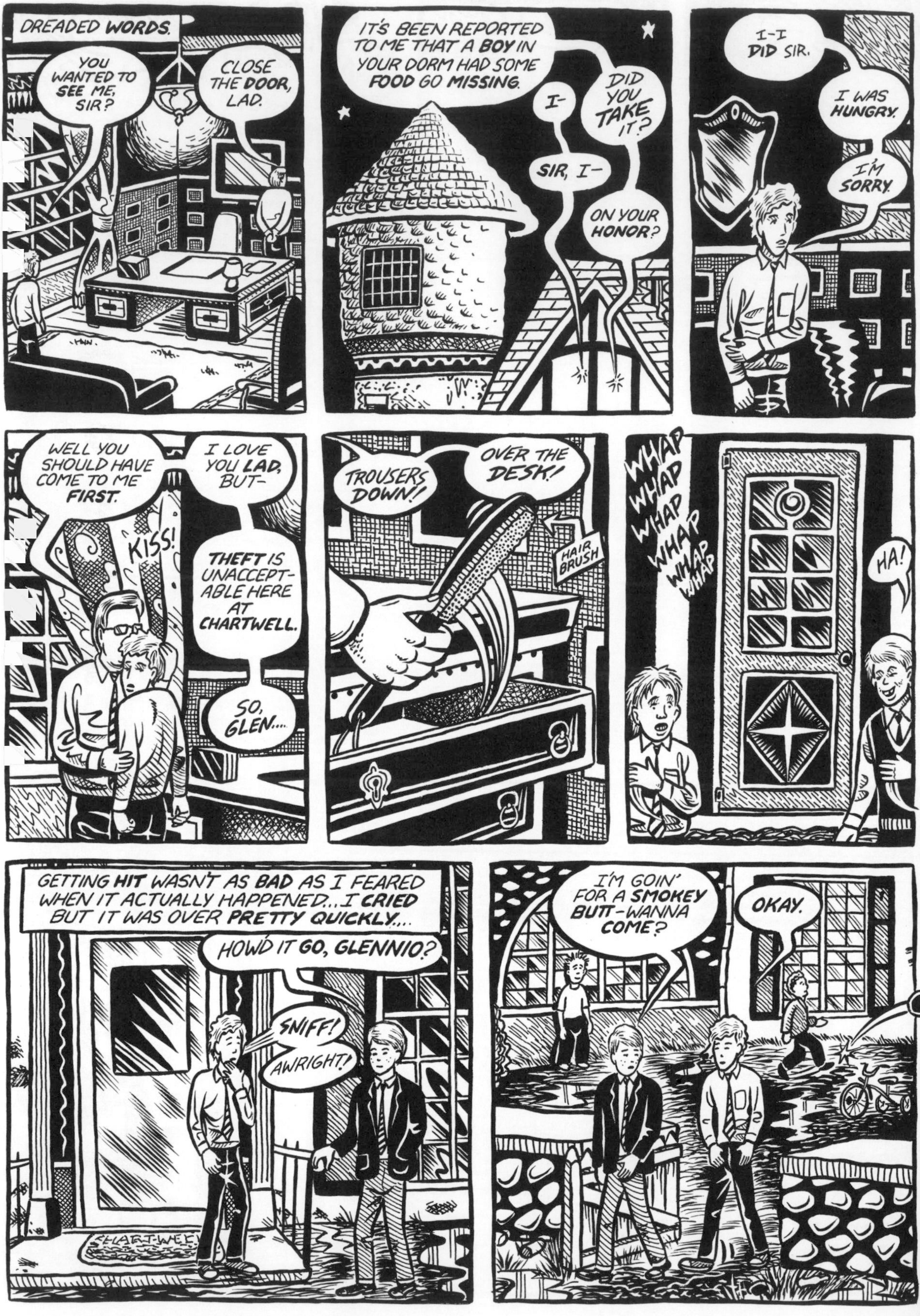

DREADED WORDS.
YOU WANTED TO SEE ME, SIR?
CLOSE THE DOOR, LAD.
IT'S BEEN REPORTED TO ME THAT A BOY IN YOUR DORM HAD SOME FOOD GO MISSING.
I-
DID YOU TAKE IT?
SIR, I-
ON YOUR HONOR?
I-I DID SIR.
I WAS HUNGRY.
I'M SORRY.
WELL YOU SHOULD HAVE COME TO ME FIRST.
I LOVE YOU LAD, BUT-
KISS!
THEFT IS UNACCEPTABLE HERE AT CHARTWELL.
SO, GLEN....
TROUSERS DOWN!
OVER THE DESK!
HAIR BRUSH
WHAP WHAP WHAP WHAP WHAP WHAP
HA!
GETTING HIT WASN'T AS BAD AS I FEARED WHEN IT ACTUALLY HAPPENED... I CRIED BUT IT WAS OVER PRETTY QUICKLY....
HOW'D IT GO, GLENNIO?
SNIFF!
AWRIGHT!
I'M GOIN' FOR A SMOKEY BUTT-WANNA COME?
OKAY.

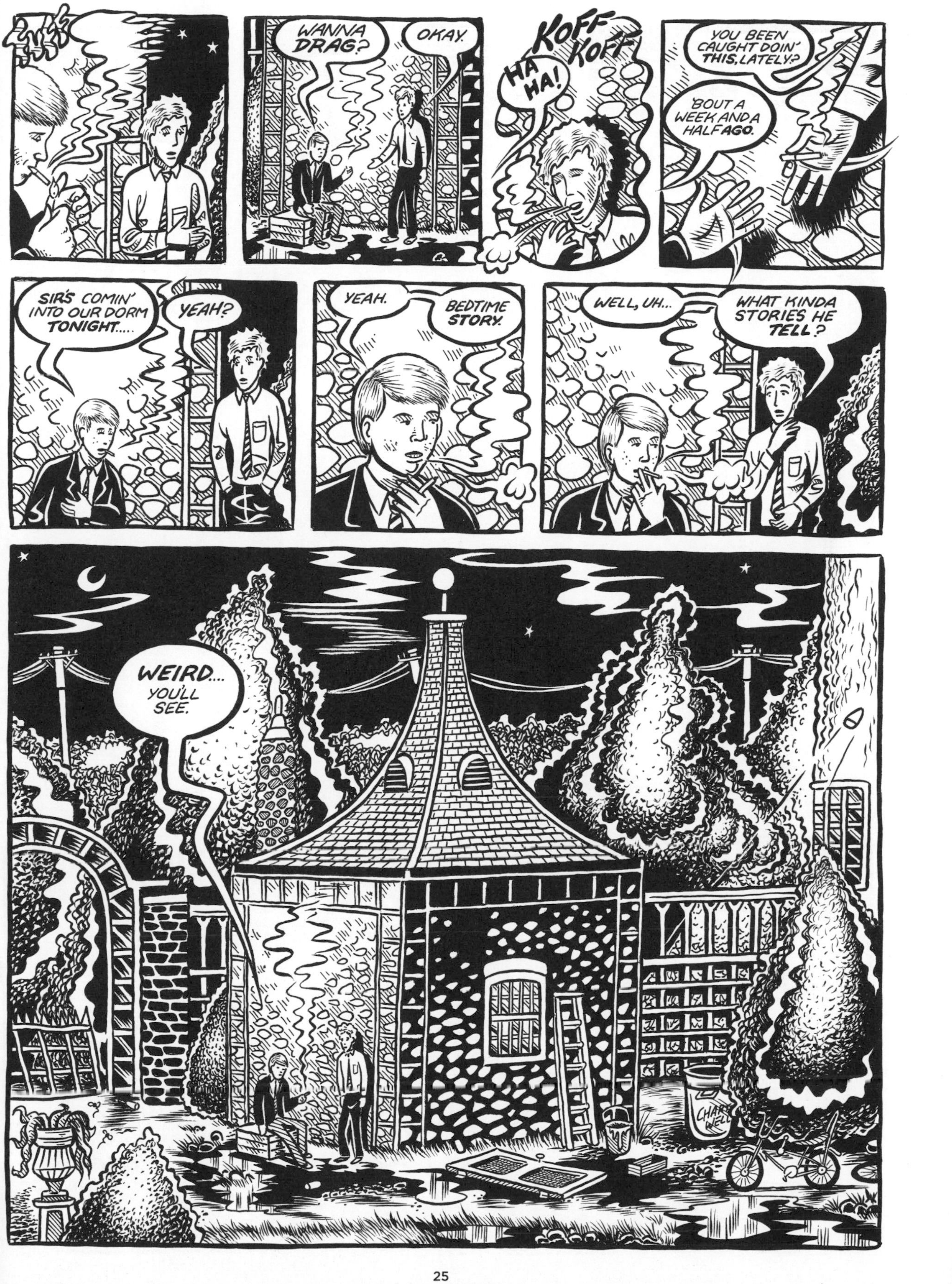

WANNA DRAG?
OKAY.
KOFF KOFF
HA HA!
YOU BEEN CAUGHT DOIN' THIS, LATELY?
'BOUT A WEEK AND A HALF AGO.
SIR'S COMIN' INTO OUR DORM TONIGHT.....
YEAH?
YEAH.
BEDTIME STORY.
WELL, UH...
WHAT KINDA STORIES HE TELL?
WEIRD.... YOU'LL SEE.

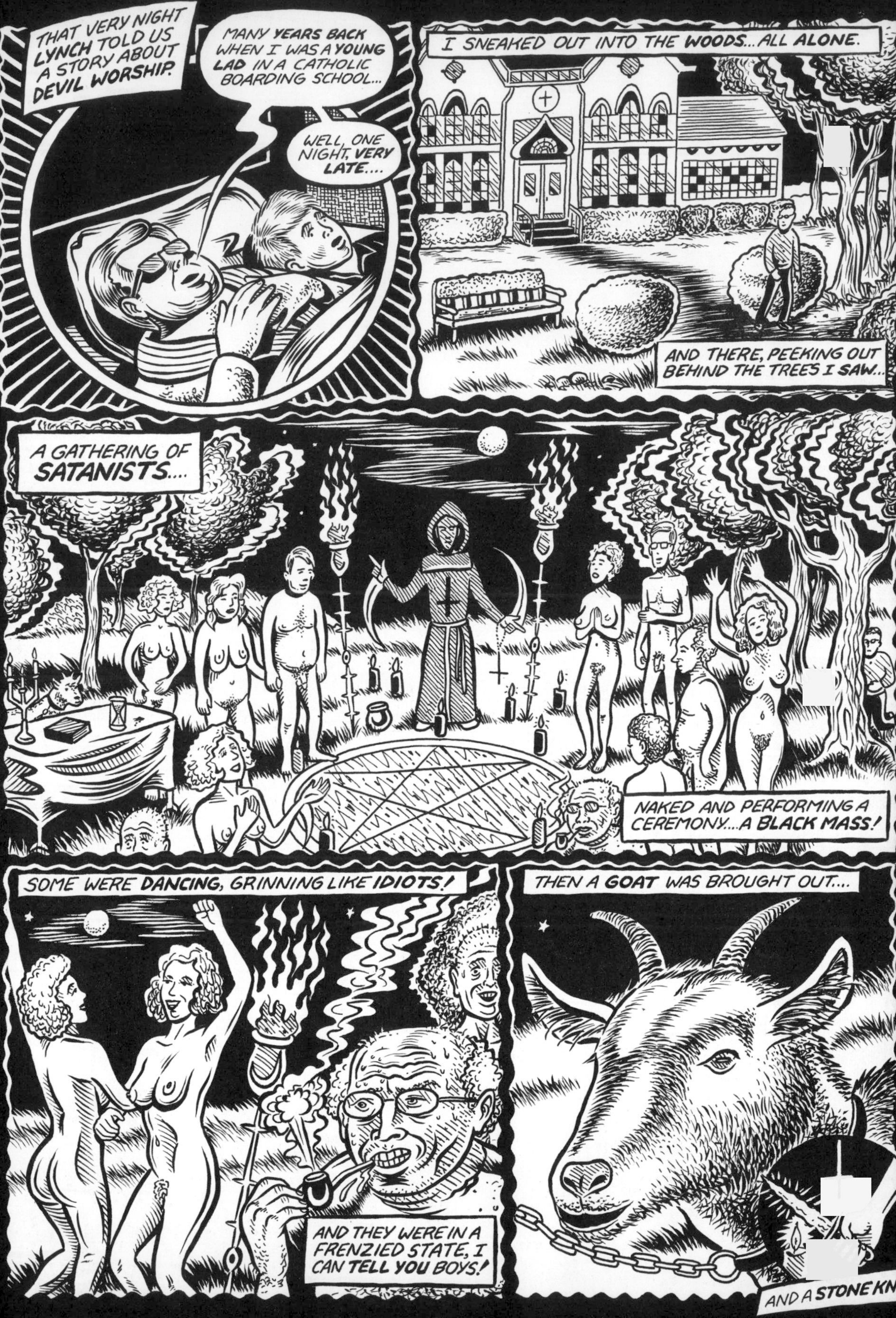
THAT VERY NIGHT LYNCH TOLD US A STORY ABOUT DEVIL WORSHIP.
MANY YEARS BACK WHEN I WAS A YOUNG LAD IN A CATHOLIC BOARDING SCHOOL...
WELL, ONE NIGHT, VERY LATE....
I SNEAKED OUT INTO THE WOODS... ALL ALONE.
AND THERE, PEEKING OUT BEHIND THE TREES I SAW...
A GATHERING OF SATANISTS....
NAKED AND PERFORMING A CEREMONY... A BLACK MASS!
SOME WERE DANCING, GRINNING LIKE IDIOTS!
AND THEY WERE IN A FRENZIED STATE, I CAN TELL YOU BOYS!
THEN A GOAT WAS BROUGHT OUT....
AND A STONE KN

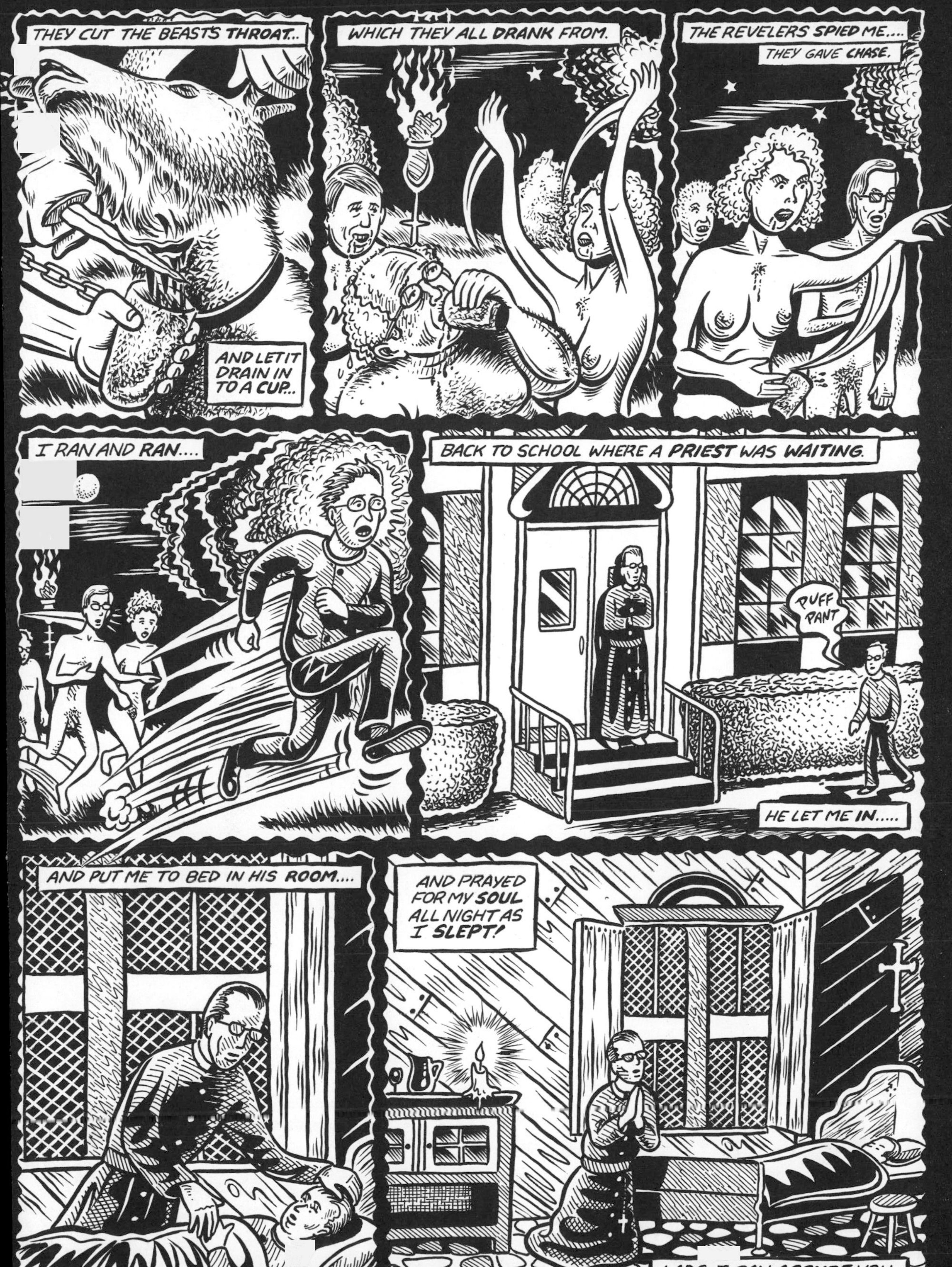
THEY CUT THE BEAST'S THROAT...
AND LET IT DRAIN IN TO A CUP...
WHICH THEY ALL DRANK FROM.
THE REVELERS SPIED ME....
THEY GAVE CHASE.
I RAN AND RAN....
BACK TO SCHOOL WHERE A PRIEST WAS WAITING.
PUFF PANT
HE LET ME IN.....
AND PUT ME TO BED IN HIS ROOM....
AND PRAYED FOR MY SOUL ALL NIGHT AS I SLEPT!
LADS, I CAN ASSURE YOU...

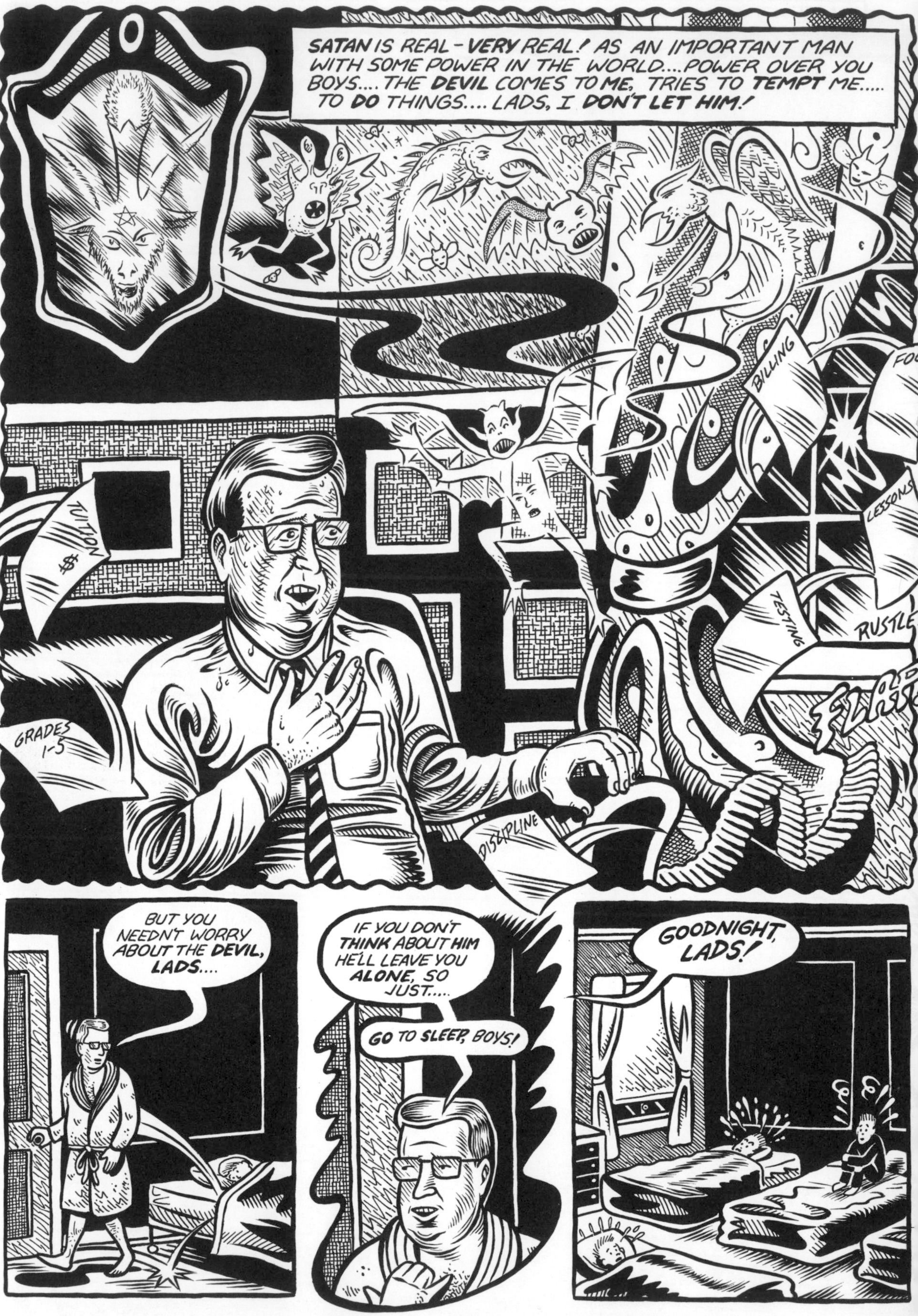

SATAN IS REAL - VERY REAL! AS AN IMPORTANT MAN WITH SOME POWER IN THE WORLD.... POWER OVER YOU BOYS.... THE DEVIL COMES TO ME, TRIES TO TEMPT ME..... TO DO THINGS.... LADS, I DON'T LET HIM!
TUITION
BILLING
LESSONS
TESTING
RUSTLE
GRADES 1-5
DISCIPLINE
BUT YOU NEEDN'T WORRY ABOUT THE DEVIL, LADS....
IF YOU DON'T THINK ABOUT HIM HE'LL LEAVE YOU ALONE, SO JUST.....
GO TO SLEEP, BOYS!
GOODNIGHT, LADS!

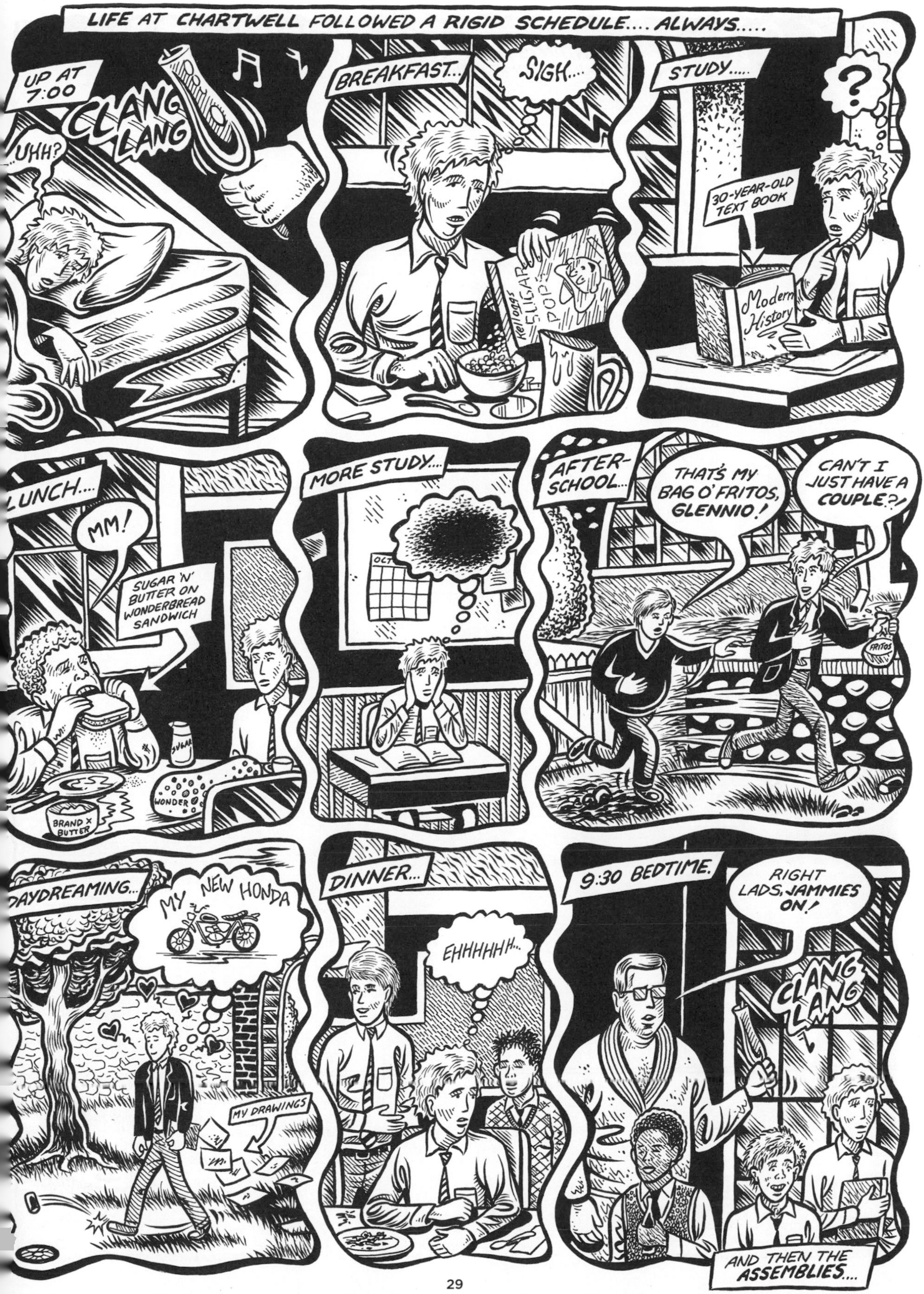

LIFE AT CHARTWELL FOLLOWED A RIGID SCHEDULE.... ALWAYS.....
UP AT 7:00
CLANG LANG
UHH?
BREAKFAST...
SIGH...
Kellogg's SUGAR POPS
STUDY.....
?
30-YEAR-OLD TEXT BOOK
Modern History
LUNCH....
MM!
SUGAR 'N' BUTTER ON WONDERBREAD SANDWICH
SUGAR
WONDER
BRAND X BUTTER
MORE STUDY....
OCT
AFTER-SCHOOL...
THAT'S MY BAG O' FRITOS, GLENNIO!
CAN'T I JUST HAVE A COUPLE?!
FRITOS
DAYDREAMING...
MY NEW HONDA
MY DRAWINGS
DINNER...
EHHHHHH...
9:30 BEDTIME.
RIGHT LADS, JAMMIES ON!
CLANG LANG
AND THEN THE ASSEMBLIES....

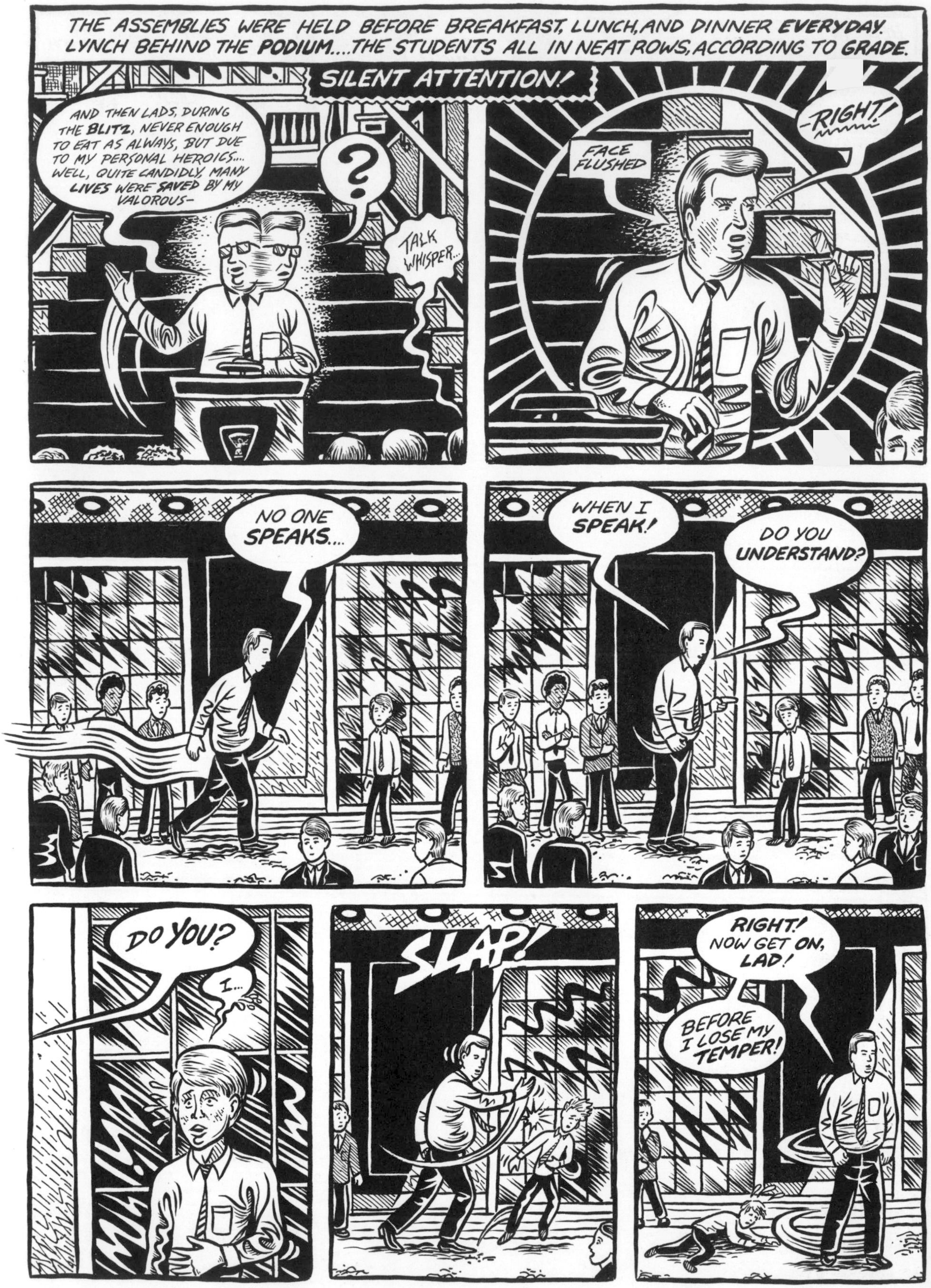
THE ASSEMBLIES WERE HELD BEFORE BREAKFAST, LUNCH, AND DINNER EVERYDAY. LYNCH BEHIND THE PODIUM....THE STUDENTS ALL IN NEAT ROWS, ACCORDING TO GRADE.
SILENT ATTENTION!
AND THEN LADS, DURING THE BLITZ, NEVER ENOUGH TO EAT AS ALWAYS, BUT DUE TO MY PERSONAL HEROICS.... WELL, QUITE CANDIDLY, MANY LIVES WERE SAVED BY MY VALOROUS-
?
TALK WHISPER...
FACE FLUSHED
-RIGHT!-
NO ONE SPEAKS....
WHEN I SPEAK!
DO YOU UNDERSTAND?
DO YOU?
I...
SLAP!
RIGHT! NOW GET ON, LAD!
BEFORE I LOSE MY TEMPER!

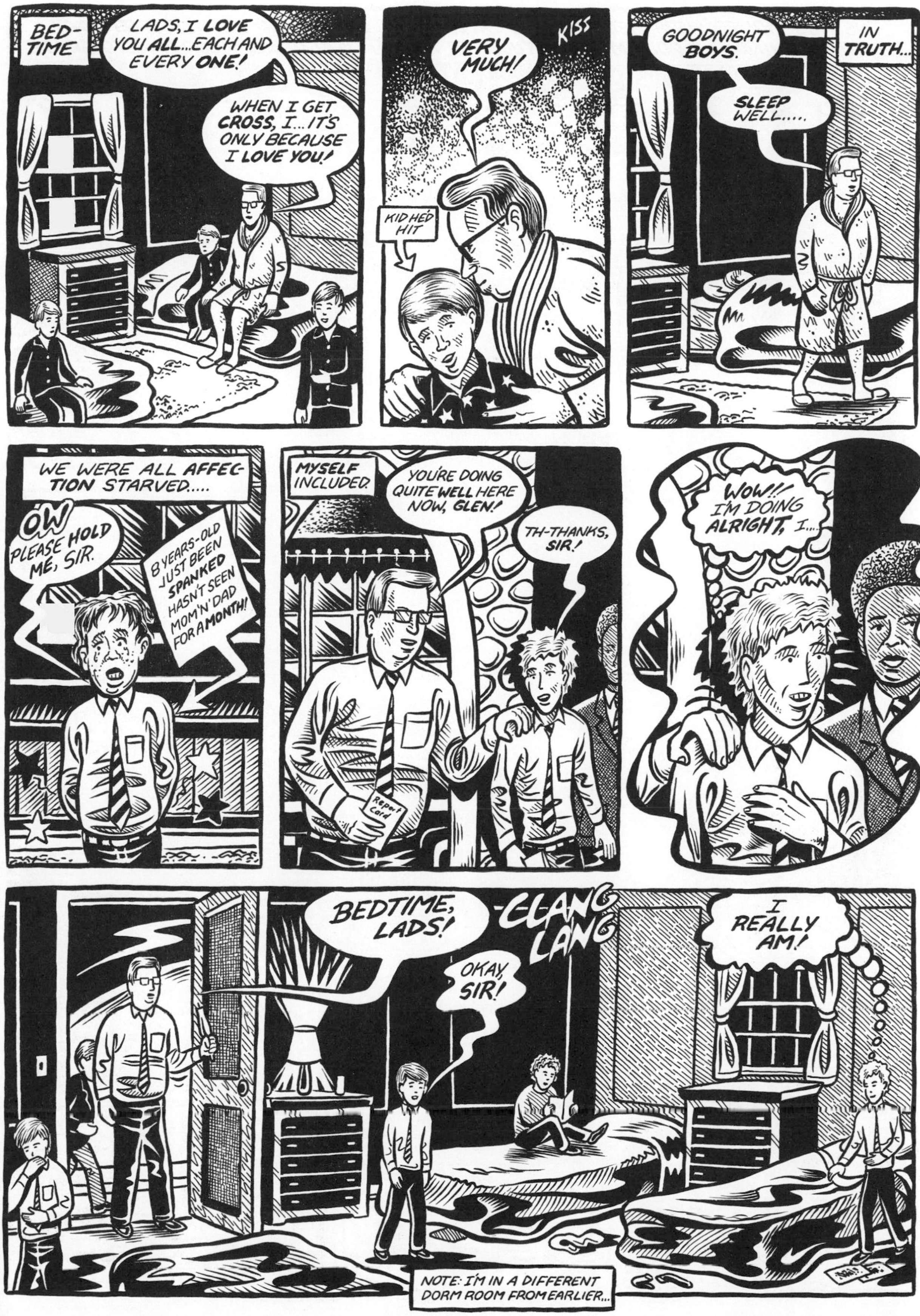
BED-TIME
LADS, I LOVE YOU ALL...EACH AND EVERY ONE!
WHEN I GET CROSS, I...IT'S ONLY BECAUSE I LOVE YOU!
VERY MUCH!
KISS
KID HE'D HIT
GOODNIGHT BOYS.
SLEEP WELL.....
IN TRUTH...
WE WERE ALL AFFEC-TION STARVED.....
OW
PLEASE HOLD ME, SIR.
8 YEARS-OLD JUST BEEN SPANKED HASN'T SEEN MOM 'N' DAD FOR A MONTH!
MYSELF INCLUDED.
YOU'RE DOING QUITE WELL HERE NOW, GLEN!
TH-THANKS, SIR!
Report Card
WOW!! I'M DOING ALRIGHT, I...
BEDTIME, LADS!
CLANG
CLANG
OKAY, SIR!
I REALLY AM!
NOTE: I'M IN A DIFFERENT DORM ROOM FROM EARLIER...

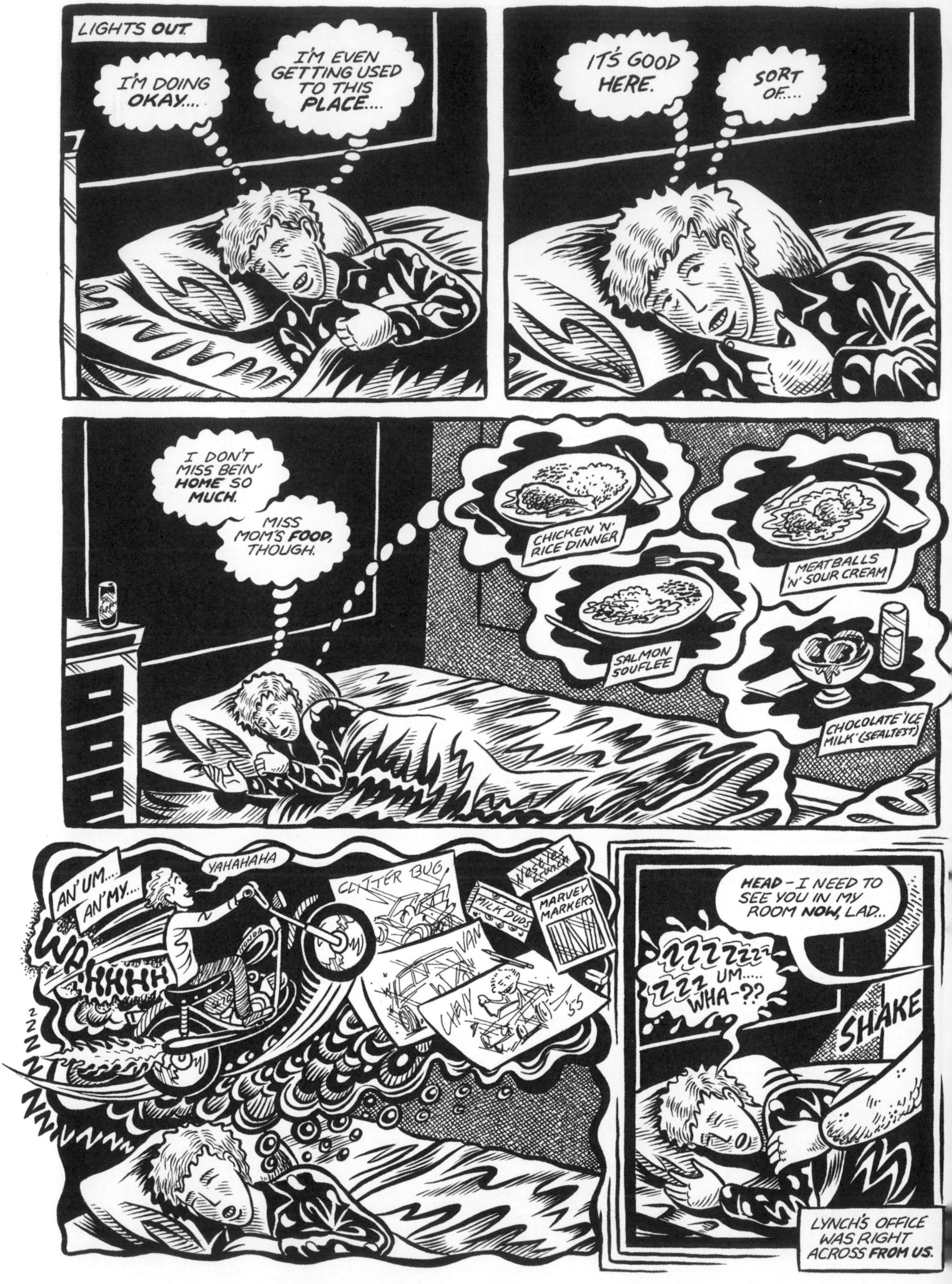
LIGHTS OUT.
I'M DOING OKAY....
I'M EVEN GETTING USED TO THIS PLACE....
IT'S GOOD HERE.
SORT OF....
I DON'T MISS BEIN' HOME SO MUCH.
MISS MOM'S FOOD, THOUGH.
CHICKEN 'N' RICE DINNER
MEATBALLS 'N' SOUR CREAM
SALMON SOUFLEE
CHOCOLATE 'ICE MILK' (SEALTEST)
AN'UM....
AN'MY....
YAHAHAHA
WAHHHHH
CLUTTER BUG
Nestles Crunch
MILK DUDS
MARVEY MARKERS
VAN
CHEVY
55
HEAD - I NEED TO SEE YOU IN MY ROOM NOW, LAD...
ZZZZZZZ UM..... ZZZ WHA-??
SHAKE
LYNCH'S OFFICE WAS RIGHT ACROSS FROM US.

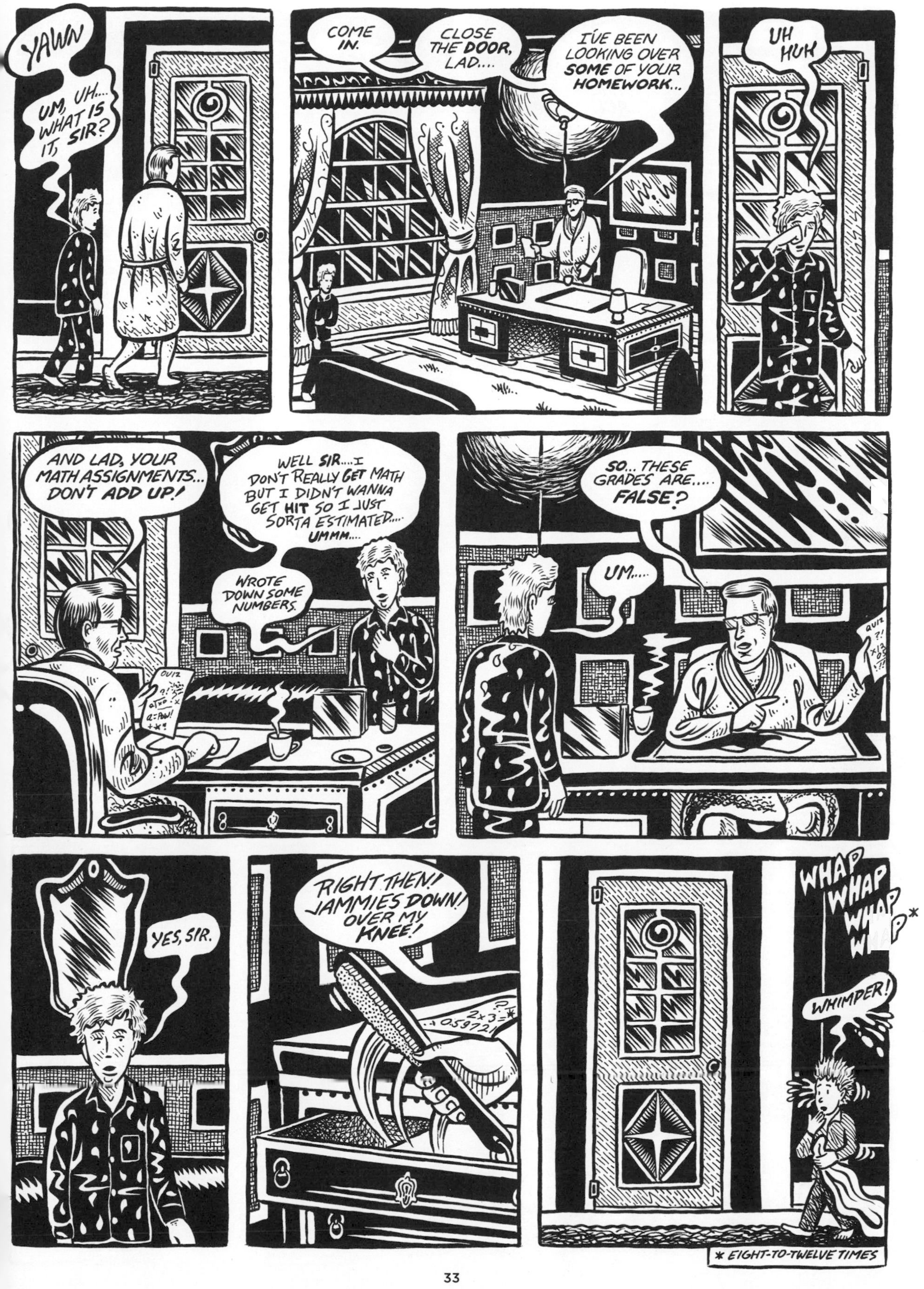
YAWN
UM, UH.... WHAT IS IT, SIR?
COME IN.
CLOSE THE DOOR, LAD....
I'VE BEEN LOOKING OVER SOME OF YOUR HOMEWORK...
UH HUH
AND LAD, YOUR MATH ASSIGNMENTS... DON'T ADD UP!
WELL SIR....I DON'T REALLY GET MATH BUT I DIDN'T WANNA GET HIT SO I JUST SORTA ESTIMATED.... UMMM....
WROTE DOWN SOME NUMBERS.
SO... THESE GRADES ARE..... FALSE?
UM.....
YES, SIR.
RIGHT THEN! JAMMIES DOWN! OVER MY KNEE!
WHAP WHAP WHAP*
WHIMPER!
* EIGHT-TO-TWELVE TIMES

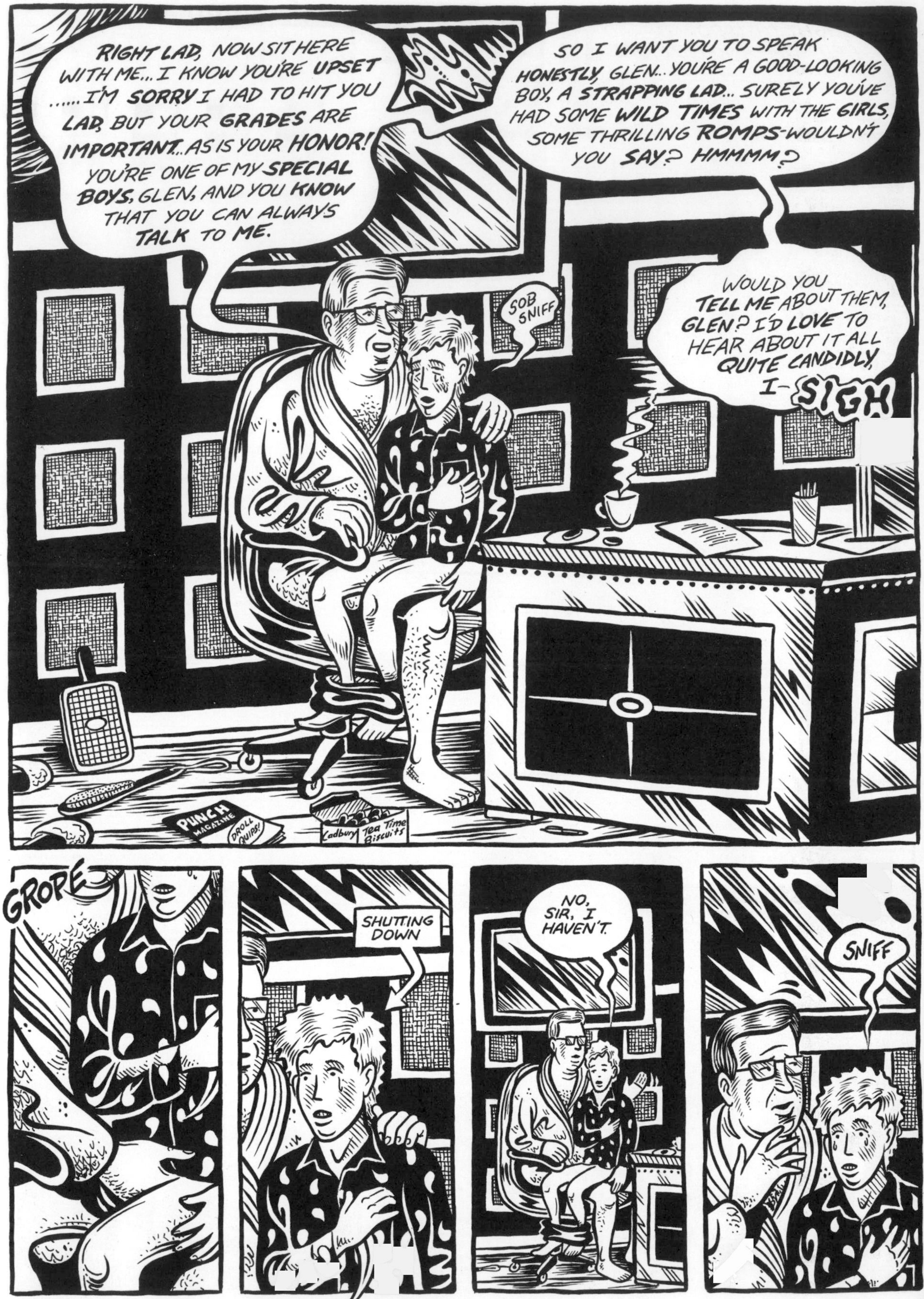
RIGHT LAD, NOW SIT HERE WITH ME... I KNOW YOU'RE UPSET ...... I'M SORRY I HAD TO HIT YOU LAD, BUT YOUR GRADES ARE IMPORTANT... AS IS YOUR HONOR! YOU'RE ONE OF MY SPECIAL BOYS, GLEN, AND YOU KNOW THAT YOU CAN ALWAYS TALK TO ME.
SO I WANT YOU TO SPEAK HONESTLY, GLEN... YOU'RE A GOOD-LOOKING BOY, A STRAPPING LAD... SURELY YOU'VE HAD SOME WILD TIMES WITH THE GIRLS, SOME THRILLING ROMPS-WOULDN'T YOU SAY? HMMMM?
SOB SNIFF
WOULD YOU TELL ME ABOUT THEM, GLEN? I'D LOVE TO HEAR ABOUT IT ALL QUITE CANDIDLY, I- SIGH
PUNCH MAGAZINE
DROLL QUIPS!
Cadbury Tea Time Biscuits
GROPE
SHUTTING DOWN
NO, SIR, I HAVEN'T.
SNIFF

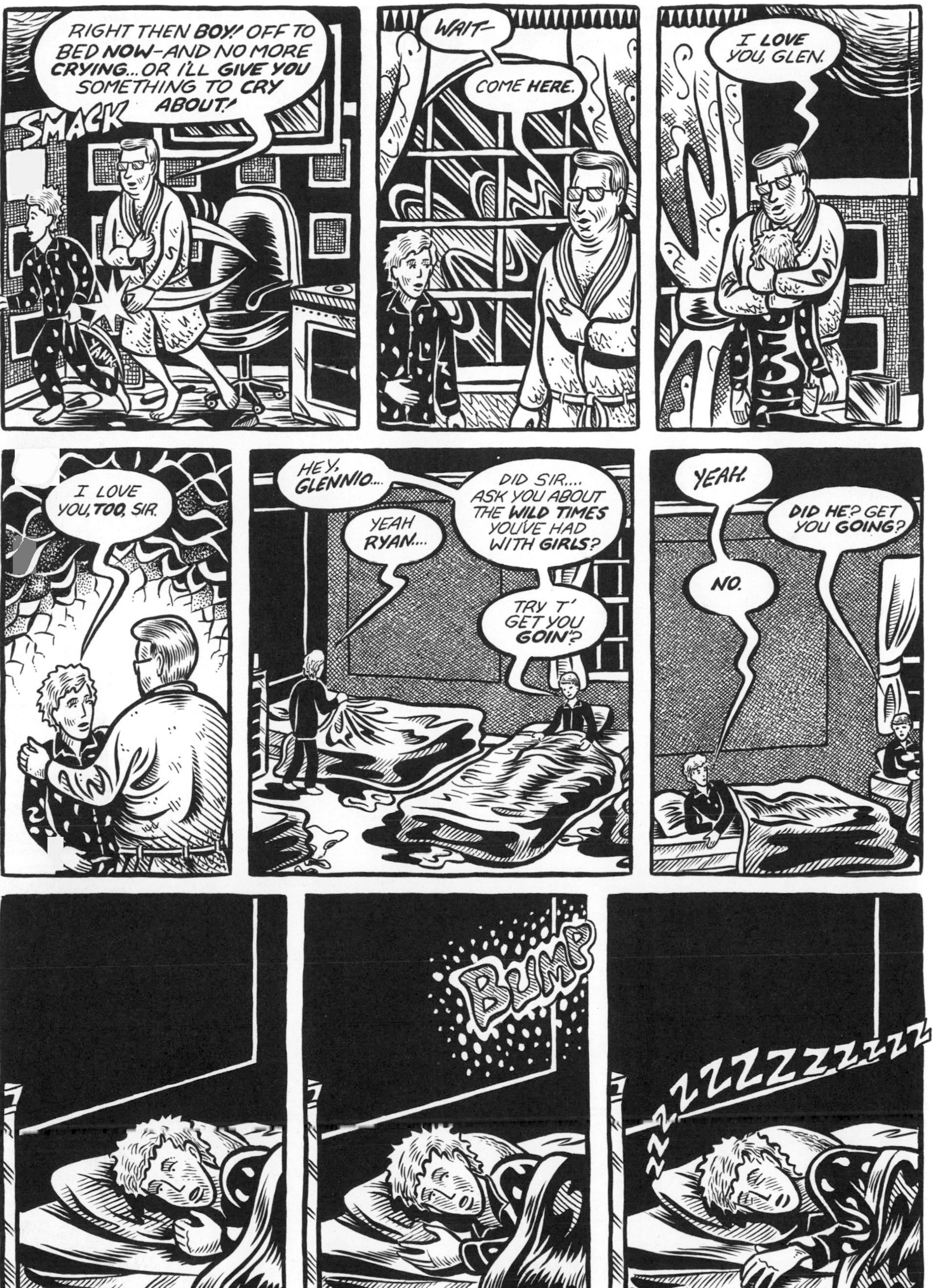
RIGHT THEN BOY! OFF TO BED NOW–AND NO MORE CRYING...OR I'LL GIVE YOU SOMETHING TO CRY ABOUT!
SMACK
YANK
WAIT–
COME HERE.
I LOVE YOU, GLEN.
I LOVE YOU, TOO, SIR.
HEY, GLENNIO...
YEAH RYAN...
DID SIR.... ASK YOU ABOUT THE WILD TIMES YOU'VE HAD WITH GIRLS?
TRY T' GET YOU GOIN'?
YEAH.
DID HE? GET YOU GOING?
NO.
BUMP
ZZZZZZZZZZZZZZZ

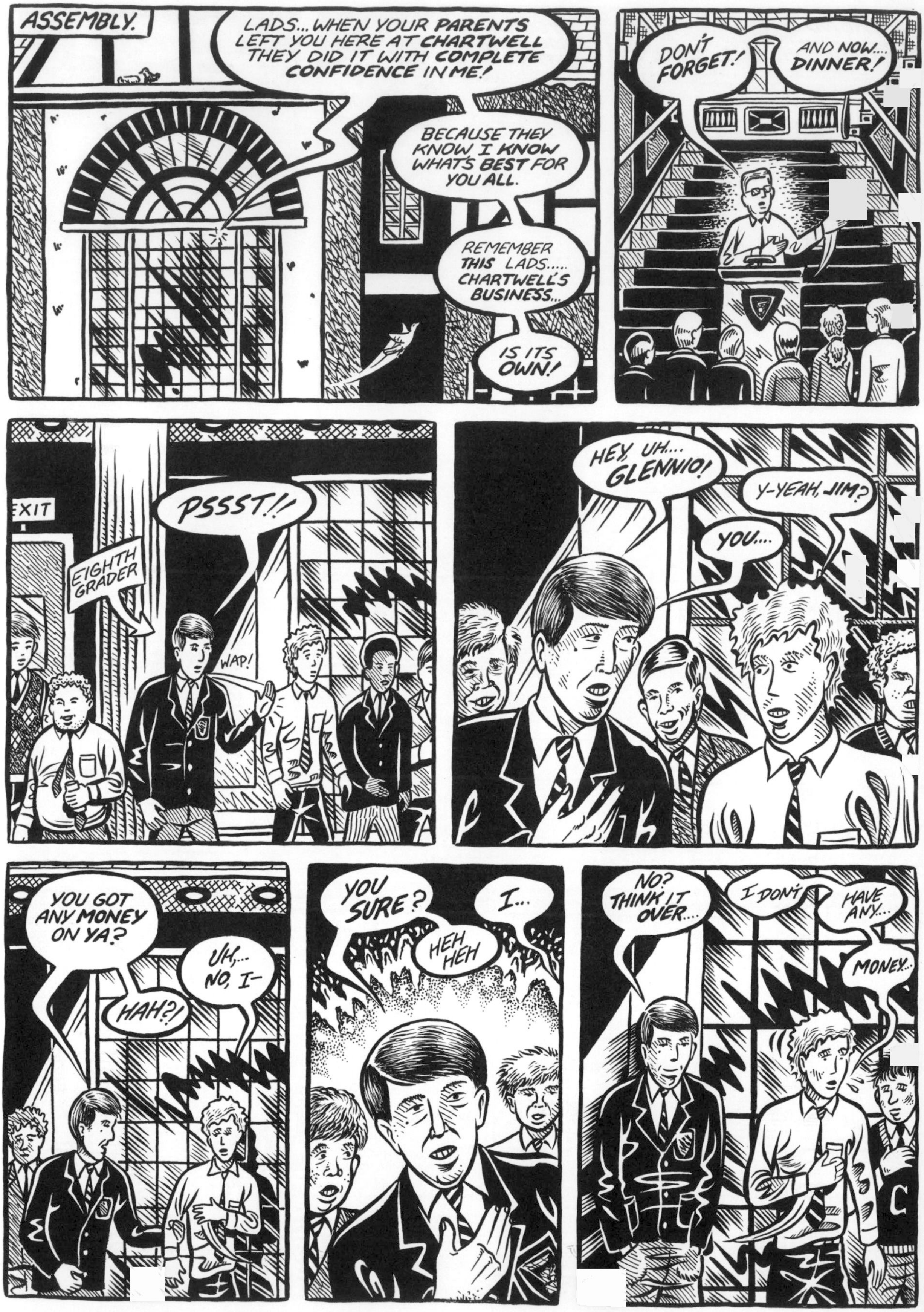
ASSEMBLY.
LADS... WHEN YOUR PARENTS LEFT YOU HERE AT CHARTWELL THEY DID IT WITH COMPLETE CONFIDENCE IN ME!
BECAUSE THEY KNOW I KNOW WHAT'S BEST FOR YOU ALL.
REMEMBER THIS LADS..... CHARTWELL'S BUSINESS...
IS ITS OWN!
DON'T FORGET!
AND NOW.... DINNER!
EXIT
EIGHTH GRADER
PSSST!!
WAP!
HEY, UH.... GLENNIO!
Y-YEAH, JIM?
YOU....
YOU GOT ANY MONEY ON YA?
HAH?!
UH,... NO, I-
YOU SURE?
I...
HEH HEH
NO? THINK IT OVER....
I DON'T
HAVE ANY...
MONEY...

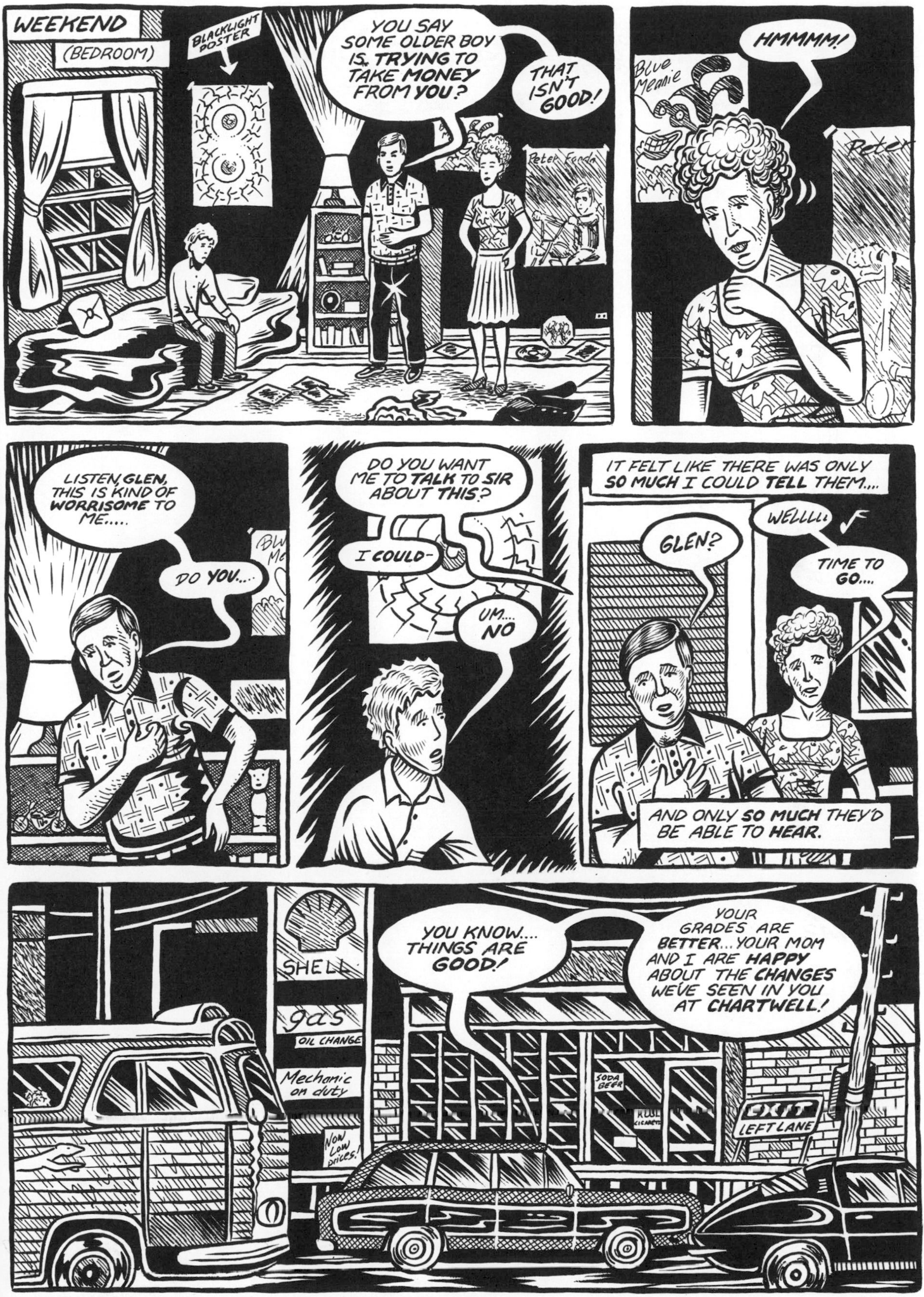
WEEKEND
(BEDROOM)
BLACKLIGHT POSTER
YOU SAY SOME OLDER BOY IS TRYING TO TAKE MONEY FROM YOU?
THAT ISN'T GOOD!
Peter Fonda
Blue Meanie
HMMMM!
LISTEN, GLEN, THIS IS KIND OF WORRISOME TO ME.....
DO YOU....
DO YOU WANT ME TO TALK TO SIR ABOUT THIS?
I COULD-
UM.... NO
IT FELT LIKE THERE WAS ONLY SO MUCH I COULD TELL THEM....
GLEN?
WELLLLL
TIME TO GO....
AND ONLY SO MUCH THEY'D BE ABLE TO HEAR.
SHELL
gas
OIL CHANGE
Mechanic on duty
NOW LOW prices!
SODA BEER
EXIT
LEFT LANE
YOU KNOW.... THINGS ARE GOOD!
YOUR GRADES ARE BETTER... YOUR MOM AND I ARE HAPPY ABOUT THE CHANGES WE'VE SEEN IN YOU AT CHARTWELL!

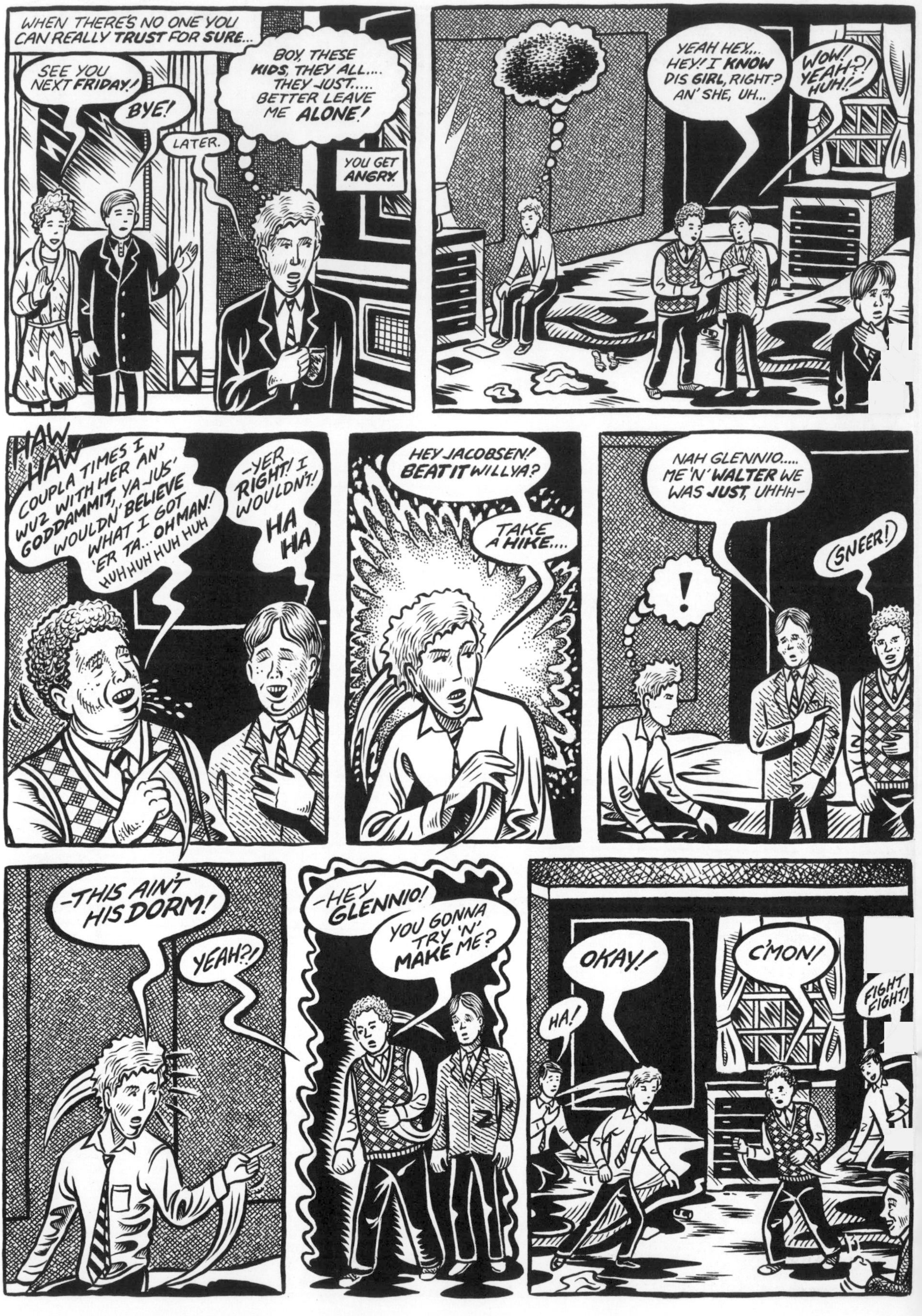
WHEN THERE'S NO ONE YOU CAN REALLY TRUST FOR SURE...
SEE YOU NEXT FRIDAY!
BYE!
LATER.
BOY, THESE KIDS, THEY ALL.... THEY JUST..... BETTER LEAVE ME ALONE!
YOU GET ANGRY.
YEAH HEY... HEY! I KNOW DIS GIRL, RIGHT? AN' SHE, UH...
WOW! YEAH?! HUH!!
HAW HAW
COUPLA TIMES I WUZ WITH HER AN' GODDAMMIT, YA JUS' WOULDN' BELIEVE WHAT I GOT 'ER TA... OH MAN! HUH HUH HUH HUH
-YER RIGHT! I WOULDN'T!
HA HA
HEY JACOBSEN! BEAT IT WILLYA?
TAKE A HIKE....
NAH GLENNIO..... ME 'N' WALTER WE WAS JUST, UHHH-
!
(SNEER!)
-THIS AIN'T HIS DORM!
YEAH?!
-HEY GLENNIO!
YOU GONNA TRY 'N' MAKE ME?
HA!
OKAY!
C'MON!
FIGHT FIGHT!

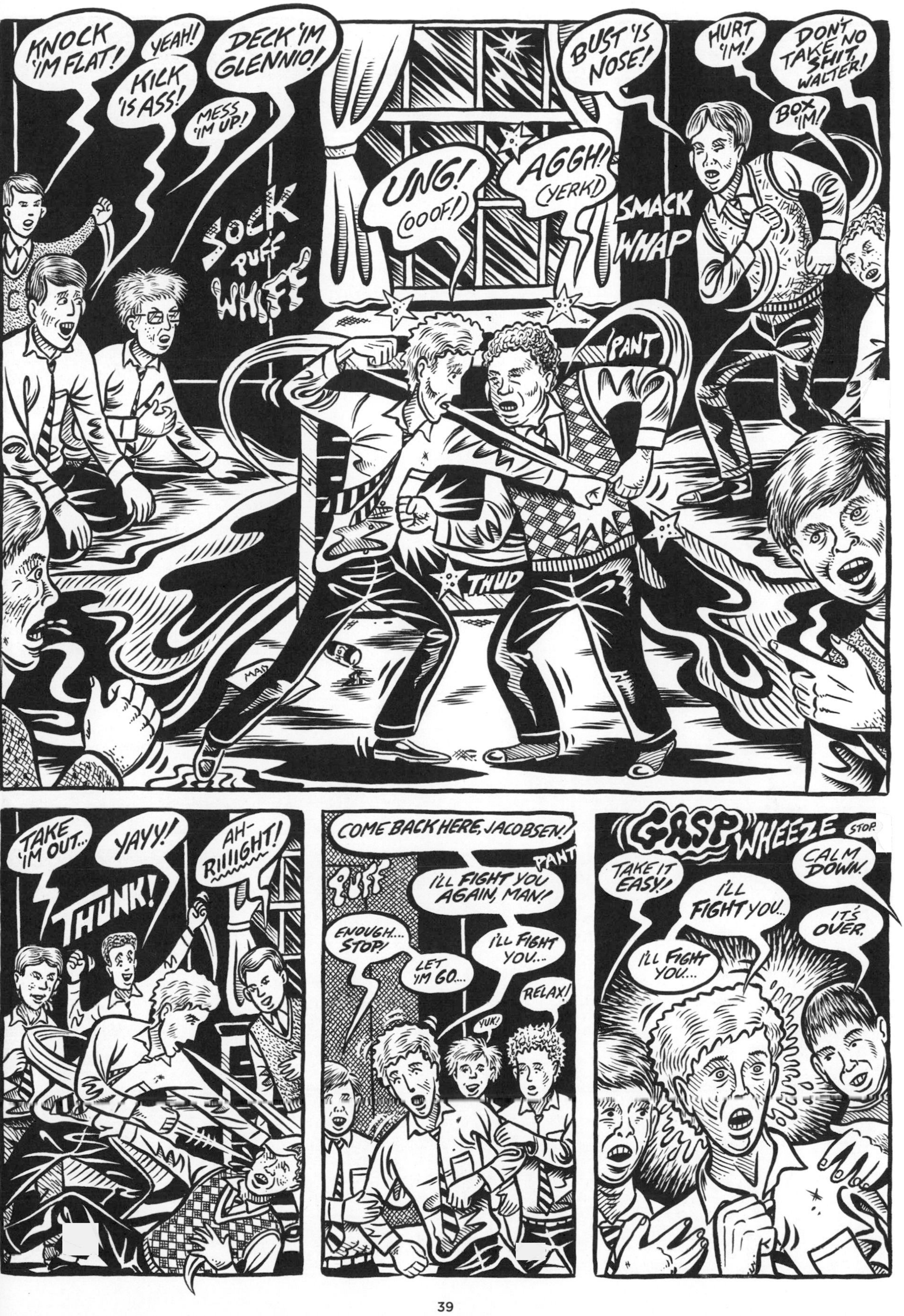
KNOCK 'IM FLAT!
YEAH!
KICK 'IS ASS!
DECK 'IM GLENNIO!
MESS 'IM UP!
SOCK
PUFF
WHIFF
UNG! (OOOF!)
AGGH! (YERK!)
BUST 'IS NOSE!
SMACK
WHAP
HURT 'IM!
DON'T TAKE NO SHIT, WALTER!
BOX 'IM!
PANT
THUD
TAKE 'IM OUT...
YAYY!
AH-RIIIIGHT!
THUNK!
COME BACK HERE, JACOBSEN!
PANT
PUFF
I'LL FIGHT YOU AGAIN, MAN!
ENOUGH... STOP!
LET 'IM GO...
I'LL FIGHT YOU...
RELAX!
YUK!
GASP
WHEEZE
STOP
TAKE IT EASY!
CALM DOWN.
I'LL FIGHT YOU...
IT'S OVER.
I'LL FIGHT YOU...

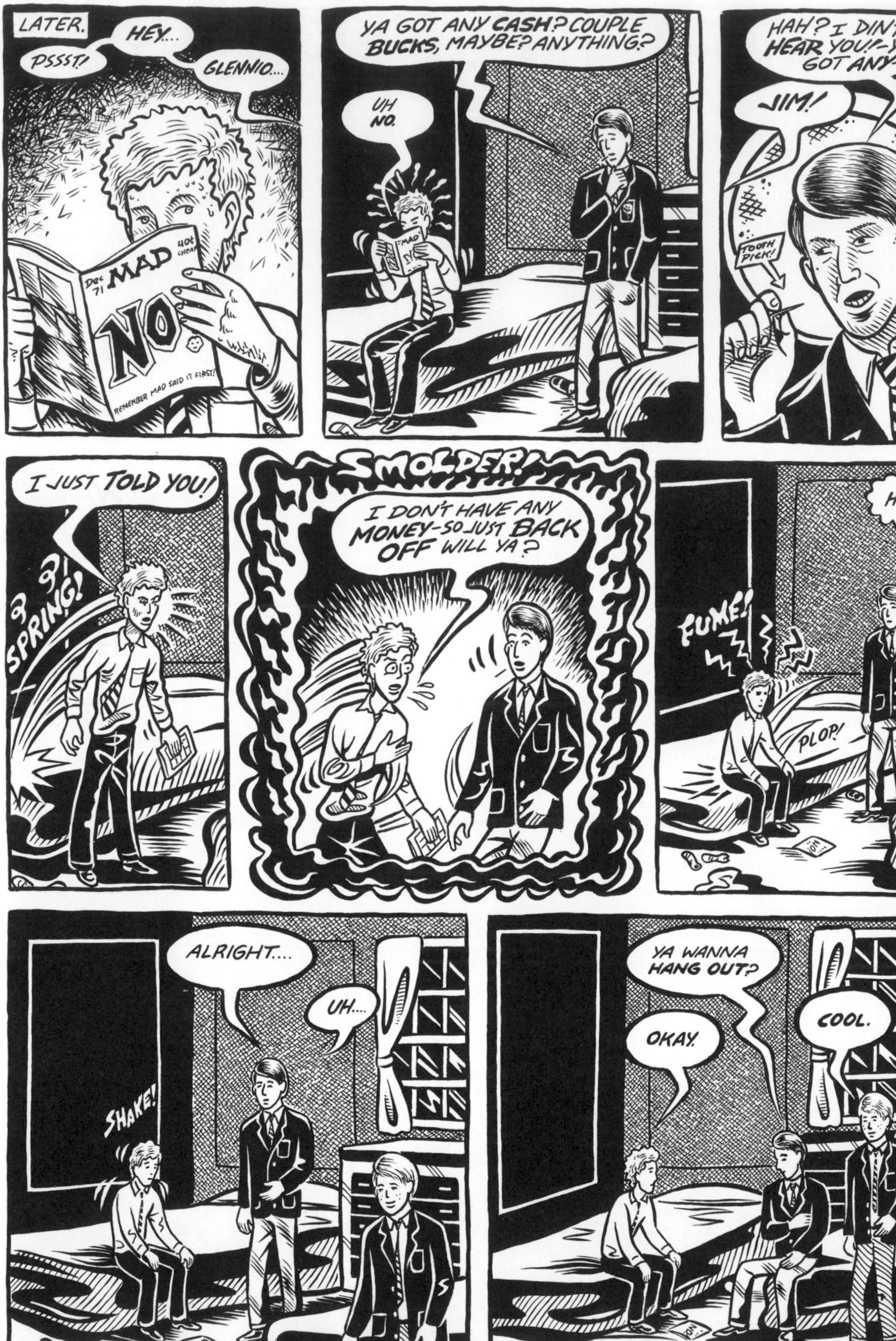
LATER.
PSSST!
HEY....
GLENNIO....
Dec 71 MAD 40¢ CHEAP
NO
REMEMBER MAD SAID IT FIRST!
YA GOT ANY CASH? COUPLE BUCKS, MAYBE? ANYTHING?
UH NO.
HAH? I DIN'T HEAR YOU!-YOU GOT ANY-
JIM!
TOOTH PICK!
I JUST TOLD YOU!
SPRING!
SMOLDER!
I DON'T HAVE ANY MONEY-SO JUST BACK OFF WILL YA?
HUH!
FUME!
PLOP!
ALRIGHT....
UH....
SHAKE!
YA WANNA HANG OUT?
OKAY.
COOL.

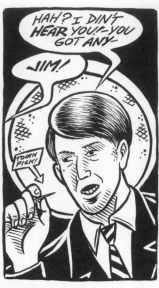

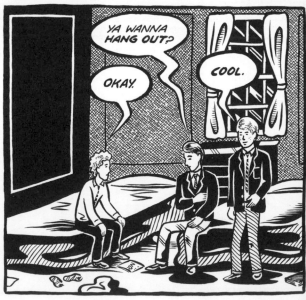

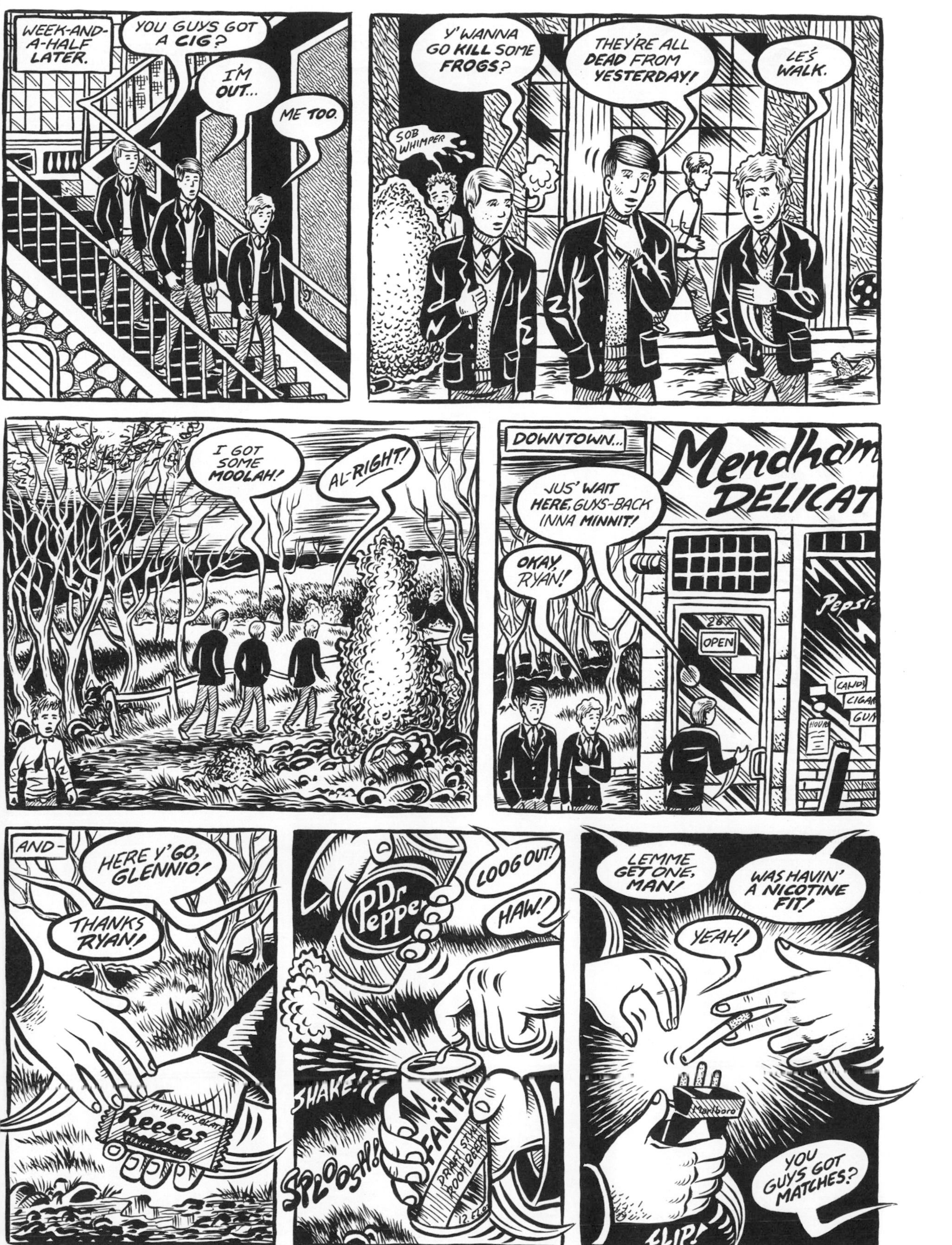
WEEK-AND-A-HALF LATER.
YOU GUYS GOT A CIG?
I'M OUT...
ME TOO.
SOB WHIMPER
Y'WANNA GO KILL SOME FROGS?
THEY'RE ALL DEAD FROM YESTERDAY!
LE'S WALK.
I GOT SOME MOOLAH!
AL-RIGHT!
DOWNTOWN...
Mendham DELICAT
JUS' WAIT HERE, GUYS-BACK INNA MINNIT!
OKAY, RYAN!
OPEN
Pepsi
CANDY
CIGAR
GUM
AND-
HERE Y'GO, GLENNIO!
THANKS RYAN!
MILK CHOCOLATE Reeses
LOOG OUT!
HAW!
Dr Pepper
SHAKE!
SPLOOSH!
FANTA
LEMME GET ONE, MAN!
WAS HAVIN' A NICOTINE FIT!
YEAH!
Marlboro
YOU GUYS GOT MATCHES?
FLIP!

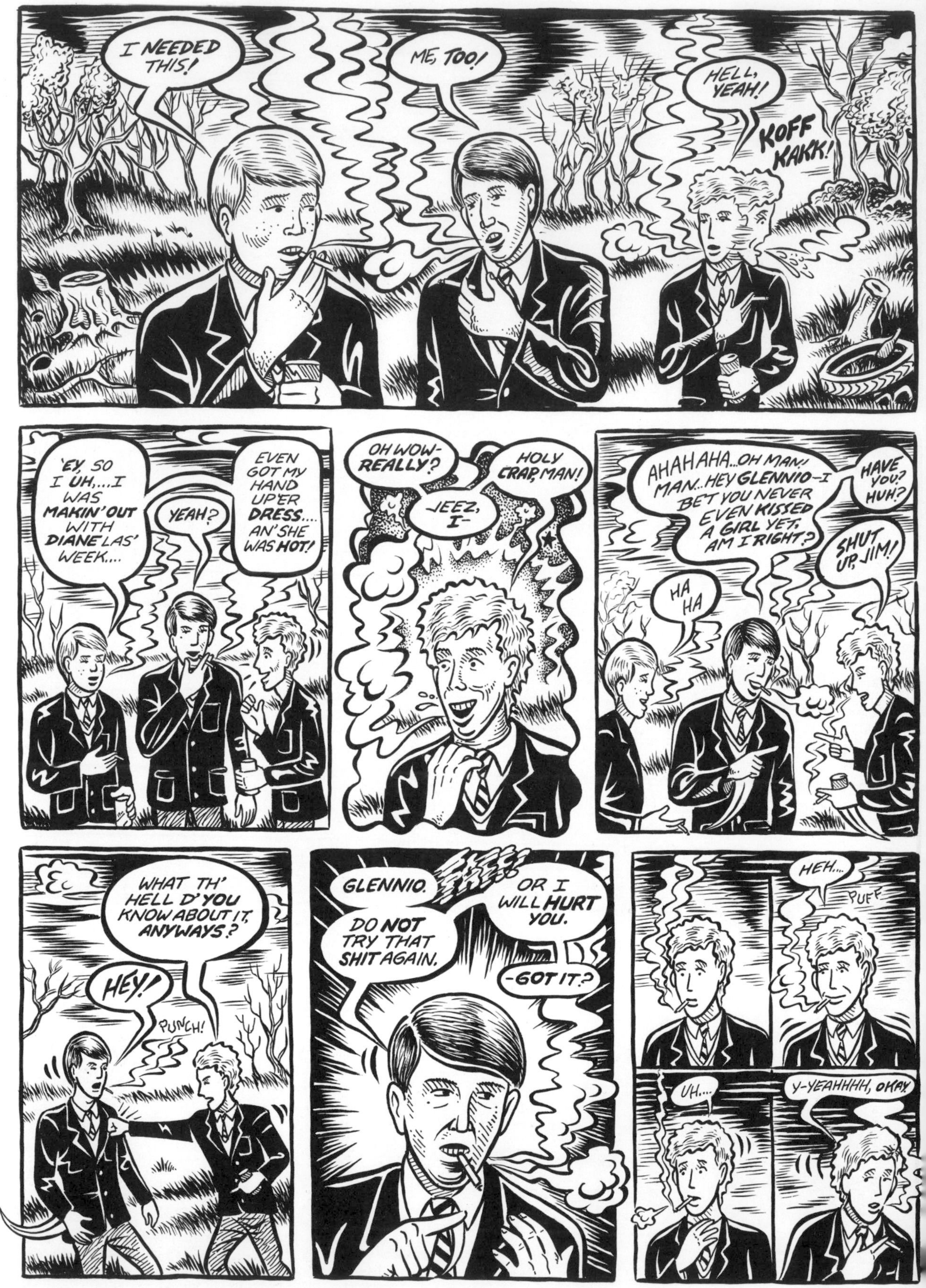
I NEEDED THIS!
ME, TOO!
HELL, YEAH!
KOFF KAKK!
'EY, SO I UH,...I WAS MAKIN' OUT WITH DIANE LAS' WEEK....
YEAH?
EVEN GOT MY HAND UP 'ER DRESS.... AN' SHE WAS HOT!
OH WOW- REALLY?
HOLY CRAP, MAN!
-JEEZ, I-
AHAHAHA...OH MAN! MAN...HEY GLENNIO-I BET YOU NEVER EVEN KISSED A GIRL YET, AM I RIGHT?
HAVE YOU? HUH?
HA HA
SHUT UP, JIM!
WHAT TH' HELL D'YOU KNOW ABOUT IT, ANYWAYS?
HEY!
PUNCH!
GLENNIO.
DO NOT TRY THAT SHIT AGAIN.
OR I WILL HURT YOU.
-GOT IT?
HEH...
PUFF
UH....
Y-YEAHHHH, OKAY.

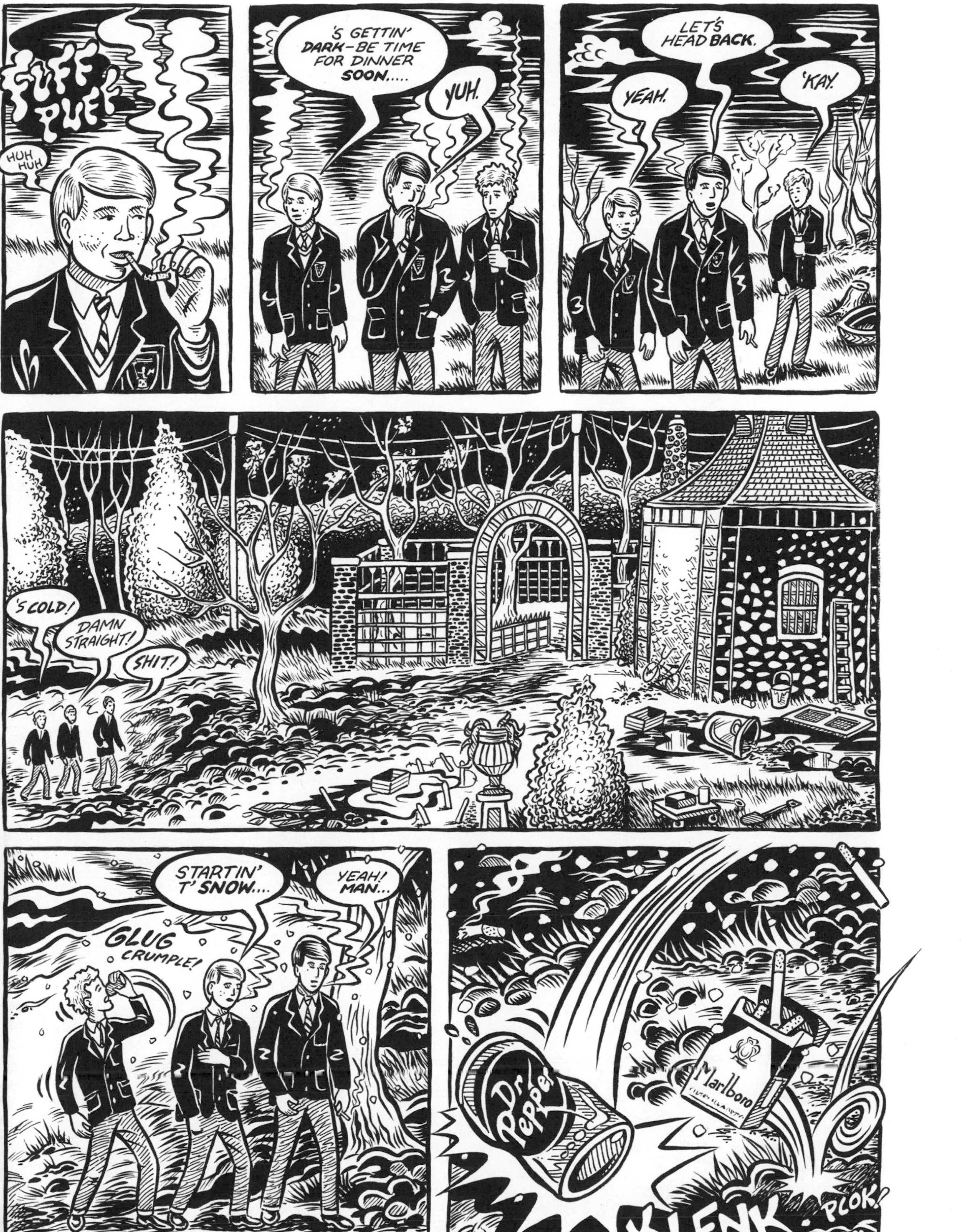

PUFF PUFF
HUH HUH
'S GETTIN' DARK—BE TIME FOR DINNER SOON.....
YUH.
LET'S HEAD BACK.
YEAH.
'KAY.
'S COLD!
DAMN STRAIGHT!
SHIT!
STARTIN' T' SNOW....
YEAH! MAN...
GLUG
CRUMPLE!
Dr Pepper
Marlboro
KLENK
PLOK!

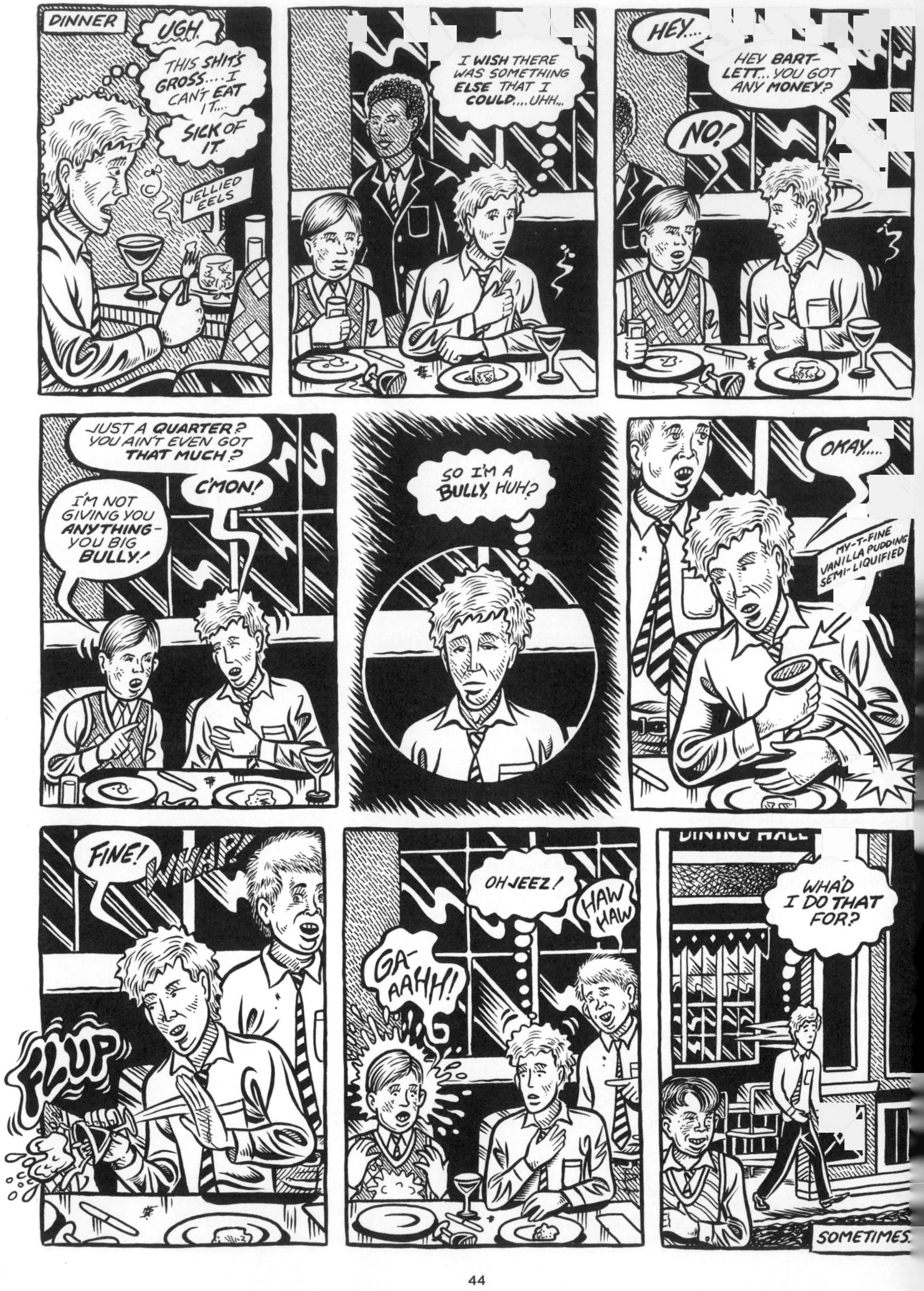

DINNER
UGH.
THIS SHIT'S GROSS.... I CAN'T EAT IT...
SICK OF IT.
JELLIED EELS
I WISH THERE WAS SOMETHING ELSE THAT I COULD.... UHH...
HEY....
HEY BARTLETT... YOU GOT ANY MONEY?
NO!
-JUST A QUARTER? YOU AIN'T EVEN GOT THAT MUCH?
C'MON!
I'M NOT GIVING YOU ANYTHING- YOU BIG BULLY!
SO I'M A BULLY, HUH?
OKAY.....
MY-T-FINE VANILLA PUDDING SEMI-LIQUIFIED
FINE!
WHAT?
FLUP
OH JEEZ!
HAW HAW
GA-AAHH!
DINING HALL
WHA'D I DO THAT FOR?
SOMETIMES.

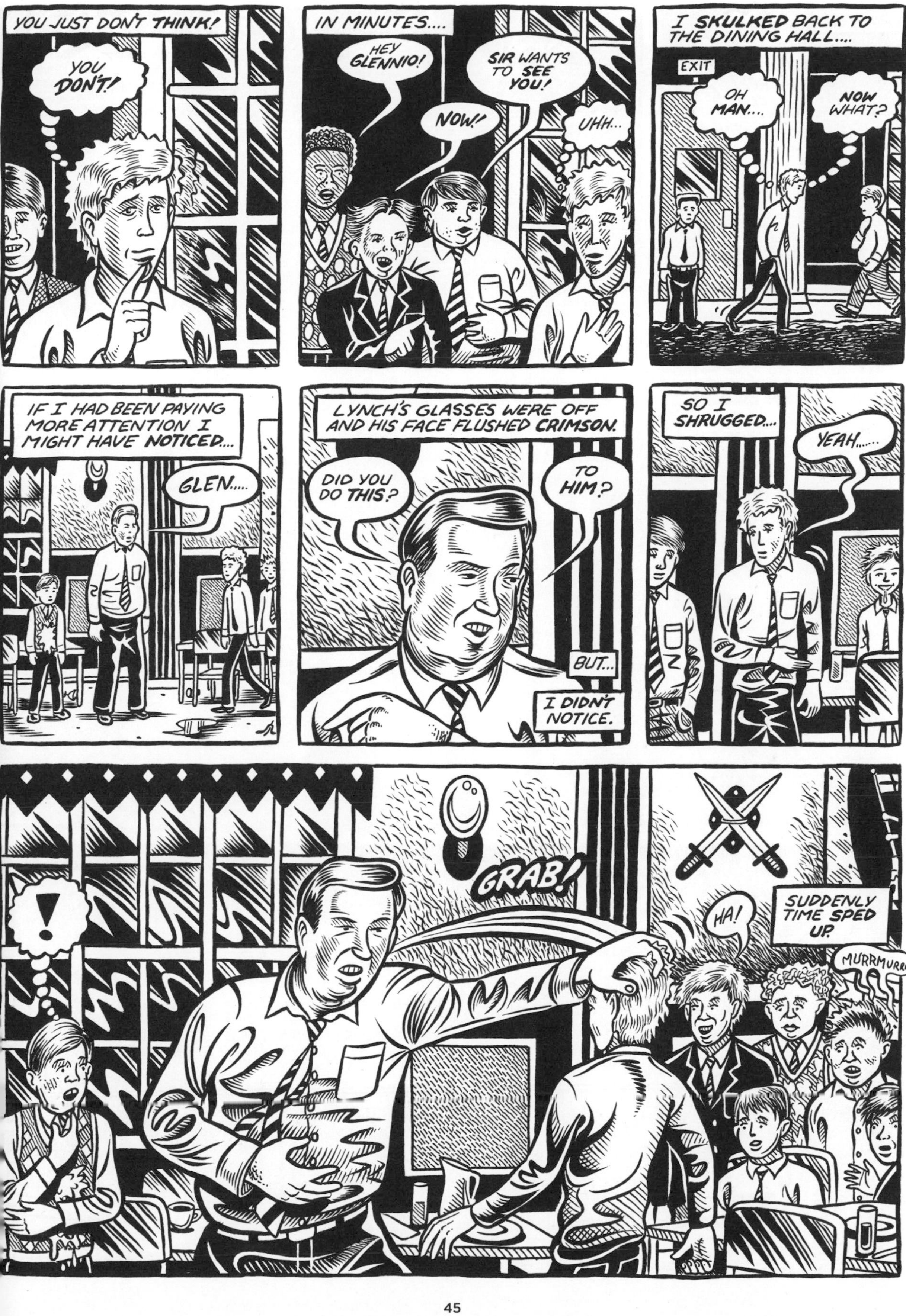

YOU JUST DON'T THINK!
YOU DON'T!
IN MINUTES....
HEY GLENNIO!
NOW!
SIR WANTS TO SEE YOU!
UHH...
I SKULKED BACK TO THE DINING HALL....
EXIT
OH MAN....
NOW WHAT?
IF I HAD BEEN PAYING MORE ATTENTION I MIGHT HAVE NOTICED....
GLEN.....
LYNCH'S GLASSES WERE OFF AND HIS FACE FLUSHED CRIMSON.
DID YOU DO THIS?
TO HIM?
BUT...
I DIDN'T NOTICE.
SO I SHRUGGED....
YEAH.......
!
GRAB!
HA!
SUDDENLY TIME SPED UP.
MURRMURRR

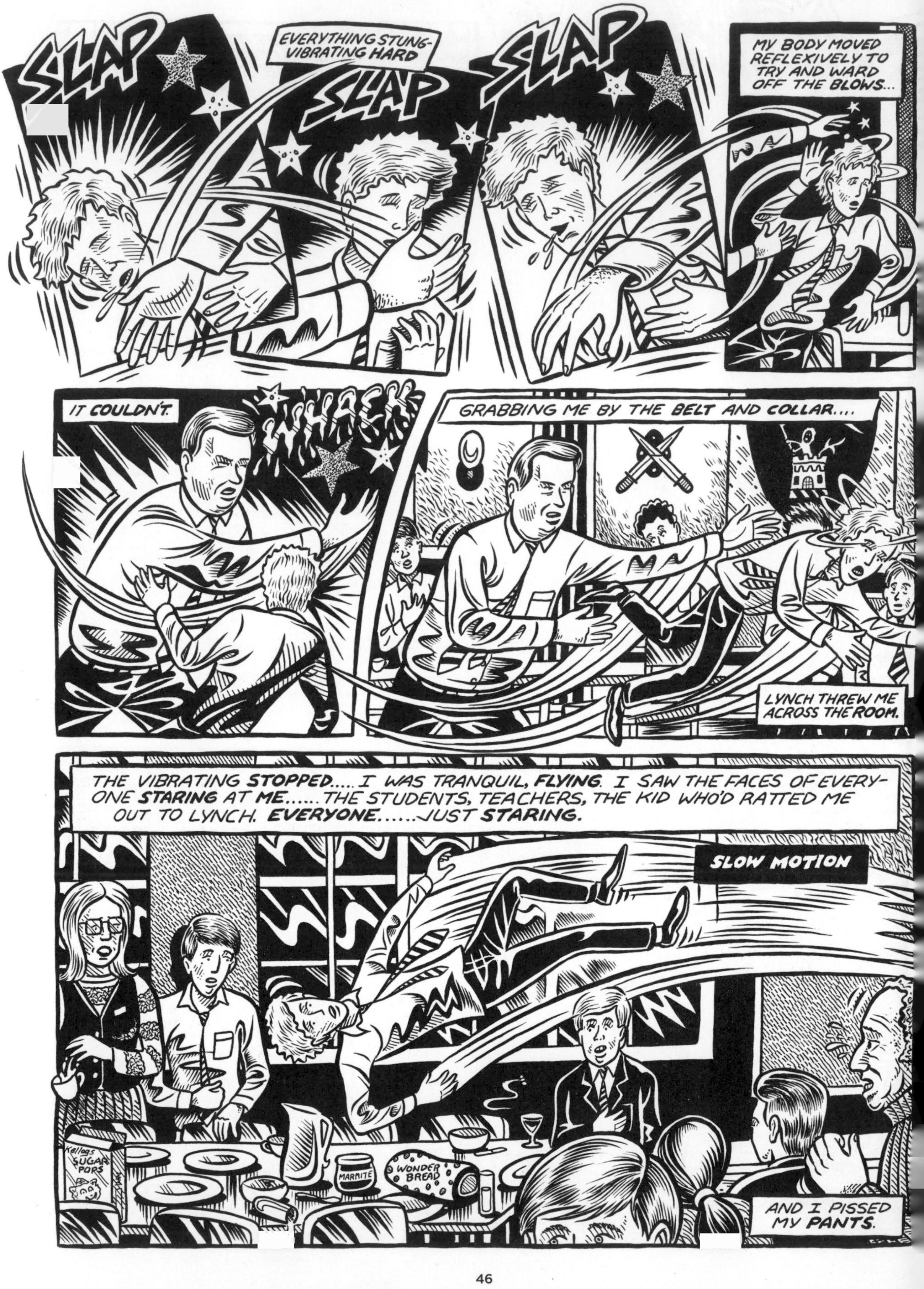
SLAP
EVERYTHING STUNG-VIBRATING HARD
SLAP
SLAP
MY BODY MOVED REFLEXIVELY TO TRY AND WARD OFF THE BLOWS...
IT COULDN'T.
WHACK
GRABBING ME BY THE BELT AND COLLAR....
LYNCH THREW ME ACROSS THE ROOM.
THE VIBRATING STOPPED..... I WAS TRANQUIL, FLYING. I SAW THE FACES OF EVERYONE STARING AT ME...... THE STUDENTS, TEACHERS, THE KID WHO'D RATTED ME OUT TO LYNCH. EVERYONE...... JUST STARING.
SLOW MOTION
Kellogg's SUGAR POPS
MARMITE
WONDER BREAD
AND I PISSED MY PANTS.

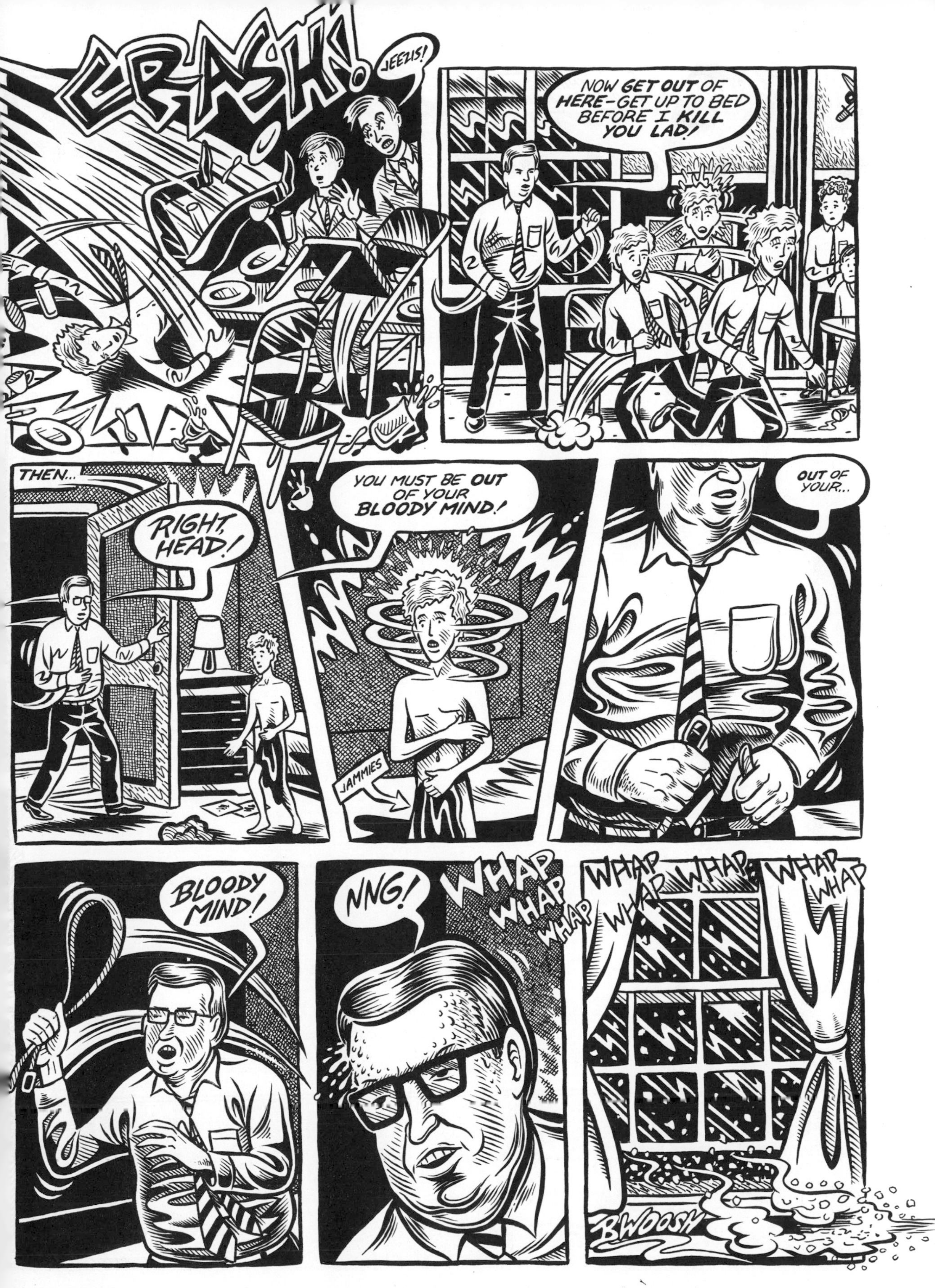
CRASH!
JEEZIS!
NOW GET OUT OF HERE-GET UP TO BED BEFORE I KILL YOU LAD!
THEN...
RIGHT, HEAD!
YOU MUST BE OUT OF YOUR BLOODY MIND!
JAMMIES
OUT OF YOUR...
BLOODY MIND!
NNG!
WHAP WHAP WHAP
WHAP WHAP WHAP WHAP WHAP WHAP
BWOOSH

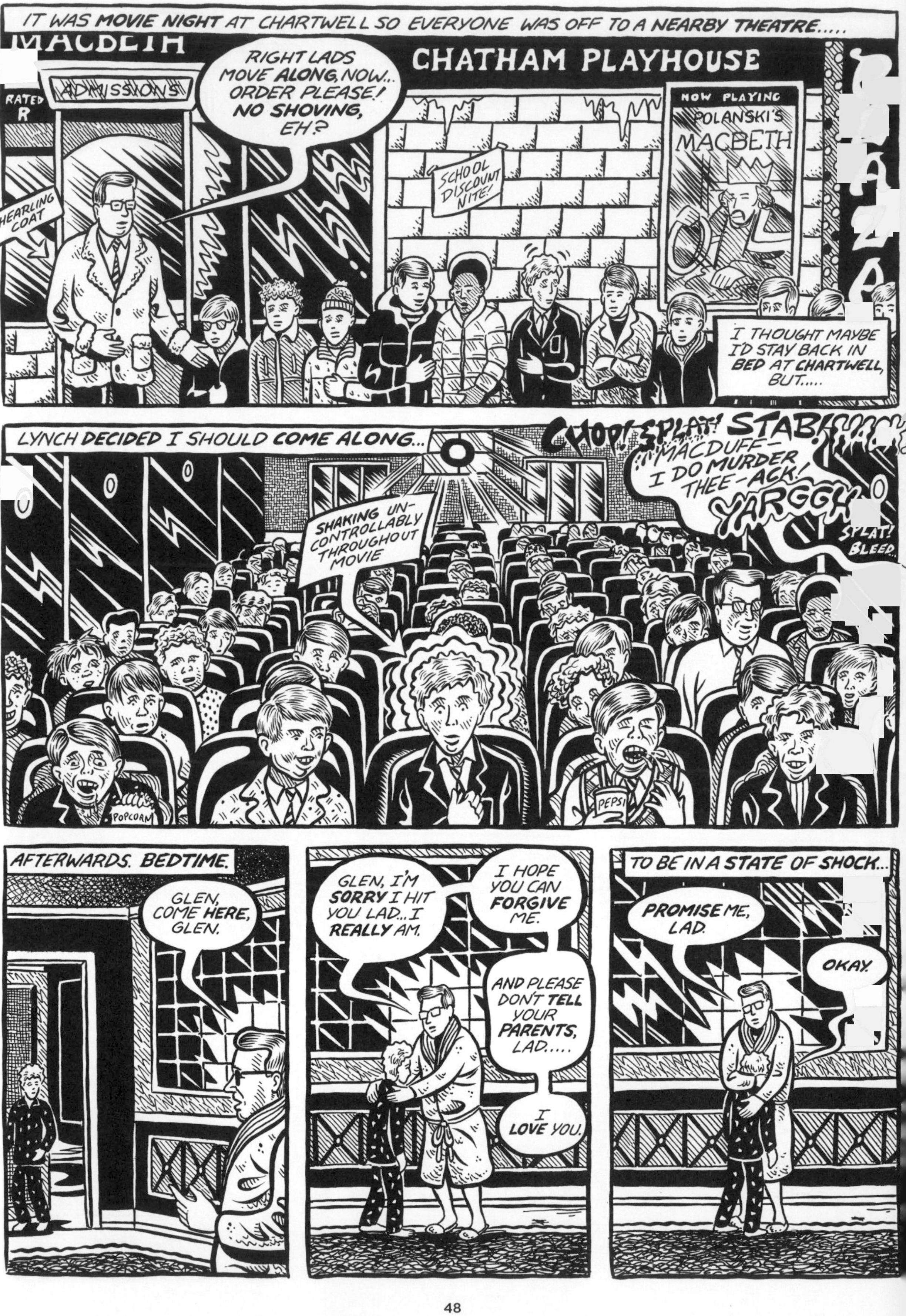
IT WAS MOVIE NIGHT AT CHARTWELL SO EVERYONE WAS OFF TO A NEARBY THEATRE.....
MACBETH
ADMISSIONS
RATED R
RIGHT LADS MOVE ALONG, NOW... ORDER PLEASE! NO SHOVING, EH?
CHATHAM PLAYHOUSE
NOW PLAYING POLANSKI'S MACBETH
SCHOOL DISCOUNT NITE!
SHEARLING COAT
I THOUGHT MAYBE I'D STAY BACK IN BED AT CHARTWELL, BUT.....
LYNCH DECIDED I SHOULD COME ALONG...
CHOP! SPLAT! STAB!
MACDUFF- I DO MURDER THEE-ACK!
YARGGH
SPLAT! BLEED...
SHAKING UN-CONTROLLABLY THROUGHOUT MOVIE
POPCORN
PEPSI
AFTERWARDS. BEDTIME.
GLEN, COME HERE, GLEN.
GLEN, I'M SORRY I HIT YOU LAD... I REALLY AM.
I HOPE YOU CAN FORGIVE ME.
AND PLEASE DON'T TELL YOUR PARENTS, LAD.....
I LOVE YOU.
TO BE IN A STATE OF SHOCK...
PROMISE ME, LAD.
OKAY.

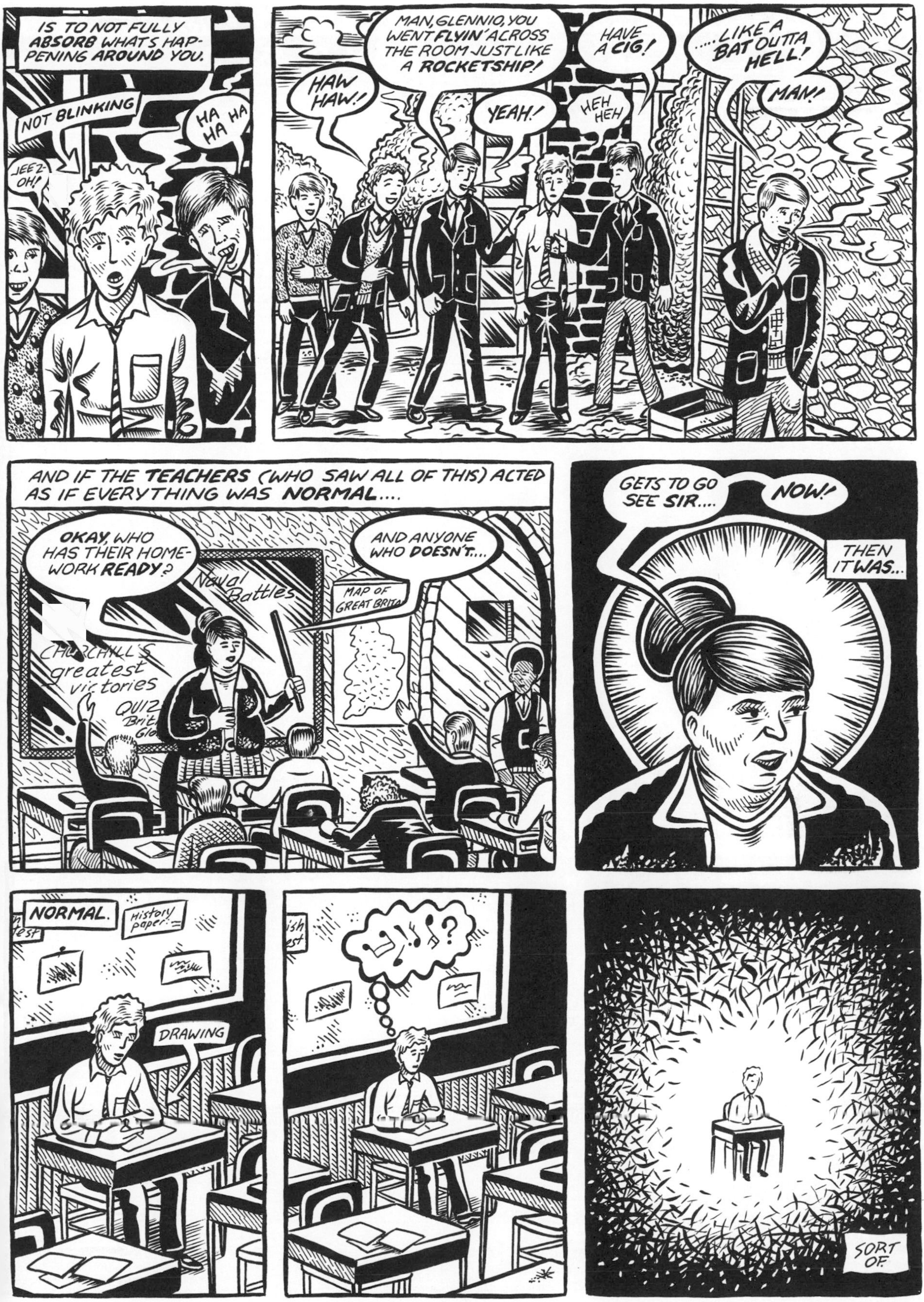
IS TO NOT FULLY ABSORB WHAT'S HAPPENING AROUND YOU.
NOT BLINKING
HA HA HA
JEEZ-OH!
MAN, GLENNIO, YOU WENT FLYIN' ACROSS THE ROOM JUST LIKE A ROCKETSHIP!
HAW HAW!
YEAH!
HAVE A CIG!
HEH HEH
....LIKE A BAT OUTTA HELL!
MAN!
AND IF THE TEACHERS (WHO SAW ALL OF THIS) ACTED AS IF EVERYTHING WAS NORMAL....
OKAY, WHO HAS THEIR HOMEWORK READY?
AND ANYONE WHO DOESN'T...
Naval Battles
MAP OF GREAT BRIT
CHURCHILL'S greatest victories
QUIZ
GETS TO GO SEE SIR....
NOW!
THEN IT WAS...
NORMAL.
History paper
DRAWING
SORT OF.

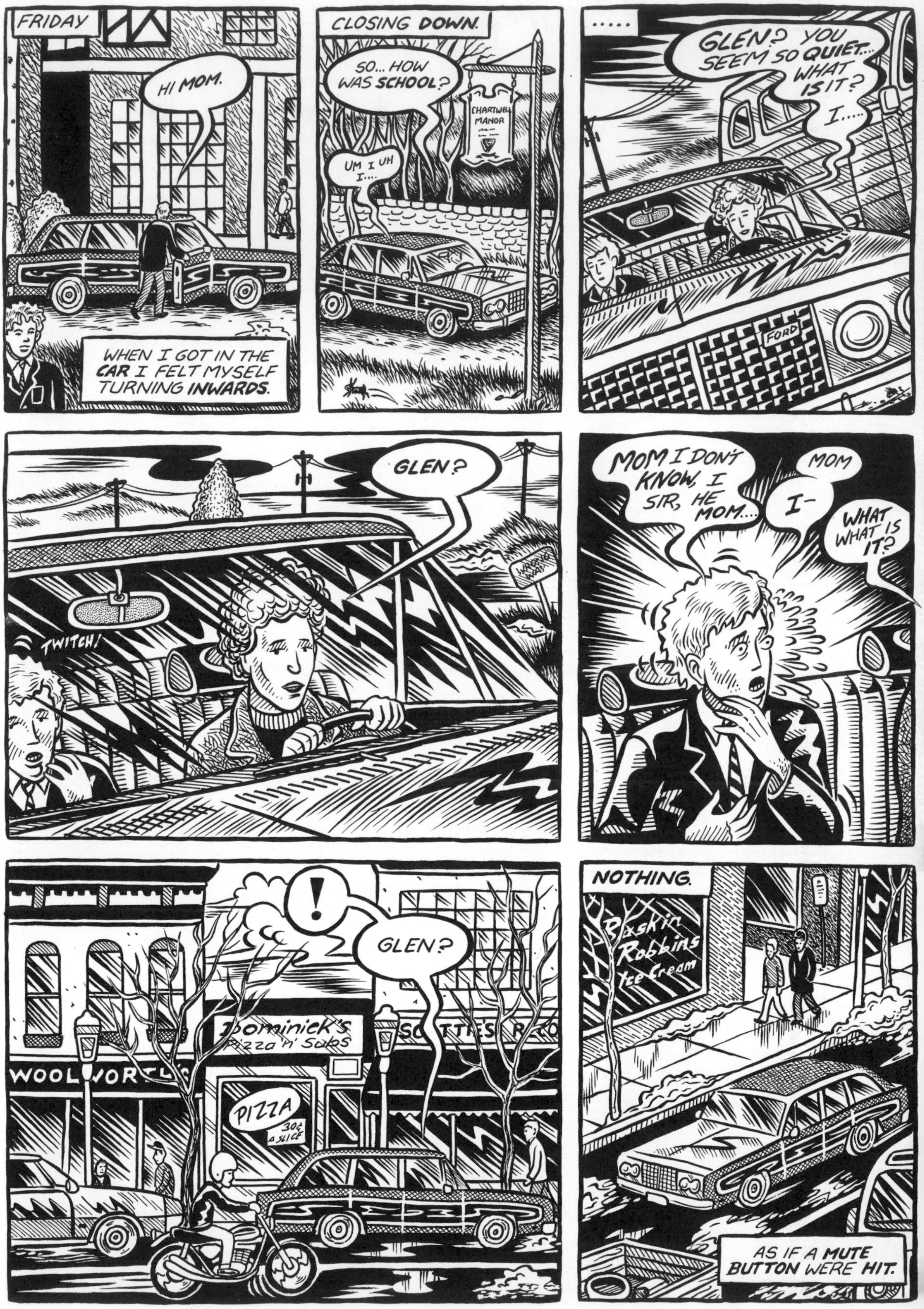
FRIDAY
HI MOM.
WHEN I GOT IN THE CAR I FELT MYSELF TURNING INWARDS.
CLOSING DOWN.
SO... HOW WAS SCHOOL?
CHARTWELL MANOR
UM I UH I....
.....
GLEN? YOU SEEM SO QUIET... WHAT IS IT?
I.....
FORD
GLEN?
TWITCH!
MOM I DON'T KNOW, I SIR, HE MOM....
MOM
I-
WHAT WHAT IS IT?
!
GLEN?
Dominick's Pizza 'n' Subs
WOOLWORTH
PIZZA
30¢ A SLICE
NOTHING.
Baskin Robbins Ice Cream
AS IF A MUTE BUTTON WERE HIT.

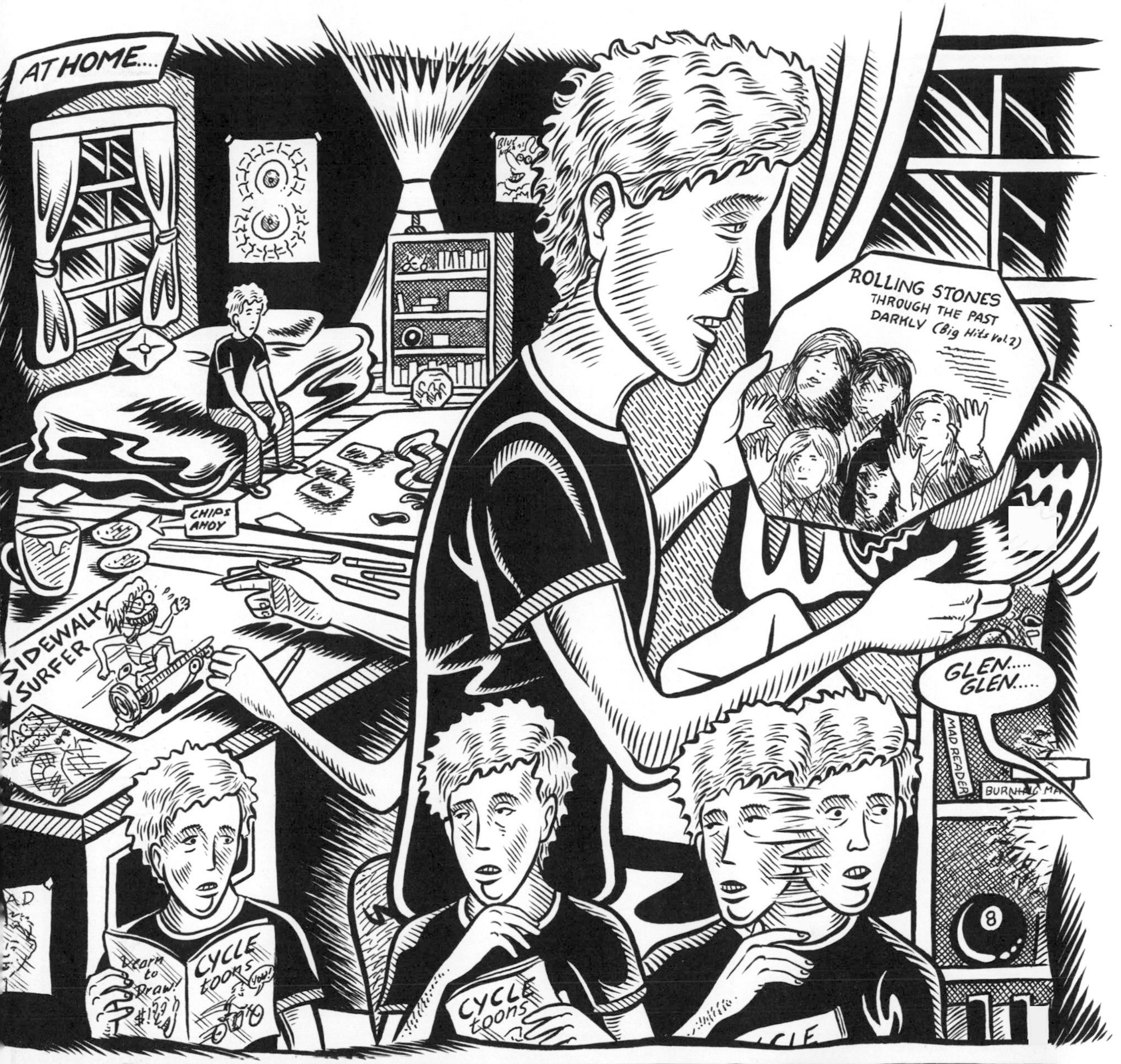
AT HOME....
CHIPS AHOY
SIDEWALK SURFER
ROLLING STONES THROUGH THE PAST DARKLY (Big Hits Vol 2)
GLEN.... GLEN.....
MAD READER
Learn to Draw!
CYCLE toons
CYCLE toons
8
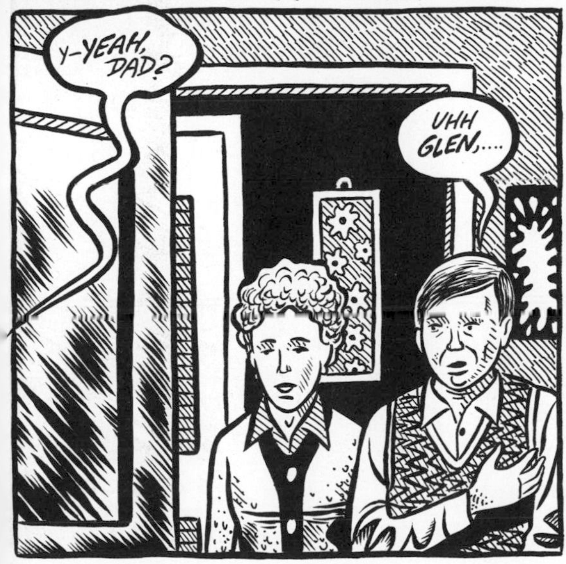
Y-YEAH, DAD?
UHH GLEN,....
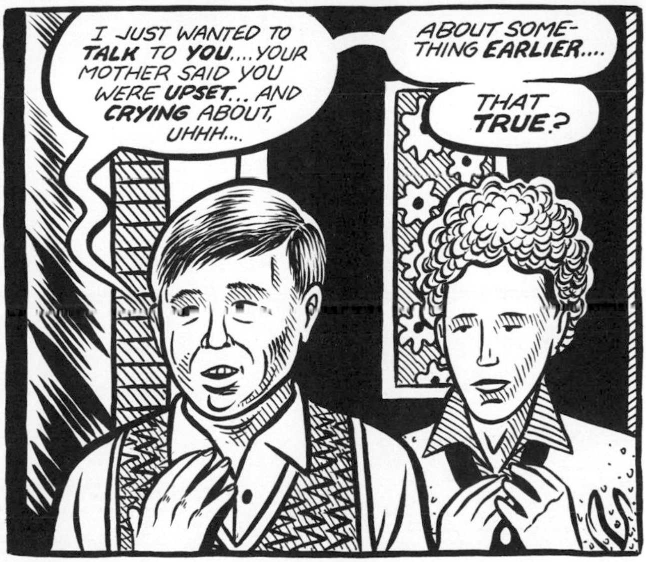
I JUST WANTED TO TALK TO YOU....YOUR MOTHER SAID YOU WERE UPSET... AND CRYING ABOUT, UHHH....
ABOUT SOMETHING EARLIER....
THAT TRUE?

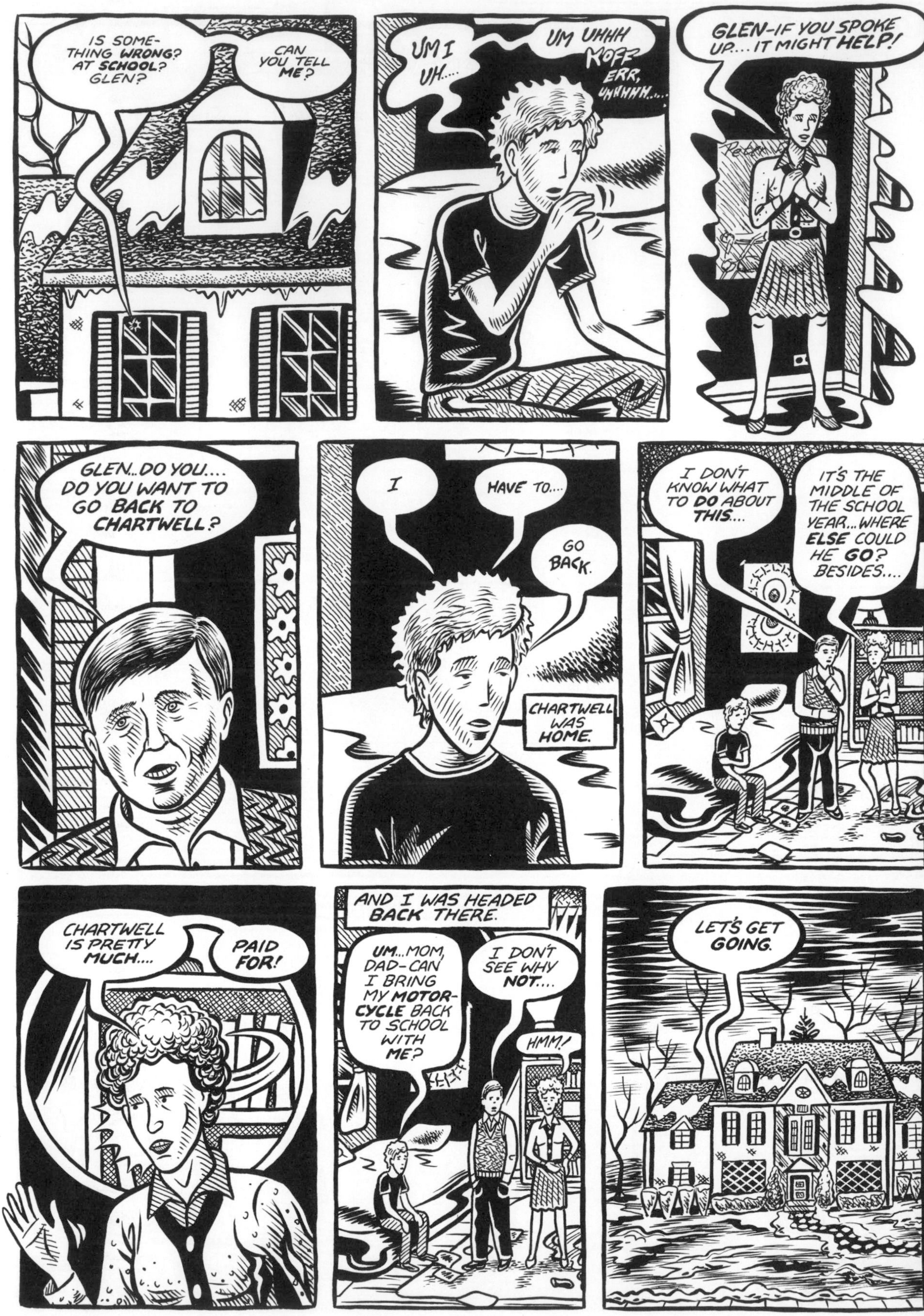
IS SOMETHING WRONG? AT SCHOOL? GLEN?
CAN YOU TELL ME?
UM I UH....
UM UHHH KOFF ERR, UHHHHH.....
GLEN–IF YOU SPOKE UP.... IT MIGHT HELP!
GLEN...DO YOU.... DO YOU WANT TO GO BACK TO CHARTWELL?
I
HAVE TO....
GO BACK.
CHARTWELL WAS HOME.
I DON'T KNOW WHAT TO DO ABOUT THIS....
IT'S THE MIDDLE OF THE SCHOOL YEAR... WHERE ELSE COULD HE GO? BESIDES....
CHARTWELL IS PRETTY MUCH....
PAID FOR!
AND I WAS HEADED BACK THERE.
UM...MOM, DAD–CAN I BRING MY MOTORCYCLE BACK TO SCHOOL WITH ME?
I DON'T SEE WHY NOT....
HMM!
LET'S GET GOING.

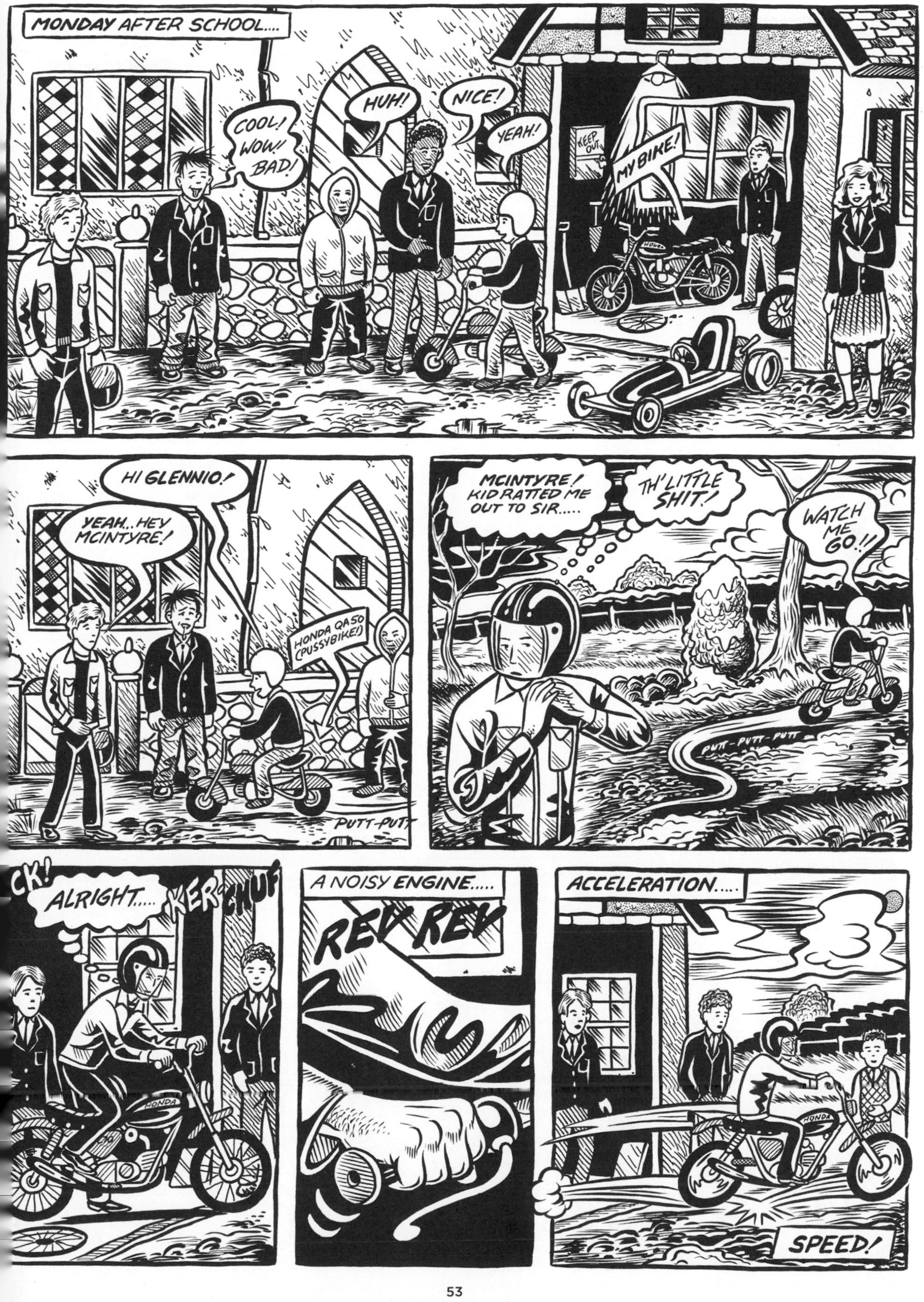
MONDAY AFTER SCHOOL....
COOL! WOW! BAD!
HUH!
NICE!
YEAH!
KEEP OUT
MY BIKE!
HI GLENNIO!
YEAH...HEY MCINTYRE!
HONDA QA50 (PUSSYBIKE!)
PUTT-PUTT
MCINTYRE! KID RATTED ME OUT TO SIR.....
TH'LITTLE SHIT!
WATCH ME GO!!
PUTT-PUTT-PUTT
CK!
ALRIGHT.....
KER-CHUF
HONDA
A NOISY ENGINE.....
REV REV
ACCELERATION.....
HONDA
SPEED!

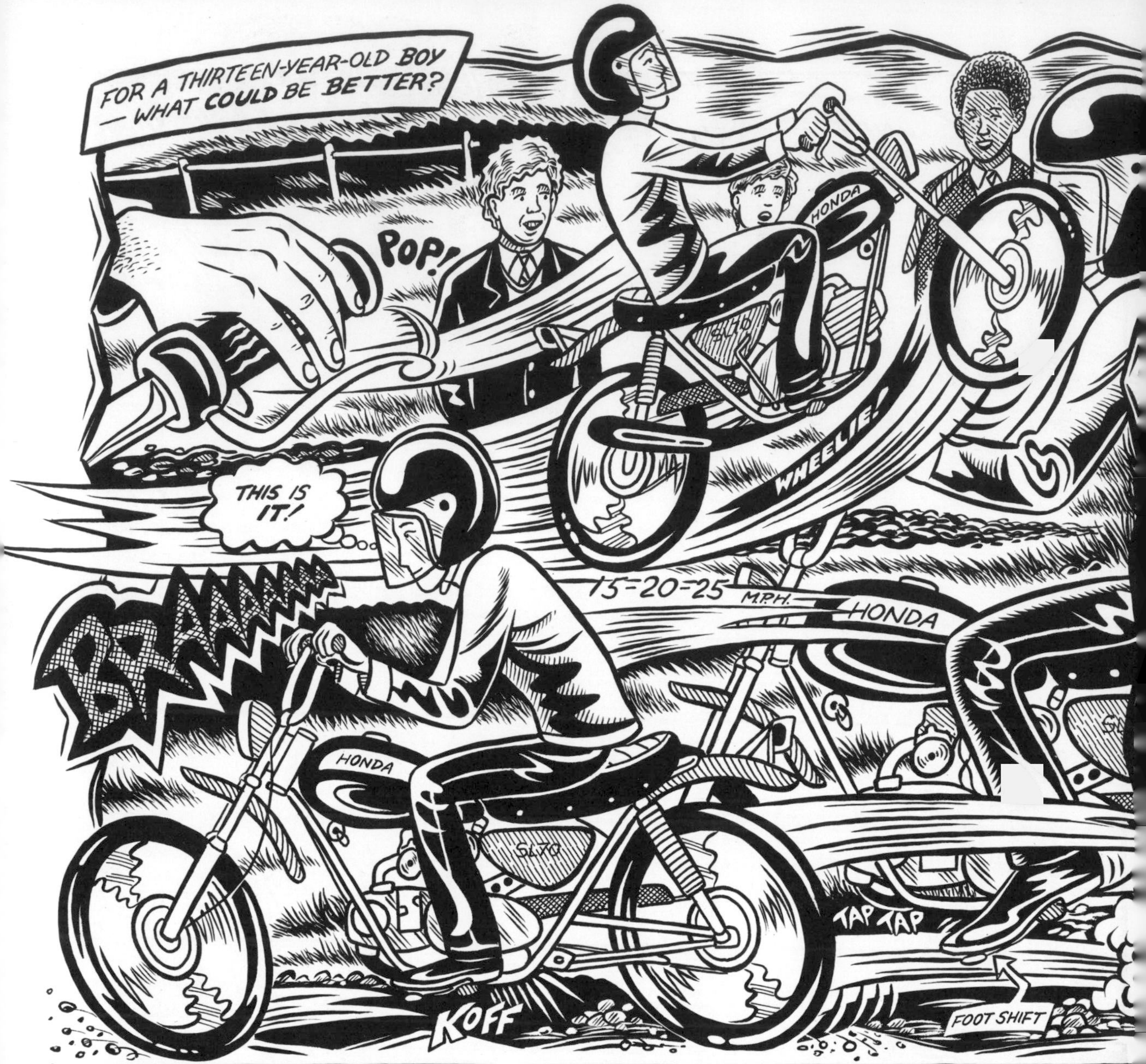
FOR A THIRTEEN-YEAR-OLD BOY — WHAT COULD BE BETTER?
POP!
HONDA
WHEELIE!
THIS IS IT!
15-20-25 M.P.H.
HONDA
HONDA
SL70
TAP TAP
FOOT SHIFT
KOFF

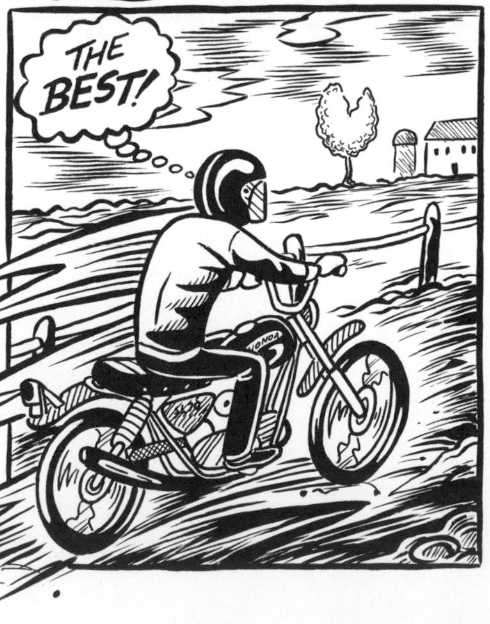
THE BEST!

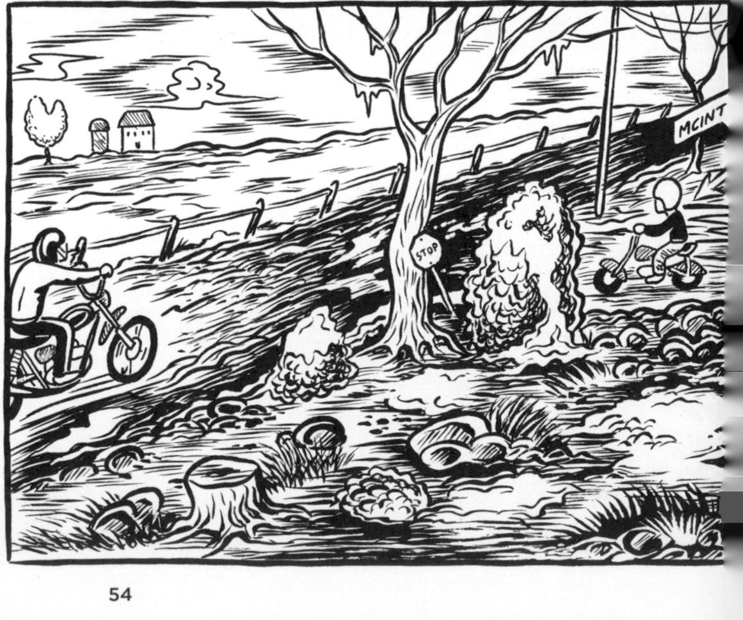

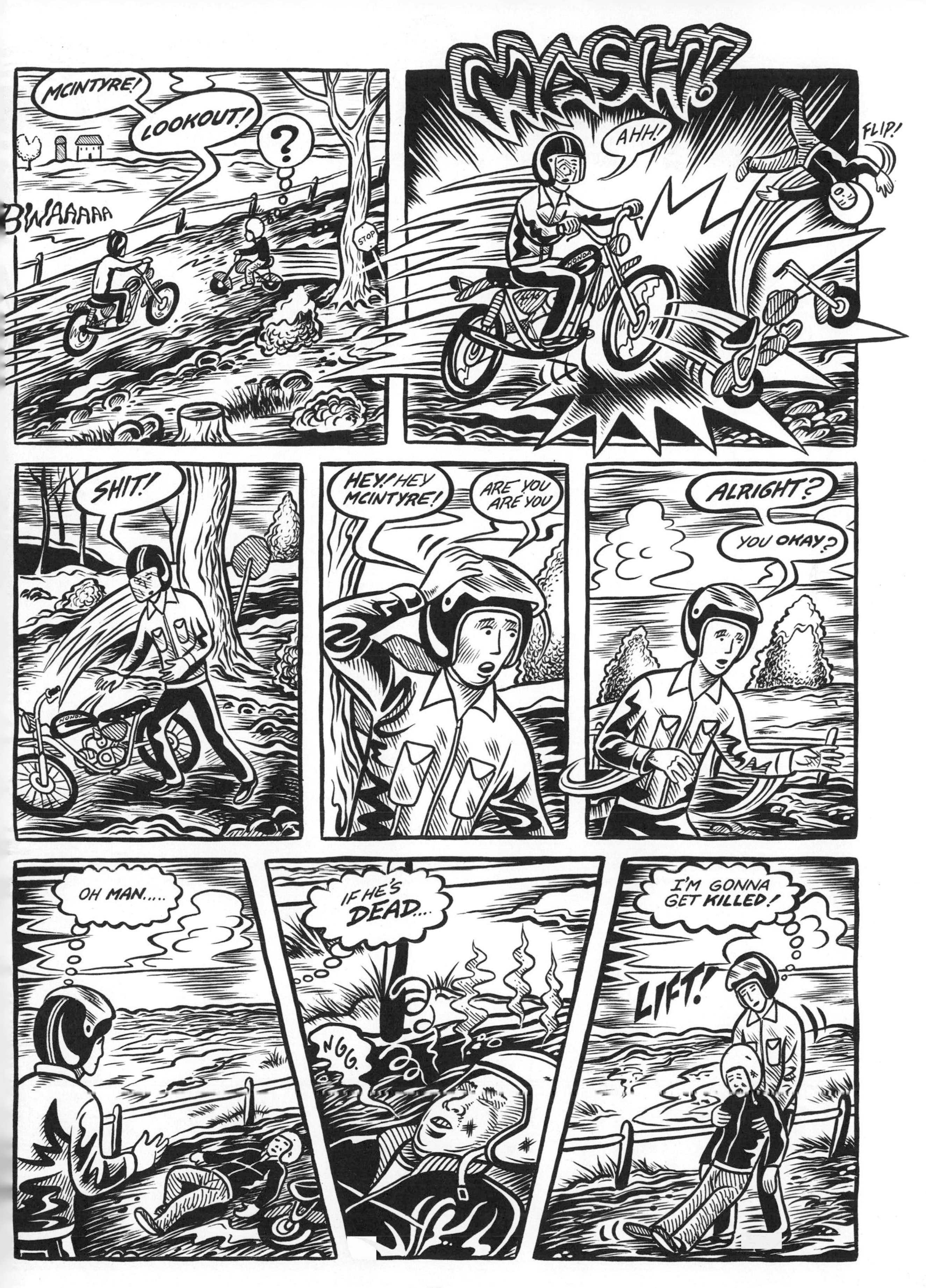

MCINTYRE!
LOOKOUT!
?
BWAAAAAA
STOP
MASH!
AHH!
FLIP!
HONDA
SHIT!
HONDA
HEY! HEY MCINTYRE!
ARE YOU ARE YOU
ALRIGHT?
YOU OKAY?
OH MAN.....
IF HE'S DEAD...
NGG.
I'M GONNA GET KILLED!
LIFT!

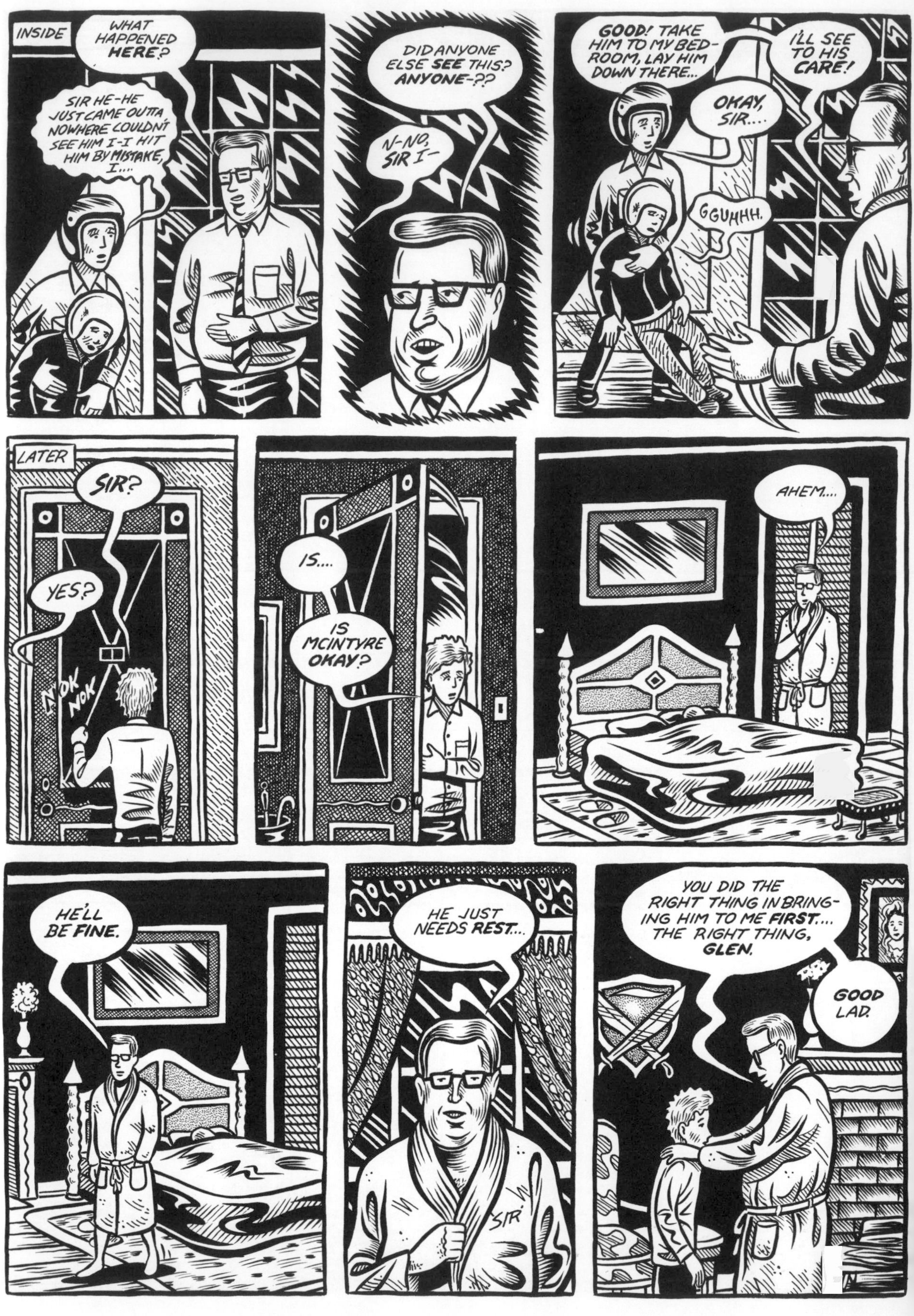
INSIDE
WHAT HAPPENED HERE?
SIR HE-HE JUST CAME OUTTA NOWHERE COULDN'T SEE HIM I-I HIT HIM BY MISTAKE, I....
DID ANYONE ELSE SEE THIS? ANYONE-??
N-NO, SIR I-
GOOD! TAKE HIM TO MY BED-ROOM, LAY HIM DOWN THERE...
I'LL SEE TO HIS CARE!
OKAY, SIR....
GGUHHH.
LATER
SIR?
YES?
NOK NOK
IS....
IS MCINTYRE OKAY?
AHEM....
HE'LL BE FINE.
HE JUST NEEDS REST....
SIR
YOU DID THE RIGHT THING IN BRING-ING HIM TO ME FIRST.... THE RIGHT THING, GLEN.
GOOD LAD.

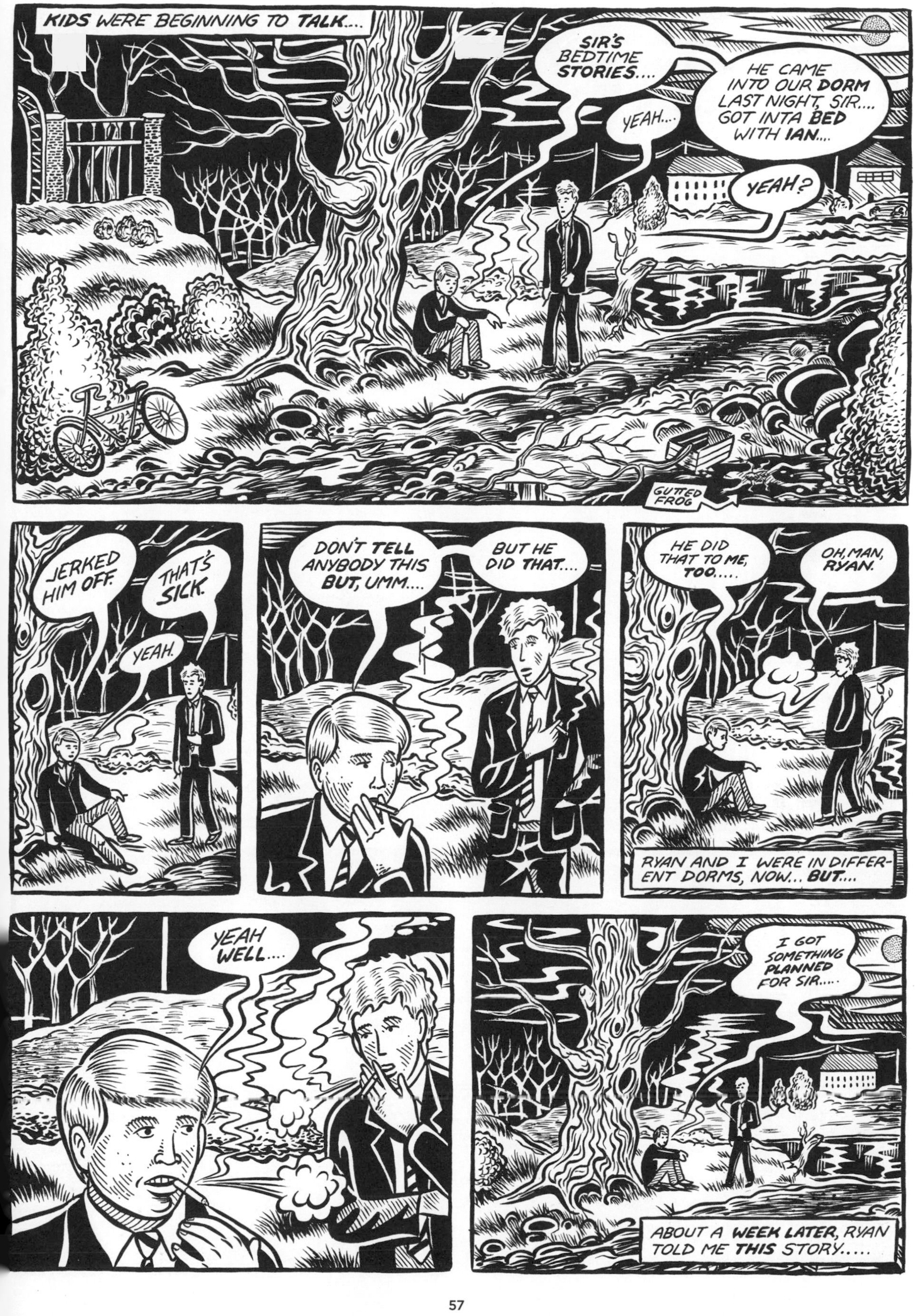
KIDS WERE BEGINNING TO TALK....
SIR'S BEDTIME STORIES....
YEAH...
HE CAME INTO OUR DORM LAST NIGHT, SIR.... GOT INTA BED WITH IAN....
YEAH?
GUTTED FROG
JERKED HIM OFF.
THAT'S SICK.
YEAH.
DON'T TELL ANYBODY THIS BUT, UMM....
BUT HE DID THAT....
HE DID THAT TO ME, TOO.....
OH, MAN, RYAN.
RYAN AND I WERE IN DIFFERENT DORMS, NOW... BUT....
YEAH WELL....
I GOT SOMETHING PLANNED FOR SIR.....
ABOUT A WEEK LATER, RYAN TOLD ME THIS STORY.....

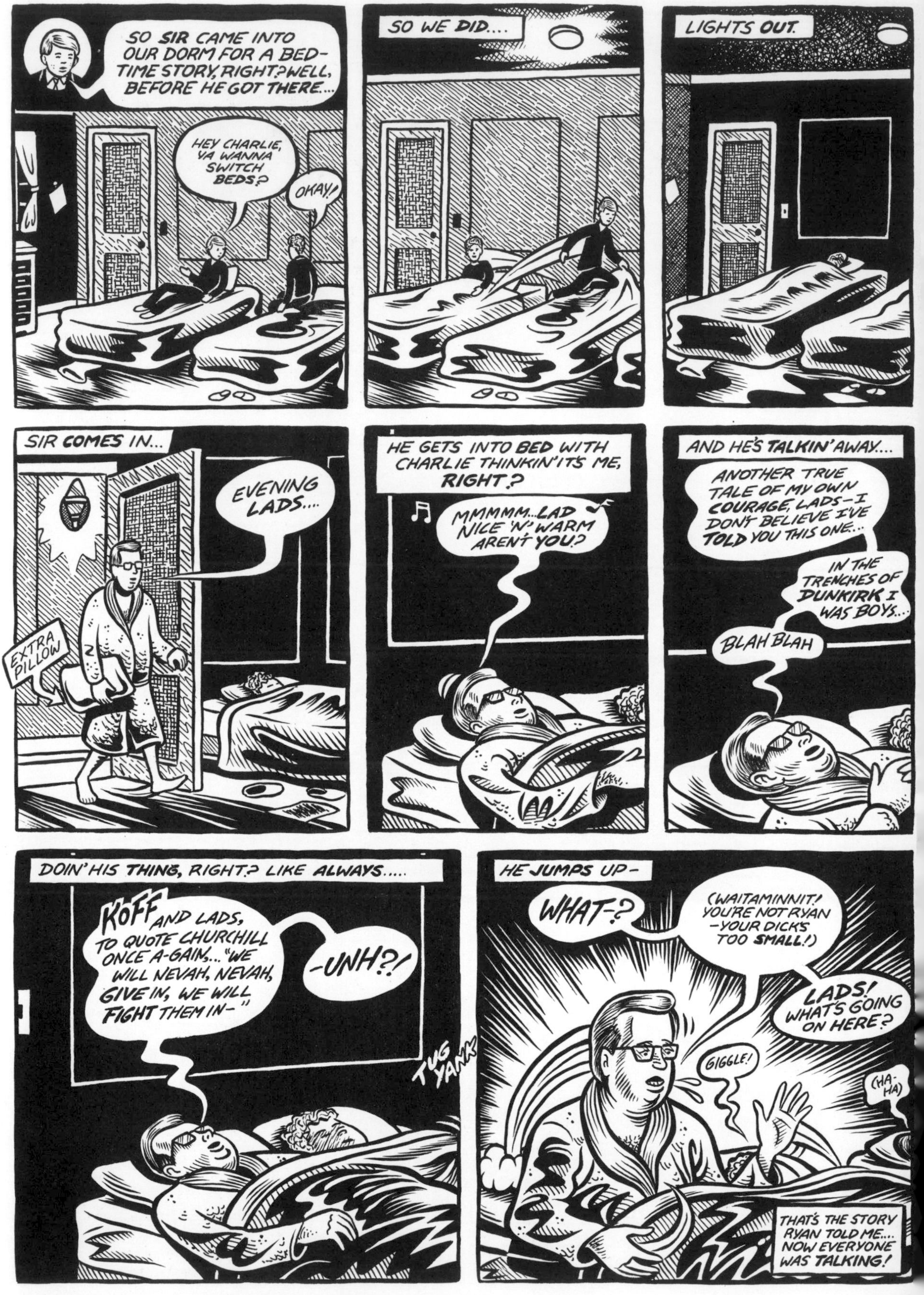
SO SIR CAME INTO OUR DORM FOR A BED-TIME STORY, RIGHT? WELL, BEFORE HE GOT THERE....
HEY CHARLIE, YA WANNA SWITCH BEDS?
OKAY!
SO WE DID....
LIGHTS OUT.
SIR COMES IN...
EVENING LADS....
EXTRA PILLOW
HE GETS INTO BED WITH CHARLIE THINKIN' IT'S ME, RIGHT?
MMMMM...LAD NICE 'N' WARM AREN'T YOU?
AND HE'S TALKIN' AWAY....
ANOTHER TRUE TALE OF MY OWN COURAGE, LADS—I DON'T BELIEVE I'VE TOLD YOU THIS ONE...
IN THE TRENCHES OF DUNKIRK I WAS BOYS...
BLAH BLAH
DOIN' HIS THING, RIGHT? LIKE ALWAYS.....
KOFF AND LADS, TO QUOTE CHURCHILL ONCE A-GAIN..."WE WILL NEVAH, NEVAH, GIVE IN, WE WILL FIGHT THEM IN-"
-UNH?!
TUG YANK
HE JUMPS UP-
WHAT-?
(WAITAMINNIT! YOU'RE NOT RYAN -YOUR DICK'S TOO SMALL!)
LADS! WHAT'S GOING ON HERE?
GIGGLE!
(HA-HA)
THAT'S THE STORY RYAN TOLD ME.... NOW EVERYONE WAS TALKING!

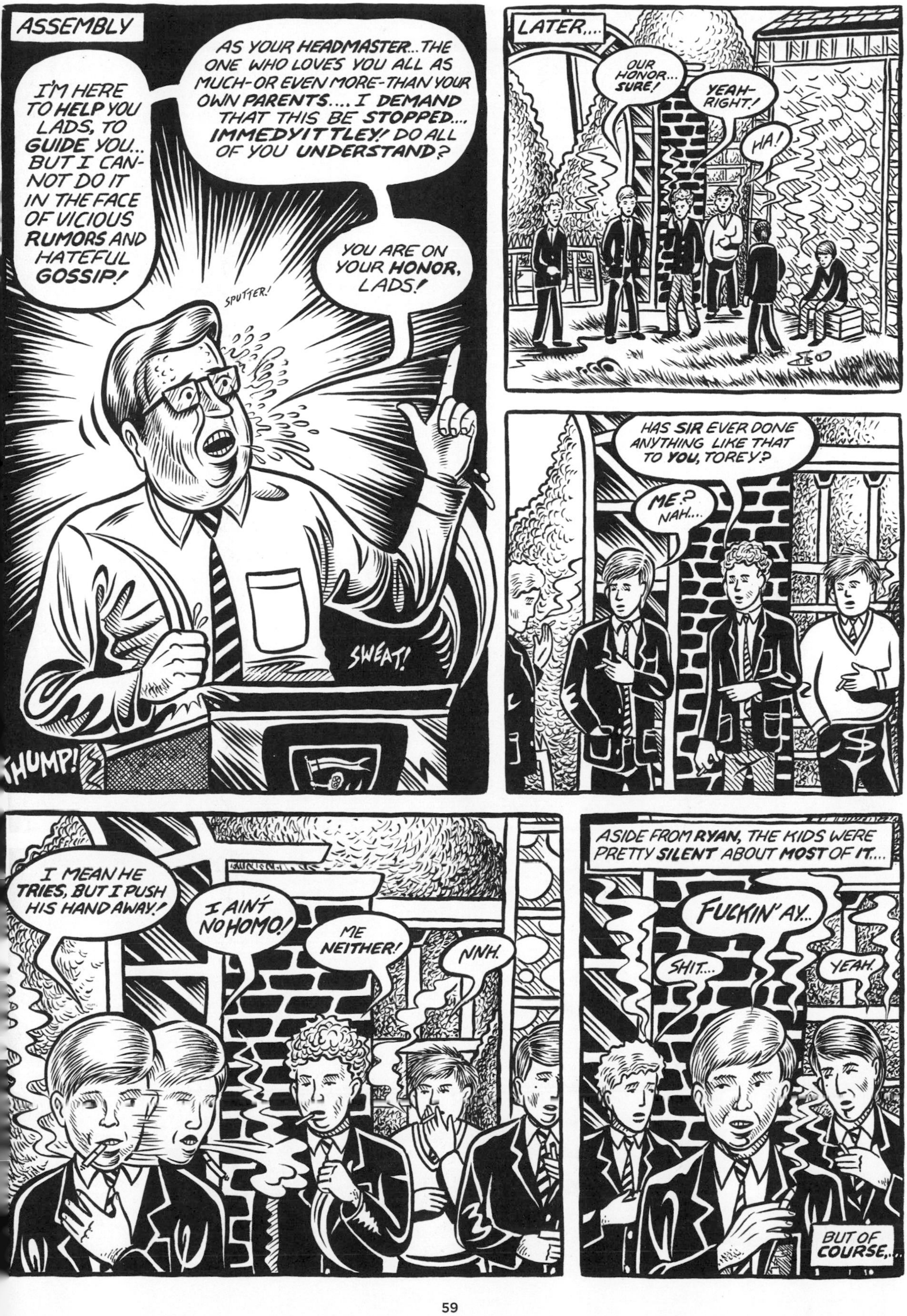
ASSEMBLY
I'M HERE TO HELP YOU LADS, TO GUIDE YOU... BUT I CANNOT DO IT IN THE FACE OF VICIOUS RUMORS AND HATEFUL GOSSIP!
AS YOUR HEADMASTER... THE ONE WHO LOVES YOU ALL AS MUCH-OR EVEN MORE-THAN YOUR OWN PARENTS.... I DEMAND THAT THIS BE STOPPED.... IMMEDYITTLEY! DO ALL OF YOU UNDERSTAND?
YOU ARE ON YOUR HONOR, LADS!
SPUTTER!
SWEAT!
THUMP!
LATER....
OUR HONOR... SURE!
YEAH-RIGHT!
HA!
HAS SIR EVER DONE ANYTHING LIKE THAT TO YOU, TOREY?
ME? NAH...
I MEAN HE TRIES, BUT I PUSH HIS HAND AWAY!
I AIN'T NO HOMO!
ME NEITHER!
NNH.
ASIDE FROM RYAN, THE KIDS WERE PRETTY SILENT ABOUT MOST OF IT...
FUCKIN' AY...
SHIT...
YEAH.
BUT OF COURSE,...

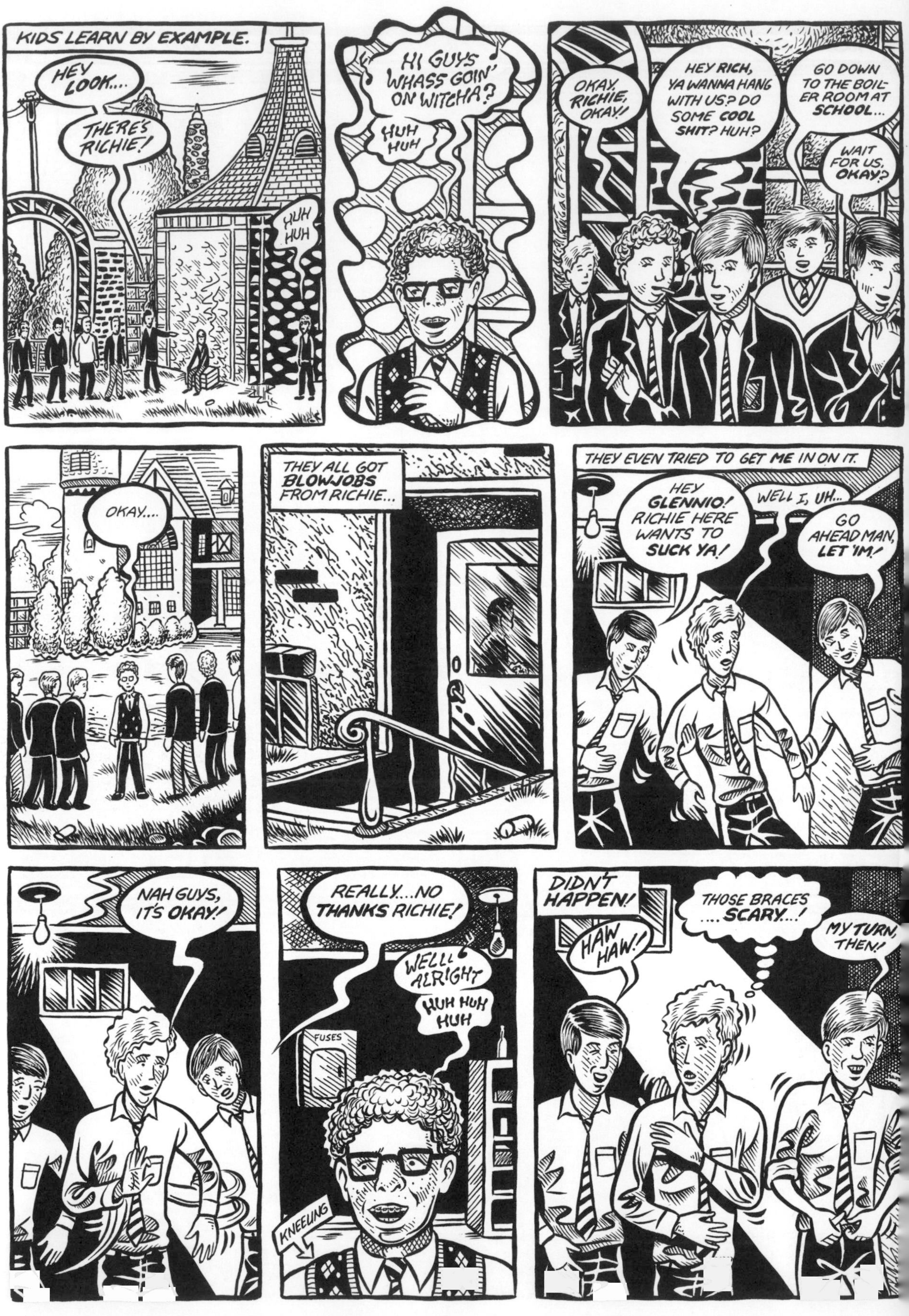
KIDS LEARN BY EXAMPLE.
HEY LOOK....
THERE'S RICHIE!
HUH HUH
HI GUYS WHASS GOIN' ON WITCHA?
HUH HUH
OKAY, RICHIE, OKAY!
HEY RICH, YA WANNA HANG WITH US? DO SOME COOL SHIT? HUH?
GO DOWN TO THE BOIL-ER ROOM AT SCHOOL...
WAIT FOR US, OKAY?
OKAY....
THEY ALL GOT BLOWJOBS FROM RICHIE...
THEY EVEN TRIED TO GET ME IN ON IT.
HEY GLENNIO! RICHIE HERE WANTS TO SUCK YA!
WELL I, UH...
GO AHEAD MAN, LET 'IM!
NAH GUYS, IT'S OKAY!
REALLY....NO THANKS RICHIE!
WELLL ALRIGHT
HUH HUH HUH
FUSES
KNEELING
DIDN'T HAPPEN!
HAW HAW!
THOSE BRACES .... SCARY....!
MY TURN, THEN!

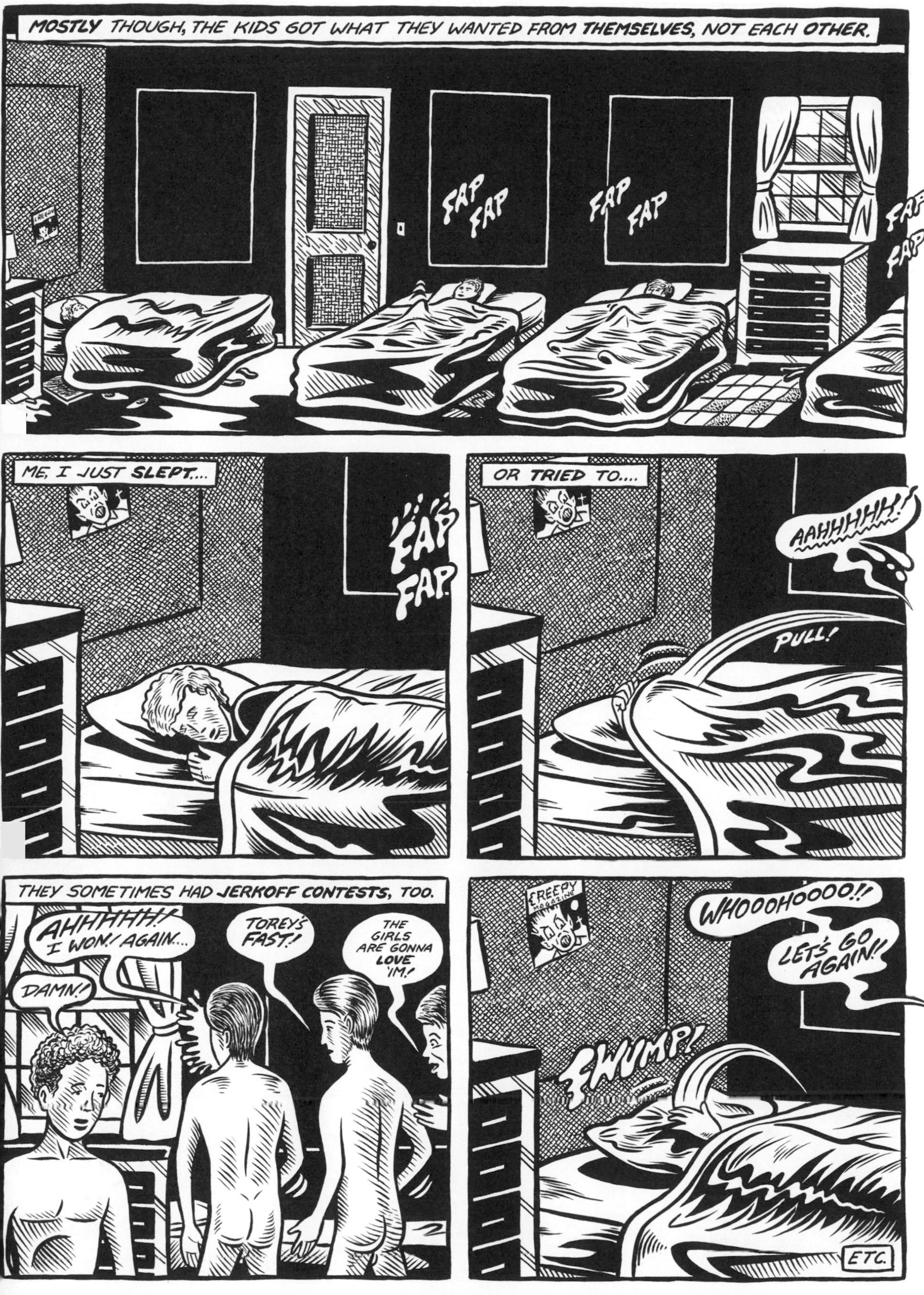
MOSTLY THOUGH, THE KIDS GOT WHAT THEY WANTED FROM THEMSELVES, NOT EACH OTHER.
FAP FAP
FAP FAP
FAP FAP
ME, I JUST SLEPT....
FAP FAP
OR TRIED TO....
AAHHHHH!
PULL!
THEY SOMETIMES HAD JERKOFF CONTESTS, TOO.
AHHHHHH! I WON! AGAIN....
DAMN!
TOREY'S FAST!
THE GIRLS ARE GONNA LOVE 'IM!
WHOOOHOOOO!!
LET'S GO AGAIN!!
FWUMP!
ETC.

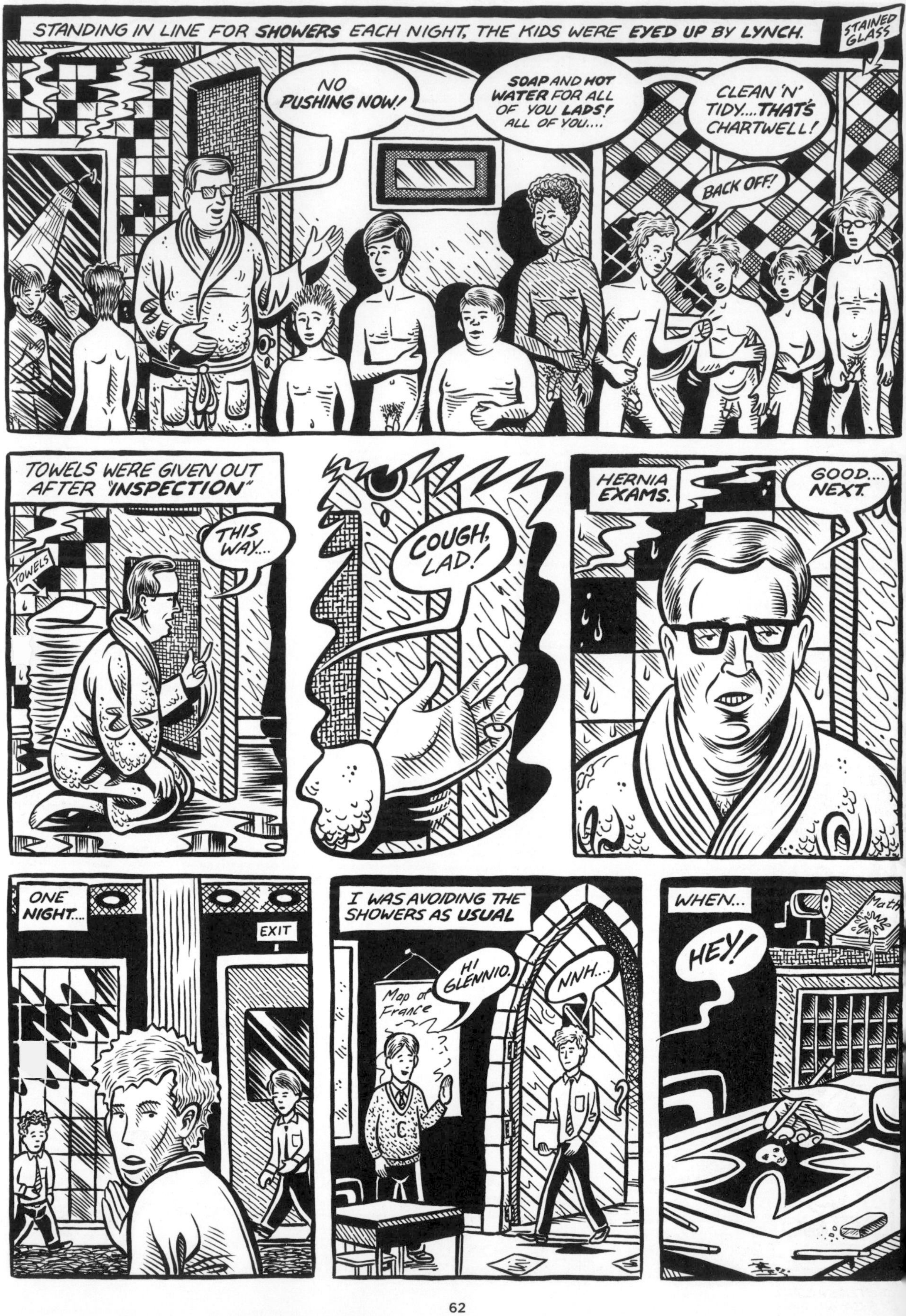

STANDING IN LINE FOR SHOWERS EACH NIGHT, THE KIDS WERE EYED UP BY LYNCH.
STAINED GLASS
NO PUSHING NOW!
SOAP AND HOT WATER FOR ALL OF YOU LADS! ALL OF YOU....
CLEAN 'N' TIDY....THAT'S CHARTWELL!
BACK OFF!
TOWELS WERE GIVEN OUT AFTER "INSPECTION"
TOWELS
THIS WAY....
COUGH, LAD!
HERNIA EXAMS.
GOOD.... NEXT.
ONE NIGHT....
EXIT
I WAS AVOIDING THE SHOWERS AS USUAL
Map of France
HI GLENNIO.
NNH....
WHEN...
Math
HEY!

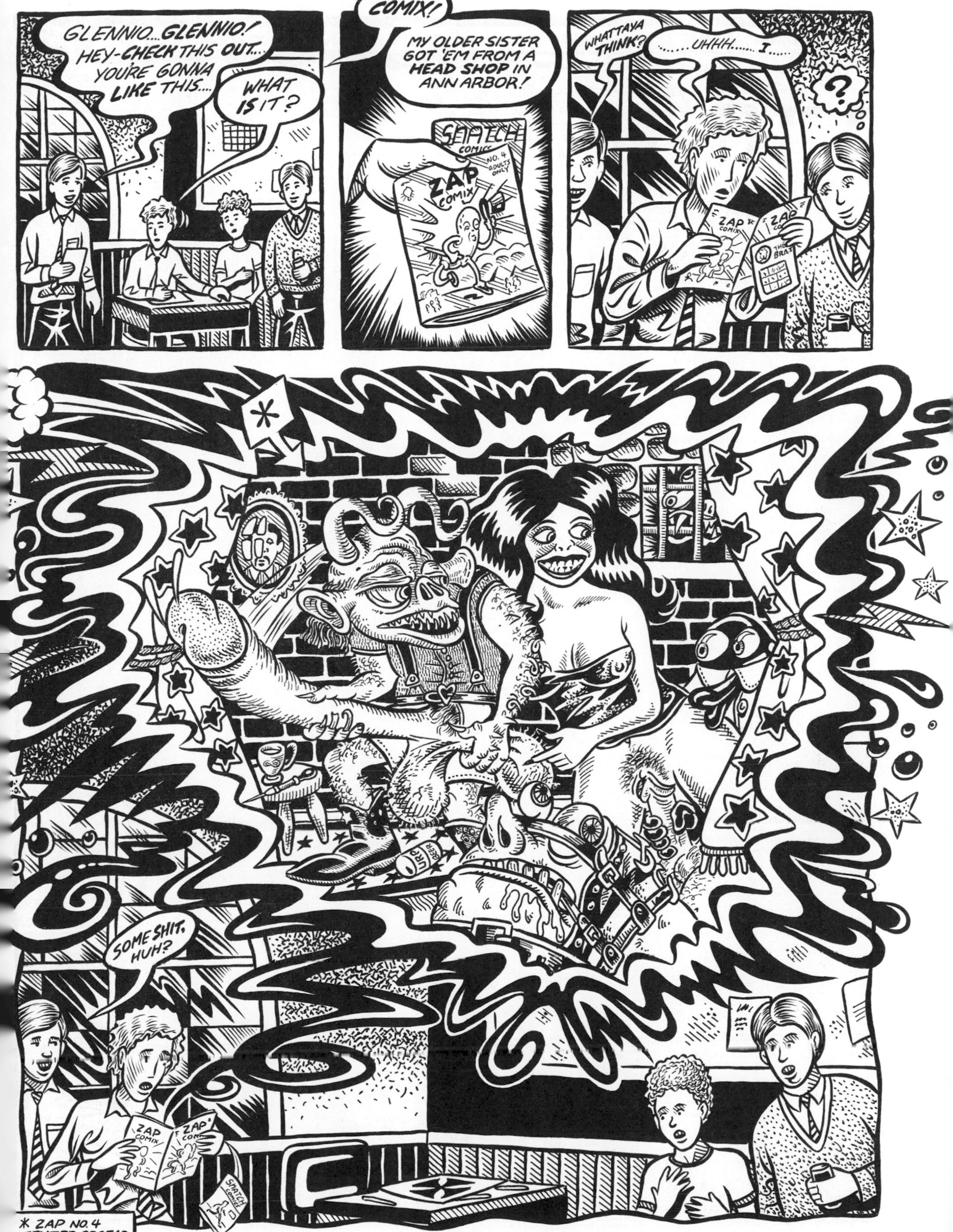
GLENNIO...GLENNIO! HEY-CHECK THIS OUT... YOU'RE GONNA LIKE THIS....
WHAT IS IT?
COMIX!
MY OLDER SISTER GOT 'EM FROM A HEAD SHOP IN ANN ARBOR!
SNATCH COMICS NO. 4 ADULTS ONLY
ZAP COMIX
WHATTAYA THINK?
......UHHH...... I.......
?
ZAP COMIX
ZAP
*
SOME SHIT, HUH?
ZAP COMIX
ZAP
SNATCH COMICS
* ZAP NO. 4 CENTER SPREAD BY S. CLAY WILSON

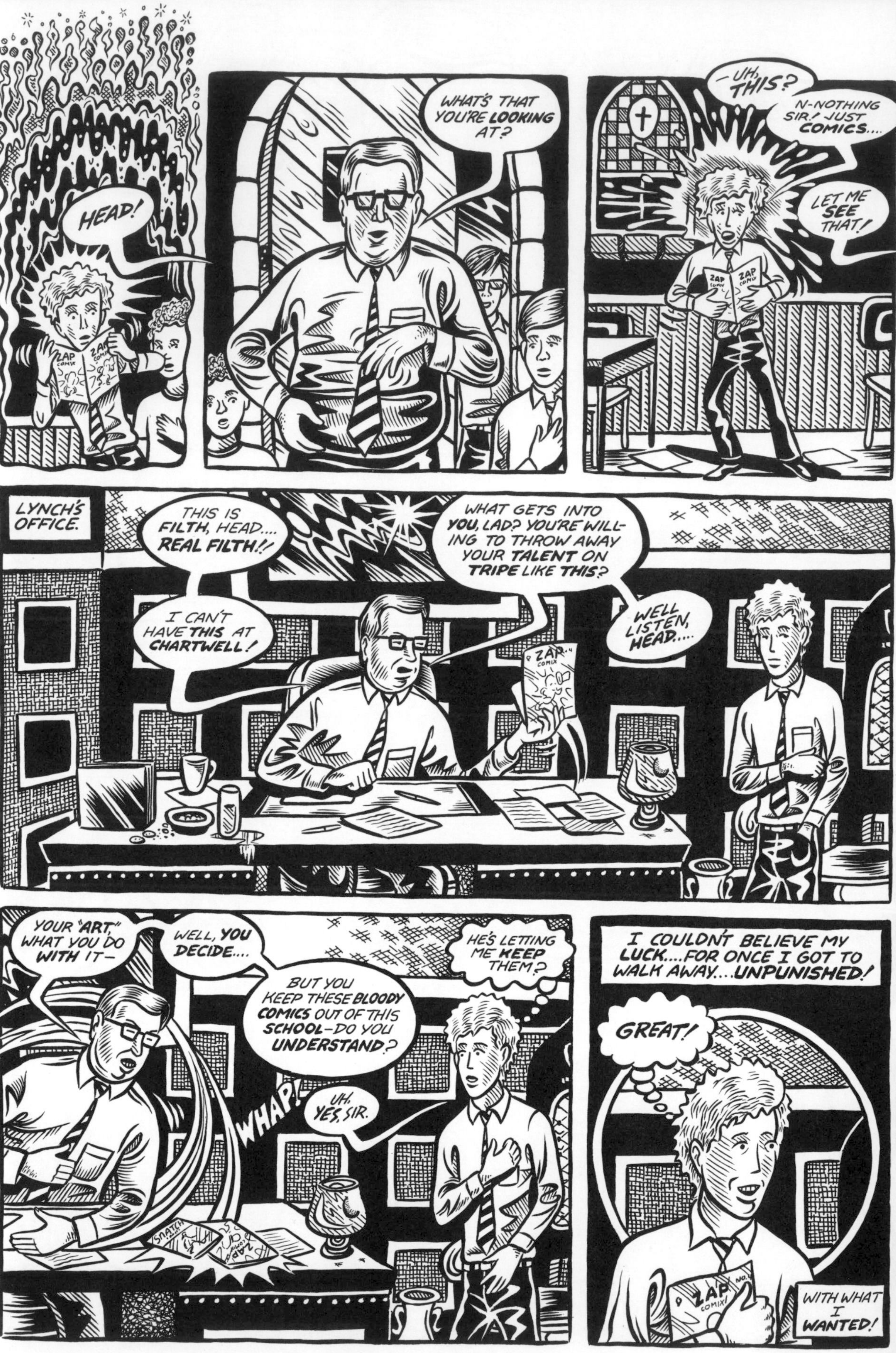
HEAD!
WHAT'S THAT YOU'RE LOOKING AT?
–UH, THIS?
N-NOTHING SIR! JUST COMICS....
LET ME SEE THAT!
LYNCH'S OFFICE.
THIS IS FILTH, HEAD.... REAL FILTH!!
I CAN'T HAVE THIS AT CHARTWELL!
WHAT GETS INTO YOU, LAD? YOU'RE WILLING TO THROW AWAY YOUR TALENT ON TRIPE LIKE THIS?
WELL LISTEN, HEAD.....
YOUR "ART," WHAT YOU DO WITH IT–
WELL, YOU DECIDE....
BUT YOU KEEP THESE BLOODY COMICS OUT OF THIS SCHOOL–DO YOU UNDERSTAND?
HE'S LETTING ME KEEP THEM?
WHAP!
UH, YES, SIR.
I COULDN'T BELIEVE MY LUCK....FOR ONCE I GOT TO WALK AWAY....UNPUNISHED!
GREAT!
WITH WHAT I WANTED!

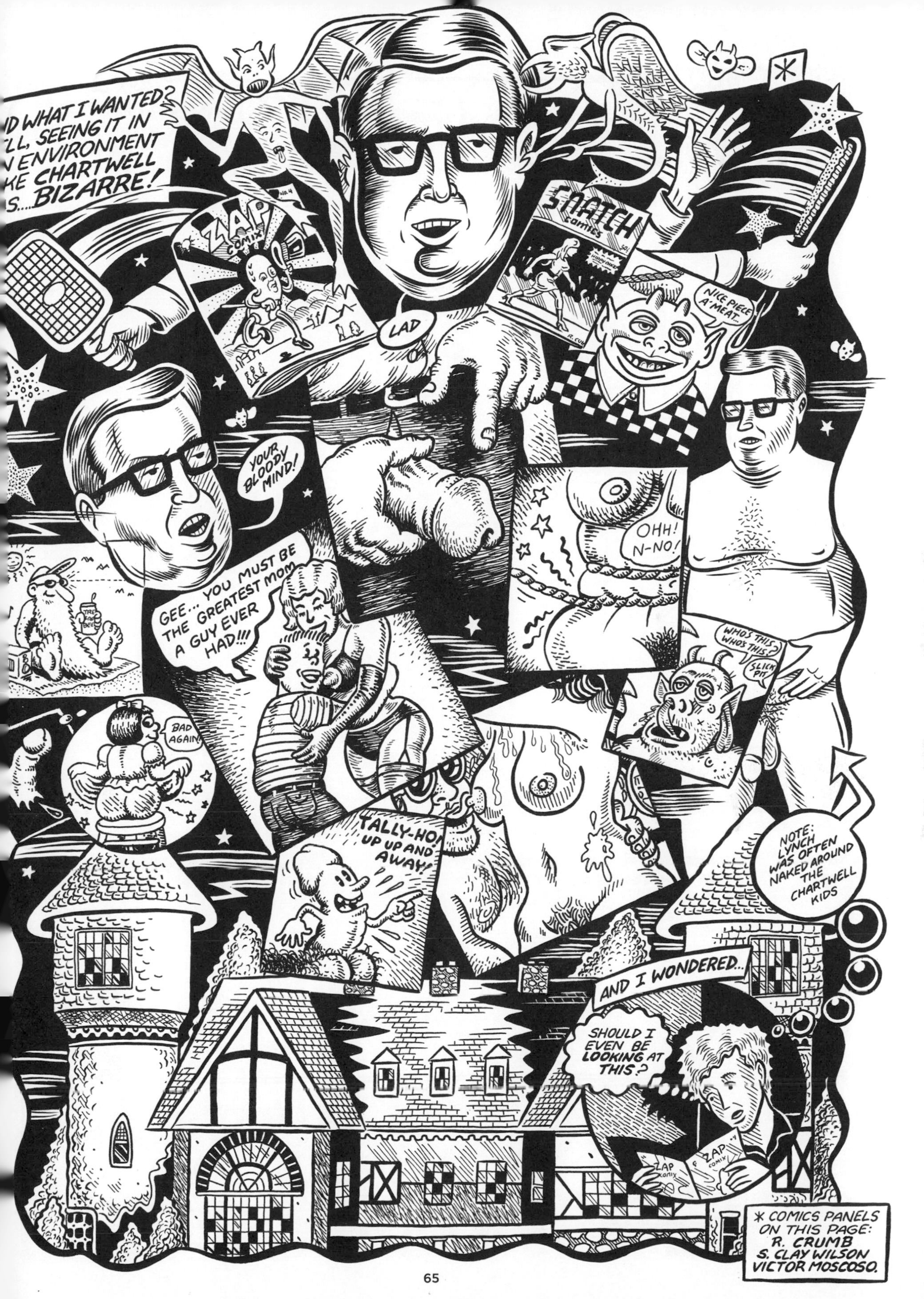
D WHAT I WANTED? LL, SEEING IT IN N ENVIRONMENT KE CHARTWELL S....BIZARRE!
ZAP COMIX
SNATCH COMICS
LAD
NICE PIECE A'MEAT..
YOUR BLOODY MIND!
OHH! N-NO!
GEE... YOU MUST BE THE GREATEST MOM A GUY EVER HAD!!!
WHO'S THIS, WHO'S THIS?
SLICK PIT
BAD AGAIN!
TALLY-HO! UP UP AND AWAY!
NOTE: LYNCH WAS OFTEN NAKED AROUND THE CHARTWELL KIDS
AND I WONDERED...
SHOULD I EVEN BE LOOKING AT THIS?
ZAP COMIX
* COMICS PANELS ON THIS PAGE: R. CRUMB S. CLAY WILSON VICTOR MOSCOSO.

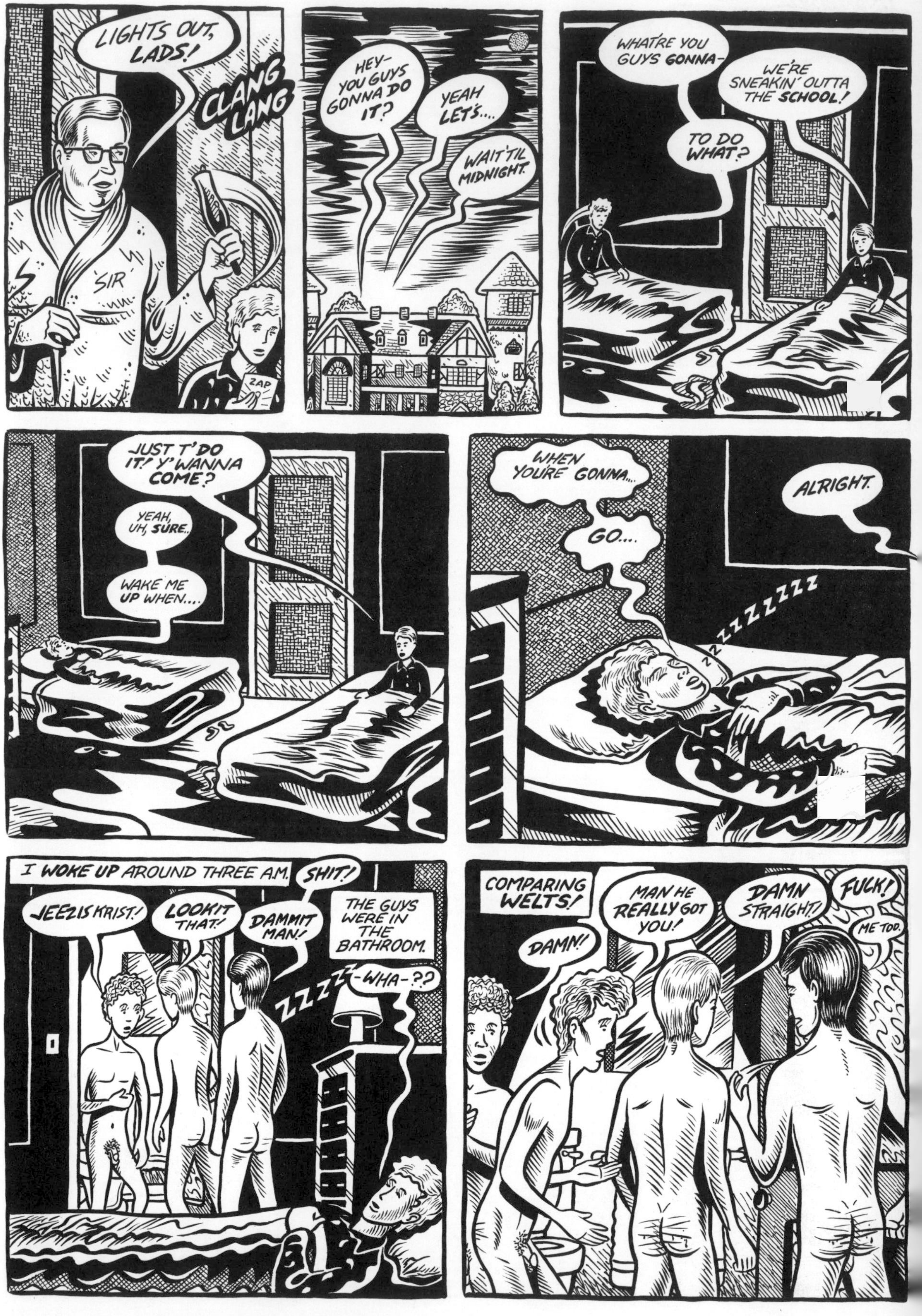
LIGHTS OUT, LADS!
CLANG CLANG
SIR
ZAP
HEY- YOU GUYS GONNA DO IT?
YEAH LET'S...
WAIT'TIL MIDNIGHT.
WHAT'RE YOU GUYS GONNA-
WE'RE SNEAKIN' OUTTA THE SCHOOL!
TO DO WHAT?
JUST T' DO IT! Y' WANNA COME?
YEAH, UH, SURE..
WAKE ME UP WHEN....
WHEN YOU'RE GONNA...
GO....
ALRIGHT.
ZZZZZZZZ
I WOKE UP AROUND THREE A.M.
SHIT!
JEEZIS KRIST!
LOOKIT THAT!
DAMMIT MAN!
THE GUYS WERE IN THE BATHROOM.
ZZZZ-WHA-??
COMPARING WELTS!
DAMN!
MAN HE REALLY GOT YOU!
DAMN STRAIGHT!
FUCK!
ME TOO.

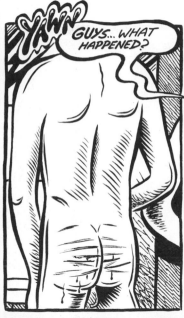

YAWN GUYS... WHAT HAPPENED?

WE SNUCK OUT, MAN!

YEAH!

WE TRIED T' WAKE YOU UP 'N' COME WITH US......

REMEMBER?

YOU WOULDN'T!

WE GOT OUT AN' WE WENT DOWNTOWN!

YEAH!

A COP PICKED US UP!

BUT THERE'S A CURFEW!

'N' DROVE US BACK TO SCHOOL!

OH....

AN' WOKE UP SIR!

HE SAW EACH ONE OF US!

OH MAN— HAHA

GODDAMN HE DID!

WHAT DID YOU GET?

TWENTY WITH THE CANE!

EACH!

HARD!

REAL HARD!

MAN!

YOU GUYS...YOU SHOULD HAVE BANDAGES!

BANDAGES, SHIT!

HA! WHERE'LL WE GET 'EM?

HELL!

THIS IS BAD!

OH MAN!

GLAD I STAYED IN!

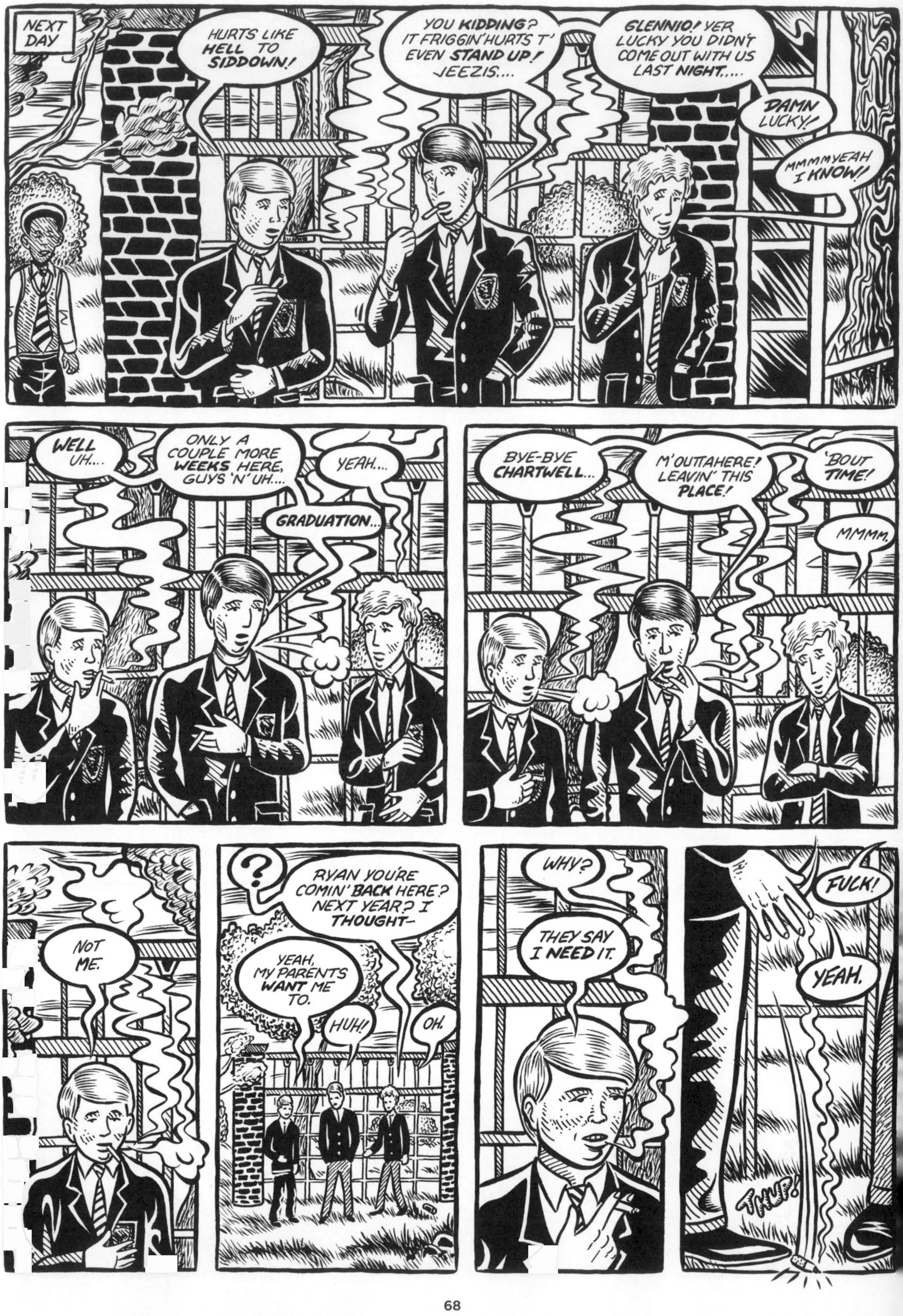
NEXT DAY
HURTS LIKE HELL TO SIDDOWN!
YOU KIDDING? IT FRIGGIN' HURTS T' EVEN STAND UP! JEEZIS....
GLENNIO! YER LUCKY YOU DIDN'T COME OUT WITH US LAST NIGHT.....
DAMN LUCKY!
MMMMYEAH I KNOW!
WELL UH...
ONLY A COUPLE MORE WEEKS HERE, GUYS 'N' UH....
YEAH....
GRADUATION...
BYE-BYE CHARTWELL...
M'OUTTAHERE! LEAVIN' THIS PLACE!
'BOUT TIME!
MMMM.
NOT ME.
?
RYAN YOU'RE COMIN' BACK HERE? NEXT YEAR? I THOUGHT-
YEAH, MY PARENTS WANT ME TO.
HUH!
OH.
WHY?
THEY SAY I NEED IT.
FUCK!
YEAH.
THWIP!

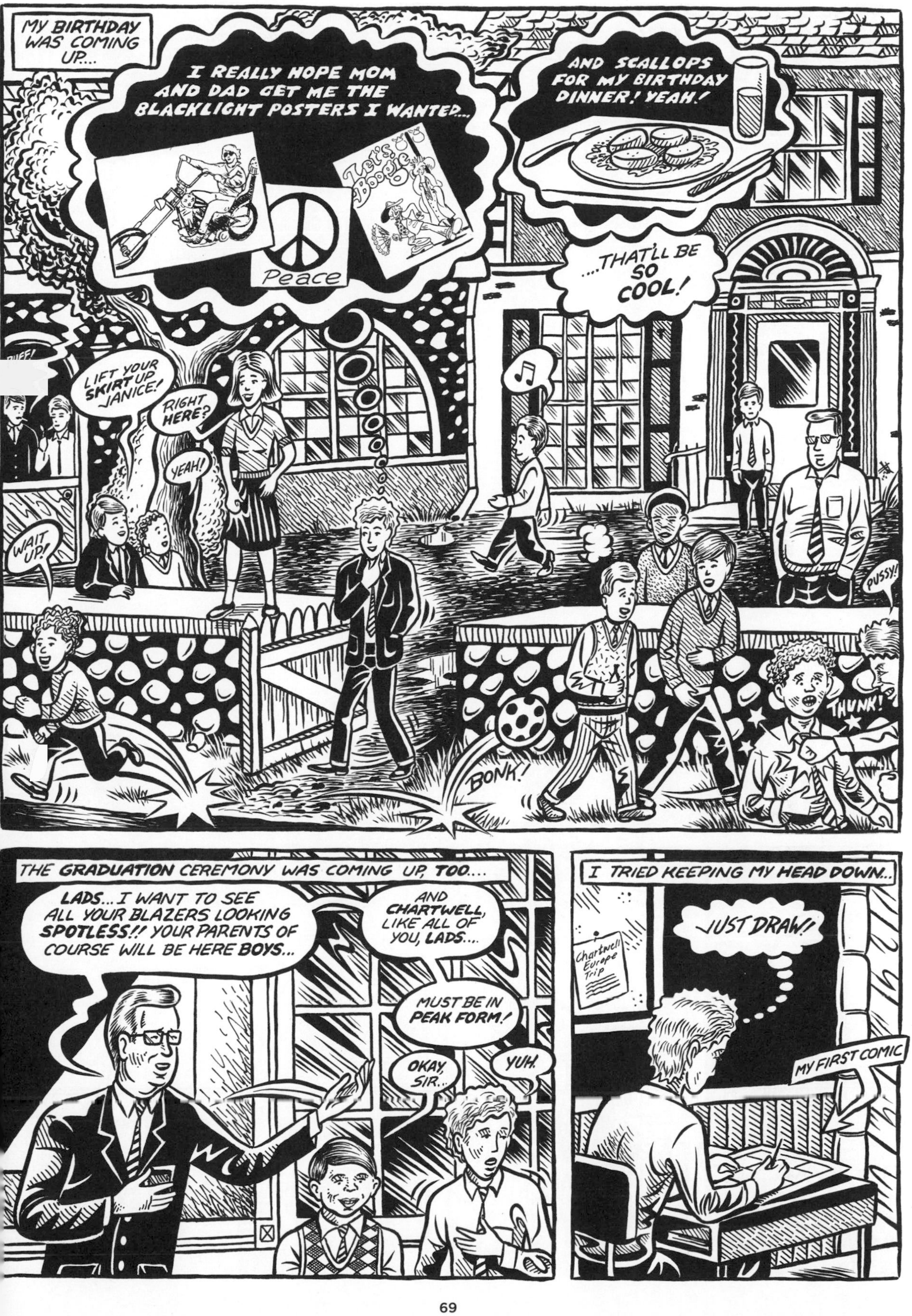
MY BIRTHDAY WAS COMING UP...
I REALLY HOPE MOM AND DAD GET ME THE BLACKLIGHT POSTERS I WANTED...
Let's Boogie
Peace
AND SCALLOPS FOR MY BIRTHDAY DINNER! YEAH!
...THAT'LL BE SO COOL!
LIFT YOUR SKIRT UP JANICE!
RIGHT HERE?
YEAH!
WAIT UP!
PUSSY!
THUNK!
BONK!
THE GRADUATION CEREMONY WAS COMING UP, TOO....
LADS... I WANT TO SEE ALL YOUR BLAZERS LOOKING SPOTLESS!! YOUR PARENTS OF COURSE WILL BE HERE BOYS...
AND CHARTWELL, LIKE ALL OF YOU, LADS....
MUST BE IN PEAK FORM!
OKAY, SIR...
YUH.
I TRIED KEEPING MY HEAD DOWN...
JUST DRAW!
Chartwell Europe Trip
MY FIRST COMIC

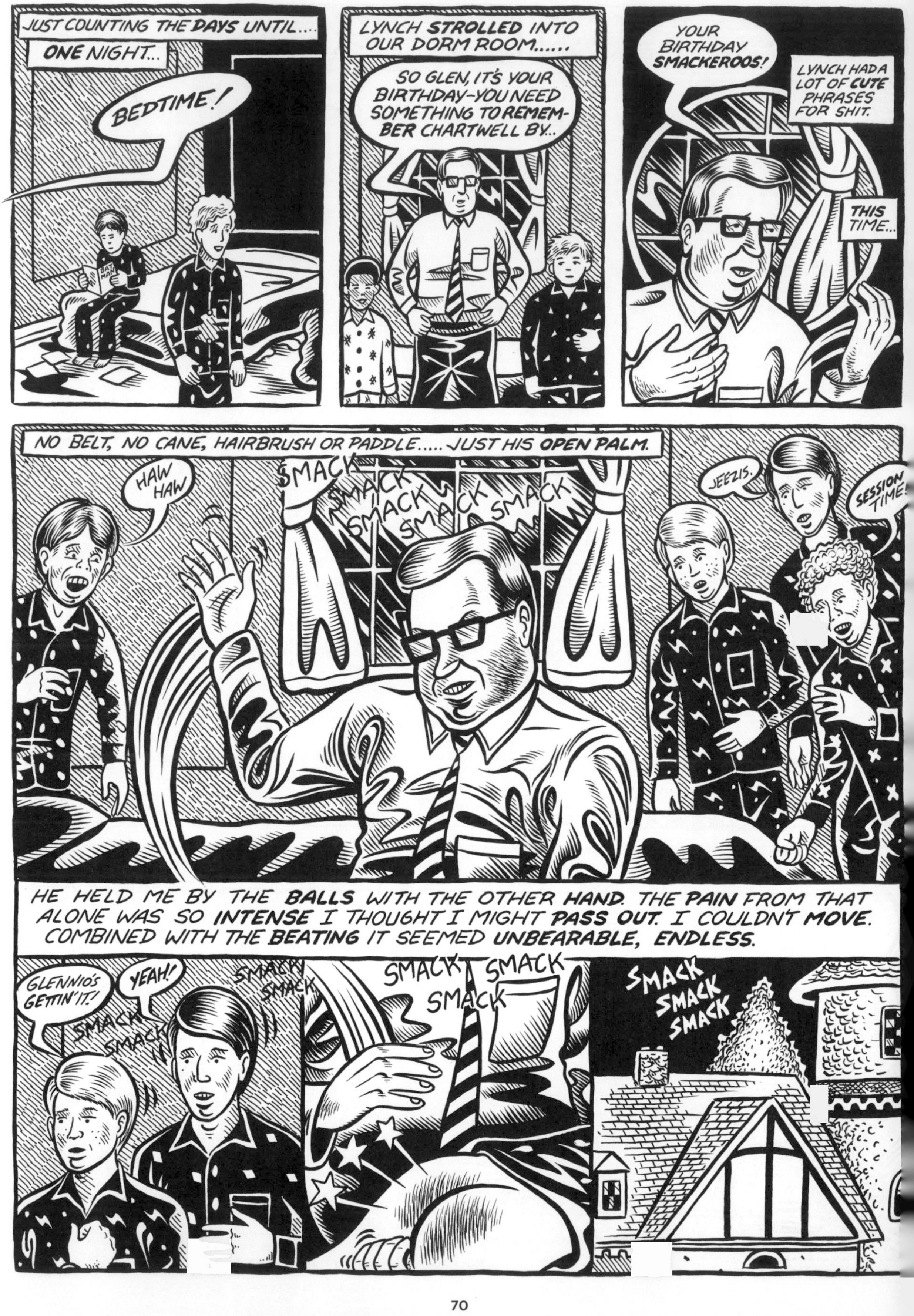
JUST COUNTING THE DAYS UNTIL....
ONE NIGHT...
BEDTIME!
BAT MAN
LYNCH STROLLED INTO OUR DORM ROOM......
SO GLEN, IT'S YOUR BIRTHDAY–YOU NEED SOMETHING TO REMEMBER CHARTWELL BY...
YOUR BIRTHDAY SMACKEROOS!
LYNCH HAD A LOT OF CUTE PHRASES FOR SHIT.
THIS TIME...
NO BELT, NO CANE, HAIRBRUSH OR PADDLE..... JUST HIS OPEN PALM.
HAW HAW
SMACK SMACK SMACK SMACK SMACK
JEEZIS.
SESSION TIME!
HE HELD ME BY THE BALLS WITH THE OTHER HAND. THE PAIN FROM THAT ALONE WAS SO INTENSE I THOUGHT I MIGHT PASS OUT. I COULDN'T MOVE. COMBINED WITH THE BEATING IT SEEMED UNBEARABLE, ENDLESS.
GLENNIO'S GETTIN' IT!
YEAH!
SMACK SMACK
SMACK SMACK
SMACK SMACK SMACK
SMACK SMACK SMACK

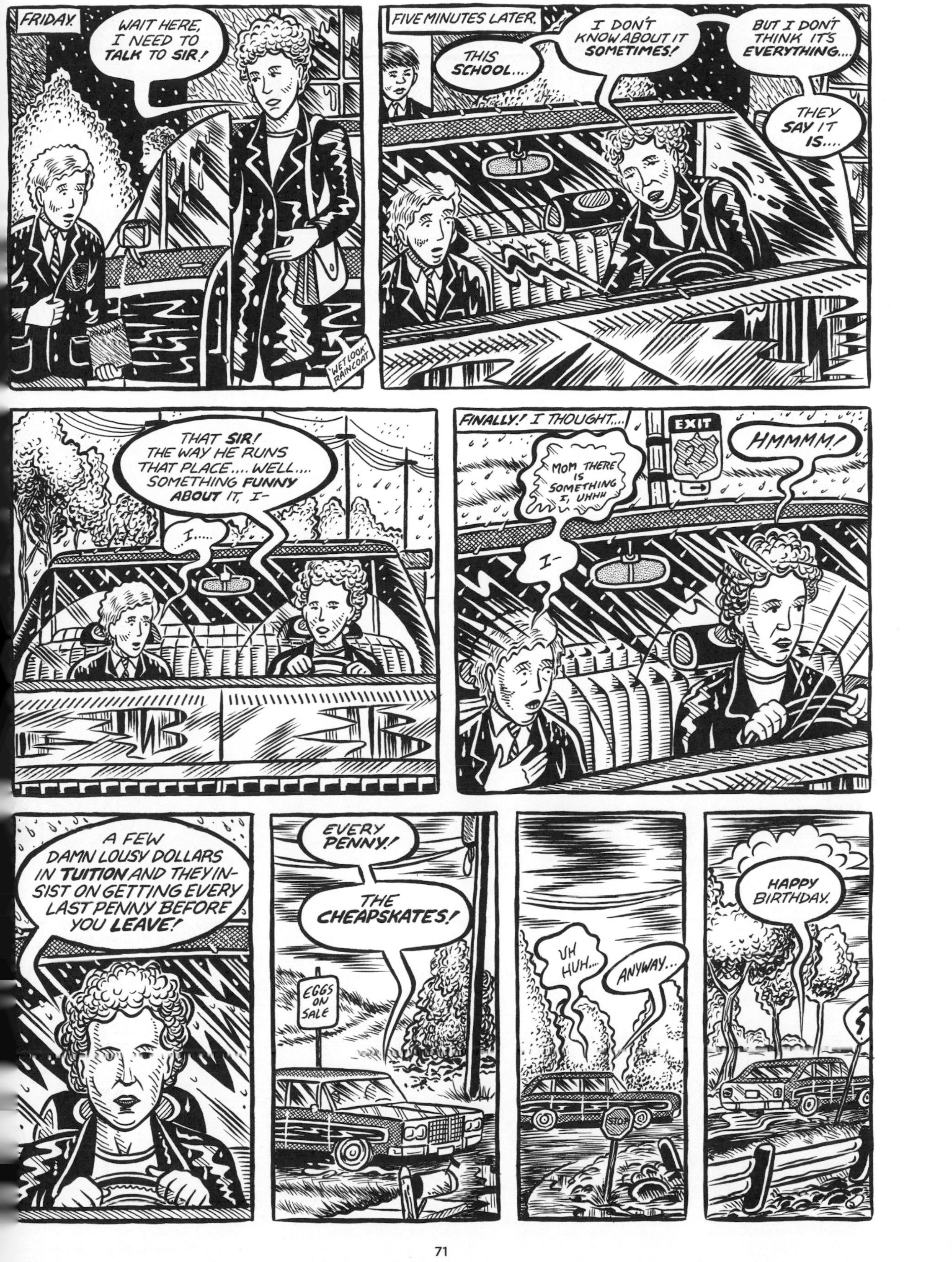
FRIDAY.
WAIT HERE, I NEED TO TALK TO SIR!
'WET LOOK' RAINCOAT
FIVE MINUTES LATER.
THIS SCHOOL....
I DON'T KNOW ABOUT IT SOMETIMES!
BUT I DON'T THINK IT'S EVERYTHING....
THEY SAY IT IS....
THAT SIR! THE WAY HE RUNS THAT PLACE.... WELL.... SOMETHING FUNNY ABOUT IT, I-
...I.....
FINALLY! I THOUGHT....
EXIT
22
MOM THERE IS SOMETHING I, UHHH
HMMMM!
I-
A FEW DAMN LOUSY DOLLARS IN TUITION AND THEY IN-SIST ON GETTING EVERY LAST PENNY BEFORE YOU LEAVE!
EVERY PENNY!
THE CHEAPSKATES!
EGGS ON SALE
UH HUH....
ANYWAY...
HAPPY BIRTHDAY.

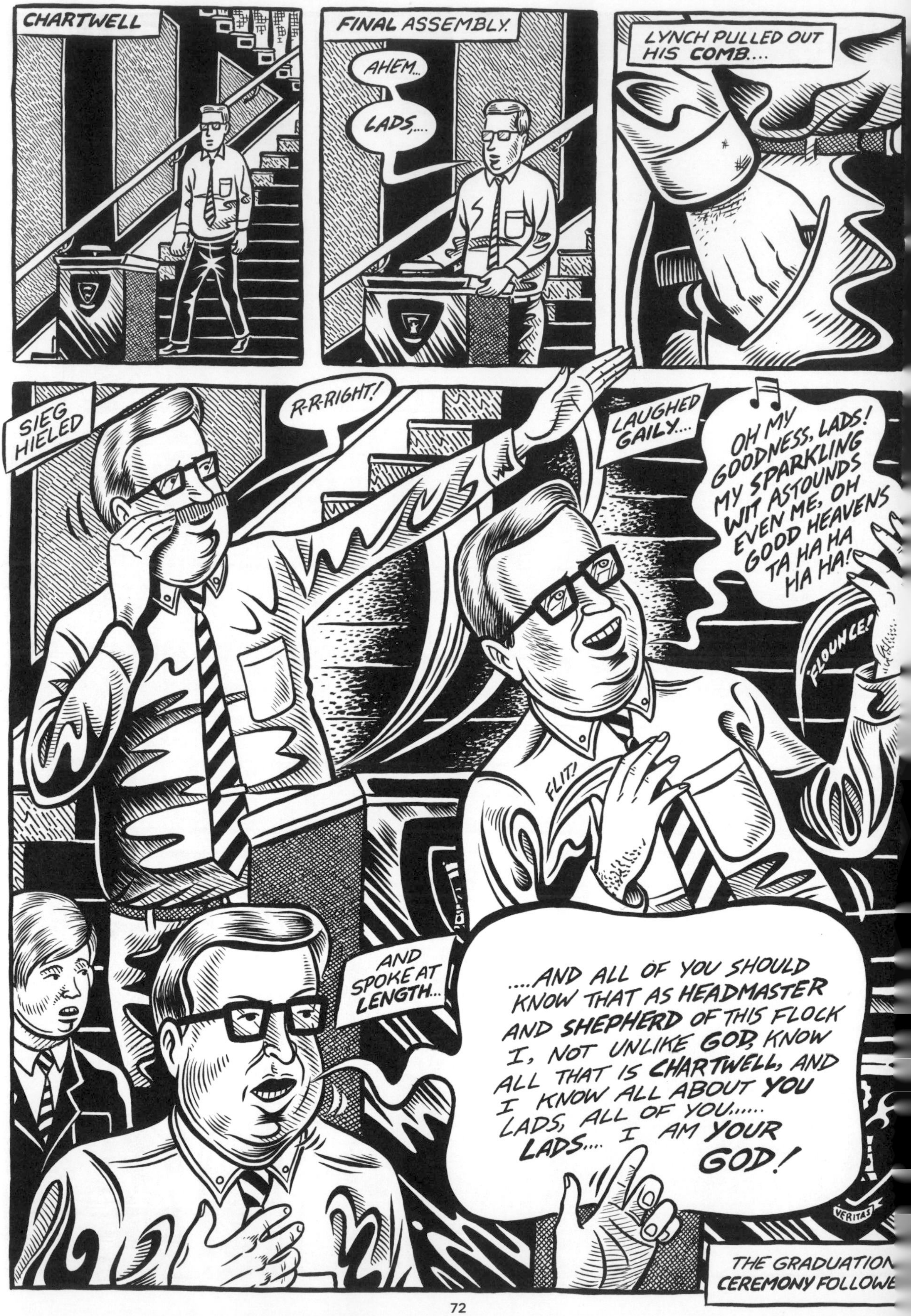
CHARTWELL
FINAL ASSEMBLY.
AHEM...
LADS,....
LYNCH PULLED OUT HIS COMB....
SIEG HIELED
R-R-RIGHT!
LAUGHED GAILY....
OH MY GOODNESS, LADS! MY SPARKLING WIT ASTOUNDS EVEN ME, OH GOOD HEAVENS TA HA HA HA HA!
FLOUNCE!
FLIT!
AND SPOKE AT LENGTH...
....AND ALL OF YOU SHOULD KNOW THAT AS HEADMASTER AND SHEPHERD OF THIS FLOCK I, NOT UNLIKE GOD, KNOW ALL THAT IS CHARTWELL, AND I KNOW ALL ABOUT YOU LADS, ALL OF YOU...... LADS.... I AM YOUR GOD!
VERITAS
THE GRADUATION CEREMONY FOLLOWE

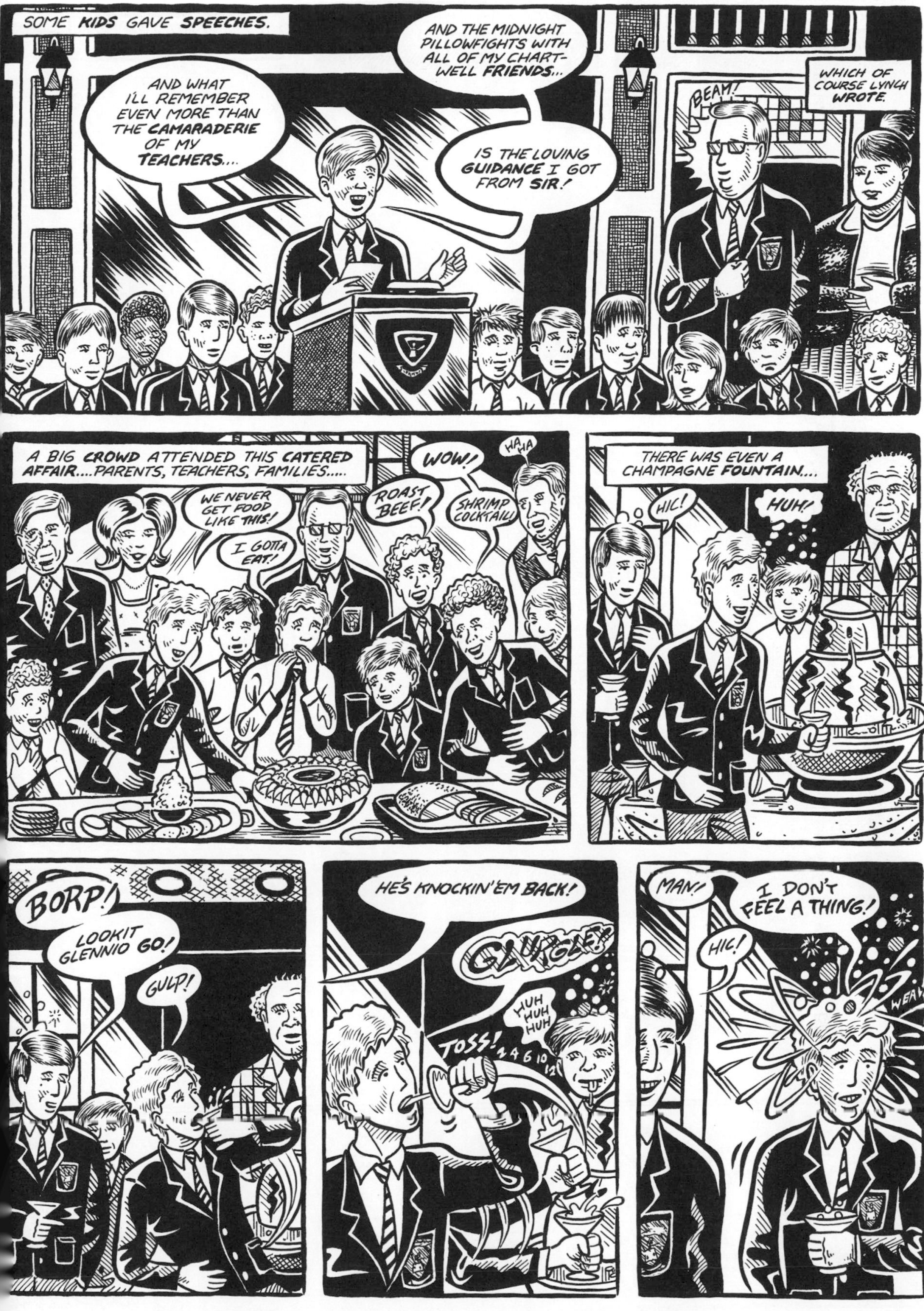
SOME KIDS GAVE SPEECHES.
AND WHAT I'LL REMEMBER EVEN MORE THAN THE CAMARADERIE OF MY TEACHERS....
AND THE MIDNIGHT PILLOWFIGHTS WITH ALL OF MY CHARTWELL FRIENDS...
IS THE LOVING GUIDANCE I GOT FROM SIR!
WHICH OF COURSE LYNCH WROTE.
BEAM!
A BIG CROWD ATTENDED THIS CATERED AFFAIR.... PARENTS, TEACHERS, FAMILIES.....
WE NEVER GET FOOD LIKE THIS!
I GOTTA EAT!
ROAST BEEF!
WOW!
SHRIMP COCKTAIL!
HA HA
THERE WAS EVEN A CHAMPAGNE FOUNTAIN....
HIC!
HUH!
BORP!
LOOKIT GLENNIO GO!
GULP!
HE'S KNOCKIN' 'EM BACK!
GLUGGLEY!
HUH HUH HUH
TOSS!
2 4 6 10 12
MAN!
I DON'T FEEL A THING!
HIC!
WEAVE

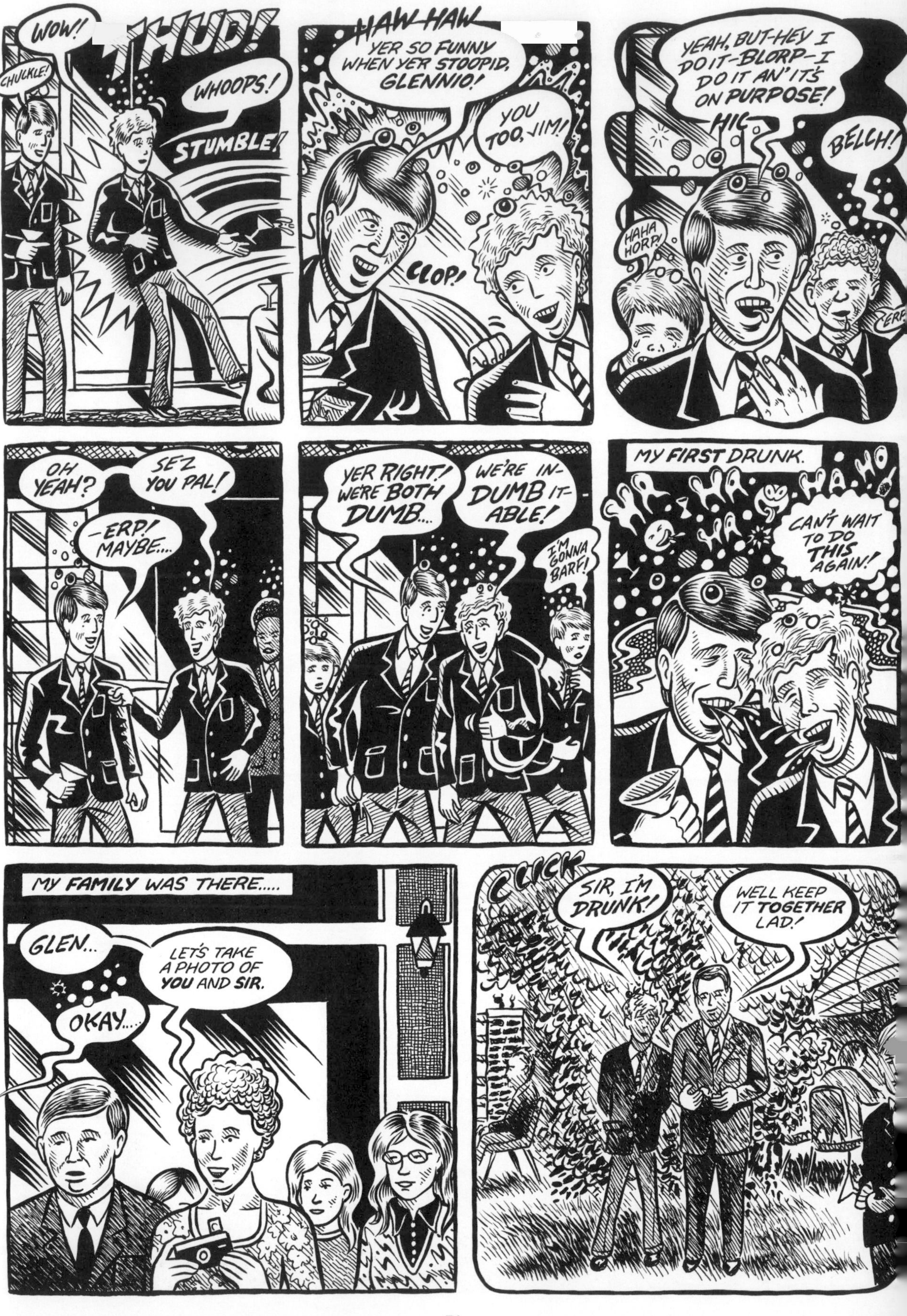
WOW!
CHUCKLE!
THUD!
WHOOPS!
STUMBLE!
HAW HAW
YER SO FUNNY WHEN YER STOOPID, GLENNIO!
YOU TOO, JIM!
CLOP!
YEAH, BUT-HEY I DO IT-BLORP-I DO IT AN' IT'S ON PURPOSE!
HIC
BELCH!
HAHA HORP!
ERP
OH YEAH?
SEZ YOU PAL!
-ERP! MAYBE....
YER RIGHT! WE'RE BOTH DUMB...
WE'RE IN-DUMB IT-ABLE!
I'M GONNA BARF!
MY FIRST DRUNK.
HA HA HA HA HO
CAN'T WAIT TO DO THIS AGAIN!
MY FAMILY WAS THERE.....
GLEN...
LET'S TAKE A PHOTO OF YOU AND SIR.
OKAY.....
CLICK
SIR, I'M DRUNK!
WELL KEEP IT TOGETHER LAD!

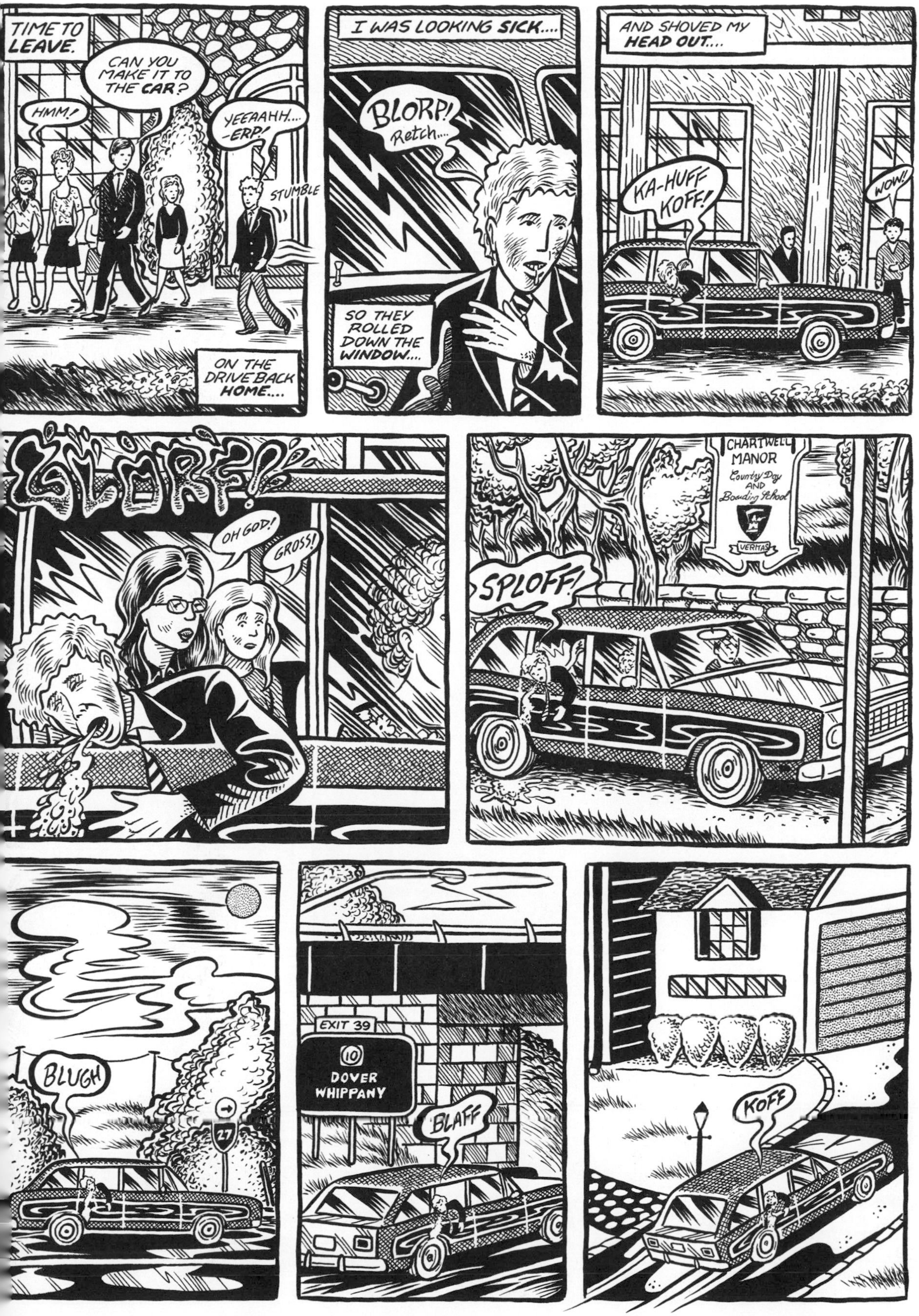
TIME TO LEAVE.
HMM!
CAN YOU MAKE IT TO THE CAR?
YEEAAHH.... -ERP!
STUMBLE
ON THE DRIVE BACK HOME....
I WAS LOOKING SICK....
BLORP! Retch....
SO THEY ROLLED DOWN THE WINDOW....
AND SHOVED MY HEAD OUT....
KA-HUFF KOFF!
WOW!
GLORF!
OH GOD!
GROSS!
CHARTWELL MANOR
Country Day AND Boarding School
VERITAS
SPLOFF!
BLUGH
27
EXIT 39
10
DOVER
WHIPPANY
BLAFF
KOFF

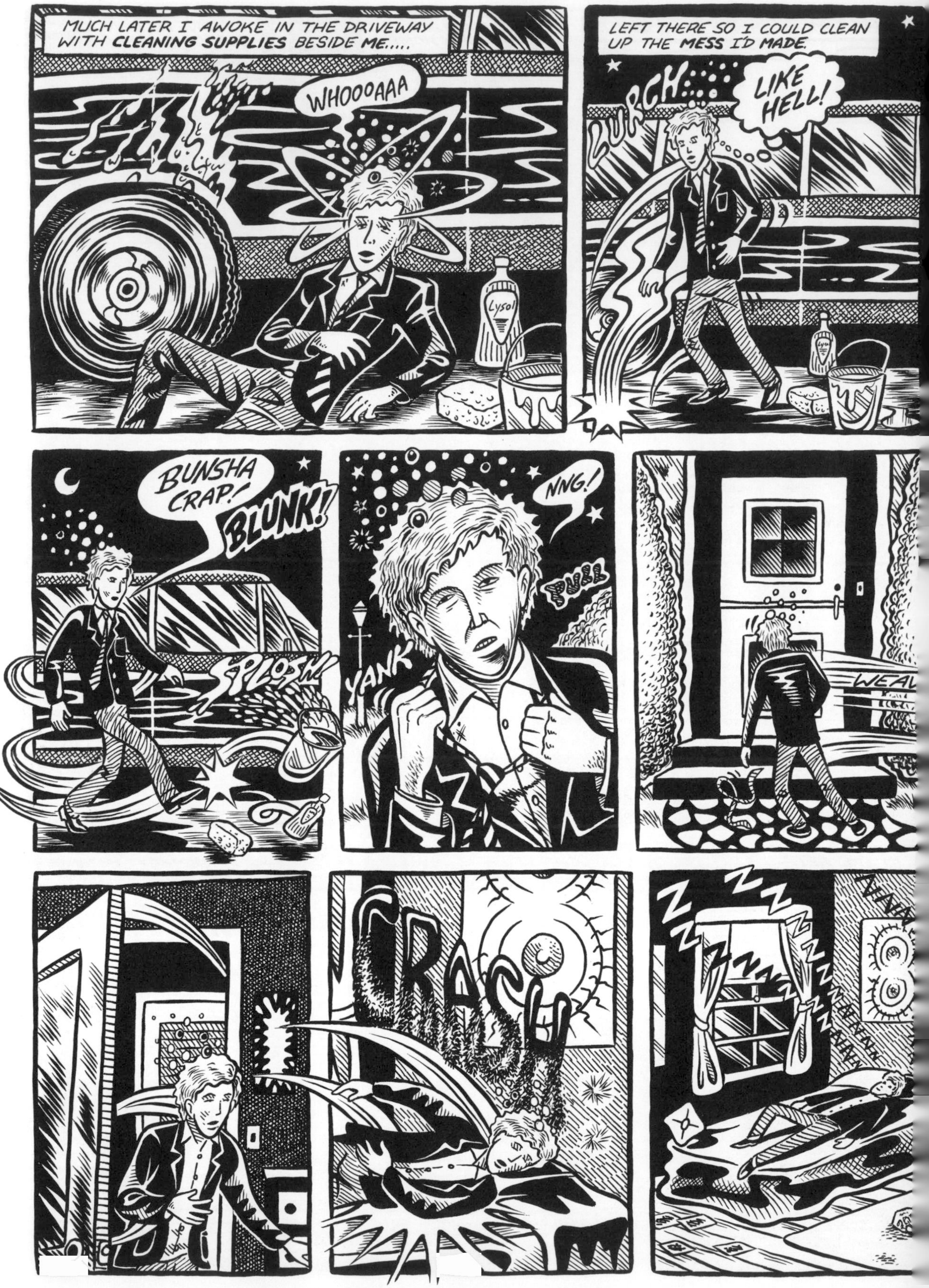
MUCH LATER I AWOKE IN THE DRIVEWAY WITH **CLEANING SUPPLIES** BESIDE **ME**.....
WHOOOAAA
Lysol
LEFT THERE SO I COULD CLEAN UP THE **MESS** I'D **MADE**.
LURCH
LIKE HELL!
BUNSHA CRAP!
BLUNK!
SPLOSH!
NNG!
YANK
PULL
CRASH

THAT SUMMER THINGS WERE **QUIET.**

IT WAS NICE TO BE **BACK HOME.**

TO HAVE MY OWN **BEDROOM** AGAIN.

I RODE MY **MOTORCYCLE** IN A NEIGHBOR'S **BACK YARD.**

THERE WAS ROOM ENOUGH TO REALLY OPEN IT UP.

IN THE AFTERNOONS I'D TAKE A **LONG WALK**.......

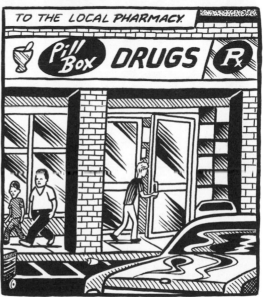

TO THE LOCAL **PHARMACY.**

Pill Box DRUGS ℞

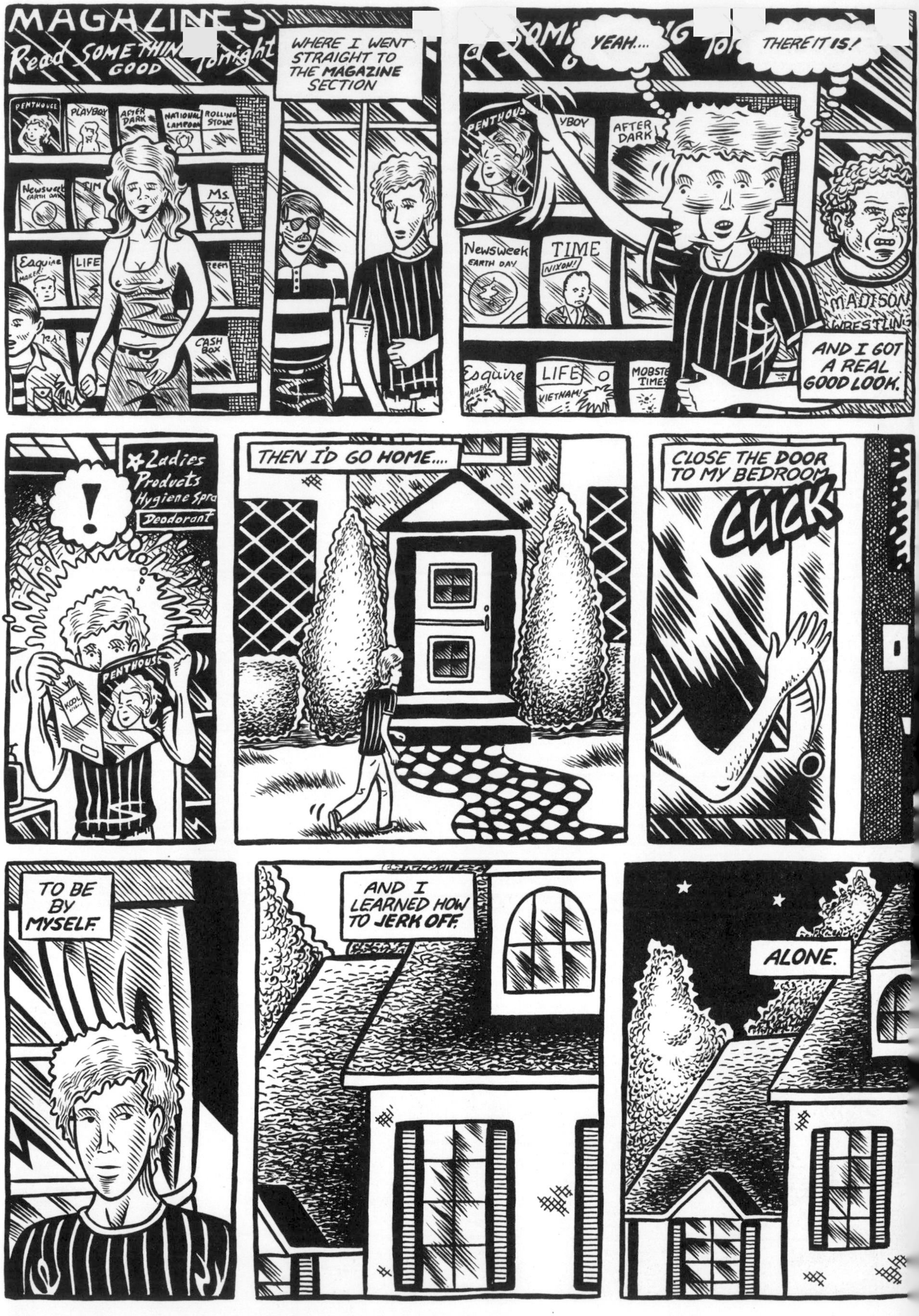
MAGAZINES
Read SOMETHIN
GOOD
Tonight
PENTHOUSE
PLAYBOY
AFTER DARK
NATIONAL LAMPOON
ROLLING STONE
Ms.
Esquire
LIFE
CASH BOX
WHERE I WENT STRAIGHT TO THE MAGAZINE SECTION
YEAH....
THERE IT IS!
AFTER DARK
Newsweek EARTH DAY
TIME NIXON!
LIFE VIETNAM!
MADISON WRESTLING
AND I GOT A REAL GOOD LOOK.
!
Ladies Products
Deodorant
PENTHOUSE
THEN I'D GO HOME....
CLOSE THE DOOR TO MY BEDROOM
CLICK
TO BE BY MYSELF.
AND I LEARNED HOW TO JERK OFF.
ALONE.

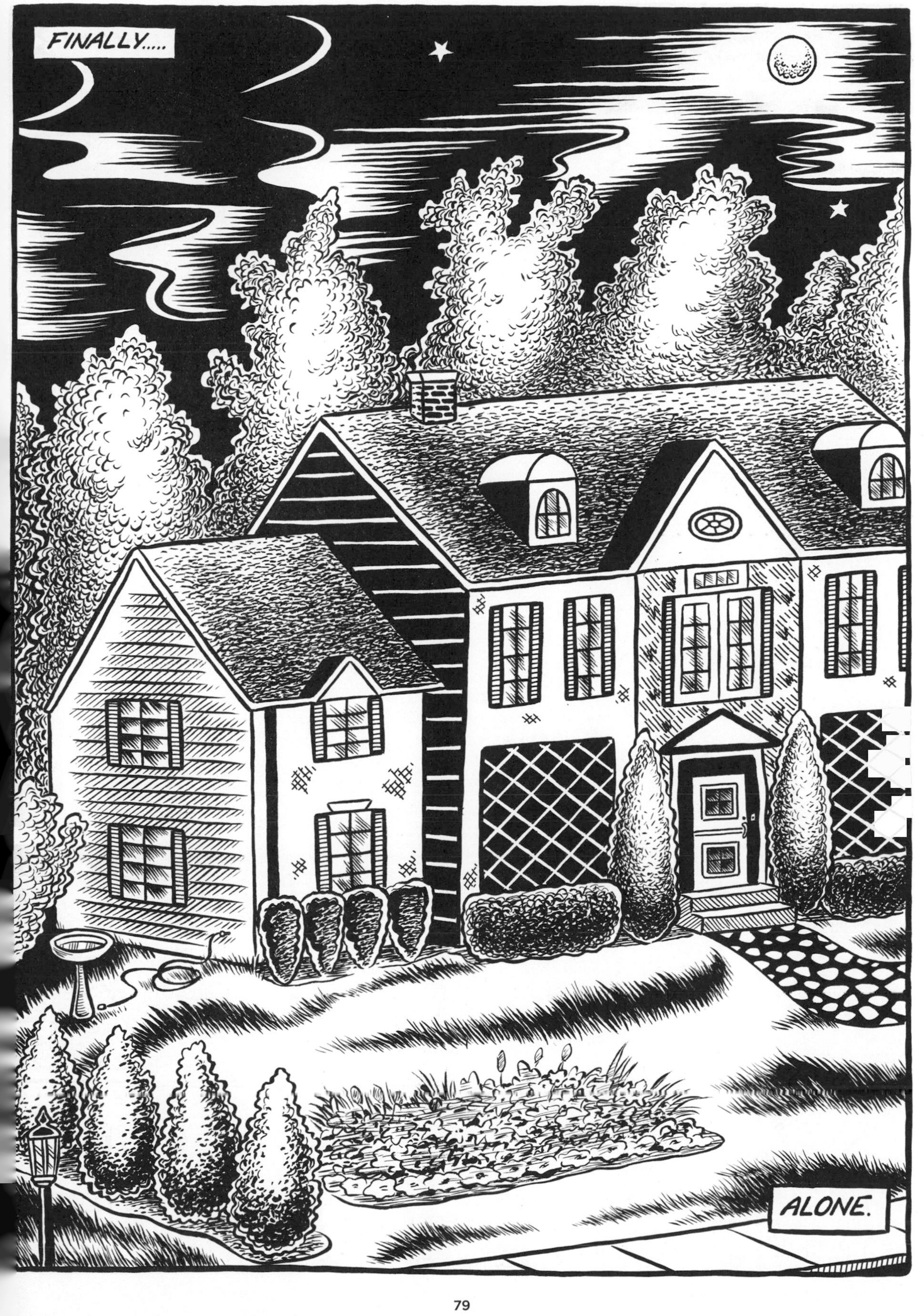
FINALLY.....
ALONE.

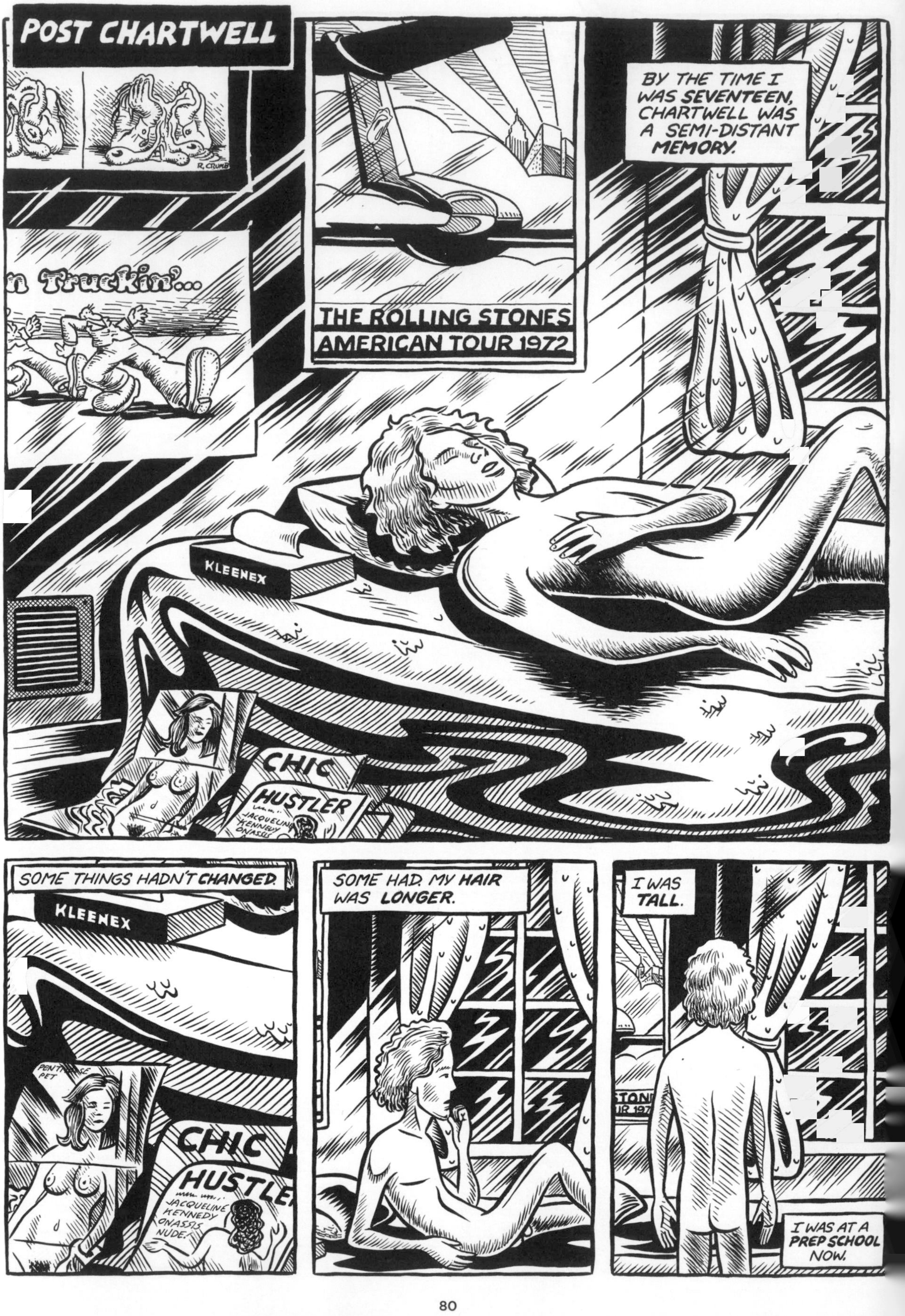
POST CHARTWELL
R. CRUMB
Truckin'...
THE ROLLING STONES
AMERICAN TOUR 1972
BY THE TIME I WAS SEVENTEEN, CHARTWELL WAS A SEMI-DISTANT MEMORY.
KLEENEX
CHIC
HUSTLER
SOME THINGS HADN'T CHANGED.
KLEENEX
PENTHOUSE PET
CHIC
HUSTLE
JACQUELINE KENNEDY ONASSIS NUDE!
SOME HAD. MY HAIR WAS LONGER.
I WAS TALL.
I WAS AT A PREP SCHOOL NOW.

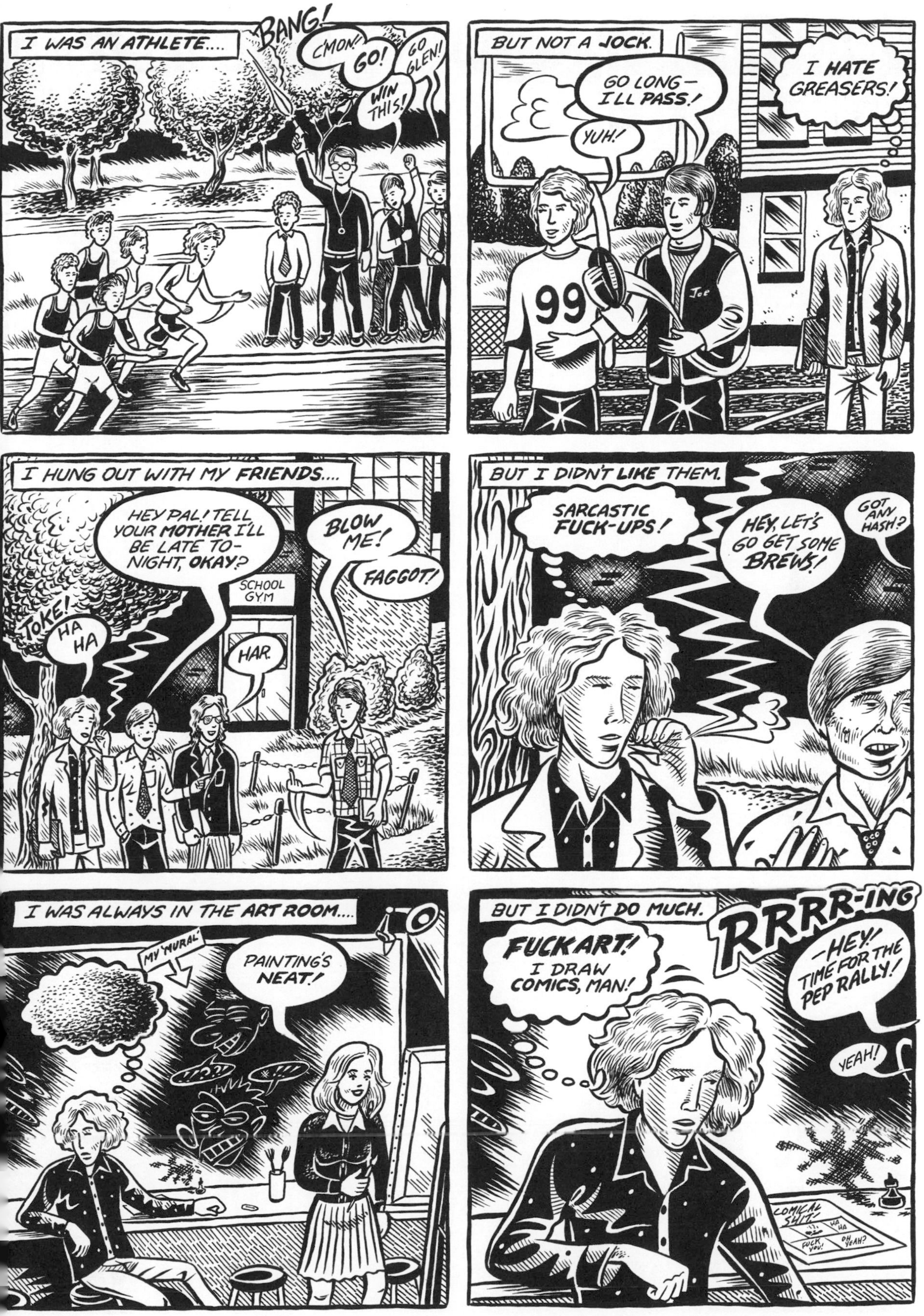
I WAS AN ATHLETE....
BANG!
C'MON!
GO!
GO GLEN!
WIN THIS!
BUT NOT A JOCK.
GO LONG— I'LL PASS!
YUH!
I HATE GREASERS!
Joe
99
I HUNG OUT WITH MY FRIENDS....
HEY PAL! TELL YOUR MOTHER I'LL BE LATE TO-NIGHT, OKAY?
BLOW ME!
FAGGOT!
SCHOOL GYM
TOKE!
HA HA
HAR.
BUT I DIDN'T LIKE THEM.
SARCASTIC FUCK-UPS!
HEY, LET'S GO GET SOME BREWS!
GOT ANY HASH?
I WAS ALWAYS IN THE ART ROOM....
MY 'MURAL'
PAINTING'S NEAT!
BUT I DIDN'T DO MUCH.
RRRR-ING
FUCK ART! I DRAW COMICS, MAN!
—HEY! TIME FOR THE PEP RALLY!
YEAH!
COMICAL SHIT
HA HA
FUCK YOU!
OH YEAH?

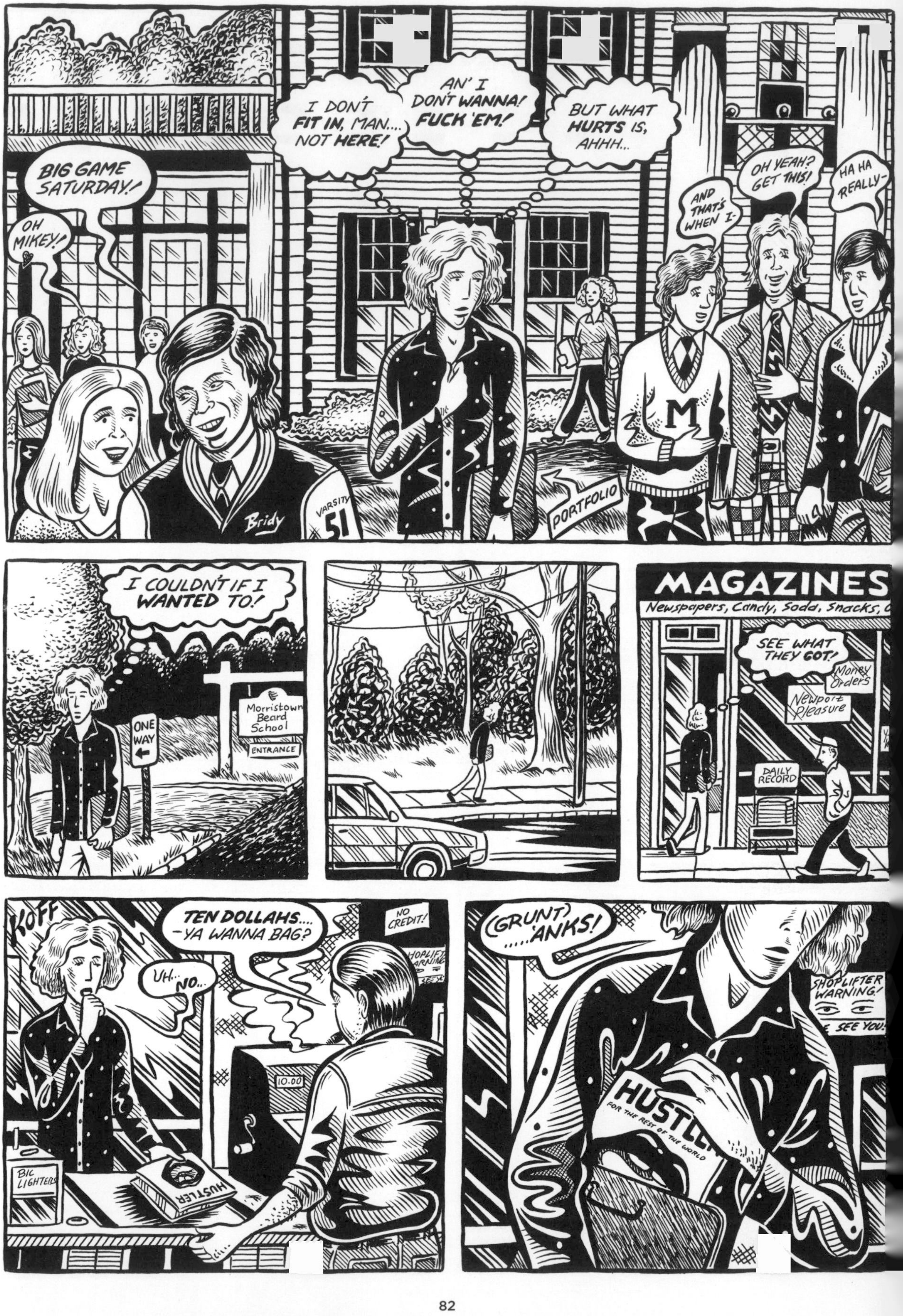

OH MIKEY!
BIG GAME SATURDAY!
Bridy
VARSITY 51
I DON'T FIT IN, MAN.... NOT HERE!
AN' I DON'T WANNA! FUCK 'EM!
BUT WHAT HURTS IS, AHHH...
PORTFOLIO
AND THAT'S WHEN I-
OH YEAH? GET THIS!
HA HA REALLY-
M
I COULDN'T IF I WANTED TO!
Morristown Beard School
ENTRANCE
ONE WAY
MAGAZINES
Newspapers, Candy, Soda, Snacks,
SEE WHAT THEY GOT!
Money Orders
Newport Pleasure
DAILY RECORD
KOFF
TEN DOLLAHS.... -YA WANNA BAG?
UH... NO...
NO CREDIT!
10.00
BIC LIGHTERS
HUSTLER
(GRUNT) ......'ANKS!
SHOPLIFTER WARNING! SEE YOU!
HUSTLER
FOR THE REST OF THE WORLD

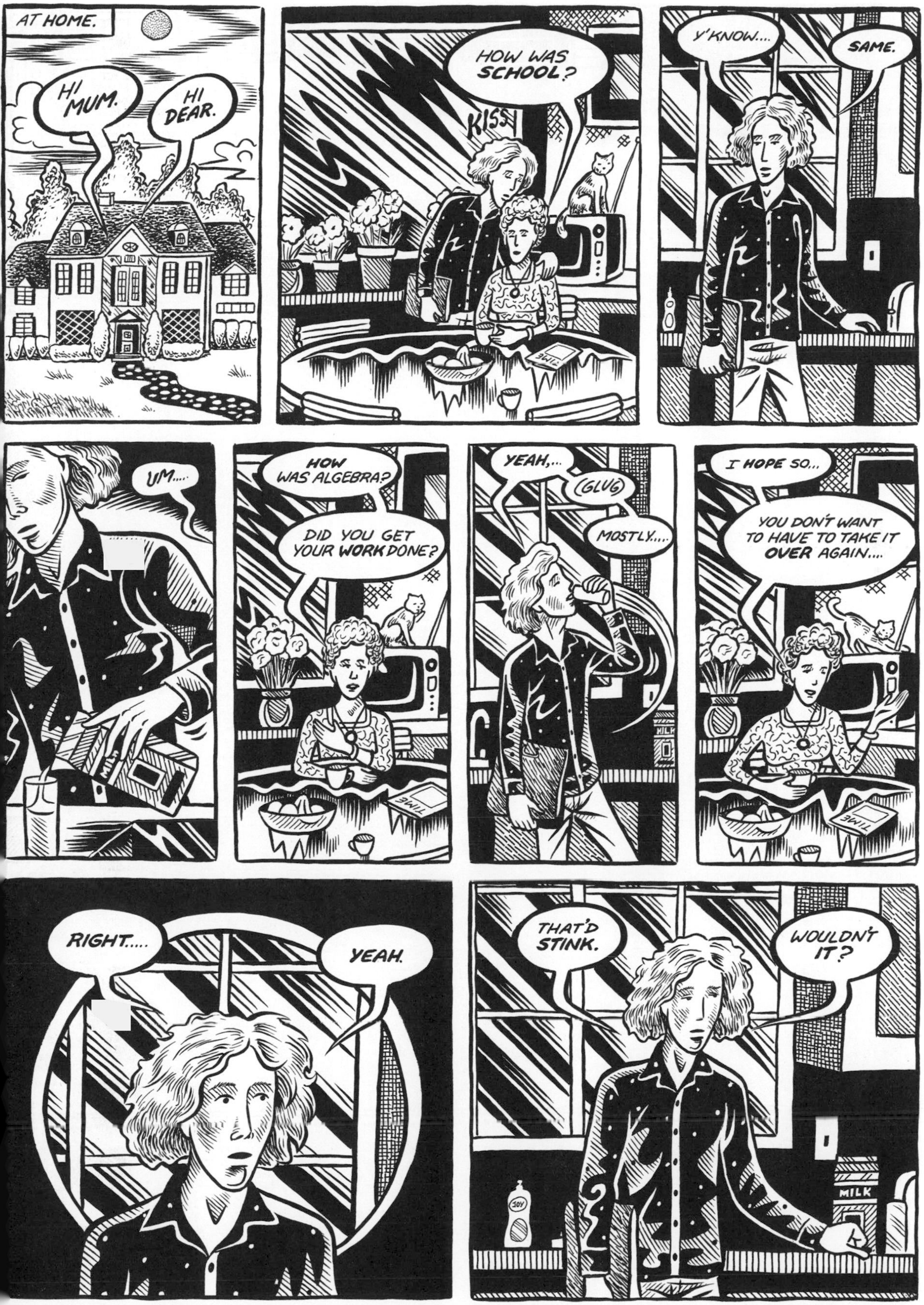
AT HOME.
HI MUM.
HI DEAR.
HOW WAS SCHOOL?
KISS
Y'KNOW....
SAME.
UM.....
HOW WAS ALGEBRA?
DID YOU GET YOUR WORK DONE?
YEAH,...
(GLUG)
MOSTLY.....
I HOPE SO...
YOU DON'T WANT TO HAVE TO TAKE IT OVER AGAIN....
RIGHT.....
YEAH.
THAT'D STINK.
WOULDN'T IT?

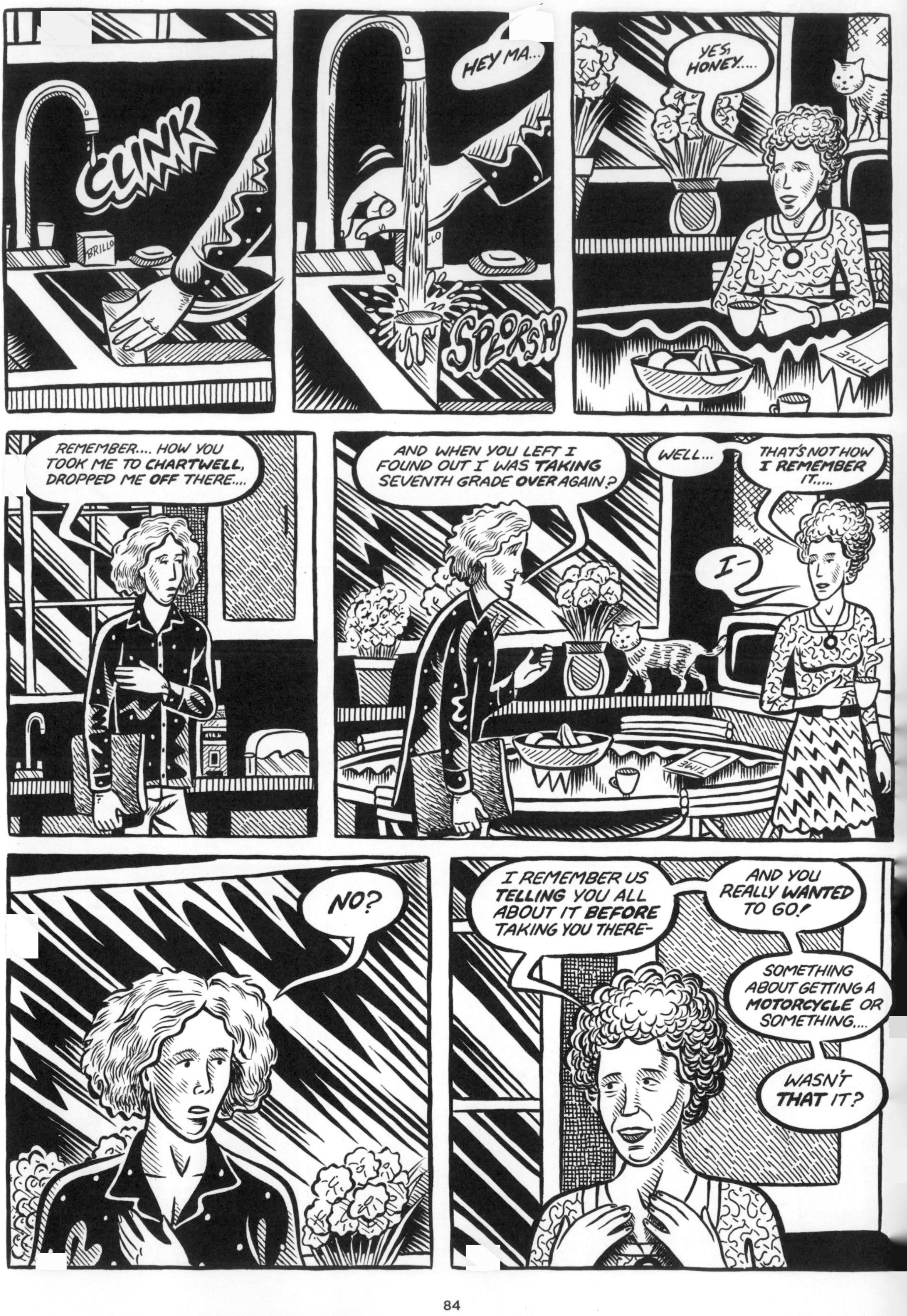
CLINK
HEY MA...
SPLORSH
YES, HONEY.....
REMEMBER.... HOW YOU TOOK ME TO CHARTWELL, DROPPED ME OFF THERE....
AND WHEN YOU LEFT I FOUND OUT I WAS TAKING SEVENTH GRADE OVER AGAIN?
WELL...
THAT'S NOT HOW I REMEMBER IT.....
I-
NO?
I REMEMBER US TELLING YOU ALL ABOUT IT BEFORE TAKING YOU THERE-
AND YOU REALLY WANTED TO GO!
SOMETHING ABOUT GETTING A MOTORCYCLE OR SOMETHING....
WASN'T THAT IT?

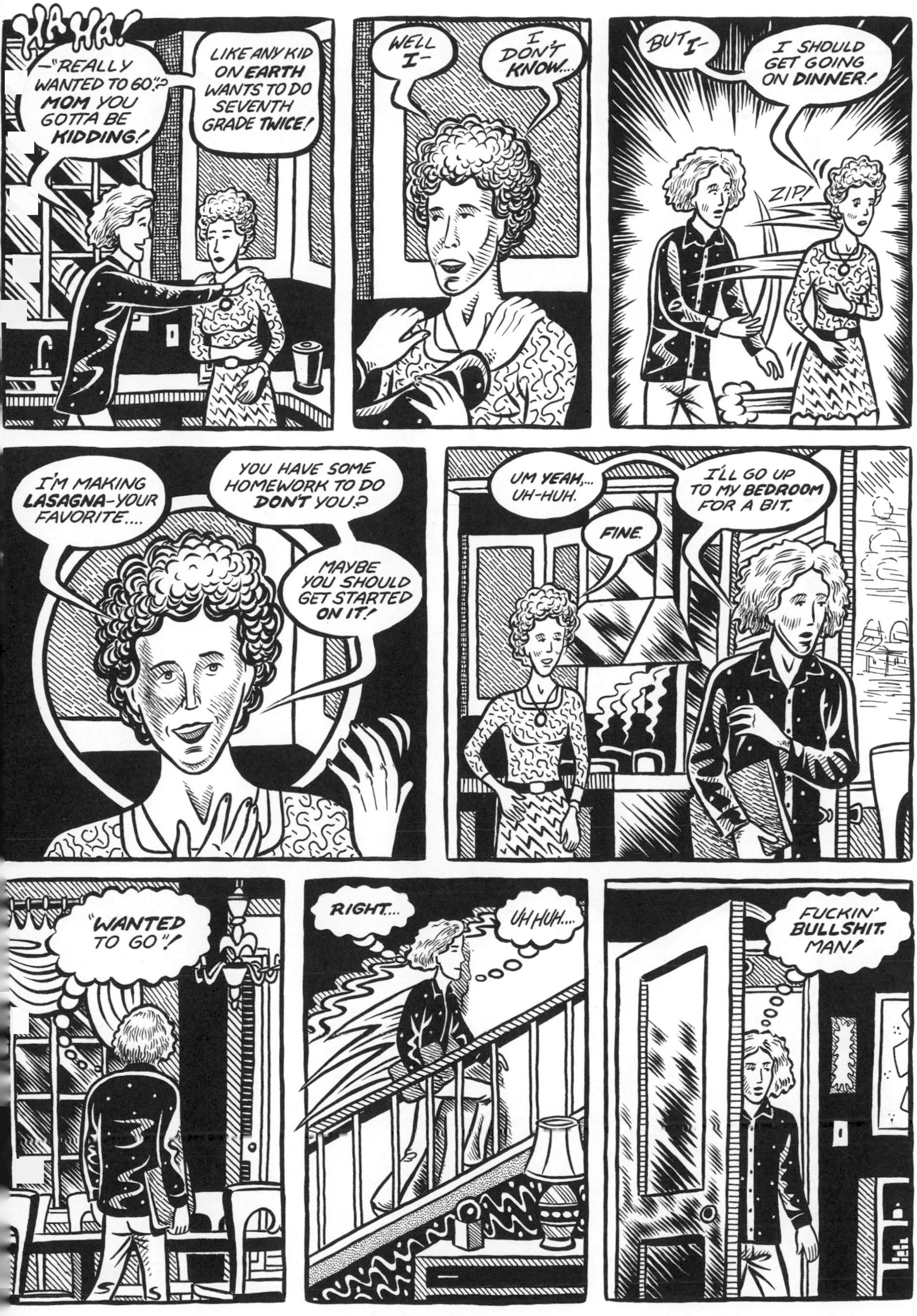
HA HA!
—"REALLY WANTED TO GO"? MOM YOU GOTTA BE KIDDING!
LIKE ANY KID ON EARTH WANTS TO DO SEVENTH GRADE TWICE!
WELL I-
I DON'T KNOW....
BUT I-
I SHOULD GET GOING ON DINNER!
ZIP!
I'M MAKING LASAGNA-YOUR FAVORITE....
YOU HAVE SOME HOMEWORK TO DO DON'T YOU?
MAYBE YOU SHOULD GET STARTED ON IT!
UM YEAH,... UH-HUH.
FINE.
I'LL GO UP TO MY BEDROOM FOR A BIT.
"WANTED TO GO"!
RIGHT....
UH HUH....
FUCKIN' BULLSHIT, MAN!

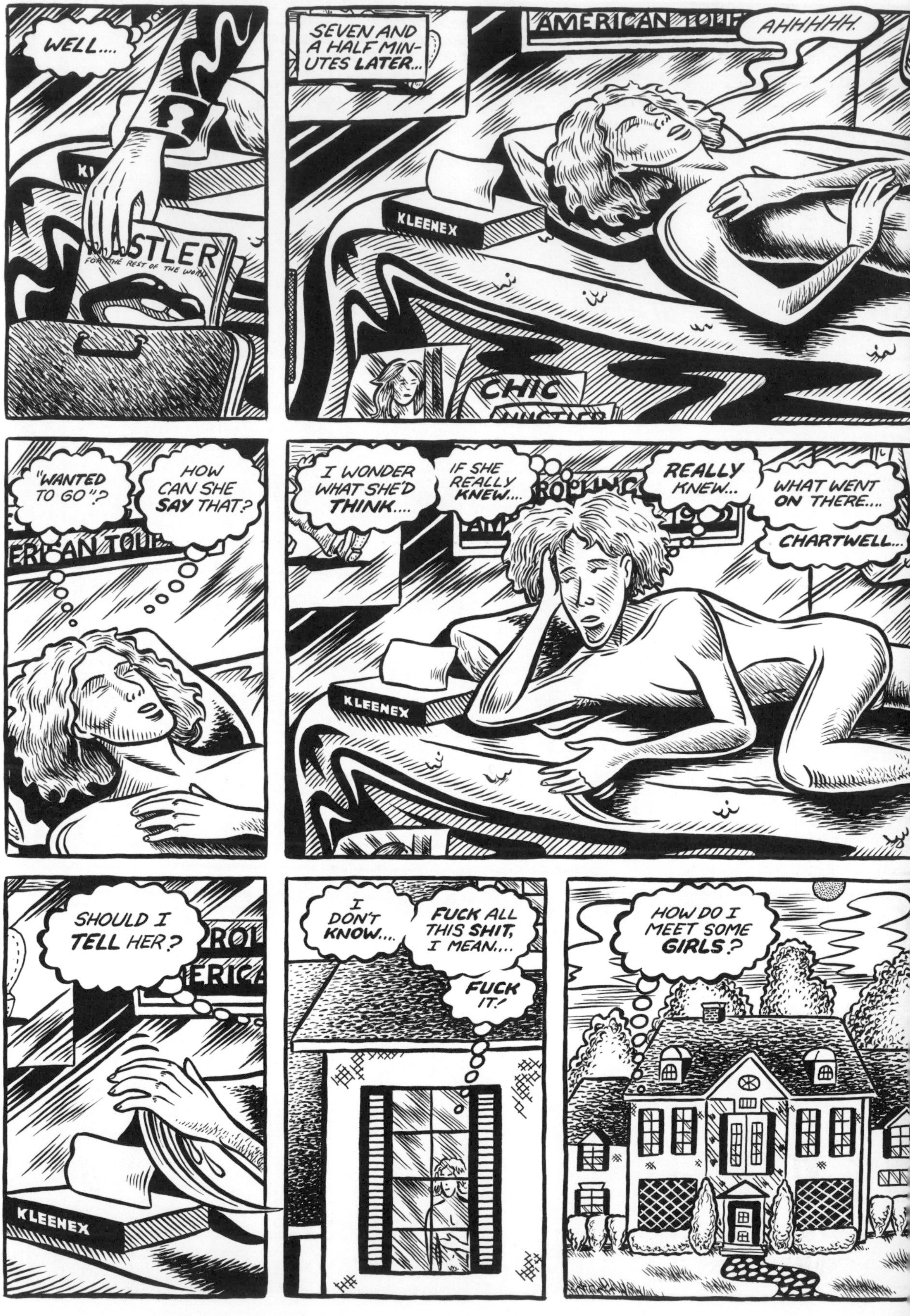
WELL....
HUSTLER
FOR THE REST OF THE WORLD
SEVEN AND A HALF MINUTES LATER...
AMERICAN TOUR
AHHHHH.
KLEENEX
CHIC
"WANTED TO GO"?
HOW CAN SHE SAY THAT?
I WONDER WHAT SHE'D THINK....
IF SHE REALLY KNEW....
REALLY KNEW...
WHAT WENT ON THERE....
CHARTWELL...
KLEENEX
SHOULD I TELL HER?
KLEENEX
I DON'T KNOW....
FUCK ALL THIS SHIT, I MEAN....
FUCK IT!
HOW DO I MEET SOME GIRLS?

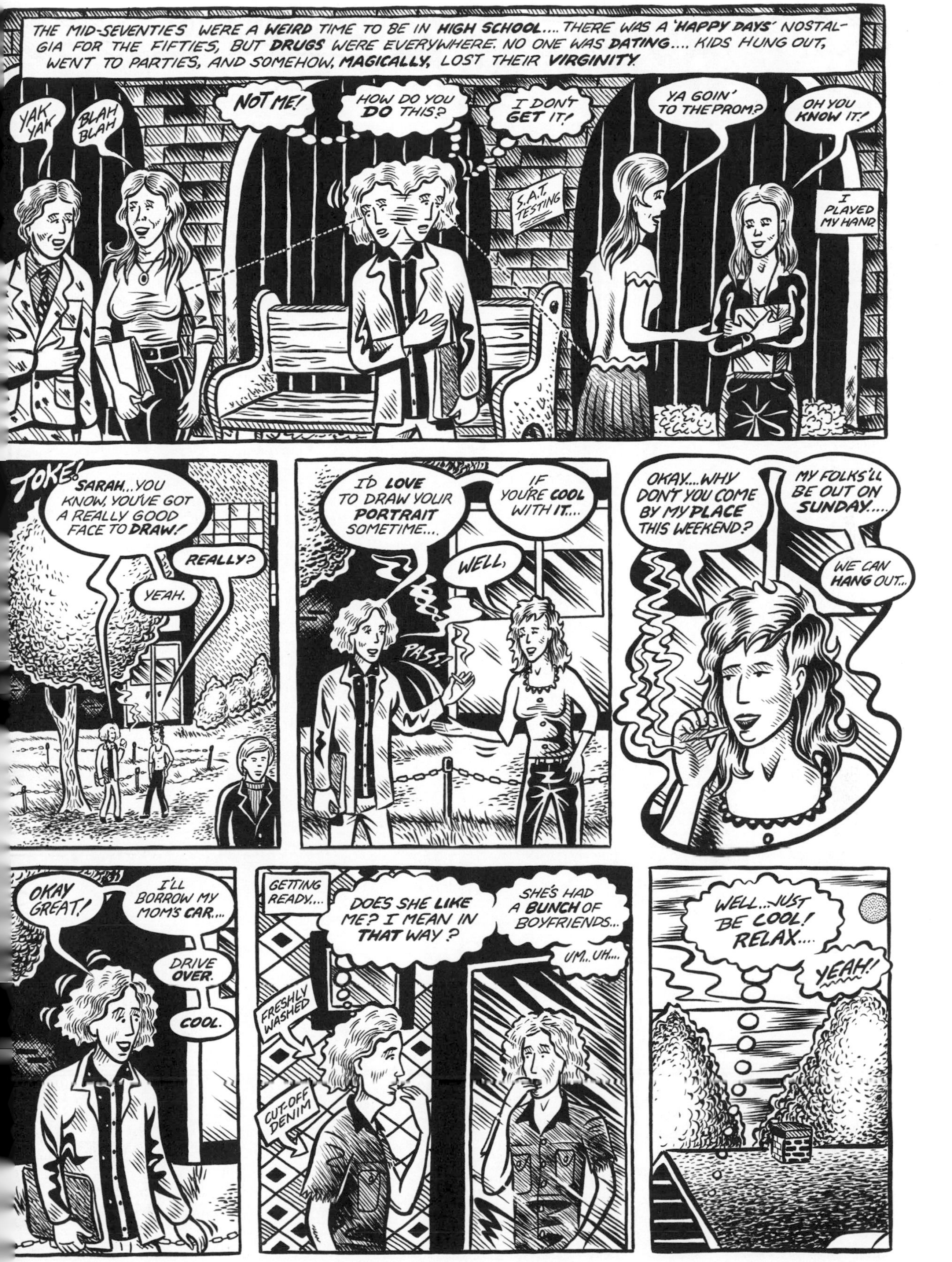
THE MID-SEVENTIES WERE A **WEIRD** TIME TO BE IN **HIGH SCHOOL**.... THERE WAS A **'HAPPY DAYS'** NOSTALGIA FOR THE FIFTIES, BUT **DRUGS** WERE EVERYWHERE. NO ONE WAS **DATING**.... KIDS HUNG OUT, WENT TO PARTIES, AND SOMEHOW, **MAGICALLY**, LOST THEIR **VIRGINITY**.
YAK YAK
BLAH BLAH
NOT ME!
HOW DO YOU **DO** THIS?
I DON'T **GET** IT!
S.A.T. TESTING
YA GOIN' TO THE PROM?
OH YOU **KNOW** IT!
I PLAYED MY HAND
TOKE!
SARAH...YOU KNOW, YOU'VE GOT A REALLY GOOD FACE TO **DRAW**!
REALLY?
YEAH.
I'D **LOVE** TO DRAW YOUR **PORTRAIT** SOMETIME....
IF YOU'RE **COOL** WITH **IT**....
WELL,
PASS!
OKAY....WHY DON'T YOU COME BY MY **PLACE** THIS WEEKEND?
MY FOLKS'LL BE OUT ON **SUNDAY**.....
WE CAN **HANG** OUT...
OKAY GREAT!
I'LL BORROW MY MOM'S **CAR**....
DRIVE **OVER**.
COOL.
GETTING READY...
DOES SHE **LIKE** ME? I MEAN IN **THAT** WAY?
SHE'S HAD A **BUNCH** OF BOYFRIENDS...
UM...UH...
FRESHLY WASHED
CUT-OFF DENIM
WELL...JUST BE **COOL**! RELAX....
YEAH!

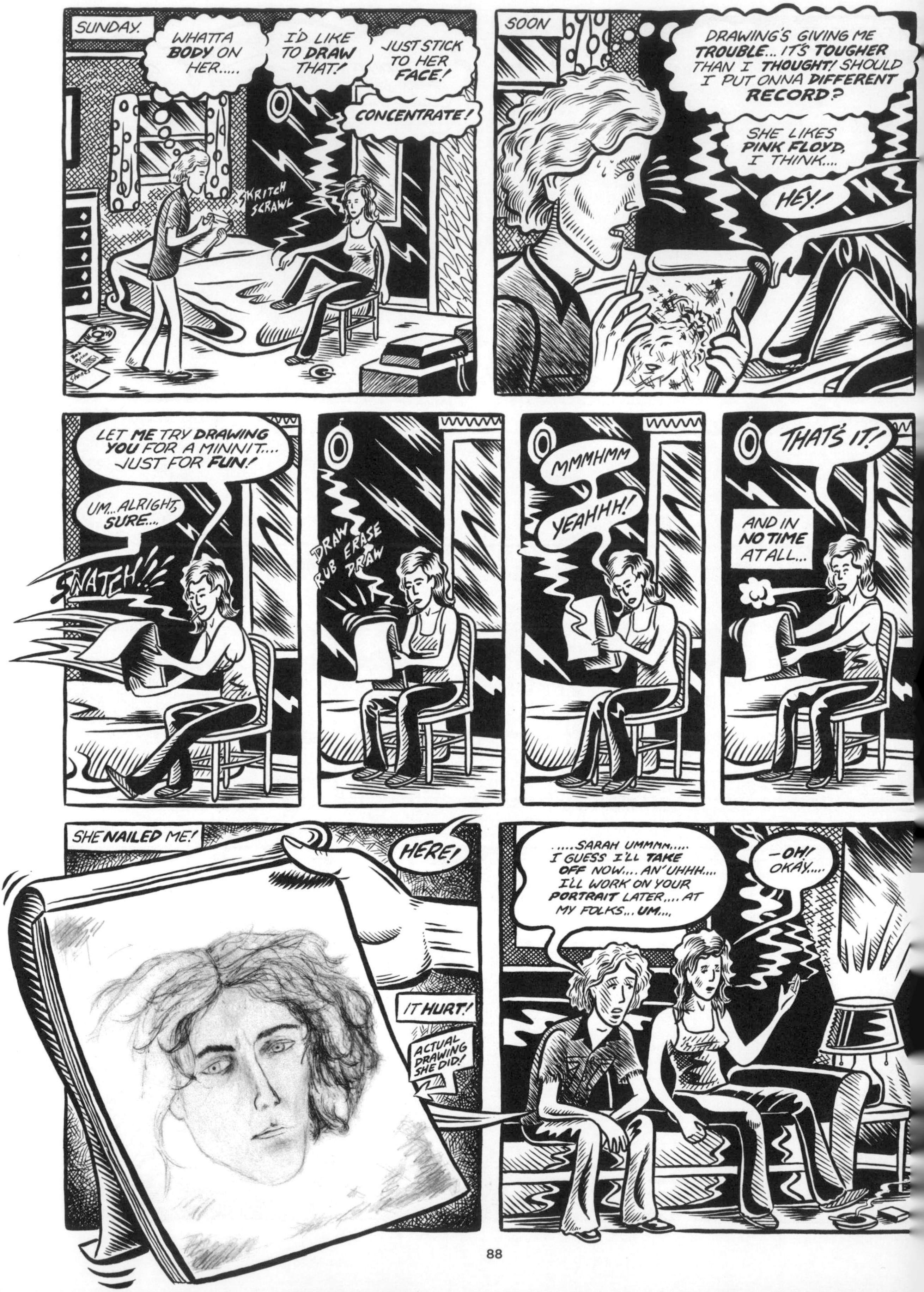
SUNDAY.
WHATTA BODY ON HER.....
I'D LIKE TO DRAW THAT!
JUST STICK TO HER FACE!
CONCENTRATE!
SKRITCH SCRAWL
SOON
DRAWING'S GIVING ME TROUBLE... IT'S TOUGHER THAN I THOUGHT! SHOULD I PUT ONNA DIFFERENT RECORD?
SHE LIKES PINK FLOYD, I THINK....
HEY!
LET ME TRY DRAWING YOU FOR A MINNIT.... JUST FOR FUN!
UM... ALRIGHT, SURE....
SNATCH!
DRAW RUB ERASE DRAW
MMMHMM
YEAHHH!
THAT'S IT!
AND IN NO TIME AT ALL...
SHE NAILED ME!
HERE!
IT HURT!
ACTUAL DRAWING SHE DID!
.....SARAH UMMMM..... I GUESS I'LL TAKE OFF NOW.... AN' UHHH... I'LL WORK ON YOUR PORTRAIT LATER,... AT MY FOLKS... UM...,
-OH! OKAY....

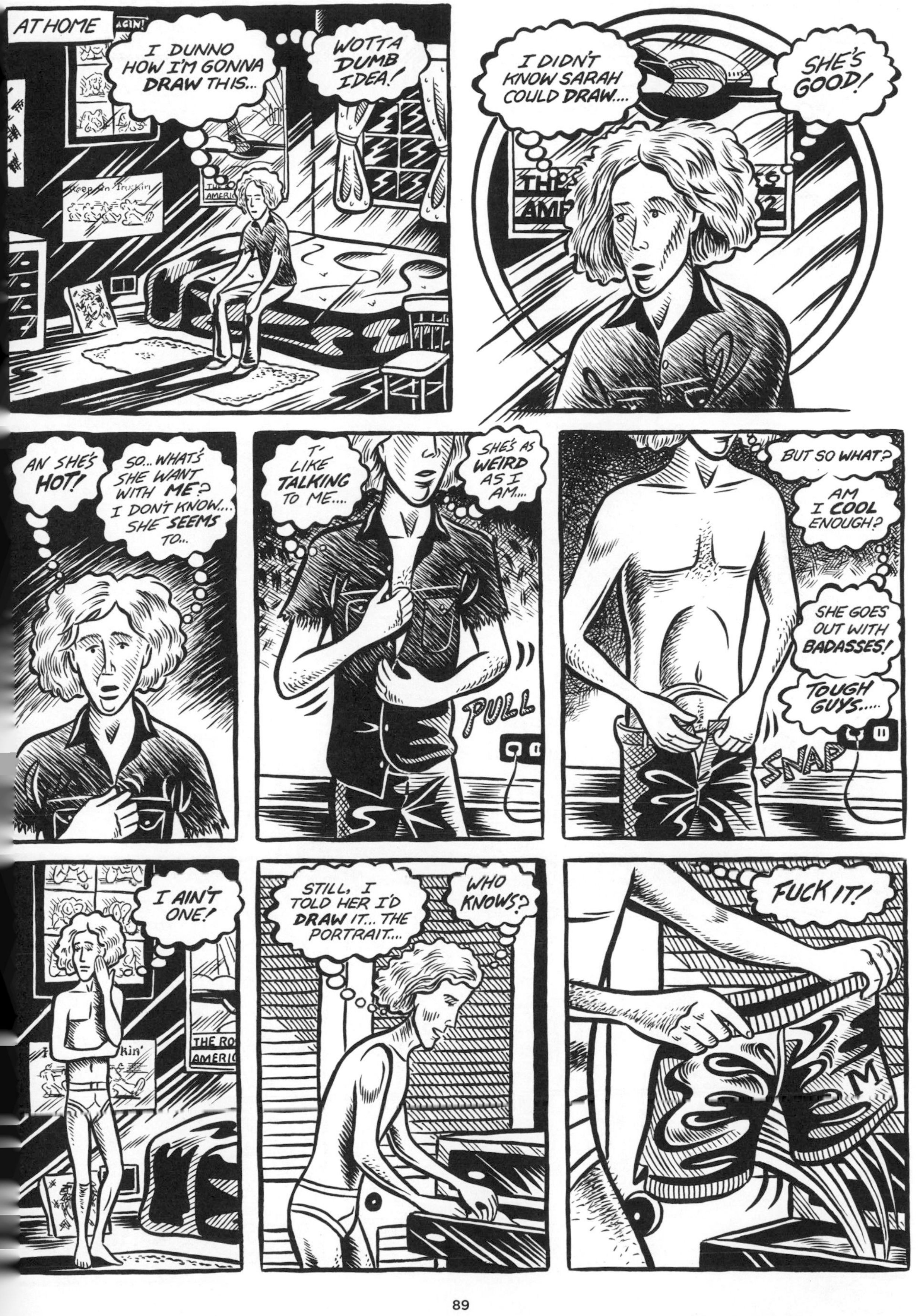

AT HOME
AGIN!
I DUNNO HOW I'M GONNA DRAW THIS...
WOTTA DUMB IDEA!
Keep on Truckin
I DIDN'T KNOW SARAH COULD DRAW....
SHE'S GOOD!
AN SHE'S HOT!
SO... WHAT'S SHE WANT WITH ME? I DON'T KNOW.... SHE SEEMS TO...
T' LIKE TALKING TO ME....
SHE'S AS WEIRD AS I AM....
PULL
BUT SO WHAT?
AM I COOL ENOUGH?
SHE GOES OUT WITH BADASSES!
TOUGH GUYS.....
SNAP
I AIN'T ONE!
STILL, I TOLD HER I'D DRAW IT... THE PORTRAIT....
WHO KNOWS?
FUCK IT!

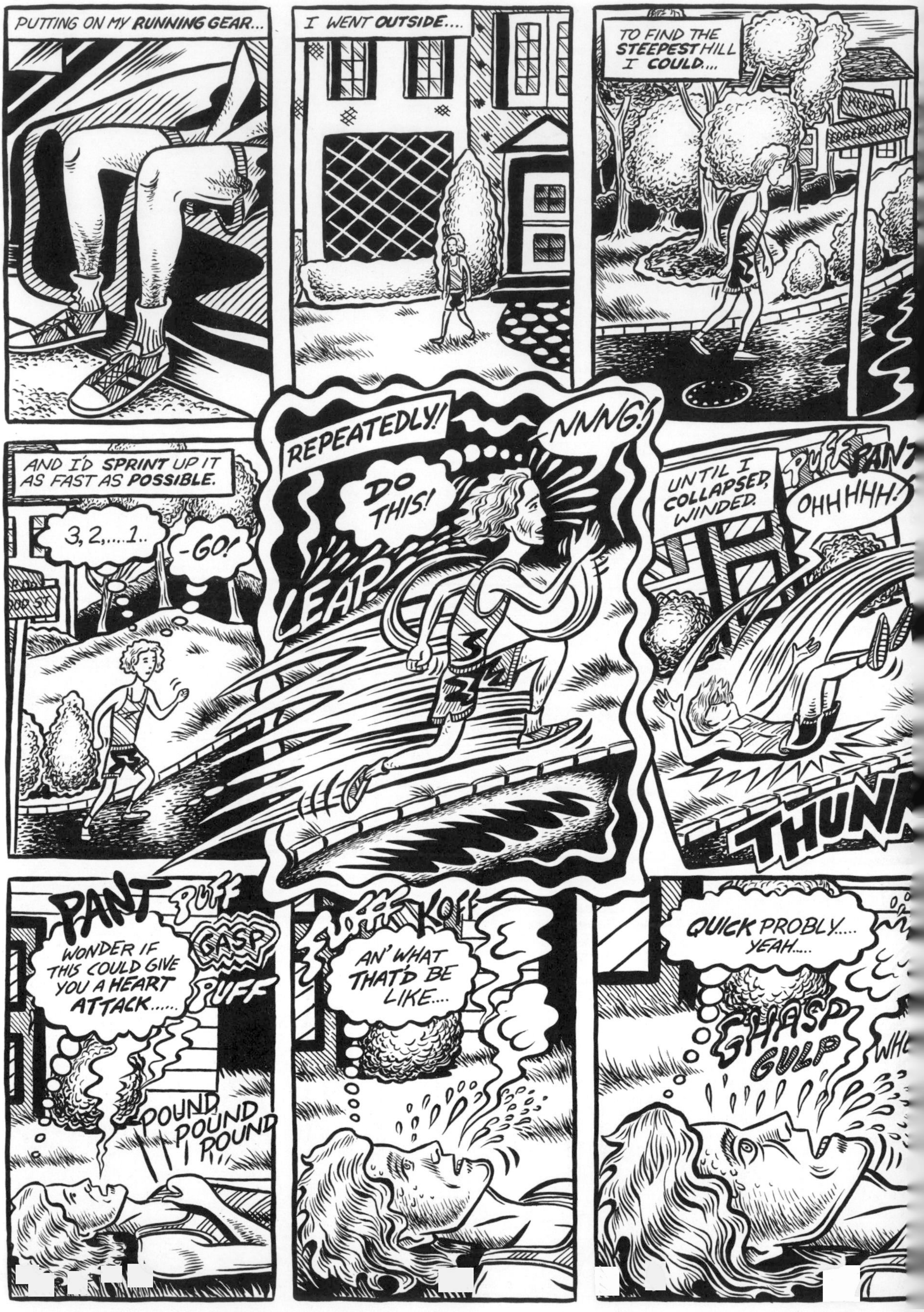
PUTTING ON MY RUNNING GEAR...
I WENT OUTSIDE....
TO FIND THE STEEPEST HILL I COULD....
AND I'D SPRINT UP IT AS FAST AS POSSIBLE.
3,2,....1..
-GO!
REPEATEDLY!
DO THIS!
NNNG!
LEAP
UNTIL I COLLAPSED, WINDED.
PUFF
OHHHHH!
PANT
PUFF
WONDER IF THIS COULD GIVE YOU A HEART ATTACK......
GASP
PUFF
POUND POUND POUND
KOFF
AN' WHAT THAT'D BE LIKE...
QUICK PROBLY.... YEAH.....
GHASP
GULP

BACK HOME.

HI MUM.

HELLO DEAR

WHAT'S UP, MA?

THIS CAME IN THE MAIL...

WHIP!

WHAT IS IT?

A WARNING NOTICE FROM SCHOOL—

DISCIPLINARY NOTICE- ALGEBRA- CON TEST LATE AT

OBNOX MOUTHS OFF

YANK!

IT SAYS YOU'RE FAILING ALGEBRA!

YEAH WELL....

HEY....

SHRUG

IS THAT ALL YOU'VE GOT TO SAY?

WHAT CAN I SAY, MA? MATH'S GARBAGE.

I HATE IT!

YOU DON'T NEED MATH T' DRAW!!

DO YOU EVEN CARE IF YOU GRADUATE?

WELL, I DUNNO, MA-

MAYBE YOU CAN JUST BOUNCE ME INTO SOME OTHER SCHOOL THAT HANDLES ME BETTER!

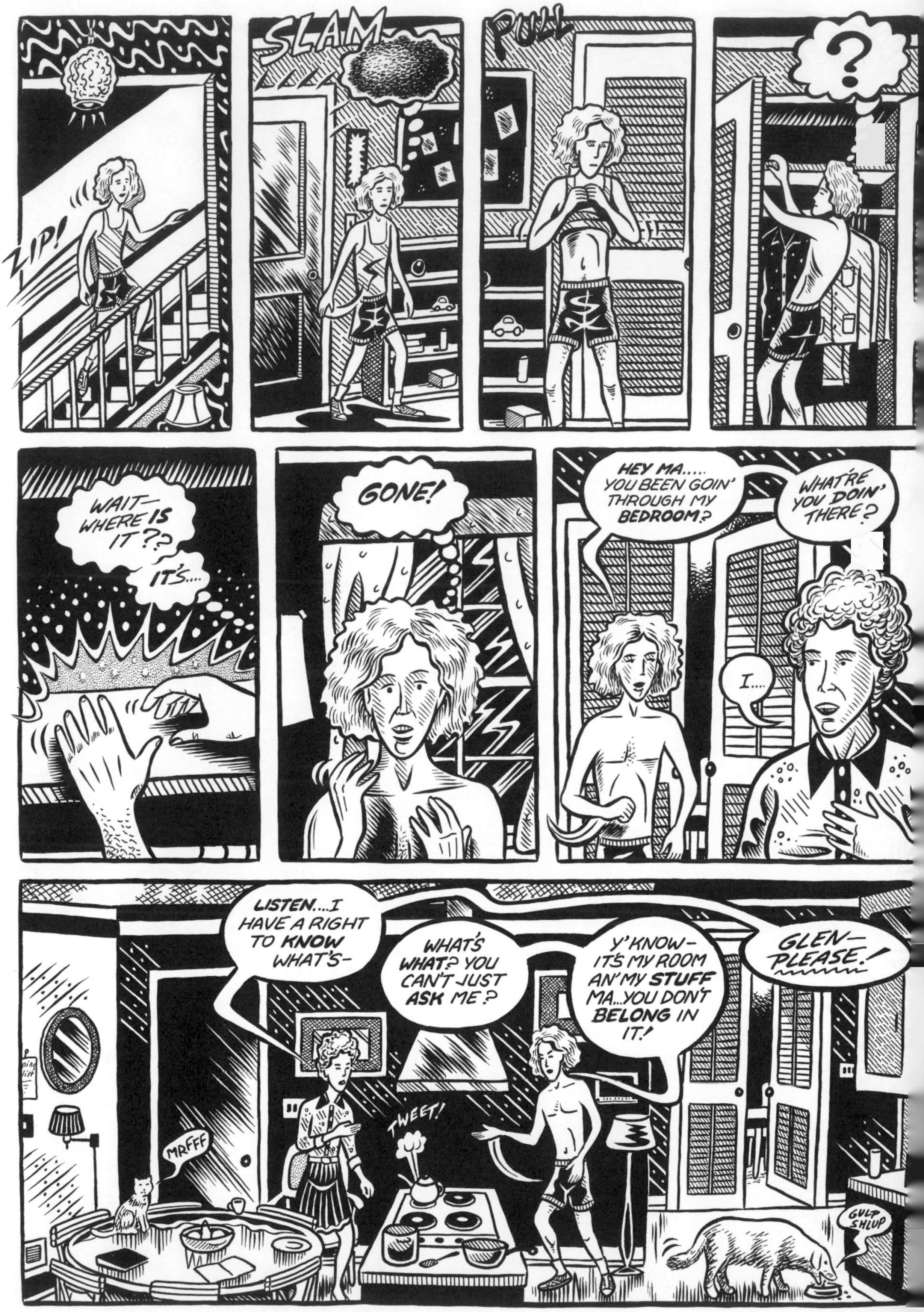
ZIP!
SLAM
PULL
?
WAIT— WHERE IS IT??
IT'S....
GONE!
HEY MA..... YOU BEEN GOIN' THROUGH MY BEDROOM?
WHAT'RE YOU DOIN' THERE?
I....
LISTEN....I HAVE A RIGHT TO KNOW WHAT'S-
WHAT'S WHAT? YOU CAN'T JUST ASK ME?
Y'KNOW- IT'S MY ROOM AN' MY STUFF MA...YOU DON'T BELONG IN IT!
GLEN— PLEASE!
MRFFF
TWEET!
GULP SHLUP

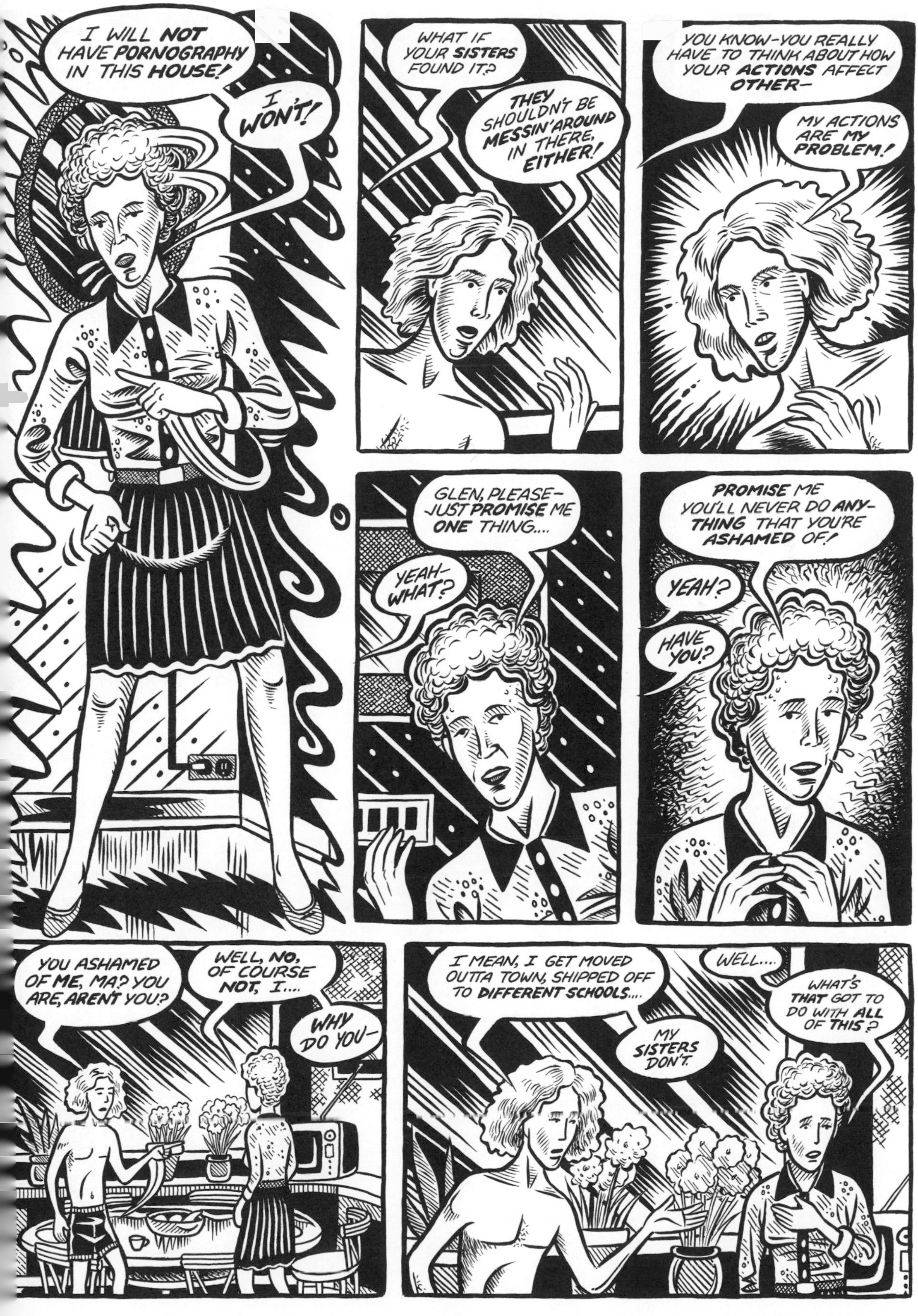
I WILL NOT HAVE PORNOGRAPHY IN THIS HOUSE!
I WON'T!
WHAT IF YOUR SISTERS FOUND IT?
THEY SHOULDN'T BE MESSIN' AROUND IN THERE, EITHER!
YOU KNOW-YOU REALLY HAVE TO THINK ABOUT HOW YOUR ACTIONS AFFECT OTHER-
MY ACTIONS ARE MY PROBLEM!
GLEN, PLEASE-JUST PROMISE ME ONE THING....
YEAH-WHAT?
PROMISE ME YOU'LL NEVER DO ANY-THING THAT YOU'RE ASHAMED OF!
YEAH?
HAVE YOU?
YOU ASHAMED OF ME, MA? YOU ARE, AREN'T YOU?
WELL, NO, OF COURSE NOT, I....
WHY DO YOU-
I MEAN, I GET MOVED OUTTA TOWN, SHIPPED OFF TO DIFFERENT SCHOOLS....
MY SISTERS DON'T.
WELL....
WHAT'S THAT GOT TO DO WITH ALL OF THIS?

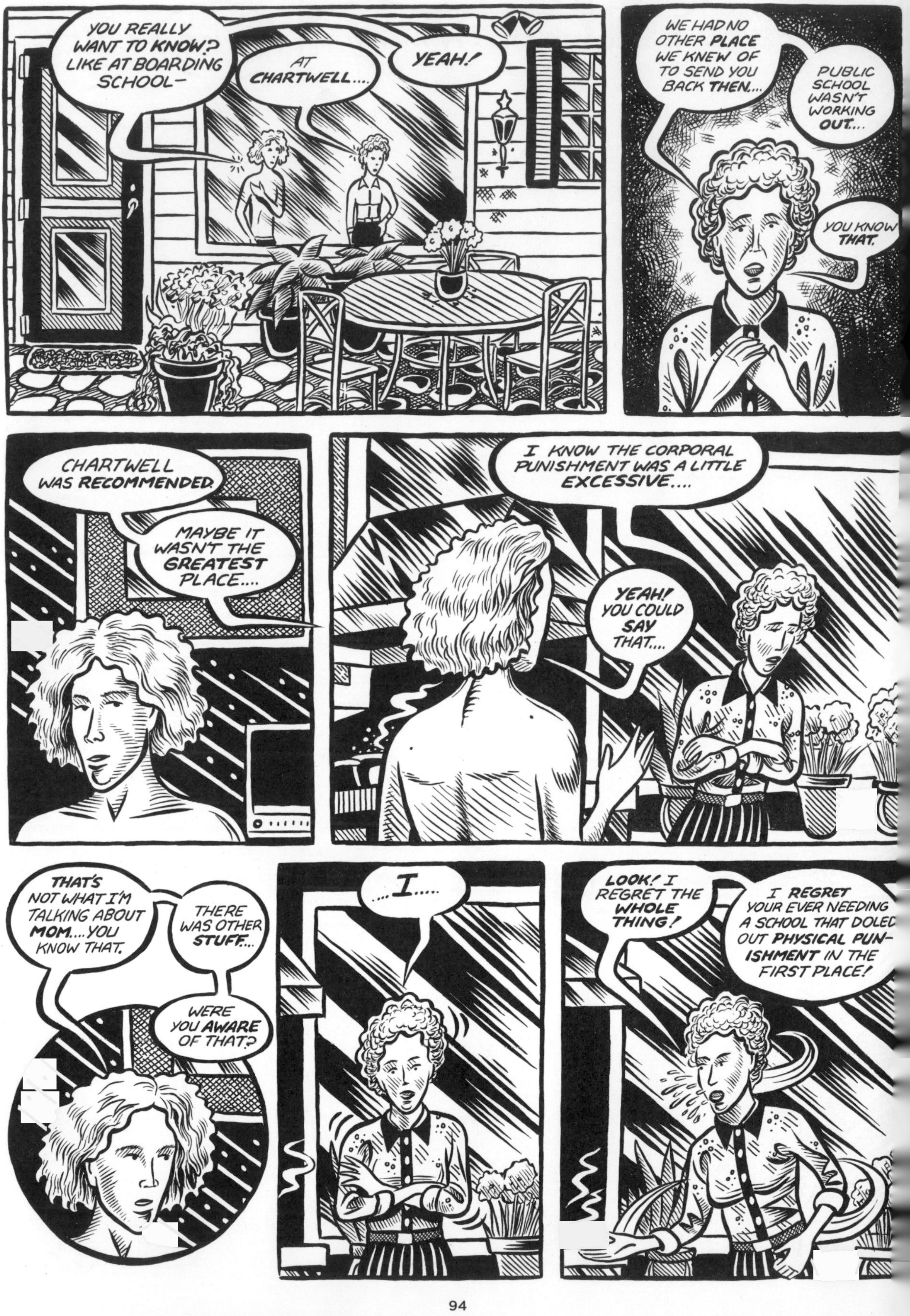
YOU REALLY WANT TO KNOW? LIKE AT BOARDING SCHOOL-
AT CHARTWELL....
YEAH!
WE HAD NO OTHER PLACE WE KNEW OF TO SEND YOU BACK THEN....
PUBLIC SCHOOL WASN'T WORKING OUT....
YOU KNOW THAT.
CHARTWELL WAS RECOMMENDED.
MAYBE IT WASN'T THE GREATEST PLACE....
I KNOW THE CORPORAL PUNISHMENT WAS A LITTLE EXCESSIVE....
YEAH! YOU COULD SAY THAT....
THAT'S NOT WHAT I'M TALKING ABOUT MOM....YOU KNOW THAT.
THERE WAS OTHER STUFF...
WERE YOU AWARE OF THAT?
...I.....
LOOK! I REGRET THE WHOLE THING!
I REGRET YOUR EVER NEEDING A SCHOOL THAT DOLED OUT PHYSICAL PUNISHMENT IN THE FIRST PLACE!

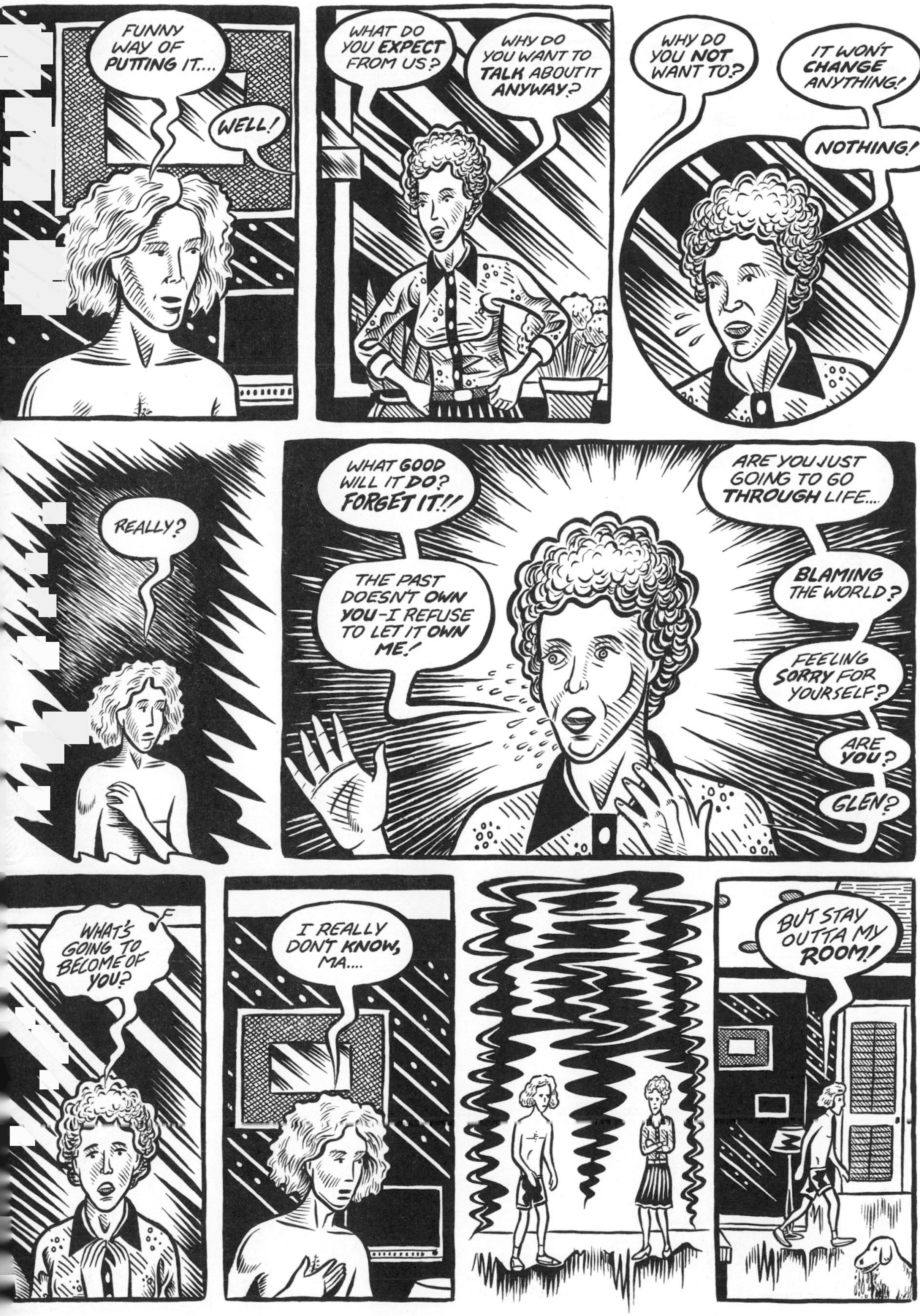
FUNNY WAY OF PUTTING IT....
WELL!
WHAT DO YOU EXPECT FROM US?
WHY DO YOU WANT TO TALK ABOUT IT ANYWAY?
WHY DO YOU NOT WANT TO?
IT WON'T CHANGE ANYTHING!
NOTHING!
REALLY?
WHAT GOOD WILL IT DO? FORGET IT!!
THE PAST DOESN'T OWN YOU–I REFUSE TO LET IT OWN ME!
ARE YOU JUST GOING TO GO THROUGH LIFE....
BLAMING THE WORLD?
FEELING SORRY FOR YOURSELF?
ARE YOU?
GLEN?
WHAT'S GOING TO BECOME OF YOU?
I REALLY DON'T KNOW, MA....
BUT STAY OUTTA MY ROOM!

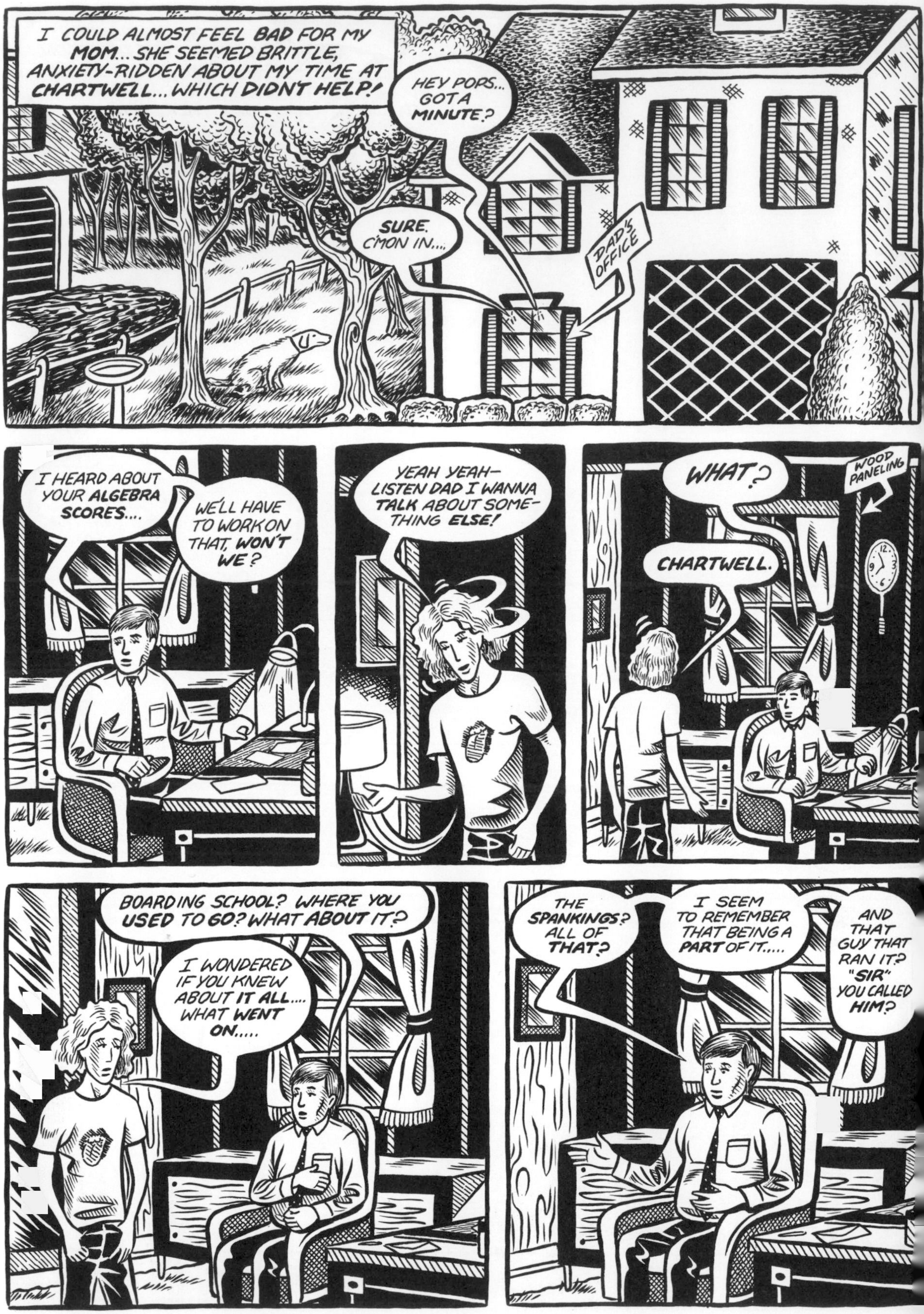
I COULD ALMOST FEEL BAD FOR MY MOM... SHE SEEMED BRITTLE, ANXIETY-RIDDEN ABOUT MY TIME AT CHARTWELL... WHICH DIDN'T HELP!
HEY POPS... GOT A MINUTE?
SURE. C'MON IN....
DAD'S OFFICE
I HEARD ABOUT YOUR ALGEBRA SCORES....
WE'LL HAVE TO WORK ON THAT, WON'T WE?
YEAH YEAH-- LISTEN DAD I WANNA TALK ABOUT SOMETHING ELSE!
WHAT?
WOOD PANELING
CHARTWELL.
BOARDING SCHOOL? WHERE YOU USED TO GO? WHAT ABOUT IT?
I WONDERED IF YOU KNEW ABOUT IT ALL.... WHAT WENT ON.....
THE SPANKINGS? ALL OF THAT?
I SEEM TO REMEMBER THAT BEING A PART OF IT.....
AND THAT GUY THAT RAN IT? "SIR" YOU CALLED HIM?

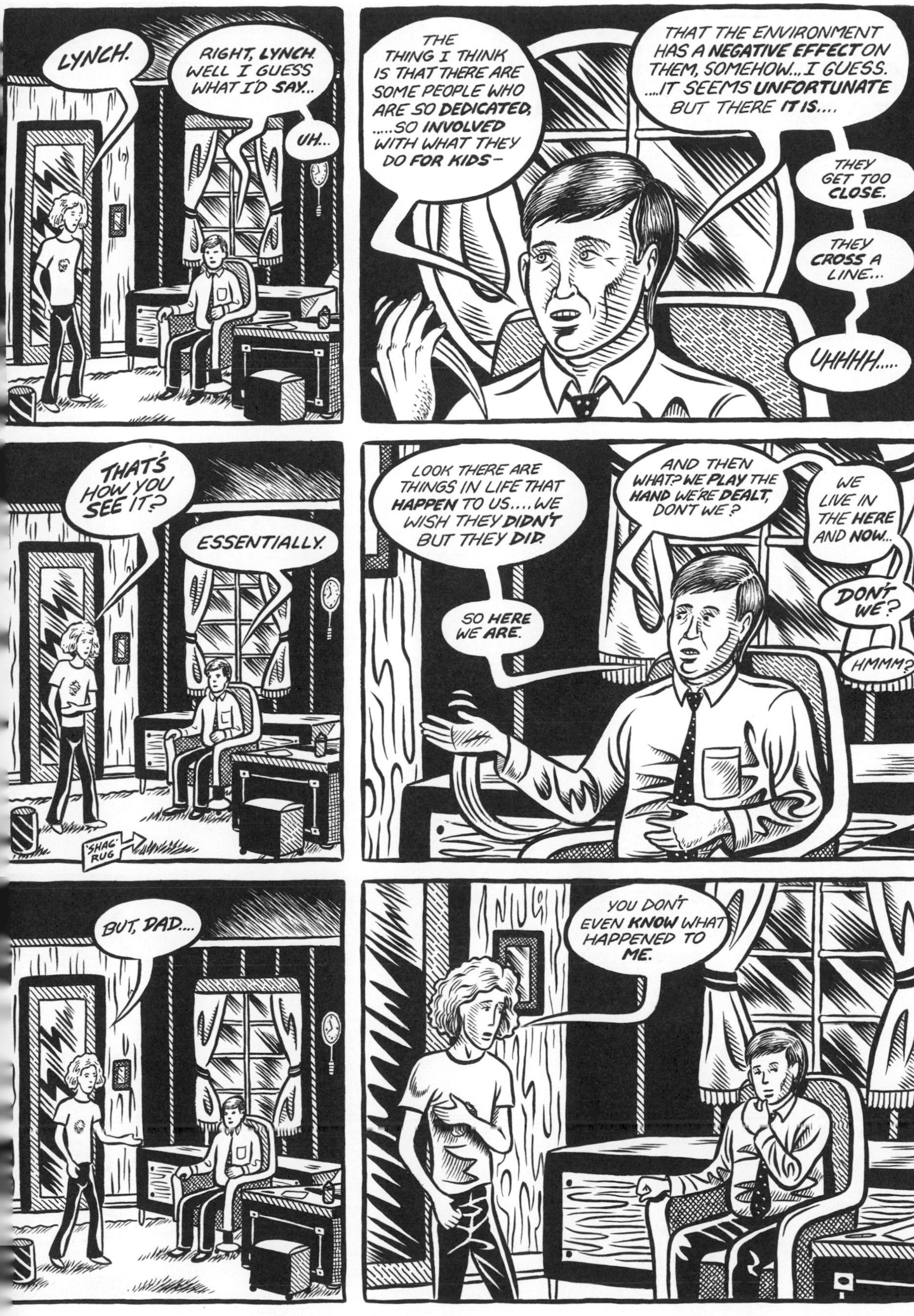
LYNCH.
RIGHT, LYNCH. WELL I GUESS WHAT I'D SAY...
UH...
THE THING I THINK IS THAT THERE ARE SOME PEOPLE WHO ARE SO DEDICATED, ...SO INVOLVED WITH WHAT THEY DO FOR KIDS–
THAT THE ENVIRONMENT HAS A NEGATIVE EFFECT ON THEM, SOMEHOW... I GUESS. ...IT SEEMS UNFORTUNATE BUT THERE IT IS....
THEY GET TOO CLOSE.
THEY CROSS A LINE...
UHHHH.....
THAT'S HOW YOU SEE IT?
ESSENTIALLY.
'SHAG' RUG
LOOK THERE ARE THINGS IN LIFE THAT HAPPEN TO US.... WE WISH THEY DIDN'T BUT THEY DID.
SO HERE WE ARE.
AND THEN WHAT? WE PLAY THE HAND WE'RE DEALT, DON'T WE?
WE LIVE IN THE HERE AND NOW...
DON'T WE?
HMMM?
BUT, DAD....
YOU DON'T EVEN KNOW WHAT HAPPENED TO ME.

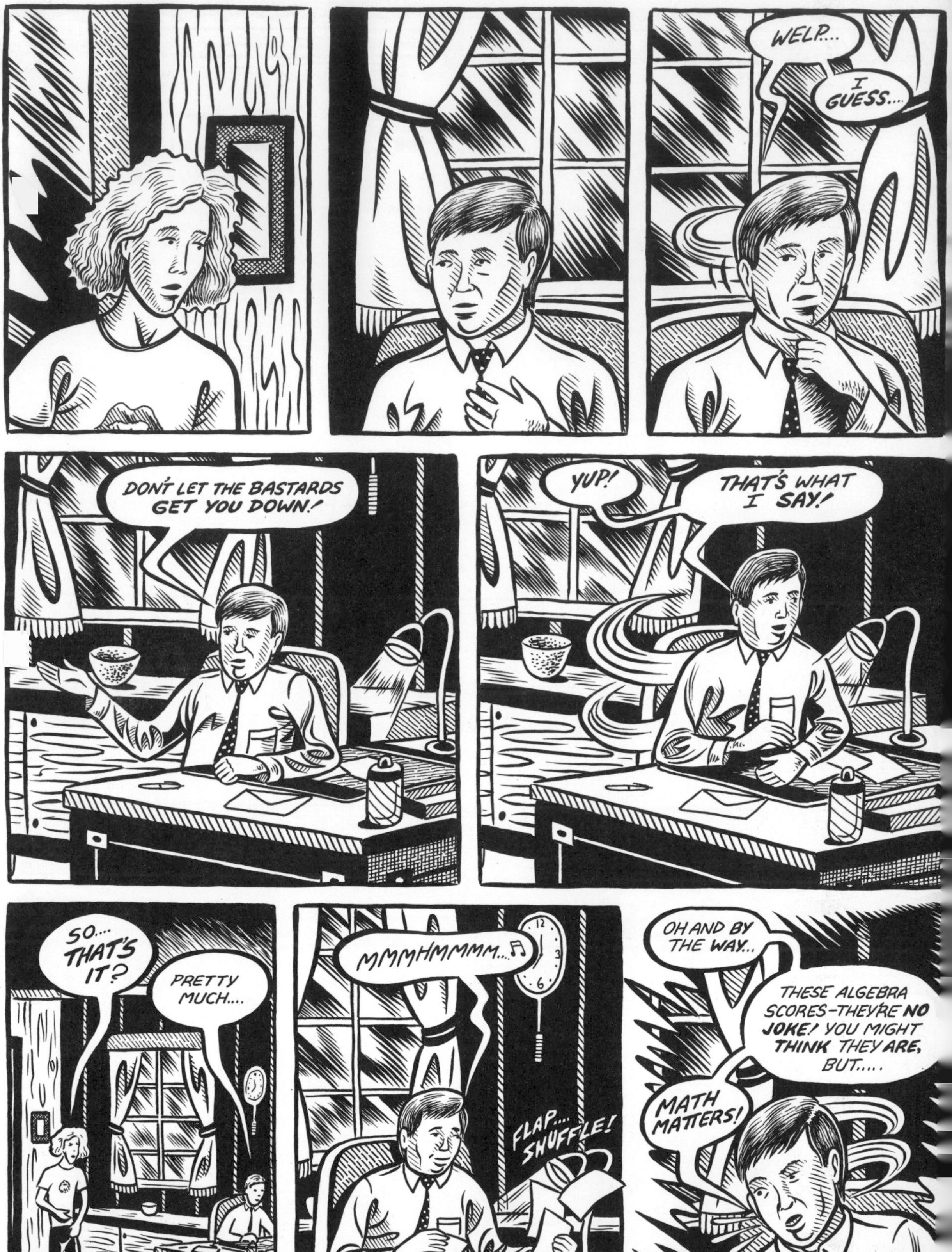
WELP....
I GUESS....
DON'T LET THE BASTARDS GET YOU DOWN!
YUP!
THAT'S WHAT I SAY!
SO.... THAT'S IT?
PRETTY MUCH....
MMMHMMMM....♫
FLAP.... SHUFFLE!
OH AND BY THE WAY...
THESE ALGEBRA SCORES–THEY'RE **NO JOKE!** YOU MIGHT **THINK** THEY **ARE**, BUT.....
MATH MATTERS!

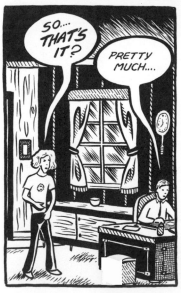

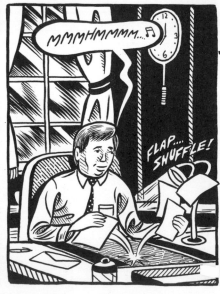

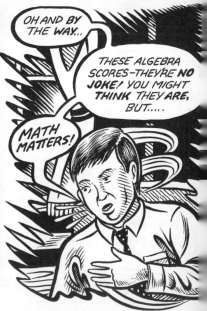

A DIGRESSION....

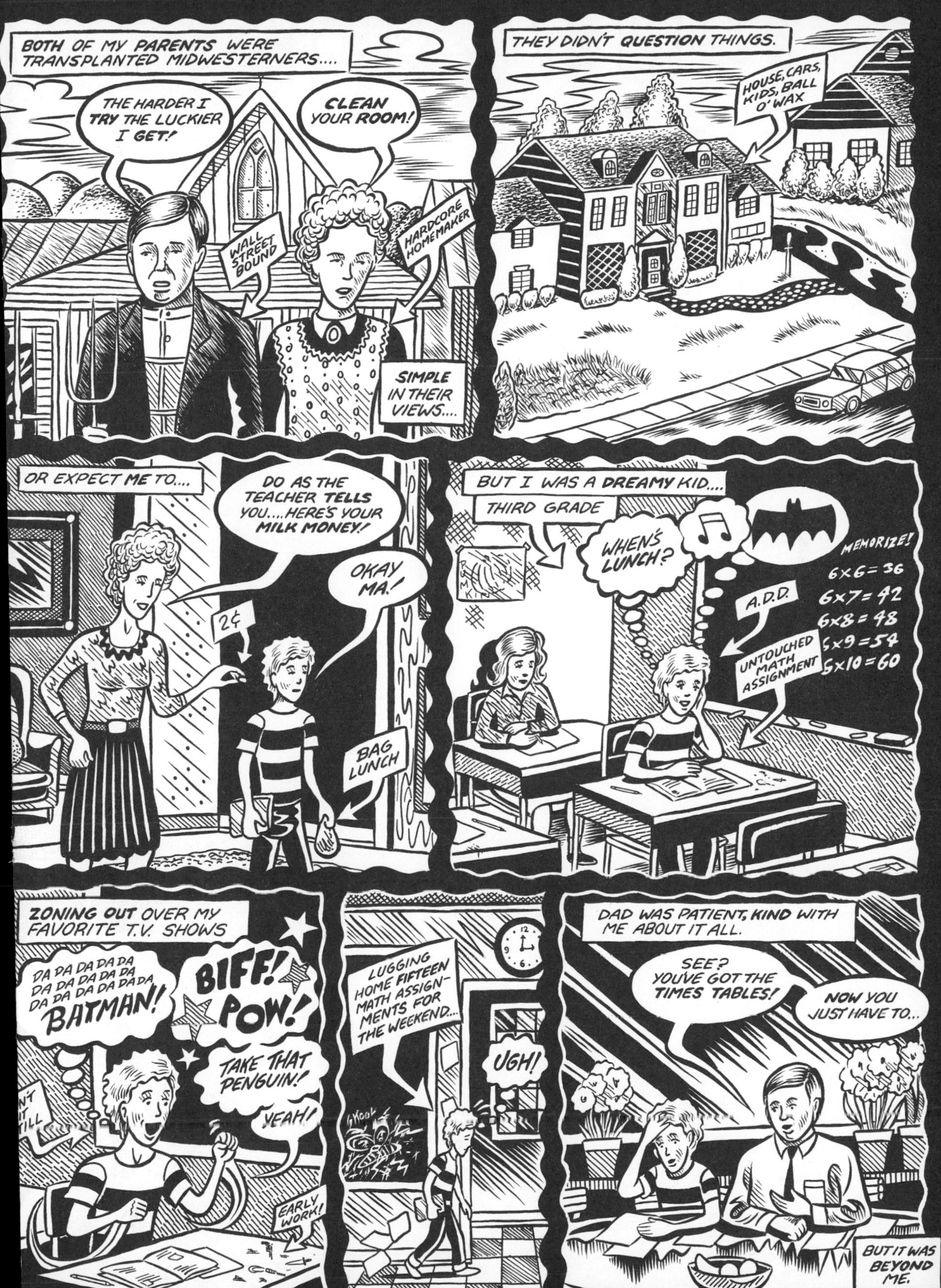
BOTH OF MY PARENTS WERE TRANSPLANTED MIDWESTERNERS....
THE HARDER I TRY THE LUCKIER I GET!
CLEAN YOUR ROOM!
WALL STREET BOUND
HARDCORE HOMEMAKER
SIMPLE IN THEIR VIEWS....
THEY DIDN'T QUESTION THINGS.
HOUSE, CARS, KIDS, BALL O' WAX
OR EXPECT ME TO....
DO AS THE TEACHER TELLS YOU....HERE'S YOUR MILK MONEY!
OKAY MA!
2¢
BAG LUNCH
BUT I WAS A DREAMY KID....
THIRD GRADE
WHEN'S LUNCH?
A.D.D.
UNTOUCHED MATH ASSIGNMENT
MEMORIZE!
6×6=36
6×7=42
6×8=48
6×9=54
6×10=60
ZONING OUT OVER MY FAVORITE T.V. SHOWS
DA DA DA DA DA DA DA DA DA DA DA DA DA DA DA DA BATMAN!
BIFF! POW!
TAKE THAT PENGUIN!
YEAH!
EARLY WORK!
LUGGING HOME FIFTEEN MATH ASSIGN-MENTS FOR THE WEEKEND...
UGH!
DAD WAS PATIENT, KIND WITH ME ABOUT IT ALL.
SEE? YOU'VE GOT THE TIMES TABLES!
NOW YOU JUST HAVE TO...
BUT IT WAS BEYOND ME.

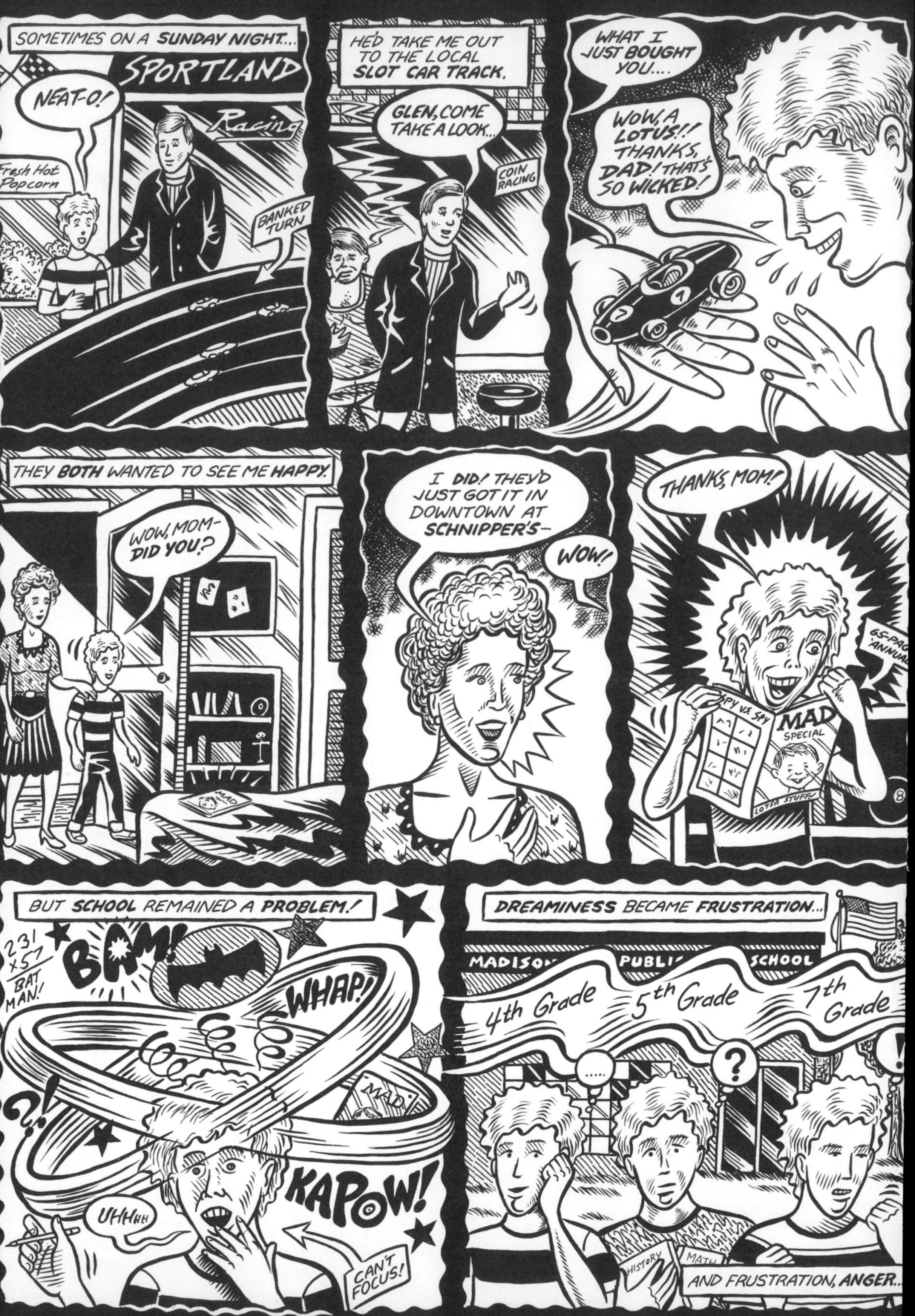
SOMETIMES ON A SUNDAY NIGHT...
SPORTLAND
Racing
NEAT-O!
Fresh Hot Popcorn
BANKED TURN
HE'D TAKE ME OUT TO THE LOCAL SLOT CAR TRACK.
GLEN, COME TAKE A LOOK...
COIN RACING
WHAT I JUST BOUGHT YOU....
WOW, A LOTUS!! THANKS, DAD! THAT'S SO WICKED!
THEY BOTH WANTED TO SEE ME HAPPY.
WOW, MOM- DID YOU?
MAD
I DID! THEY'D JUST GOT IT IN DOWNTOWN AT SCHNIPPER'S-
WOW!
THANKS, MOM!
SPY VS. SPY
MAD SPECIAL
LOTSA STUFF!
BUT SCHOOL REMAINED A PROBLEM!
231 x57
BATMAN!
BAM!
WHAP!
MAD
?!
KAPOW!
UHHhh
CAN'T FOCUS!
DREAMINESS BECAME FRUSTRATION...
MADISON PUBLIC SCHOOL
4th Grade
5th Grade
7th Grade
?
HISTORY
MATH
AND FRUSTRATION, ANGER...

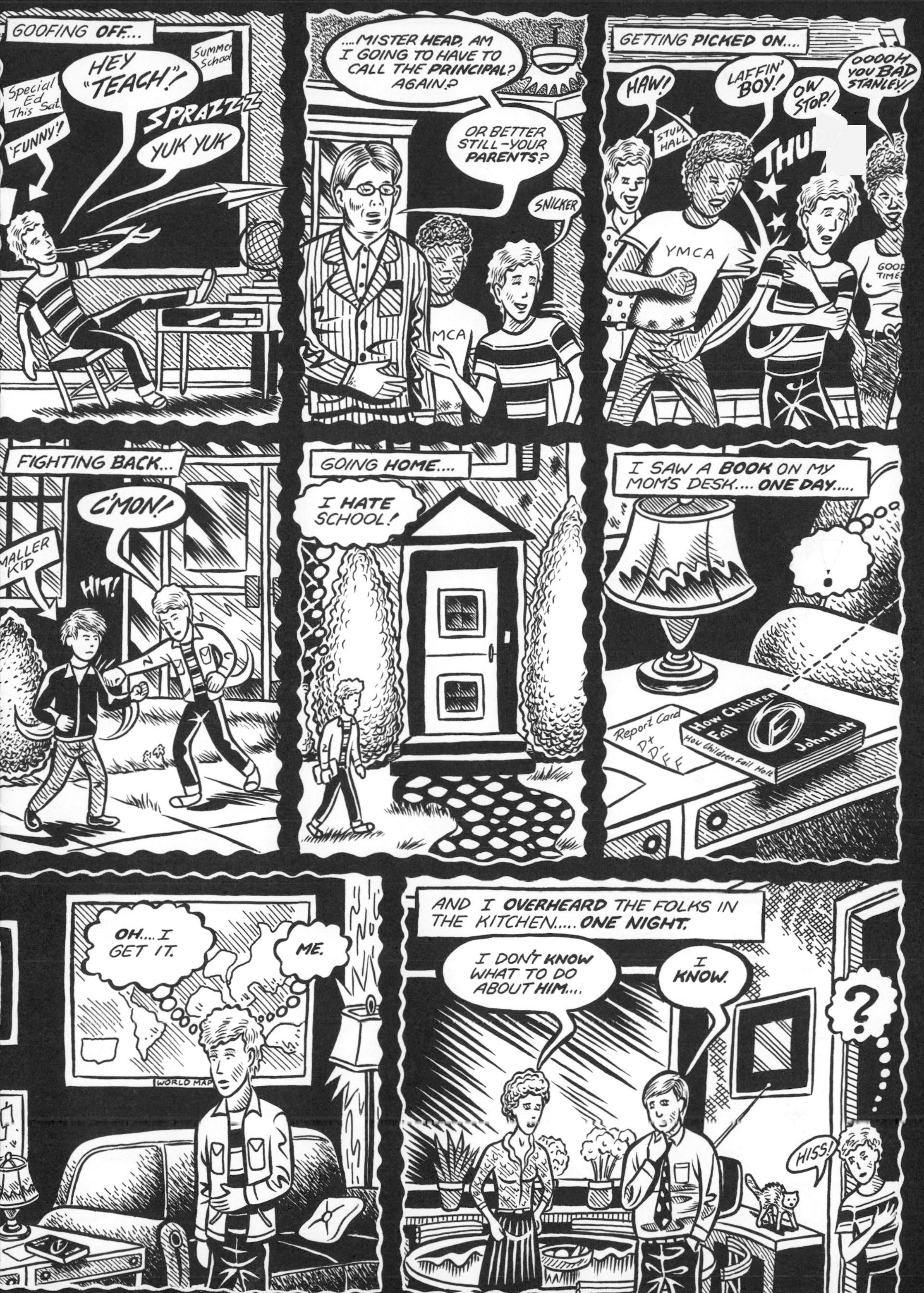
GOOFING OFF....
Summer School
HEY "TEACH"!
Special Ed This Sat.
SPRAZZZZ
"FUNNY"!
YUK YUK
...MISTER HEAD, AM I GOING TO HAVE TO CALL THE PRINCIPAL? AGAIN?
OR BETTER STILL-YOUR PARENTS?
SNICKER
YMCA
GETTING PICKED ON....
HAW!
LAFFIN' BOY!
OW STOP!
OOOOH YOU BAD STANLEY!
THU
YMCA
GOOD TIMES
FIGHTING BACK...
C'MON!
MALLER KID
HIT!
GOING HOME....
I HATE SCHOOL!
I SAW A BOOK ON MY MOM'S DESK.... ONE DAY.....
!
Report Card
How Children Fail
John Holt
How Children Fail Holt
OH.... I GET IT.
ME.
WORLD MAP
AND I OVERHEARD THE FOLKS IN THE KITCHEN..... ONE NIGHT.
I DON'T KNOW WHAT TO DO ABOUT HIM....
I KNOW.
?
HISS!

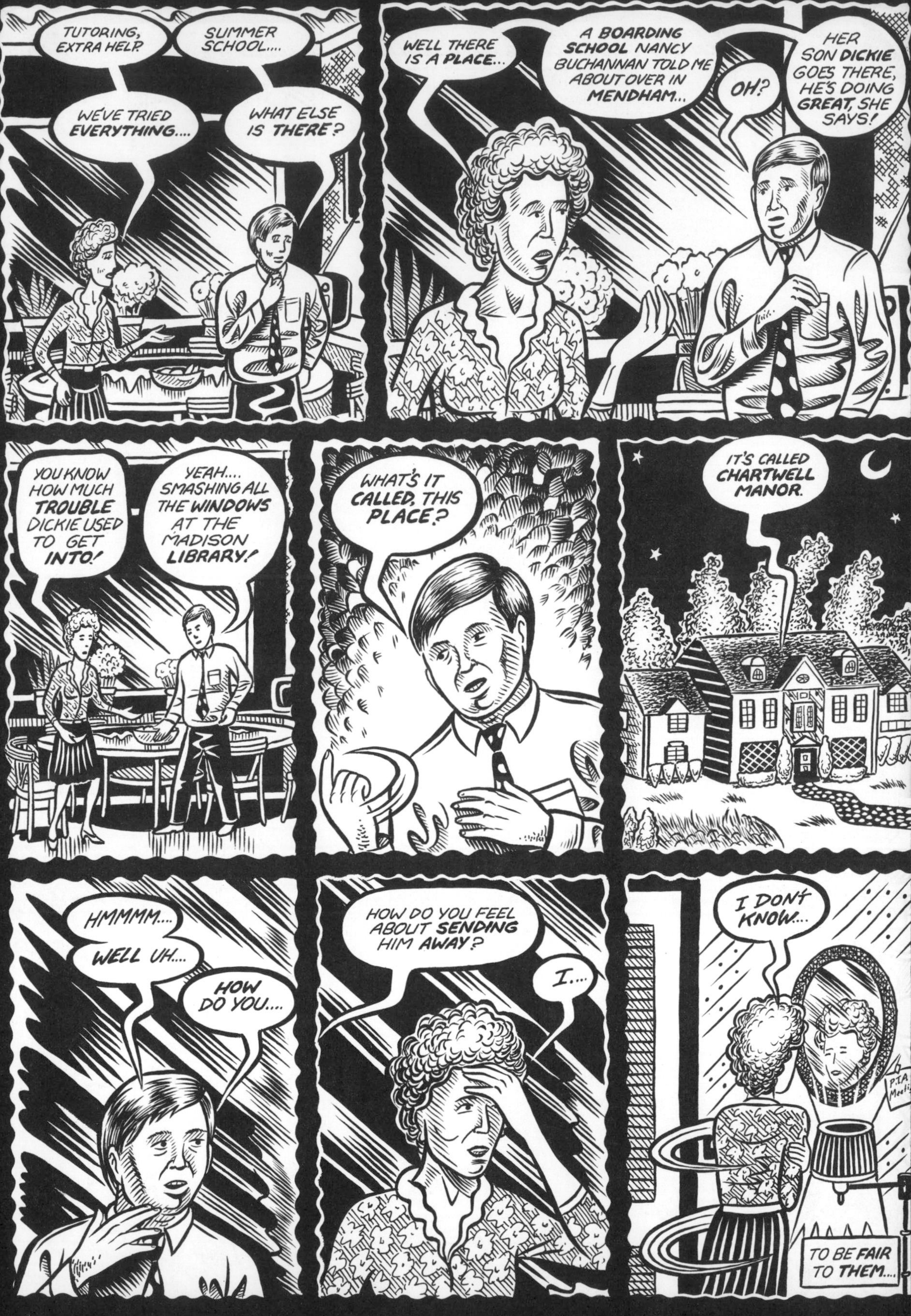
TUTORING, EXTRA HELP?
SUMMER SCHOOL....
WE'VE TRIED EVERYTHING....
WHAT ELSE IS THERE?
WELL THERE IS A PLACE...
A BOARDING SCHOOL NANCY BUCHANNAN TOLD ME ABOUT OVER IN MENDHAM...
OH?
HER SON DICKIE GOES THERE, HE'S DOING GREAT, SHE SAYS!
YOU KNOW HOW MUCH TROUBLE DICKIE USED TO GET INTO!
YEAH.... SMASHING ALL THE WINDOWS AT THE MADISON LIBRARY!
WHAT'S IT CALLED, THIS PLACE?
IT'S CALLED CHARTWELL MANOR.
HMMMM....
WELL UH....
HOW DO YOU....
HOW DO YOU FEEL ABOUT SENDING HIM AWAY?
I....
I DON'T KNOW....
TO BE FAIR TO THEM....

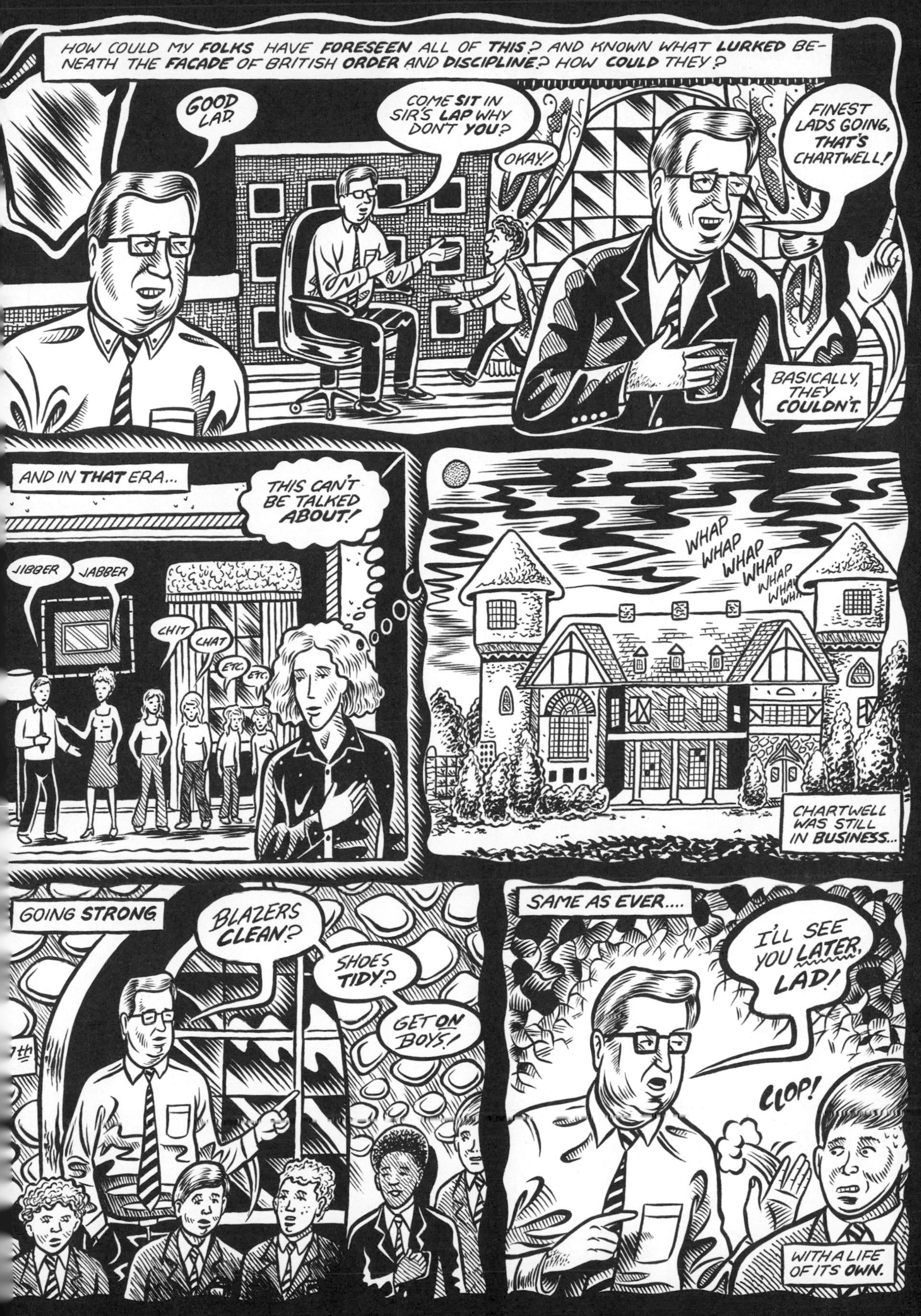
HOW COULD MY FOLKS HAVE FORESEEN ALL OF THIS? AND KNOWN WHAT LURKED BENEATH THE FACADE OF BRITISH ORDER AND DISCIPLINE? HOW COULD THEY?
GOOD LAD.
COME SIT IN SIR'S LAP WHY DON'T YOU?
OKAY!
FINEST LADS GOING, THAT'S CHARTWELL!
BASICALLY, THEY COULDN'T.
AND IN THAT ERA...
THIS CAN'T BE TALKED ABOUT!
JIBBER
JABBER
CHIT
CHAT
ETC.
ETC.
WHAP WHAP WHAP WHAP WHAP WHAP
CHARTWELL WAS STILL IN BUSINESS...
GOING STRONG.
BLAZERS CLEAN?
SHOES TIDY?
GET ON BOYS!
SAME AS EVER....
I'LL SEE YOU LATER, LAD!
CLOP!
WITH A LIFE OF ITS OWN.

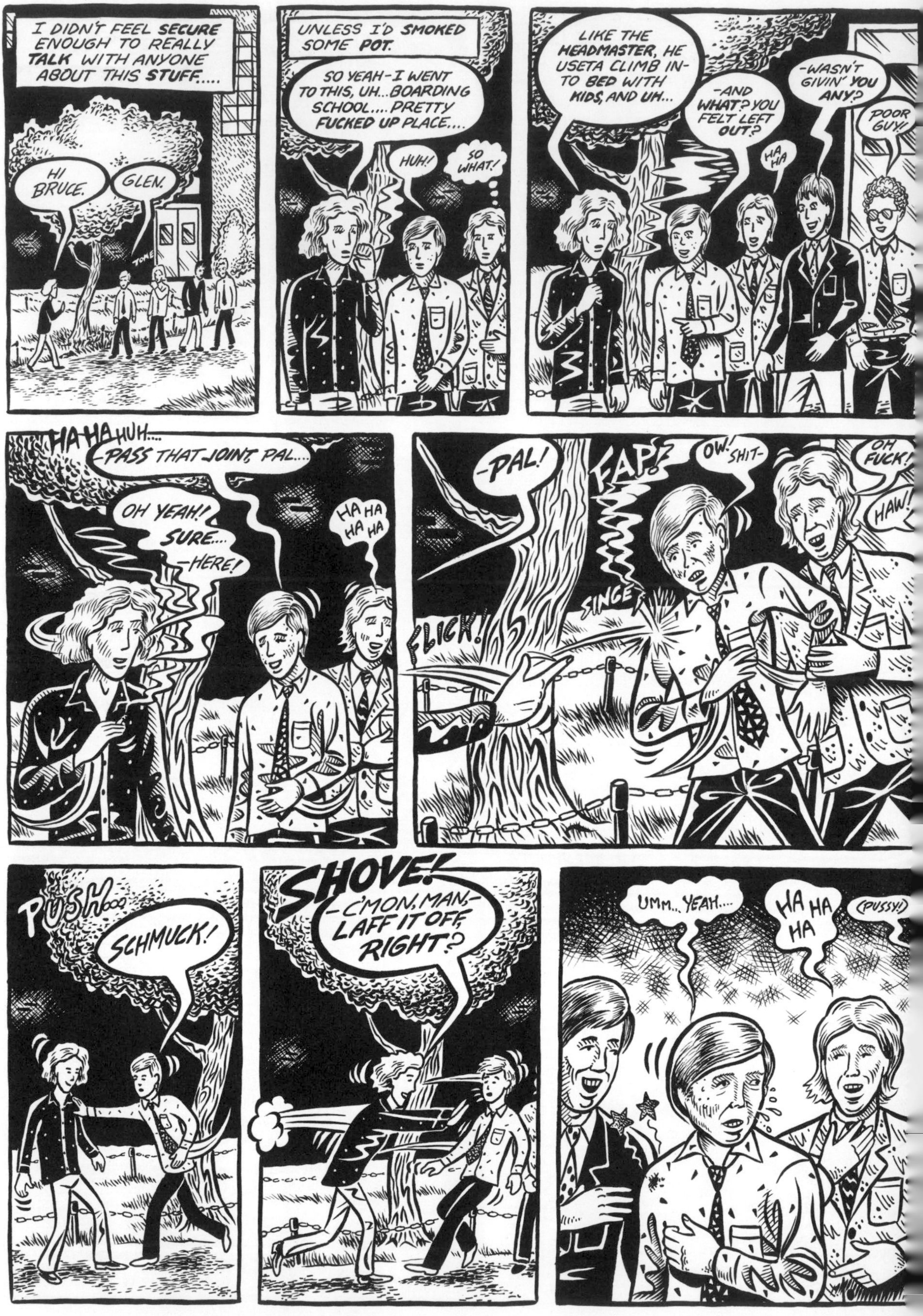
I DIDN'T FEEL SECURE ENOUGH TO REALLY TALK WITH ANYONE ABOUT THIS STUFF....
HI BRUCE.
GLEN.
TOKE
UNLESS I'D SMOKED SOME POT.
SO YEAH-I WENT TO THIS, UH...BOARDING SCHOOL....PRETTY FUCKED UP PLACE....
HUH!
SO WHAT!
LIKE THE HEADMASTER, HE USETA CLIMB IN-TO BED WITH KIDS, AND UH...
-AND WHAT? YOU FELT LEFT OUT?
HA HA
-WASN'T GIVIN' YOU ANY?
POOR GUY!
HA HA HUH....
-PASS THAT JOINT, PAL....
OH YEAH! SURE.... -HERE!
HA HA HA HA
-PAL!
FAP!
OW! SHIT-
OH FUCK!
HAW!
SINGE
FLICK!
PUSH
SCHMUCK!
SHOVE!
-C'MON, MAN, LAFF IT OFF, RIGHT?
UMM... YEAH....
HA HA HA
(PUSSY!)

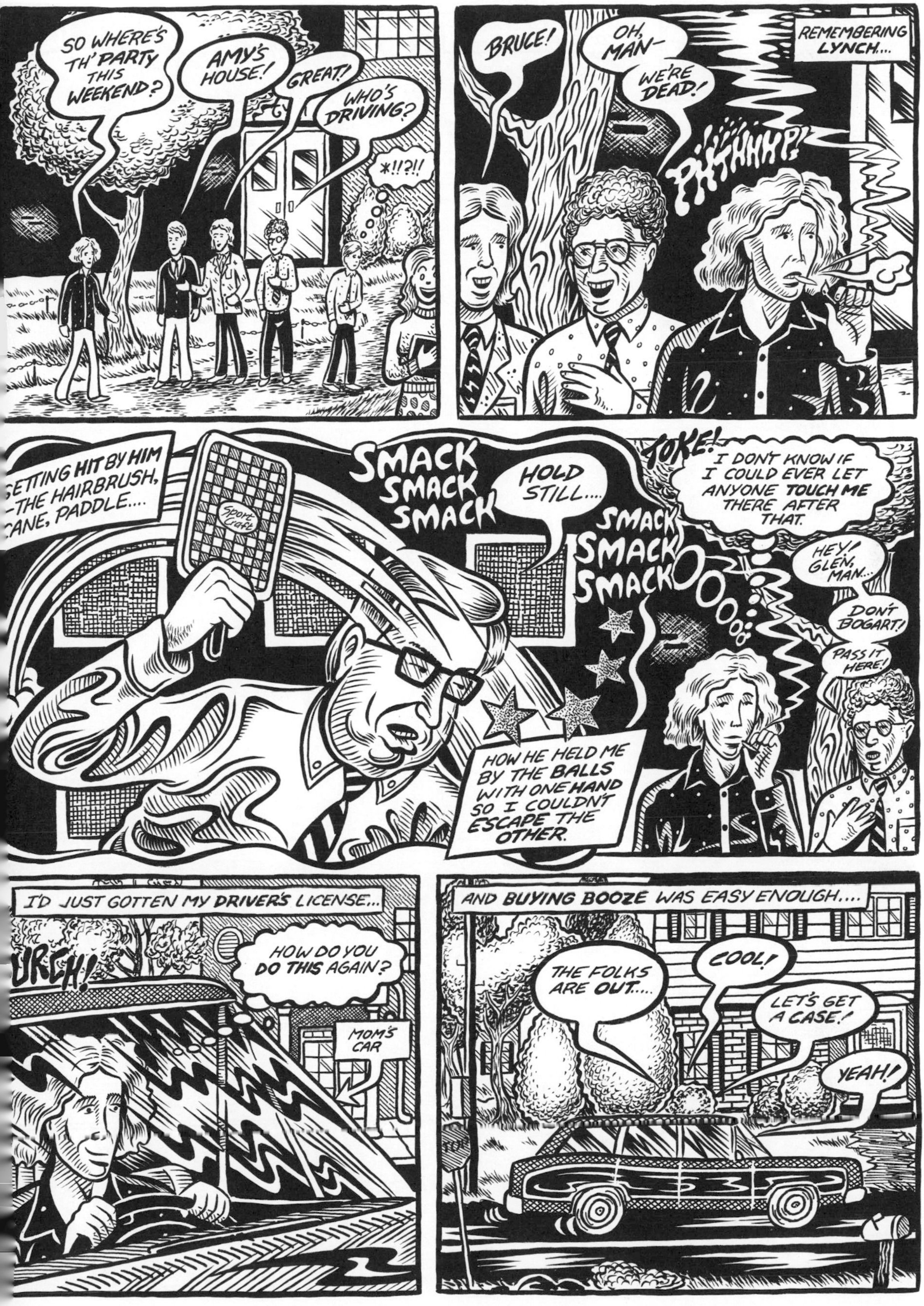
SO WHERE'S TH' PARTY THIS WEEKEND?
AMY'S HOUSE!
GREAT!
WHO'S DRIVING?
*!!?!!
BRUCE!
OH, MAN-
WE'RE DEAD!
REMEMBERING LYNCH...
PHTHHHP!
GETTING HIT BY HIM —THE HAIRBRUSH, CANE, PADDLE....
SMACK SMACK SMACK
HOLD STILL....
SMACK SMACK SMACK
TOKE!
I DON'T KNOW IF I COULD EVER LET ANYONE TOUCH ME THERE AFTER THAT.
HEY! GLEN, MAN...
DON'T BOGART!
PASS IT HERE!
HOW HE HELD ME BY THE BALLS WITH ONE HAND SO I COULDN'T ESCAPE THE OTHER.
I'D JUST GOTTEN MY DRIVER'S LICENSE...
URCH!
HOW DO YOU DO THIS AGAIN?
MOM'S CAR
AND BUYING BOOZE WAS EASY ENOUGH....
THE FOLKS ARE OUT....
COOL!
LET'S GET A CASE!
YEAH!

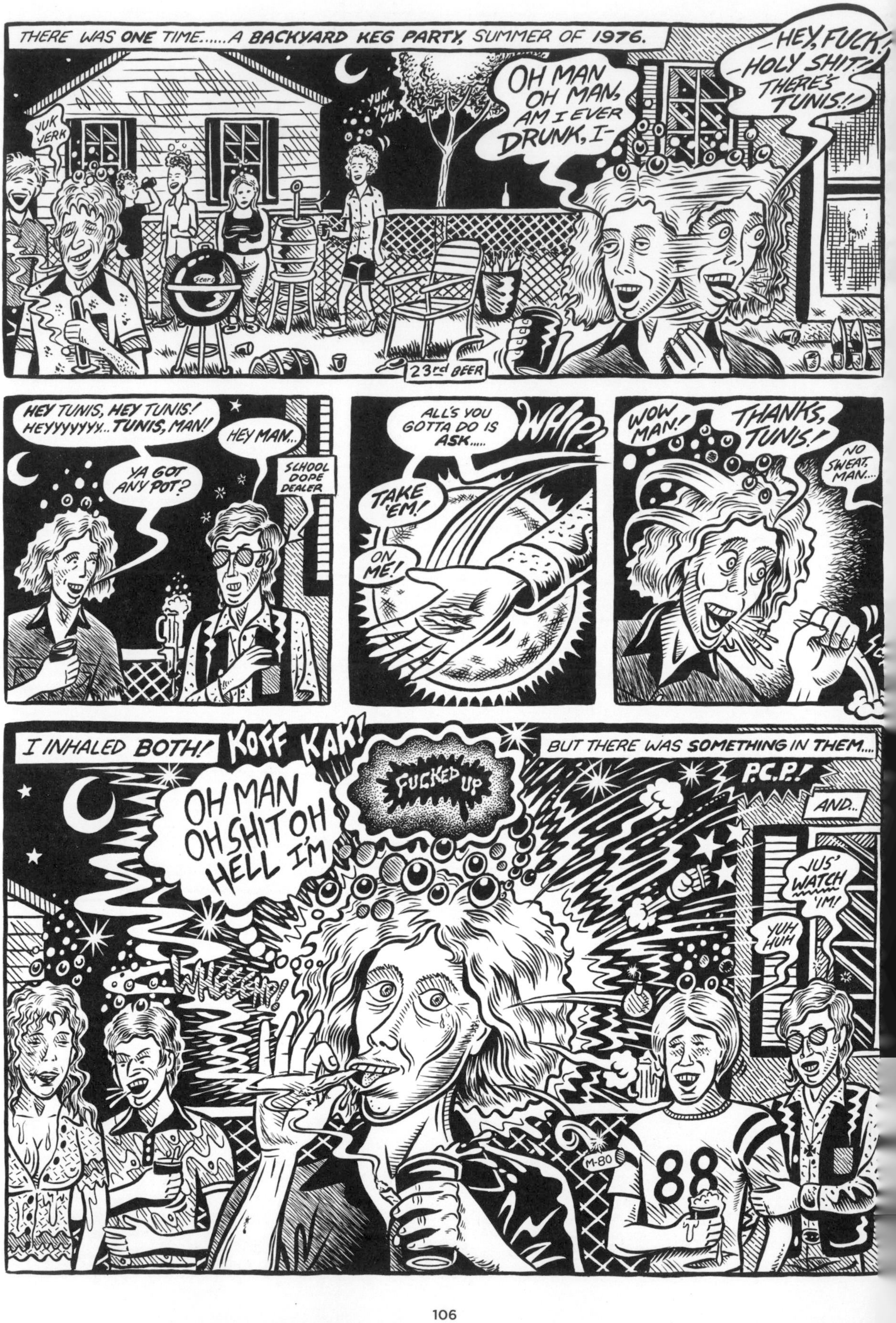
THERE WAS ONE TIME......A BACKYARD KEG PARTY, SUMMER OF 1976.
YUK YERK
YUK YUK YUK
OH MAN OH MAN, AM I EVER DRUNK, I-
-HEY, FUCK! -HOLY SHIT! THERE'S TUNIS!!
23rd BEER
HEY TUNIS, HEY TUNIS! HEYYYYYYY...TUNIS, MAN!
YA GOT ANY POT?
HEY MAN...
SCHOOL DOPE DEALER
ALL'S YOU GOTTA DO IS ASK.....
WHIP!
TAKE 'EM!
ON ME!
WOW MAN!
THANKS, TUNIS!
NO SWEAT, MAN....
I INHALED BOTH!
KOFF KAK!
BUT THERE WAS SOMETHING IN THEM...
FUCKED UP
OH MAN OH SHIT OH HELL I'M
P.C.P.!
AND...
JUS' WATCH 'IM!
YUH HUH
WHEEEH!
M-80
88

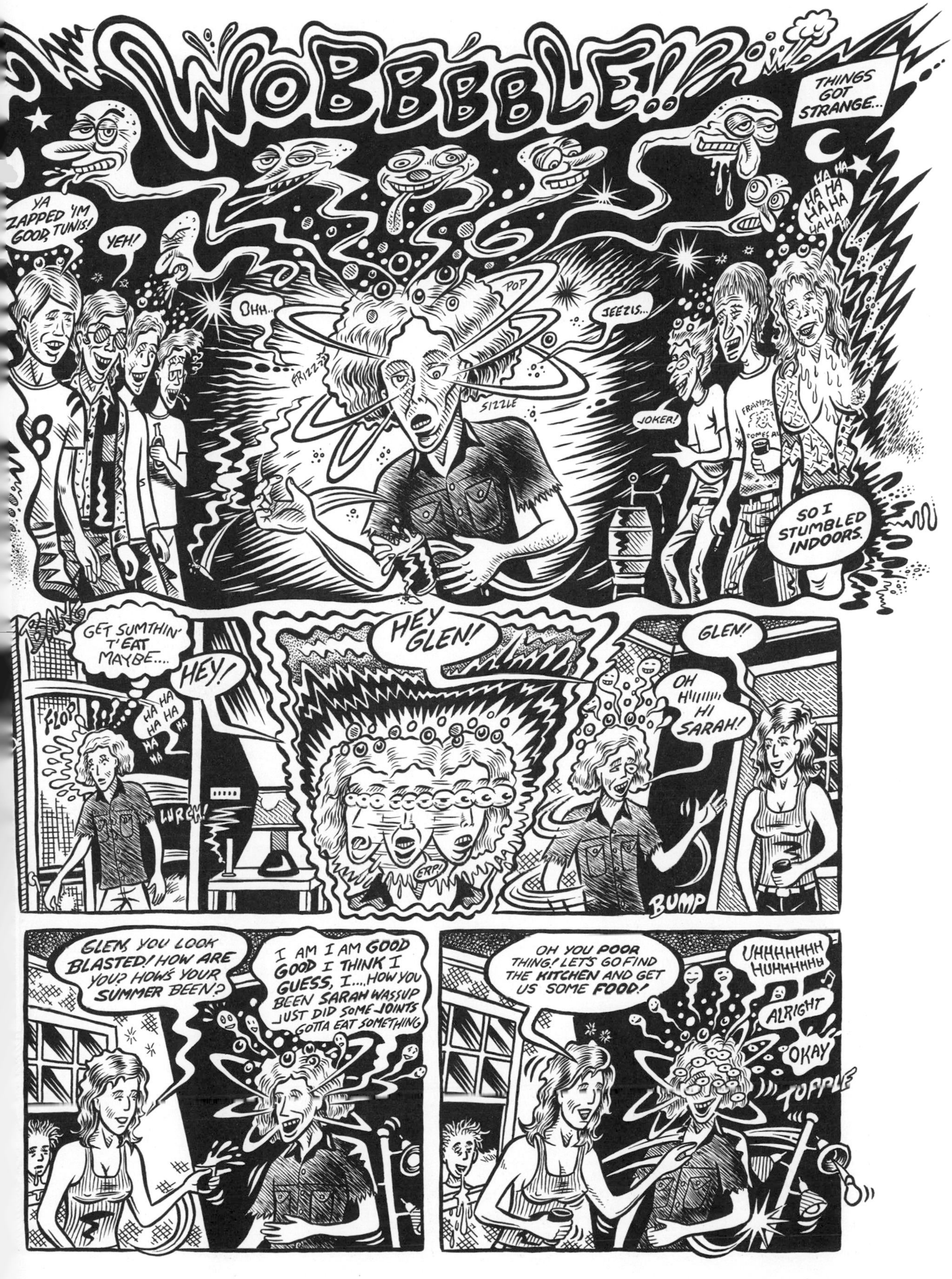
WOBBBBLE!!
THINGS GOT STRANGE...
YA ZAPPED 'IM GOOD, TUNIS!
YEH!
HA HA HA HA HA HA HA HA HA
OHH...
POP
JEEZIS...
FRIZZZ
SIZZLE
JOKER!
SO I STUMBLED INDOORS.
GET SUMTHIN' T'EAT MAYBE....
HEY!
HA HA HA HA HA HA HA
FLOP
LURCH!
HEY GLEN!
ERP!
GLEN!
OH H!!!!!! HI SARAH!
BUMP
GLEN, YOU LOOK BLASTED! HOW ARE YOU? HOW'S YOUR SUMMER BEEN?
I AM I AM GOOD GOOD I THINK I GUESS, I....HOW YOU BEEN SARAH WASSUP JUST DID SOME JOINTS GOTTA EAT SOMETHING
OH YOU POOR THING! LET'S GO FIND THE KITCHEN AND GET US SOME FOOD!
UHHHHHHH HUHHHHHH
ALRIGHT
OKAY
TOPPLE

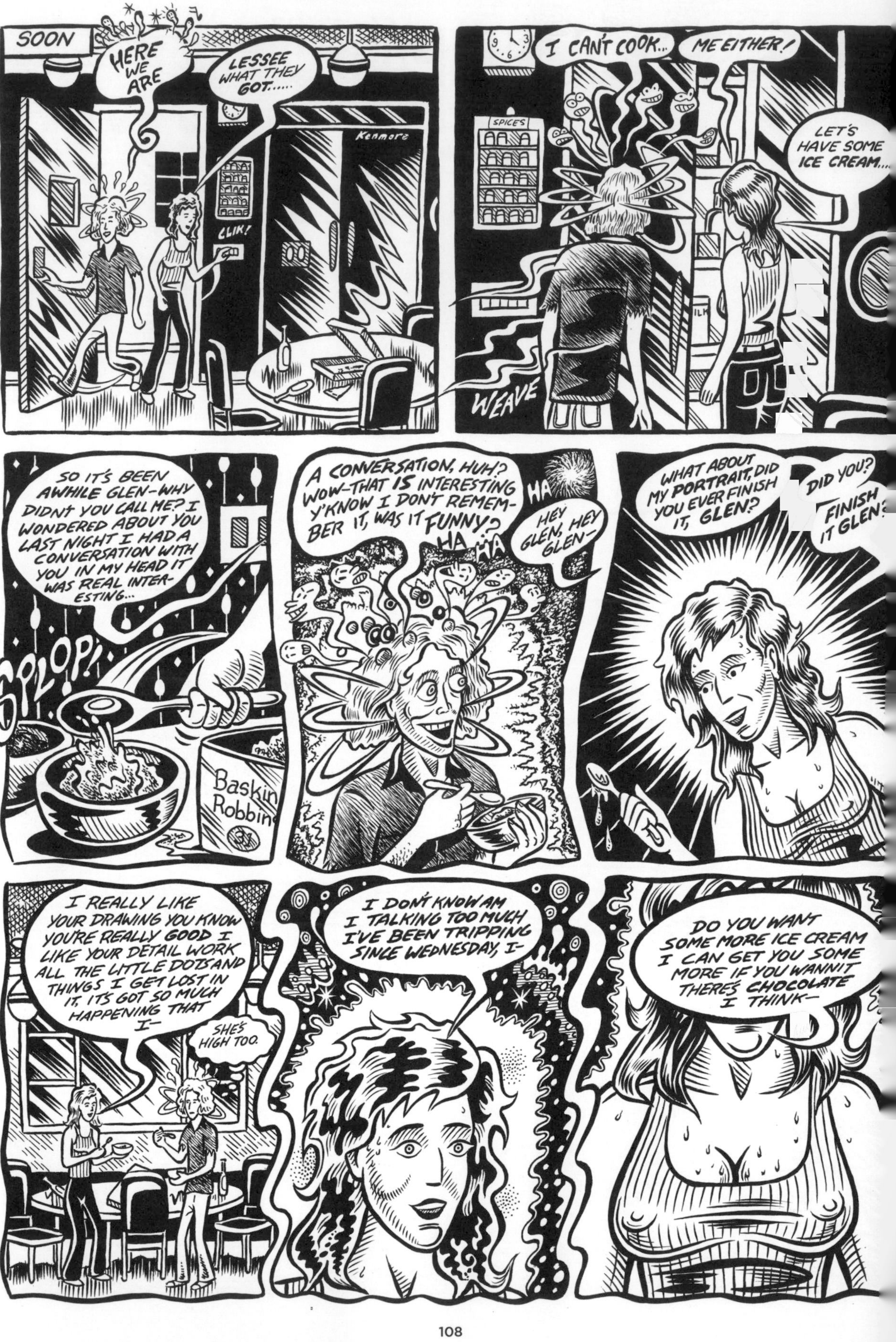
SOON
HERE WE ARE
LESSEE WHAT THEY GOT......
Kenmore
CLIK!
I CAN'T COOK...
ME EITHER!
SPICE'S
LET'S HAVE SOME ICE CREAM....
WEAVE
SO IT'S BEEN AWHILE GLEN-WHY DIDN'T YOU CALL ME? I WONDERED ABOUT YOU LAST NIGHT I HAD A CONVERSATION WITH YOU IN MY HEAD IT WAS REAL INTER-ESTING...
SPLOP!
Baskin Robbins
A CONVERSATION, HUH? WOW-THAT IS INTERESTING Y'KNOW I DON'T REMEM-BER IT, WAS IT FUNNY?
HA
HA HA
HEY GLEN, HEY GLEN-
WHAT ABOUT MY PORTRAIT, DID YOU EVER FINISH IT, GLEN?
DID YOU?
FINISH IT GLEN?
I REALLY LIKE YOUR DRAWING YOU KNOW YOU'RE REALLY GOOD I LIKE YOUR DETAIL WORK ALL THE LITTLE DOTS AND THINGS I GET LOST IN IT, IT'S GOT SO MUCH HAPPENING THAT I-
SHE'S HIGH TOO.
I DON'T KNOW AM I TALKING TOO MUCH I'VE BEEN TRIPPING SINCE WEDNESDAY, I-
DO YOU WANT SOME MORE ICE CREAM I CAN GET YOU SOME MORE IF YOU WANNIT THERE'S CHOCOLATE I THINK-

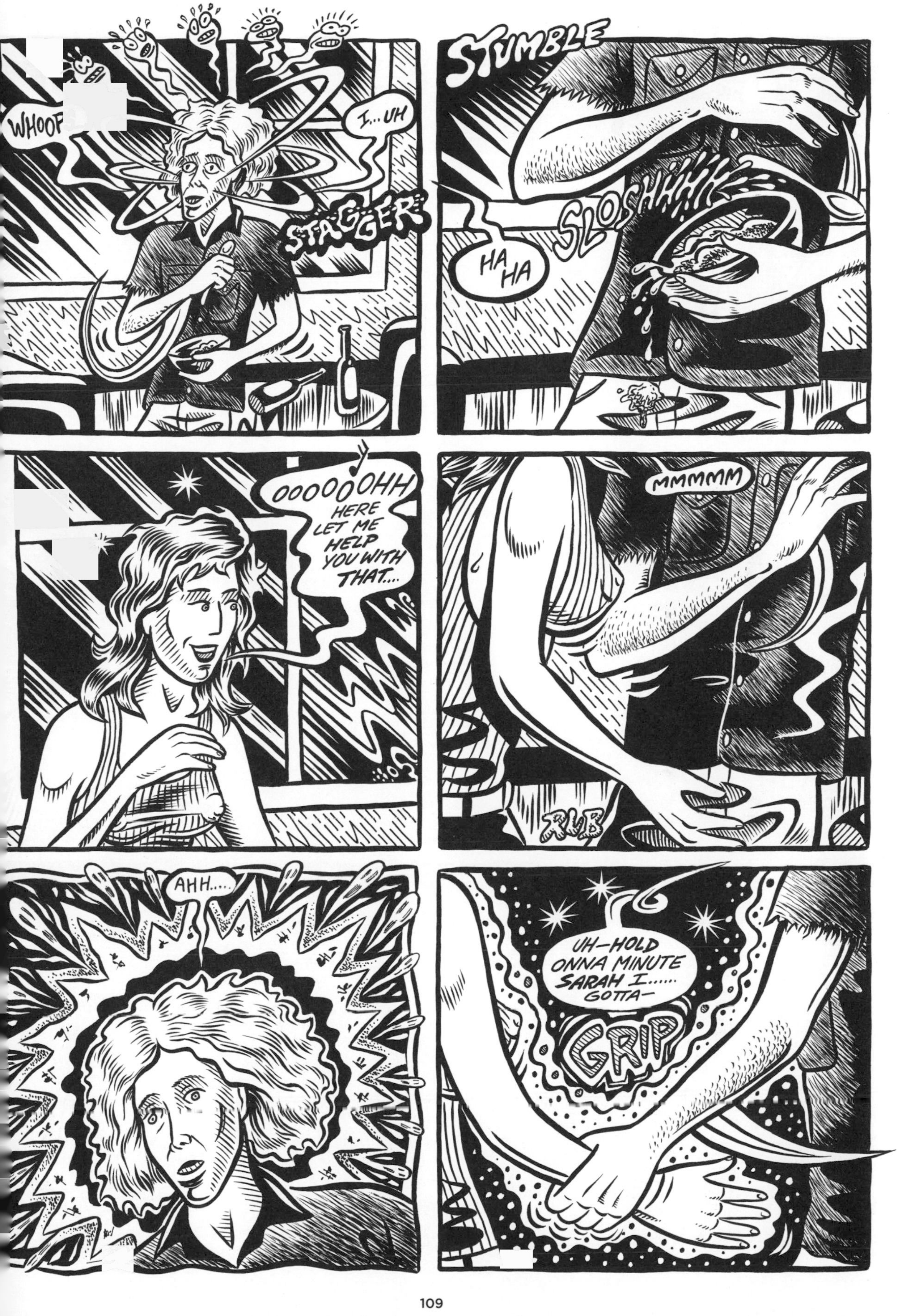
WHOOF
I...UH
STAGGER
STUMBLE
HA HA
SLOSHHHH
OOOOOOHH HERE LET ME HELP YOU WITH THAT....
MMMMM
RUB
AHH.....
UH-HOLD ONNA MINUTE SARAH I...... GOTTA-
GRIP

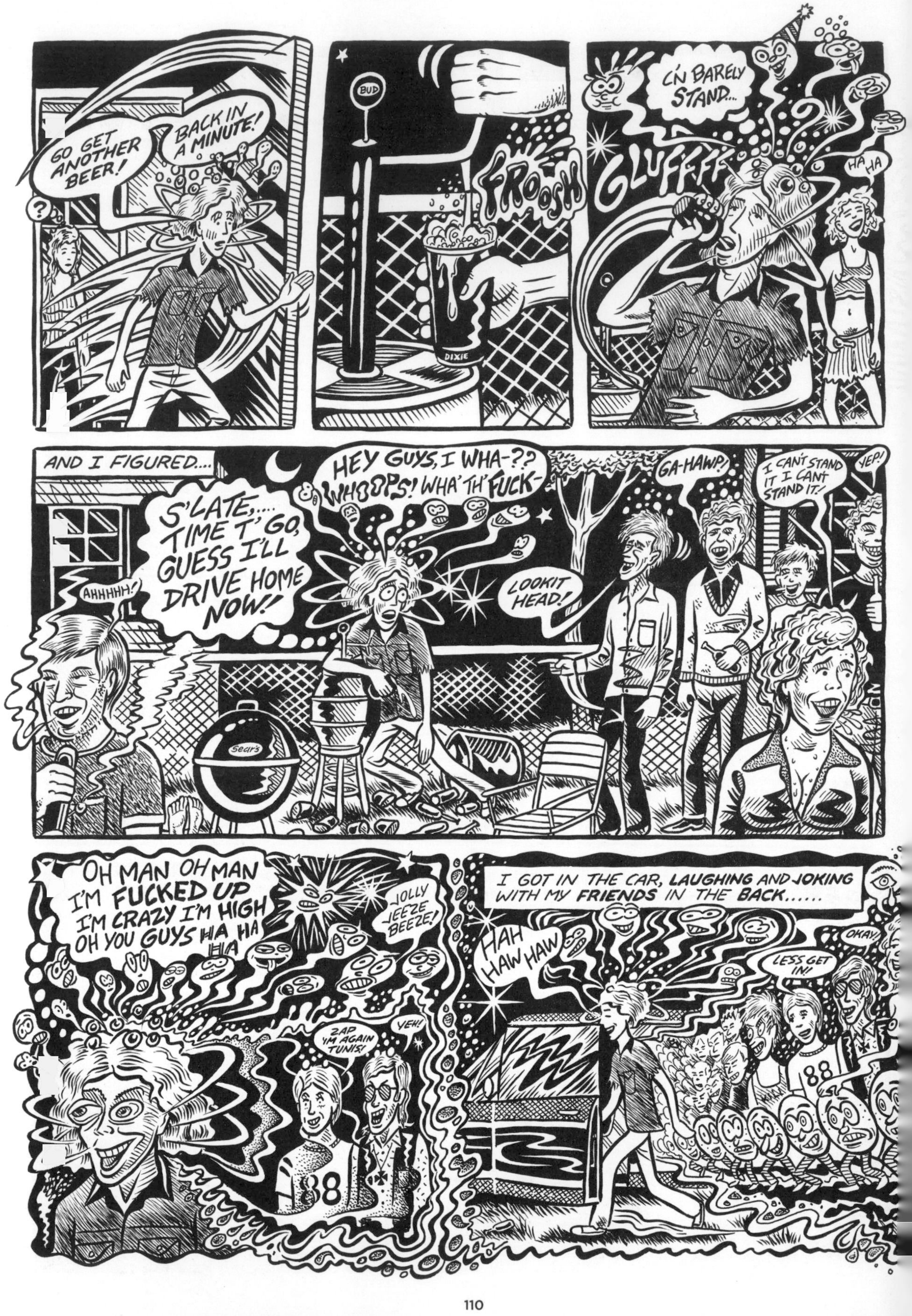
GO GET ANOTHER BEER!
BACK IN A MINUTE!
?
BUD
FROOSH
DIXIE
C'N BARELY STAND...
GLUFFFF
HA HA
AND I FIGURED....
S'LATE,.... TIME T' GO, GUESS I'LL DRIVE HOME NOW!
HEY GUYS, I WHA-?? WHOOPS! WHA' TH' FUCK-
GA-HAWP!
I CAN'T STAND IT I CAN'T STAND IT!
YEP!
AHHHHH!
LOOKIT HEAD!
Sear's
OH MAN OH MAN I'M FUCKED UP I'M CRAZY I'M HIGH OH YOU GUYS HA HA HA
JOLLY JEEZE BEEZE!
ZAP 'M AGAIN TUNIS!
YEH!
88
I GOT IN THE CAR, LAUGHING AND JOKING WITH MY FRIENDS IN THE BACK......
HAH HAW HAW
OKAY!
LESS GET IN!
88

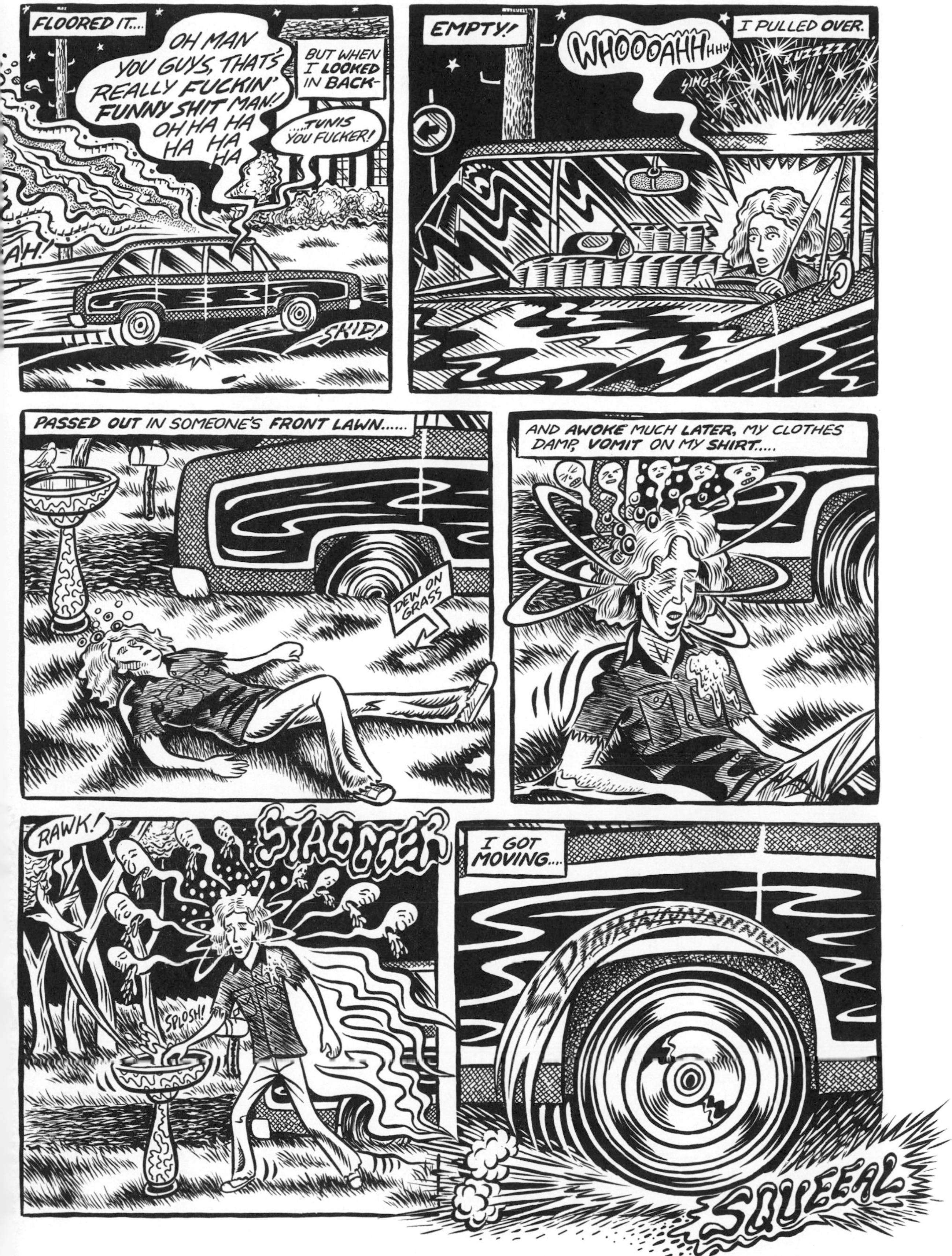

FLOORED IT....
OH MAN YOU GUYS, THAT'S REALLY FUCKIN' FUNNY SHIT MAN! OH HA HA HA HA HA
BUT WHEN I LOOKED IN BACK-
....TUNIS YOU FUCKER!
AH!
SKID!
EMPTY!
WHOOOOAHHhhh
I PULLED OVER.
SINGE!
BUZZZZ
PASSED OUT IN SOMEONE'S FRONT LAWN......
DEW ON GRASS
AND AWOKE MUCH LATER, MY CLOTHES DAMP, VOMIT ON MY SHIRT.....
RAWK!
STAGGGER
SPLOSH!
I GOT MOVING....
SQUEEAL

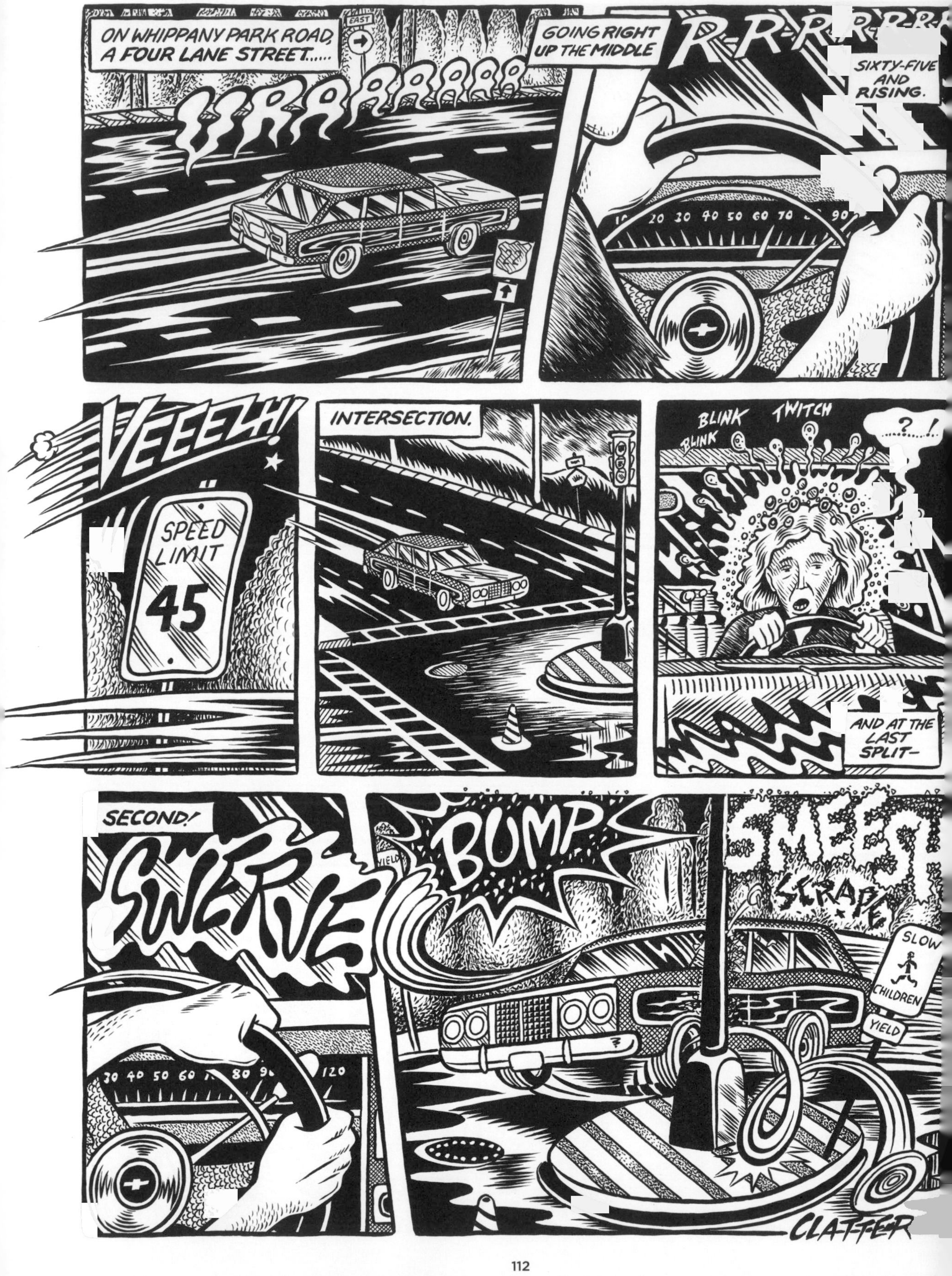
ON WHIPPANY PARK ROAD, A FOUR LANE STREET.....
EAST
GOING RIGHT UP THE MIDDLE
SIXTY-FIVE AND RISING.
SPEED LIMIT 45
INTERSECTION.
BLINK
BLINK
TWITCH
?!
AND AT THE LAST SPLIT-
SECOND!
SWERVE
BUMP
SCRAPE
SLOW
CHILDREN
YIELD
YIELD
CLATTER

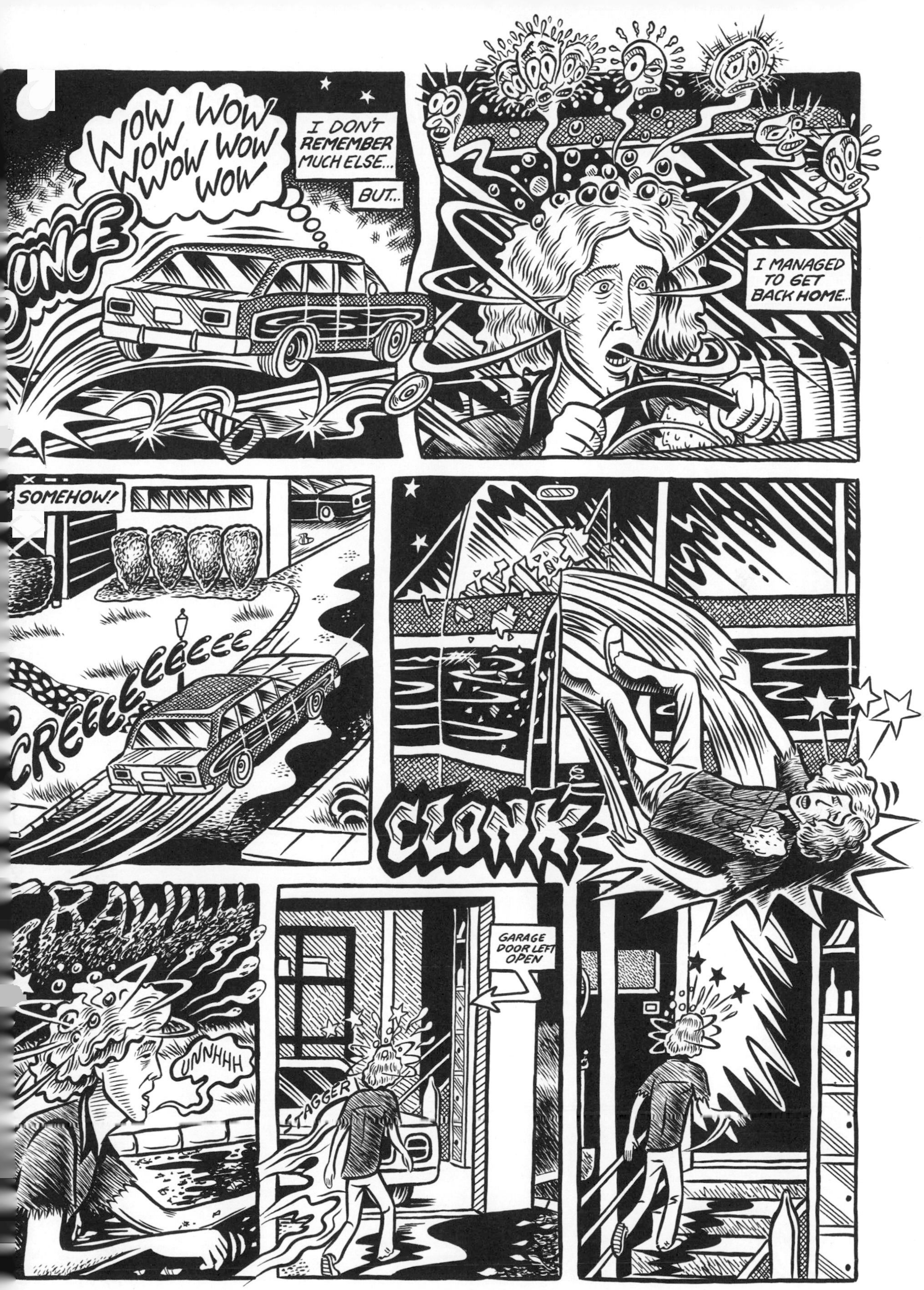

BOUNCE
WOW WOW WOW WOW WOW WOW WOW
I DON'T REMEMBER MUCH ELSE...
BUT...
I MANAGED TO GET BACK HOME...
SOMEHOW!
CREEEEEEEEEEEE
CLONK
UNNHHH
GARAGE DOOR LEFT OPEN
STAGGER

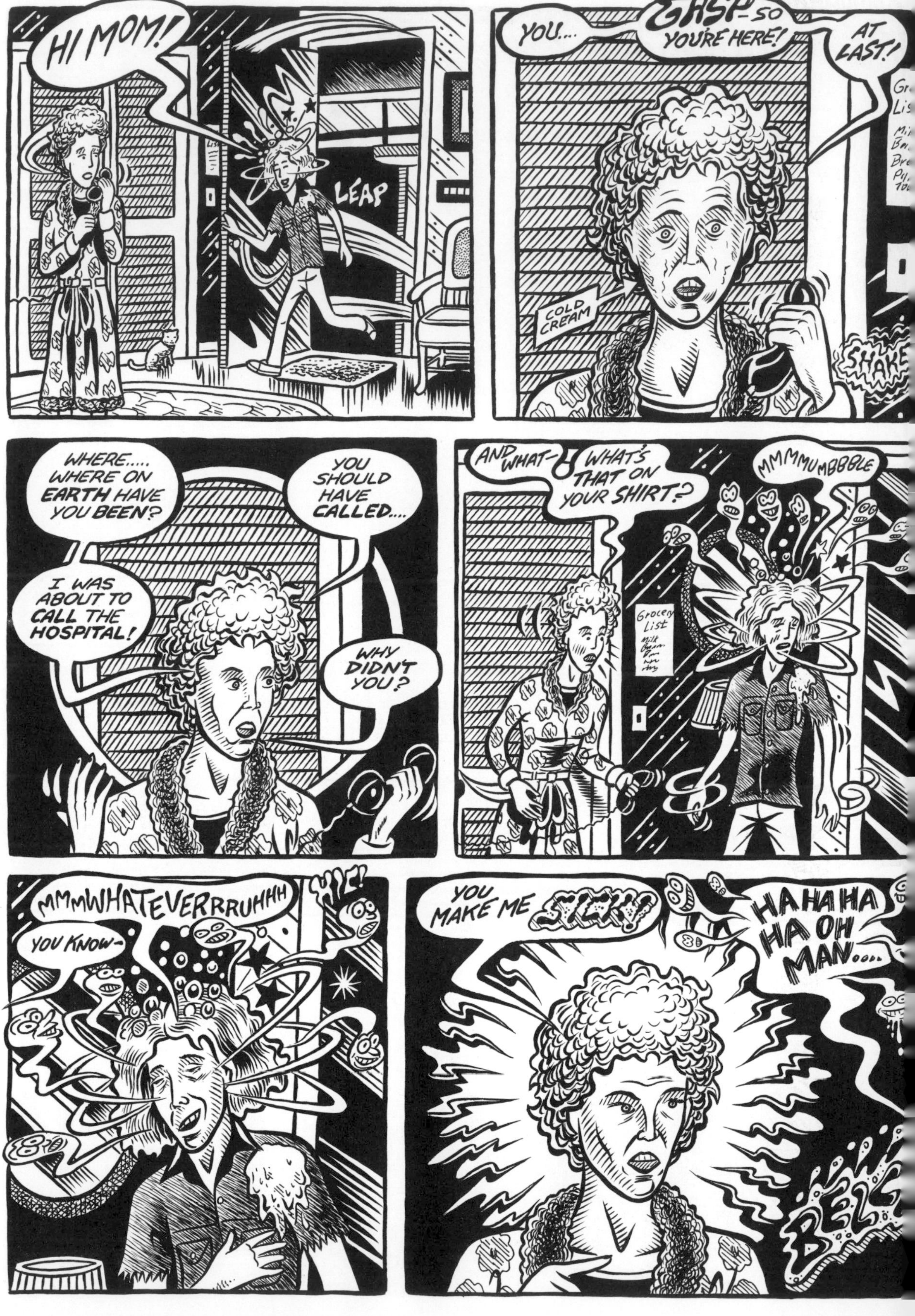
HI MOM!
LEAP
YOU....
GASP-SO YOU'RE HERE!
AT LAST!
COLD CREAM
SHAKE
WHERE..... WHERE ON EARTH HAVE YOU BEEN?
YOU SHOULD HAVE CALLED....
I WAS ABOUT TO CALL THE HOSPITAL!
WHY DIDN'T YOU?
AND WHAT-
WHAT'S THAT ON YOUR SHIRT?
MMMMUMBBBLE
Grocery List
MMMWHATEVERRRUHHH
YOU KNOW-
HIC!
YOU MAKE ME SICK!
HA HA HA HA HA OH MAN...

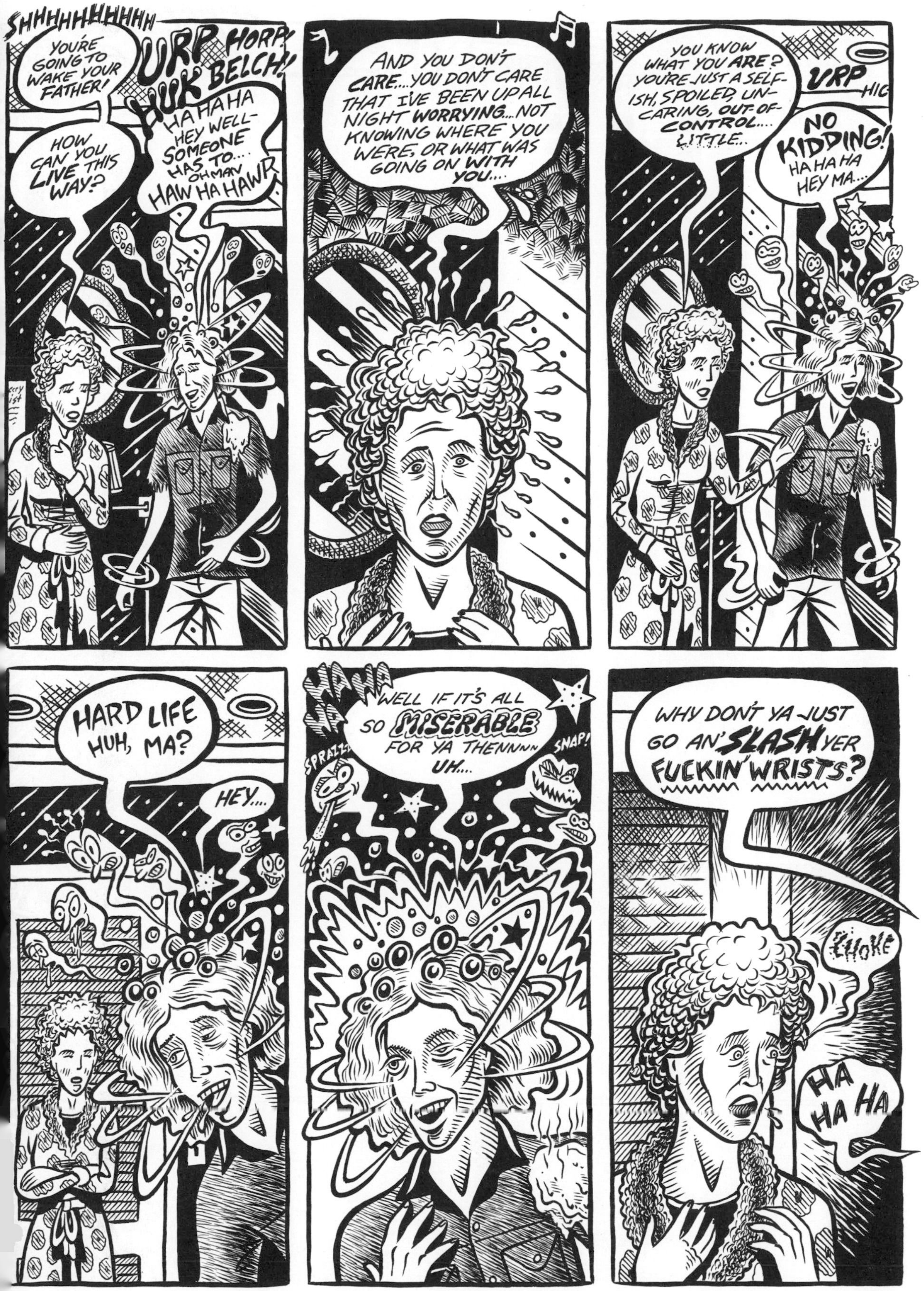
SHHHHHHHHHH
YOU'RE GOING TO WAKE YOUR FATHER!
URP HORP! HUK BELCH!
HOW CAN YOU LIVE THIS WAY?
HA HA HA HEY WELL- SOMEONE HAS TO.... OH MAN HAW HA HAWR
AND YOU DON'T CARE... YOU DON'T CARE THAT I'VE BEEN UP ALL NIGHT WORRYING... NOT KNOWING WHERE YOU WERE, OR WHAT WAS GOING ON WITH YOU....
YOU KNOW WHAT YOU ARE? YOU'RE JUST A SELFISH, SPOILED, UNCARING, OUT-OF-CONTROL.... LITTLE...
URP HIC
NO KIDDING! HA HA HA HEY MA....
HARD LIFE HUH, MA?
HEY....
HA HA
WELL IF IT'S ALL SO MISERABLE FOR YA THENNNN UH....
SPRAZZ
SNAP!
WHY DON'T YA JUST GO AN' SLASH YER FUCKIN' WRISTS?
CHOKE
HA HA HA

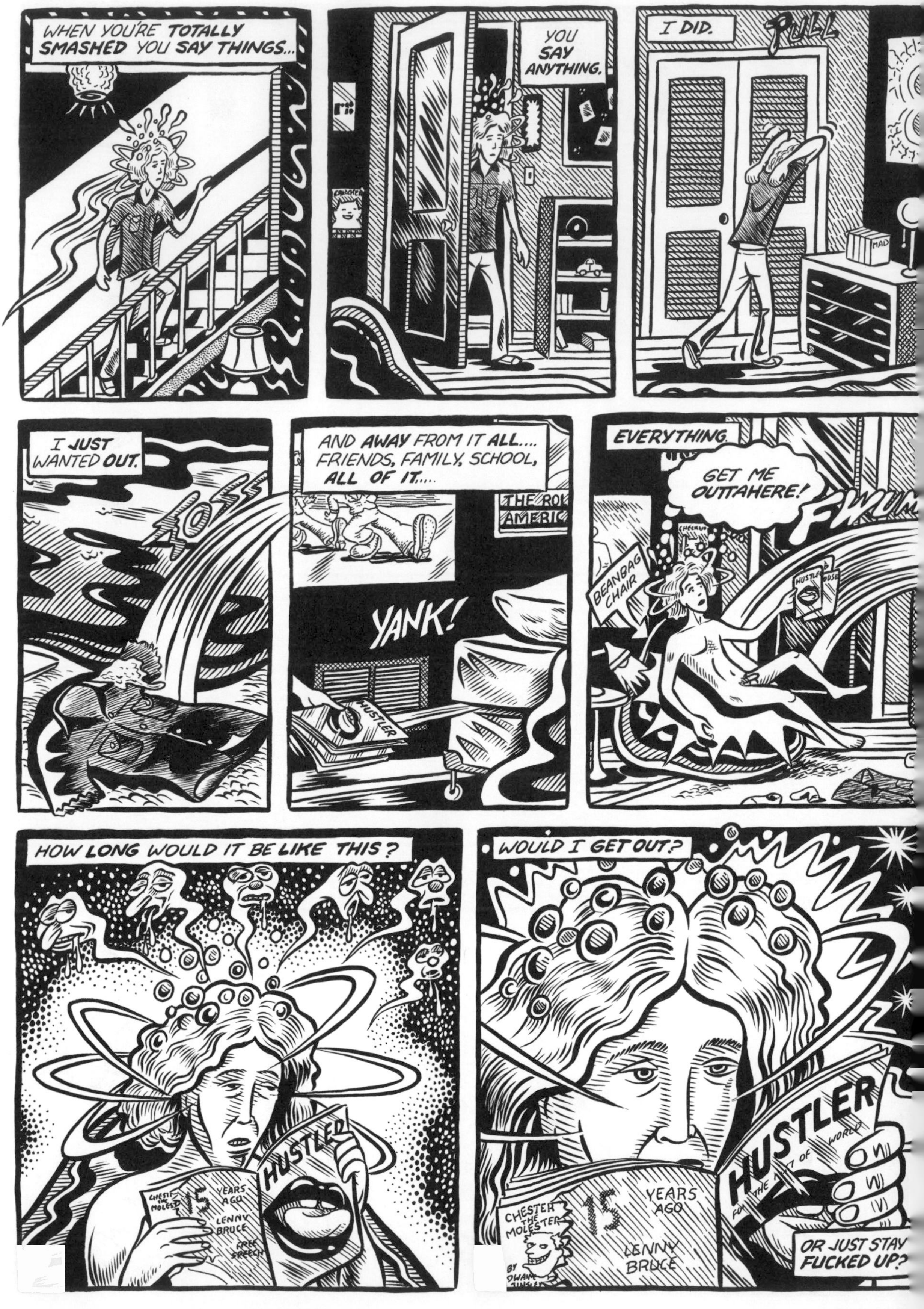
WHEN YOU'RE TOTALLY SMASHED YOU SAY THINGS...
YOU SAY ANYTHING.
I DID.
PULL
MAD
I JUST WANTED OUT.
AND AWAY FROM IT ALL.... FRIENDS, FAMILY, SCHOOL, ALL OF IT.....
YANK!
HUSTLER
EVERYTHING.
GET ME OUTTAHERE!
FWUM
BEANBAG CHAIR
HOW LONG WOULD IT BE LIKE THIS?
HUSTLER
15 YEARS AGO
LENNY BRUCE
WOULD I GET OUT?
HUSTLER
CHESTER THE MOLESTER
15 YEARS AGO
LENNY BRUCE
OR JUST STAY FUCKED UP?

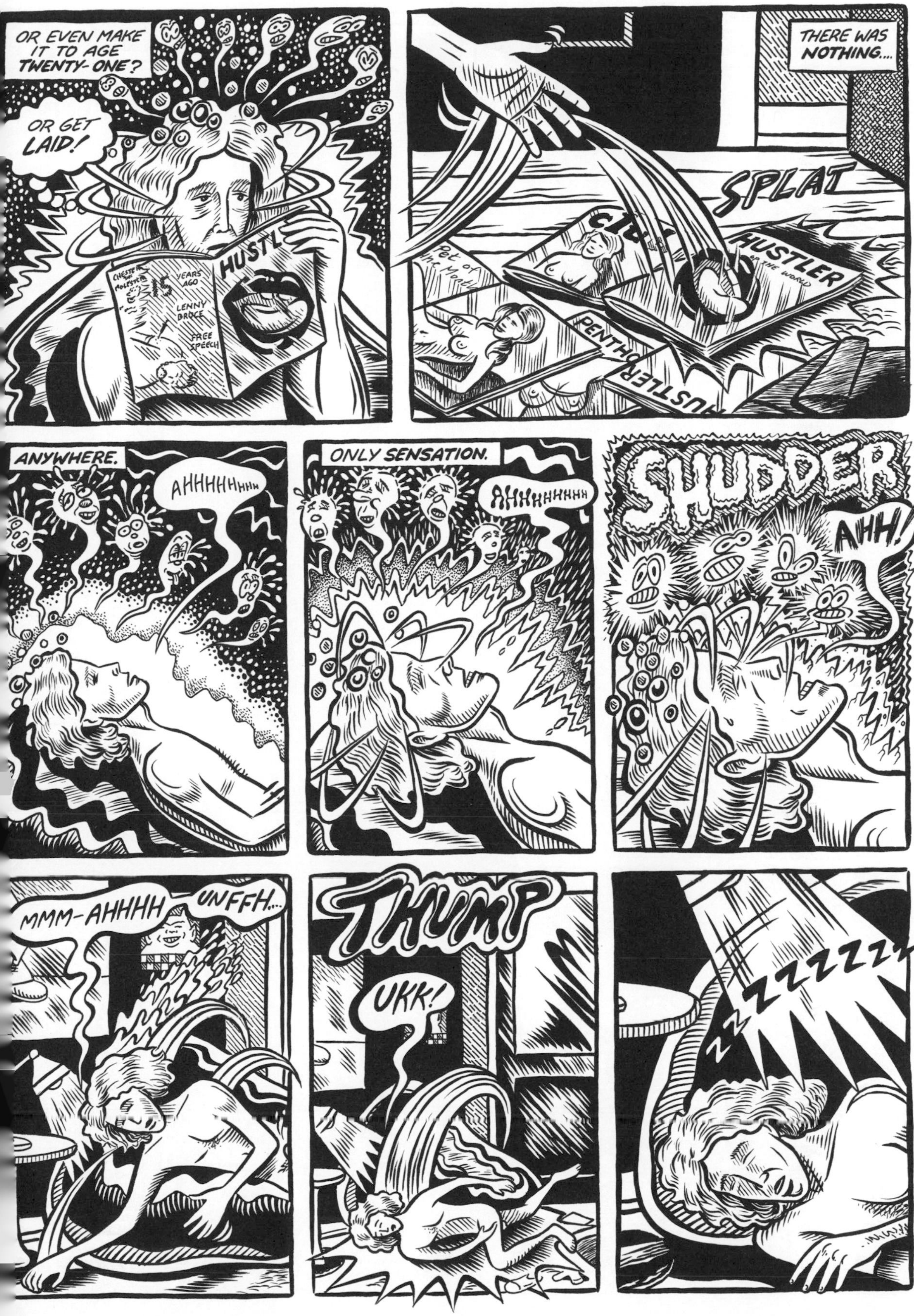
OR EVEN MAKE IT TO AGE TWENTY-ONE?
OR GET LAID!
HUSTL
15 YEARS AGO
LENNY BRUCE
FREE SPEECH
THERE WAS NOTHING...
SPLAT
HUSTLER
PENTHO
HUSTLER
ANYWHERE.
AHHHHHhhhh
ONLY SENSATION.
AHHHHHHHH
SHUDDER
AHH!
MMM-AHHHH
UNFFH...
THUMP
UKK!
ZZZZZZZZZ

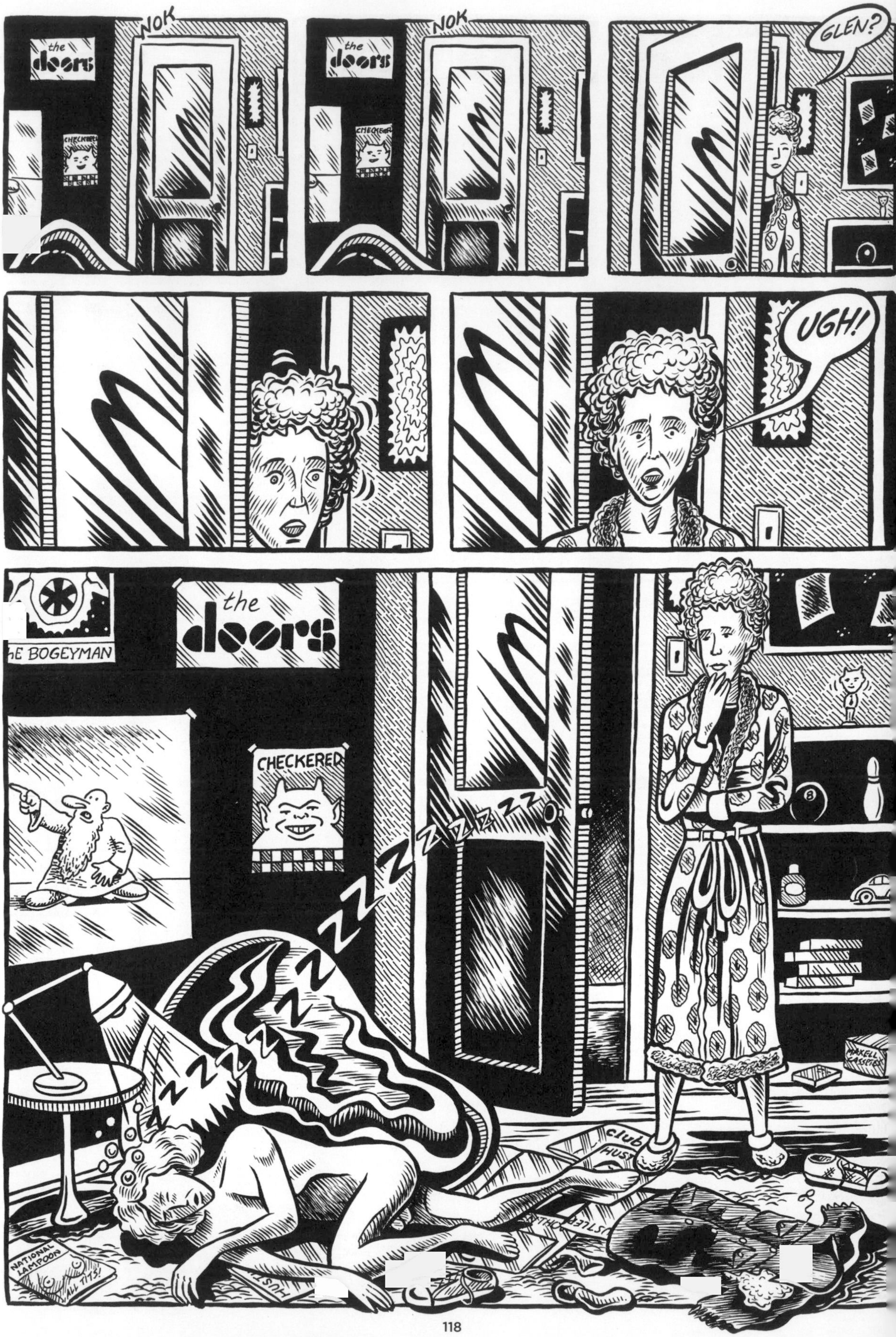

NOK
NOK
GLEN?
UGH!
the doors
CHECKERED
HE BOGEYMAN
NATIONAL LAMPOON
ALL TITS!
club

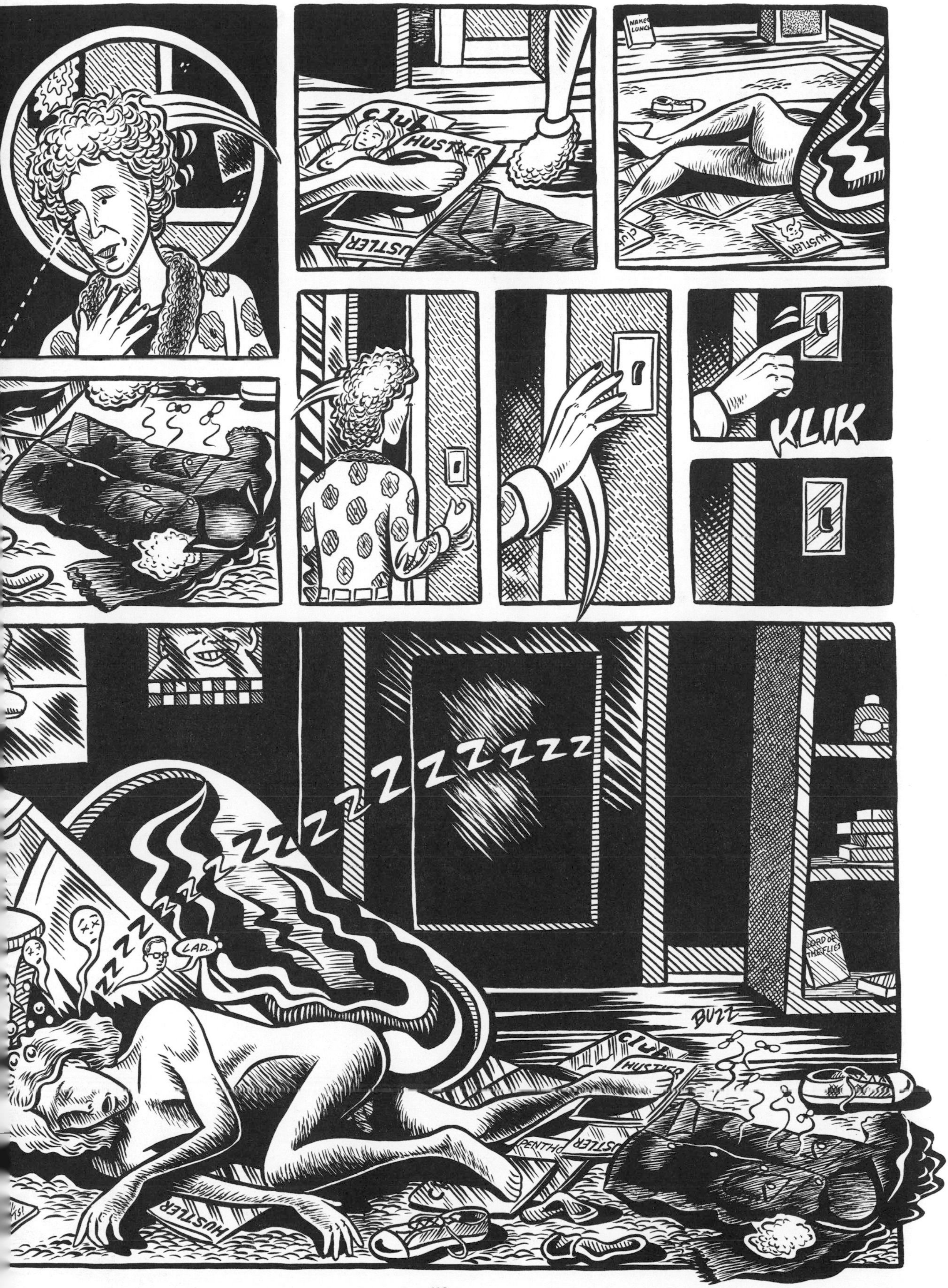
Club
HUSTLER
HUSTLER
NAKED LUNCH
HUSTLER
KLIK
ZZZZZZZZZZZZZZZ
ZZZZ
LAD...
BUZZ
LORD OF THE FLIES
Club
HUSTLER
PENTHO
HUSTLER
HUSTLER

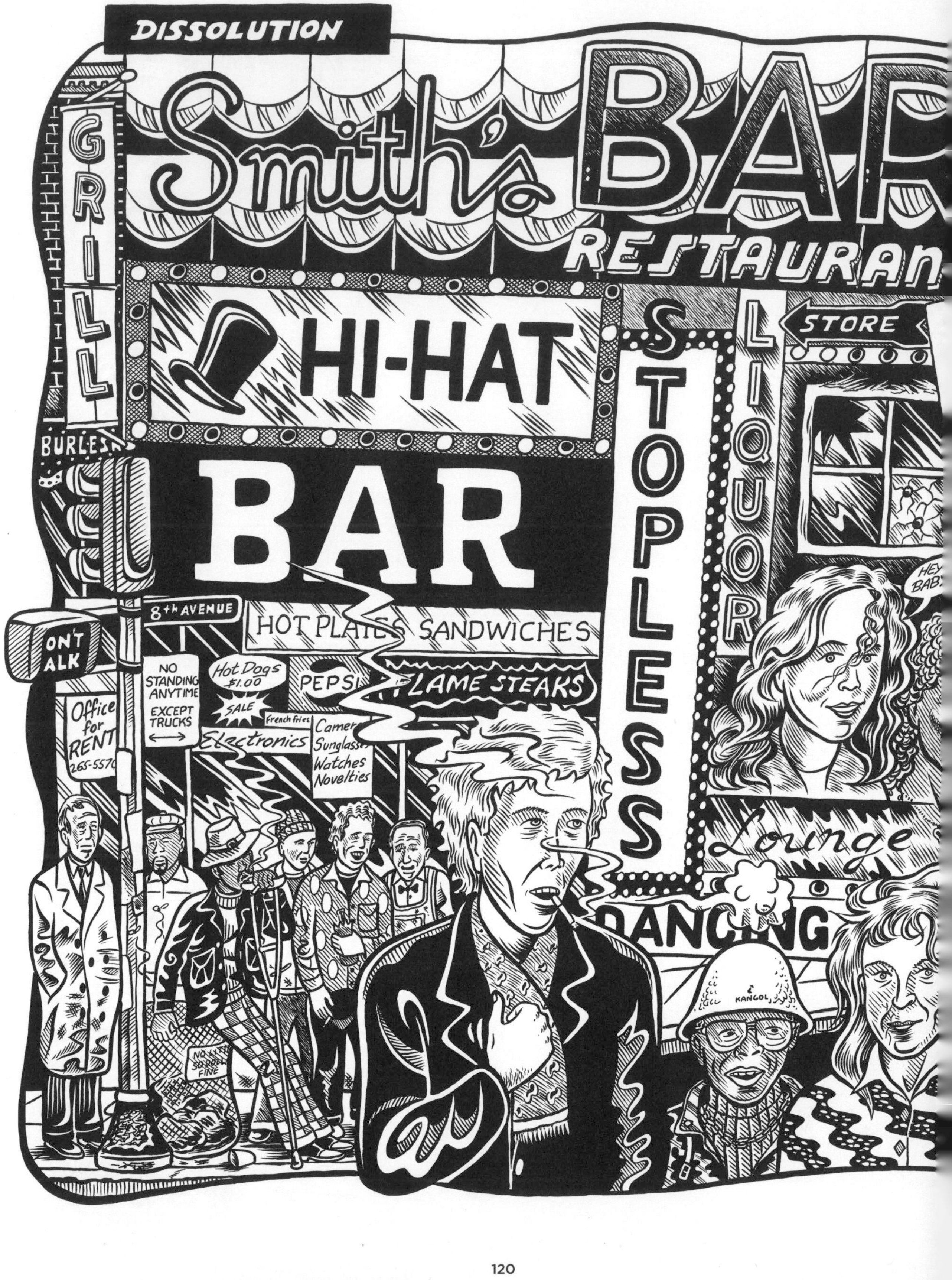
DISSOLUTION
Smith's BAR
RESTAURAN
GRILL
HI-HAT
BAR
STOPLESS
LIQUOR
STORE
BURLES
8th AVENUE
HOT PLATES SANDWICHES
ON'T ALK
HEY BAB
NO STANDING ANYTIME EXCEPT TRUCKS
Hot Dogs $1.00
SALE
French fries
PEPSI
FLAME STEAKS
Office for RENT 265-557
Electronics
Camer Sunglasse Watches Novelties
Lounge
DANCING
KANGOL

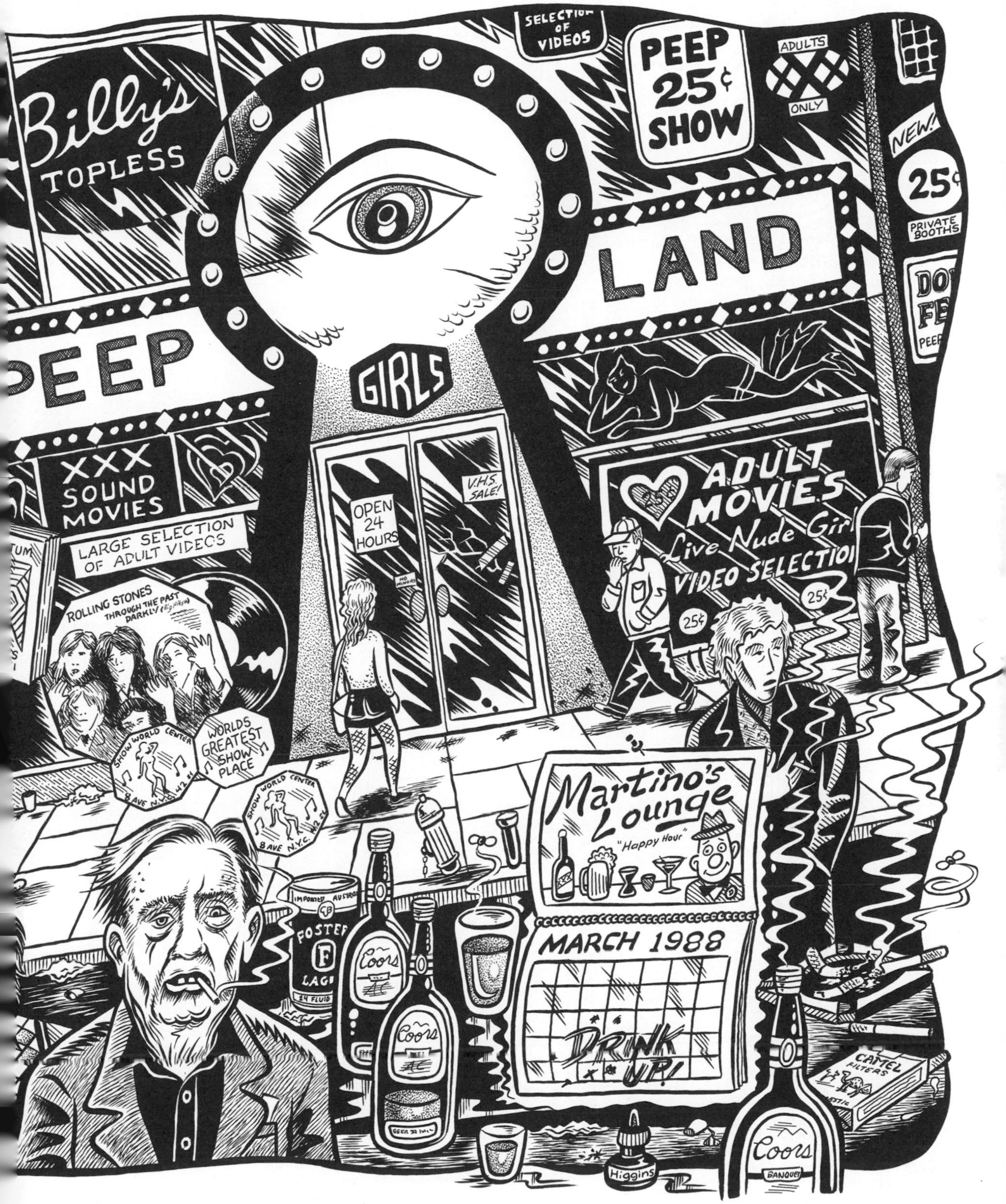
SELECTION OF VIDEOS
PEEP 25¢ SHOW
ADULTS XXX ONLY
Billy's TOPLESS
NEW!
25¢ PRIVATE BOOTHS
PEEP
LAND
GIRLS
XXX SOUND MOVIES
LARGE SELECTION OF ADULT VIDEOS
OPEN 24 HOURS
V.H.S SALE!
ADULT MOVIES
Live Nude Girl
VIDEO SELECTIO
25¢
25¢
ROLLING STONES THROUGH THE PAST DARKLY
SHOW WORLD CENTER 8 AVE N.Y.C.
WORLDS GREATEST SHOW PLACE
SHOW WORLD CENTER 8 AVE N.Y.C.
Martino's Lounge
"Happy Hour"
MARCH 1988
DRINK UP!
Coors
Coors
CAMEL FILTERS
Higgins
Coors
BANQUET

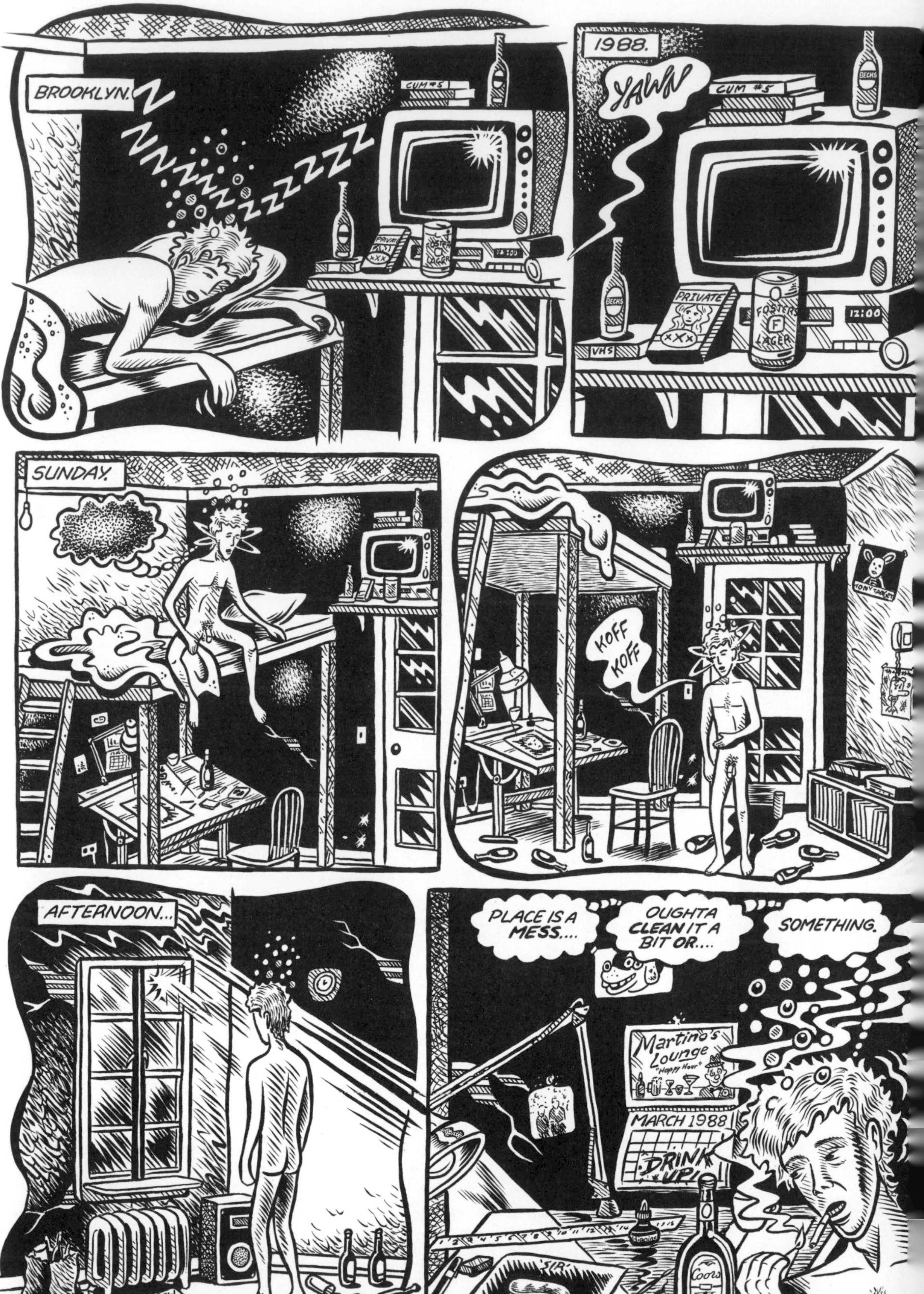
BROOKLYN.
CUM #5
PRIVATE
1988.
YAWN
CUM #5
BECKS
PRIVATE
XXX
FOSTERS LAGER
VHS
12:00
SUNDAY.
KOFF KOFF
AFTERNOON...
SCREW
PLACE IS A MESS....
OUGHTA CLEAN IT A BIT OR....
SOMETHING.
Martino's Lounge
"Happy Hour"
MARCH 1988
DRINK UP!
Coors

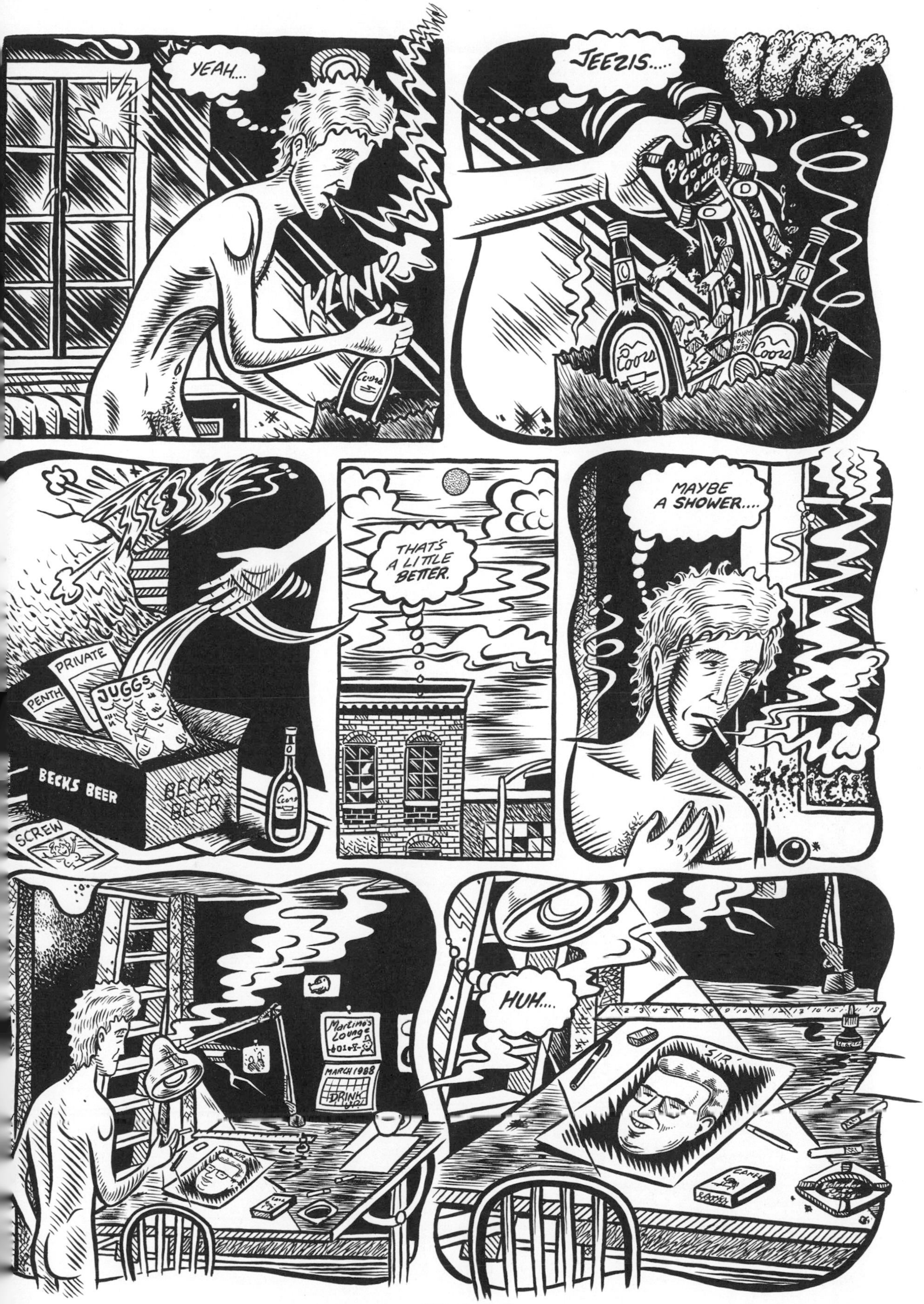
YEAH....
KLINK
JEEZIS....
Belinda's Go-Go Lounge
Coors
Coors
THAT'S A LITTLE BETTER.
PRIVATE
PENTH
JUGGS
BECKS BEER
BECKS BEER
SCREW
MAYBE A SHOWER....
SKRITCH
Martino's Lounge
MARCH 1988
DRINK UP!
HUH....
'SIR'
CAMEL

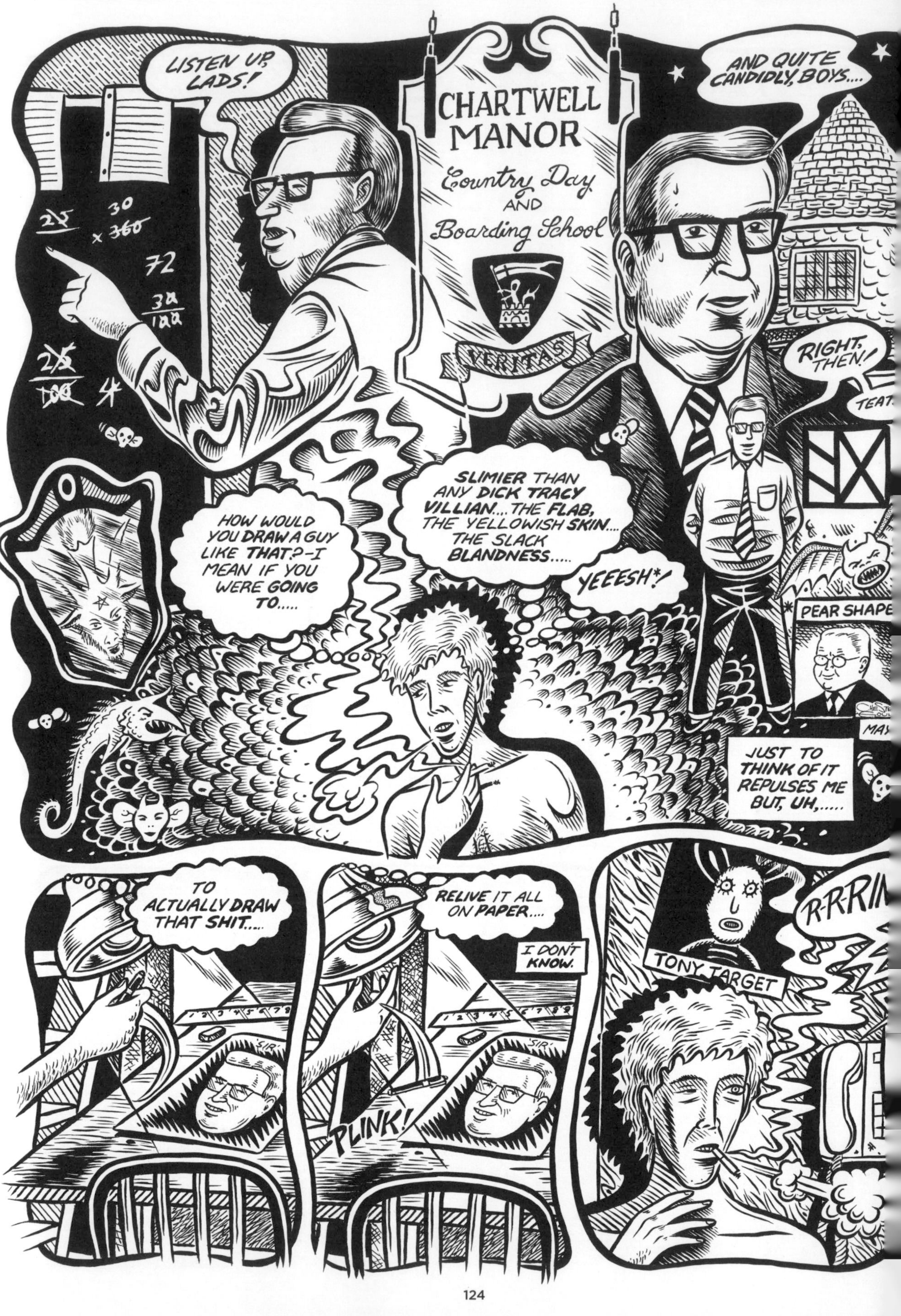

LISTEN UP, LADS!
CHARTWELL MANOR
Country Day AND Boarding School
VERITAS
AND QUITE CANDIDLY, BOYS....
RIGHT, THEN!
SLIMIER THAN ANY DICK TRACY VILLIAN.... THE FLAB, THE YELLOWISH SKIN.... THE SLACK BLANDNESS.....
HOW WOULD YOU DRAW A GUY LIKE THAT?-I MEAN IF YOU WERE GOING TO.....
YEEESH*!
PEAR SHAPE
JUST TO THINK OF IT REPULSES ME BUT, UH,.....
TO ACTUALLY DRAW THAT SHIT.....
'SIR'
RELIVE IT ALL ON PAPER....
I DONT KNOW.
PLINK!
'SIR'
TONY TARGET
R-R-RIN

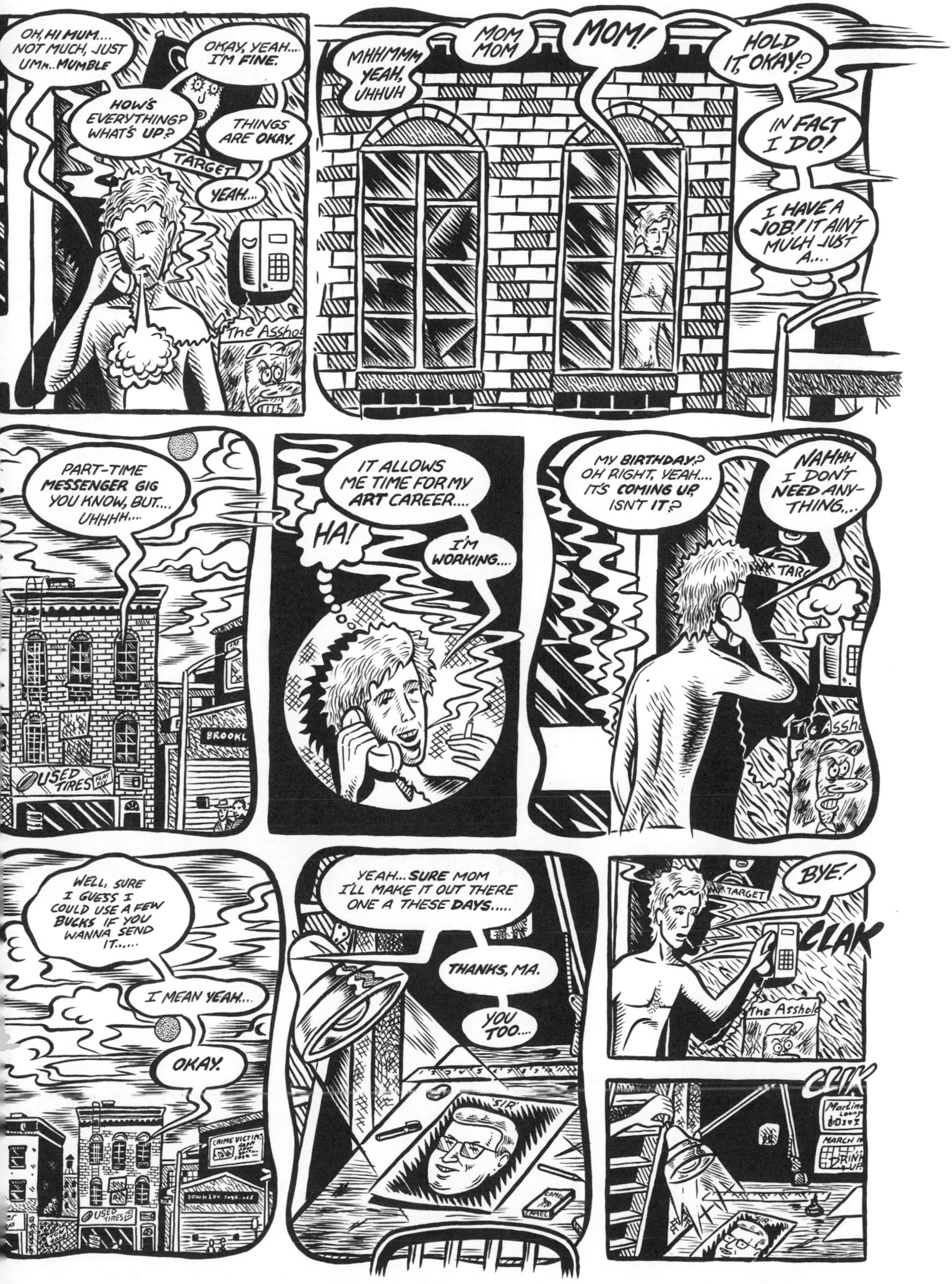
OH, HI MUM.... NOT MUCH, JUST UMM...MUMBLE
OKAY, YEAH.... I'M FINE.
HOW'S EVERYTHING? WHAT'S UP?
THINGS ARE OKAY.
TARGET
YEAH....
The Assho
MHHMMM YEAH, UHHUH
MOM MOM
MOM!
HOLD IT, OKAY?
IN FACT I DO!
I HAVE A JOB! IT AIN'T MUCH JUST A....
PART-TIME MESSENGER GIG YOU KNOW, BUT.... UHHHH....
USED TIRES
BROOKL
IT ALLOWS ME TIME FOR MY ART CAREER....
HA!
I'M WORKING....
MY BIRTHDAY? OH RIGHT, YEAH.... IT'S COMING UP, ISN'T IT?
NAHHH I DON'T NEED ANY-THING....
WELL, SURE I GUESS I COULD USE A FEW BUCKS IF YOU WANNA SEND IT.....
I MEAN YEAH...
OKAY.
USED TIRES
YEAH... SURE MOM I'LL MAKE IT OUT THERE ONE A THESE DAYS.....
THANKS, MA.
YOU TOO....
'SIR'
CAMEL
BYE!
TARGET
CLAK
The Asshol
CLIK

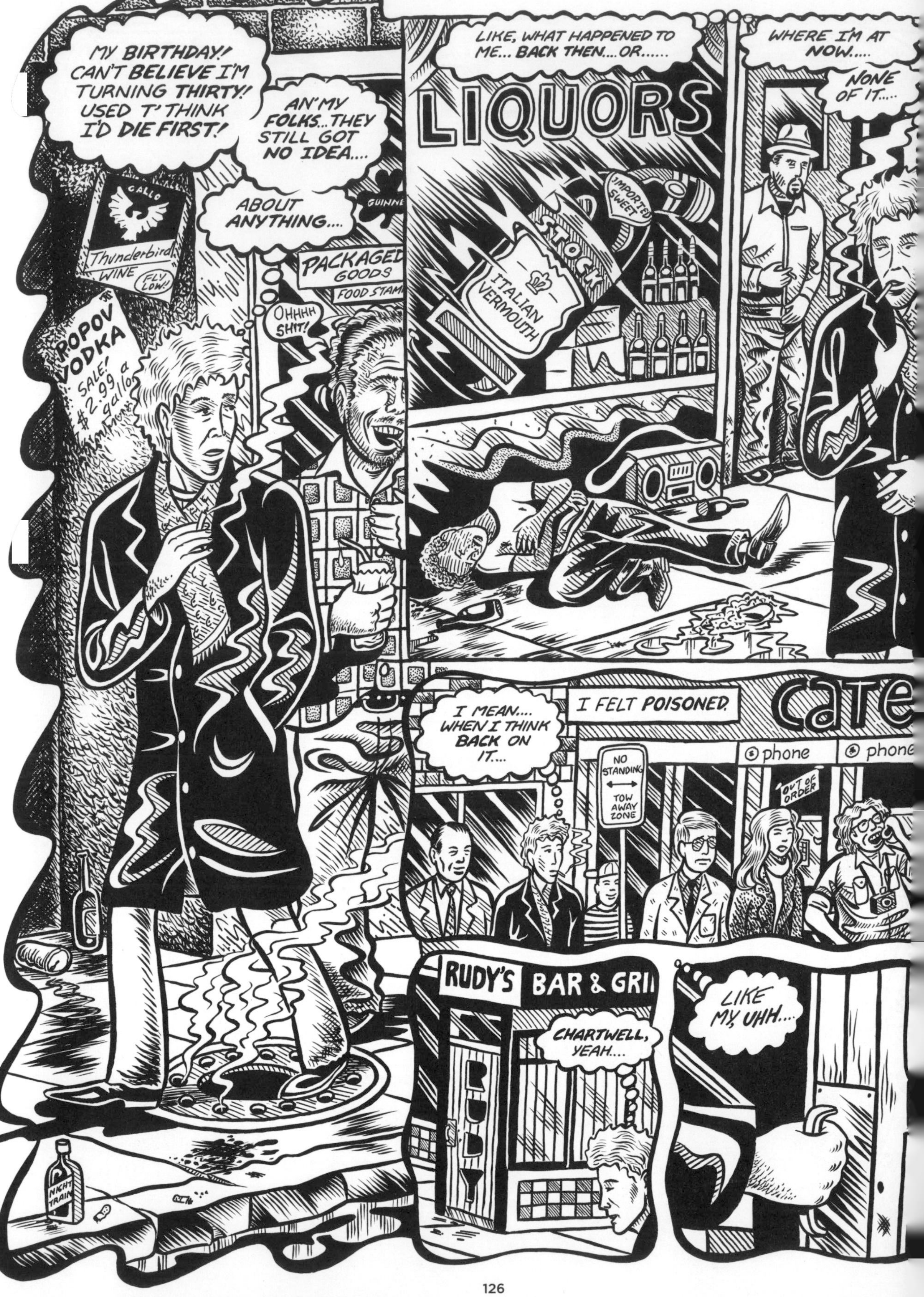
MY BIRTHDAY! CAN'T BELIEVE I'M TURNING THIRTY! USED T' THINK I'D DIE FIRST!
AN' MY FOLKS... THEY STILL GOT NO IDEA....
ABOUT ANYTHING....
GALLO
Thunderbird WINE
FLY LOW!
POPOV VODKA
SALE! $2.99 a gallon
PACKAGED GOODS
FOOD STAMPS
OHHHH SHIT!
LIKE, WHAT HAPPENED TO ME... BACK THEN.... OR......
LIQUORS
IMPORTED SWEET
STOCK
ITALIAN VERMOUTH
WHERE I'M AT NOW.....
NONE OF IT....
I MEAN.... WHEN I THINK BACK ON IT....
I FELT POISONED.
phone
phone
NO STANDING
TOW AWAY ZONE
OUT OF ORDER
RUDY'S BAR & GRI
CHARTWELL, YEAH....
LIKE MY, UHH....
NIGHT TRAIN

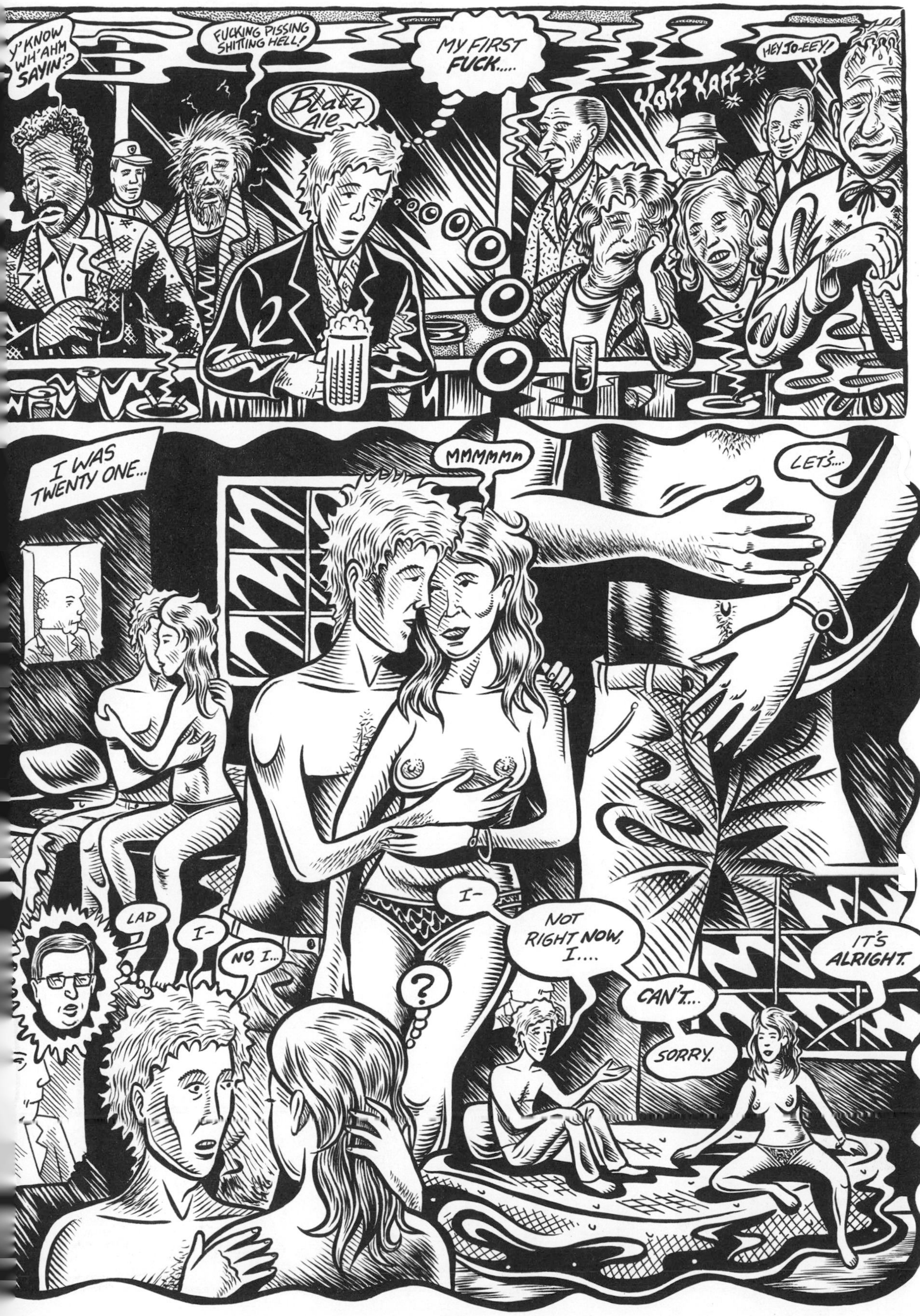
Y'KNOW WH'AH'M SAYIN'?
FUCKING PISSING SHITTING HELL!
Blatz Ale
MY FIRST FUCK.....
KOFF KAFF
HEY JO-EEY!
I WAS TWENTY ONE...
MMMMMM
LET'S....
I-
LAD
I-
NO, I...
?
NOT RIGHT NOW, I....
CAN'T...
SORRY.
IT'S ALRIGHT.

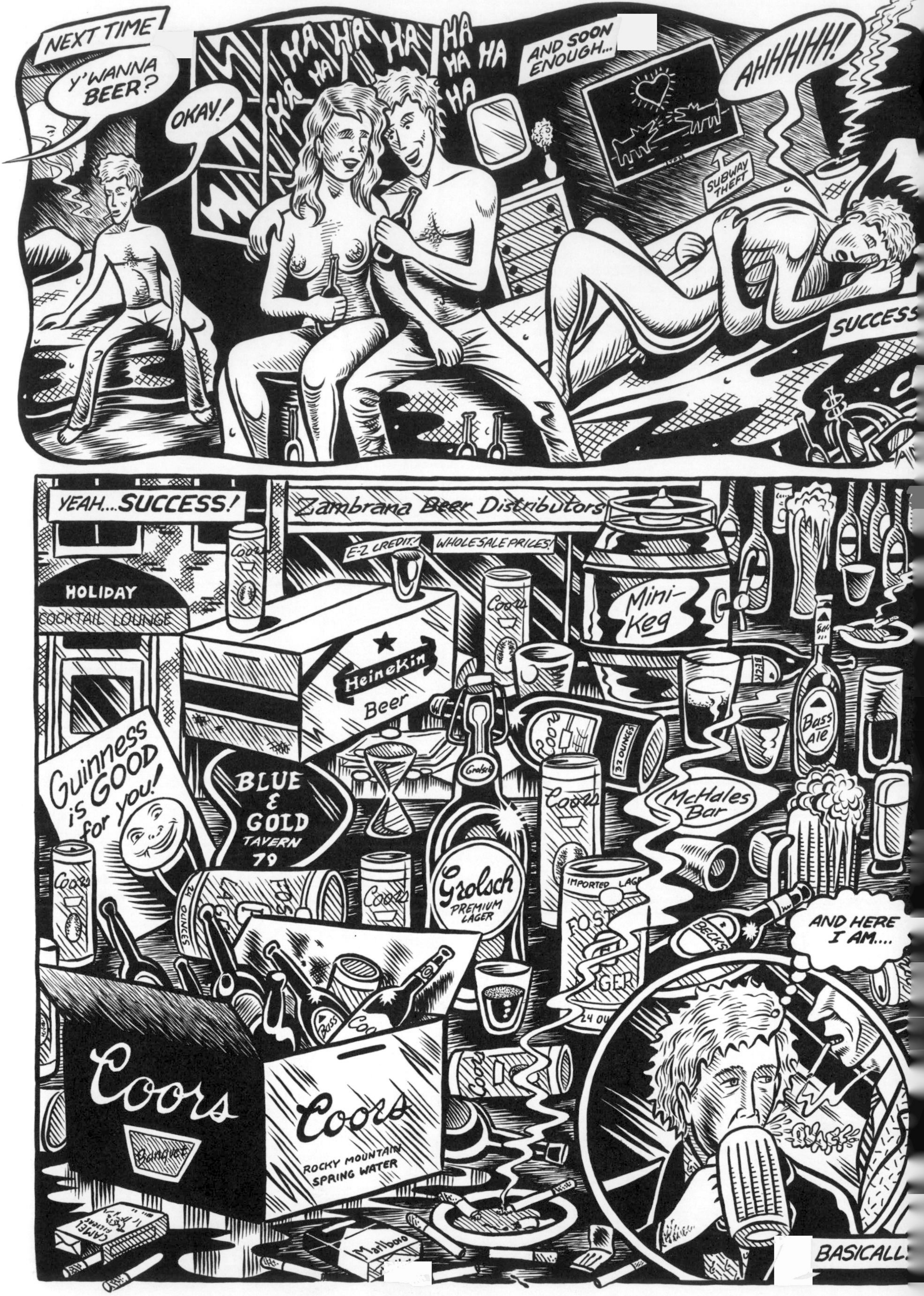
NEXT TIME
Y'WANNA BEER?
OKAY!
HA HA HA HA HA HA HA HA HA HA
AND SOON ENOUGH...
AHHHHH!
SUBWAY THEFT
SUCCESS
YEAH...SUCCESS!
Zambrana Beer Distributors
E-Z CREDIT!
WHOLESALE PRICES!
HOLIDAY
COCKTAIL LOUNGE
Mini-Keg
Heineken
Beer
Guinness is GOOD for you!
BLUE & GOLD TAVERN 79
McHales Bar
Grolsch
PREMIUM LAGER
IMPORTED LAGER
Bass Ale
Coors
Banquet
Coors
ROCKY MOUNTAIN SPRING WATER
AND HERE I AM....
BASICALL

DAILY GRIND

MESSENGER GIG...

GRUMBLE GRITCH GRIPE.....

Keep hands off the door

HUNGOVER

COFFEE.

FIFTY CENTS.....

I ♥ NY

BREAKFAST SPECIAL
SCRAMBLED EGGS
OMELET
PANCAKES
OATMEAL

RUNNING ERRANDS...

PICKING UP LUNCH.

JOB SUCKS....

I NEED THREE B.L.T.s NO MAYO ON ONE.

COLD DRINKS

PLEASE CLOSE DOOR

SANDWICH CHOPPED LIVER

BAGEL + A SHMEER 50¢

GETTING THE SHITS.. SQUIRT?

UNH...

HOPE THERE'S NO BLOOD.

Roll

SWEATING IT OUT....

FEEL LOUSY.....

ALCOHOL COMING THROUGH PORES

Design Studio

Reception

QUITTING TIME.

BUCK FIFTY!!

Ribbed Condoms

CIGARETTES

$1.50

32 OUNCES

HEADING HOME.....

FASCINATION

Eros Books

KING TIME

WE GOT IT! TRY US!

KIT KAT KLUB BURLESK

N.Y.P.D.

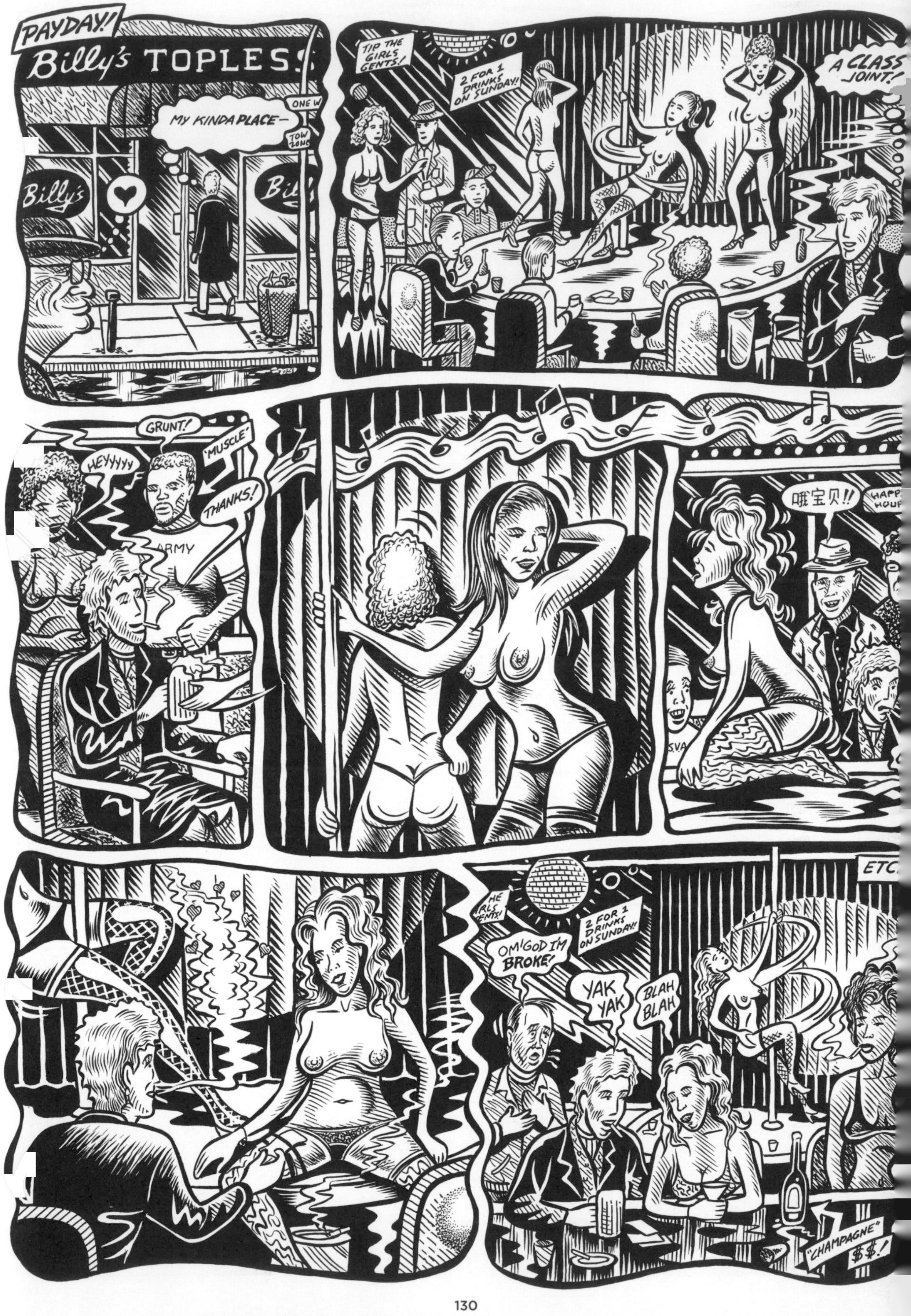
PAYDAY!
Billy's TOPLES
MY KINDA PLACE—
Billy's
TIP THE GIRLS GENTS!
2 FOR 1 DRINKS ON SUNDAY!
A CLASS JOINT!
GRUNT!
HEYYYYY
"MUSCLE"
THANKS!
ARMY
哦宝贝!!
OM'GOD I'M BROKE!
2 FOR 1 DRINKS ON SUNDAY!!
YAK YAK
BLAH BLAH
ETC
"CHAMPAGNE" $$!

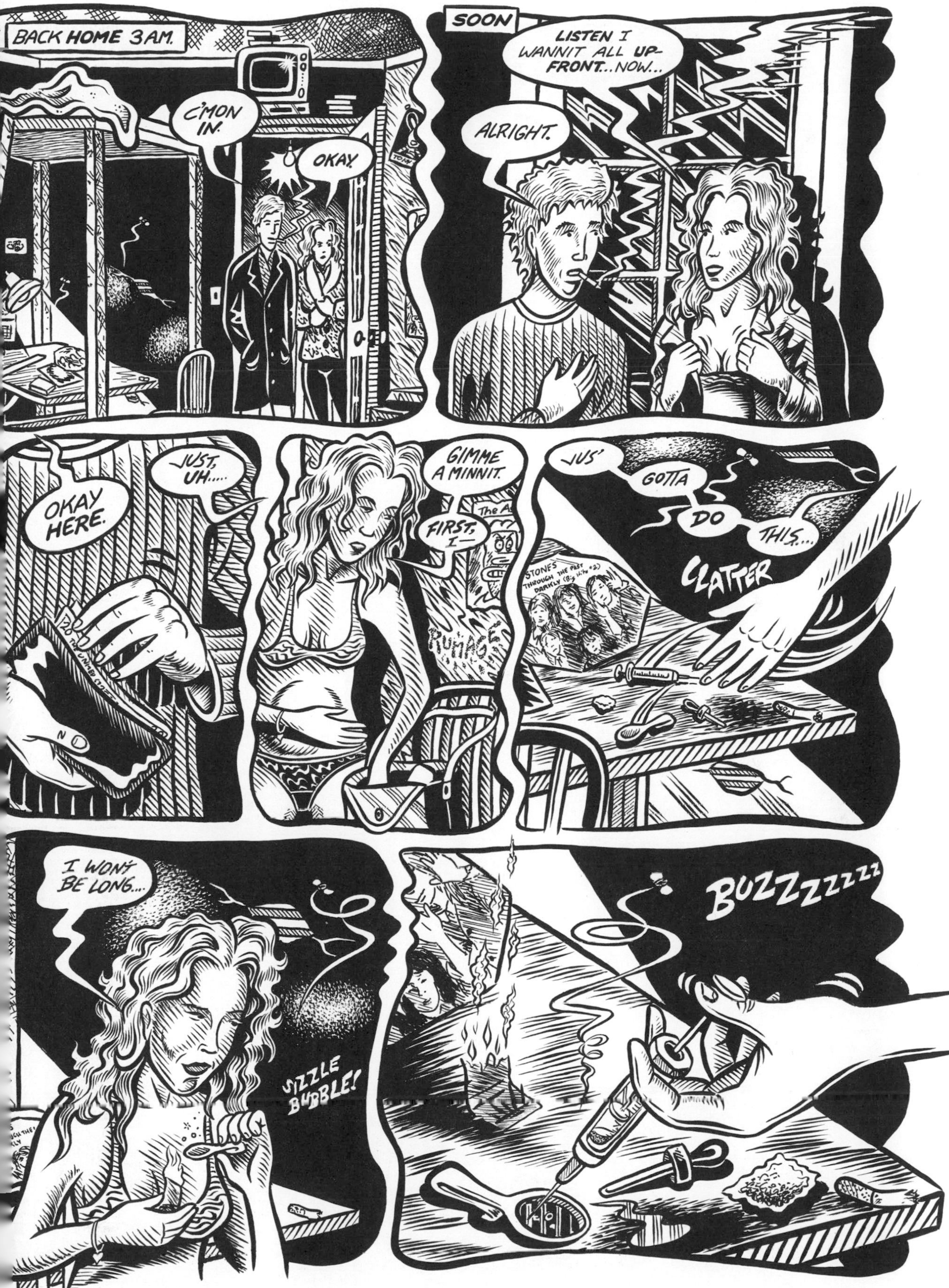
BACK HOME 3 AM.
C'MON IN.
OKAY.
SOON
LISTEN I WANNIT ALL UP FRONT... NOW...
ALRIGHT.
OKAY HERE.
JUST, UH.....
GIMME A MINNIT.
FIRST, I—
JUS'
GOTTA
DO
THIS...
CLATTER
I WON'T BE LONG...
SIZZLE BUBBLE!
BUZZzzzzz

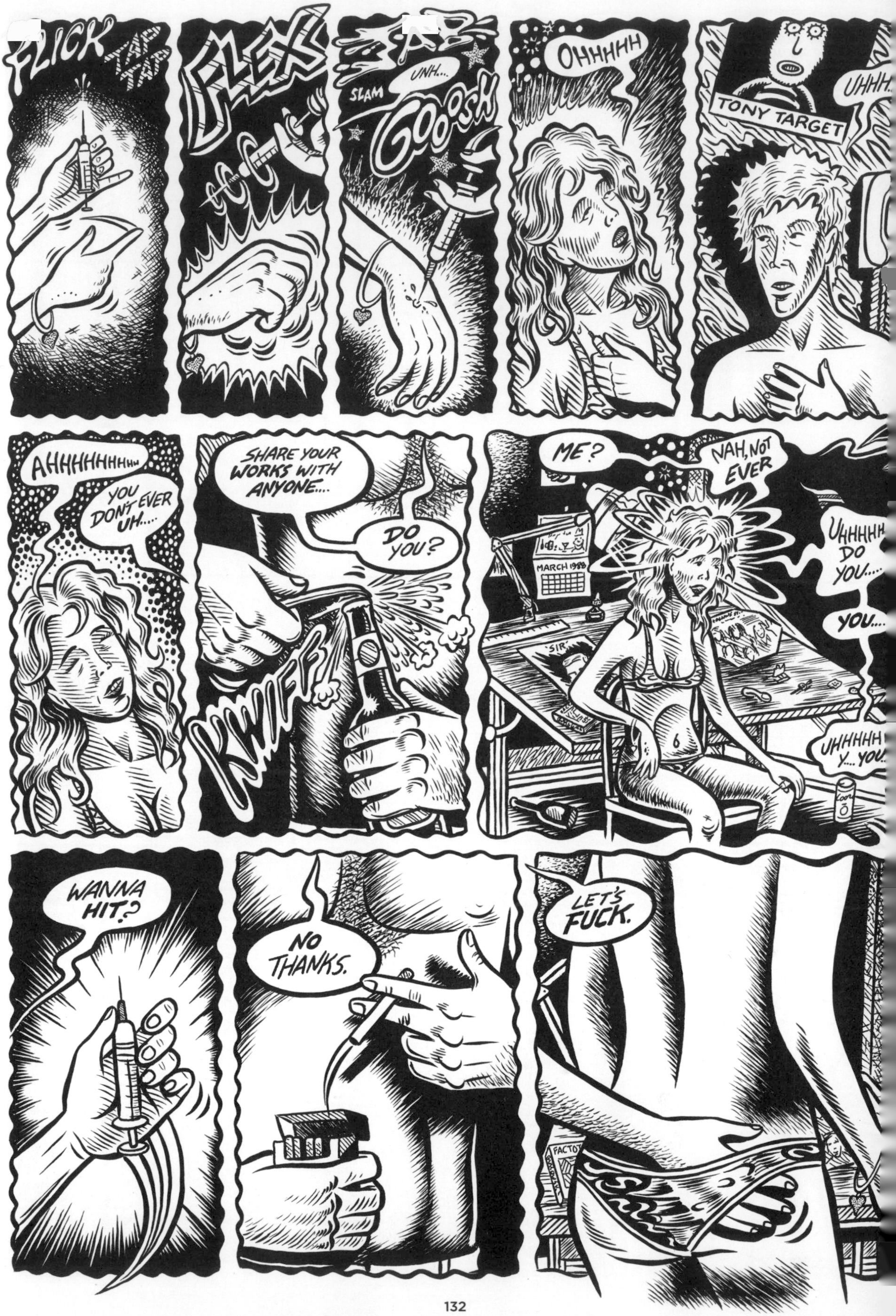
FLICK
TAP TAP
FLEX
SLAM
UNH...
GOOOSH
OHHHHH
TONY TARGET
UHHH...
AHHHHHHhhhh
YOU DON'T EVER UH.....
SHARE YOUR WORKS WITH ANYONE...
DO YOU?
KWIFF
ME?
NAH, NOT EVER
MARCH 1988
UHHHHH DO YOU.....
YOU....
UHHHHH Y... YOU
WANNA HIT?
NO THANKS.
LET'S FUCK.

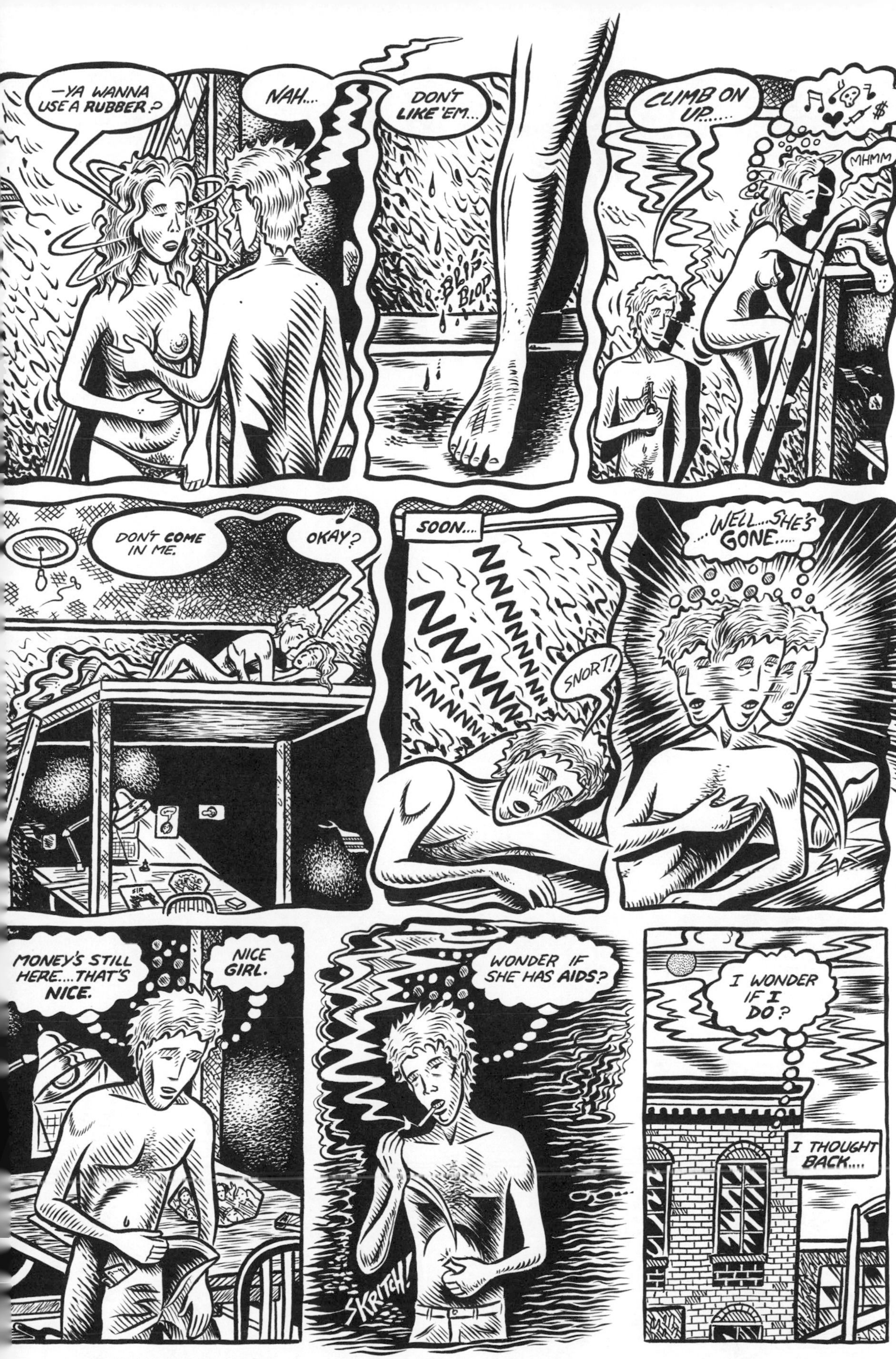
—YA WANNA USE A RUBBER?
NAH...
DON'T LIKE 'EM...
BLIP BLOP
CLIMB ON UP......
MHMM
DON'T COME IN ME.
OKAY?
SOON....
NNNNNNNNN
NNNNN
NNNNNNNN
SNORT!
...WELL...SHE'S GONE.....
MONEY'S STILL HERE....THAT'S NICE.
NICE GIRL.
WONDER IF SHE HAS AIDS?
SKRITCH!
I WONDER IF I DO?
I THOUGHT BACK....

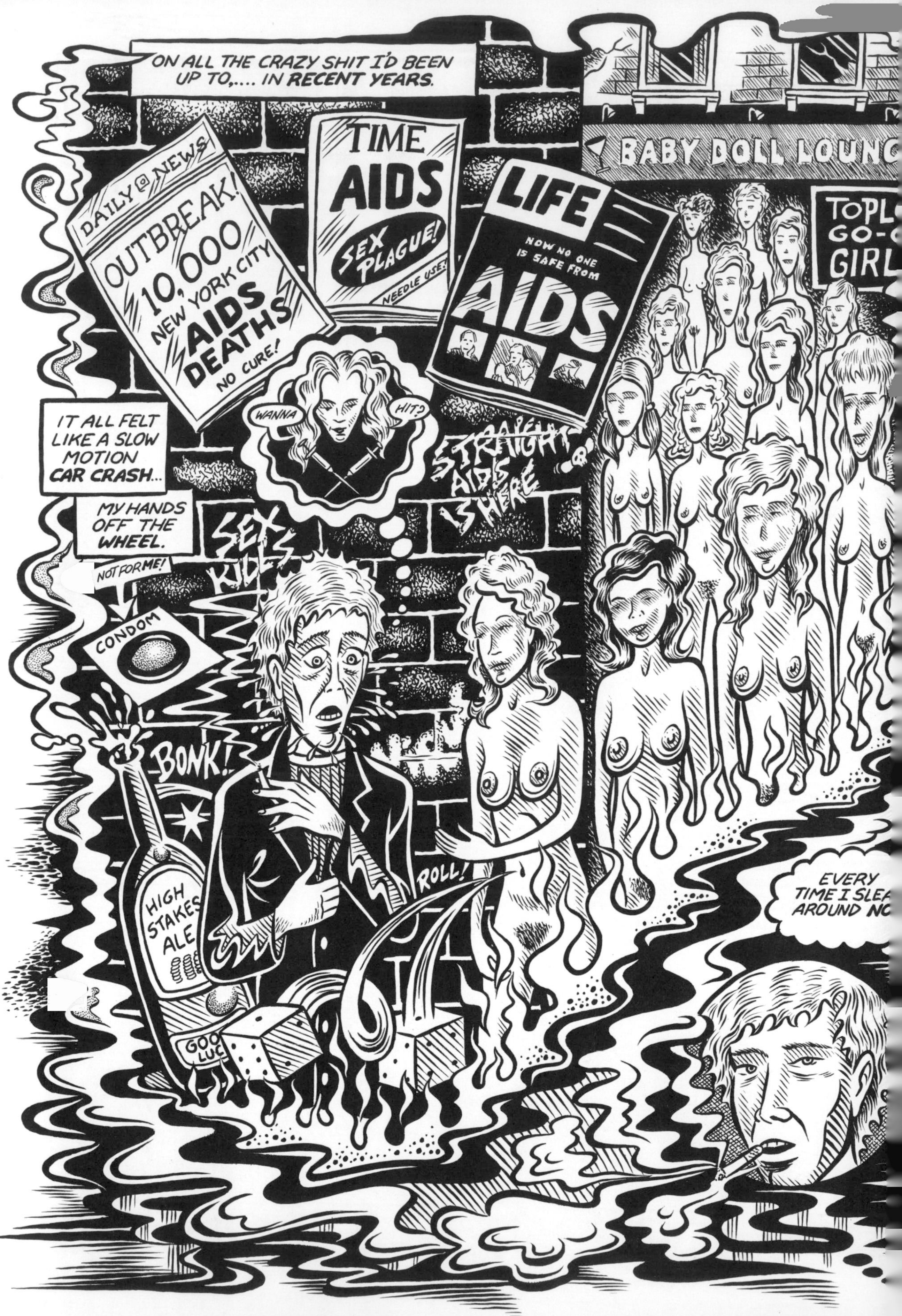
ON ALL THE CRAZY SHIT I'D BEEN UP TO,.... IN RECENT YEARS.
DAILY NEWS
OUTBREAK! 10,000 NEW YORK CITY AIDS DEATHS
NO CURE!
TIME
AIDS
SEX PLAGUE!
NEEDLE USE!
LIFE
NOW NO ONE IS SAFE FROM
AIDS
BABY DOLL LOUNG
TOPL GO-G GIRL
IT ALL FELT LIKE A SLOW MOTION CAR CRASH...
MY HANDS OFF THE WHEEL.
WANNA
HIT?
STRAIGHT AIDS IS HERE
SEX KILLS
NOT FOR ME!
CONDOM
BONK!
HIGH STAKES ALE
GOO LUC
ROLL!
EVERY TIME I SLEA AROUND NO

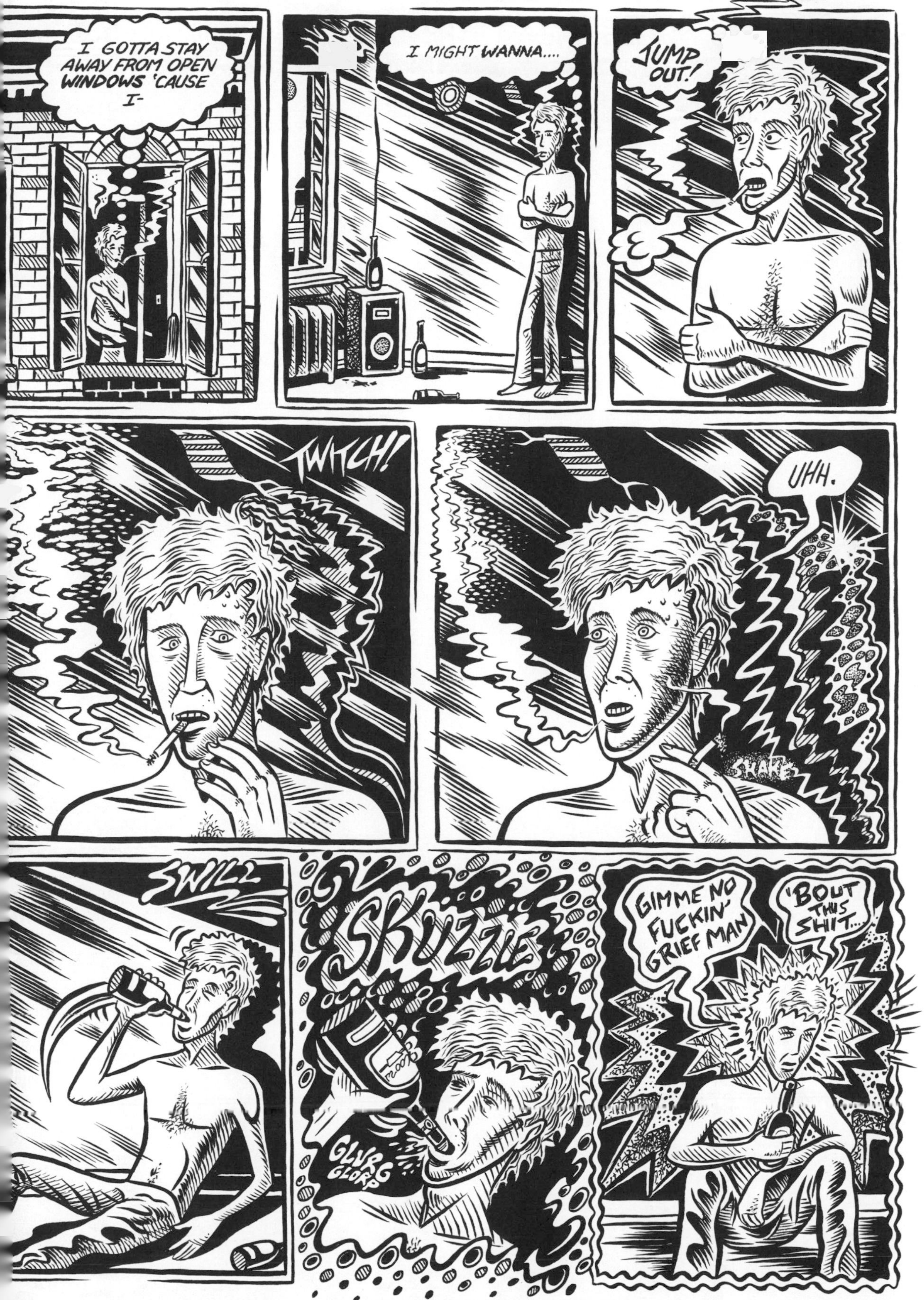
I GOTTA STAY AWAY FROM OPEN WINDOWS 'CAUSE I-
I MIGHT WANNA....
JUMP OUT!
TWITCH!
UHH.
SWILL
SKUZZLE
GLURG GLORP
GIMME NO FUCKIN' GRIEF MAN
'BOUT THIS SHIT...

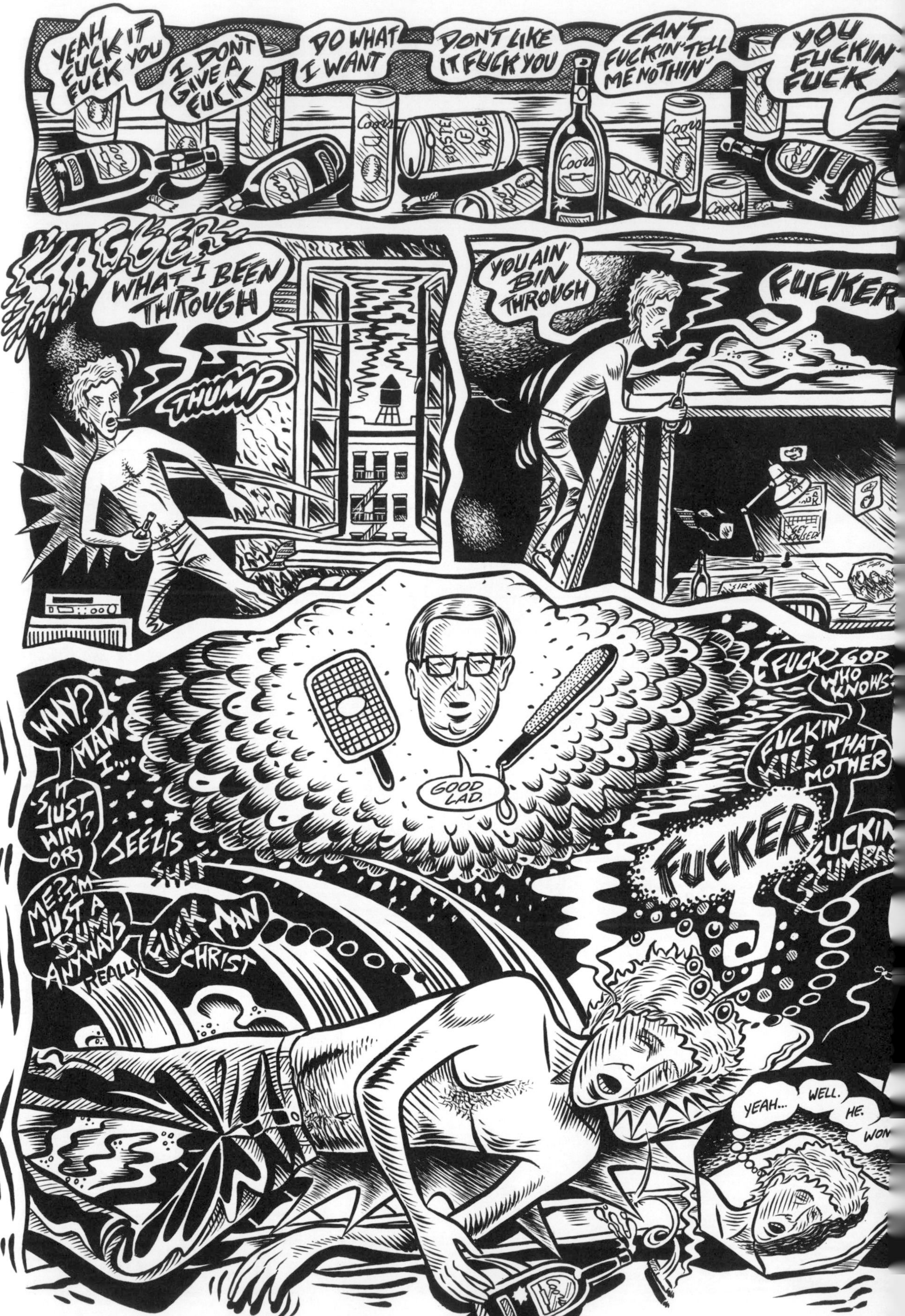
YEAH FUCK IT FUCK YOU
I DON'T GIVE A FUCK
DO WHAT I WANT
DON'T LIKE IT FUCK YOU
CAN'T FUCKIN' TELL ME NOTHIN'
YOU FUCKIN' FUCK
WHAT I BEEN THROUGH
THUMP
YOU AIN' BIN THROUGH
FUCKER
GOOD LAD.
WHY?
MAN I...
'S IT JUST HIM? OR
JEEZ IS SHIT
ME? I'M JUST A BUMS ANYWAYS REALLY
FUCK MAN CHRIST
FUCK GOD WHO KNOWS
FUCKIN' KILL THAT MOTHER
FUCKER
YEAH... WELL. HE.

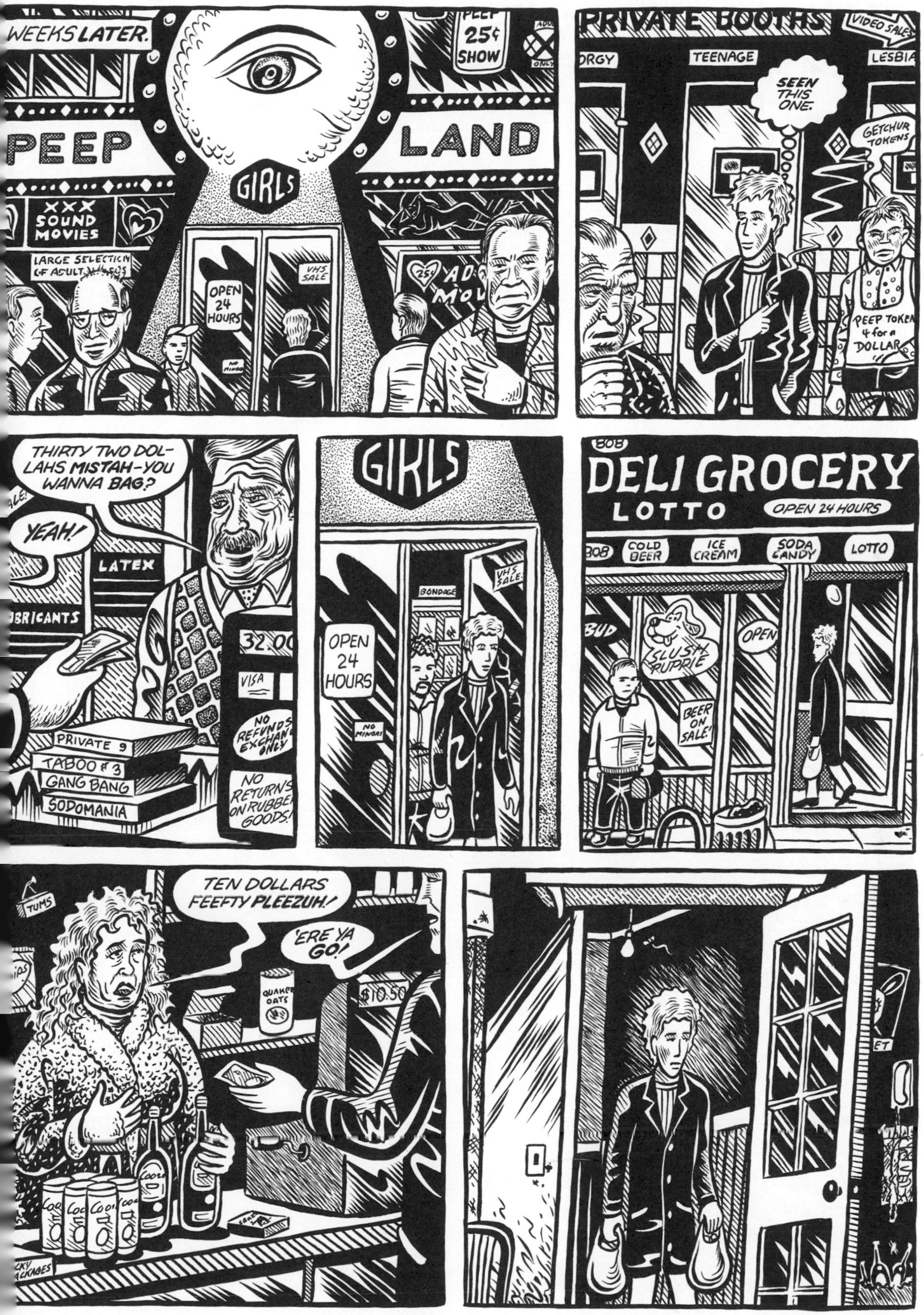
WEEKS LATER.
PEEP
LAND
GIRLS
PEEP 25¢ SHOW
XXX SOUND MOVIES
OPEN 24 HOURS
VHS SALE
PRIVATE BOOTHS
VIDEO SALES
ORGY
TEENAGE
SEEN THIS ONE.
GETCHUR TOKENS
PEEP TOKEN 4 for a DOLLAR
THIRTY TWO DOL-LAHS MISTAH–YOU WANNA BAG?
YEAH!
LATEX
32.00
VISA
NO REFUNDS EXCHANGE ONLY
NO RETURNS ON RUBBER GOODS!
PRIVATE 9
TABOO # 3
GANG BANG
SODOMANIA
GIRLS
BONDAGE
VHS SALE
OPEN 24 HOURS
808
DELI GROCERY
LOTTO
OPEN 24 HOURS
COLD BEER
ICE CREAM
SODA CANDY
LOTTO
BUD
OPEN
SLUSH PUPPIE
BEER ON SALE!
TUMS
TEN DOLLARS FEEFTY PLEEZUH!
'ERE YA GO!
QUAKER OATS
$10.50

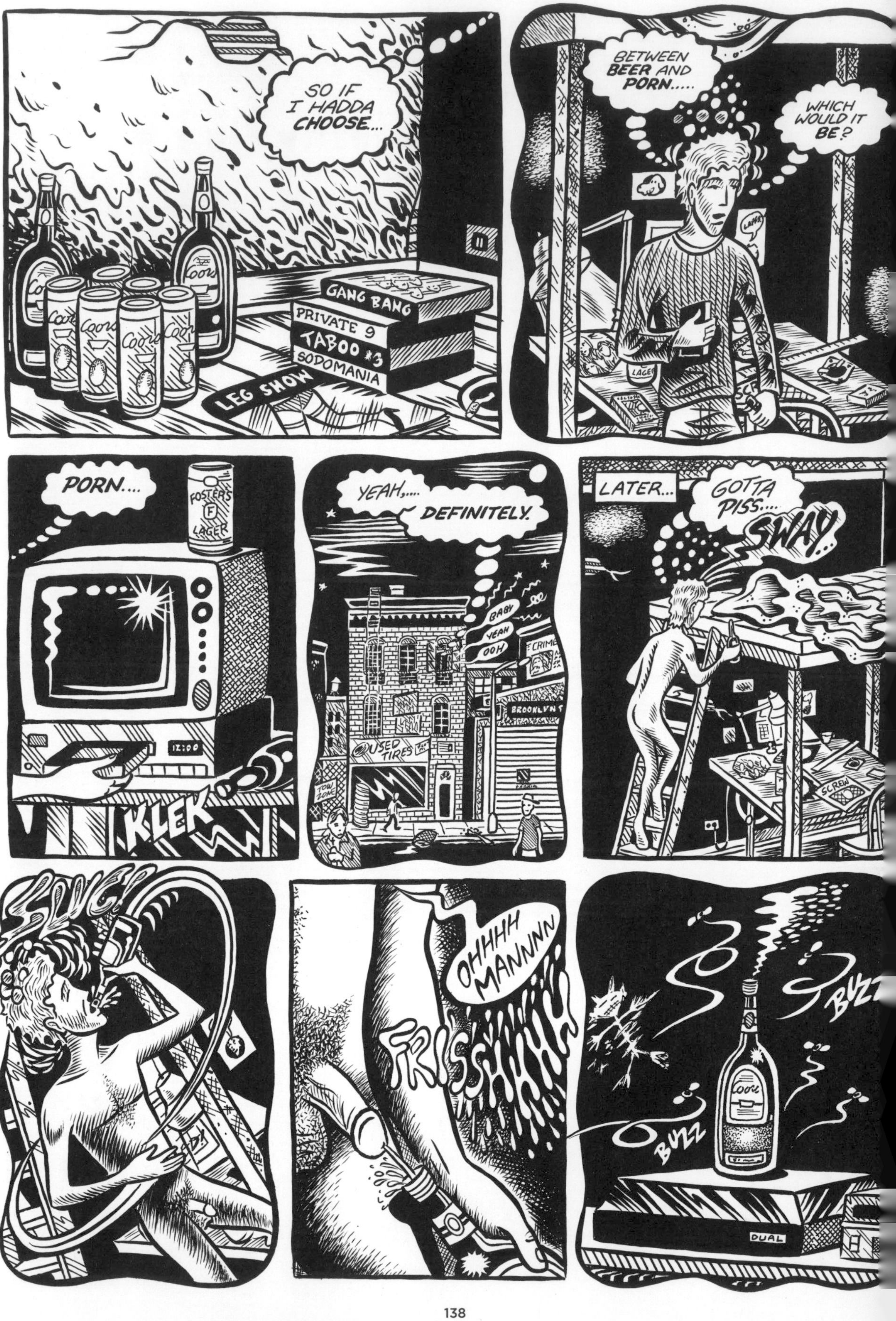
SO IF I HADDA CHOOSE...
GANG BANG
PRIVATE 9
TABOO #3
SODOMANIA
LEG SHOW
BETWEEN BEER AND PORN.....
WHICH WOULD IT BE?
LAGER
PORN....
FOSTER'S LAGER
12:00
KLEK
YEAH,.... DEFINITELY.
BABY
YEAH
OOH
CRIME
BROOKLYN
USED TIRES
TOW ZONE
LATER...
GOTTA PISS.....
SWAY
SCREW
OHHHH MANNNN
FRISSHHH
BUZZ
BUZZ
DUAL

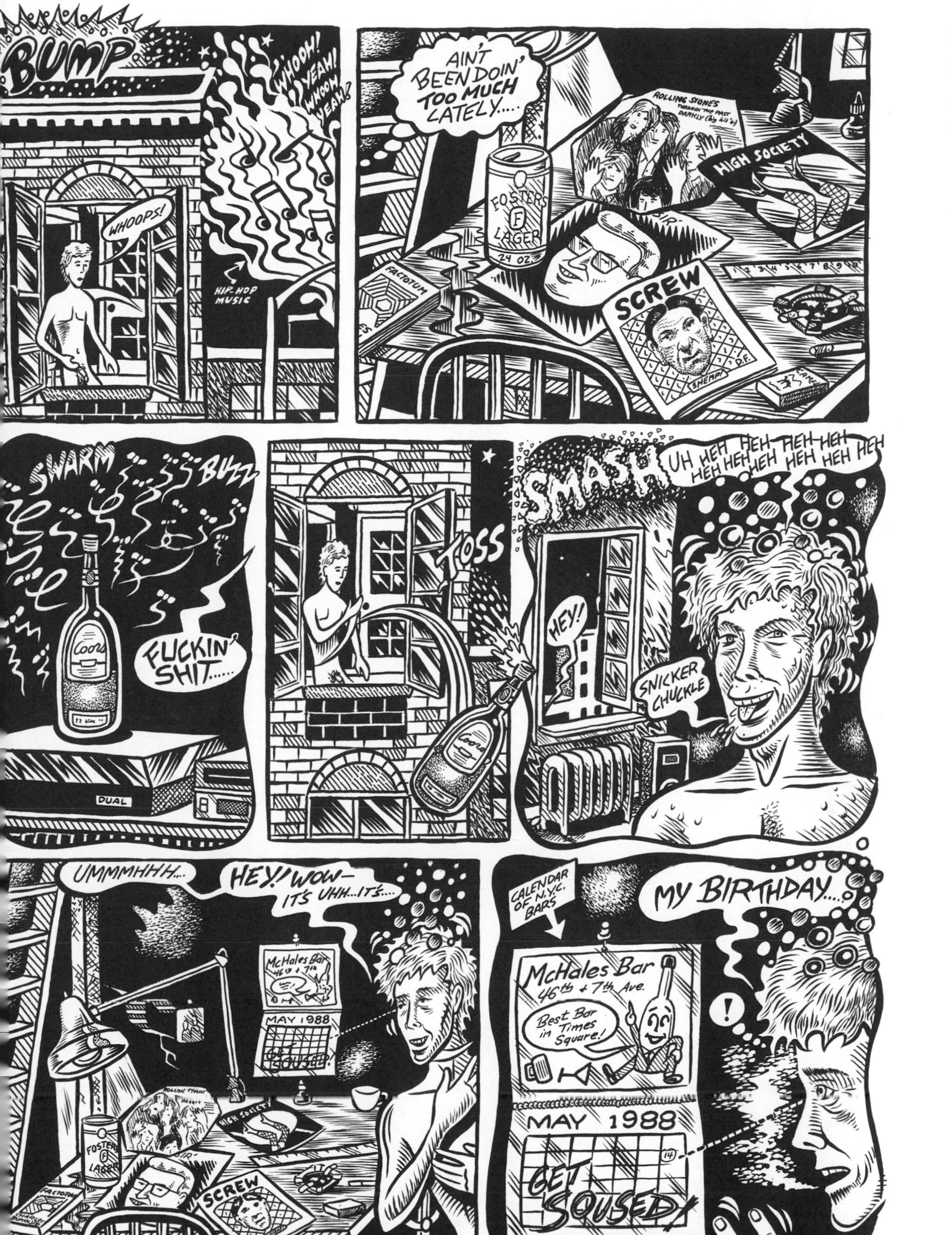
BUMP
WHOOH! YEAH! WHOOH YEAH!
WHOOPS!
HIP-HOP MUSIC
AIN'T BEEN DOIN' TOO MUCH LATELY.....
ROLLING STONES THROUGH THE PAST DARKLY (big hit's)
HIGH SOCIETY
FOSTERS LAGER 24 OZ.
FACTOTUM
SCREW
SHEMP!
SWARM BUZZ
Coors
FUCKIN' SHIT......
DUAL
TOSS
SMASH
UH HEH HEH HEH HEH HEH HEH HEH HEH HEH HEH HEH HEH
HEY!
SNICKER CHUCKLE
UMMMHHH...
HEY! WOW— IT'S UHH...IT'S...
CALENDAR OF N.Y.C. BARS
MY BIRTHDAY.....
McHales Bar 46th + 7th Ave.
Best Bar in Times Square!
MAY 1988
14
GET SOUSED!
!

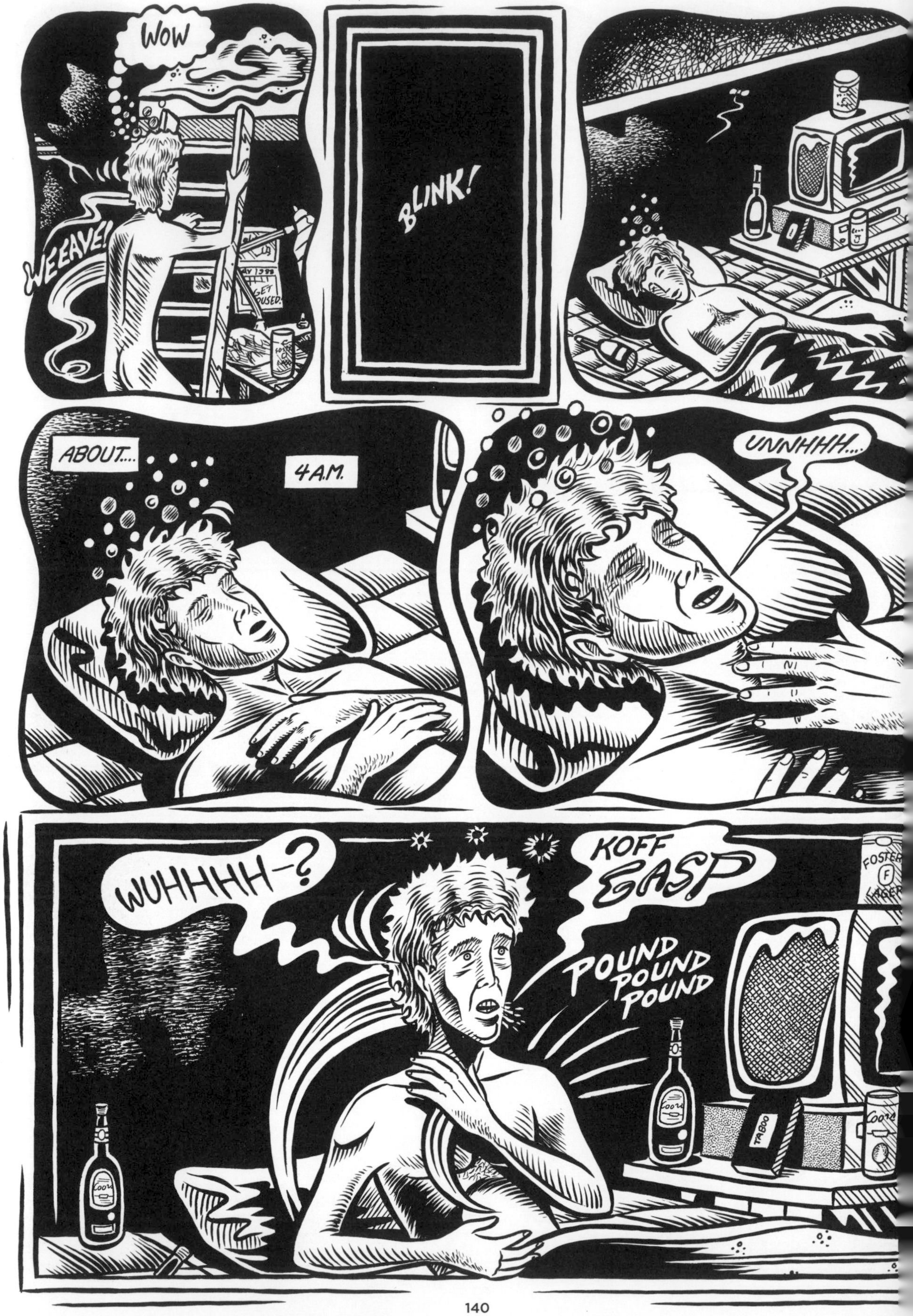
WOW
WEEAVE!
BLINK!
ABOUT....
4 A.M.
UNNHHH...
WUHHHH-?
KOFF
GASP
POUND
POUND
POUND
FOSTER'S
LAGER
TABOO

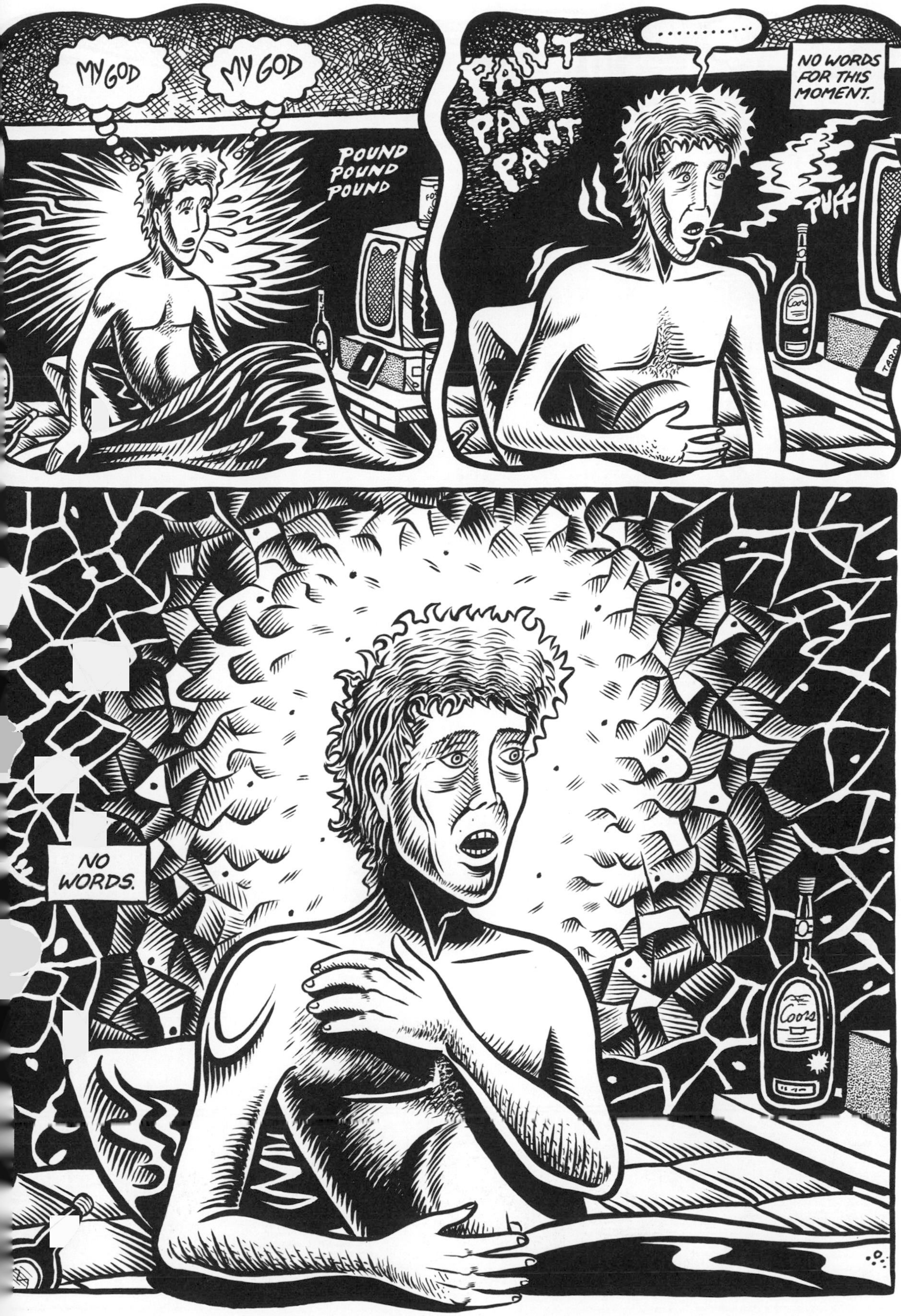
MY GOD
MY GOD
POUND POUND POUND
PANT PANT PANT
. . . .
NO WORDS FOR THIS MOMENT.
PUFF
NO WORDS.

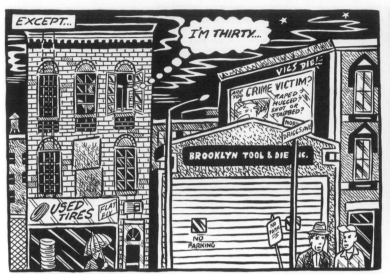

EXCEPT...

I'M THIRTY...

VICS DIE

ARE YOU A CRIME VICTIM?
RAPED? MUGGED? SHOT OR STABBED?
NO. DRIGGS AVE.

BROOKLYN TOOL & DIE INC.

NO PARKING

I GOT DRESSED.

AND WALKED...

NORTH NINTH

ONE WAY

NO PARKING

ALL OVER BROOKLYN...

LUNCHEONETTE FOUNTAIN

Coca Cola

Daily News on sale

NYNEX Phone

Ice Cream

OTB OFF TRACK B

WIN BIG!

HAD BREAKFAST...

WELL....

BACON & EGGS 99¢ SPECIAL

HERE IT IS....

AA

EVEN IF THEY'RE A BUNCH OF CRAZY PEOPLE—MOONIES, WHATEVER....IT REALLY DON'T MATTER...

I GOTTA GO IN!

AA

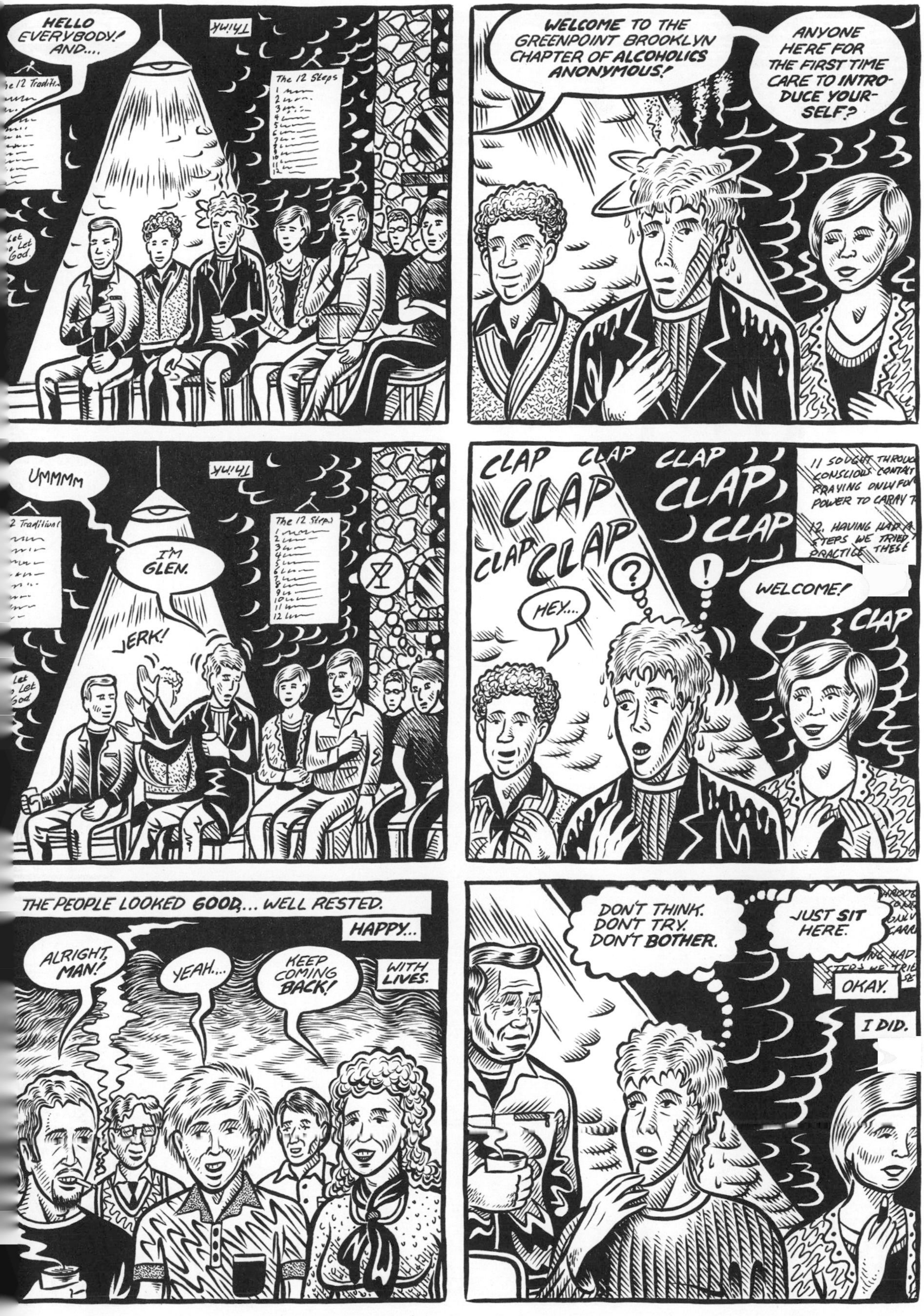
HELLO EVERYBODY! AND....
Think
The 12 Steps
WELCOME TO THE GREENPOINT BROOKLYN CHAPTER OF ALCOHOLICS ANONYMOUS!
ANYONE HERE FOR THE FIRST TIME CARE TO INTRODUCE YOURSELF?
UMMMM
Think
The 12 Steps
I'M GLEN.
JERK!
CLAP CLAP CLAP CLAP CLAP CLAP CLAP
?
!
HEY...
WELCOME!
CLAP
THE PEOPLE LOOKED GOOD... WELL RESTED.
HAPPY...
ALRIGHT, MAN!
YEAH...
KEEP COMING BACK!
WITH LIVES.
DON'T THINK. DON'T TRY. DON'T BOTHER.
JUST SIT HERE.
OKAY.
I DID.

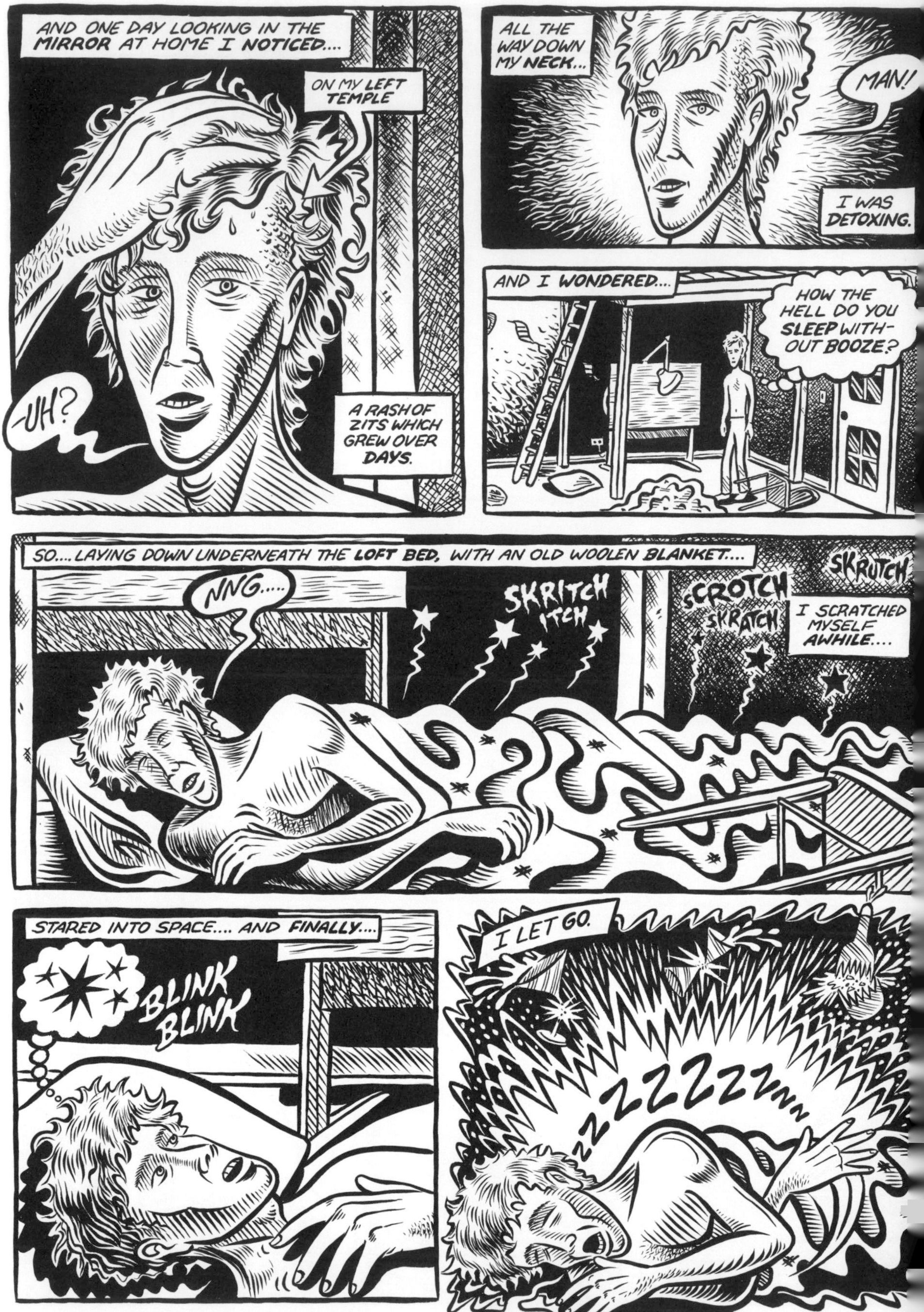
AND ONE DAY LOOKING IN THE MIRROR AT HOME I NOTICED....
ON MY LEFT TEMPLE
-UH?
A RASH OF ZITS WHICH GREW OVER DAYS.
ALL THE WAY DOWN MY NECK...
MAN!
I WAS DETOXING.
AND I WONDERED....
HOW THE HELL DO YOU SLEEP WITH-OUT BOOZE?
SO.... LAYING DOWN UNDERNEATH THE LOFT BED, WITH AN OLD WOOLEN BLANKET....
NNG.....
SKRITCH ITCH
SCROTCH
SKRATCH
SKRUTCH
I SCRATCHED MYSELF AWHILE....
STARED INTO SPACE.... AND FINALLY....
BLINK BLINK
I LET GO.
ZZZZZZZZZzzzz
AGHHH.

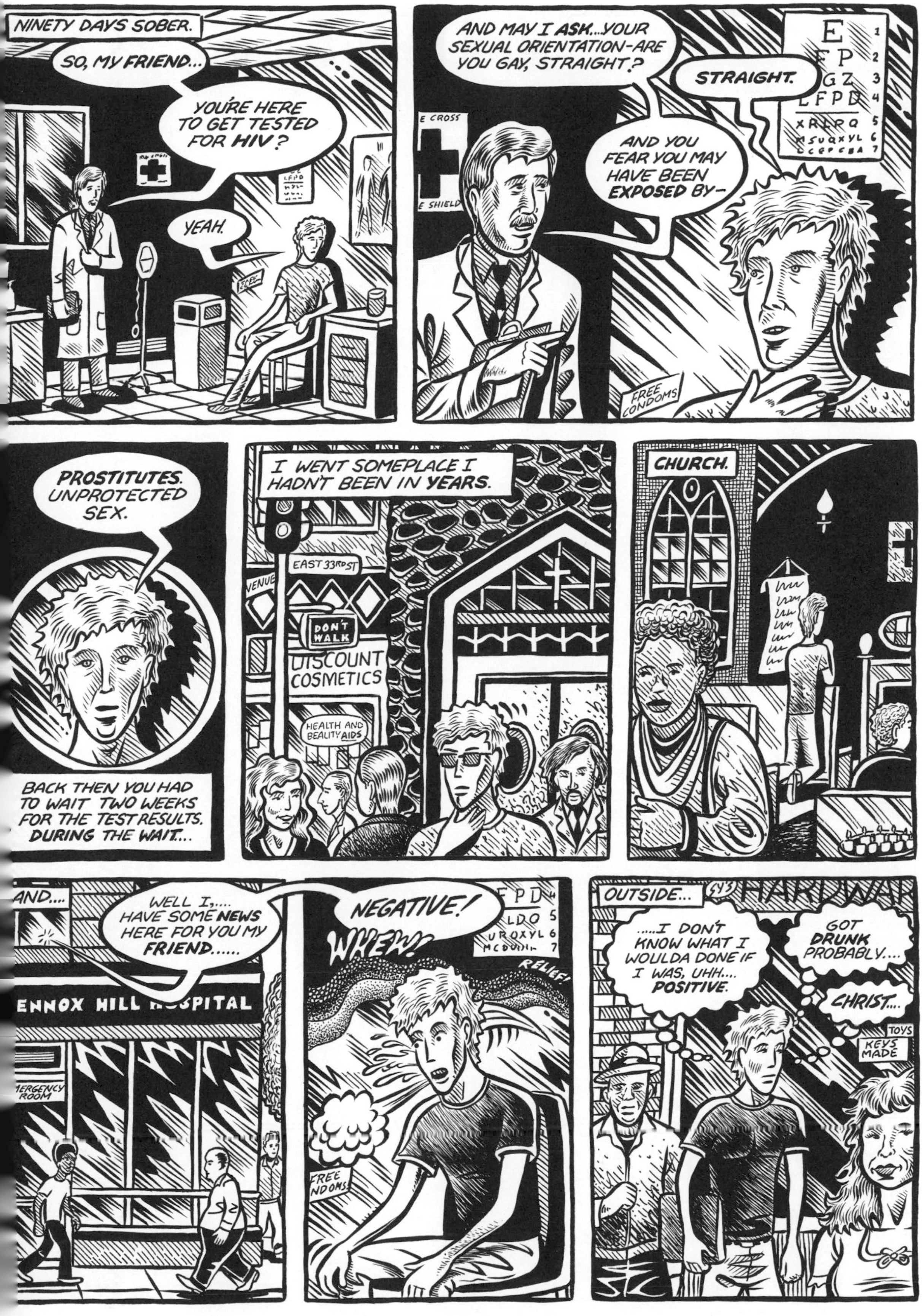

NINETY DAYS SOBER.
SO, MY FRIEND...
YOU'RE HERE TO GET TESTED FOR HIV?
YEAH.
AND MAY I ASK...YOUR SEXUAL ORIENTATION-ARE YOU GAY, STRAIGHT?
STRAIGHT.
AND YOU FEAR YOU MAY HAVE BEEN EXPOSED BY-
FREE CONDOMS
PROSTITUTES. UNPROTECTED SEX.
BACK THEN YOU HAD TO WAIT TWO WEEKS FOR THE TEST RESULTS. DURING THE WAIT...
I WENT SOMEPLACE I HADN'T BEEN IN YEARS.
EAST 33RD ST
DON'T WALK
DISCOUNT COSMETICS
HEALTH AND BEAUTY AIDS
CHURCH.
AND....
WELL I.... HAVE SOME NEWS HERE FOR YOU MY FRIEND......
ENNOX HILL HOSPITAL
MERGENCY ROOM
NEGATIVE!
WHEW!
RELIEF!
OUTSIDE...
HARDWAR
.....I DON'T KNOW WHAT I WOULDA DONE IF I WAS, UHH.... POSITIVE.
GOT DRUNK PROBABLY....
CHRIST....
TOYS
KEYS MADE

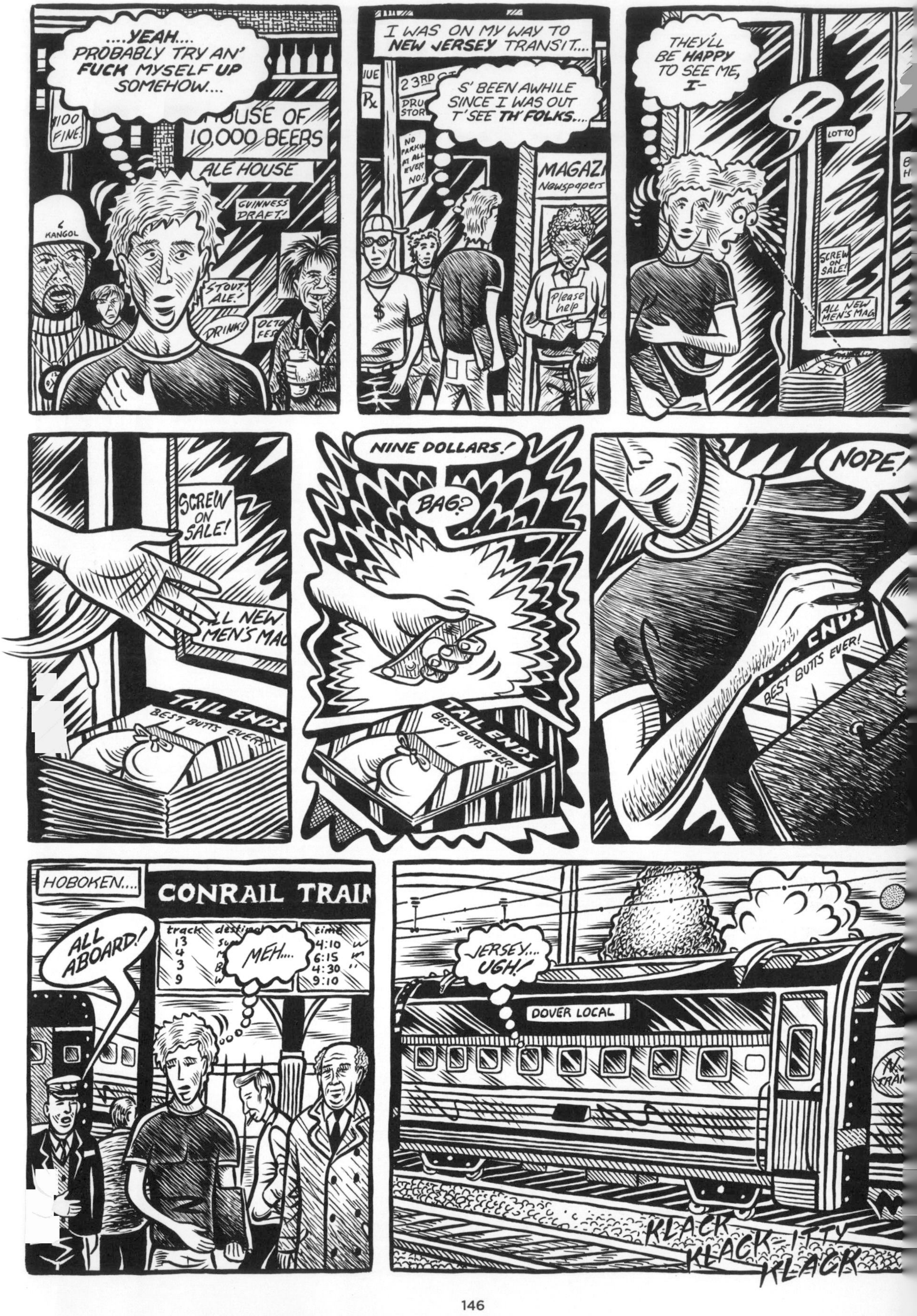
....YEAH.... PROBABLY TRY AN' FUCK MYSELF UP SOMEHOW....
HOUSE OF 10,000 BEERS
ALE HOUSE
GUINNESS DRAFT!
KANGOL
STOUT! ALE!
DRINK!
I WAS ON MY WAY TO NEW JERSEY TRANSIT....
S' BEEN AWHILE SINCE I WAS OUT T' SEE TH' FOLKS....
Newspapers
Please help
THEY'LL BE HAPPY TO SEE ME, I-
!!
LOTTO
SCREW ON SALE!
SCREW ON SALE!
TAIL ENDS
BEST BUTTS EVER!
NINE DOLLARS!
BAG?
NOPE!
BEST BUTTS EVER!
HOBOKEN....
ALL ABOARD!
MEH....
4:10
6:15
4:30
9:10
JERSEY.... UGH!
DOVER LOCAL
KLACK KLACK ITTY KLACK

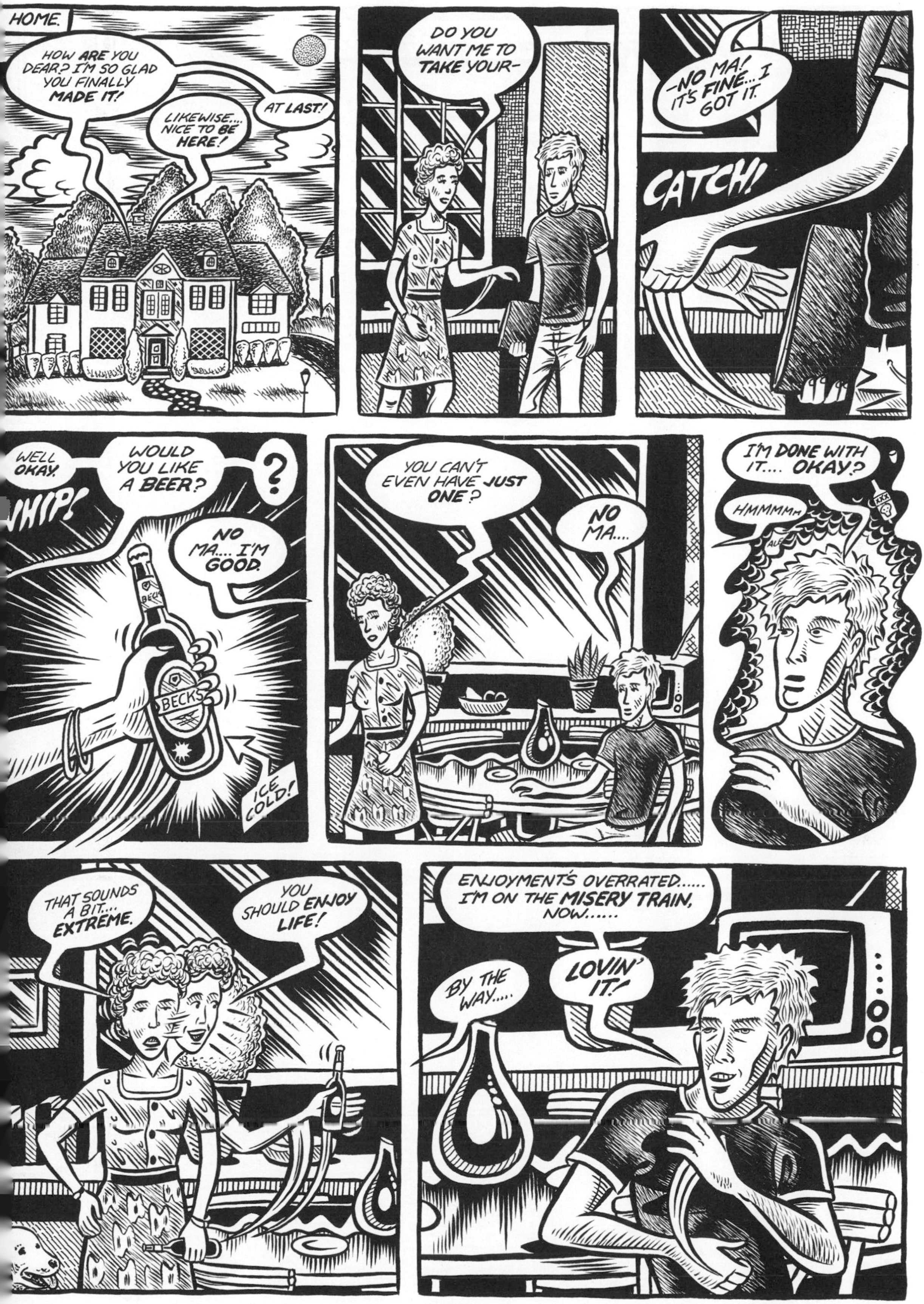
HOME.
HOW ARE YOU DEAR? I'M SO GLAD YOU FINALLY MADE IT!
AT LAST!
LIKEWISE.... NICE TO BE HERE!
DO YOU WANT ME TO TAKE YOUR-
-NO MA! IT'S FINE... I GOT IT.
CATCH!
WELL OKAY.
WOULD YOU LIKE A BEER?
?
WHIP!
NO MA.... I'M GOOD.
BECKS
ICE COLD!
YOU CAN'T EVEN HAVE JUST ONE?
NO MA....
I'M DONE WITH IT.... OKAY?
HMMMMm
THAT SOUNDS A BIT.... EXTREME.
YOU SHOULD ENJOY LIFE!
ENJOYMENT'S OVERRATED..... I'M ON THE MISERY TRAIN, NOW......
BY THE WAY.....
LOVIN' IT!

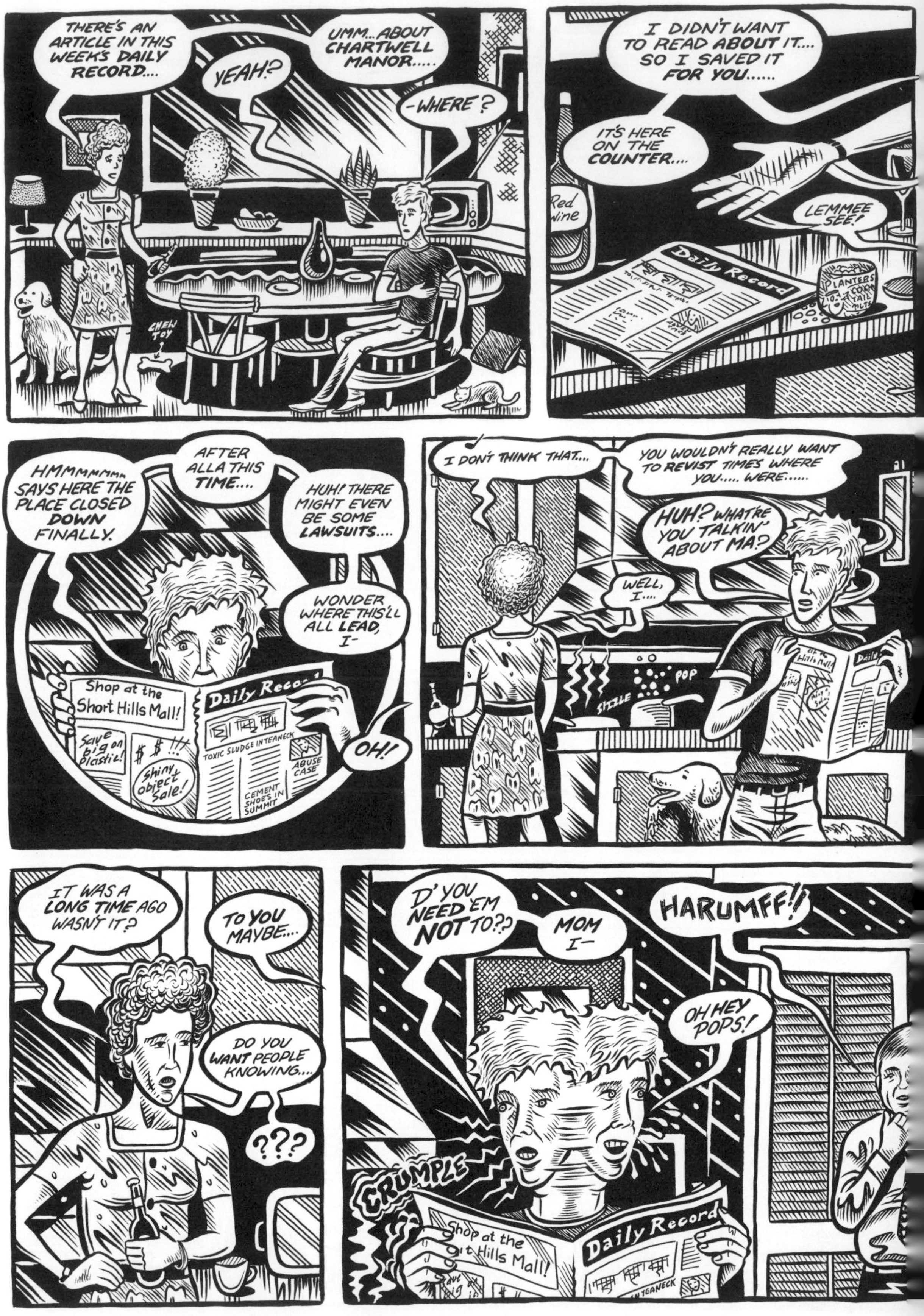
THERE'S AN ARTICLE IN THIS WEEK'S DAILY RECORD....
YEAH?
UMM...ABOUT CHARTWELL MANOR.....
-WHERE?
CHEW TOY
I DIDN'T WANT TO READ ABOUT IT.... SO I SAVED IT FOR YOU......
IT'S HERE ON THE COUNTER....
Red Wine
LEMMEE SEE!
Daily Record
PLANTERS COCKTAIL NUTS
HMMMMMM SAYS HERE THE PLACE CLOSED DOWN FINALLY.
AFTER ALLA THIS TIME....
HUH! THERE MIGHT EVEN BE SOME LAWSUITS....
WONDER WHERE THIS'LL ALL LEAD, I-
OH!
Shop at the Short Hills Mall!
Save big on plastic!
Shiny object Sale!
Daily Reco
TOXIC SLUDGE IN TEANECK
ABUSE CASE
CEMENT SHOES IN SUMMIT
I DON'T THINK THAT....
YOU WOULDN'T REALLY WANT TO REVIST TIMES WHERE YOU..... WERE......
HUH? WHAT'RE YOU TALKIN' ABOUT MA?
WELL, I....
POP
SIZZLE
IT WAS A LONG TIME AGO WASN'T IT?
TO YOU MAYBE....
DO YOU WANT PEOPLE KNOWING....
???
D' YOU NEED 'EM NOT TO??
MOM I-
HARUMFF!!
OH HEY POPS!
CRUMPLE
Daily Record
Shop at the ...t Hills Mall!

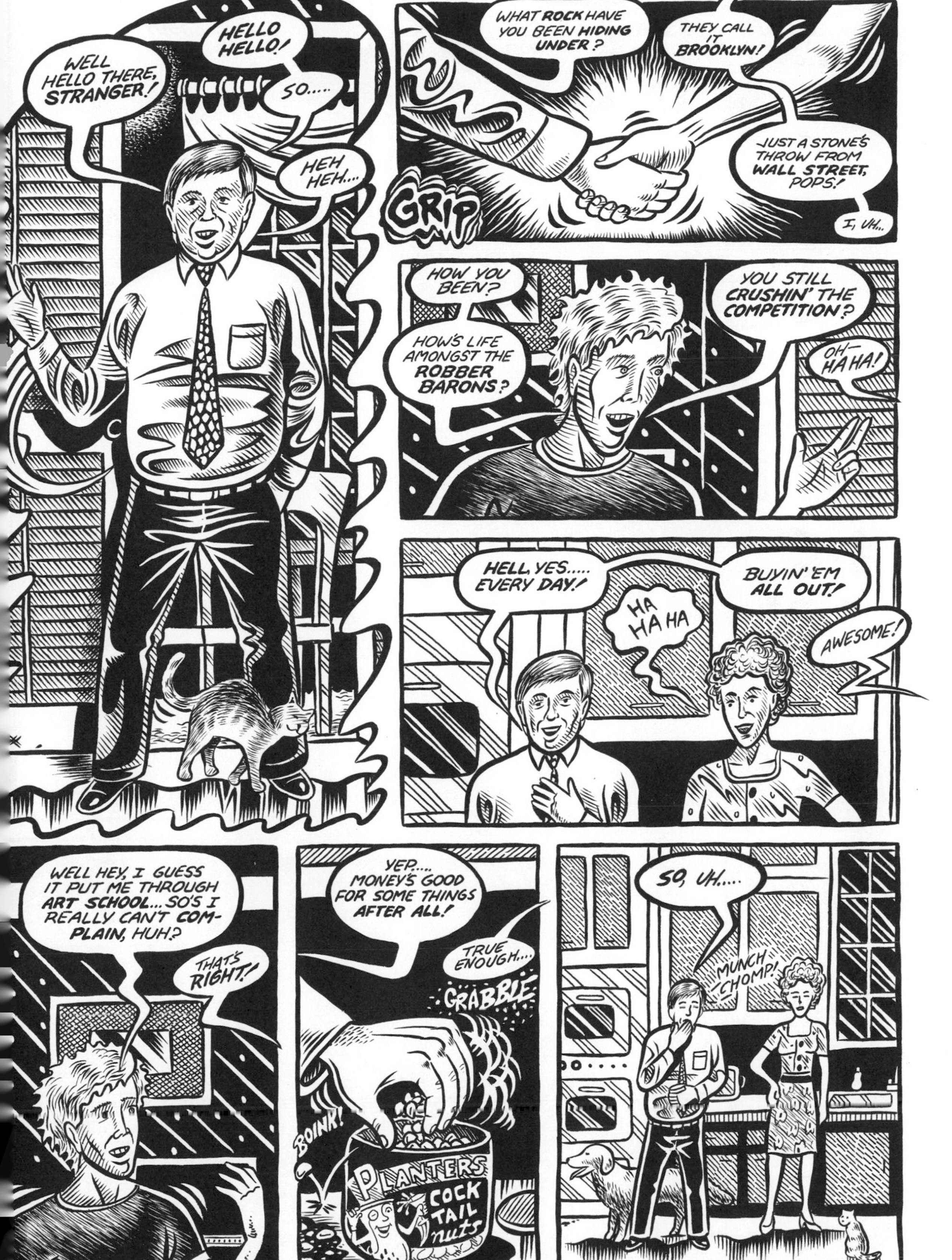
WELL HELLO THERE, STRANGER!
HELLO HELLO!
SO.....
HEH HEH...
GRIP
WHAT ROCK HAVE YOU BEEN HIDING UNDER?
THEY CALL IT BROOKLYN!
JUST A STONE'S THROW FROM WALL STREET, POPS!
I, UH...
HOW YOU BEEN?
HOW'S LIFE AMONGST THE ROBBER BARONS?
YOU STILL CRUSHIN' THE COMPETITION?
OH-HA HA!
HELL, YES..... EVERY DAY!
BUYIN' 'EM ALL OUT!
HA HA HA
AWESOME!
WELL HEY, I GUESS IT PUT ME THROUGH ART SCHOOL... SO'S I REALLY CAN'T COMPLAIN, HUH?
THAT'S RIGHT!
YEP.... MONEY'S GOOD FOR SOME THINGS AFTER ALL!
TRUE ENOUGH....
GRABBLE
BOINK!
PLANTERS COCKTAIL nuts
SO, UH.....
MUNCH CHOMP!

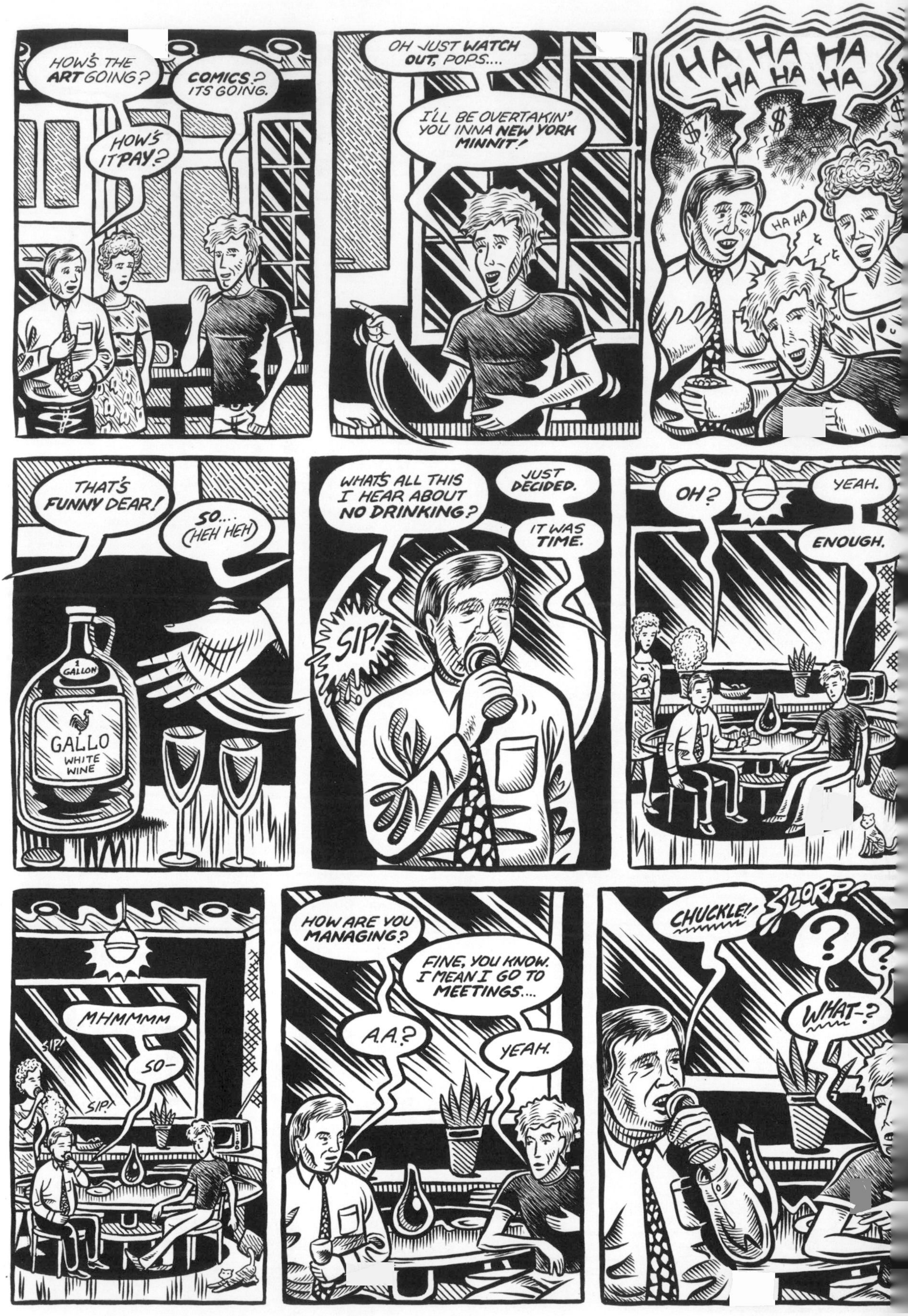
HOW'S THE ART GOING?
COMICS? ITS GOING.
HOW'S IT PAY?
OH JUST WATCH OUT, POPS....
I'LL BE OVERTAKIN' YOU INNA NEW YORK MINNIT!
HA HA HA HA HA HA
HA HA
THAT'S FUNNY DEAR!
SO.... (HEH HEH)
1 GALLON
GALLO WHITE WINE
WHAT'S ALL THIS I HEAR ABOUT NO DRINKING?
JUST DECIDED.
IT WAS TIME.
SIP!
OH?
YEAH.
ENOUGH.
MHMMMM
SO-
SIP!
SIP!
HOW ARE YOU MANAGING?
FINE, YOU KNOW. I MEAN I GO TO MEETINGS....
A.A.?
YEAH.
CHUCKLE!!
SLORP!
?
?
WHAT-?

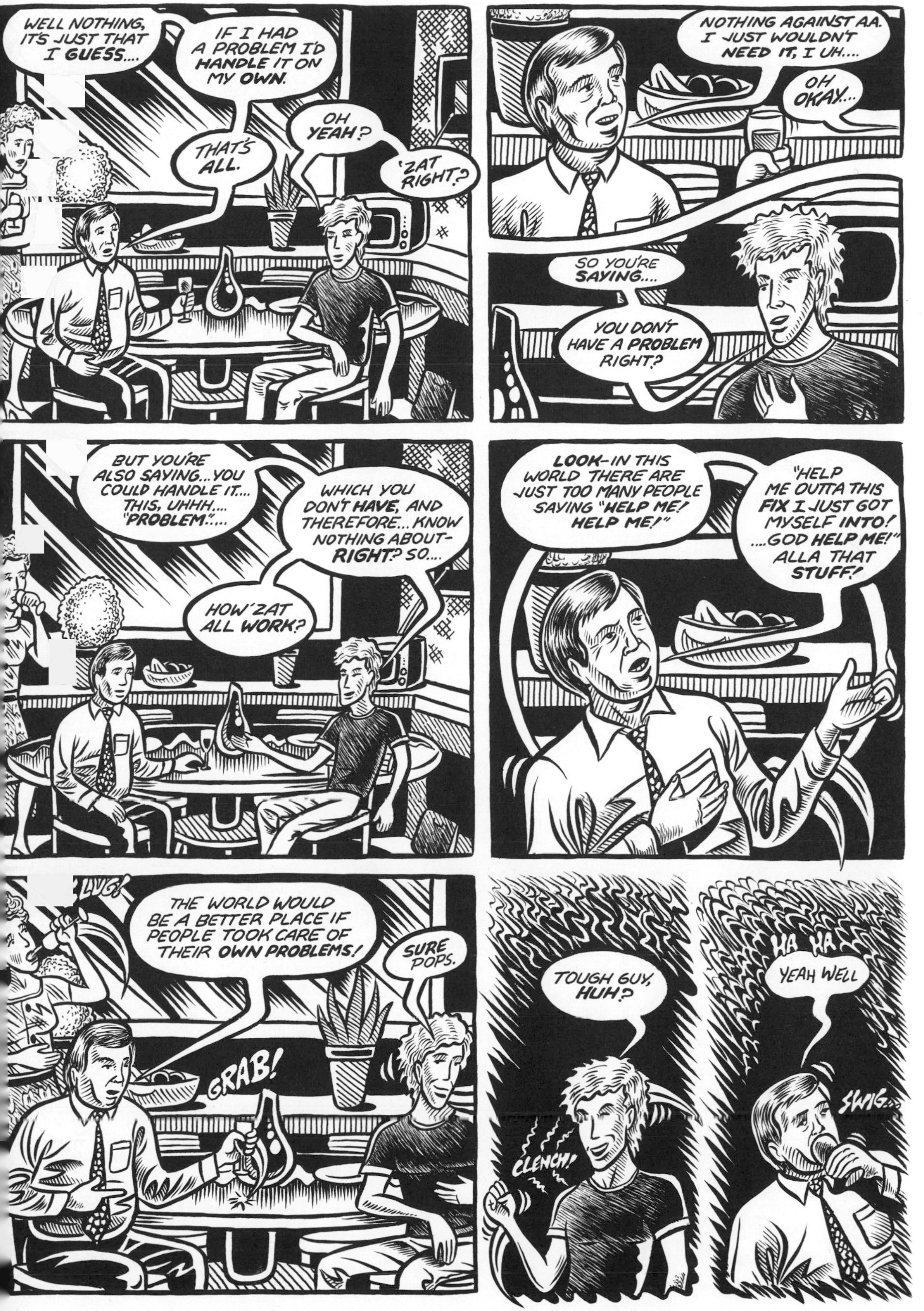
WELL NOTHING, IT'S JUST THAT I GUESS....
IF I HAD A PROBLEM I'D HANDLE IT ON MY OWN.
THAT'S ALL.
OH YEAH?
'ZAT RIGHT?
NOTHING AGAINST AA. I JUST WOULDN'T NEED IT, I UH....
OH OKAY...
SO YOU'RE SAYING....
YOU DON'T HAVE A PROBLEM RIGHT?
BUT YOU'RE ALSO SAYING...YOU COULD HANDLE IT.... THIS, UHHH.... "PROBLEM."....
WHICH YOU DON'T HAVE, AND THEREFORE... KNOW NOTHING ABOUT- RIGHT? SO....
HOW'ZAT ALL WORK?
LOOK- IN THIS WORLD THERE ARE JUST TOO MANY PEOPLE SAYING "HELP ME! HELP ME!"
"HELP ME OUTTA THIS FIX I JUST GOT MYSELF INTO! ...GOD HELP ME!" ALLA THAT STUFF!
LUG!
THE WORLD WOULD BE A BETTER PLACE IF PEOPLE TOOK CARE OF THEIR OWN PROBLEMS!
SURE POPS.
GRAB!
TOUGH GUY, HUH?
CLENCH!
HA HA
YEAH WELL
SWIG...

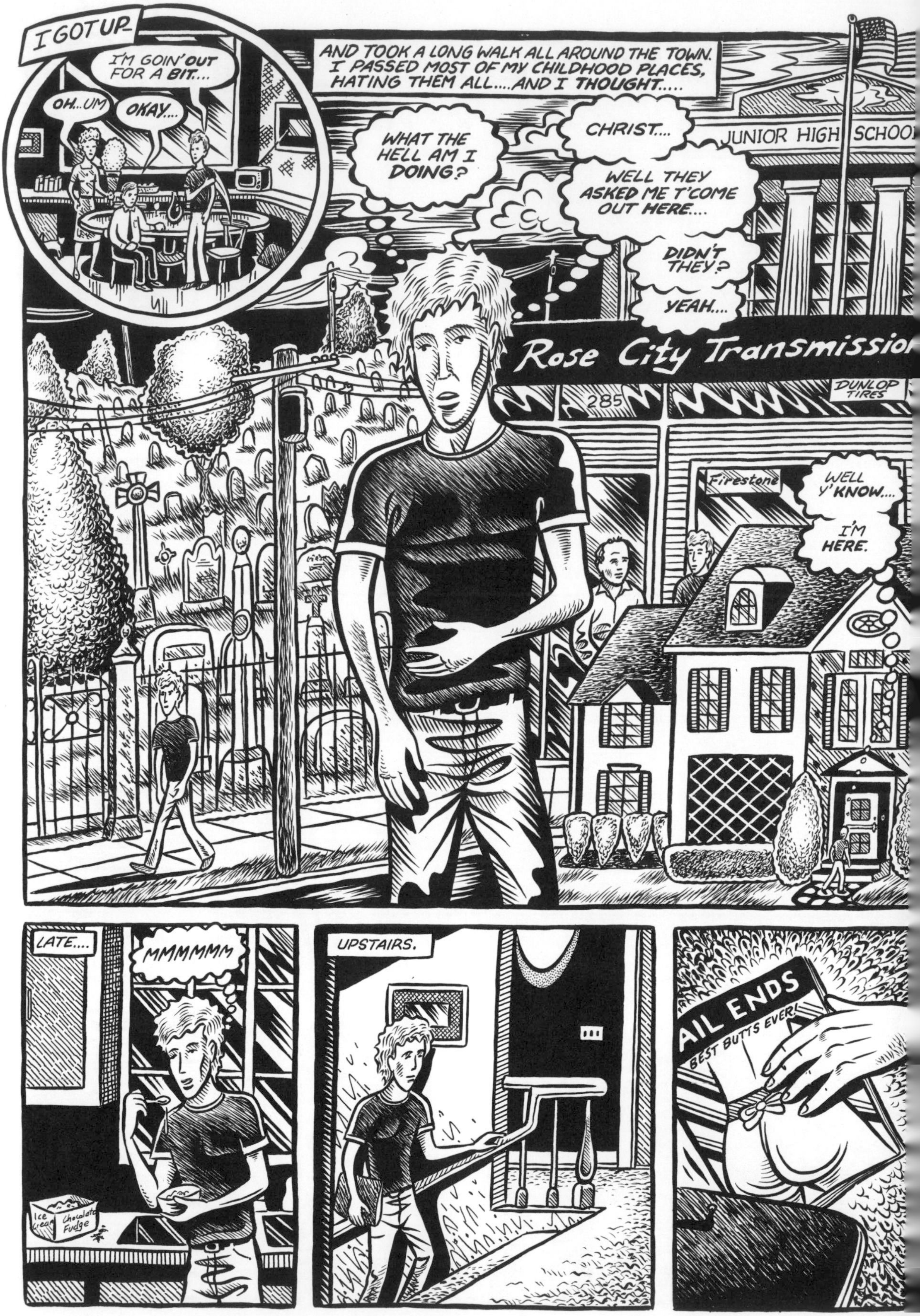
I GOT UP.
I'M GOIN' OUT FOR A BIT....
OH...UM
OKAY....
AND TOOK A LONG WALK ALL AROUND THE TOWN. I PASSED MOST OF MY CHILDHOOD PLACES, HATING THEM ALL....AND I THOUGHT.....
WHAT THE HELL AM I DOING?
CHRIST....
WELL THEY ASKED ME T'COME OUT HERE....
DIDN'T THEY?
YEAH....
JUNIOR HIGH SCHOOL
Rose City Transmission
285
DUNLOP TIRES
Firestone
WELL Y'KNOW....
I'M HERE.
LATE....
MMMMMM
Ice Cream
Chocolate Fudge
UPSTAIRS.
AIL ENDS
BEST BUTTS EVER!

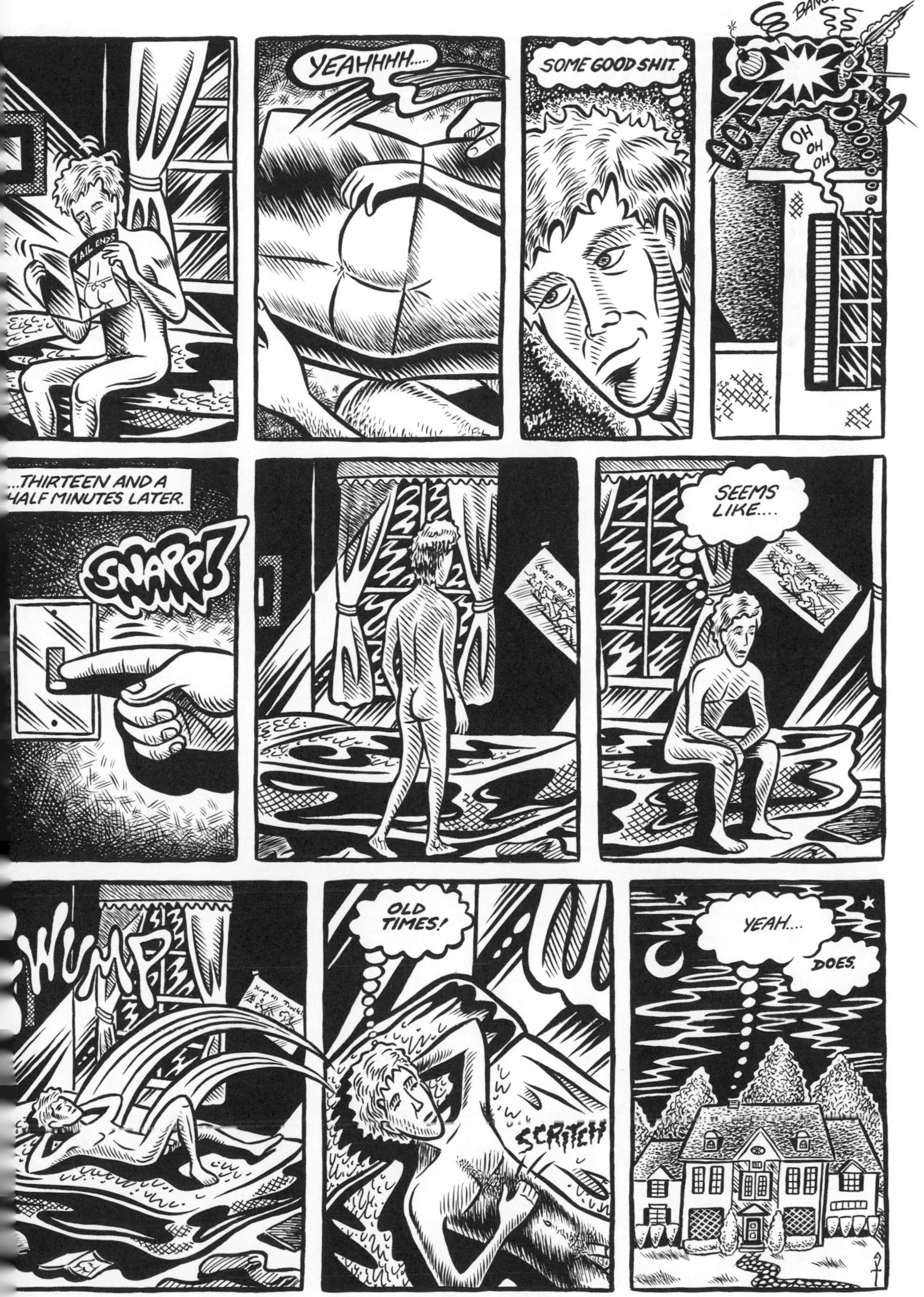
TAIL ENDS
YEAHHHH.....
SOME GOOD SHIT.
BUZZ
BANG!
OH OH OH!
...THIRTEEN AND A HALF MINUTES LATER.
SNAPP!
SEEMS LIKE....
WUMP
OLD TIMES!
SCRITCH
YEAH....
DOES.

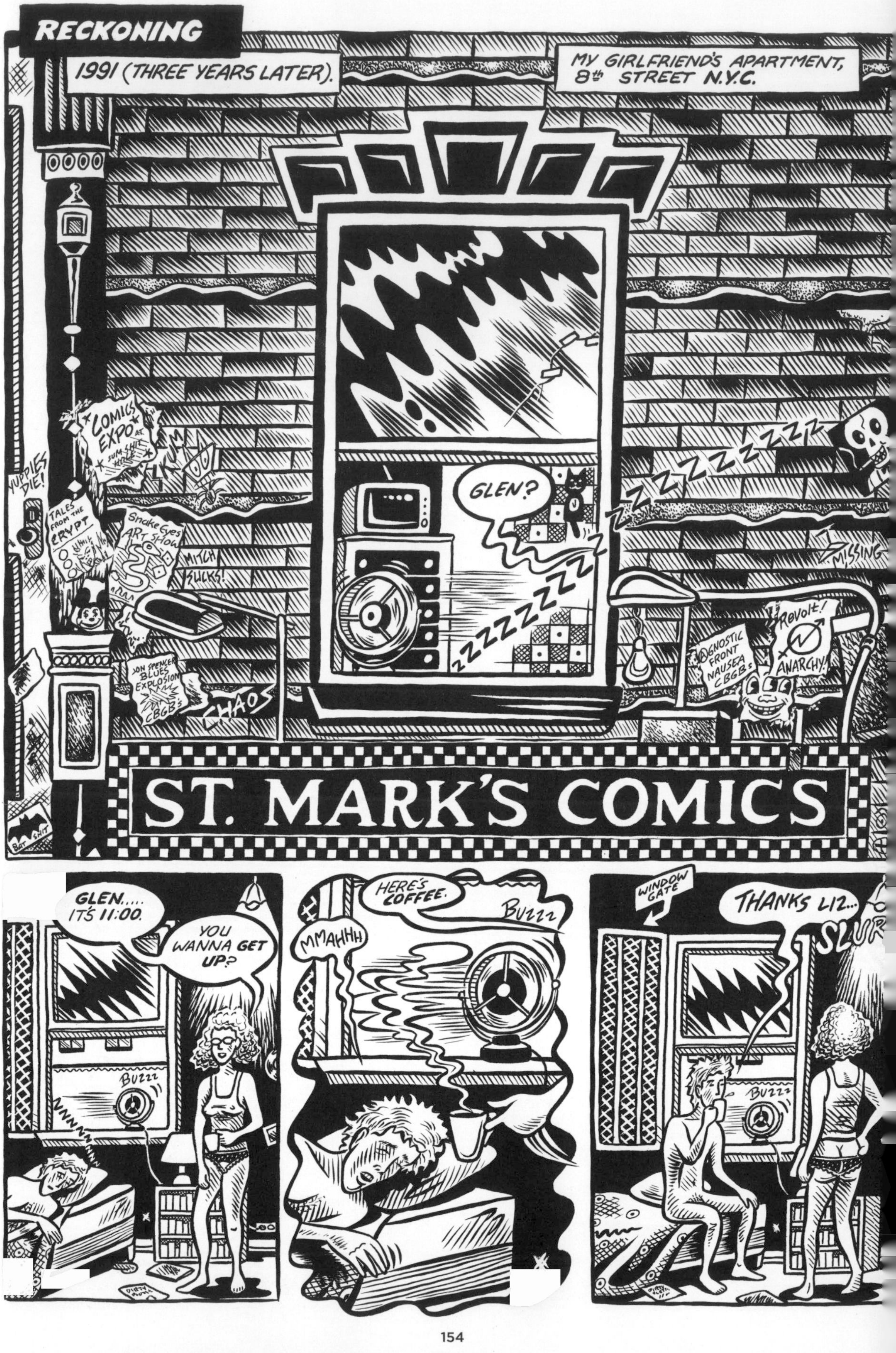

RECKONING
1991 (THREE YEARS LATER).
MY GIRLFRIEND'S APARTMENT, 8th STREET N.Y.C.
GLEN?
ZZZZZZZZZZZZ
COMICS EXPO
YUPPIES DIE!
TALES FROM THE CRYPT
Snake Eyes ART Show
MITCH SUCKS!
JON SPENCER BLUES EXPLOSION CBGB's
CHAOS
AGNOSTIC FRONT NAUSEA CBGBs
Revolt! ANARCHY!
MISSING
ST. MARK'S COMICS
GLEN..... IT'S 11:00.
YOU WANNA GET UP?
BUZZZ
HERE'S COFFEE.
BUZZZ
MMAHHH
WINDOW GATE
THANKS LIZ...
SLUR
BUZZZ

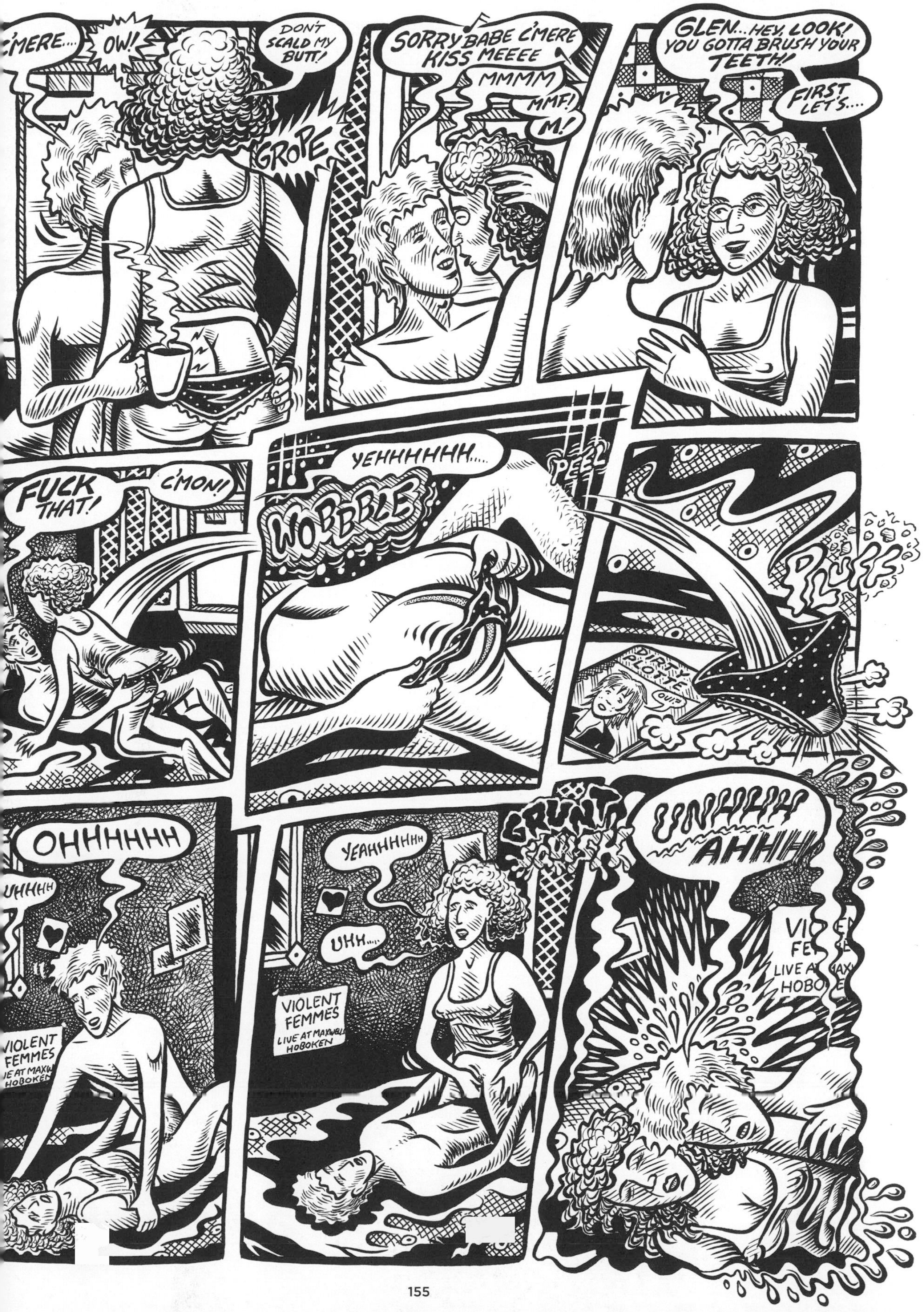
C'MERE....
OW!
DON'T SCALD MY BUTT!
GROPE
SORRY BABE C'MERE KISS MEEEE
MMMM
MMF!
M!
GLEN... HEY, LOOK! YOU GOTTA BRUSH YOUR TEETH!
FIRST LET'S....
FUCK THAT!
C'MON!
YEHHHHHH....
WOBBBLE
PEEL
PLUFF
DIRTY PLOTTE
OUI?
OHHHHHH
UHHHH
VIOLENT FEMMES
YEAHHHHHH
UHH....
VIOLENT FEMMES
LIVE AT MAXWELL'S HOBOKEN
GRUNT!
UNHHH
AHHH

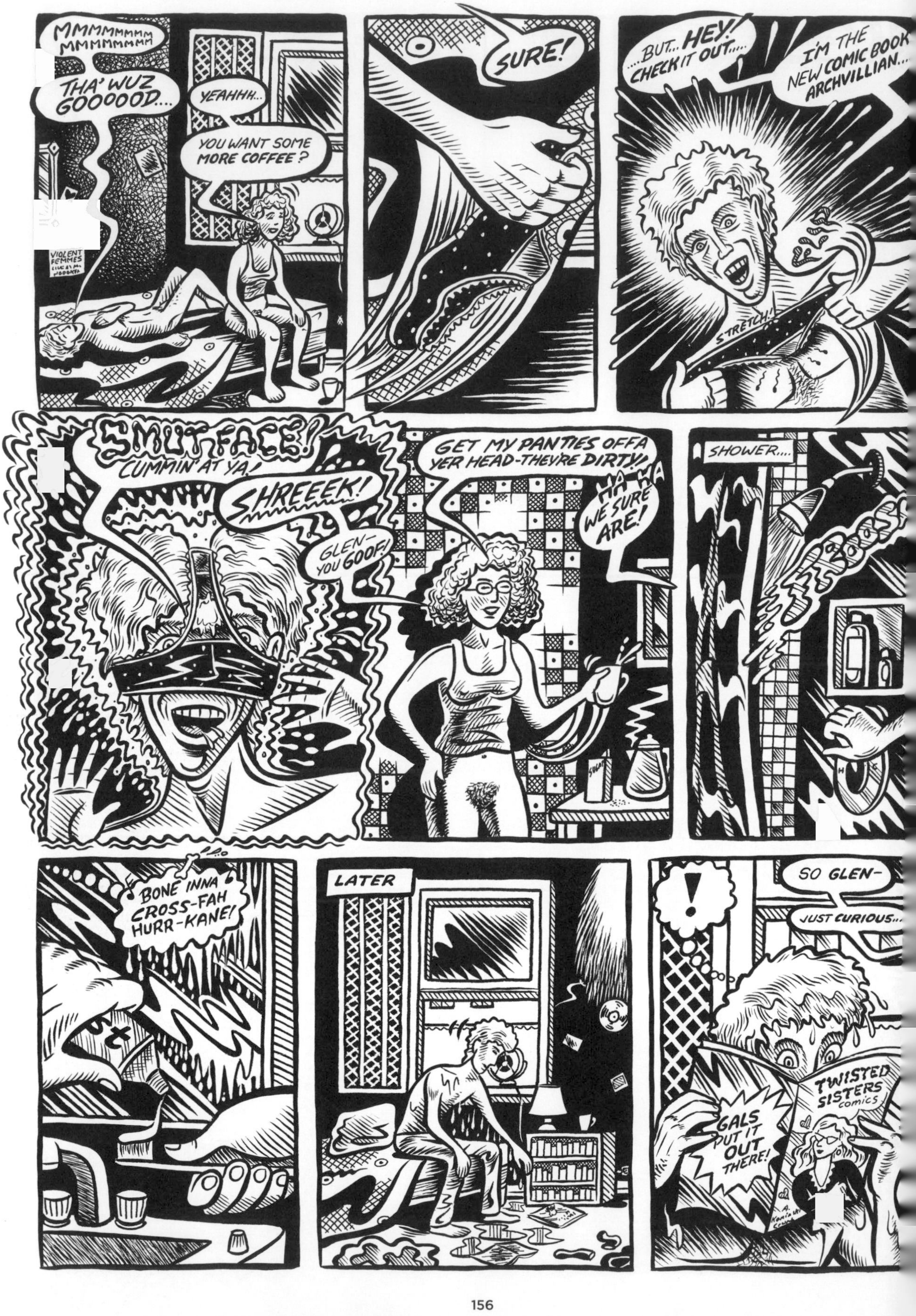

MMMMMMMM MMMMMMMM
THA' WUZ GOOOOOD....
YEAHHH...
YOU WANT SOME MORE COFFEE ?
VIOLENT FEMMES
SURE!
....BUT... HEY! CHECK IT OUT.....
I'M THE NEW COMIC BOOK ARCHVILLIAN....
STRETCH!
SMUT-FACE! CUMMIN' AT YA!
SHREEEK!
GLEN-YOU GOOF!
GET MY PANTIES OFFA YER HEAD-THEY'RE DIRTY!
HA HA WE SURE ARE!
SUGAR
SHOWER....
WHOOSH
BONE INNA CROSS-FAH HURR-KANE!
LATER
!
SO GLEN-
JUST CURIOUS...
TWISTED SISTERS comics
GALS PUT IT OUT THERE!

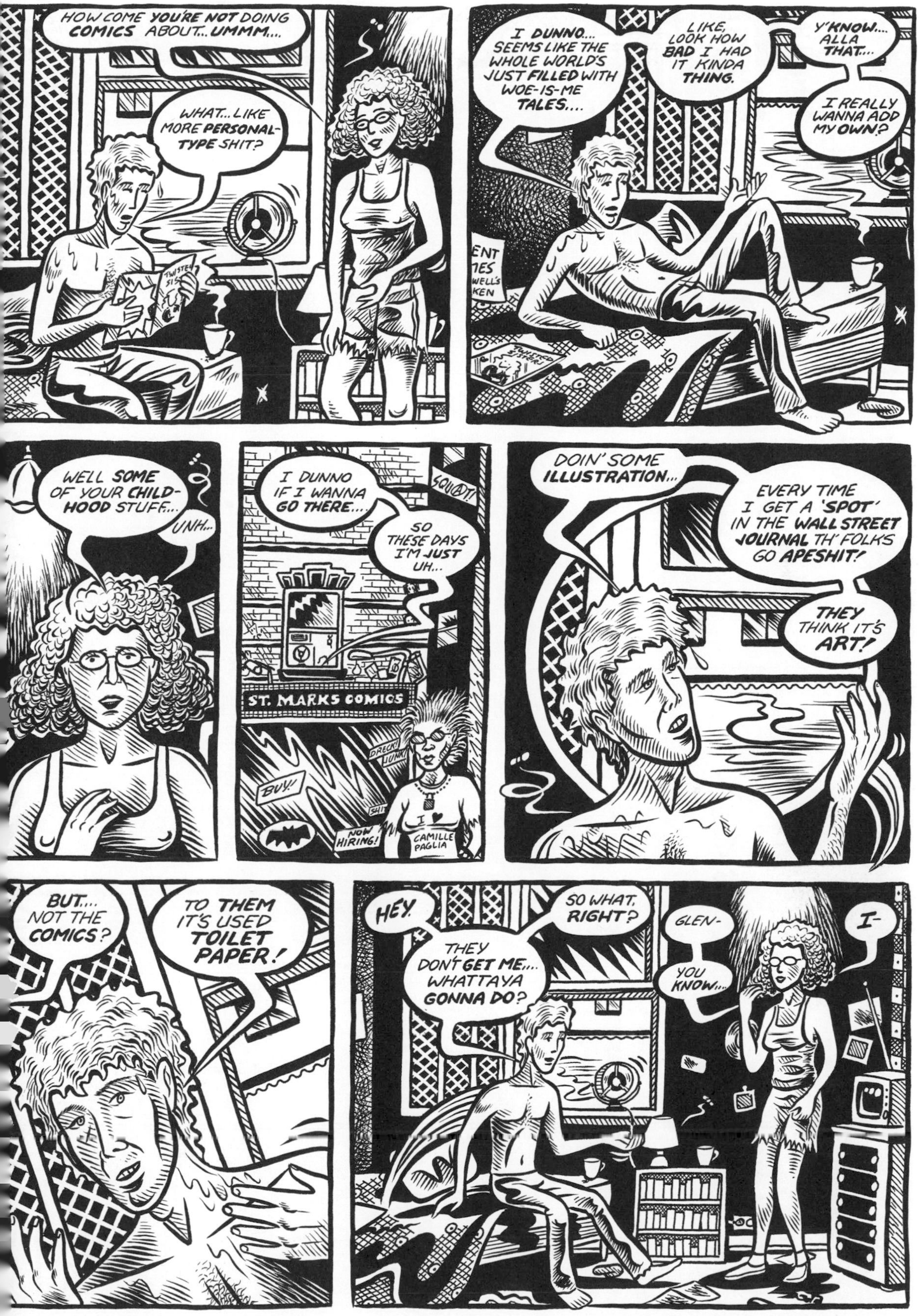
HOW COME YOU'RE NOT DOING COMICS ABOUT... UMMM....
WHAT... LIKE MORE PERSONAL-TYPE SHIT?
I DUNNO.... SEEMS LIKE THE WHOLE WORLD'S JUST FILLED WITH WOE-IS-ME TALES....
LIKE, LOOK HOW BAD I HAD IT KINDA THING.
Y'KNOW.... ALLA THAT....
I REALLY WANNA ADD MY OWN?
WELL SOME OF YOUR CHILDHOOD STUFF....
UNH...
I DUNNO IF I WANNA GO THERE....
SO THESE DAYS I'M JUST UH...
SQU@T!
ST. MARKS COMICS
BUY!
DRECK!
JUNK!
NOW HIRING!
I ♥ CAMILLE PAGLIA
DOIN' SOME ILLUSTRATION...
EVERY TIME I GET A 'SPOT' IN THE WALL STREET JOURNAL TH' FOLKS GO APESHIT!
THEY THINK IT'S ART!
BUT... NOT THE COMICS?
TO THEM IT'S USED TOILET PAPER!
HEY.
SO WHAT, RIGHT?
THEY DON'T GET ME... WHATTAYA GONNA DO?
GLEN-
YOU KNOW...
I-

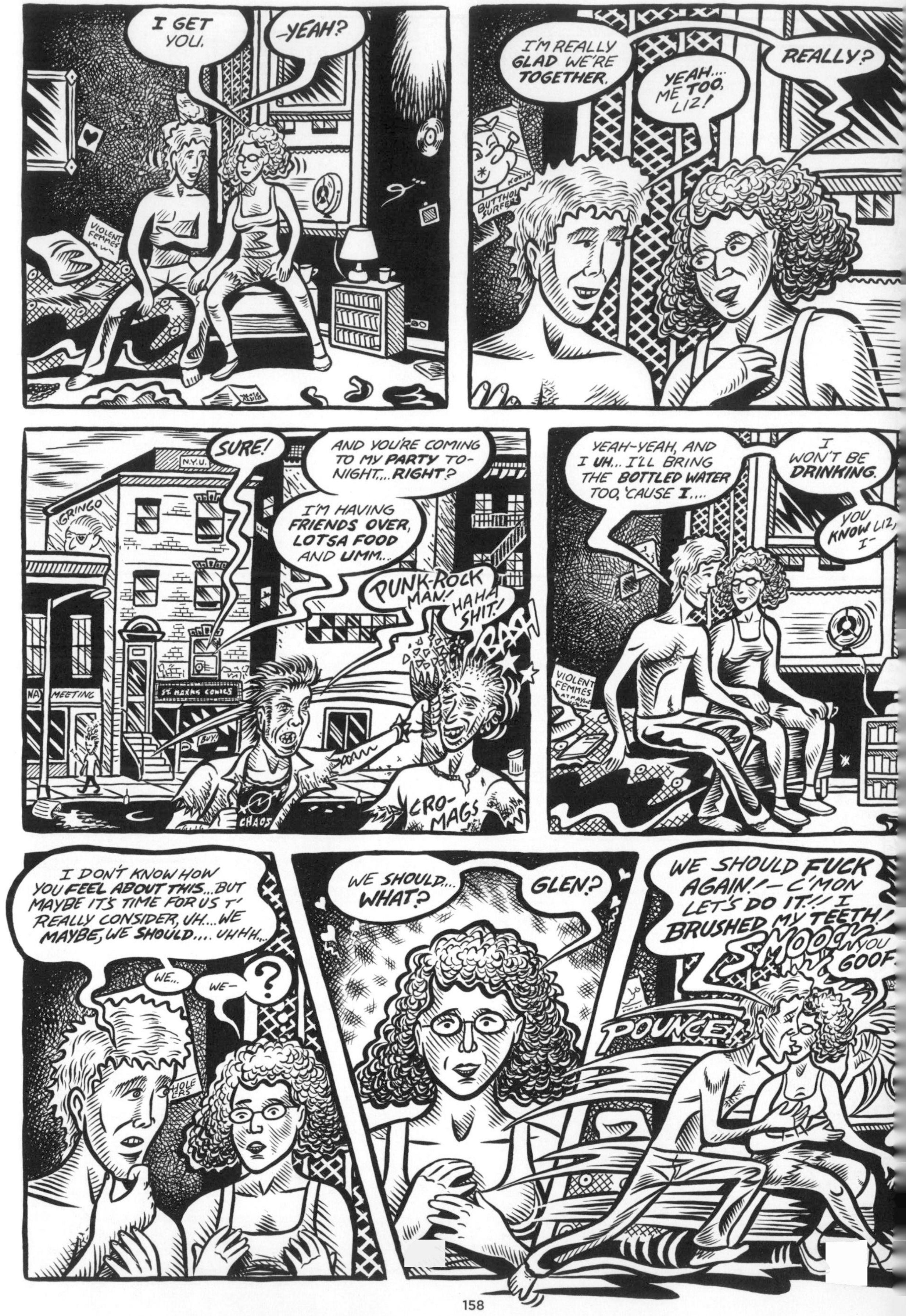

I GET YOU.
-YEAH?
VIOLENT FEMMES
I'M REALLY GLAD WE'RE TOGETHER.
YEAH.... ME TOO, LIZ!
REALLY?
SURE!
AND YOU'RE COMING TO MY PARTY TO-NIGHT,...RIGHT?
I'M HAVING FRIENDS OVER, LOTSA FOOD AND UMM...
PUNK-ROCK MAN!
HAHA SHIT!
BASH
N.Y.U.
GRINGO
ST. MARKS COMICS
MEETING
BUY!
CHAOS
CRO-MAGS
YEAH-YEAH, AND I UH... I'LL BRING THE BOTTLED WATER TOO, 'CAUSE I....
I WON'T BE DRINKING.
YOU KNOW LIZ, I-
VIOLENT FEMMES
I DON'T KNOW HOW YOU FEEL ABOUT THIS...BUT MAYBE IT'S TIME FOR US T' REALLY CONSIDER, UH....WE MAYBE, WE SHOULD.... UHHH...
WE...
WE-
?
WE SHOULD... WHAT?
GLEN?
WE SHOULD FUCK AGAIN!-C'MON LET'S DO IT!!! I BRUSHED MY TEETH!
YOU GOOF
POUNCE!

LATER, TOMPKINS SQUARE PARK....
HAVE TO REMEMBER TO...
GET LIZ SOMETHING...
BIRTHDAY GIFT....
YEAH.
HA HA
KING TUT'S
WA WA HUT
AVE A
SHUT UP!
WAH!
RIOT!
SKETCHBOOK
PUNK'S DEAD!
NOW!
UM...
DRAW THIS GUY.
PYRAMID CLUB
PYRAMID CLUB
SKRATCH!
JESUS....
LOOKS A BIT LIKE LYNCH!
OH WELL....
Stromboli's PIZZA
PUBLIC ENEMY
WORLD WAR 3

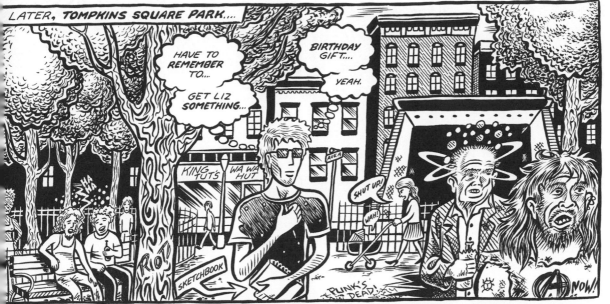

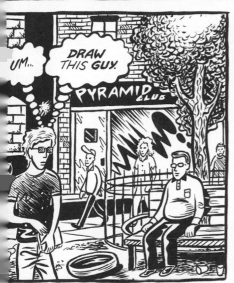

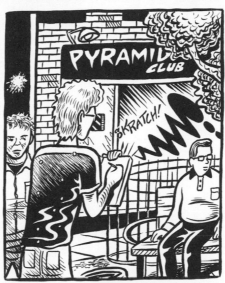

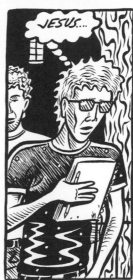

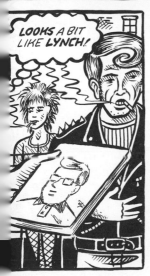

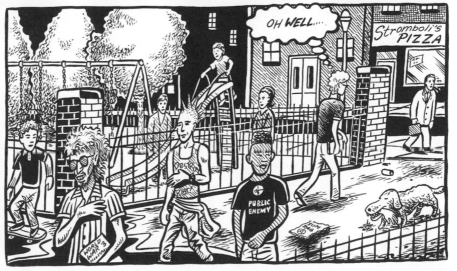

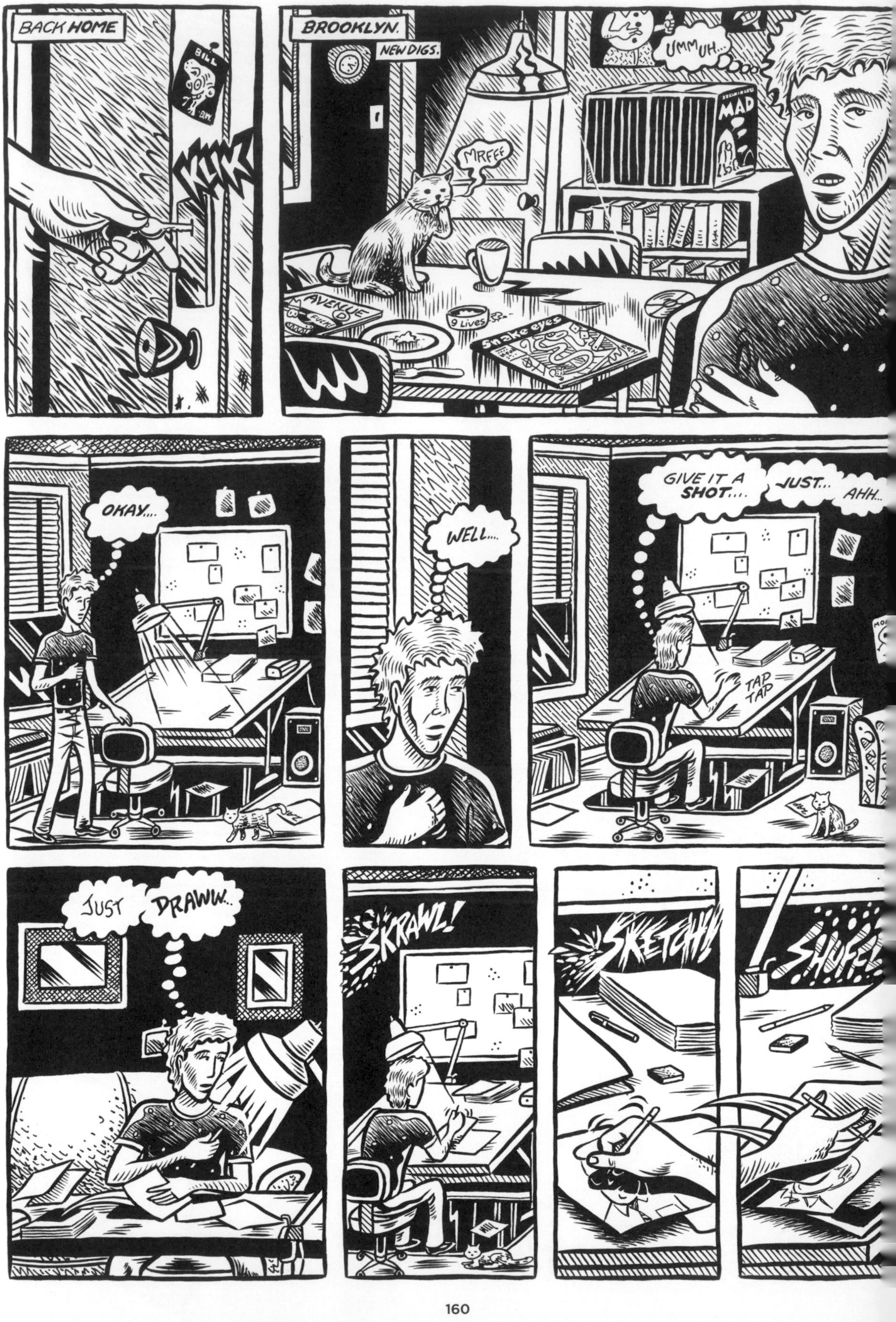

BACK HOME
BILL
KLIK
BROOKLYN.
NEW DIGS.
UMMUH...
MRFEE
MAD
AVENUE D
9 Lives
Snake eyes
OKAY...
WELL...
GIVE IT A SHOT....
JUST...
AHH...
TAP TAP
JUST
DRAWW...
SKRAWL!
SKETCH!
SHUFF!

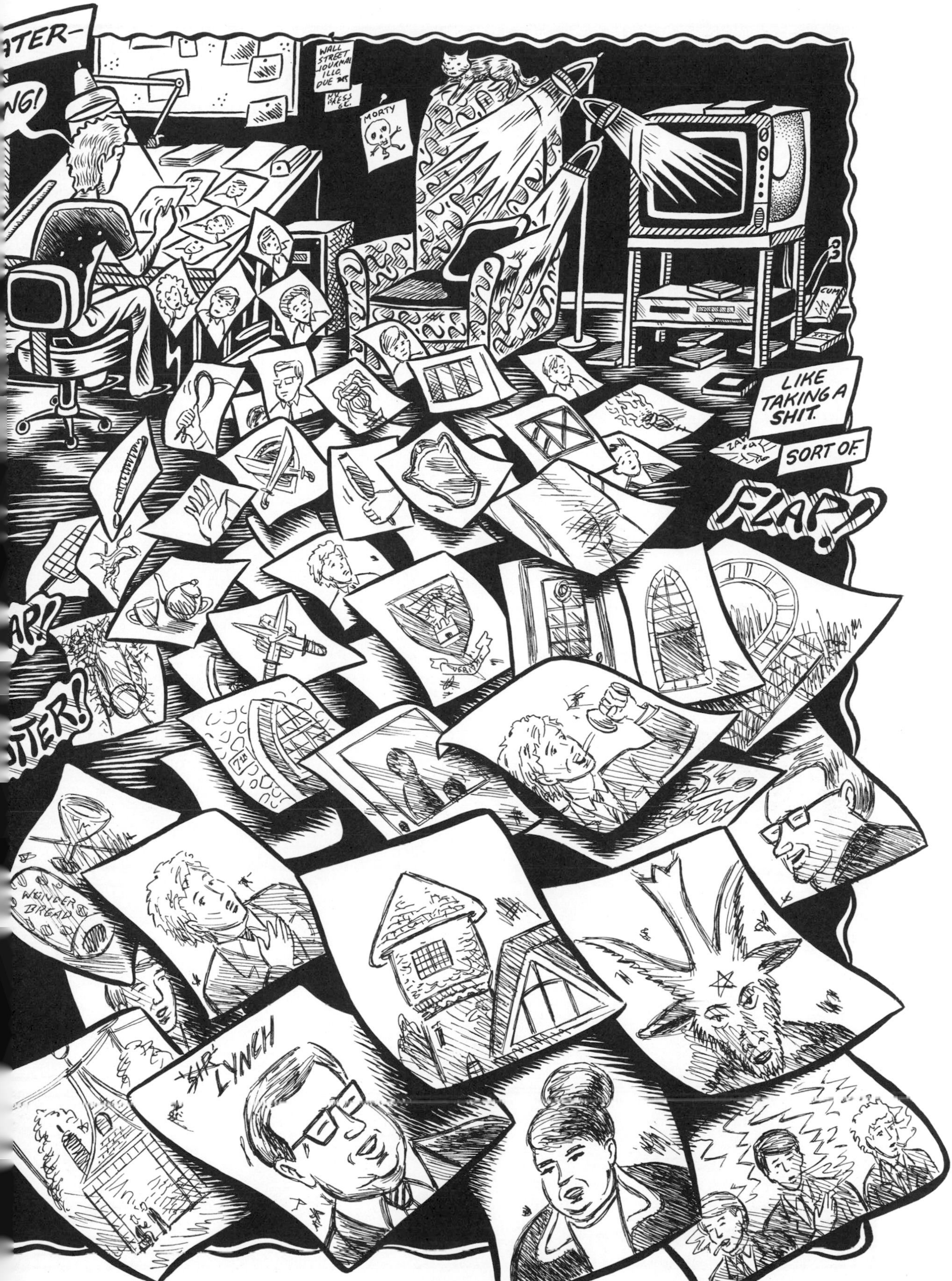
WALL STREET JOURNAL ILLO. DUE 3RD
MORTY
LIKE TAKING A SHIT.
SORT OF.
FLAP!
LYNCH

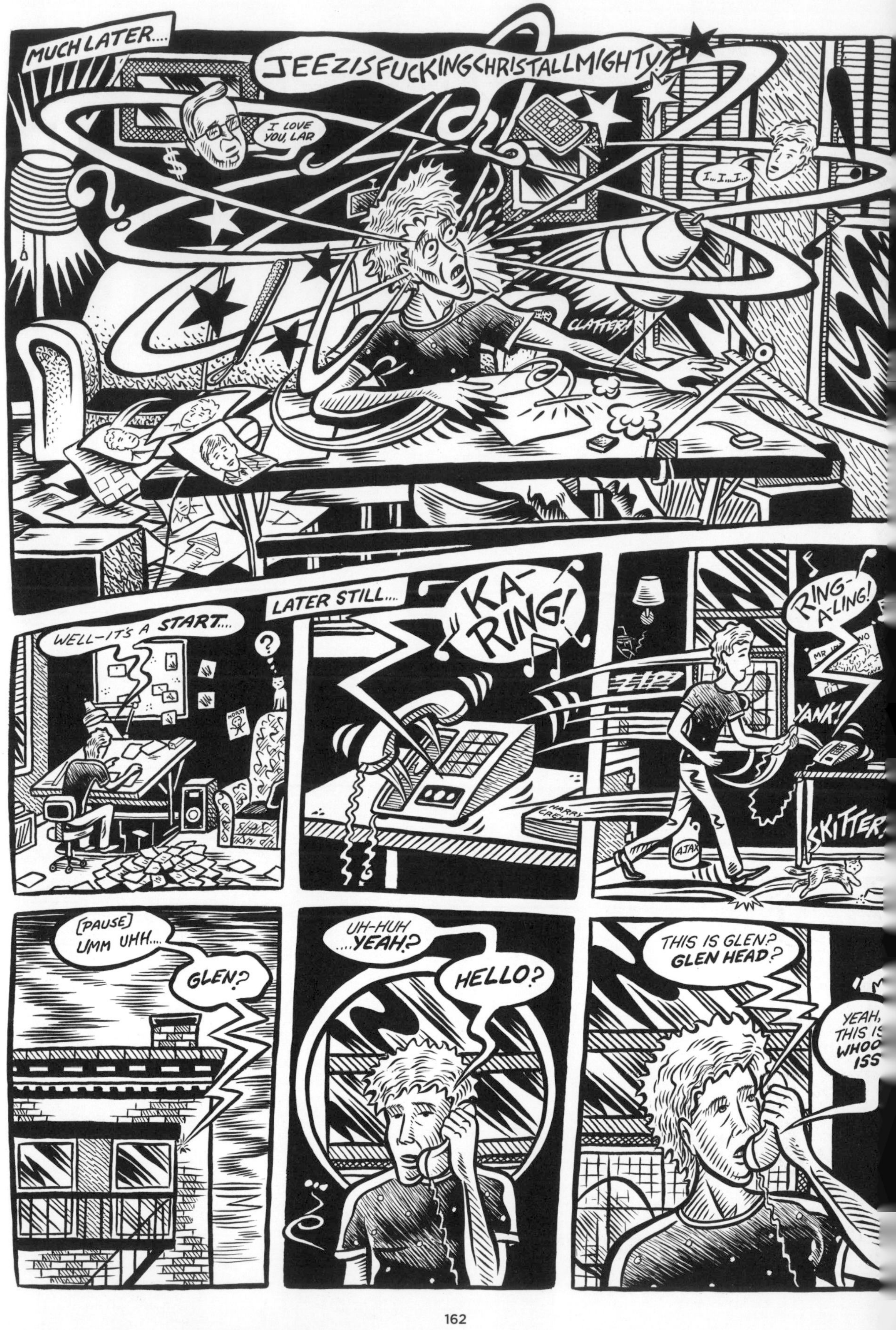
MUCH LATER....
JEEZISFUCKINGCHRISTALLMIGHTY!
I LOVE YOU, LAR
I...I...I...
CLATTER!
LATER STILL....
WELL—IT'S A START....
KA-RING!
ZIP!
RING-A-LING!
YANK!
SKITTER!
[PAUSE] UMM UHH....
GLEN?
UH-HUH ....YEAH?
HELLO?
THIS IS GLEN? GLEN HEAD?
YEAH, THIS IS WHOO ISS

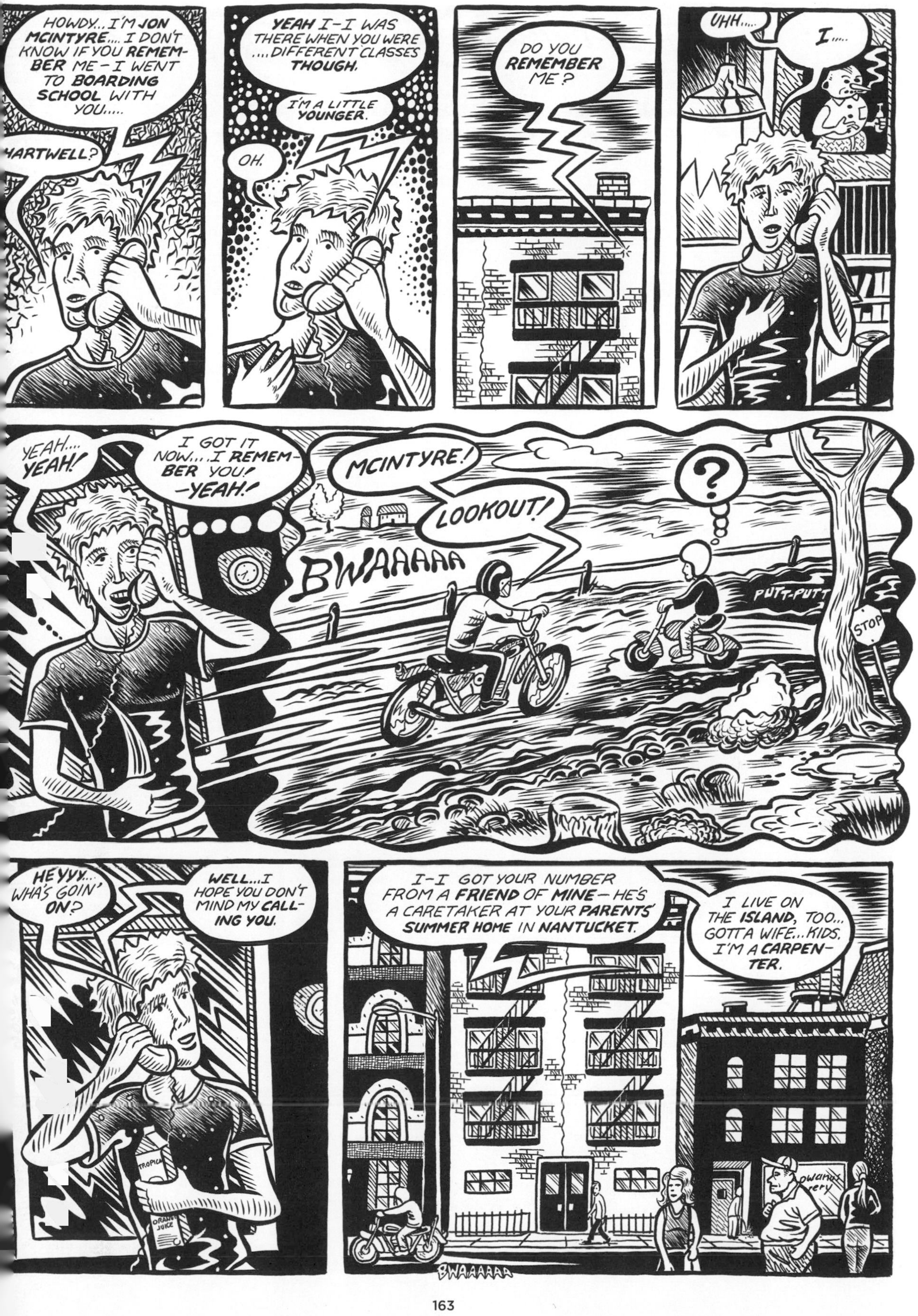

HOWDY... I'M JON MCINTYRE.... I DON'T KNOW IF YOU REMEMBER ME – I WENT TO BOARDING SCHOOL WITH YOU.....
HARTWELL?
YEAH I–I WAS THERE WHEN YOU WERE .....DIFFERENT CLASSES THOUGH.
I'M A LITTLE YOUNGER.
OH.
DO YOU REMEMBER ME?
UHH.....
I....
YEAH.... YEAH!
I GOT IT NOW.....I REMEMBER YOU! –YEAH!
MCINTYRE!
LOOKOUT!
?
BWAAAAA
PUTT-PUTT
STOP
HEYYY... WHA'S GOIN' ON?
WELL...I HOPE YOU DON'T MIND MY CALLING YOU.
I–I GOT YOUR NUMBER FROM A FRIEND OF MINE – HE'S A CARETAKER AT YOUR PARENTS' SUMMER HOME IN NANTUCKET.
I LIVE ON THE ISLAND, TOO... GOTTA WIFE...KIDS. I'M A CARPENTER.
BWAAAAAA

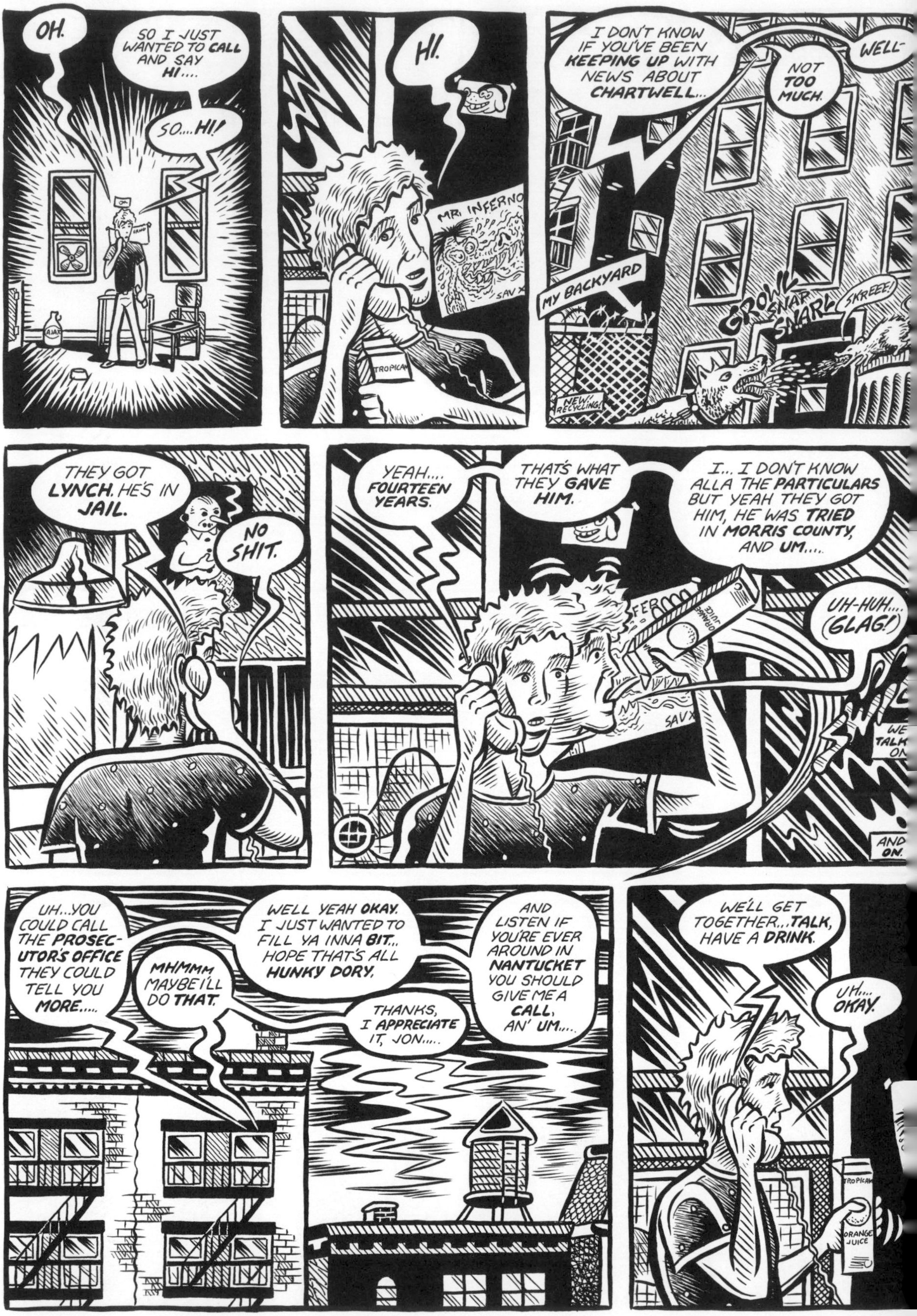
OH.
SO I JUST WANTED TO CALL AND SAY HI....
SO....HI!
HI.
MR. INFERNO
SAVX
TROPICAN
I DON'T KNOW IF YOU'VE BEEN KEEPING UP WITH NEWS ABOUT CHARTWELL...
NOT TOO MUCH.
WELL-
MY BACKYARD
GROWL SNAP SNARL
SKREEE!
NEW! RECYCLING!
THEY GOT LYNCH. HE'S IN JAIL.
NO SHIT.
YEAH.... FOURTEEN YEARS.
THAT'S WHAT THEY GAVE HIM.
I... I DON'T KNOW ALLA THE PARTICULARS BUT YEAH THEY GOT HIM, HE WAS TRIED IN MORRIS COUNTY, AND UM....
UH-HUH.... (GLAG!)
ORANGE JUICE
SAVX
AND ON.
UH...YOU COULD CALL THE PROSECUTOR'S OFFICE THEY COULD TELL YOU MORE.....
MHMMM MAYBE I'LL DO THAT.
WELL YEAH OKAY. I JUST WANTED TO FILL YA INNA BIT... HOPE THAT'S ALL HUNKY DORY.
THANKS, I APPRECIATE IT, JON.....
AND LISTEN IF YOU'RE EVER AROUND IN NANTUCKET YOU SHOULD GIVE ME A CALL, AN' UM....
WE'LL GET TOGETHER...TALK, HAVE A DRINK.
UH... OKAY.
TROPICAN
ORANGE JUICE

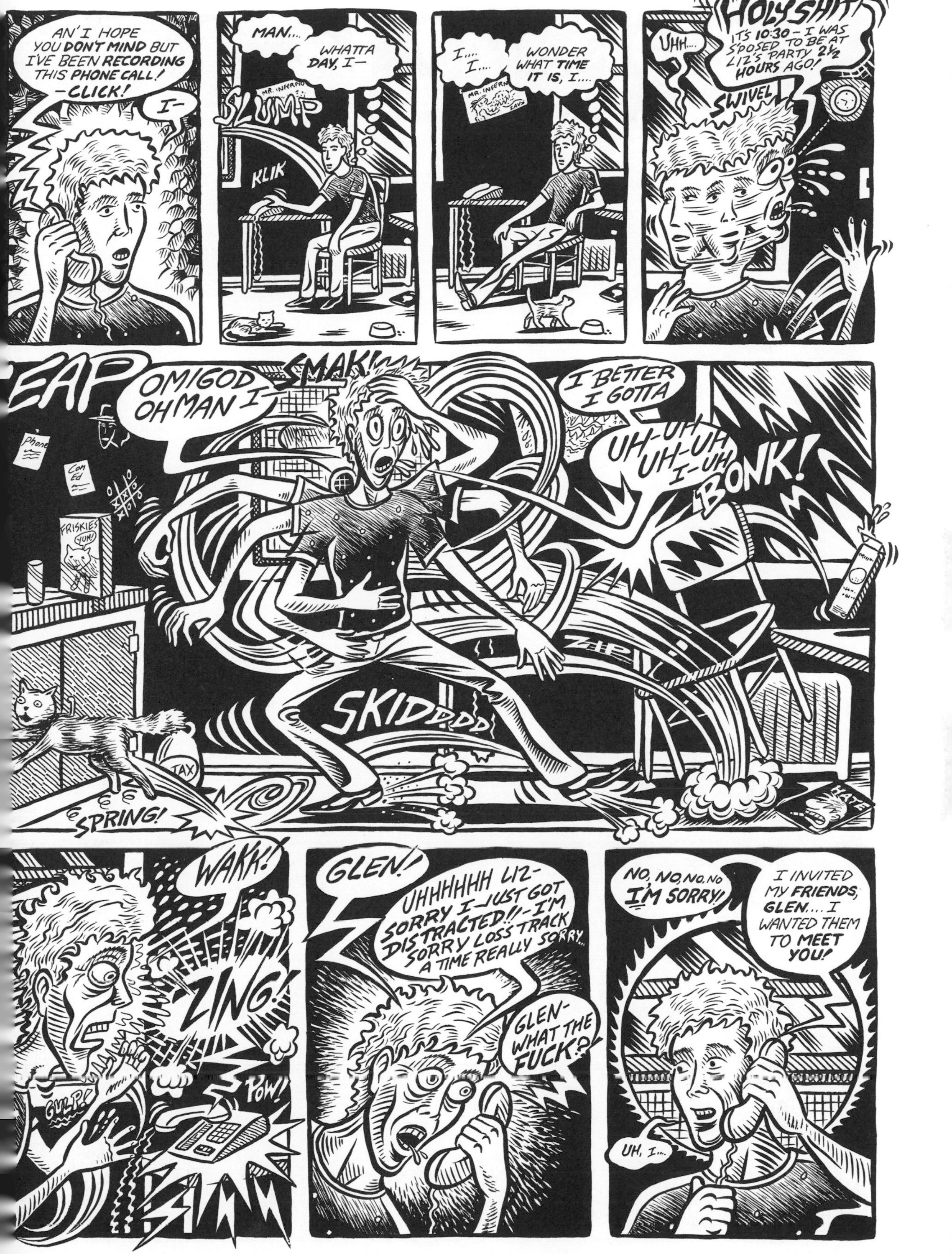

AN' I HOPE YOU DON'T MIND BUT I'VE BEEN RECORDING THIS PHONE CALL! —CLICK!
I-
MAN...
WHATTA DAY, I—
SLUMP
KLIK
I....
I....
WONDER WHAT TIME IT IS, I....
UHH...
HOLY SHIT!
IT'S 10:30 - I WAS S'POSED TO BE AT LIZ'S PARTY 2½ HOURS AGO!
SWIVEL
EAP
OMIGOD OH MAN I-
SMAK!
I BETTER I GOTTA
UH-UH UH-UH I-UH
BONK!
ZIP
SKIDDDD
SPRING!
TAX
FRISKIES
WAKK!
ZING!
POW!
GULP
GLEN!
UHHHHHH LIZ- SORRY I-JUST GOT DISTRACTED!!-I'M SORRY LOSS TRACK A TIME REALLY SORRY...
GLEN- WHAT THE FUCK?!
NO, NO, NO, NO I'M SORRY!
I INVITED MY FRIENDS, GLEN.... I WANTED THEM TO MEET YOU!
UH, I...

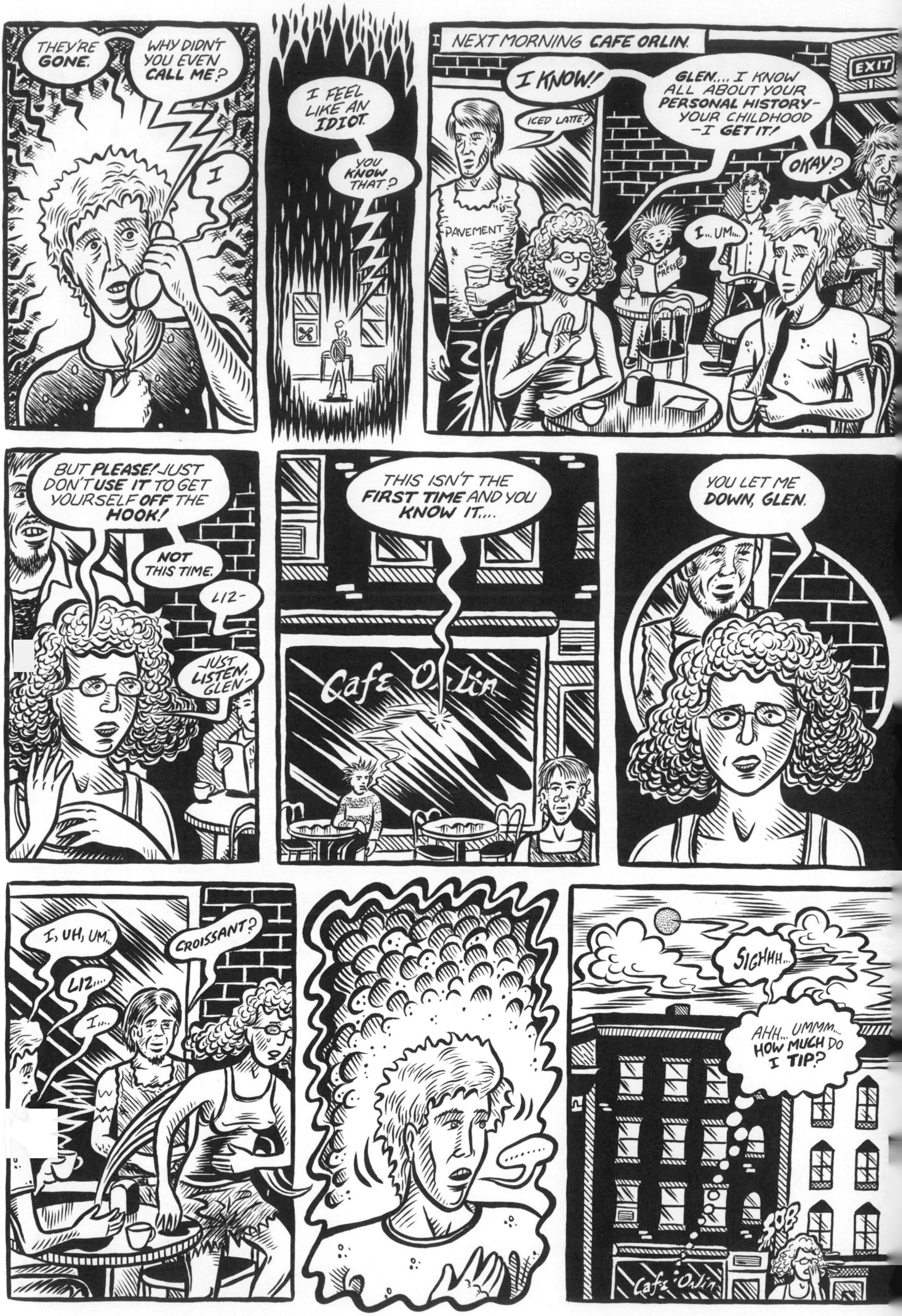

THEY'RE GONE.
WHY DIDN'T YOU EVEN CALL ME?
I
I FEEL LIKE AN IDIOT.
YOU KNOW THAT?
NEXT MORNING CAFE ORLIN.
I KNOW!
ICED LATTE?
GLEN.... I KNOW ALL ABOUT YOUR PERSONAL HISTORY- YOUR CHILDHOOD -I GET IT!
OKAY?
I... UM...
EXIT
PAVEMENT
NY PRESS
BUT PLEASE! JUST DON'T USE IT TO GET YOURSELF OFF THE HOOK!
NOT THIS TIME.
LIZ-
JUST LISTEN, GLEN-
THIS ISN'T THE FIRST TIME AND YOU KNOW IT....
Cafe Orlin
YOU LET ME DOWN, GLEN.
I, UH, UM...
CROISSANT?
LIZ....
I...
SIGHHH...
AHH... UMMM... HOW MUCH DO I TIP?
SOB
Cafe Orlin

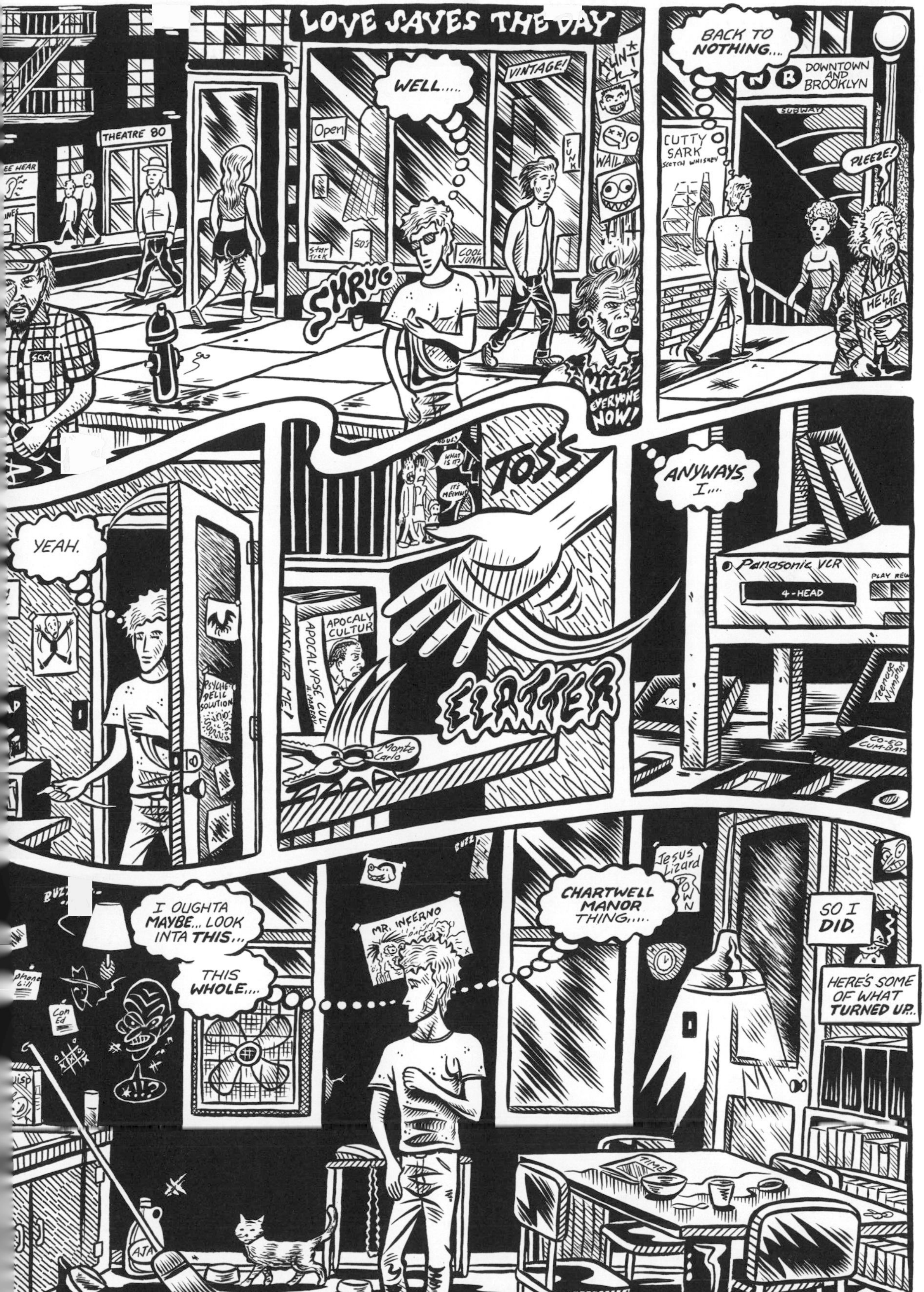

LOVE SAVES THE DAY
THEATRE 80
Open
VINTAGE!
WELL.....
FUNK
WAIL
Star Trek
50's
COOL JUNK
SHRUG
KILL EVERYONE NOW!
BACK TO NOTHING....
N R DOWNTOWN AND BROOKLYN
SUBWAY
CUTTY SARK SCOTCH WHISKEY
PLEEZE!
HELP ME!
YEAH.
PSYCHEDELIC SOLUTION
WHAT IS IT?
IT'S MELVINS
TOSS
APOCALYPSE CULTURE
ANSWER ME!
Monte Carlo
ANYWAYS, I....
Panasonic VCR
4-HEAD
Teenage Nymphos
BUZZ
I OUGHTA MAYBE... LOOK INTA THIS...
THIS WHOLE....
MR. INFERNO
Jesus Lizard
DOWN
CHARTWELL MANOR THING.....
Phone Bill
Con Ed
TIME
SO I DID.
HERE'S SOME OF WHAT TURNED UP..

IN THE NEW JERSEY PAPERS...

Daily Record

FRIDAY, JUNE 13, 1986 A THE PAPER THAT CARES ABOUT YOU VOL. 86 NO. 354

Indictments in school sex cas

Headmaster, teachers accused of molesting 14 students

By BRIAN MURRAY and PHIL GARBER
Daily Record Staff Writers

The British headmaster and two instructors of a now-defunct, exclusive Mendham Township boarding school were charged with sexually molesting 14 students over a three-year period in an indictment unsealed yesterday.

The Morris County indictment named Terrence Lynch, 52, headmaster and owner of the Chartwell Manor school, in 102 of the 109 counts.

The indictment said Lynch performed the sexual acts under the guise of corporal punishment and medical treatment.

"The more students we talked to, the more information we obtained about a pattern of corporal punishment where the students were stripped half-naked . . . and sexually abused," said Assistant Morris County Prosecutor John O'Reilly of the 18-month investigation.

The co-educational school charged tuition of $10,000-a-year and operated in a Georgian mansion on Route 24 from 1969 through June 1984. It housed about 200 students between the ages of 10 and 16, many with learning disabilities. Students from as far away as Turkey, Nigeria and South America were enrolled.

All but two of 14 students identified in the indictment were young boys.

O'Reilly said Lynch, formerly of Morristown, has returned to England.

"He has been made aware of the charges through his attorney. If we have to, we'll extradict him," O'Reilly said.

Former school coach Peter Ahlers, 32, now of New York City, was charged in the indictment with endangering the welfare of a child and with performing oral sex on a 14-year-old boy in 1983. Ahlers surrendered to authorities when informed of the charges and was lodged in Morris County Jail on $10,000 bail.

Former instructor Pamela Lamar, 26, of Massachusetts, indicted on two counts of persuading a 16-year-old girl to smoke marijuana and three counts of sexually touching her ...

to be arrested last night, O'Reilly said.

Lynch's attorney, Stephen Weinstein of Morristown, said Lynch ha... "dedicated his professional life t... young and troubled children. He ... forthrightly accepted those that ... been rejects of others."

Weinstein said parents of chi... who attended the school will "c... out in batallion support" of Lyn...

Lynch also was charged in a ... suit in 1979 with sexually and ph... cally assaulting a 12-year-old N...

York b... at the scho... said th... case was s... he did n... know if L... damage...

Headma... sued ag... in sex a... of a stud...

By Christopher ...

... selling the facilities for $1 million.

... charged with physically and sexually ... ting the 12-year-old New York

"Apparently such activities became an understood part of life at the school and were accepted by most of the students," he said, maintaining the pupils were **"on their honor"** not to talk about it to outsiders.

Headmaster admits sex charges over 3 years at Chartwell Manc...

... June 15, 1986

Some defend headmaster in child sex cas

and his wife, Mary, taught along w... 10 other teachers. The school was run strictly and Lynch would tolerate no variations from the rules.

Tuition was $10,000 a year, but annual payments exceeded $18,000, because of extracurricular activities, such as horseback riding, tennis lessons, trips to Europe. Students included the son of a Short Hills businessman, the daughter of a Ugandan diplomat and the brother of actress Mackenzie Phillips.

14 cases

N... Eng... me...

no sexual ... said Lynch would stand by the showers while students bathed but that this was for insurance reasons because, at one time, a student injured himself in the shower.

Randy Schaeffer, spokesman for the office of non-public schools in the state Education Department, said the only complaint the state ever received about the school was from Gloria Riley in 1983. Riley said Lynch screamed and yelled at her because she asked him why an injury ... a sporting event

fection to those children as ... seen."

Kirschenbaum said students never reported abuse nor did he see any bruises to indicate abuse.

The students and parents knew about the corporal punishment. Corporal punishment has been forbidden in New Jersey public and private schools since 1903 but it went on regularly at Chartwell Manor. Usually, Lynch would pull the student's pants down, place the student on his knee and spank him with his hand, a

...efend on Pa...

Lynch, 55, is awaiti... ing in state Superior ... Morris County. He ha... guilty to charges of ... sexual abuse, sexual abu... dangering the welfare o...

The Morristown res... indicted in May 1986 by... County grand jury and... with five counts of aggra... ual assault, 51 counts of... ed criminal sexual co... counts of sexual assault... of aggravated ... tact, an...

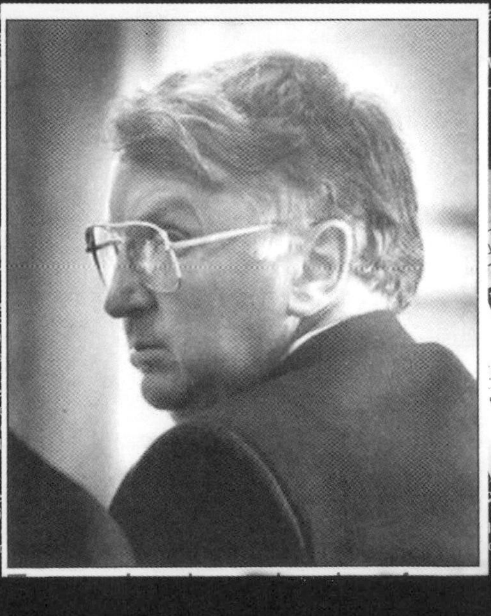

"I don't honestly think I did it for sexual gratification," he maintained, admitting his conduct may have humiliated or degraded his students, which falls under sex abuse statutes

THE STAR-LEDGER, Friday, June 13, 1986

Ex-headmaster, 2 teachers cited in sex case a...

By BILL RILEY

The former headmaster and two teachers who worked at the defunct Chartwell Manor boarding school in Mendham Township have been indicted on charges of engaging in sexual conduct with 14 students between 1981 and 1984.

The 109-count indictment, unsealed yesterday, charges Terence Lynch, 52, with 51 counts of endangering the welfare of minors, 20 counts of sexual assault, 25 counts of aggravated criminal sexual contact, five counts of aggravated sexual assault and one count of criminal sexual contact.

Former teacher Pamela Lamor, 26, now residing in Massachusetts, is charged with three counts of criminal sexual contact and two counts of persuading minors to use a controlled drug.

Peter Ahlers, 32, of New York, employed as a physical education teacher and athletic coach at Chartwell Manor, was charged with both sexual assault and endangering the welfare of a boy.

Prosecutor John O'Reilly said the indictment involves conduct committed with boys and girls aged 10-16 who attended the school at a cost of $6,000 and $8,000 per year.

He said the charges "mushroomed" from an investigation begun by the state Division of Youth and Family Services in 1984 that was turned over to the prosecutor's office early last year.

"The more students that were contacted and interviewed, the more we ... pattern developing in which ...

tered to students who were re... be nude below the waist," O'Re...

"Apparently such acti... came an understood part of... school and were accepted... the students," he said, m... pupils were "on their ... talk about it to outsiders...

"I don't think the... dents appreciated the... poral punishment or ... it took o... O'Reilly... of the s...ankings ... before ...

... according to th... ...yer, Stephen L. ... of Newark.

Another federal lawsu... three state court actions al... been filed by former Ch... Manor students, said Lync... torney, Stephen L. Weins... Morristown.

... statutes agains... ... responsibility ... ...dren and makes the... ...said Thomas Blatner, ... official within the state Division of Youth and Family Services, which ... charged with leading the state's efforts to reduce child abuse.

Blatner said many young children ...

... in 1982 to more than 47,00... DYFS files show.

... s office ... state Supreme ... ourt t... w the appellate ruling

North Jersey Advance
ents 24 Pages in 2 Sections Roxbury Township Vol. 82, No. 137 Friday, June 13, 1986

107 counts of school sex abuse cited

arsico
er

mer headmaster of a paratory school in Menship and two former ve been indicted on more unts of sexual abuse that nvolved 14 students beges of 10 and 16 between 4.

d indictment, which was June 3 in state Superior orristown, was unsealed y Judge Charles Egan. nent was sealed to give time to learn the loca- of the defendants, said ant Morris County Prosecutor John J. O'Reilly.

Those charged worked for the now-defunct Chartwell Manor preparatory school on Route 24.

The former headmaster, 52-year-old Terrence Lynch of England, is not yet under arrest because he is in England, O'Reilly said Thursday afternoon. He said he hopes Lynch will agree to surrender voluntarily. If he does not, O'Reilly said extradition proceedings would be started.

Lynch, who ran the school, is charged with five counts of aggravated sexual assault, 20 counts of sexual assault, 25 counts of aggravated criminal sexual contact, one count of criminal sexual contact, and 51 counts of endangering the welfare of a child.

Teacher Peter Ahlers, 32, of New York City, has already been arrested and arraigned, O'Reilly said, for one count of sexual assault and one count of endangering the welfare of a child. He was remanded to the Morris County Correctional Facility in lieu of the option to post 10 percent of his $10,000 bail. The assault, O'Reilly said, allegedly involved an oral sex incident with a boy.

Teacher Pamela Lamar, 26, of Massachusetts, has not yet been arrested, O'Reilly said. She is charged with three counts of criminal sexual contact and two counts of pursuading others to use narcotics, the indictment said.

O'Reilly said that, of the 14 alleged victims, 12 were boys. Although there were alleged sexual penetration incidents involving Lynch and the boys, the females are not alleged to have been abused in a similar fashion by Lynch or Lamar, O'Reilly said. The school, which had some 200 to 300 students, most of whom boarded the facility, included students from fifth grade through high school and closed in June 1984, according to O'Reilly.

O'Reilly said the abuses allegedly committed by Lynch took place either under the guise of punishing the students or false medical care. The punishment allegedly included spanking of nude buttocks, and

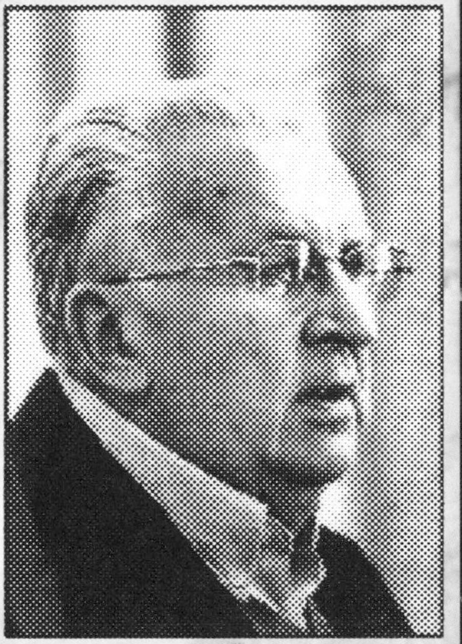

Daily Record

Northwest New Jersey
Tuesday, June 17, 1986
Page B1 Morris East

s Office.
One of the teac
would sometimes happen right
s. It became almost an accept-
g by the students. I don't be-
e parents realized it or the
s understood the sexual as-
it," O'Reilly added.

s) and completed by the Morris County Prose-
Division of Youth and Family
owed an investigation
Lynch and
ed in the indictment
when the student
he lied after
uthoriti
for

tor's office c
to face up to
arole ineligib
She noted, h
as a compulsi
fined at the state
venel. In that e
expect to spend
nent.
ynch, free on $100,000 bail, admi
ering or debauching the
f aggravated sexual
lt.
g his

be evaluat-
and could be
Treatment Center
told the defendant he
years undergoing sp

School sex charges: Scandal or mistake?

al.
"If anything
by," he mai
adult
ha

om were prepared to testify if the
admitted by Lynch involv
Assistant Prosecu

a lot stronger
he victims are
s themselves

from Engl
style" boardi
garten to the nint
sed corporal punish
sey's public and private

Lynch was always addressed as
her was a British diplo
Churchill—whose cou
anor, authorities sa
d attended school
several

provided
were
nal frie
In court
England
colle

Although 99 percent of public and private schools receive accredidation from the Middle States Association of Colleges and Schools, Chartwell Manor was not accredited and had never applied for accredidation, said Mary Ellen Dorsey, a Middle States spokeswoman.

Lynch pleaded guilty last September to 12 counts of a 102-count indictment.

that in some instances Lynch would hold students genitals with his hand while delivering a spanking with a wooden paddl r his other hand.

Former headmaster surrenders

URRAY
urthouse Writer

Mendham Township head- last week with sexually dents at his now-defunct was freed on $100,000 bail surrendering to Morris Coun- nd appearing before a Superi-

o aggressively defend himself o have the matter fully dis- said Stephen Weinstein, at- nce Lynch, 52.

Lynch, once headmaster and owner of the Chartwell Manor in Mendham Township, is named in 102 counts of a 109-count indictment charging him and two former school instructors with sexually molesting the students between 1981 and 1984 under the guise of corporal punishment and medical examinations.

Superior Court Judge Daniel Coburn in Morristown set the $100,000 bail requested by Morris County First Assistant Prosecutor John O'Reilly, setting a tentative trial date of Oct. 20.

Although the prosecutor's office originally believed Lynch was living in Dover, England, when the charges were made public last week, Weinstein indicated in court yesterday that Lynch lives on Miller Road in Morristown.

That address was also listed by Lynch when he posted a $10,000 cash option to make bail yesterday.

Lynch was not available for comment, but Weinstein said he vehemently denies the allegations and that "an onslaught" of former students and their parents are lining up in support of the former instructor, whose school closed in June 1984.

"There's been an excess of a dozen people who've contacted me at my office and at my home indicating a willingness to do what they can for him," Weinstein said.

The indictment, handed up two weeks ago, was unsealed Thursday when the prosecutor's office said it was able to track down the whereabouts of two other instructors involved.

Pamela Lamar, 26, of 133 Park St., Brookline, Mass., was arrested Friday at her home on charges she gave marijuana to
ally touched a

with molesting.

She also appeared at a bail hearing be Coburn yesterday, when her bail was set $25,000.

Her father, William Lamar of Grovenor's N.Y., posted a $2,500 cash option and she wa released yesterday afternoon.

Peter Ahlers, 32, of 4 Marc Court, Hampton Bays, N.Y., a former gym teacher at the school, was releas

Former headmaster gets 14 years for sex abuse at boarding school

arents file suit against defunct school's headmaster

N CUTLER
rd

STOWN — An Ocean couple, contending their injured during spankings cks at the defunct filed a

terday seeking damages.

The child, then 13, was placed in the private school in Mendham Township in 1983 as a special education student, and was subject to an unauthorized practice of medicine and corporal punishment, the suit contends.

During that time, the youngster was in the custody of the headmaster and school founder, Terance Lynch, who was sentenced in March to 14 years in prison for molesting 12 boys.

Last September, Lynch admitted in court that he molested the boys, ages 12 to 15, while performing unauthorized medical exams and punishment.

He pleaded guilty to two counts of sexual assault, three counts of aggravated sexual assault and 12 counts of endangering the welfare of a minor.

The incidents occurred between 1981 and 1984, when the closed.

their genitals and spanking them. He gave five youngs and made hernia check

Lynch, who was ord four years in prison eligibility, insisted the part of a well-known corporal punishment he founded.

Yesterday's lawsuit against

ou were late for class, he'd
ou with his hand," Para-
d. "If you were caught
you encouraged greater
nt, a hair brush or a

'Big deal, you got your pants pulled down and you got hit. I think it was good. You wouldn't even shed a tear.'
— Peter Altamore, former student

Chartwell Manor had the proper trappings: an elegant mansion in rural Mendham Township, a headmaster with a British accent. He claimed to specialize in troubled boys.

"At first, I thought everything was normal. I mean, he would beat us. I got hit by him, I don't know how many times — a paddle, a brush, a belt, the side of a broken

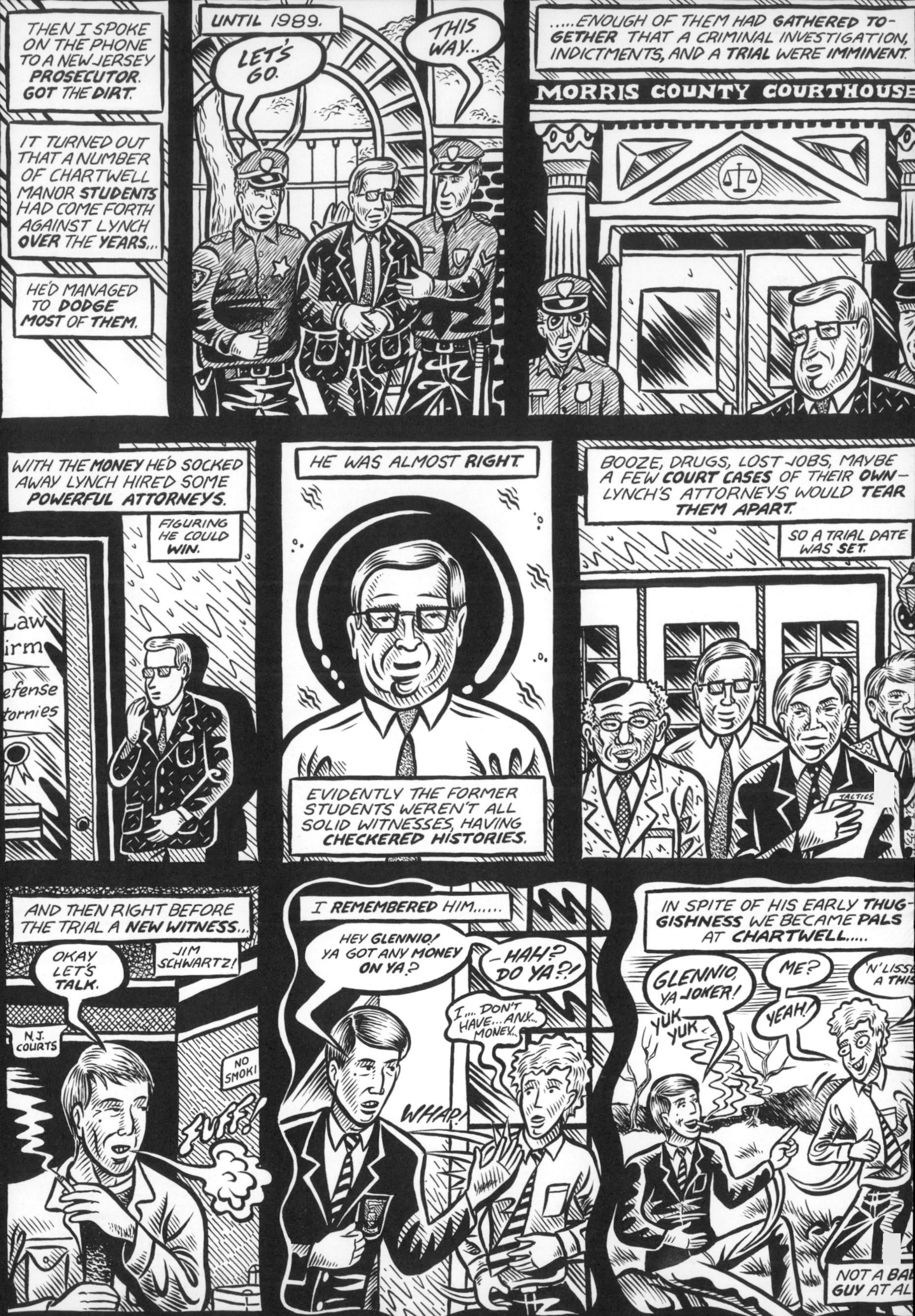
THEN I SPOKE ON THE PHONE TO A NEW JERSEY PROSECUTOR. GOT THE DIRT.
IT TURNED OUT THAT A NUMBER OF CHARTWELL MANOR STUDENTS HAD COME FORTH AGAINST LYNCH OVER THE YEARS...
HE'D MANAGED TO DODGE MOST OF THEM.
UNTIL 1989.
LET'S GO.
THIS WAY...
.....ENOUGH OF THEM HAD GATHERED TOGETHER THAT A CRIMINAL INVESTIGATION, INDICTMENTS, AND A TRIAL WERE IMMINENT.
MORRIS COUNTY COURTHOUSE
WITH THE MONEY HE'D SOCKED AWAY LYNCH HIRED SOME POWERFUL ATTORNEYS.
FIGURING HE COULD WIN.
Law
irm
efense
torneys
HE WAS ALMOST RIGHT.
EVIDENTLY THE FORMER STUDENTS WEREN'T ALL SOLID WITNESSES, HAVING CHECKERED HISTORIES.
BOOZE, DRUGS, LOST JOBS, MAYBE A FEW COURT CASES OF THEIR OWN– LYNCH'S ATTORNEYS WOULD TEAR THEM APART.
SO A TRIAL DATE WAS SET.
AND THEN RIGHT BEFORE THE TRIAL A NEW WITNESS...
JIM SCHWARTZ!
OKAY LET'S TALK.
N.J. COURTS
NO SMOKI
FUFF!
I REMEMBERED HIM......
HEY GLENNIO! YA GOT ANY MONEY ON YA?
–HAH? DO YA?!
I... DON'T HAVE... ANY... MONEY...
WHAP!
IN SPITE OF HIS EARLY THUGGISHNESS WE BECAME PALS AT CHARTWELL.....
GLENNIO, YA JOKER!
YUK YUK
ME?
YEAH!
N'LISS A THIS
NOT A BA GUY AT AL

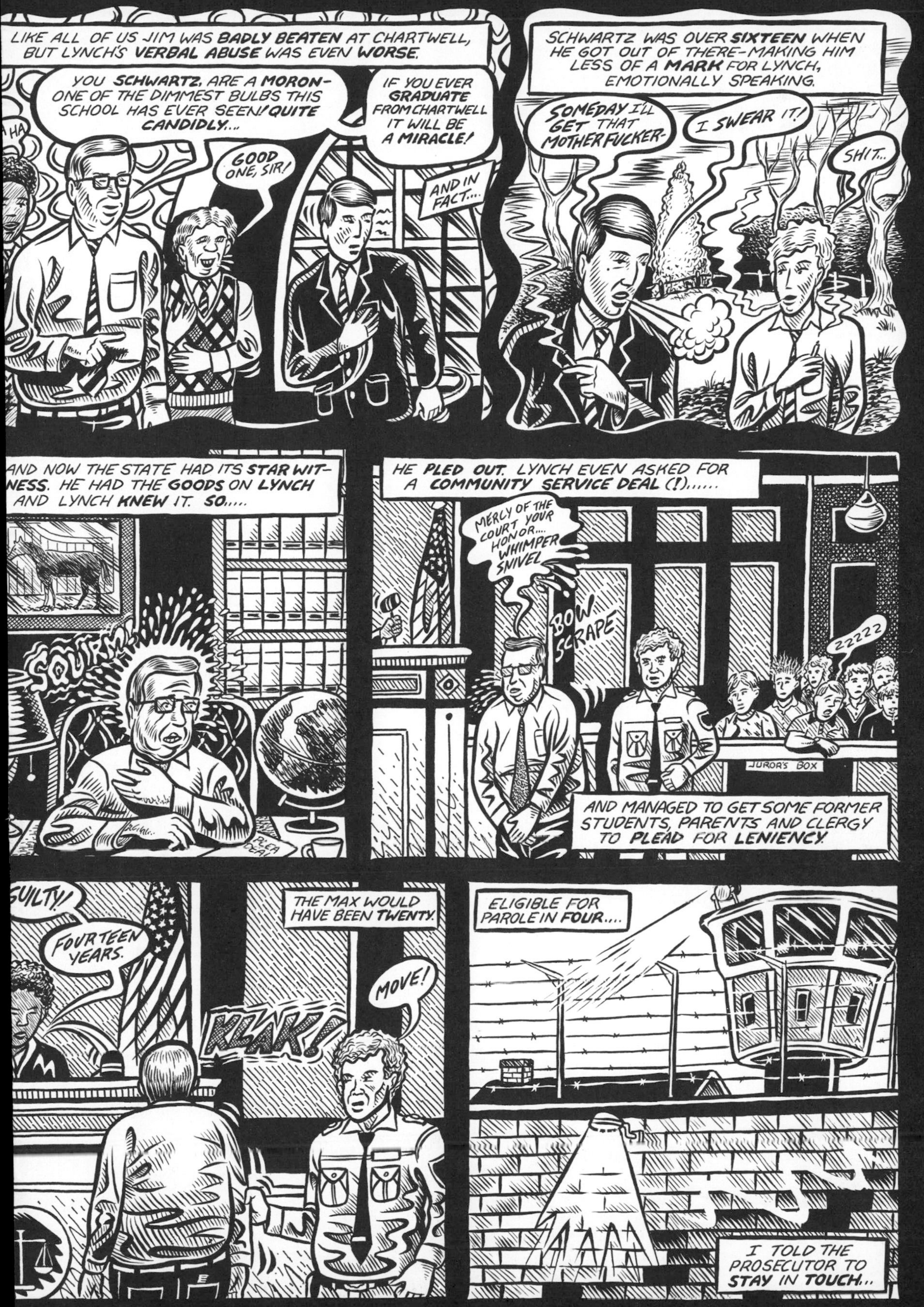

LIKE ALL OF US JIM WAS BADLY BEATEN AT CHARTWELL, BUT LYNCH'S VERBAL ABUSE WAS EVEN WORSE.
YOU SCHWARTZ, ARE A MORON- ONE OF THE DIMMEST BULBS THIS SCHOOL HAS EVER SEEN! QUITE CANDIDLY...
IF YOU EVER GRADUATE FROM CHARTWELL IT WILL BE A MIRACLE!
GOOD ONE, SIR!
AND IN FACT....
SCHWARTZ WAS OVER SIXTEEN WHEN HE GOT OUT OF THERE-MAKING HIM LESS OF A MARK FOR LYNCH, EMOTIONALLY SPEAKING.
SOMEDAY I'LL GET THAT MOTHERFUCKER-
I SWEAR IT!
SHIT...
AND NOW THE STATE HAD ITS STAR WITNESS. HE HAD THE GOODS ON LYNCH AND LYNCH KNEW IT. SO.....
SQUIRM
PLEA DEAL
HE PLED OUT. LYNCH EVEN ASKED FOR A COMMUNITY SERVICE DEAL (!)......
MERCY OF THE COURT YOUR HONOR.... WHIMPER SNIVEL
BOW SCRAPE
ZZZZZ
JUROR'S BOX
AND MANAGED TO GET SOME FORMER STUDENTS, PARENTS AND CLERGY TO PLEAD FOR LENIENCY.
GUILTY!
FOURTEEN YEARS.
THE MAX WOULD HAVE BEEN TWENTY.
MOVE!
KLAK!
ELIGIBLE FOR PAROLE IN FOUR....
I TOLD THE PROSECUTOR TO STAY IN TOUCH...

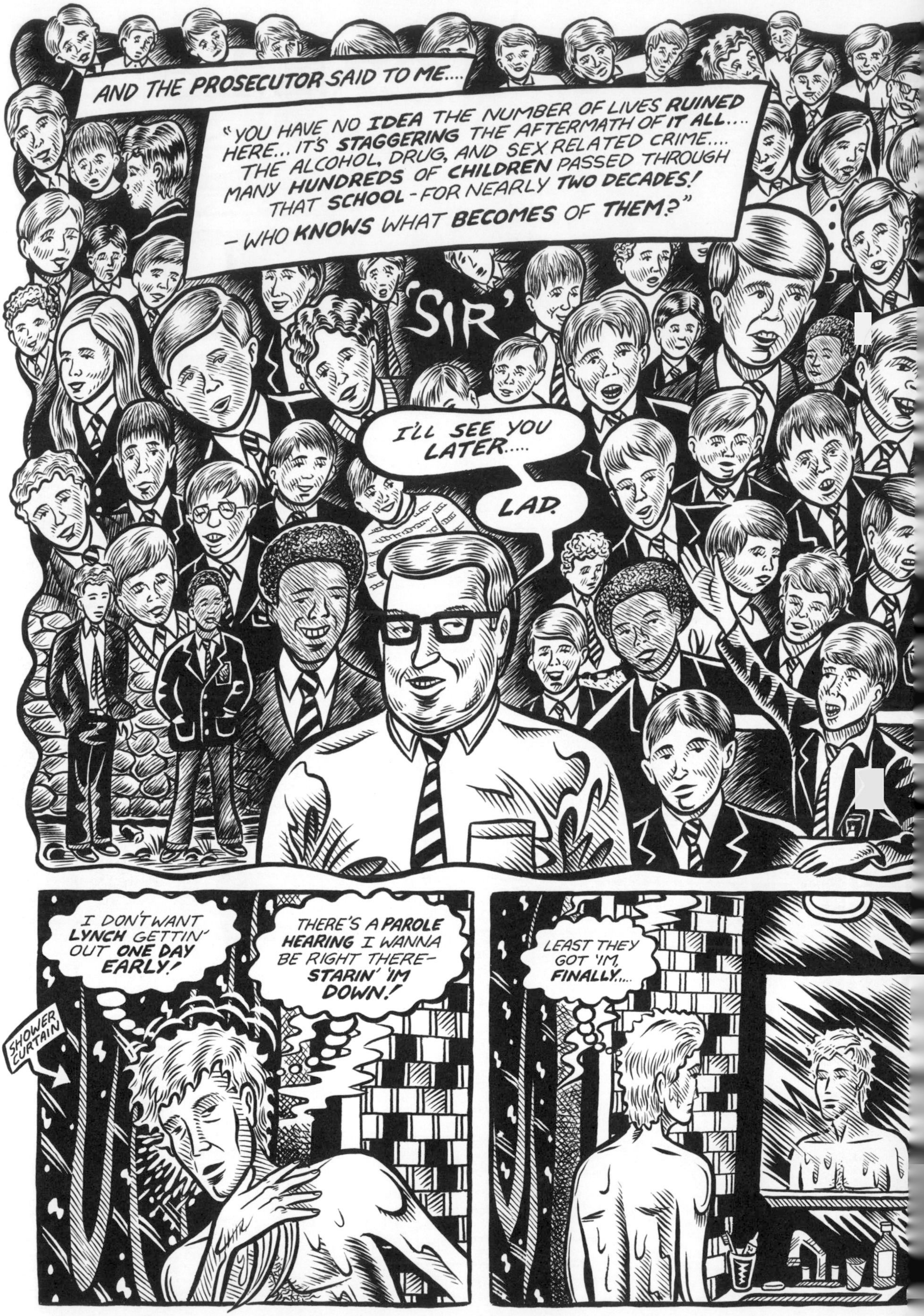
AND THE PROSECUTOR SAID TO ME....
"YOU HAVE NO IDEA THE NUMBER OF LIVES RUINED HERE... IT'S STAGGERING THE AFTERMATH OF IT ALL.... THE ALCOHOL, DRUG, AND SEX RELATED CRIME.... MANY HUNDREDS OF CHILDREN PASSED THROUGH THAT SCHOOL - FOR NEARLY TWO DECADES! - WHO KNOWS WHAT BECOMES OF THEM?"
'SIR'
I'LL SEE YOU LATER.....
LAD.
I DON'T WANT LYNCH GETTIN' OUT ONE DAY EARLY!
THERE'S A PAROLE HEARING I WANNA BE RIGHT THERE- STARIN' 'IM DOWN!
SHOWER CURTAIN
LEAST THEY GOT 'IM, FINALLY.....

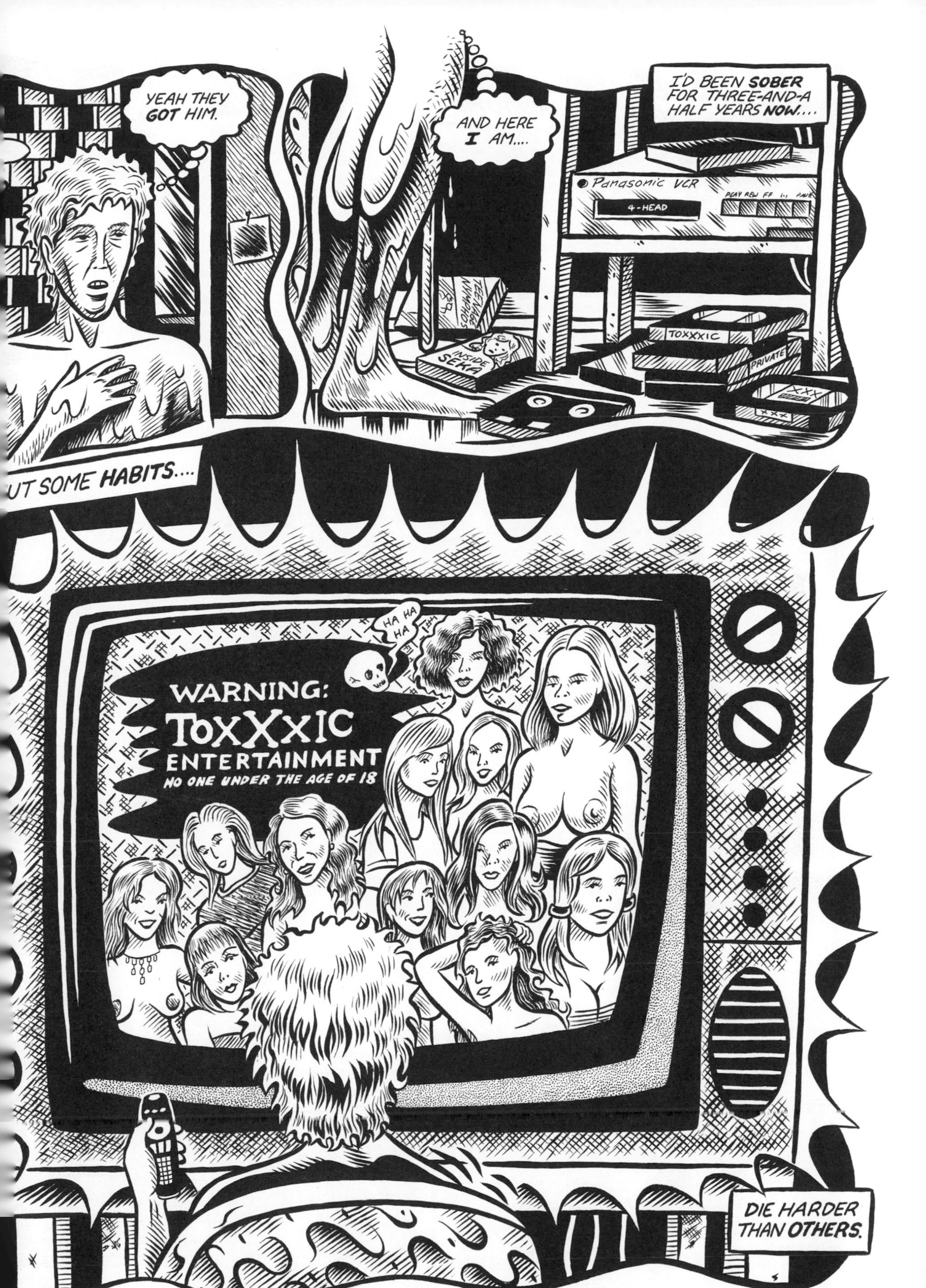

YEAH THEY GOT HIM.
AND HERE I AM....
I'D BEEN SOBER FOR THREE-AND-A HALF YEARS NOW....
Panasonic VCR
4-HEAD
TOXXXIC
PRIVATE
XXX
UT SOME HABITS....
HA HA HA
WARNING: ToXXxIC ENTERTAINMENT
NO ONE UNDER THE AGE OF 18
DIE HARDER THAN OTHERS.

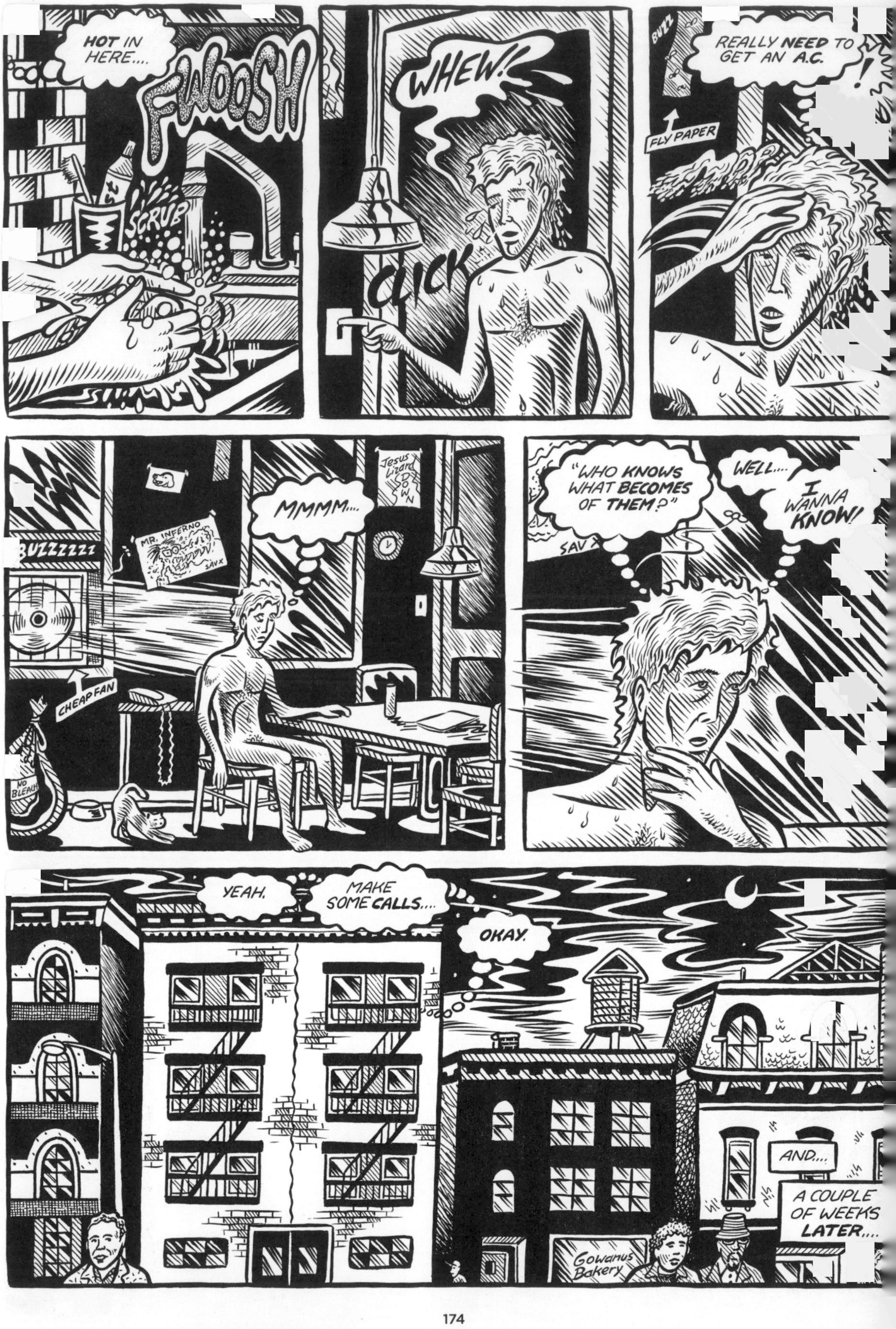
HOT IN HERE....
FWOOSH
SCRUB
WHEW!
CLICK
BUZZ
REALLY NEED TO GET AN A.C.
FLY PAPER
!
BUZZZZZZ
MR. INFERNO
SAV X
Jesus Lizard DOWN
MMMM....
CHEAP FAN
NO BLEACH
"WHO KNOWS WHAT BECOMES OF THEM?"
WELL....
I WANNA KNOW!
SAV X
YEAH.
MAKE SOME CALLS....
OKAY.
AND....
A COUPLE OF WEEKS LATER....
Gowanus Bakery

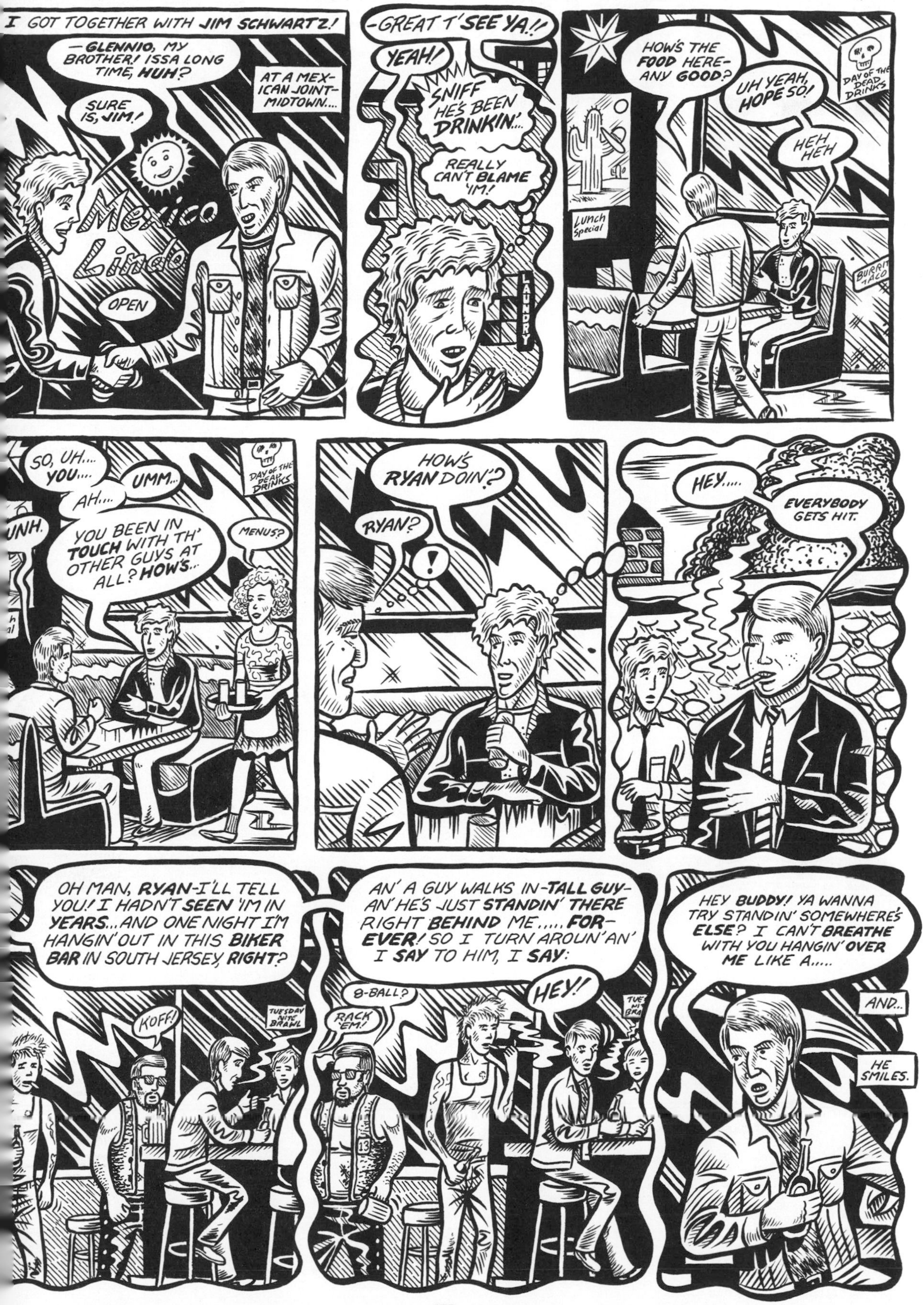
I GOT TOGETHER WITH JIM SCHWARTZ!
—GLENNIO, MY BROTHER! ISSA LONG TIME, HUH?
SURE IS, JIM!
AT A MEXICAN JOINT—MIDTOWN....
Mexico Lindo
OPEN
—GREAT T' SEE YA!!
YEAH!
SNIFF HE'S BEEN DRINKIN'...
REALLY CAN'T BLAME 'IM!
LAUNDRY
HOW'S THE FOOD HERE—ANY GOOD?
UH YEAH, HOPE SO!
HEH HEH
DAY OF THE DEAD DRINKS
Lunch Special
BURRITO TACO
SO, UH.... YOU....
AH....
UMM...
UNH.
YOU BEEN IN TOUCH WITH TH' OTHER GUYS AT ALL? HOW'S...
MENUS?
DAY OF THE DEAD DRINKS
HOW'S RYAN DOIN'?
RYAN?
!
HEY.....
EVERYBODY GETS HIT.
OH MAN, RYAN—I'LL TELL YOU! I HADN'T SEEN 'IM IN YEARS... AND ONE NIGHT I'M HANGIN' OUT IN THIS BIKER BAR IN SOUTH JERSEY, RIGHT?
KOFF!
TUESDAY NITE BRAWL
AN' A GUY WALKS IN—TALL GUY—AN' HE'S JUST STANDIN' THERE RIGHT BEHIND ME..... FOR-EVER! SO I TURN AROUN' AN' I SAY TO HIM, I SAY:
8-BALL?
RACK 'EM!
HEY!
HEY BUDDY! YA WANNA TRY STANDIN' SOMEWHERE'S ELSE? I CAN'T BREATHE WITH YOU HANGIN' OVER ME LIKE A.....
AND...
HE SMILES.

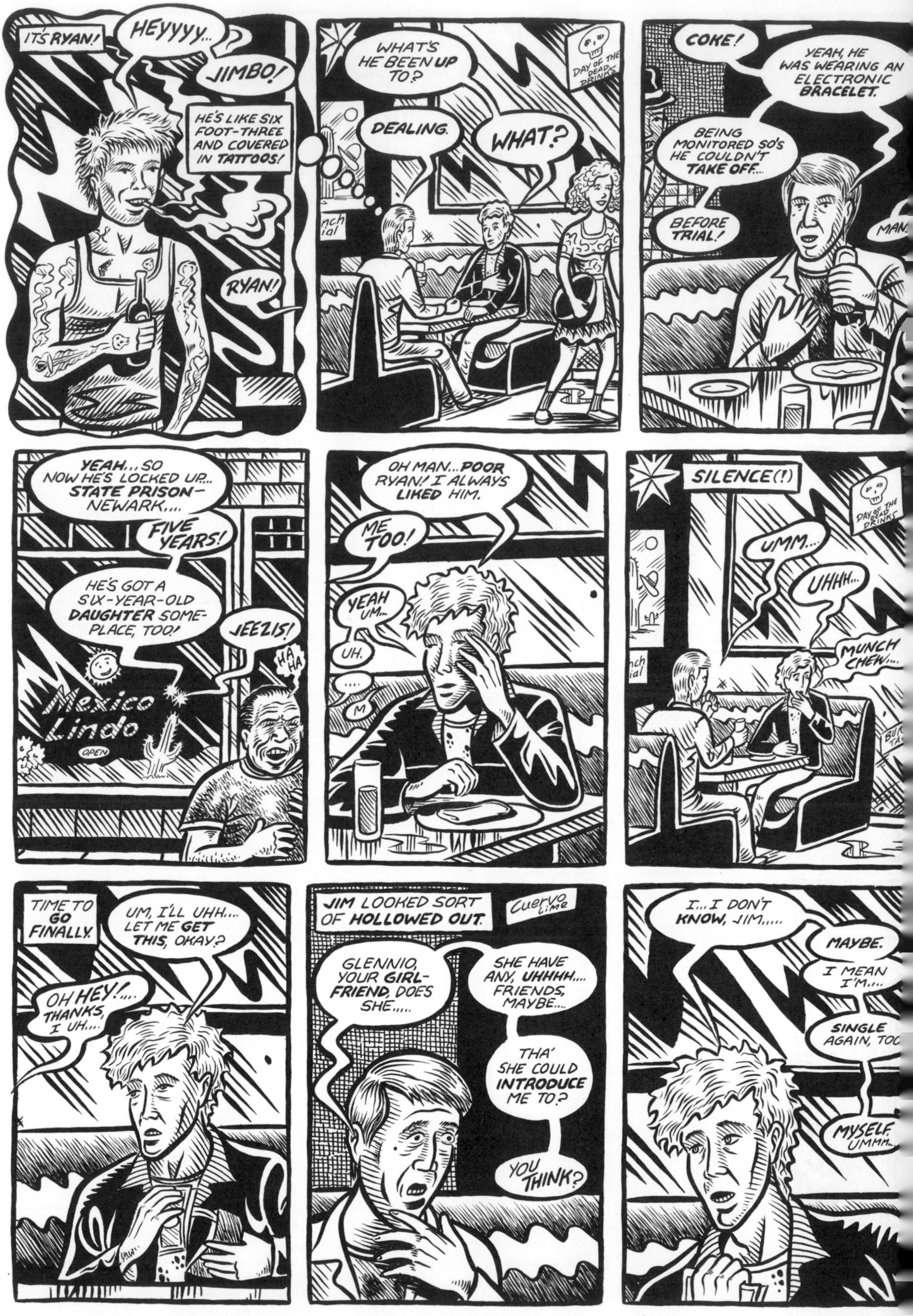
IT'S RYAN!
HEYYYY...
JIMBO!
HE'S LIKE SIX FOOT-THREE AND COVERED IN TATTOOS!
RYAN!
WHAT'S HE BEEN UP TO?
DEALING.
WHAT?
DAY OF THE DEAD DRINKS
COKE!
YEAH, HE WAS WEARING AN ELECTRONIC BRACELET.
BEING MONITORED SO'S HE COULDN'T TAKE OFF...
BEFORE TRIAL!
YEAH... SO NOW HE'S LOCKED UP... STATE PRISON— NEWARK....
FIVE YEARS!
HE'S GOT A SIX-YEAR-OLD DAUGHTER SOME-PLACE, TOO!
JEEZIS!
HA HA
Mexico Lindo
OPEN
OH MAN... POOR RYAN! I ALWAYS LIKED HIM.
ME TOO!
YEAH UM...
UH.
....
M
SILENCE(!)
DAY OF THE DEAD DRINKS
UMM...
UHHH...
MUNCH CHEW....
TIME TO GO FINALLY.
UM, I'LL UHH... LET ME GET THIS, OKAY?
OH HEY!... THANKS, I UH...
JIM LOOKED SORT OF HOLLOWED OUT.
Cuervo Lime
GLENNIO, YOUR GIRL-FRIEND, DOES SHE.....
SHE HAVE ANY, UHHHH.... FRIENDS, MAYBE....
THA' SHE COULD INTRODUCE ME TO?
YOU THINK?
I... I DON'T KNOW, JIM.....
MAYBE.
I MEAN I'M....
SINGLE AGAIN, TOO
MYSELF. UMMM...

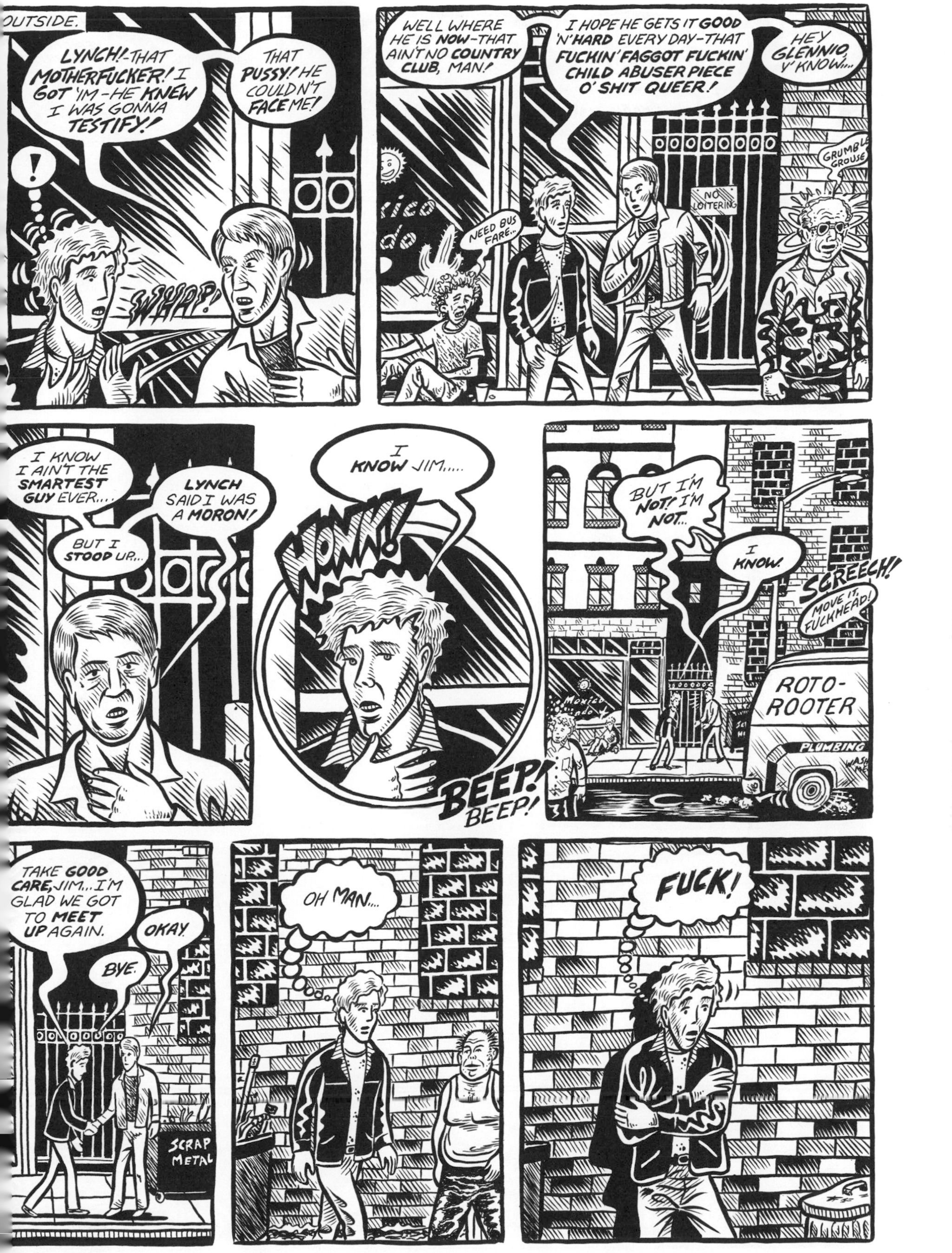
OUTSIDE.
LYNCH! -THAT MOTHERFUCKER! I GOT 'IM -HE KNEW I WAS GONNA TESTIFY!
THAT PUSSY! HE COULDN'T FACE ME!
!
WHAP!
WELL WHERE HE IS NOW-THAT AIN'T NO COUNTRY CLUB, MAN!
I HOPE HE GETS IT GOOD 'N' HARD EVERY DAY-THAT FUCKIN' FAGGOT FUCKIN' CHILD ABUSER PIECE O' SHIT QUEER!
HEY GLENNIO, Y' KNOW....
GRUMBLE GROUSE
NO LOITERING
NEED BUS FARE...
I KNOW I AIN'T THE SMARTEST GUY EVER....
LYNCH SAID I WAS A MORON!
BUT I STOOD UP....
I KNOW JIM.....
HONK!
BEEP! BEEP!
BUT I'M NOT! I'M NOT...
I KNOW.
SCREECH!
MOVE IT, FUCKHEAD!
ROTO-ROOTER
PLUMBING
TAKE GOOD CARE, JIM... I'M GLAD WE GOT TO MEET UP AGAIN.
OKAY.
BYE.
SCRAP METAL
OH MAN....
FUCK!

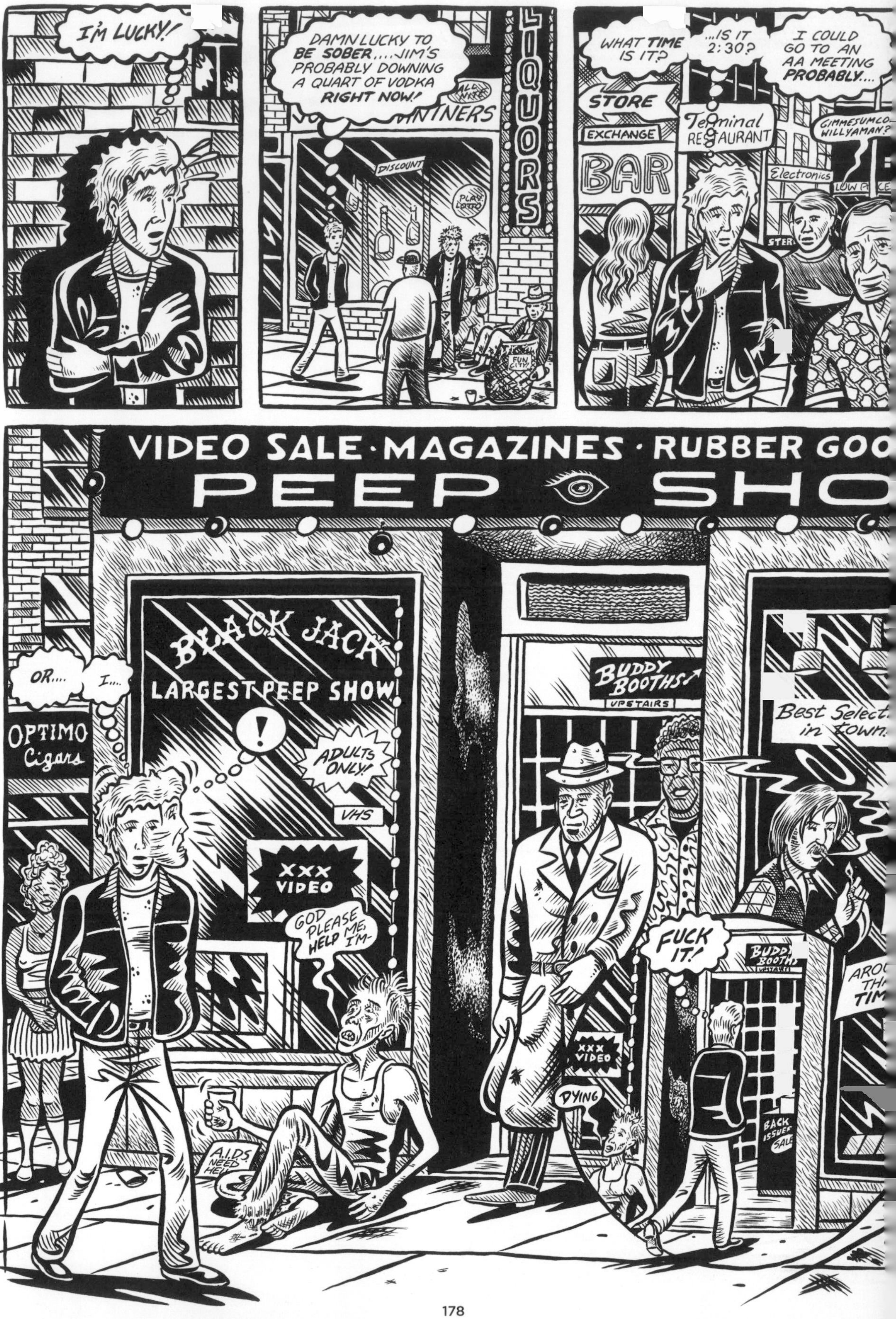

I'M LUCKY!
DAMN LUCKY TO BE SOBER....JIM'S PROBABLY DOWNING A QUART OF VODKA RIGHT NOW!
DISCOUNT
PLAY LOTTO
LIQUORS
FUN CITY
WHAT TIME IS IT?
...IS IT 2:30?
I COULD GO TO AN AA MEETING PROBABLY....
STORE
EXCHANGE
BAR
Terminal RESTAURANT
GIMMESUMCO- WILLYAMAN?
Electronics
VIDEO SALE · MAGAZINES · RUBBER GOO
PEEP SHO
OR....
I....
OPTIMO Cigars
BLACK JACK
LARGEST PEEP SHOW!
!
ADULTS ONLY!
VHS
XXX VIDEO
GOD PLEASE HELP ME, I'M-
BUDDY BOOTHS UPSTAIRS
FUCK IT!
XXX VIDEO
DYING
BACK ISSUES SALE

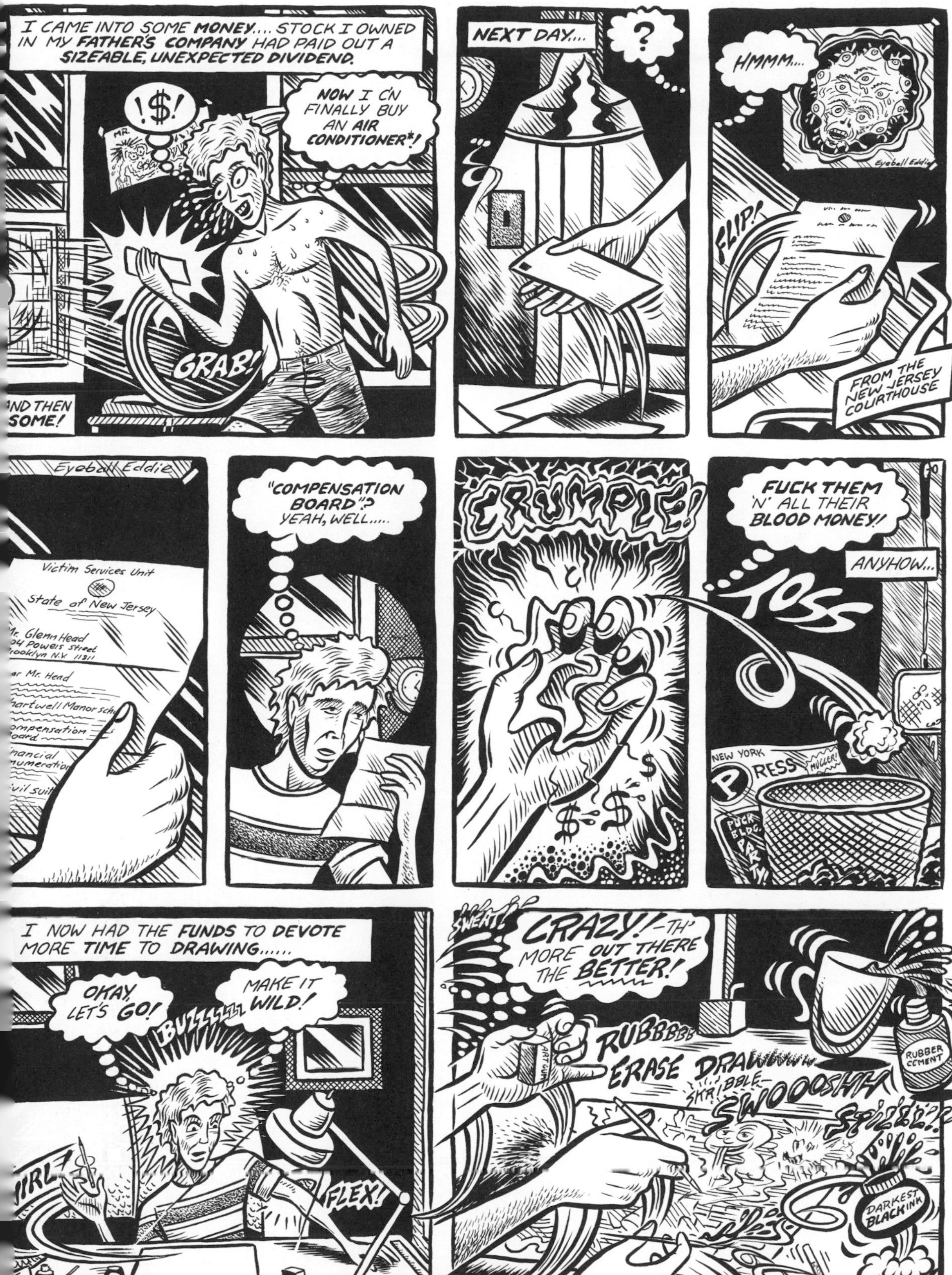

I CAME INTO SOME MONEY.... STOCK I OWNED IN MY FATHER'S COMPANY HAD PAID OUT A SIZEABLE, UNEXPECTED DIVIDEND.
!$!
NOW I C'N FINALLY BUY AN AIR CONDITIONER*!
GRAB!
AND THEN SOME!
NEXT DAY....
?
HMMM...
Eyeball Eddie
FLIP!
FROM THE NEW JERSEY COURTHOUSE
Eyeball Eddie
Victim Services Unit
State of New Jersey
Mr. Glenn Head
Powers street
Brooklyn N.Y. 11211
Mr. Head
Hartwell Manor sch
compensation board
financial remuneration
civil suit
"COMPENSATION BOARD"? YEAH, WELL.....
CRUMPLE!
FUCK THEM 'N' ALL THEIR BLOOD MONEY!
ANYHOW...
TOSS
NEW YORK PRESS
I NOW HAD THE FUNDS TO DEVOTE MORE TIME TO DRAWING......
OKAY, LET'S GO!
MAKE IT WILD!
BUZZZZZZ
FLEX!
SWEAT!
CRAZY!-TH' MORE OUT THERE THE BETTER!
RUBBBBB
ERASE
DRAWWWW
SKRIBBLE
SWOOOSHH
SPLZZZ
RUBBER CEMENT
DARKEST BLACK INK
DOINK!

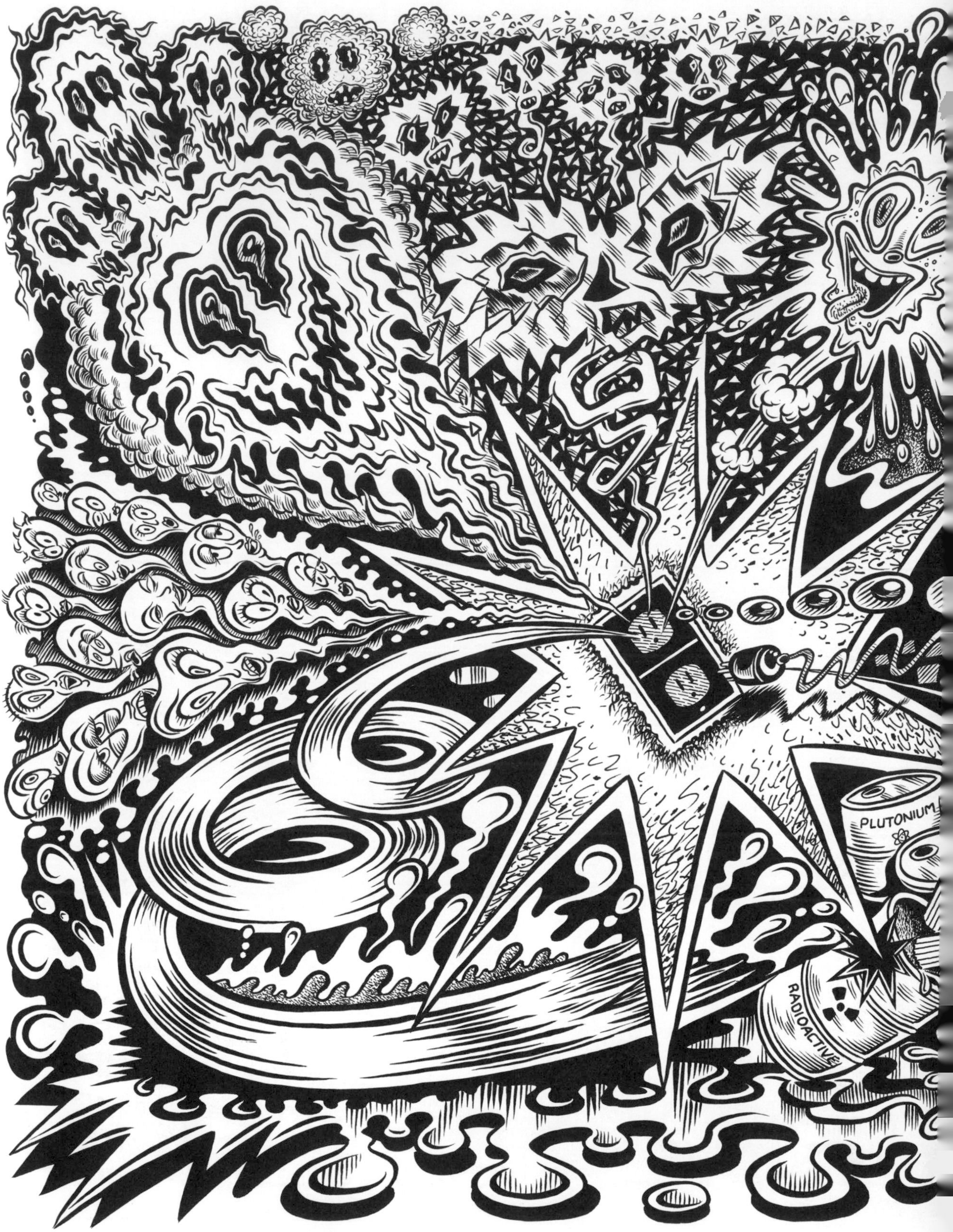
PLUTONIUM
RADIOACTIVE

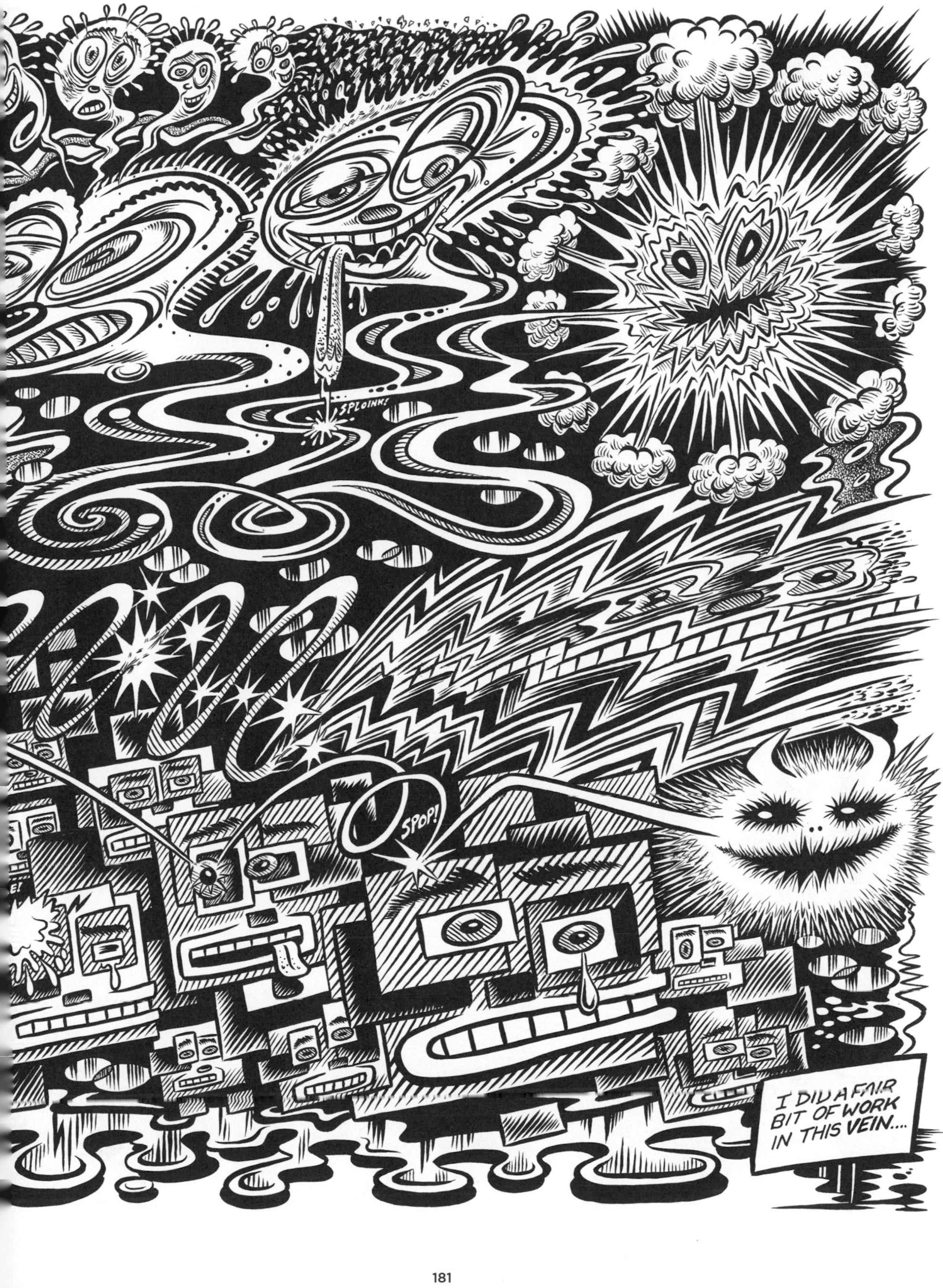
SPLOINK!
SPOP!
I DID A FAIR BIT OF WORK IN THIS VEIN....

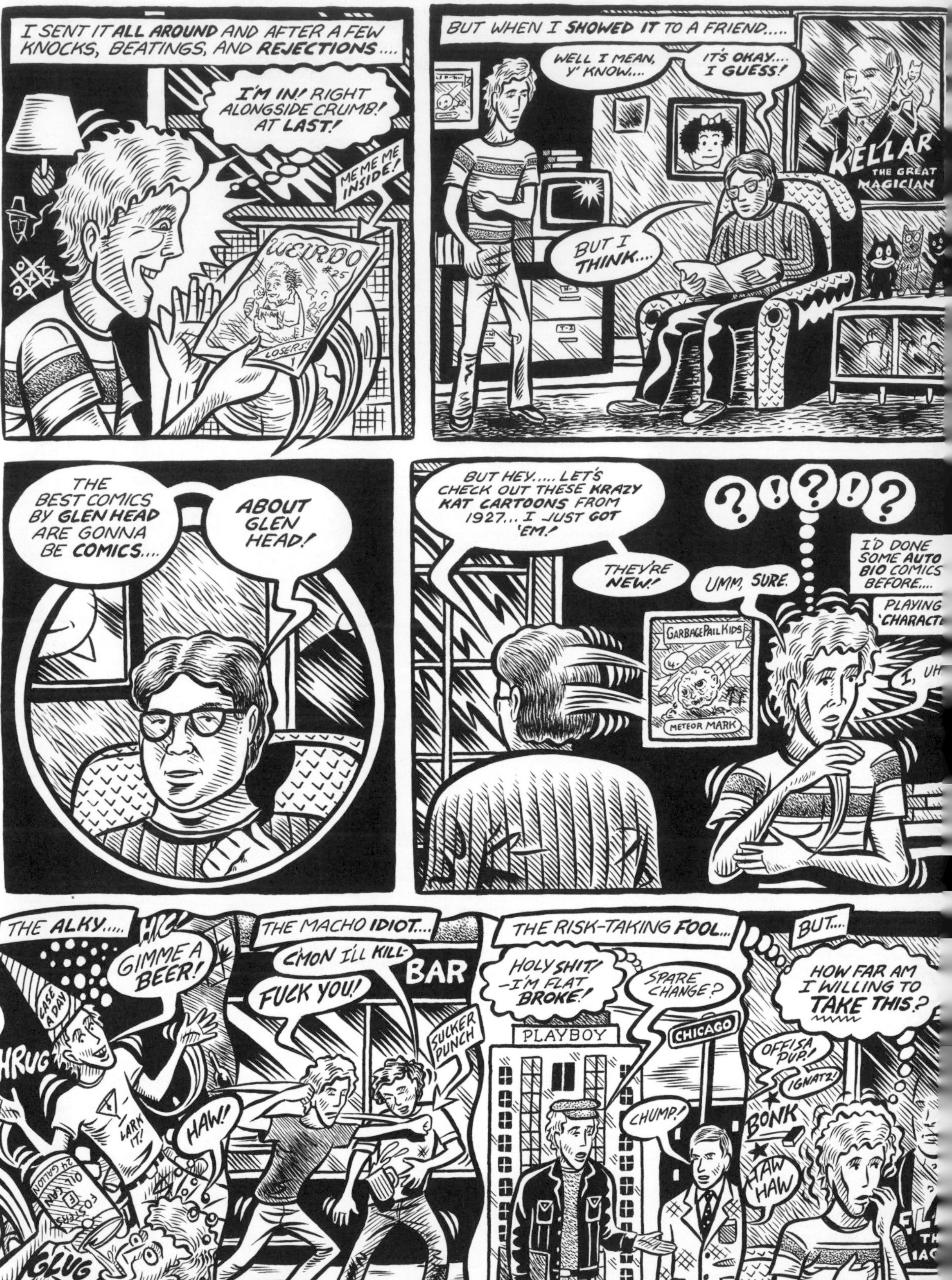

I SENT IT ALL AROUND AND AFTER A FEW KNOCKS, BEATINGS, AND REJECTIONS....
I'M IN! RIGHT ALONGSIDE CRUMB! AT LAST!
ME ME ME INSIDE!
WEIRDO #25
LOSERS!
BUT WHEN I SHOWED IT TO A FRIEND.....
WELL I MEAN, Y' KNOW....
IT'S OKAY.... I GUESS!
BUT I THINK....
KELLAR THE GREAT MAGICIAN
THE BEST COMICS BY GLEN HEAD ARE GONNA BE COMICS....
ABOUT GLEN HEAD!
BUT HEY..... LET'S CHECK OUT THESE KRAZY KAT CARTOONS FROM 1927... I JUST GOT 'EM!
THEY'RE NEW!
UMM, SURE.
?!?!?
I'D DONE SOME AUTO BIO COMICS BEFORE....
PLAYING
GARBAGE PAIL KIDS
METEOR MARK
I, UH
THE ALKY.....
HIC!
GIMME A BEER!
CASE A DAY
SHRUG
LARK IT!
HAW!
24 GALLON OIL CAN
FOSTERS
GLUG
MORE! NOW!
THE MACHO IDIOT....
C'MON I'LL KILL-
FUCK YOU!
BAR
SUCKER PUNCH
THE RISK-TAKING FOOL...
HOLY SHIT! -I'M FLAT BROKE!
SPARE CHANGE?
PLAYBOY
CHICAGO
CHUMP!
BUT....
HOW FAR AM I WILLING TO TAKE THIS?
OFFISA PUP!
IGNATZ!
BONK
HAW HAW

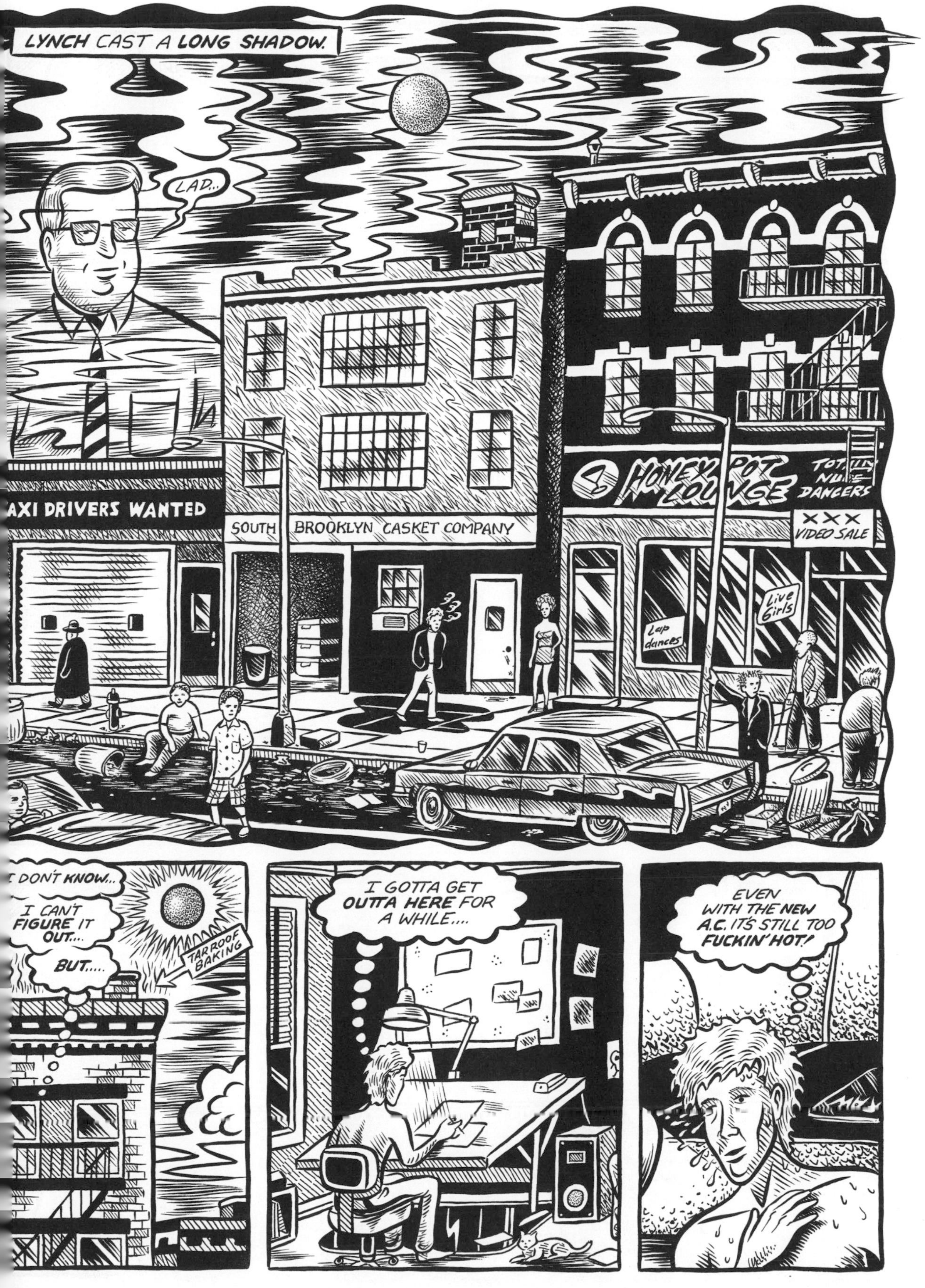
LYNCH CAST A LONG SHADOW.
LAD..
AXI DRIVERS WANTED
SOUTH BROOKLYN CASKET COMPANY
HONEY POT LOUNGE
DANCERS
XXX VIDEO SALE
Live Girls
Lap dances
I DON'T KNOW... I CAN'T FIGURE IT OUT.... BUT....
TAR ROOF BAKING
I GOTTA GET OUTTA HERE FOR A WHILE....
EVEN WITH THE NEW A.C. IT'S STILL TOO FUCKIN' HOT!

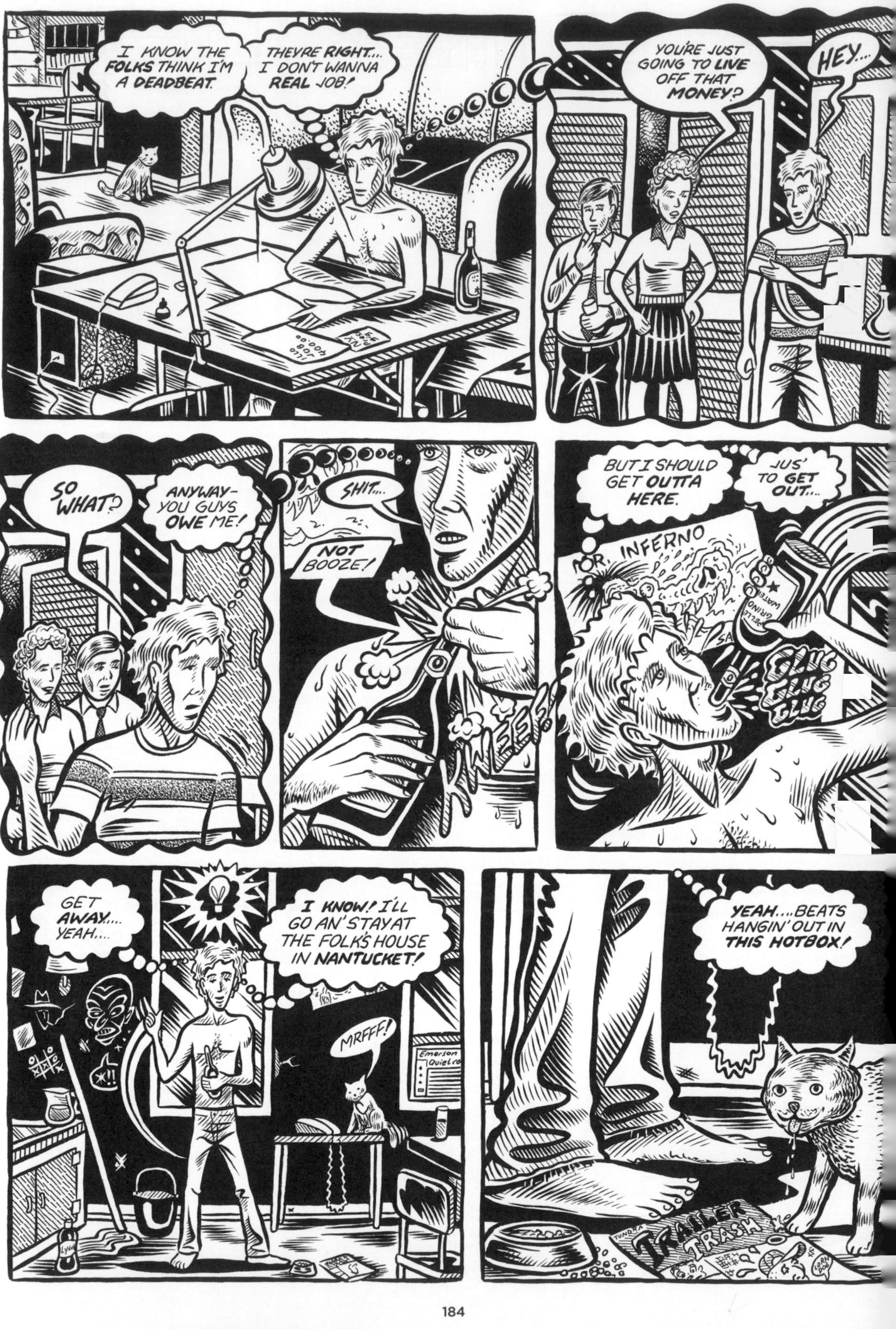

I KNOW THE FOLKS THINK I'M A DEADBEAT.
THEY'RE RIGHT.... I DON'T WANNA REAL JOB!
JOB 400.00
YOU'RE JUST GOING TO LIVE OFF THAT MONEY?
HEY...
SO WHAT?
ANYWAY- YOU GUYS OWE ME!
SHIT....
NOT BOOZE!
BUT I SHOULD GET OUTTA HERE.
JUS' TO GET OUT....
INFERNO
GET AWAY.... YEAH....
I KNOW! I'LL GO AN' STAY AT THE FOLK'S HOUSE IN NANTUCKET!
MRFFF!
Emerson
YEAH.... BEATS HANGIN' OUT IN THIS HOTBOX!
TRAILER TRASH

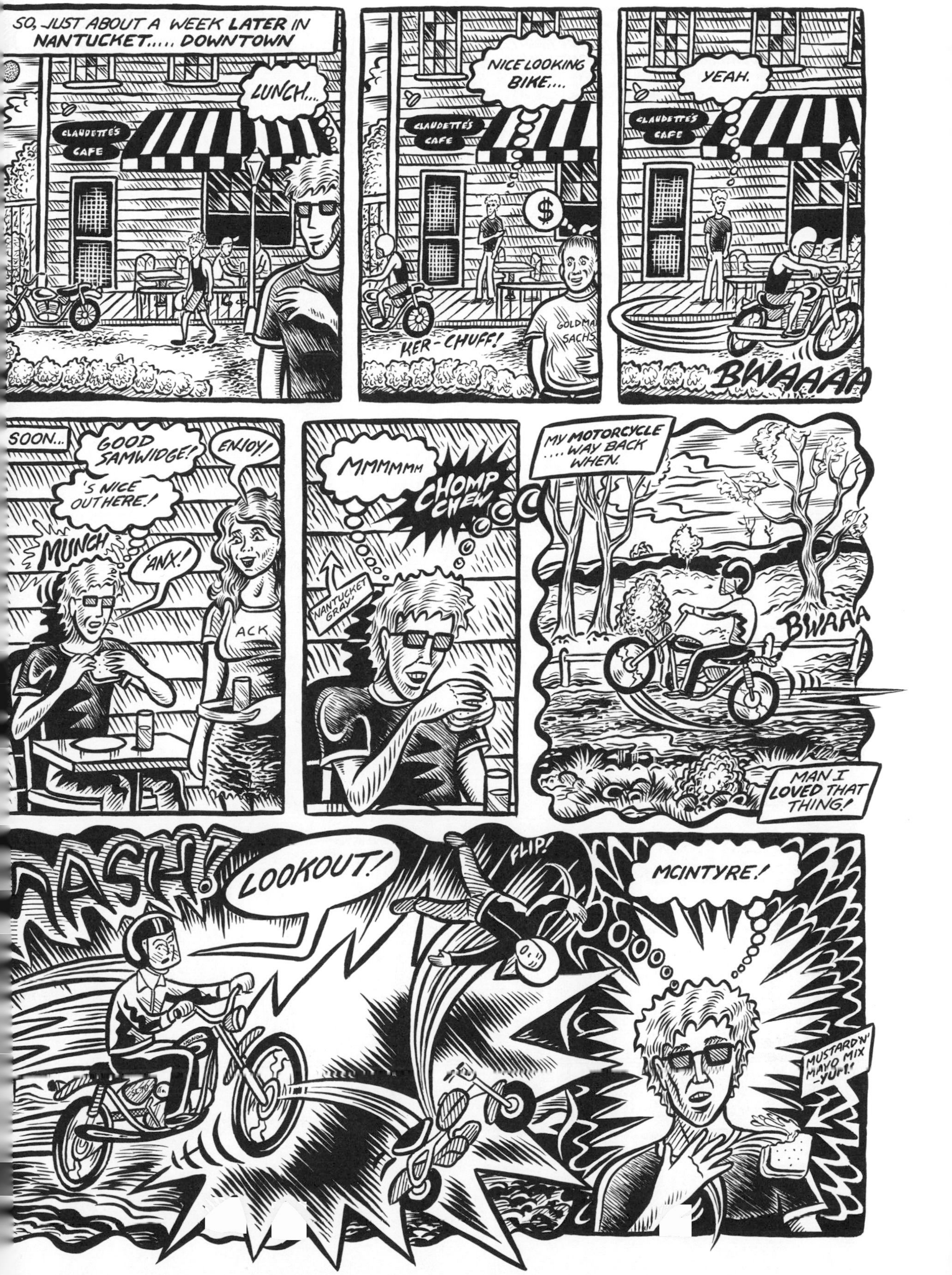
SO, JUST ABOUT A WEEK LATER IN NANTUCKET..... DOWNTOWN
CLAUDETTE'S CAFE
LUNCH...
NICE LOOKING BIKE....
$
KER-CHUFF!
GOLDMAN SACHS
YEAH.
BWAAAA
SOON...
GOOD SAMWIDGE!
ENJOY!
'S NICE OUT HERE!
MUNCH
'ANX!
ACK
MMMMMM
CHOMP CHEW
NANTUCKET GRAY
MY MOTORCYCLE .... WAY BACK WHEN.
BWAAA
MAN I LOVED THAT THING!
LOOKOUT!
FLIP!
MCINTYRE!
HONDA
MUSTARD 'N' MAYO MIX -YUM!

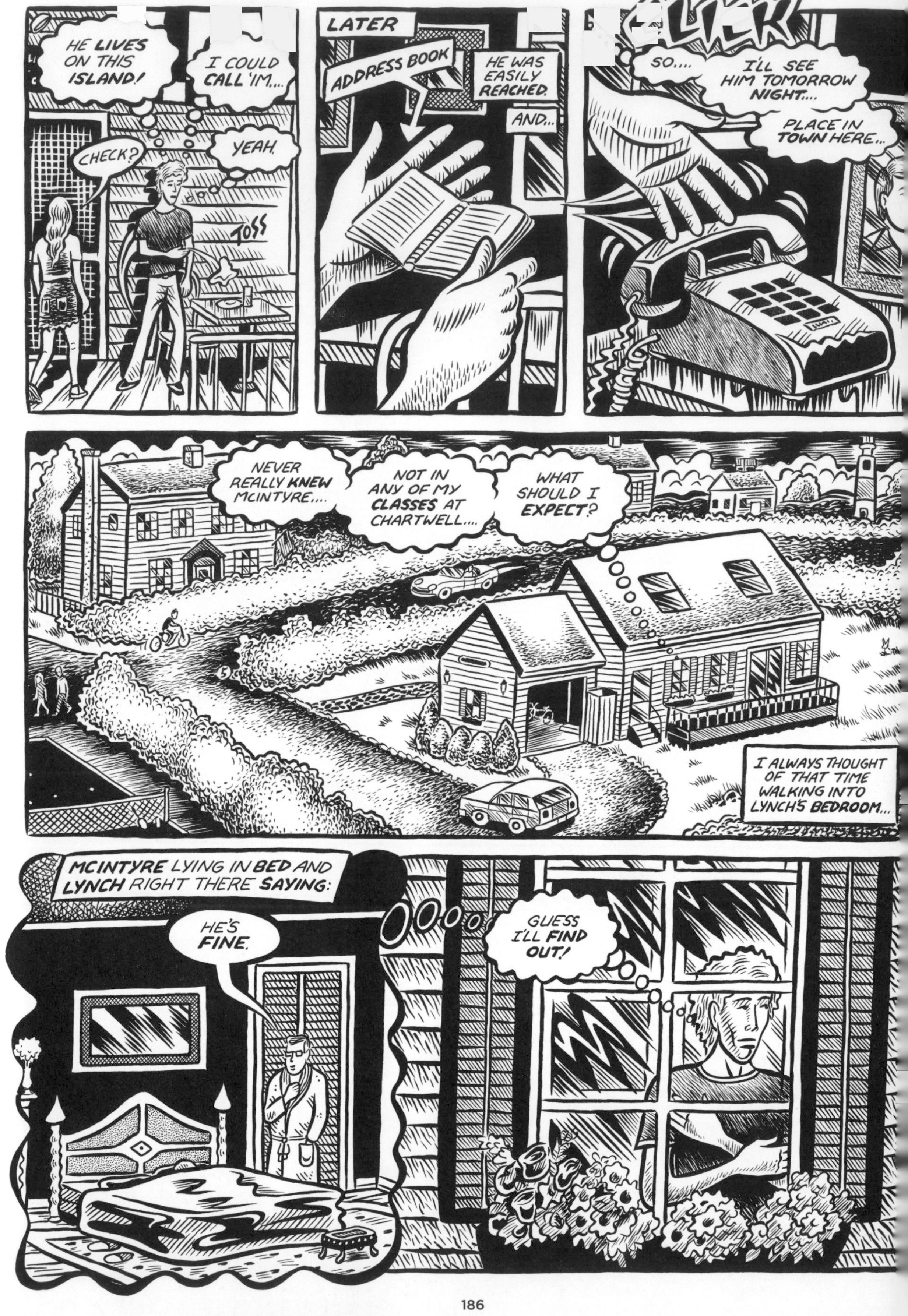
HE LIVES ON THIS ISLAND!
I COULD CALL 'IM....
CHECK?
YEAH.
LATER
ADDRESS BOOK
HE WAS EASILY REACHED.
AND...
SO....
I'LL SEE HIM TOMORROW NIGHT....
PLACE IN TOWN HERE...
NEVER REALLY KNEW MCINTYRE....
NOT IN ANY OF MY CLASSES AT CHARTWELL....
WHAT SHOULD I EXPECT?
I ALWAYS THOUGHT OF THAT TIME WALKING INTO LYNCH'S BEDROOM...
MCINTYRE LYING IN BED AND LYNCH RIGHT THERE SAYING:
HE'S FINE.
GUESS I'LL FIND OUT!

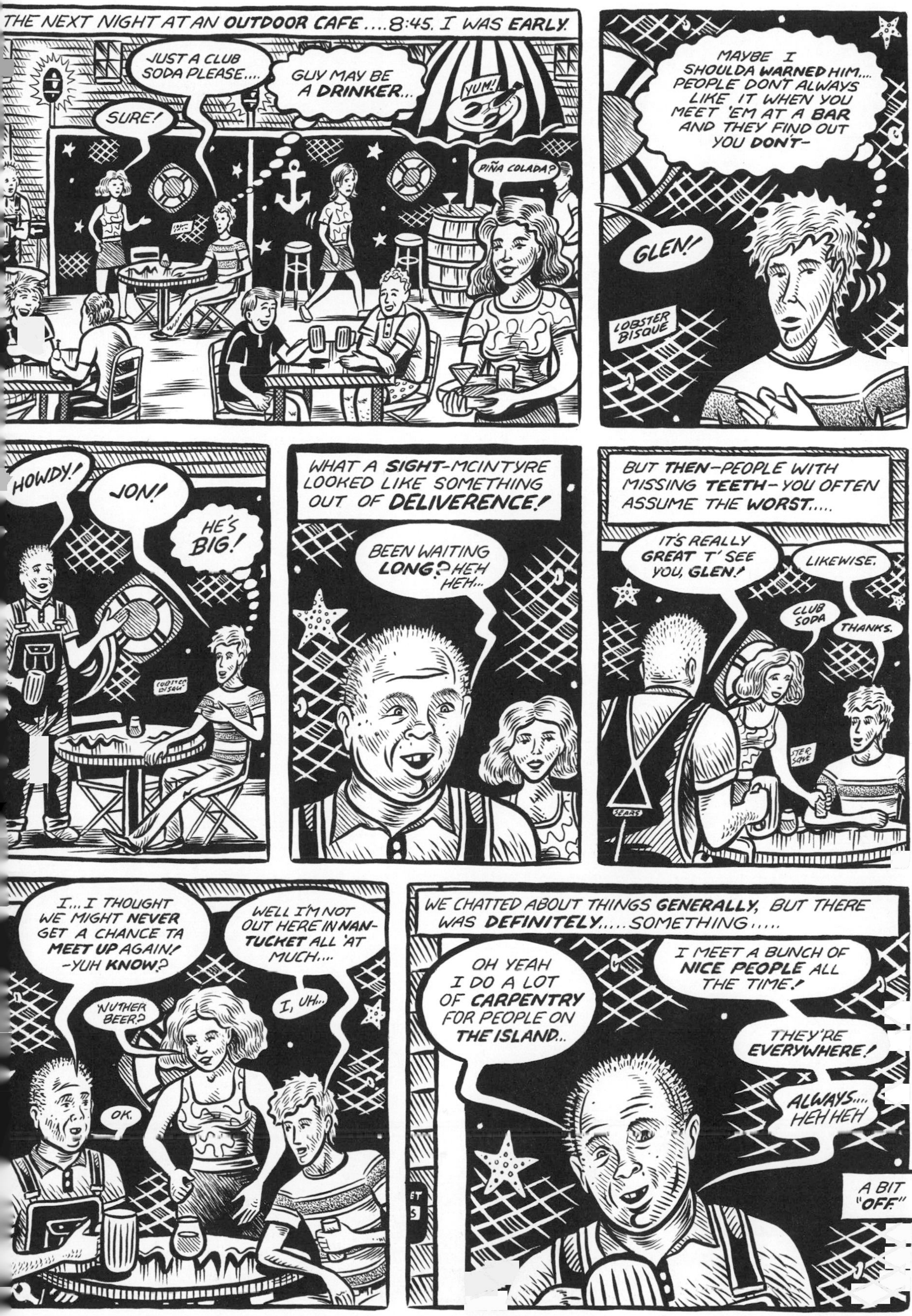
THE NEXT NIGHT AT AN OUTDOOR CAFE....8:45. I WAS EARLY.
JUST A CLUB SODA PLEASE....
SURE!
GUY MAY BE A DRINKER...
YUM!
PIÑA COLADA?
MAYBE I SHOULDA WARNED HIM... PEOPLE DONT ALWAYS LIKE IT WHEN YOU MEET 'EM AT A BAR AND THEY FIND OUT YOU DON'T-
GLEN!
LOBSTER BISQUE
HOWDY!
JON!
HE'S BIG!
WHAT A SIGHT-MCINTYRE LOOKED LIKE SOMETHING OUT OF DELIVERENCE!
BEEN WAITING LONG? HEH HEH...
BUT THEN-PEOPLE WITH MISSING TEETH-YOU OFTEN ASSUME THE WORST.....
IT'S REALLY GREAT T' SEE YOU, GLEN!
LIKEWISE.
CLUB SODA
THANKS.
I...I THOUGHT WE MIGHT NEVER GET A CHANCE TA MEET UP AGAIN! -YUH KNOW?
WELL I'M NOT OUT HERE IN NANTUCKET ALL 'AT MUCH....
I, UH...
'NUTHER BEER?
OK.
WE CHATTED ABOUT THINGS GENERALLY, BUT THERE WAS DEFINITELY.....SOMETHING.....
OH YEAH I DO A LOT OF CARPENTRY FOR PEOPLE ON THE ISLAND...
I MEET A BUNCH OF NICE PEOPLE ALL THE TIME!
THEY'RE EVERYWHERE!
ALWAYS.... HEH HEH
A BIT "OFF."

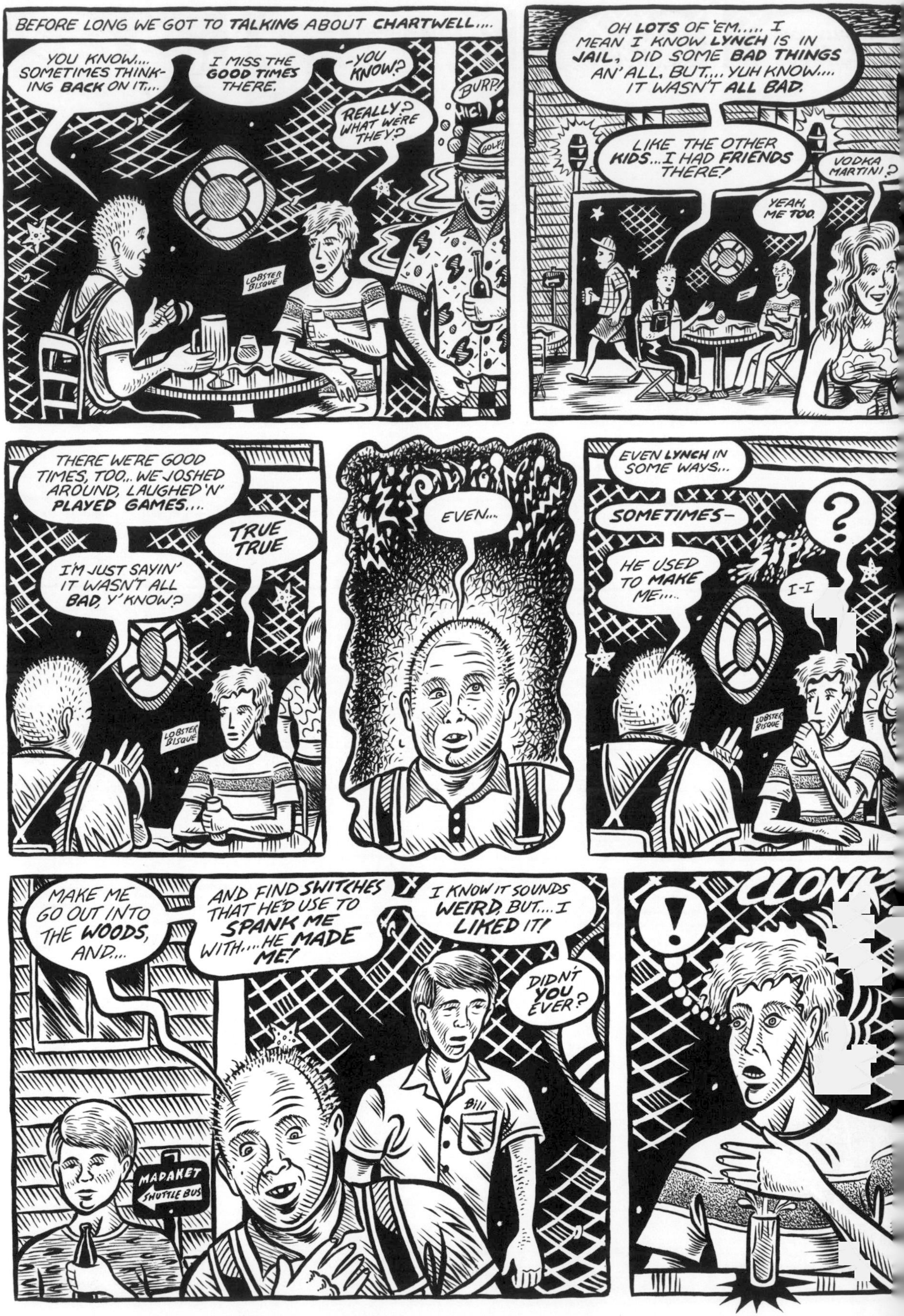

BEFORE LONG WE GOT TO TALKING ABOUT CHARTWELL....
YOU KNOW... SOMETIMES THINKING BACK ON IT...
I MISS THE GOOD TIMES THERE.
-YOU KNOW?
BURP
HIC!
REALLY? WHAT WERE THEY?
GOLF!
LOBSTER BISQUE
OH LOTS OF 'EM..... I MEAN I KNOW LYNCH IS IN JAIL, DID SOME BAD THINGS AN' ALL, BUT.... YUH KNOW.... IT WASN'T ALL BAD.
LIKE THE OTHER KIDS... I HAD FRIENDS THERE!
VODKA MARTINI?
YEAH, ME TOO.
THERE WERE GOOD TIMES, TOO... WE JOSHED AROUND, LAUGHED 'N' PLAYED GAMES....
TRUE TRUE
I'M JUST SAYIN' IT WASN'T ALL BAD, Y'KNOW?
LOBSTER BISQUE
EVEN...
EVEN LYNCH IN SOME WAYS...
SOMETIMES-
?
SIP!
HE USED TO MAKE ME....
I-I
LOBSTER BISQUE
MAKE ME GO OUT INTO THE WOODS, AND...
AND FIND SWITCHES THAT HE'D USE TO SPANK ME WITH.... HE MADE ME!
I KNOW IT SOUNDS WEIRD, BUT.... I LIKED IT!
DIDN'T YOU EVER?
Bill
MADAKET SHUTTLE BUS
CLONK
!

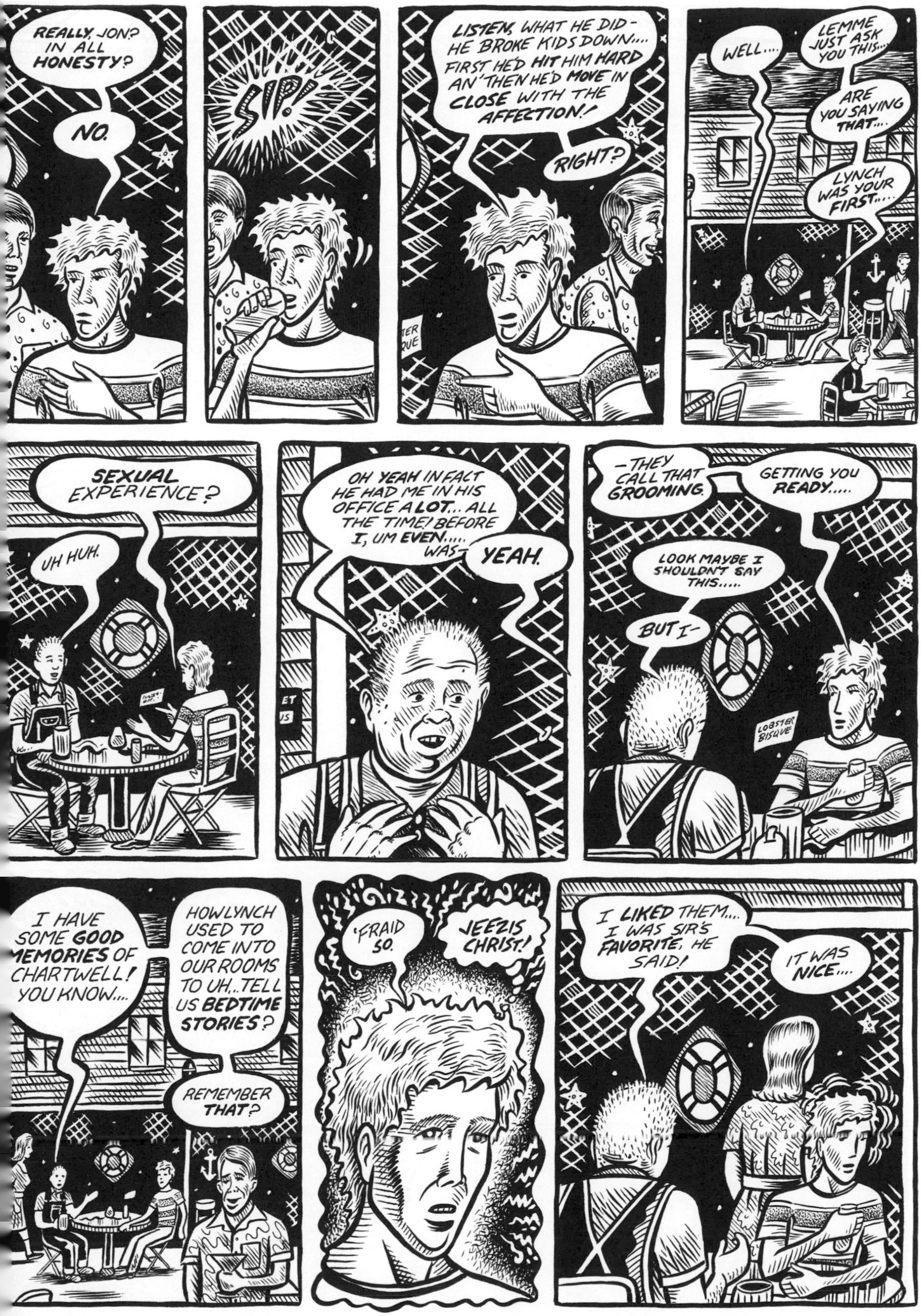
REALLY, JON? IN ALL HONESTY?
NO.
SIP!
LISTEN, WHAT HE DID- HE BROKE KIDS DOWN... FIRST HE'D HIT HIM HARD AN' THEN HE'D MOVE IN CLOSE WITH THE AFFECTION!
RIGHT?
WELL....
LEMME JUST ASK YOU THIS...
ARE YOU SAYING THAT...
LYNCH WAS YOUR FIRST.....
SEXUAL EXPERIENCE?
UH HUH.
OH YEAH IN FACT HE HAD ME IN HIS OFFICE A LOT... ALL THE TIME! BEFORE I, UM EVEN..... WAS-
YEAH.
-THEY CALL THAT GROOMING.
GETTING YOU READY.....
LOOK MAYBE I SHOULDN'T SAY THIS.....
BUT I-
LOBSTER BISQUE
I HAVE SOME GOOD MEMORIES OF CHARTWELL! YOU KNOW....
HOW LYNCH USED TO COME INTO OUR ROOMS TO UH,.. TELL US BEDTIME STORIES?
REMEMBER THAT?
'FRAID SO.
JEEZIS CHRIST!
I LIKED THEM... I WAS SIR'S FAVORITE, HE SAID!
IT WAS NICE....

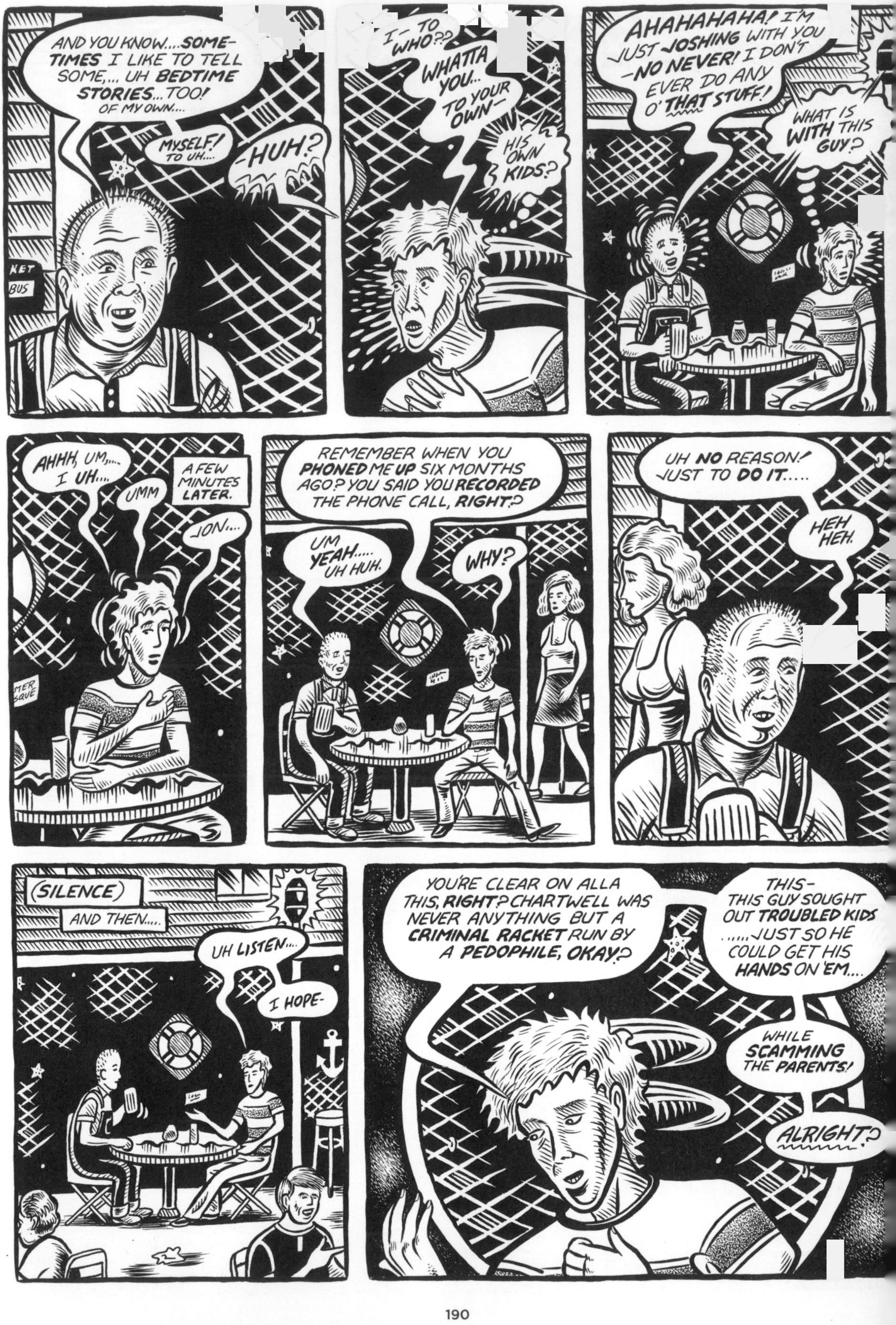
AND YOU KNOW....SOME-TIMES I LIKE TO TELL SOME,... UH BEDTIME STORIES...TOO! OF MY OWN....
MYSELF! TO UH...
-HUH?
KET
BUS
I- TO WHO??
WHATTA YOU... TO YOUR OWN-
HIS OWN KIDS?
AHAHAHAHA! I'M JUST JOSHING WITH YOU -NO NEVER! I DON'T EVER DO ANY O' THAT STUFF!
WHAT IS WITH THIS GUY?
AHHH, UM,... I UH....
A FEW MINUTES LATER.
UMM
JON...
REMEMBER WHEN YOU PHONED ME UP SIX MONTHS AGO? YOU SAID YOU RECORDED THE PHONE CALL, RIGHT?
UM YEAH..... UH HUH.
WHY?
UH NO REASON! JUST TO DO IT.....
HEH HEH.
(SILENCE)
AND THEN.....
UH LISTEN...
I HOPE-
YOU'RE CLEAR ON ALLA THIS, RIGHT? CHARTWELL WAS NEVER ANYTHING BUT A CRIMINAL RACKET RUN BY A PEDOPHILE, OKAY?
THIS- THIS GUY SOUGHT OUT TROUBLED KIDS .....JUST SO HE COULD GET HIS HANDS ON 'EM....
WHILE SCAMMING THE PARENTS!
ALRIGHT?

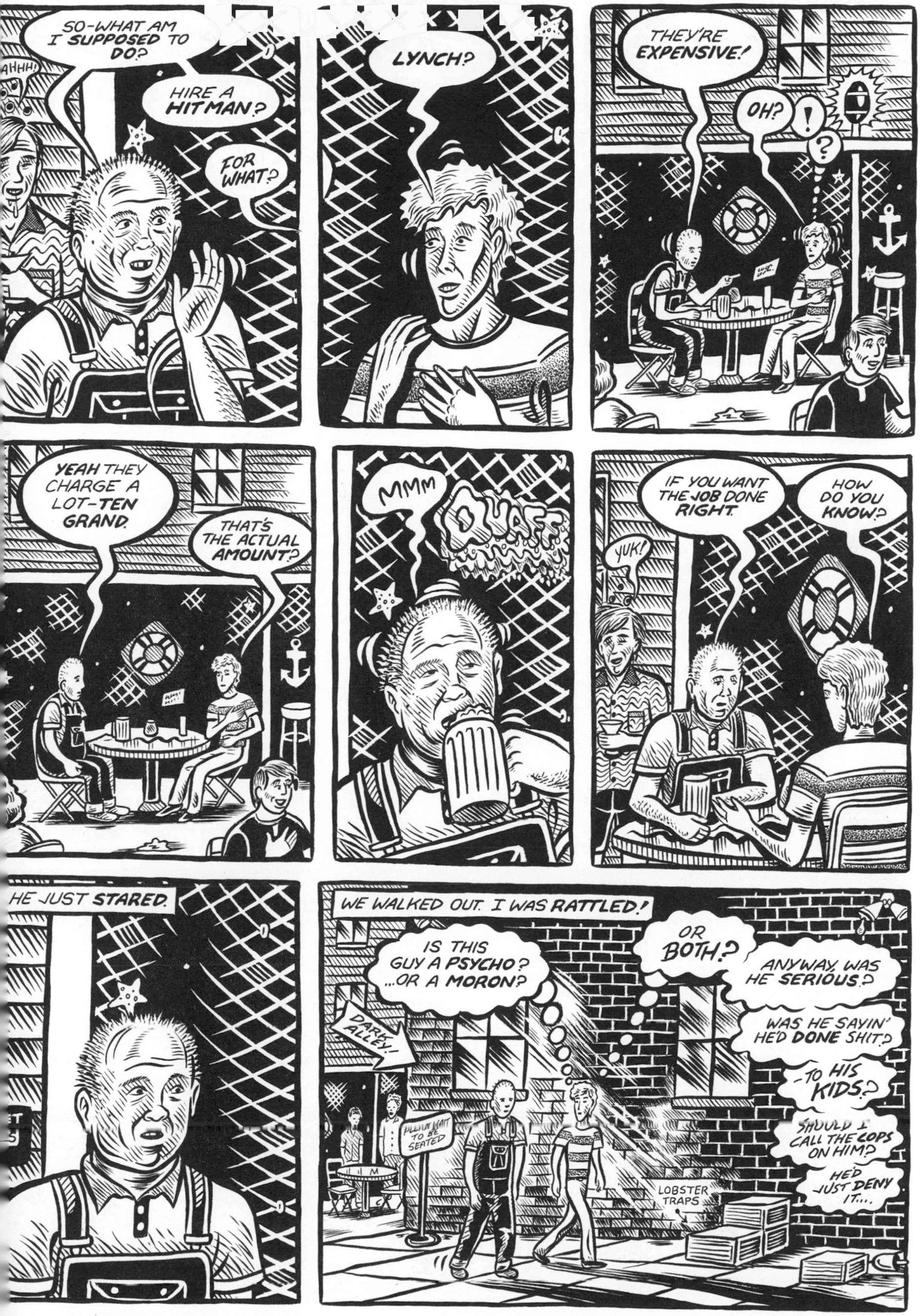

SO-WHAT AM I SUPPOSED TO DO?
HIRE A HITMAN?
FOR WHAT?
LYNCH?
THEY'RE EXPENSIVE!
OH?
!
?
YEAH THEY CHARGE A LOT-TEN GRAND.
THAT'S THE ACTUAL AMOUNT?
MMM
QUAFF
IF YOU WANT THE JOB DONE RIGHT.
HOW DO YOU KNOW?
YUK!
HE JUST STARED.
WE WALKED OUT. I WAS RATTLED!
IS THIS GUY A PSYCHO? ...OR A MORON?
OR BOTH?
ANYWAY, WAS HE SERIOUS?
WAS HE SAYIN' HE'D DONE SHIT?
-TO HIS KIDS?
SHOULD I CALL THE COPS ON HIM?
HE'D JUST DENY IT...
DARK ALLEY
PLEASE WAIT TO BE SEATED
LOBSTER TRAPS

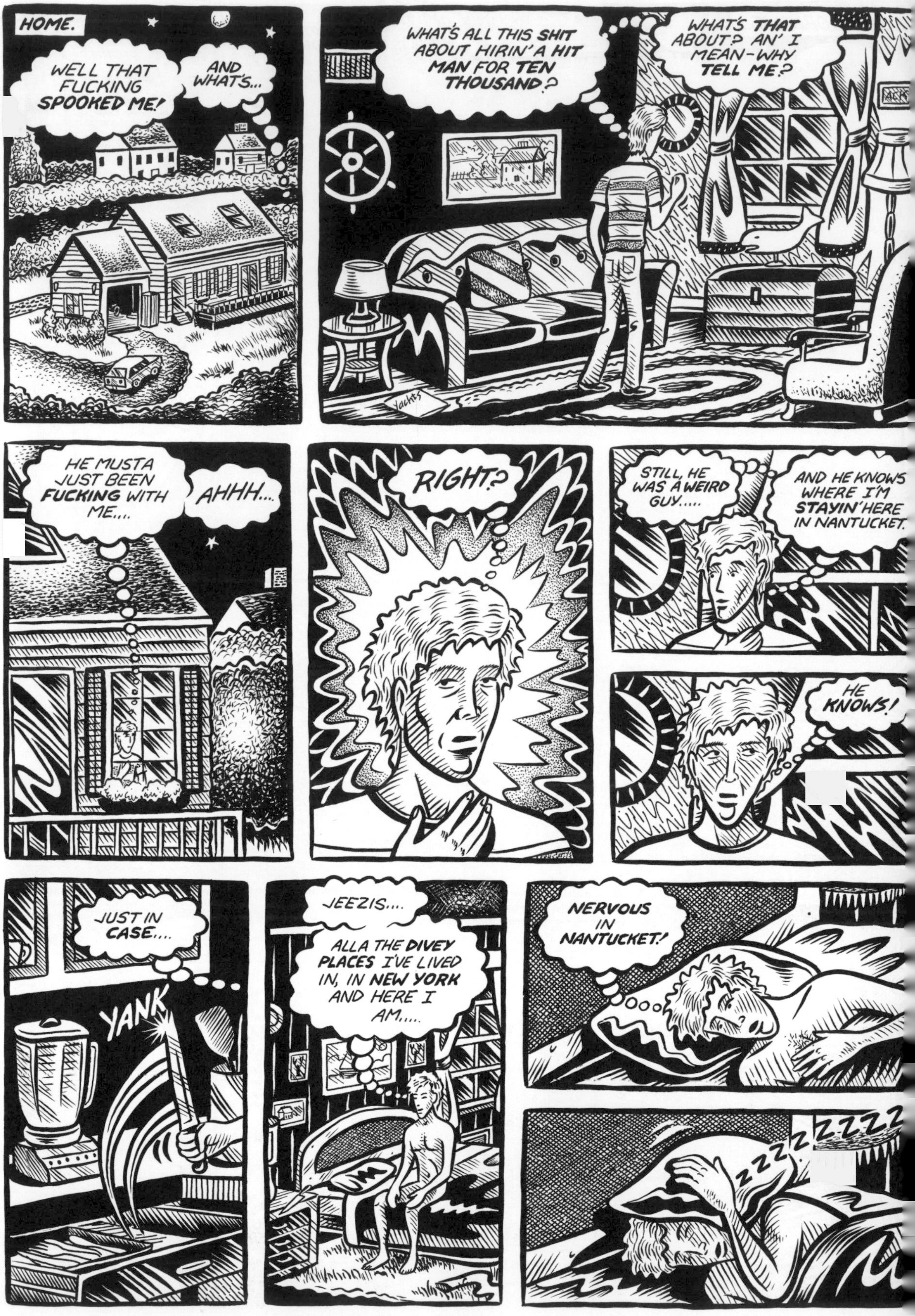
HOME.
WELL THAT FUCKING SPOOKED ME!
AND WHAT'S...
WHAT'S ALL THIS SHIT ABOUT HIRIN' A HIT MAN FOR TEN THOUSAND?
WHAT'S THAT ABOUT? AN' I MEAN-WHY TELL ME?
HE MUSTA JUST BEEN FUCKING WITH ME....
AHHH...
RIGHT?
STILL, HE WAS A WEIRD GUY.....
AND HE KNOWS WHERE I'M STAYIN' HERE IN NANTUCKET.
HE KNOWS!
JUST IN CASE....
YANK
JEEZIS....
ALLA THE DIVEY PLACES I'VE LIVED IN, IN NEW YORK AND HERE I AM....
NERVOUS IN NANTUCKET!
ZZZZZZZZZ

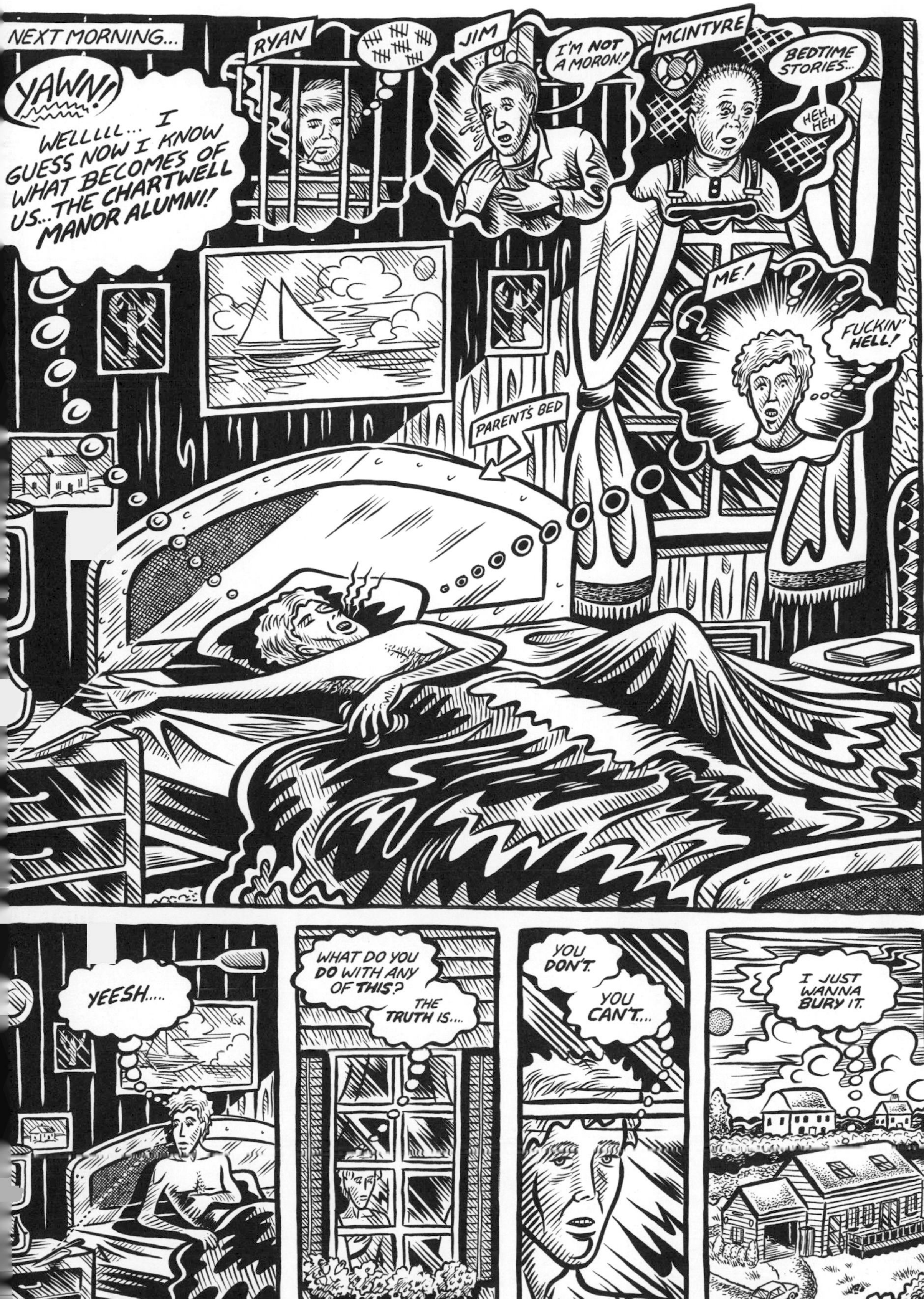
NEXT MORNING...
YAWN!!
WELLLLL... I GUESS NOW I KNOW WHAT BECOMES OF US...THE CHARTWELL MANOR ALUMNI!!
RYAN
JIM
I'M NOT A MORON!
MCINTYRE
BEDTIME STORIES...
HEH HEH
ME!
FUCKIN' HELL!
PARENT'S BED
YEESH.....
WHAT DO YOU DO WITH ANY OF THIS?
THE TRUTH IS....
YOU DON'T.
YOU CAN'T....
I JUST WANNA BURY IT.

RENEWAL

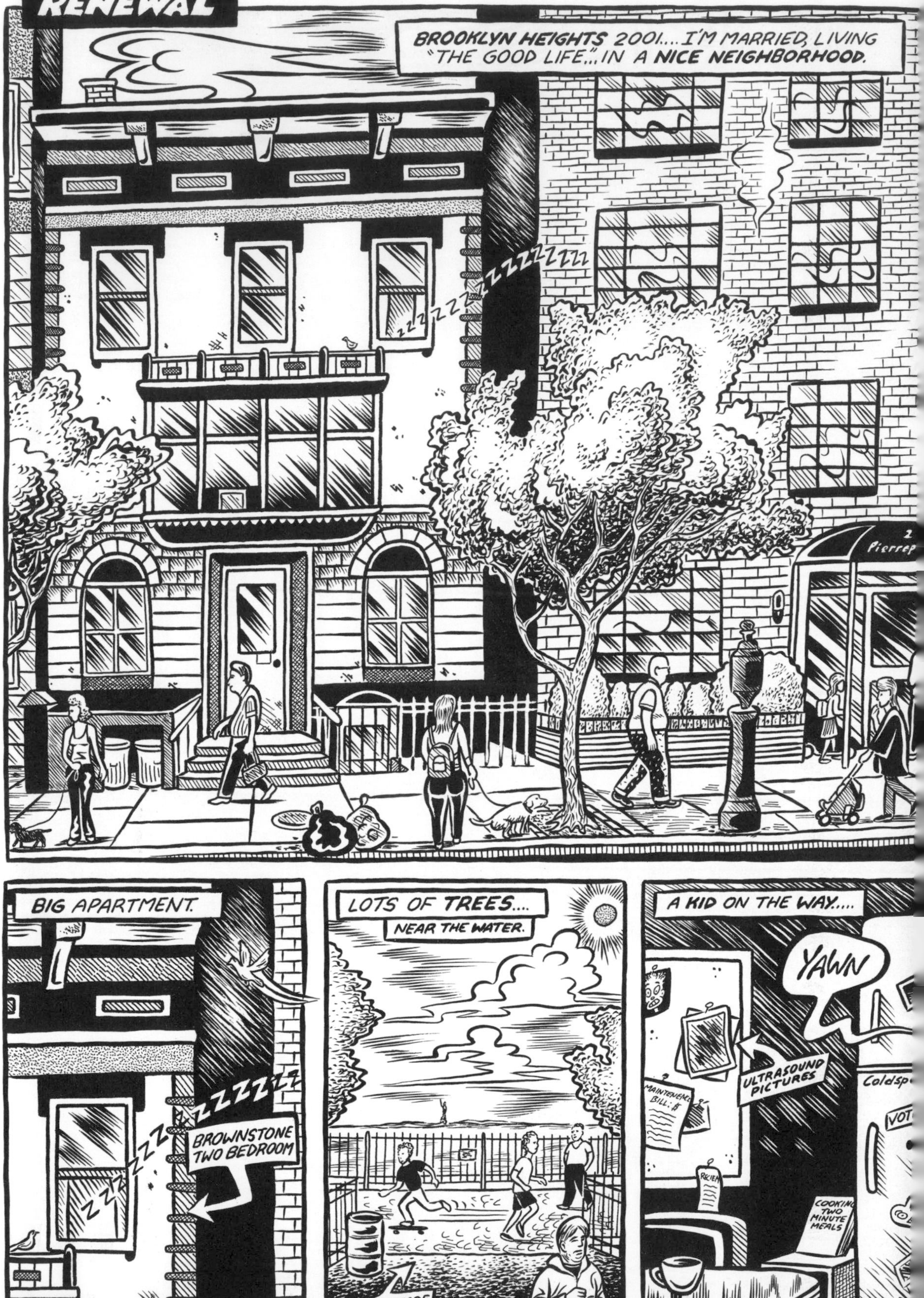
BROOKLYN HEIGHTS 2001.... I'M MARRIED, LIVING "THE GOOD LIFE"... IN A NICE NEIGHBORHOOD.
ZZZZZZZZZZZZZ
BIG APARTMENT.
ZZZZZZZZZZZZ
BROWNSTONE TWO BEDROOM
LOTS OF TREES....
NEAR THE WATER.
PROMENADE
A KID ON THE WAY.....
YAWN
ULTRASOUND PICTURES
COOKING TWO MINUTE MEALS

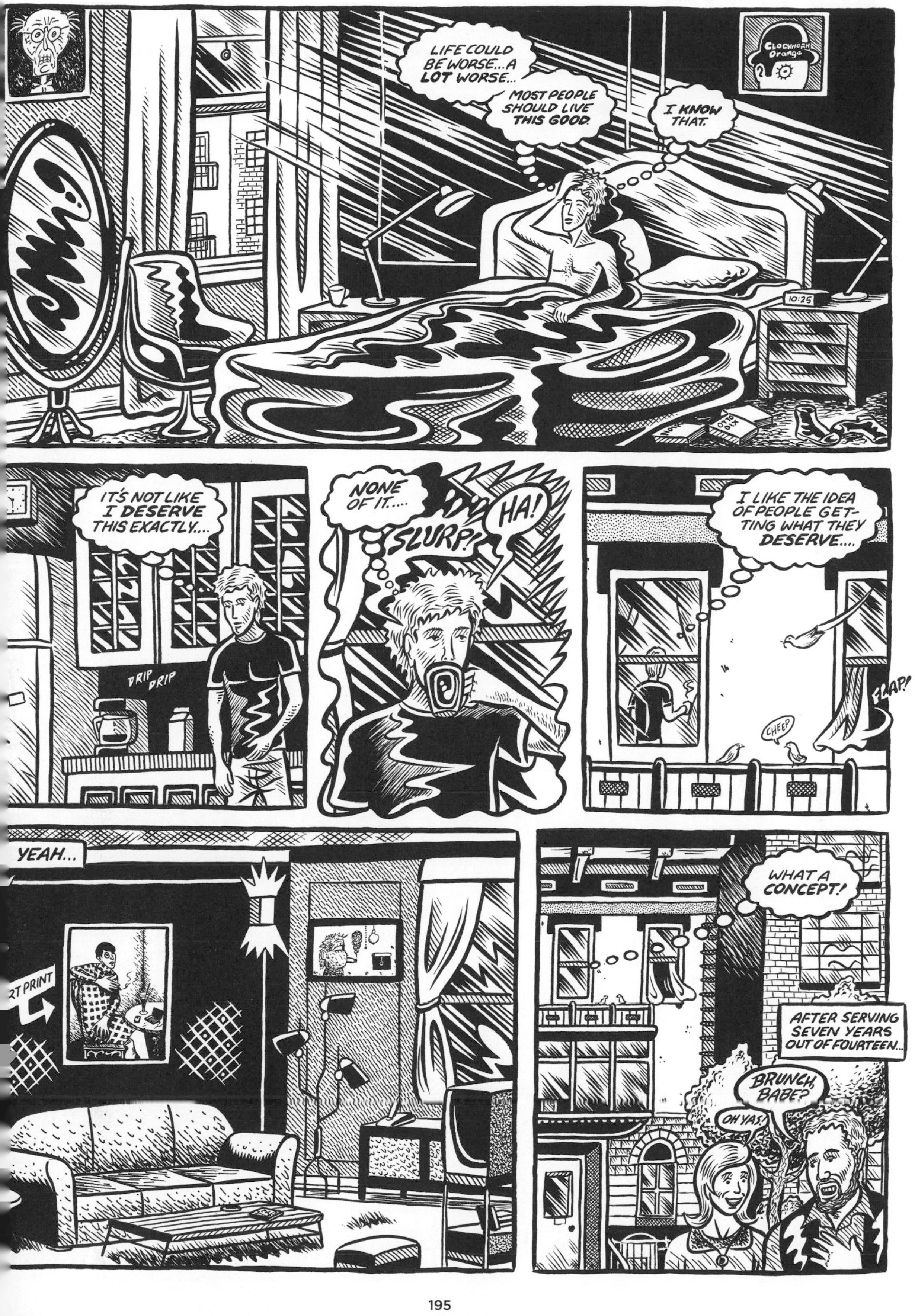

LIFE COULD BE WORSE...A LOT WORSE...
MOST PEOPLE SHOULD LIVE THIS GOOD.
I KNOW THAT.
CLOCKWORK Orange
10:25
IT'S NOT LIKE I DESERVE THIS EXACTLY....
DRIP DRIP
NONE OF IT....
SLURP!
HA!
I LIKE THE IDEA OF PEOPLE GETTING WHAT THEY DESERVE....
CHEEP
FLAP!
YEAH...
RT PRINT
WHAT A CONCEPT!
AFTER SERVING SEVEN YEARS OUT OF FOURTEEN...
BRUNCH, BABE?
OH YAS!

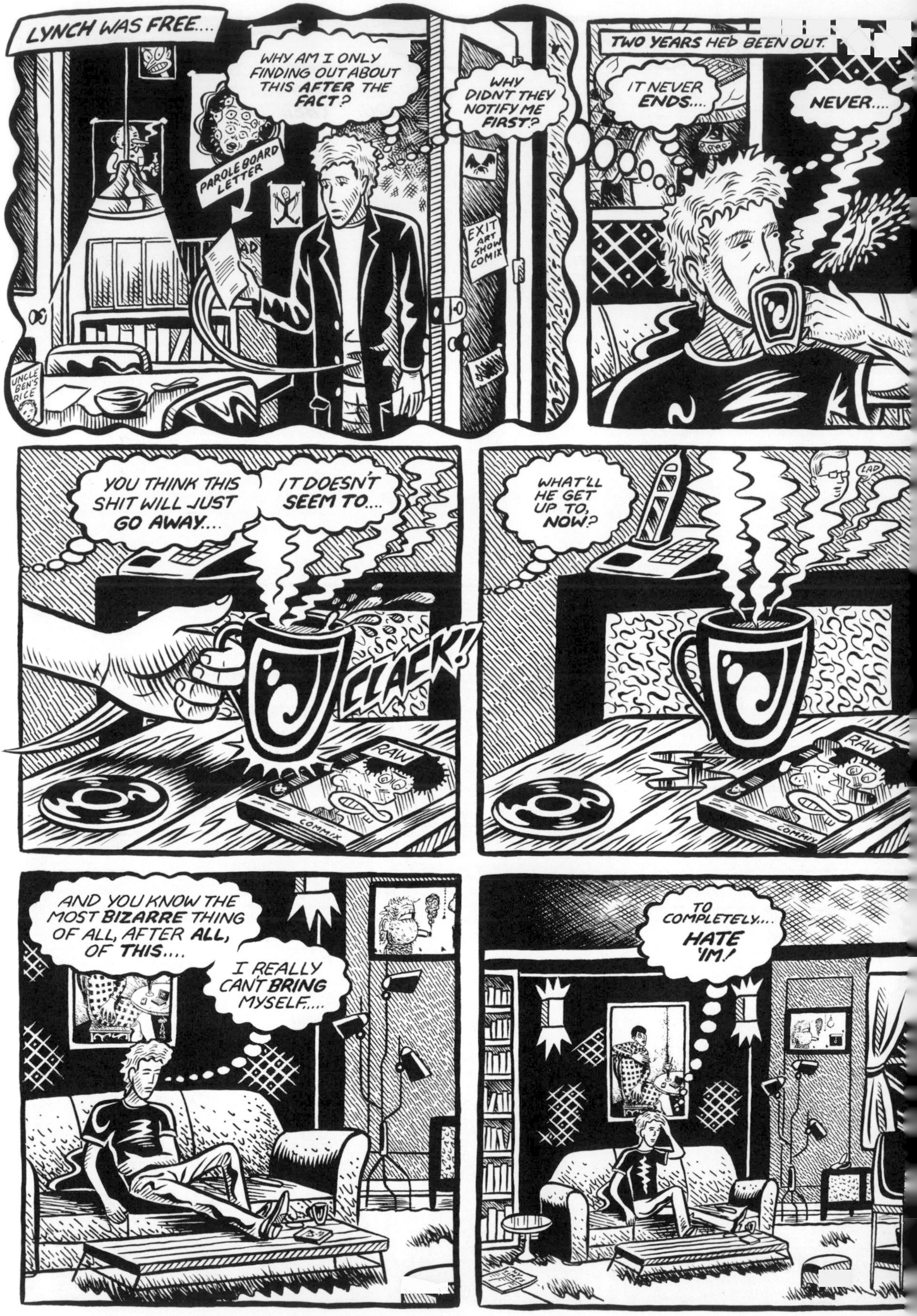

LYNCH WAS FREE....
WHY AM I ONLY FINDING OUT ABOUT THIS AFTER THE FACT?
WHY DIDN'T THEY NOTIFY ME FIRST?
PAROLE BOARD LETTER
EXIT ART SHOW COMIX
UNCLE BEN'S RICE
TWO YEARS HE'D BEEN OUT.
IT NEVER ENDS....
NEVER....
YOU THINK THIS SHIT WILL JUST GO AWAY....
IT DOESN'T SEEM TO....
CLACK!
RAW
COMMIX
WHAT'LL HE GET UP TO, NOW?
RAW
COMMIX
AND YOU KNOW THE MOST BIZARRE THING OF ALL, AFTER ALL, OF THIS....
I REALLY CAN'T BRING MYSELF....
TO COMPLETELY.... HATE 'IM!

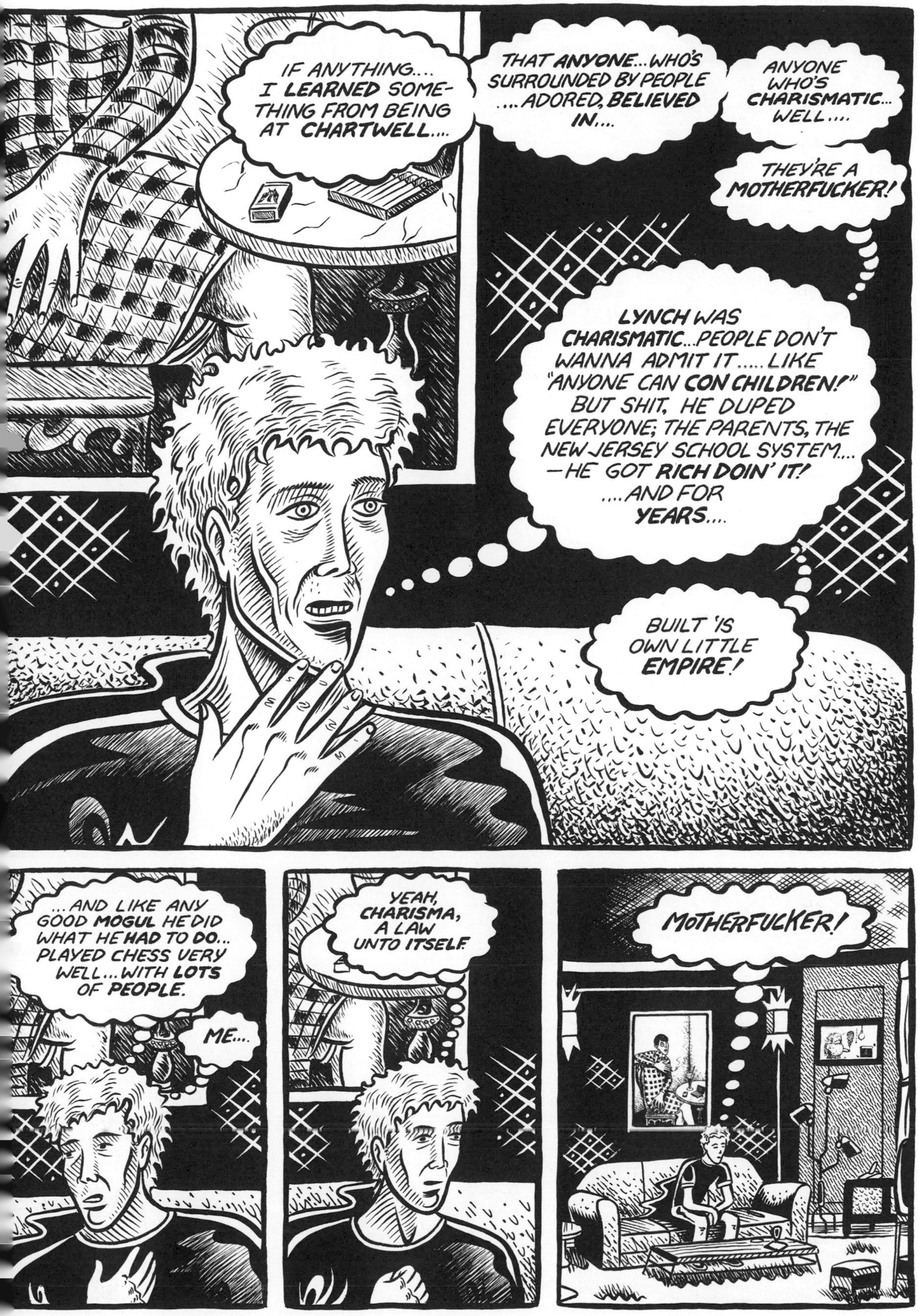
IF ANYTHING.... I LEARNED SOMETHING FROM BEING AT CHARTWELL....
THAT ANYONE...WHO'S SURROUNDED BY PEOPLE ....ADORED, BELIEVED IN....
ANYONE WHO'S CHARISMATIC... WELL....
THEY'RE A MOTHERFUCKER!
LYNCH WAS CHARISMATIC...PEOPLE DON'T WANNA ADMIT IT..... LIKE "ANYONE CAN CON CHILDREN!" BUT SHIT, HE DUPED EVERYONE; THE PARENTS, THE NEW JERSEY SCHOOL SYSTEM.... —HE GOT RICH DOIN' IT! ....AND FOR YEARS....
BUILT 'IS OWN LITTLE EMPIRE!
...AND LIKE ANY GOOD MOGUL HE DID WHAT HE HAD TO DO... PLAYED CHESS VERY WELL...WITH LOTS OF PEOPLE.
ME...
YEAH, CHARISMA, A LAW UNTO ITSELF.
MOTHERFUCKER!

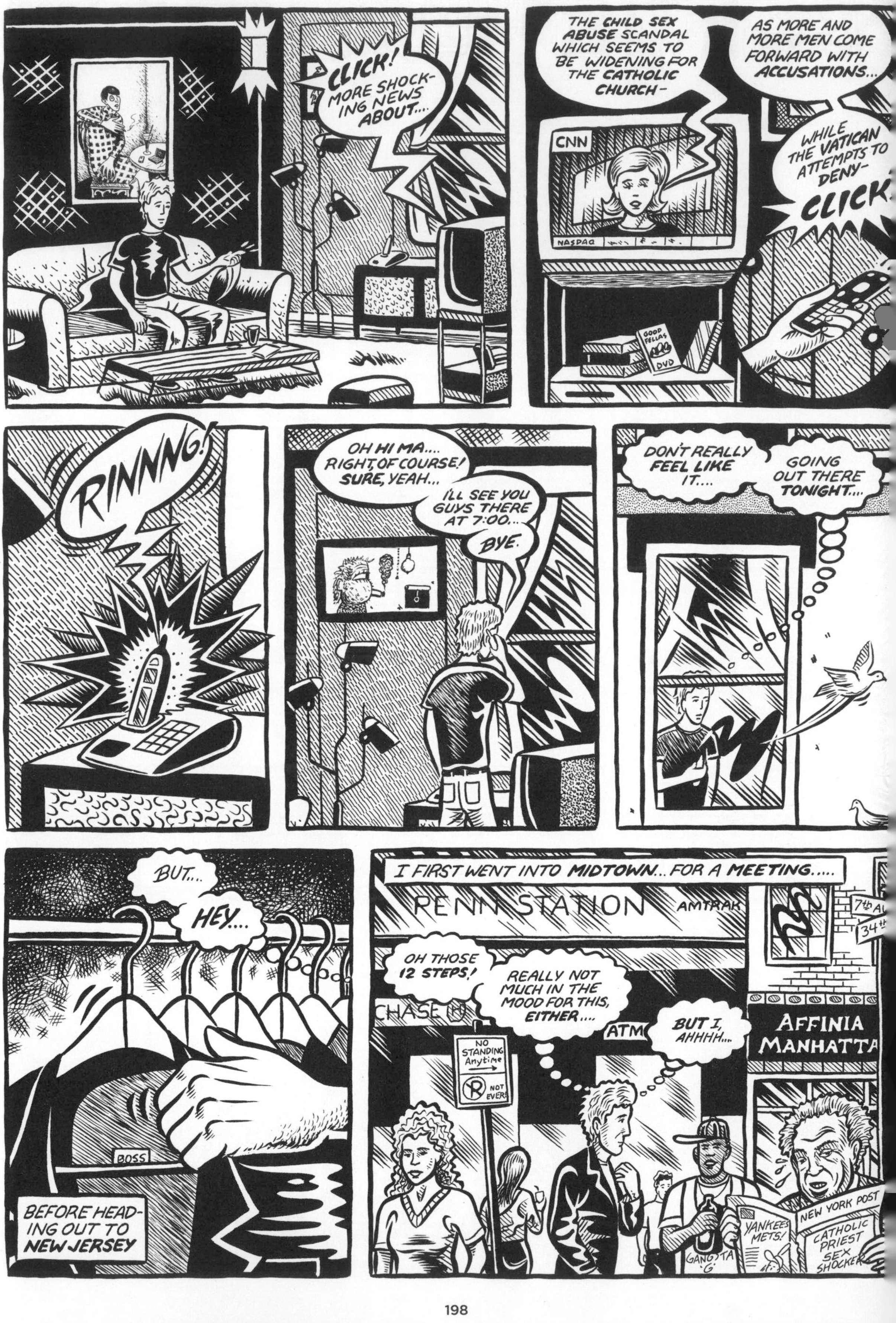
CLICK! MORE SHOCKING NEWS ABOUT....
THE CHILD SEX ABUSE SCANDAL WHICH SEEMS TO BE WIDENING FOR THE CATHOLIC CHURCH-
AS MORE AND MORE MEN COME FORWARD WITH ACCUSATIONS...
WHILE THE VATICAN ATTEMPTS TO DENY-
CLICK
CNN
NASDAQ
GOOD FELLAS DVD
RINNNG!
OH HI MA.... RIGHT, OF COURSE! SURE, YEAH...
I'LL SEE YOU GUYS THERE AT 7:00...
BYE.
DON'T REALLY FEEL LIKE IT....
GOING OUT THERE TONIGHT....
BUT...
HEY....
BOSS
BEFORE HEADING OUT TO NEW JERSEY
I FIRST WENT INTO MIDTOWN... FOR A MEETING.....
PENN STATION
AMTRAK
OH THOSE 12 STEPS!
REALLY NOT MUCH IN THE MOOD FOR THIS, EITHER....
CHASE
ATM
BUT I, AHHHH...
AFFINIA MANHATTA
NO STANDING Anytime
NOT EVER!
NEW YORK POST
YANKEES METS!
CATHOLIC PRIEST SEX SHOCKER
GANGSTA 'G'

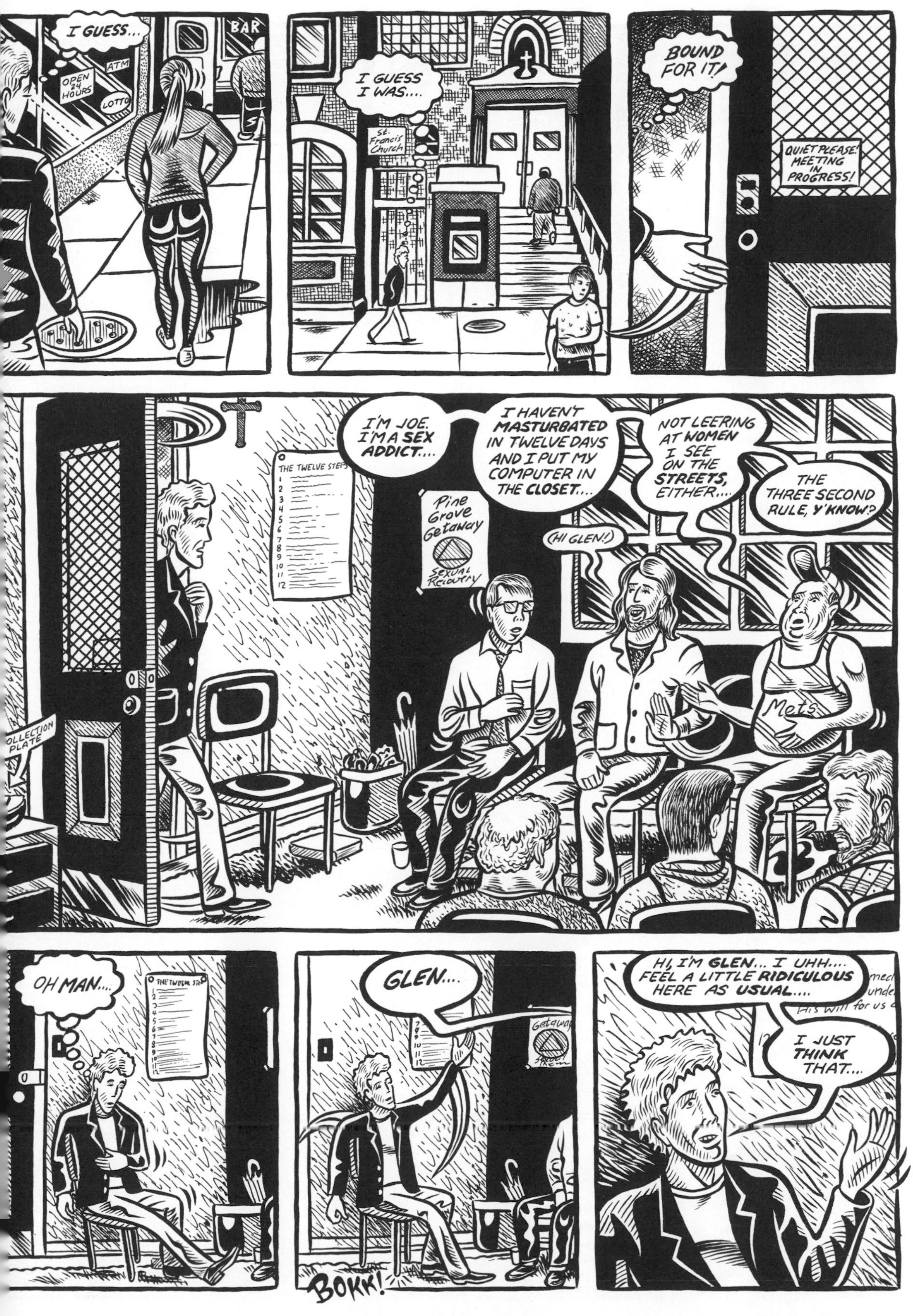
I GUESS...
BAR
OPEN 24 HOURS
ATM
LOTTO
I GUESS I WAS....
St. Francis Church
BOUND FOR IT!
QUIET PLEASE! MEETING IN PROGRESS!
I'M JOE. I'M A SEX ADDICT....
I HAVEN'T MASTURBATED IN TWELVE DAYS AND I PUT MY COMPUTER IN THE CLOSET....
NOT LEERING AT WOMEN I SEE ON THE STREETS, EITHER....
THE THREE SECOND RULE, Y'KNOW?
(HI GLEN!)
THE TWELVE STEPS
Pine Grove Getaway
SEXUAL RECOVERY
COLLECTION PLATE
Mets
OH MAN....
GLEN....
BOKK!
HI, I'M GLEN... I UHH.... FEEL A LITTLE RIDICULOUS HERE AS USUAL....
I JUST THINK THAT....

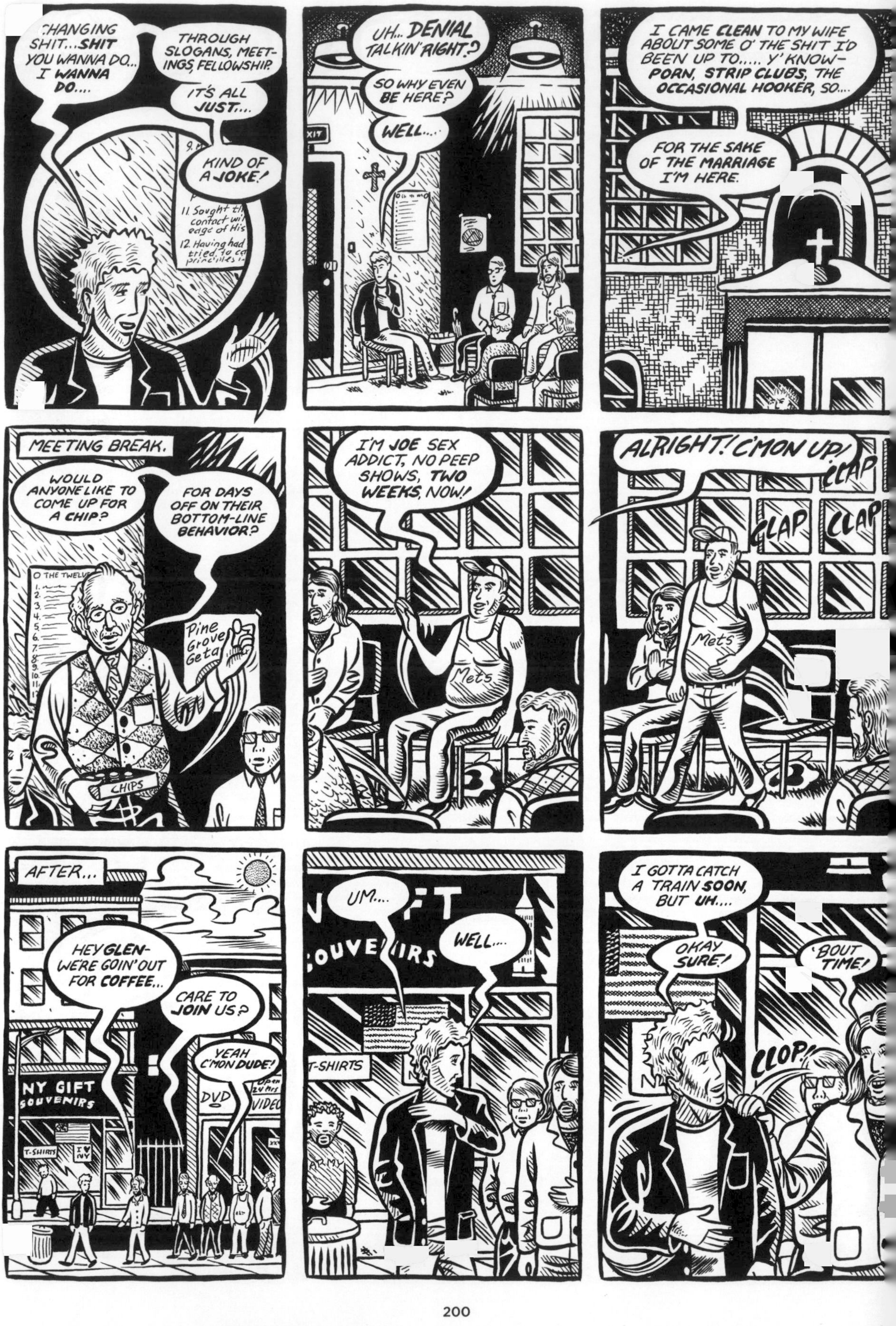
CHANGING SHIT...SHIT YOU WANNA DO... I WANNA DO....
THROUGH SLOGANS, MEETINGS, FELLOWSHIP.
IT'S ALL JUST....
KIND OF A JOKE!
11. Sought th contact wi edge of His
12. Having had tried to ca principles i
UH... DENIAL TALKIN' RIGHT?
SO WHY EVEN BE HERE?
WELL....
I CAME CLEAN TO MY WIFE ABOUT SOME O' THE SHIT I'D BEEN UP TO..... Y'KNOW– PORN, STRIP CLUBS, THE OCCASIONAL HOOKER, SO....
FOR THE SAKE OF THE MARRIAGE I'M HERE.
MEETING BREAK.
WOULD ANYONE LIKE TO COME UP FOR A CHIP?
FOR DAYS OFF ON THEIR BOTTOM-LINE BEHAVIOR?
THE TWELVE
Pine Grove Geta
CHIPS
I'M JOE SEX ADDICT, NO PEEP SHOWS, TWO WEEKS, NOW!
Mets
ALRIGHT! C'MON UP!
CLAP
CLAP
CLAP
Mets
AFTER...
HEY GLEN– WE'RE GOIN' OUT FOR COFFEE...
CARE TO JOIN US?
YEAH C'MON DUDE!
NY GIFT SOUVENIRS
DVD
VIDEO
T-SHIRTS
UM....
WELL....
SOUVENIRS
T-SHIRTS
ARMY
I GOTTA CATCH A TRAIN SOON, BUT UH....
OKAY SURE!
'BOUT TIME!
CLOP!

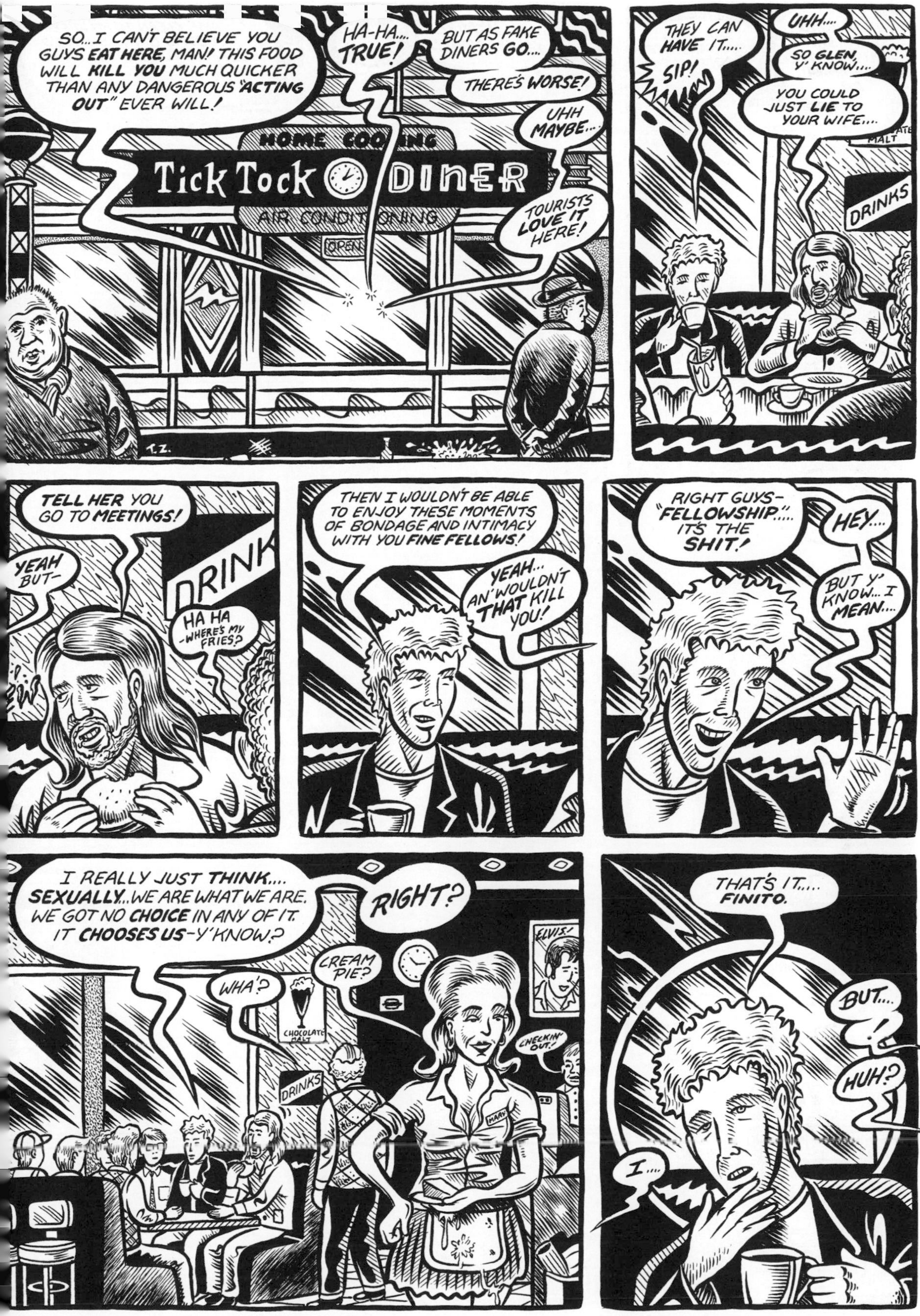

SO...I CAN'T BELIEVE YOU GUYS EAT HERE, MAN! THIS FOOD WILL KILL YOU MUCH QUICKER THAN ANY DANGEROUS "ACTING OUT" EVER WILL!
HA-HA... TRUE!
BUT AS FAKE DINERS GO....
THERE'S WORSE!
UHH MAYBE....
TOURISTS LOVE IT HERE!
HOME COOKING
Tick Tock DINER
AIR CONDITIONING
OPEN
T.Z.
THEY CAN HAVE IT.....
SIP!
UHH...
SO GLEN, Y' KNOW....
YOU COULD JUST LIE TO YOUR WIFE....
MALT
DRINKS
TELL HER YOU GO TO MEETINGS!
YEAH BUT-
DRINK
HA HA -WHERE'S MY FRIES?
THEN I WOULDN'T BE ABLE TO ENJOY THESE MOMENTS OF BONDAGE AND INTIMACY WITH YOU FINE FELLOWS!
YEAH... AN' WOULDN'T THAT KILL YOU!
RIGHT GUYS- "FELLOWSHIP"..... IT'S THE SHIT!
HEY....
BUT Y' KNOW... I MEAN....
I REALLY JUST THINK.... SEXUALLY...WE ARE WHAT WE ARE. WE GOT NO CHOICE IN ANY OF IT. IT CHOOSES US-Y'KNOW?
RIGHT?
WHA'?
CREAM PIE?
ELVIS!
CHOCOLATE MALT
CHECKIN' OUT!
DRINKS
MARY
THAT'S IT..... FINITO.
BUT....
!
HUH?
I....

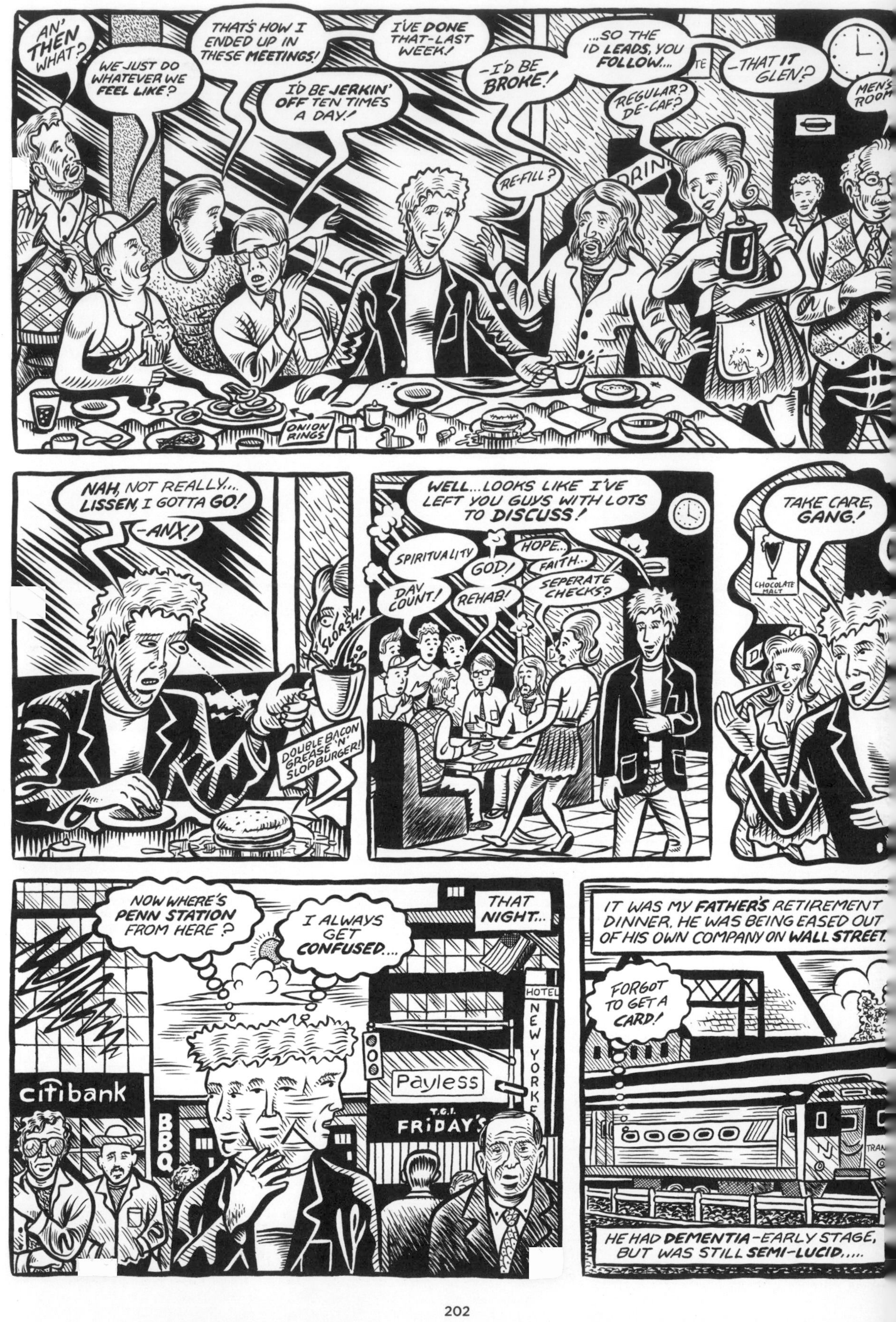
AN' THEN WHAT?
WE JUST DO WHATEVER WE FEEL LIKE?
THAT'S HOW I ENDED UP IN THESE MEETINGS!
I'VE DONE THAT-LAST WEEK!
I'D BE JERKIN' OFF TEN TIMES A DAY!
-I'D BE BROKE!
...SO THE ID LEADS, YOU FOLLOW....
-THAT IT GLEN?
REGULAR? DE-CAF?
MEN'S ROOM
RE-FILL?
ONION RINGS
NAH, NOT REALLY... LISSEN, I GOTTA GO!
-ANX!
SLORSH!
DOUBLE BACON GREASE 'N' SLOPBURGER!
WELL...LOOKS LIKE I'VE LEFT YOU GUYS WITH LOTS TO DISCUSS!
SPIRITUALITY
GOD!
HOPE..
FAITH...
DAY COUNT!
REHAB!
SEPERATE CHECKS?
TAKE CARE, GANG!
CHOCOLATE MALT
NOW WHERE'S PENN STATION FROM HERE?
I ALWAYS GET CONFUSED....
THAT NIGHT...
citibank
BBQ
Payless
T.G.I. FRIDAY'S
HOTEL NEW YORKE
IT WAS MY FATHER'S RETIREMENT DINNER. HE WAS BEING EASED OUT OF HIS OWN COMPANY ON WALL STREET.
FORGOT TO GET A CARD!
HE HAD DEMENTIA-EARLY STAGE, BUT WAS STILL SEMI-LUCID.....

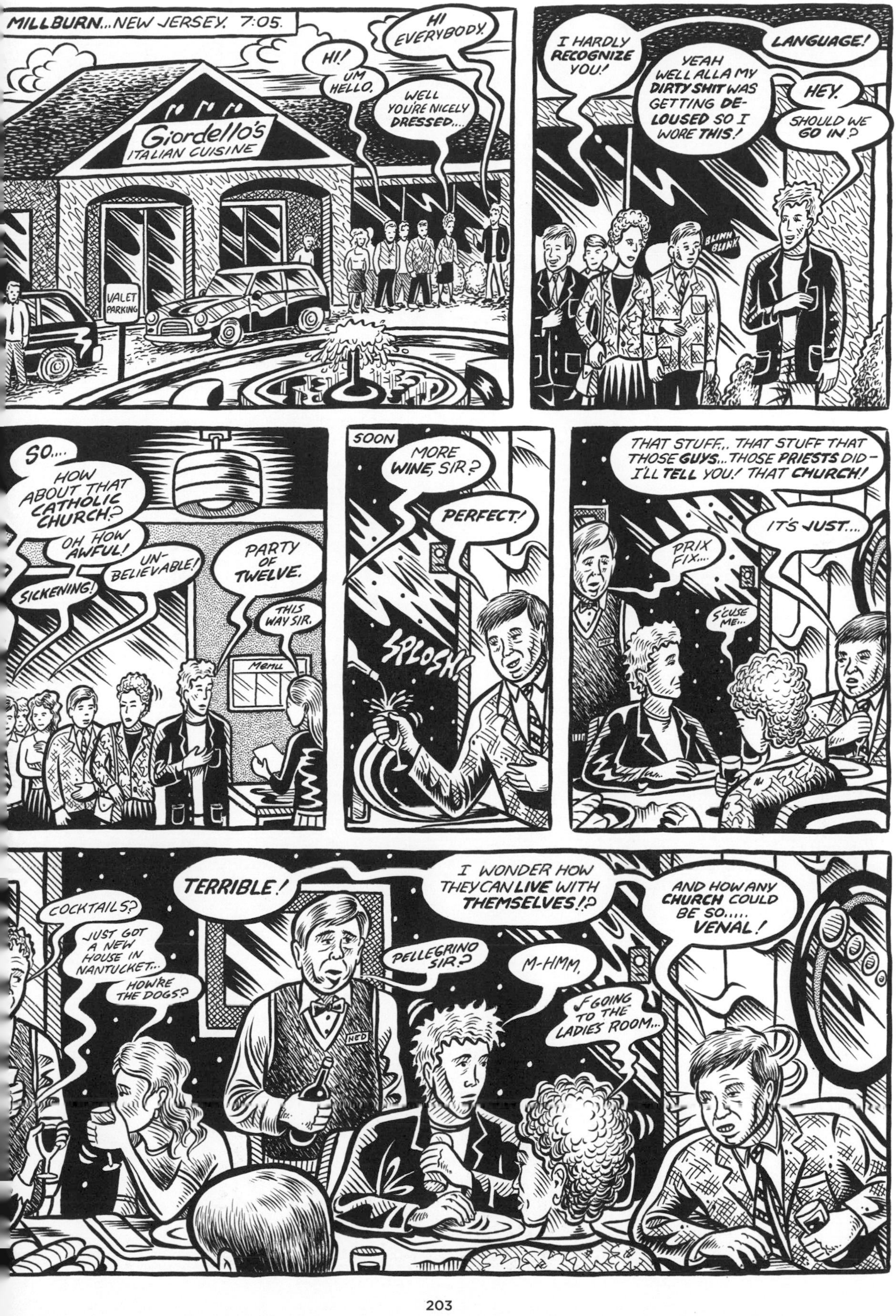

MILLBURN... NEW JERSEY. 7:05.
Giordello's ITALIAN CUISINE
VALET PARKING
HI EVERYBODY.
HI!
UM HELLO.
WELL YOU'RE NICELY DRESSED....
I HARDLY RECOGNIZE YOU!
YEAH WELL ALLA MY DIRTY SHIT WAS GETTING DE-LOUSED SO I WORE THIS!
LANGUAGE!
HEY.
SHOULD WE GO IN?
BLINK BLINK
SO.... HOW ABOUT THAT CATHOLIC CHURCH?
OH HOW AWFUL!
UN-BELIEVABLE!
SICKENING!
PARTY OF TWELVE.
THIS WAY SIR.
Menu
SOON
MORE WINE, SIR?
PERFECT!
SPLOSH!
THAT STUFF.. THAT STUFF THAT THOSE GUYS... THOSE PRIESTS DID - I'LL TELL YOU! THAT CHURCH!
IT'S JUST....
PRIX FIX...
S'CUSE ME...
NED
TERRIBLE!
I WONDER HOW THEY CAN LIVE WITH THEMSELVES!?
AND HOW ANY CHURCH COULD BE SO..... VENAL!
COCKTAILS?
JUST GOT A NEW HOUSE IN NANTUCKET...
HOW'RE THE DOGS?
PELLEGRINO SIR?
M-HMM.
GOING TO THE LADIES' ROOM...
NED

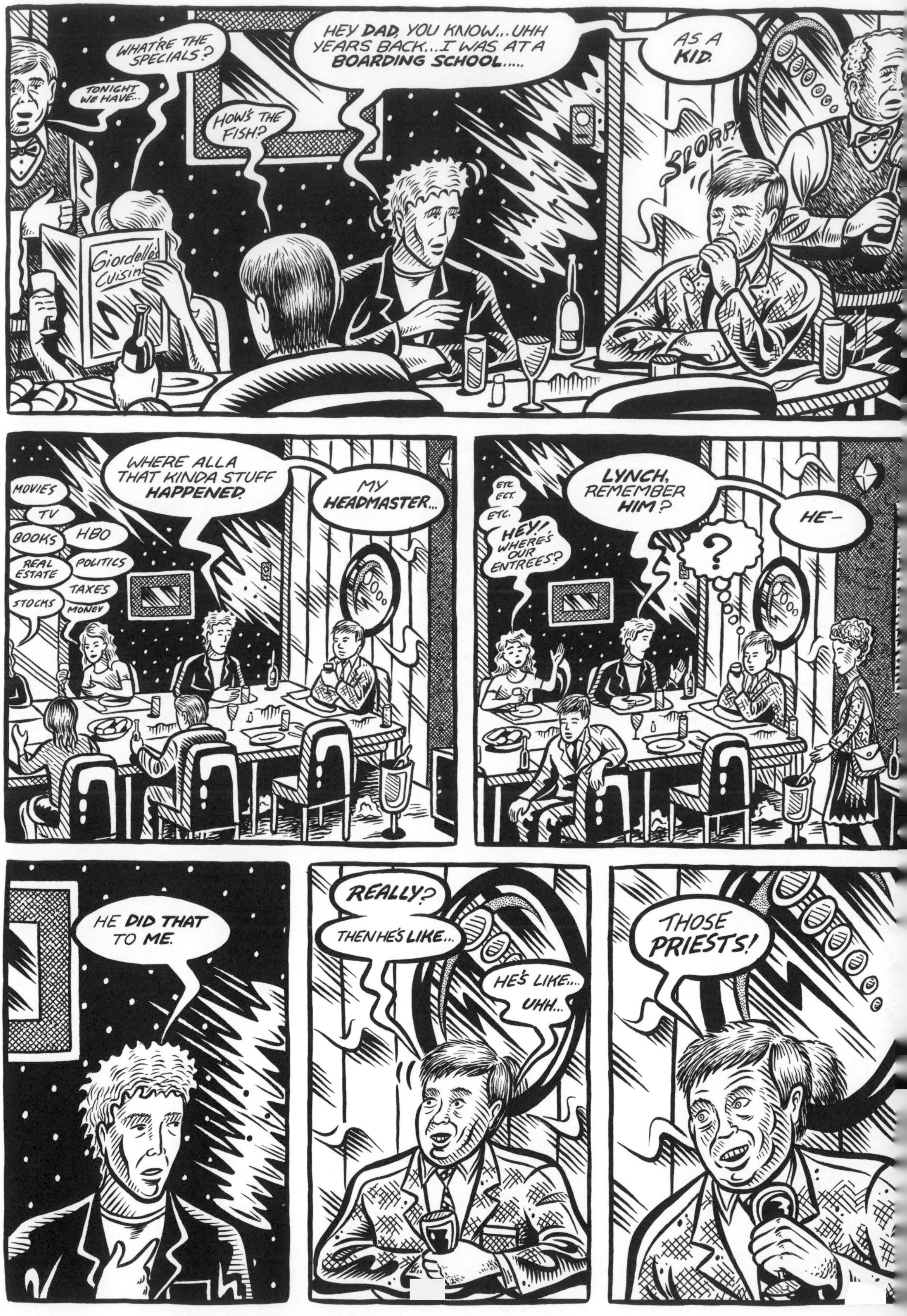
WHAT'RE THE SPECIALS?
TONIGHT WE HAVE...
HOW'S THE FISH?
HEY DAD, YOU KNOW... UHH YEARS BACK... I WAS AT A BOARDING SCHOOL.....
AS A KID.
SLORP!
GIORDELLO'S CUISIN
MOVIES
TV
BOOKS
HBO
REAL ESTATE
POLITICS
TAXES
STOCKS
MONEY
WHERE ALLA THAT KINDA STUFF HAPPENED.
MY HEADMASTER...
ETC. ETC.
ETC.
HEY! WHERE'S OUR ENTREES?
LYNCH, REMEMBER HIM?
?
HE-
HE DID THAT TO ME.
REALLY?
THEN HE'S LIKE...
HE'S LIKE... UHH...
THOSE PRIESTS!

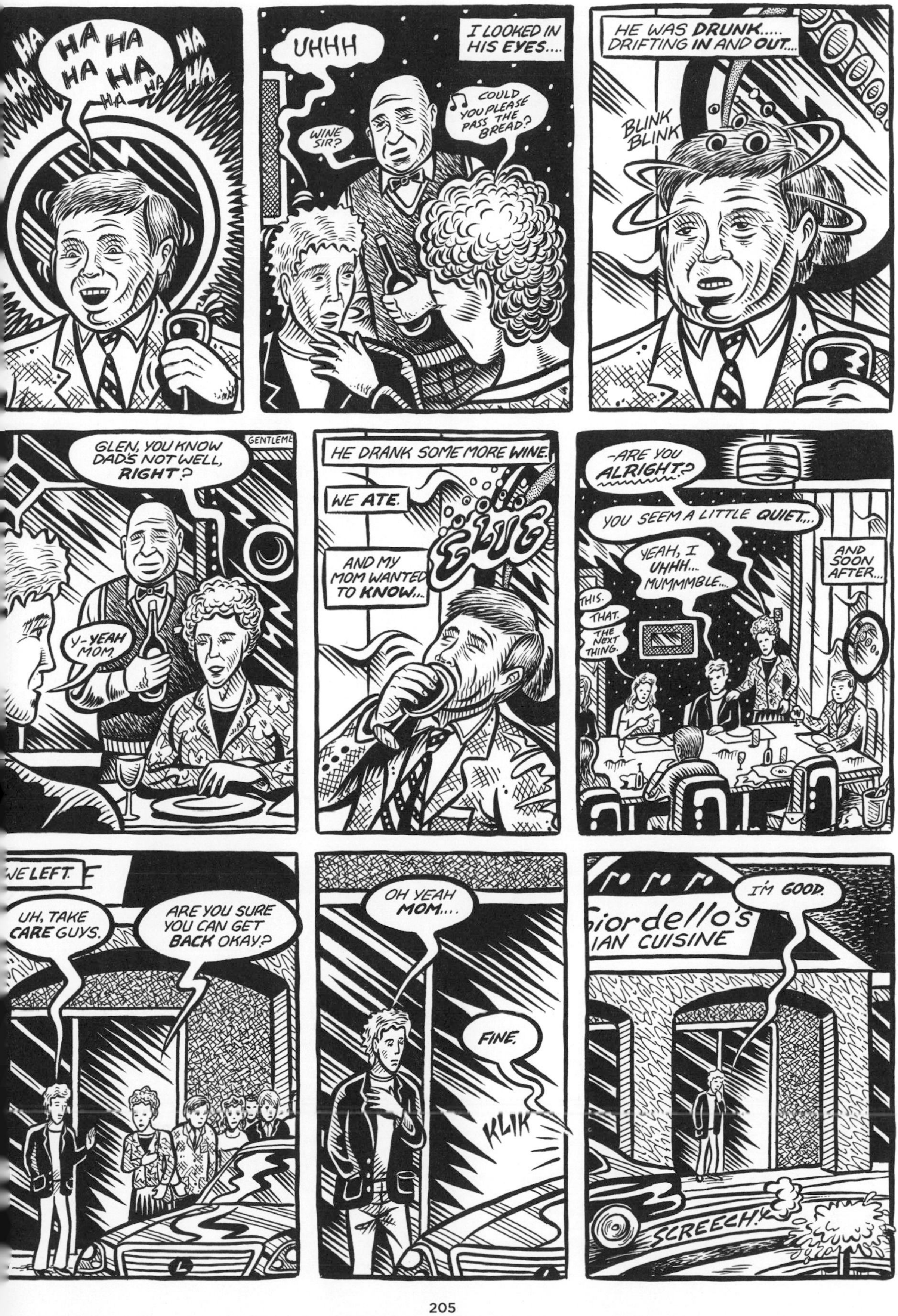
HA HA HA HA HA HA HA HA HA HA HA HA
UHHH
I LOOKED IN HIS EYES....
WINE SIR?
COULD YOU PLEASE PASS THE BREAD?
HE WAS DRUNK..... DRIFTING IN AND OUT....
BLINK BLINK
GENTLEME
GLEN, YOU KNOW DAD'S NOT WELL, RIGHT?
Y-YEAH MOM.
HE DRANK SOME MORE WINE.
WE ATE.
GLUG
AND MY MOM WANTED TO KNOW...
-ARE YOU ALRIGHT?
YOU SEEM A LITTLE QUIET....
YEAH, I UHHH... MUMMMBLE....
THIS.
THAT.
THE NEXT THING.
AND SOON AFTER...
WE LEFT.
UH, TAKE CARE GUYS.
ARE YOU SURE YOU CAN GET BACK OKAY?
OH YEAH MOM....
FINE.
KLIK
Giordello's
IAN CUISINE
I'M GOOD.
SCREECH!

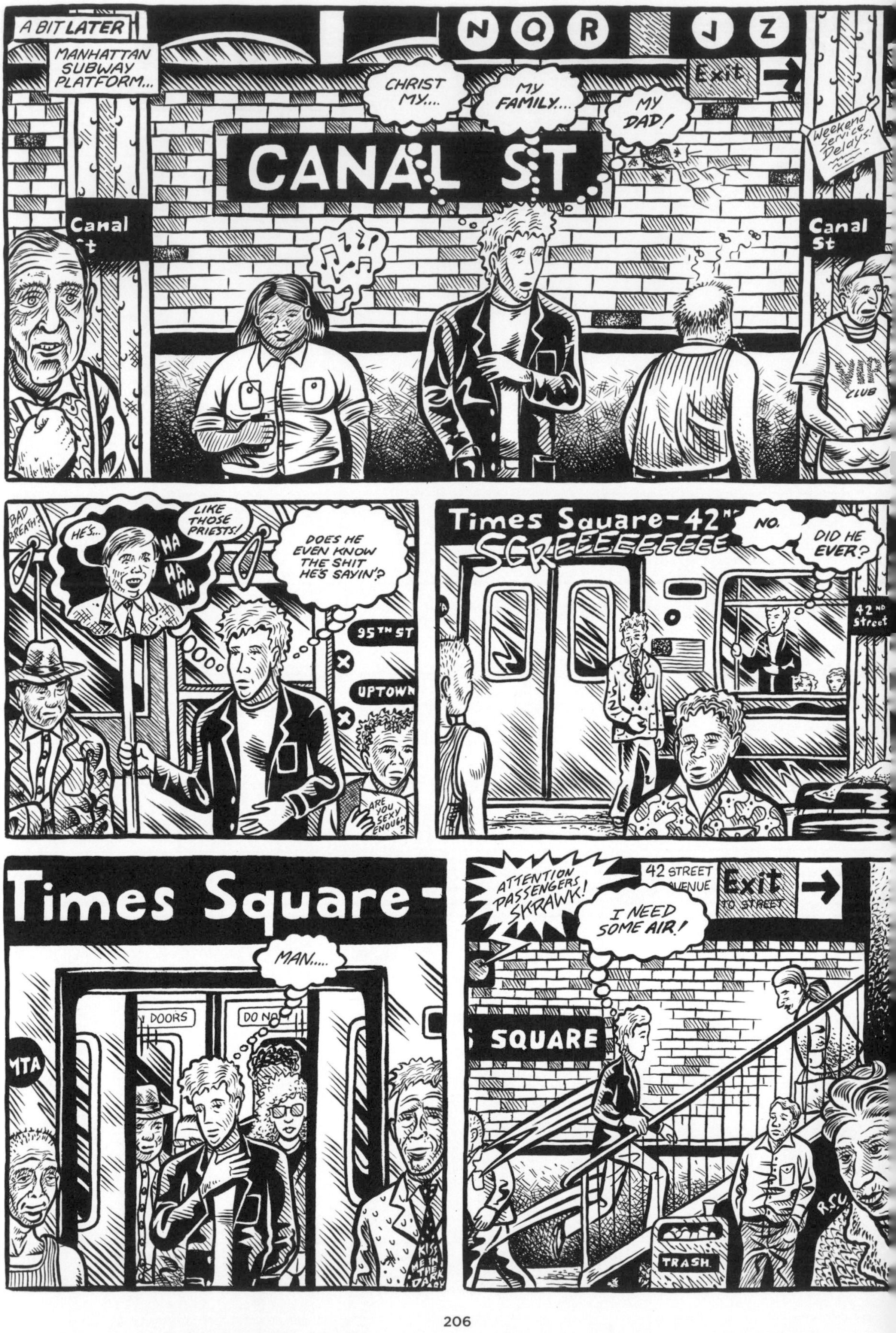
A BIT LATER
MANHATTAN SUBWAY PLATFORM...
N Q R J Z
Exit
CHRIST MY...
MY FAMILY....
MY DAD!
CANAL ST
Weekend Service Delays!
Canal St
Canal St
CLUB
BAD BREATH?
HE'S...
LIKE THOSE PRIESTS!
HA HA HA HA
DOES HE EVEN KNOW THE SHIT HE'S SAYIN'?
95TH ST
UPTOWN
ARE YOU SEXY ENOUGH?
Times Square-42
SCREEEEEEEEE
NO.
DID HE EVER?
42ND Street
Times Square-
MAN.....
DOORS
MTA
KISS ME IN THE DARK
ATTENTION PASSENGERS SKRAWK!
42 STREET
Exit
TO STREET
I NEED SOME AIR!
SQUARE
TRASH
R.S.

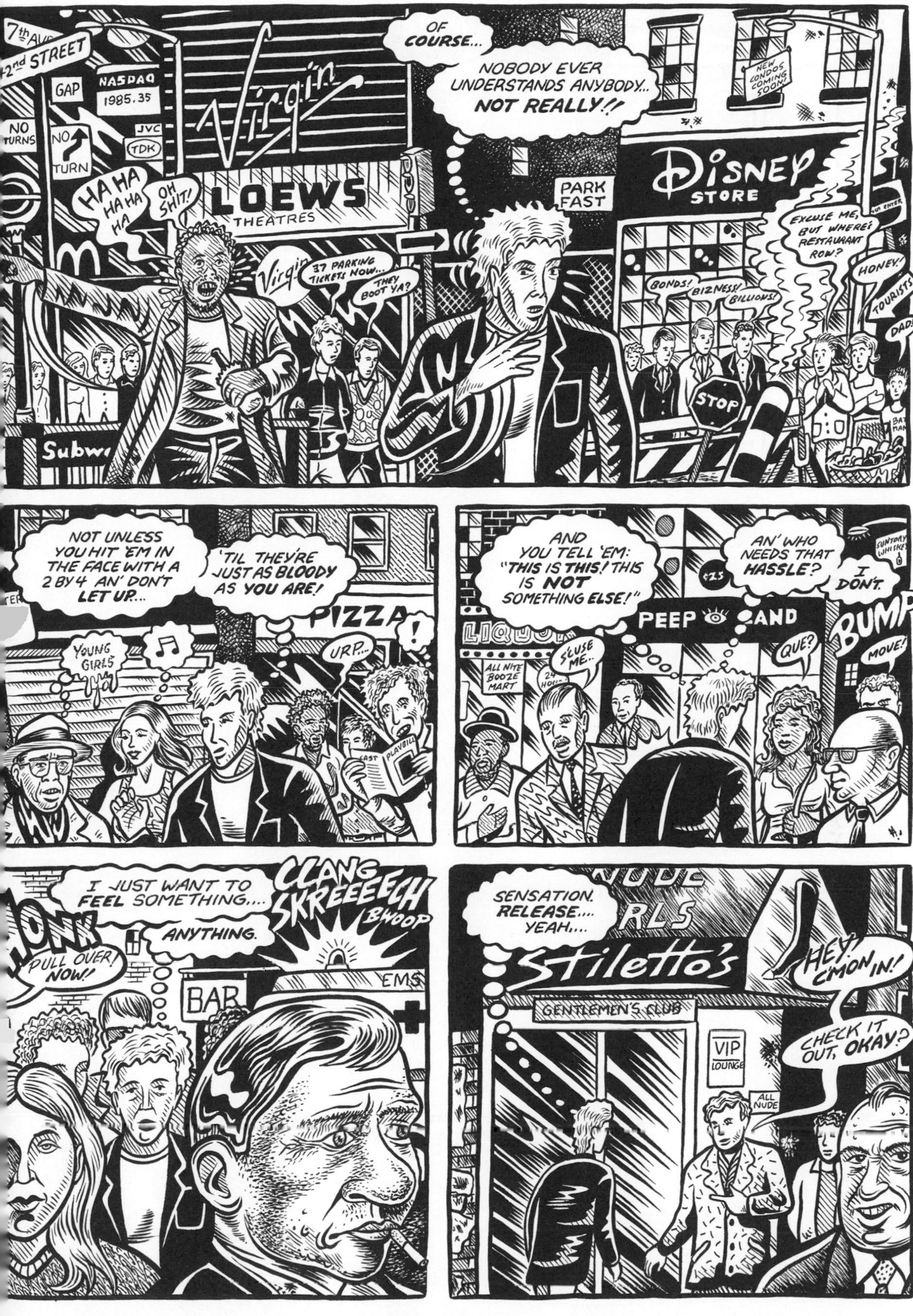

7th AVE
42nd STREET
GAP
NASDAQ 1985.35
NO TURNS
NO TURN
JVC
TDK
Virgin
LOEWS THEATRES
HA HA HA HA HA
OH SHIT!
Virgin
37 PARKING TICKETS NOW...
THEY BOOT YA?
Subw
OF COURSE...
NOBODY EVER UNDERSTANDS ANYBODY... NOT REALLY!!
PARK FAST
NEW CONDOS COMING SOON!
DISNEY STORE
EXCUSE ME, BUT WHERE: RESTAURANT ROW?
BONDS!
BIZNESS!
BILLIONS!
HONEY!
TOURISTS
DAD!
STOP
NOT UNLESS YOU HIT 'EM IN THE FACE WITH A 2 BY 4 AN' DON'T LET UP...
'TIL THEY'RE JUST AS BLOODY AS YOU ARE!
PIZZA
YOUNG GIRLS
URP...
!
PLAYBILL
AND YOU TELL 'EM: "THIS IS THIS! THIS IS NOT SOMETHING ELSE!"
AN' WHO NEEDS THAT HASSLE?
I DON'T.
SUNTORY WHISKEY
PEEP LAND
S'CUSE ME...
ALL NITE BOOZE MART
QUE?
BUMP
MOVE!
I JUST WANT TO FEEL SOMETHING....
ANYTHING.
CLANG SKREEEEECH BWOOP
PULL OVER! NOW!
BAR
EMS
SENSATION. RELEASE.... YEAH,...
Stiletto's
GENTLEMEN'S CLUB
HEY! C'MON IN!
VIP LOUNGE
ALL NUDE
CHECK IT OUT, OKAY?

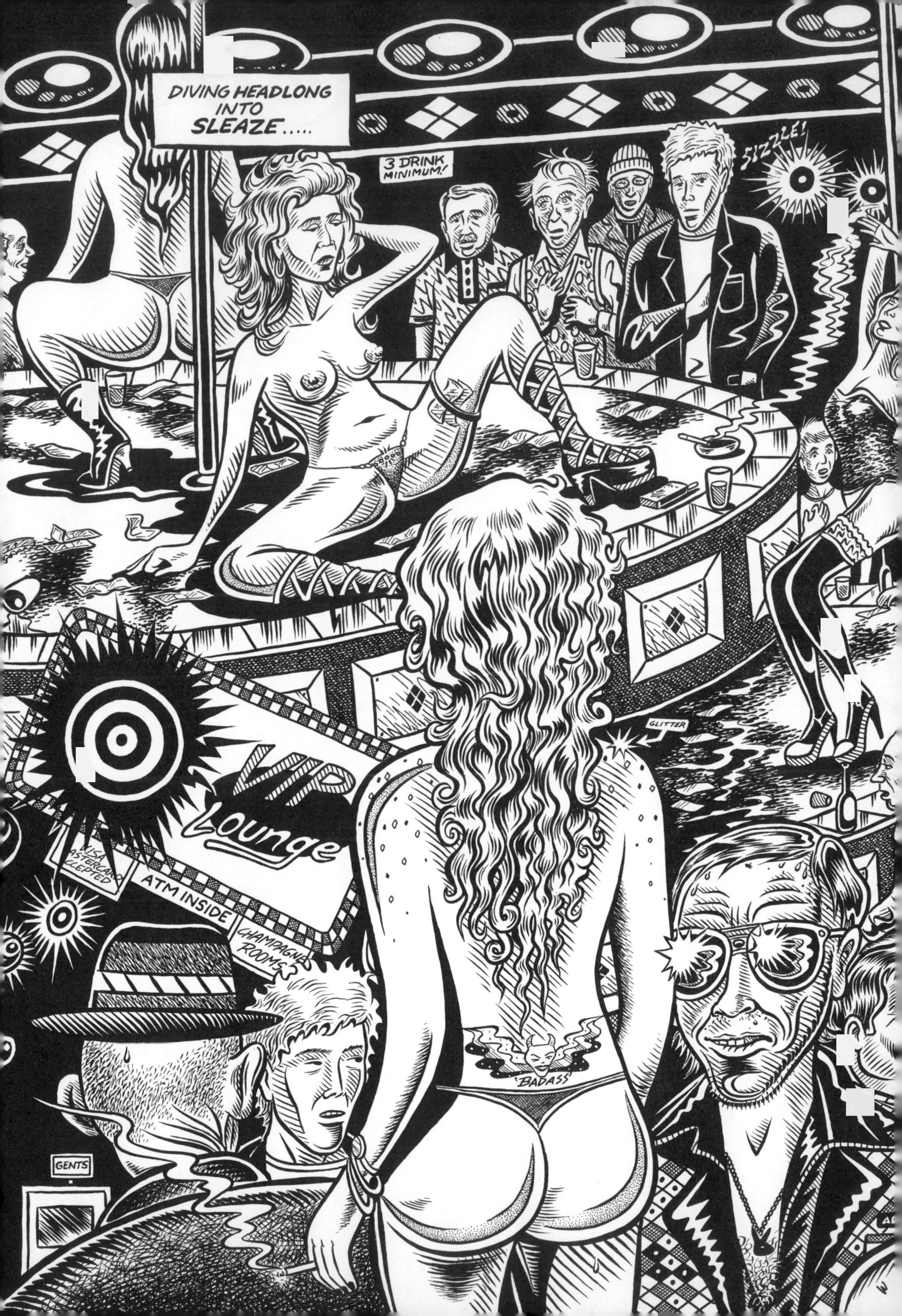

DIVING HEADLONG INTO SLEAZE.....
3 DRINK MINIMUM!
SIZZLE!
GLITTER
VIP
Lounge
ATM INSIDE
CHAMPAGNE ROOMS
BADASS
GENTS

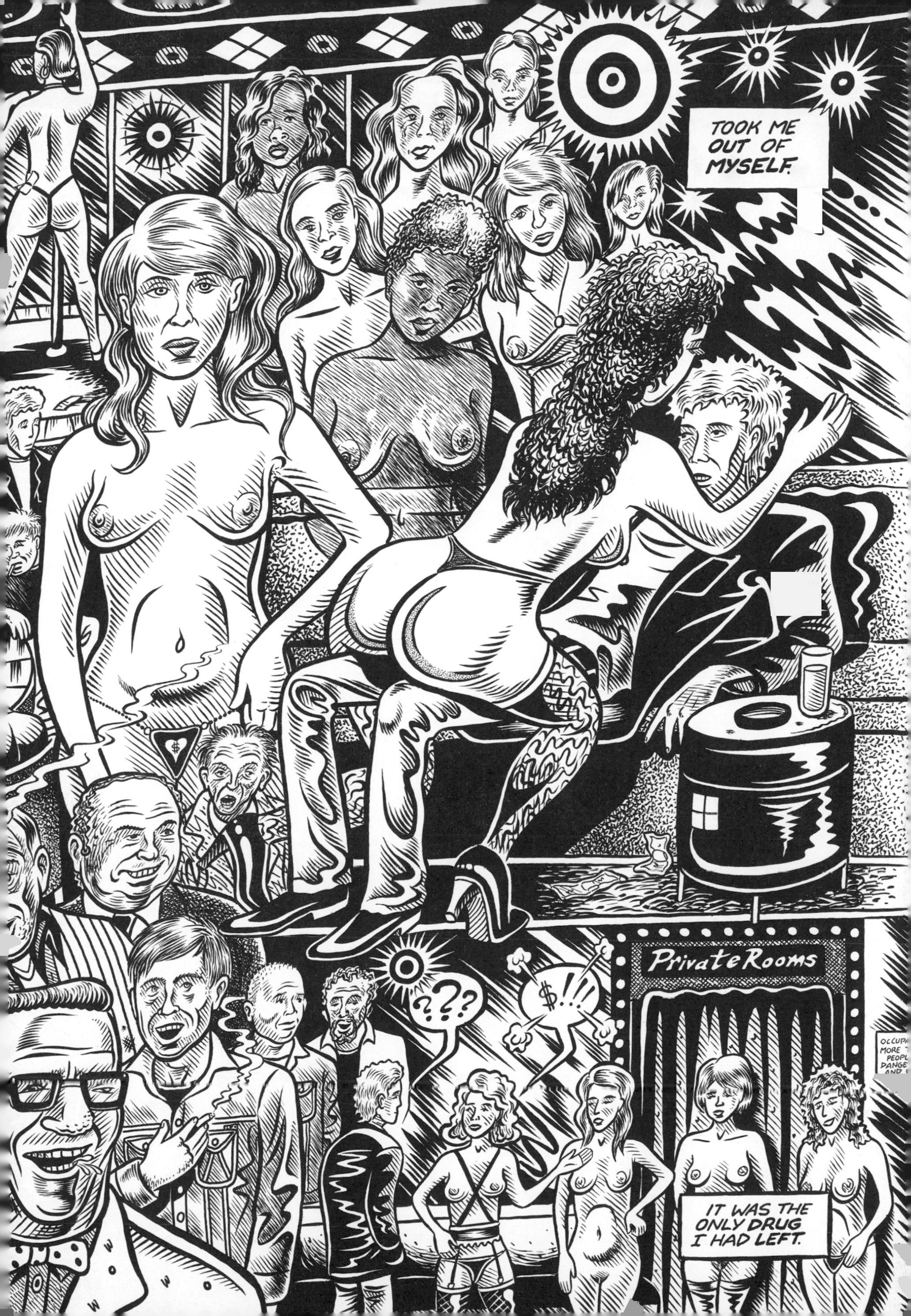
TOOK ME OUT OF MYSELF.
Private Rooms
???
$!!!
IT WAS THE ONLY DRUG I HAD LEFT.

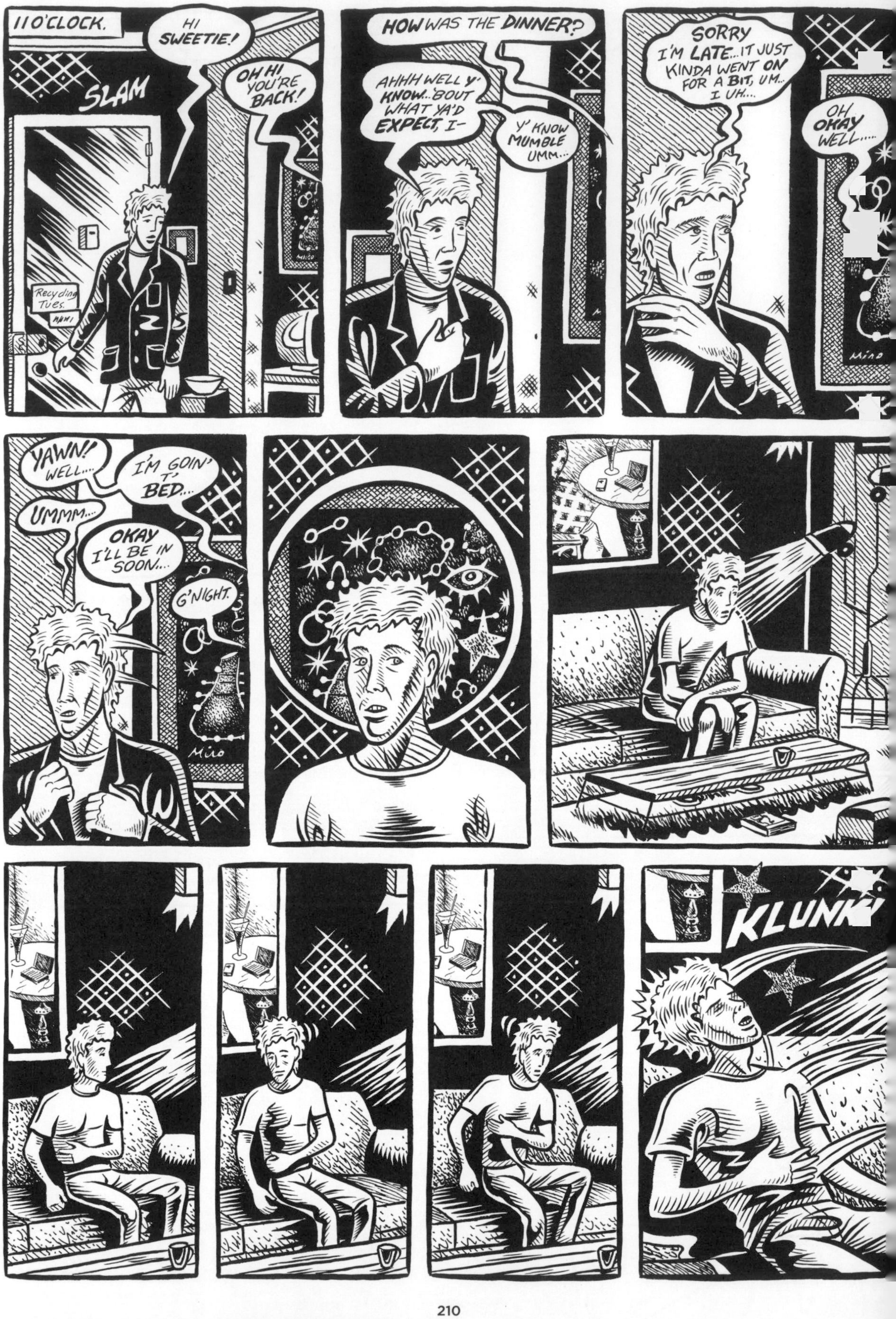
11 O'CLOCK.
HI SWEETIE!
SLAM
OH HI YOU'RE BACK!
Recycling Tues.
HOW WAS THE DINNER?
AHHH WELL Y' KNOW...'BOUT WHAT YA'D EXPECT, I-
Y' KNOW MUMBLE UMM...
SORRY I'M LATE... IT JUST KINDA WENT ON FOR A BIT, UM... I UH....
OH OKAY WELL.....
YAWN! WELL....
I'M GOIN' T' BED...
UMMM....
OKAY I'LL BE IN SOON...
G'NIGHT.
KLUNK

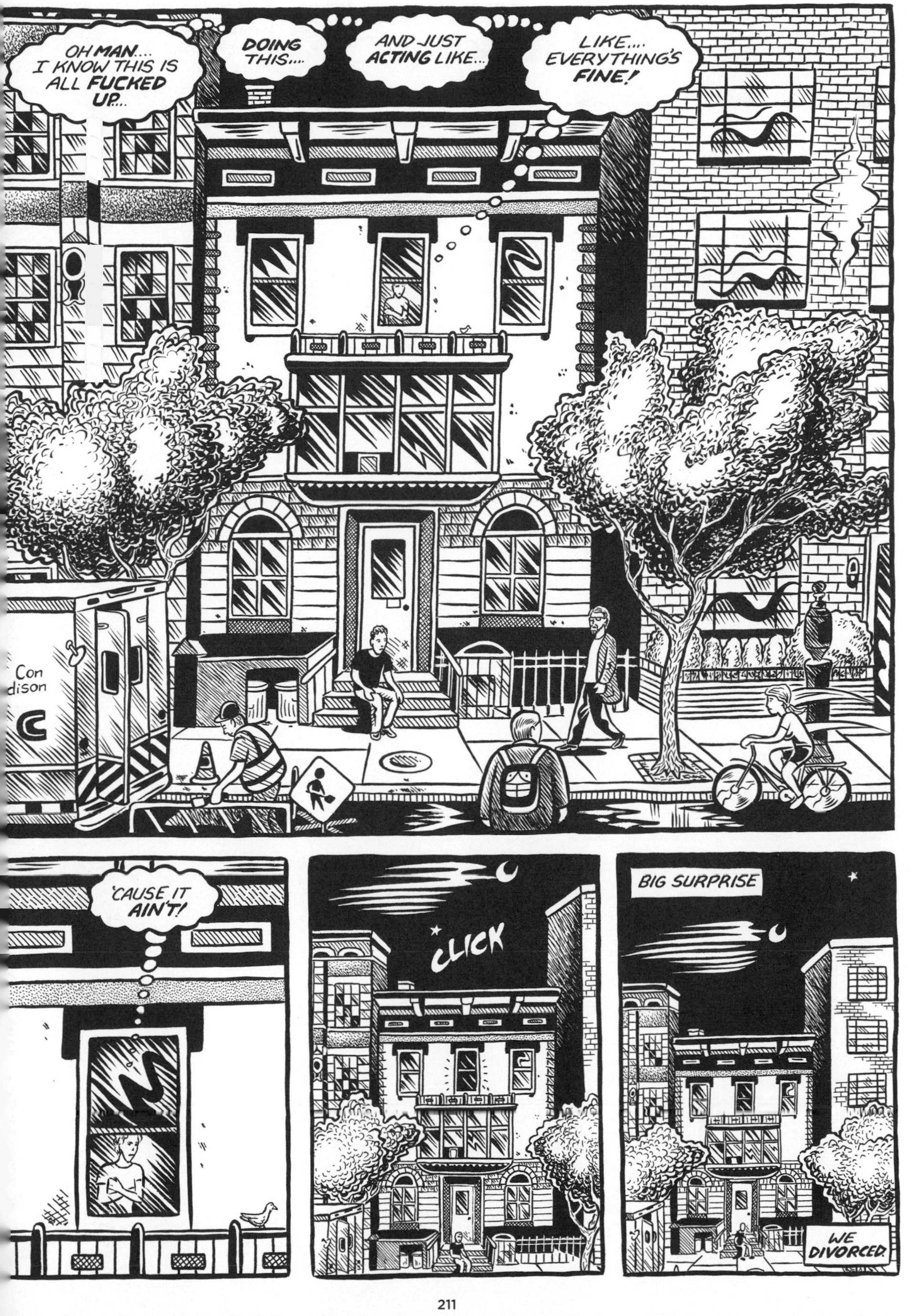
OH MAN.... I KNOW THIS IS ALL FUCKED UP....
DOING THIS....
AND JUST ACTING LIKE...
LIKE.... EVERYTHING'S FINE!
Con
dison
'CAUSE IT AIN'T!
CLICK
BIG SURPRISE
WE DIVORCED.

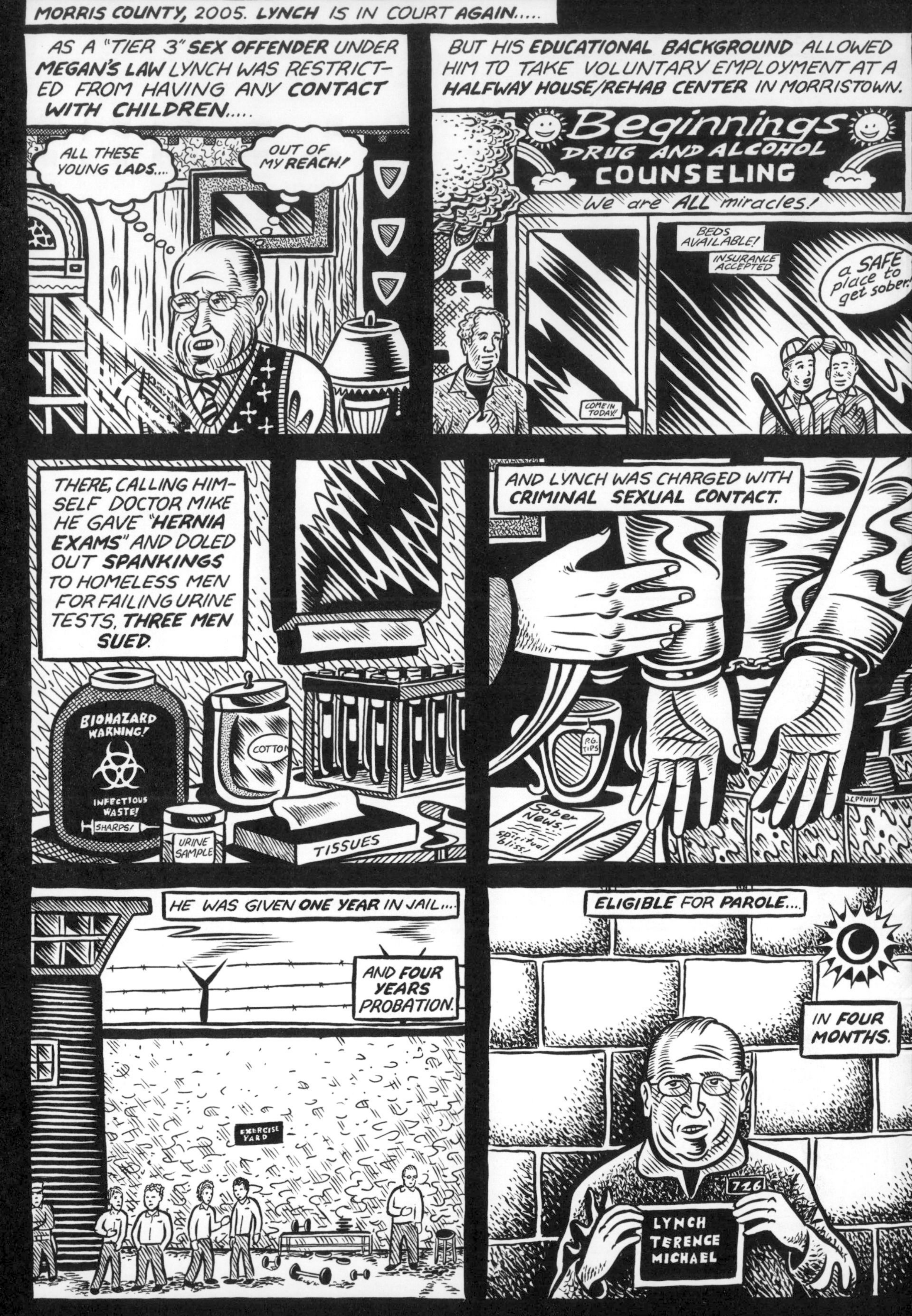
MORRIS COUNTY, 2005. LYNCH IS IN COURT AGAIN.....
AS A "TIER 3" SEX OFFENDER UNDER MEGAN'S LAW LYNCH WAS RESTRICTED FROM HAVING ANY CONTACT WITH CHILDREN.....
ALL THESE YOUNG LADS....
OUT OF MY REACH!
BUT HIS EDUCATIONAL BACKGROUND ALLOWED HIM TO TAKE VOLUNTARY EMPLOYMENT AT A HALFWAY HOUSE/REHAB CENTER IN MORRISTOWN.
Beginnings
DRUG AND ALCOHOL
COUNSELING
We are ALL miracles!
BEDS AVAILABLE!
INSURANCE ACCEPTED
a SAFE place to get sober!
COME IN TODAY!
THERE, CALLING HIMSELF DOCTOR MIKE HE GAVE "HERNIA EXAMS" AND DOLED OUT SPANKINGS TO HOMELESS MEN FOR FAILING URINE TESTS. THREE MEN SUED.
BIOHAZARD WARNING!
INFECTIOUS WASTE!
SHARPS!
COTTON
URINE SAMPLE
TISSUES
AND LYNCH WAS CHARGED WITH CRIMINAL SEXUAL CONTACT.
P.G. TIPS
Sober News!
spiritual bliss!
J.C. PENNY
HE WAS GIVEN ONE YEAR IN JAIL....
AND FOUR YEARS PROBATION.
EXERCISE YARD
ELIGIBLE FOR PAROLE....
IN FOUR MONTHS.
726
LYNCH
TERENCE
MICHAEL

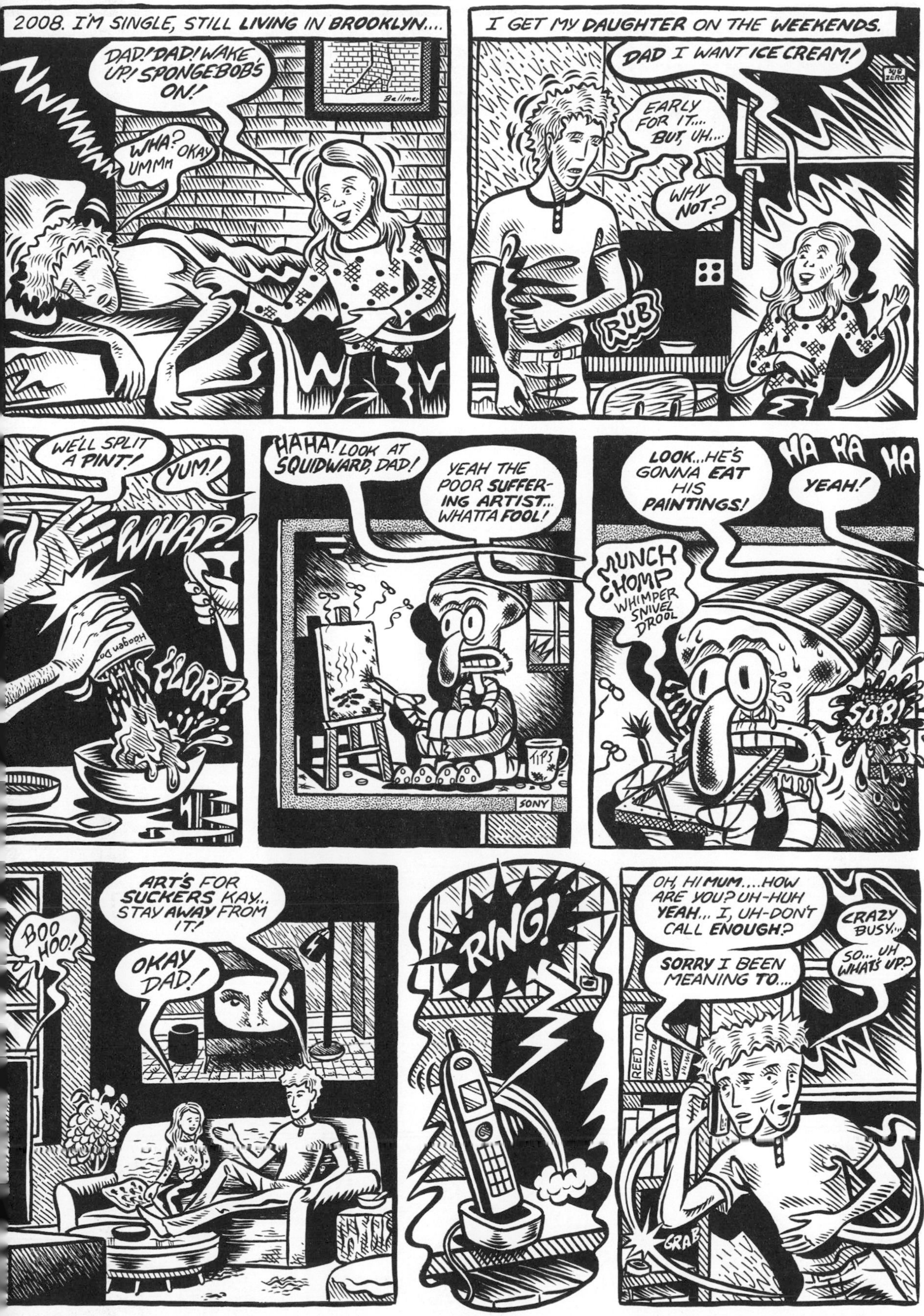
2008. I'M SINGLE, STILL LIVING IN BROOKLYN....
DAD! DAD! WAKE UP! SPONGEBOB'S ON!
WHA? UMMM OKAY
Bellmer
I GET MY DAUGHTER ON THE WEEKENDS.
DAD I WANT ICE CREAM!
EARLY FOR IT.... BUT, UH....
WHY NOT?
RUB
WE'LL SPLIT A PINT!
YUM!
WHAP!
FLORP!
HAHA! LOOK AT SQUIDWARD, DAD!
YEAH THE POOR SUFFERING ARTIST... WHATTA FOOL!
TIPS
SONY
LOOK... HE'S GONNA EAT HIS PAINTINGS!
HA HA HA
YEAH!
MUNCH CHOMP WHIMPER SNIVEL DROOL
SOB!
BOO HOO!
ART'S FOR SUCKERS KAY... STAY AWAY FROM IT!
OKAY DAD!
RING!
OH, HI MUM.... HOW ARE YOU? UH-HUH YEAH... I, UH-DON'T CALL ENOUGH?
CRAZY BUSY...
SORRY I BEEN MEANING TO....
SO... UH WHAT'S UP?
LOU REED
GRAB

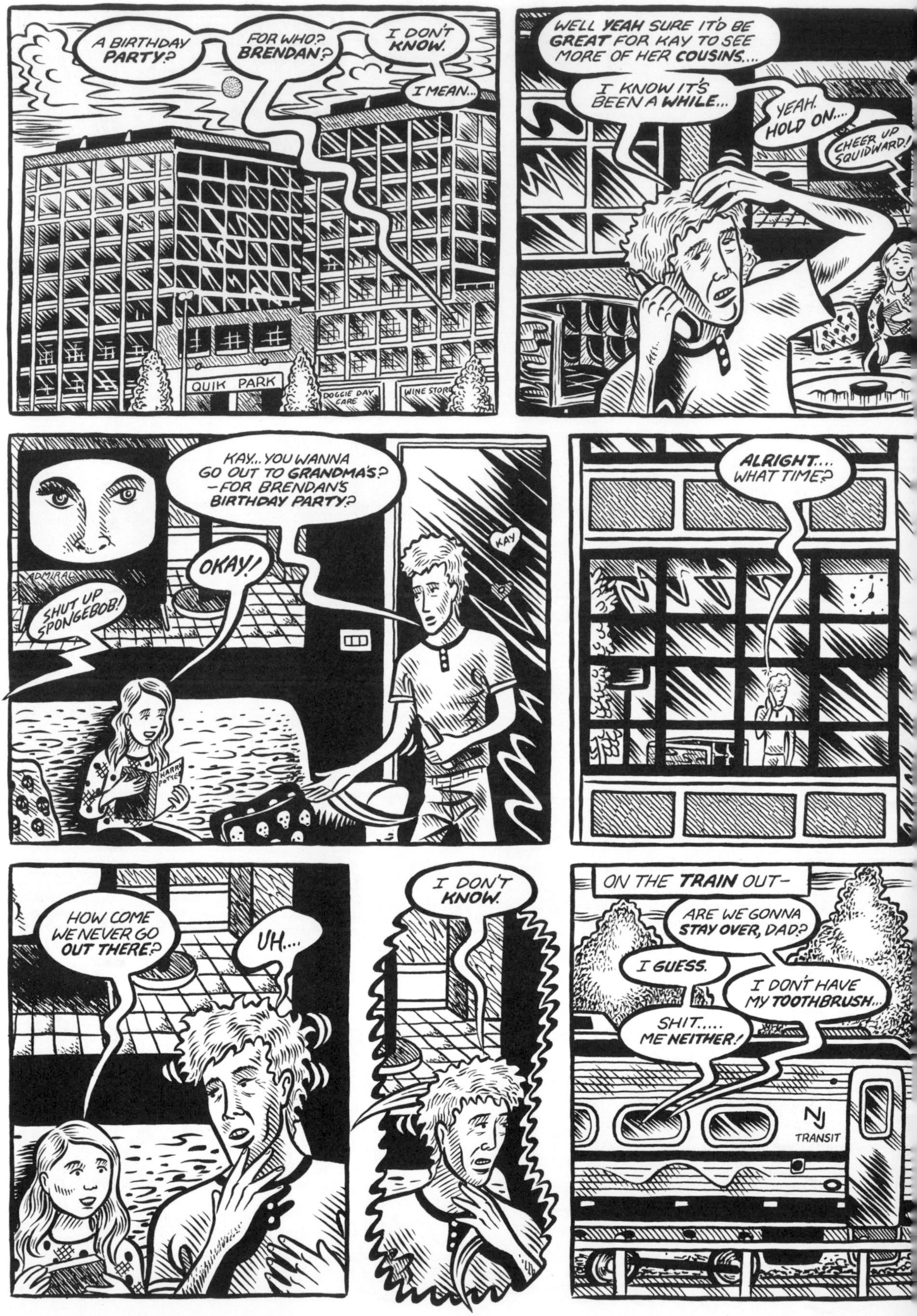
A BIRTHDAY PARTY?
FOR WHO? BRENDAN?
I DON'T KNOW.
I MEAN...
QUIK PARK
DOGGIE DAY CARE
WINE STORE
WELL YEAH SURE IT'D BE GREAT FOR KAY TO SEE MORE OF HER COUSINS....
I KNOW IT'S BEEN A WHILE...
YEAH. HOLD ON....
CHEER UP SQUIDWARD!
KAY... YOU WANNA GO OUT TO GRANDMA'S? -FOR BRENDAN'S BIRTHDAY PARTY?
ADMIRAL
SHUT UP SPONGEBOB!
OKAY!
KAY
ALRIGHT.... WHAT TIME?
HOW COME WE NEVER GO OUT THERE?
UH....
I DON'T KNOW.
ON THE TRAIN OUT-
ARE WE GONNA STAY OVER, DAD?
I GUESS.
I DON'T HAVE MY TOOTHBRUSH...
SHIT..... ME NEITHER!
NJ TRANSIT

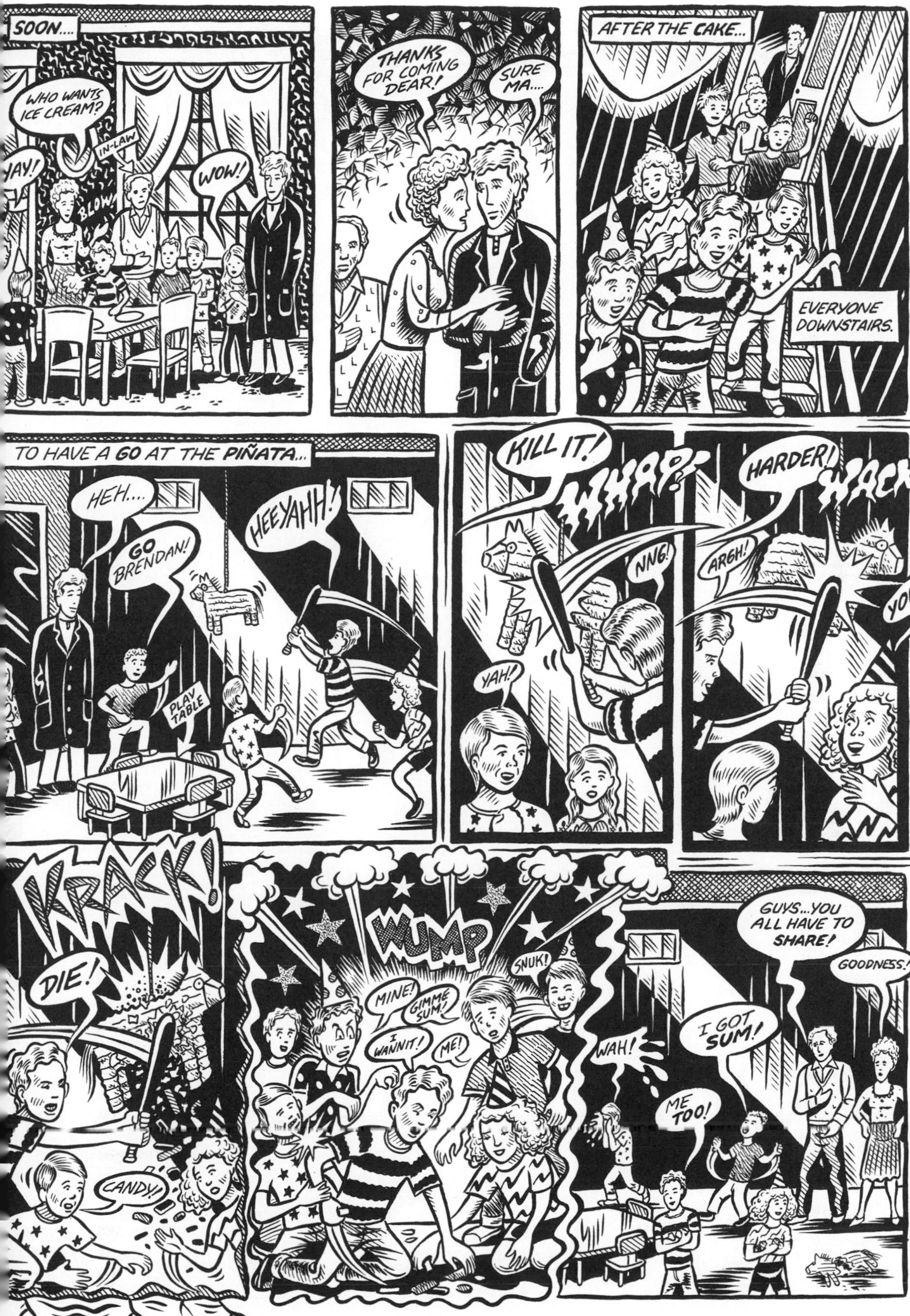
SOON....
WHO WANTS ICE CREAM?
IN-LAW
YAY!
BLOW
WOW!
THANKS FOR COMING DEAR!
SURE MA....
AFTER THE CAKE...
EVERYONE DOWNSTAIRS.
TO HAVE A GO AT THE PIÑATA...
HEH....
GO BRENDAN!
HEEYAHH!
PLAY TABLE
KILL IT!
WHAP!
NNG!
YAH!
HARDER!
WACK!
ARGH!
YOW!
KRACK!
DIE!
CANDY!
WUMP
MINE!
GIMME SUM!
I WANNIT!
ME!
SNUK!
WAH!
GUYS...YOU ALL HAVE TO SHARE!
GOODNESS!
I GOT SUM!
ME TOO!

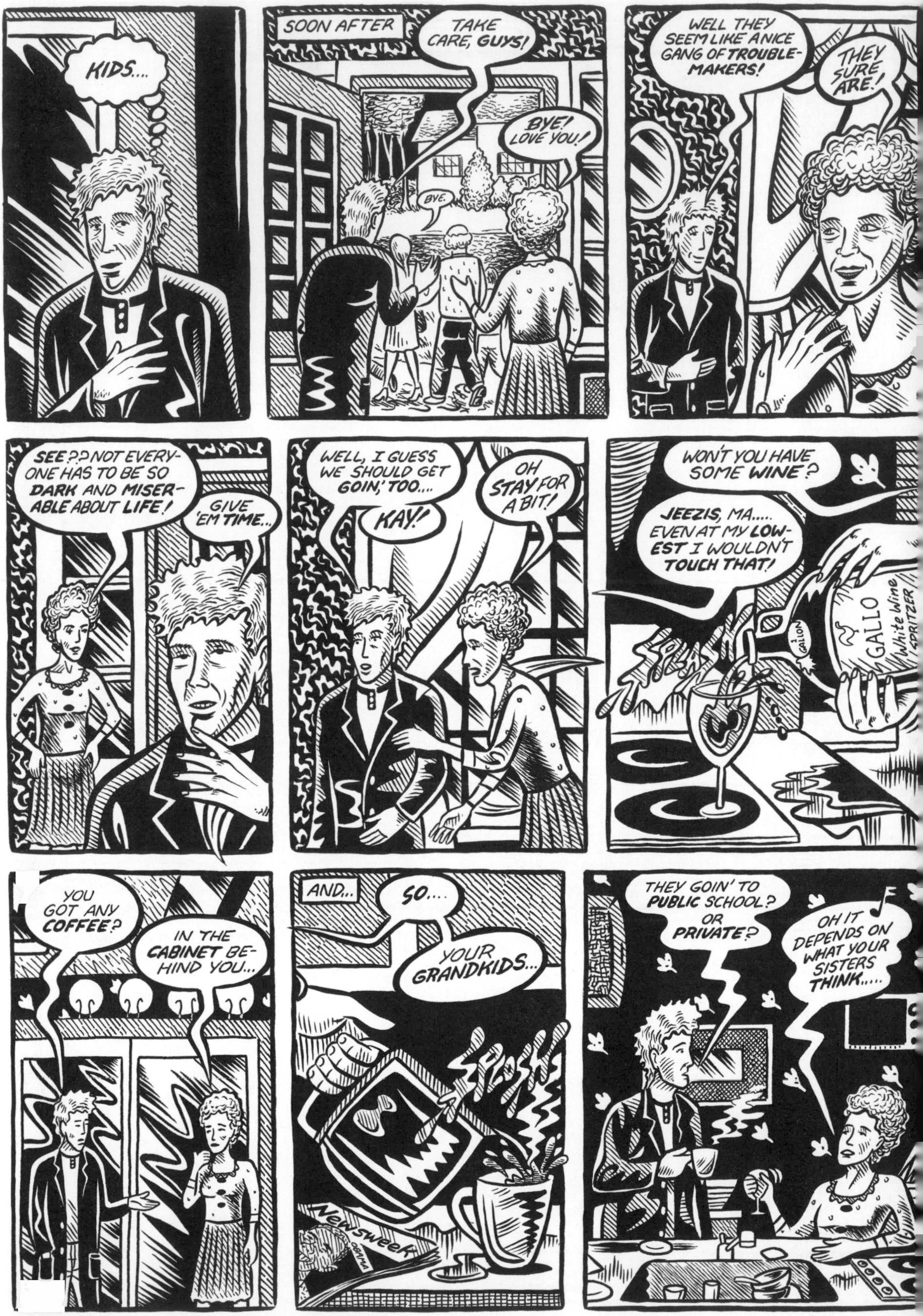
KIDS....
SOON AFTER
TAKE CARE, GUYS!
BYE.
BYE! LOVE YOU!
WELL THEY SEEM LIKE A NICE GANG OF TROUBLE-MAKERS!
THEY SURE ARE!
SEE?? NOT EVERY-ONE HAS TO BE SO DARK AND MISER-ABLE ABOUT LIFE!
GIVE 'EM TIME...
WELL, I GUESS WE SHOULD GET GOIN,' TOO....
KAY!
OH STAY FOR A BIT!
WON'T YOU HAVE SOME WINE?
JEEZIS, MA..... EVEN AT MY LOW-EST I WOULDN'T TOUCH THAT!
GALLO
White Wine SPRITZER
1 GALLON
YOU GOT ANY COFFEE?
IN THE CABINET BE-HIND YOU...
AND...
SO....
YOUR GRANDKIDS...
Newsweek
THEY GOIN' TO PUBLIC SCHOOL? OR PRIVATE?
OH IT DEPENDS ON WHAT YOUR SISTERS THINK.....

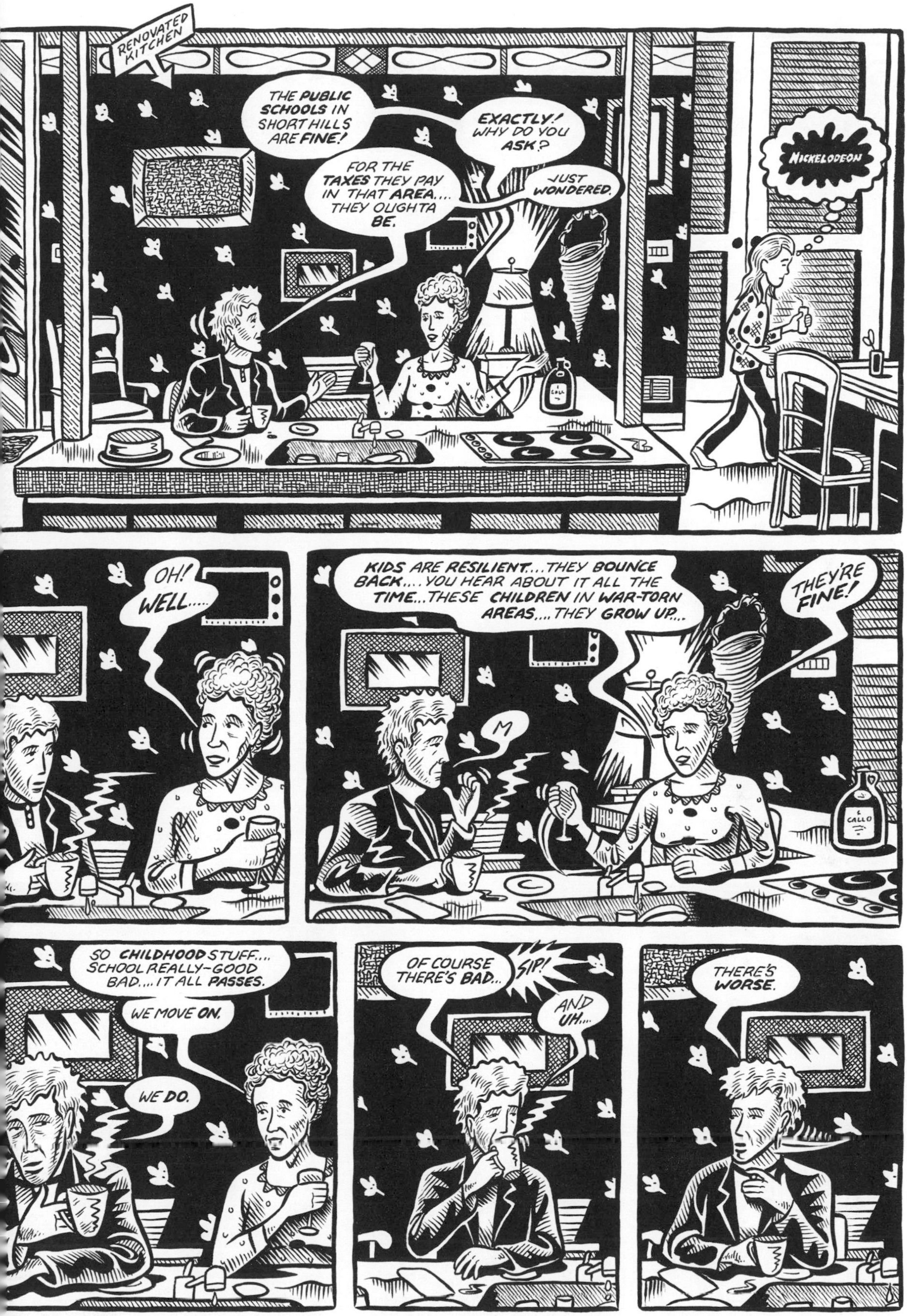
RENOVATED KITCHEN
THE PUBLIC SCHOOLS IN SHORT HILLS ARE FINE!
EXACTLY! WHY DO YOU ASK?
FOR THE TAXES THEY PAY IN THAT AREA.... THEY OUGHTA BE.
JUST WONDERED.
NICKELODEON
OH! WELL.....
KIDS ARE RESILIENT.... THEY BOUNCE BACK.... YOU HEAR ABOUT IT ALL THE TIME... THESE CHILDREN IN WAR-TORN AREAS.... THEY GROW UP....
THEY'RE FINE!
M
SO CHILDHOOD STUFF.... SCHOOL REALLY-GOOD BAD.... IT ALL PASSES.
WE MOVE ON.
WE DO.
OF COURSE THERE'S BAD...
SIP!
AND UH...
THERE'S WORSE.

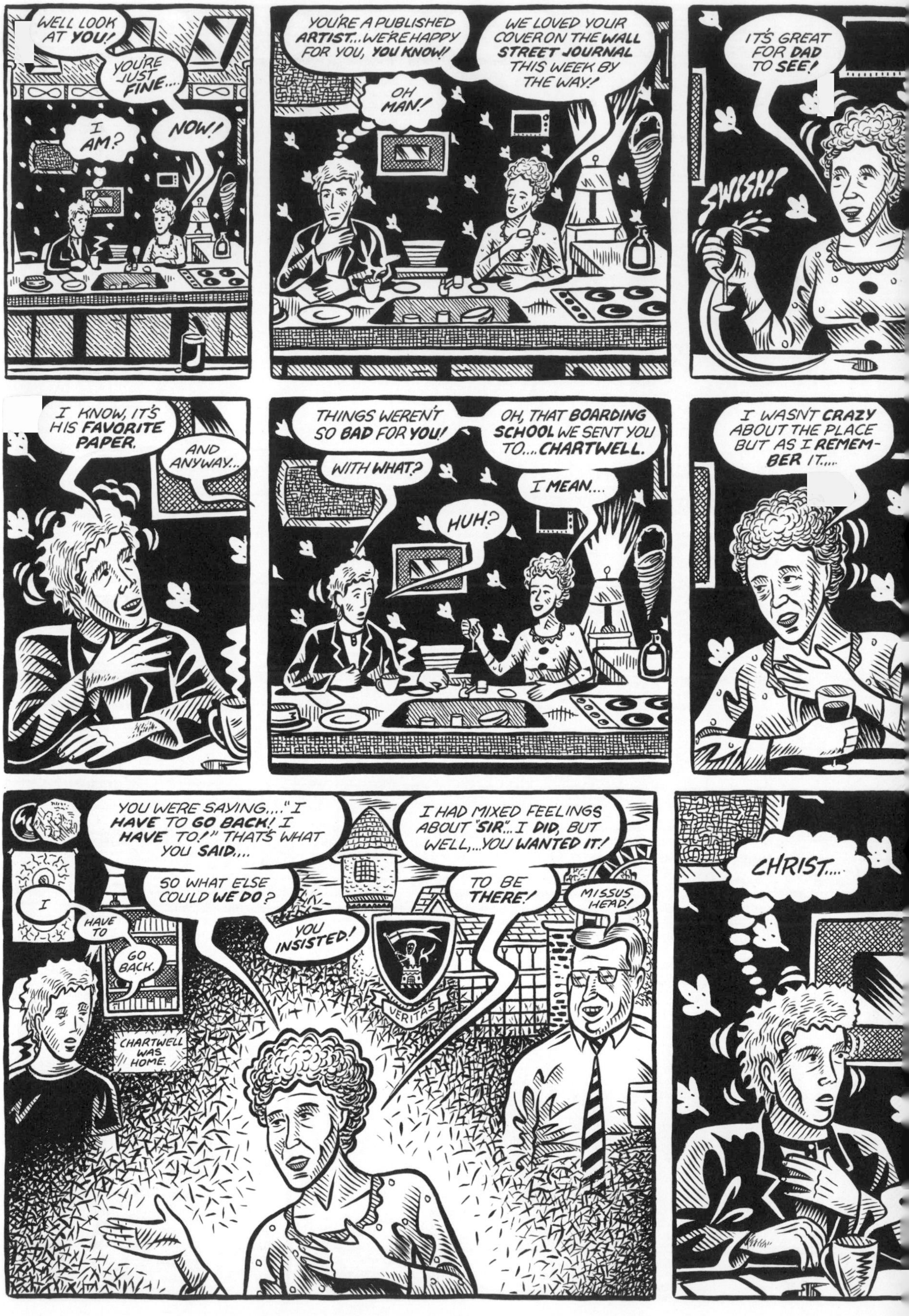
WELL LOOK AT YOU!
YOU'RE JUST FINE....
NOW!
I AM?
YOU'RE A PUBLISHED ARTIST...WE'RE HAPPY FOR YOU, YOU KNOW!
OH MAN!
WE LOVED YOUR COVER ON THE WALL STREET JOURNAL THIS WEEK BY THE WAY!
IT'S GREAT FOR DAD TO SEE!
SWISH!
I KNOW, IT'S HIS FAVORITE PAPER.
AND ANYWAY...
THINGS WEREN'T SO BAD FOR YOU!
WITH WHAT?
OH, THAT BOARDING SCHOOL WE SENT YOU TO....CHARTWELL.
I MEAN....
HUH?
I WASN'T CRAZY ABOUT THE PLACE BUT AS I REMEMBER IT....
YOU WERE SAYING...."I HAVE TO GO BACK! I HAVE TO!" THAT'S WHAT YOU SAID....
I
HAVE TO
GO BACK.
CHARTWELL WAS HOME.
SO WHAT ELSE COULD WE DO?
YOU INSISTED!
VERITAS
I HAD MIXED FEELINGS ABOUT "SIR"... I DID, BUT WELL,...YOU WANTED IT!
TO BE THERE!
MISSUS HEAD!
CHRIST....

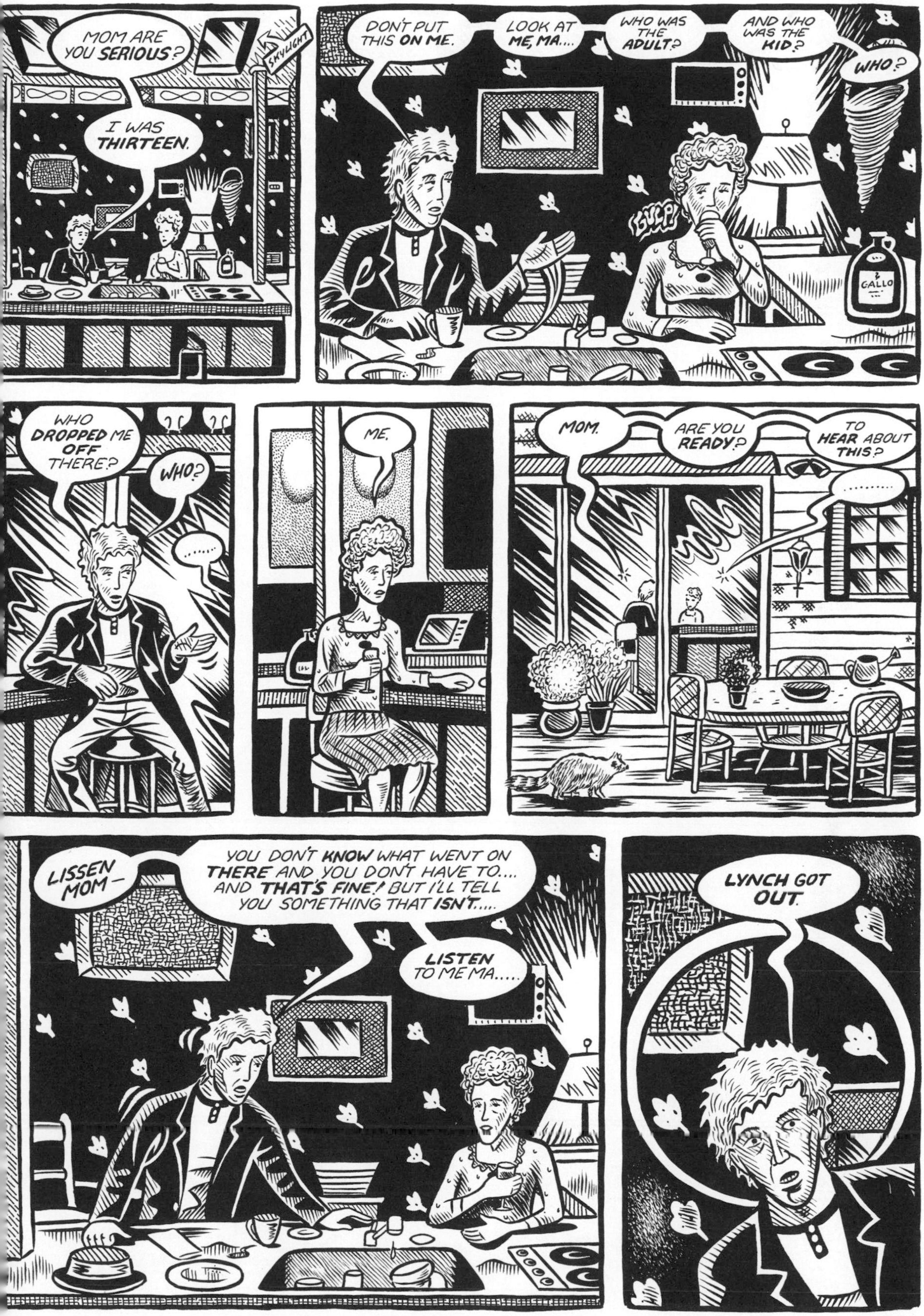
MOM ARE YOU SERIOUS?
SKYLIGHT
I WAS THIRTEEN.
DON'T PUT THIS ON ME.
LOOK AT ME, MA....
WHO WAS THE ADULT?
AND WHO WAS THE KID?
WHO?
GULP
GALLO
WHO DROPPED ME OFF THERE?
WHO?
......
ME.
MOM.
ARE YOU READY?
TO HEAR ABOUT THIS?
....
LISSEN MOM—
YOU DON'T KNOW WHAT WENT ON THERE AND YOU DON'T HAVE TO.... AND THAT'S FINE! BUT I'LL TELL YOU SOMETHING THAT ISN'T....
LISTEN TO ME MA.....
LYNCH GOT OUT.

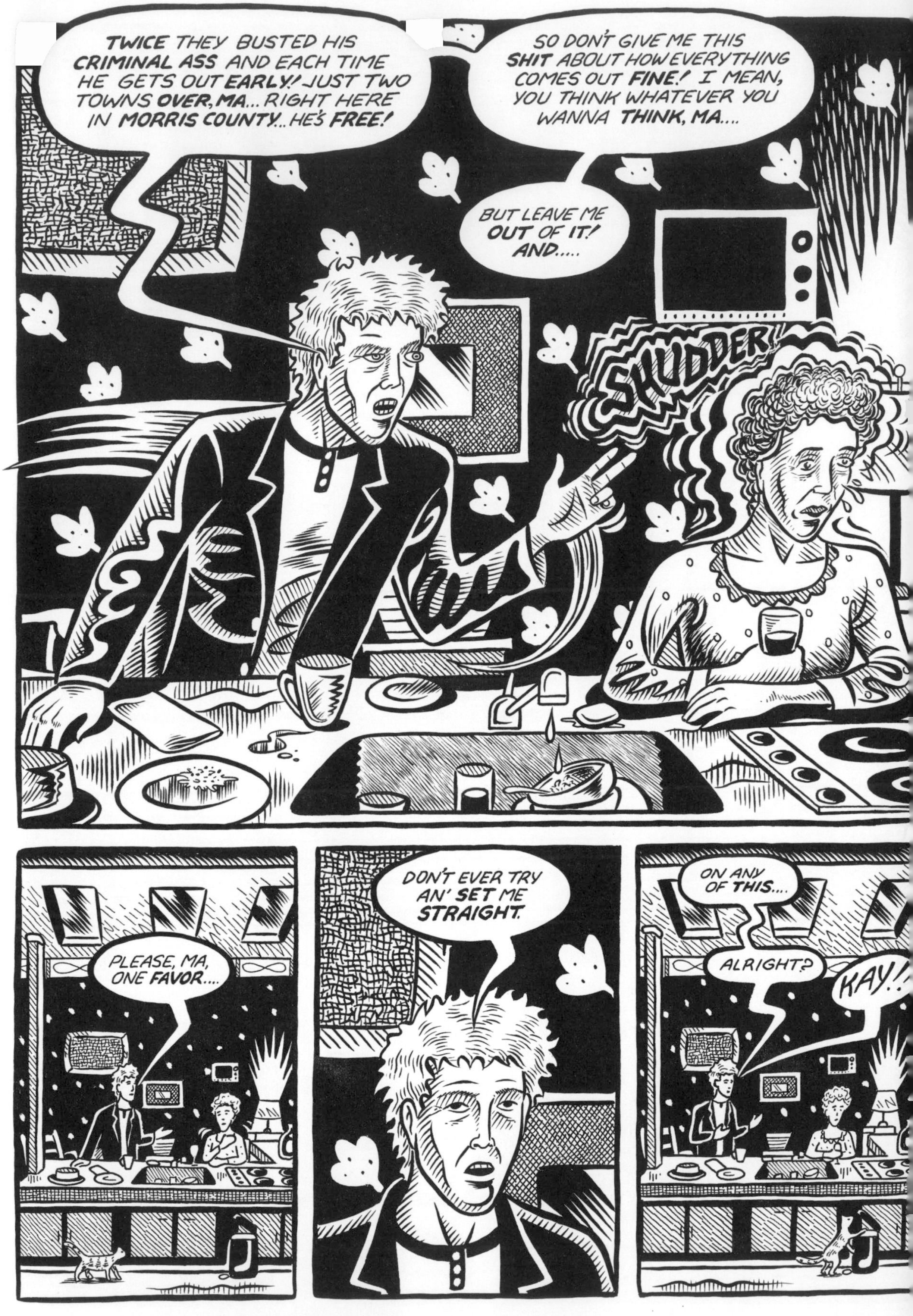
TWICE THEY BUSTED HIS CRIMINAL ASS AND EACH TIME HE GETS OUT EARLY! JUST TWO TOWNS OVER, MA... RIGHT HERE IN MORRIS COUNTY... HE'S FREE!
SO DON'T GIVE ME THIS SHIT ABOUT HOW EVERYTHING COMES OUT FINE! I MEAN, YOU THINK WHATEVER YOU WANNA THINK, MA....
BUT LEAVE ME OUT OF IT! AND.....
SHUDDER
PLEASE, MA, ONE FAVOR....
DON'T EVER TRY AN' SET ME STRAIGHT.
ON ANY OF THIS....
ALRIGHT?
KAY!!

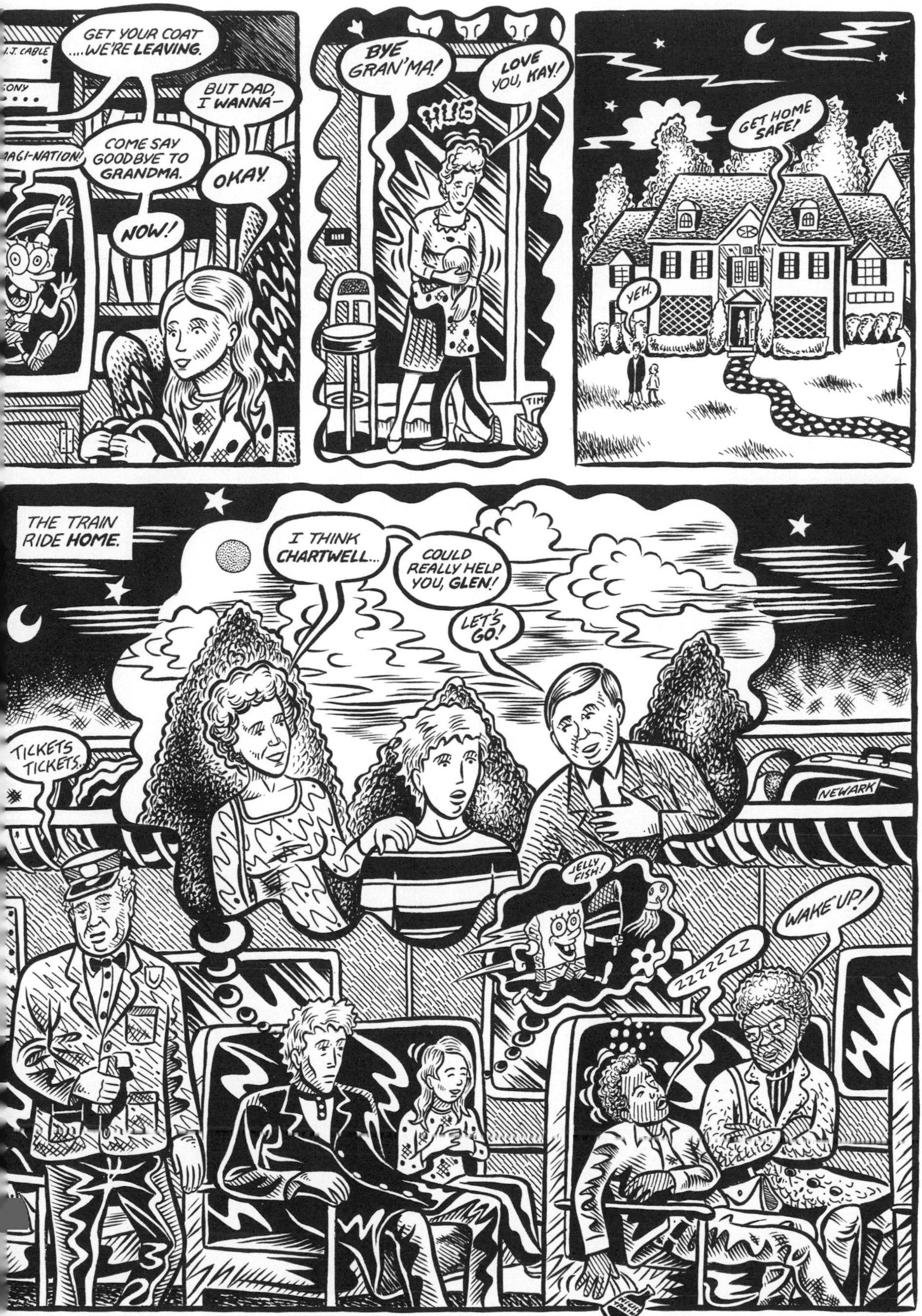
GET YOUR COAT ....WE'RE LEAVING.
BUT DAD, I WANNA–
COME SAY GOODBYE TO GRANDMA.
OKAY.
NOW!
BYE GRAN'MA!
LOVE YOU, KAY!
HUG
GET HOME SAFE!
YEH.
THE TRAIN RIDE HOME.
I THINK CHARTWELL...
COULD REALLY HELP YOU, GLEN!
LET'S GO!
TICKETS TICKETS...
NEWARK
WAKE UP!
ZZZZZZZ

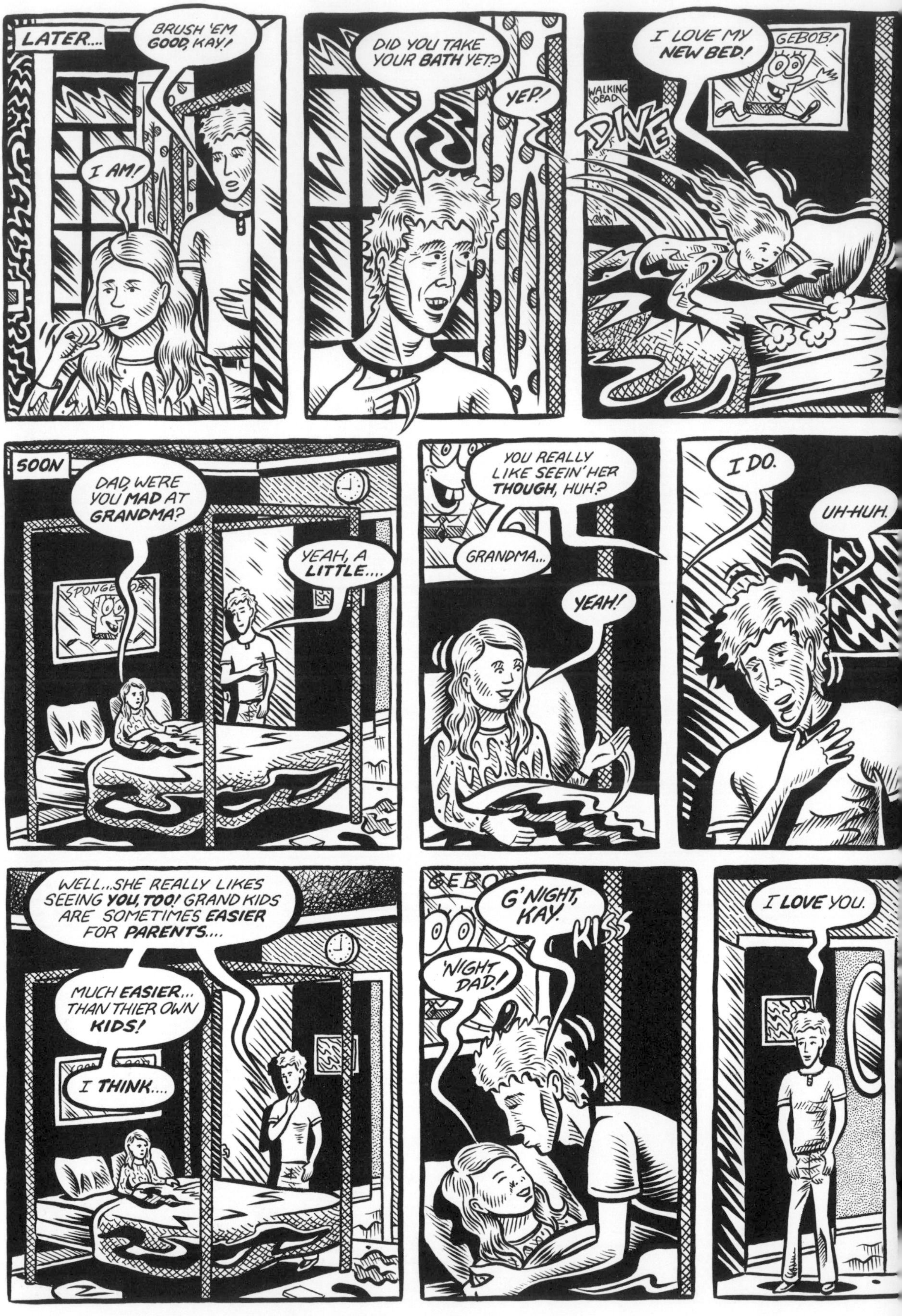
LATER....
BRUSH 'EM GOOD, KAY!
I AM!
DID YOU TAKE YOUR BATH YET?
YEP!
I LOVE MY NEW BED!
GEBOB!
WALKING DEAD
DIVE
SOON
DAD, WERE YOU MAD AT GRANDMA?
YEAH, A LITTLE....
YOU REALLY LIKE SEEIN' HER THOUGH, HUH?
GRANDMA...
YEAH!
I DO.
UH-HUH.
WELL...SHE REALLY LIKES SEEING YOU, TOO! GRAND KIDS ARE SOMETIMES EASIER FOR PARENTS....
MUCH EASIER... THAN THIER OWN KIDS!
I THINK....
G'NIGHT, KAY.
KISS
'NIGHT DAD!
I LOVE YOU.

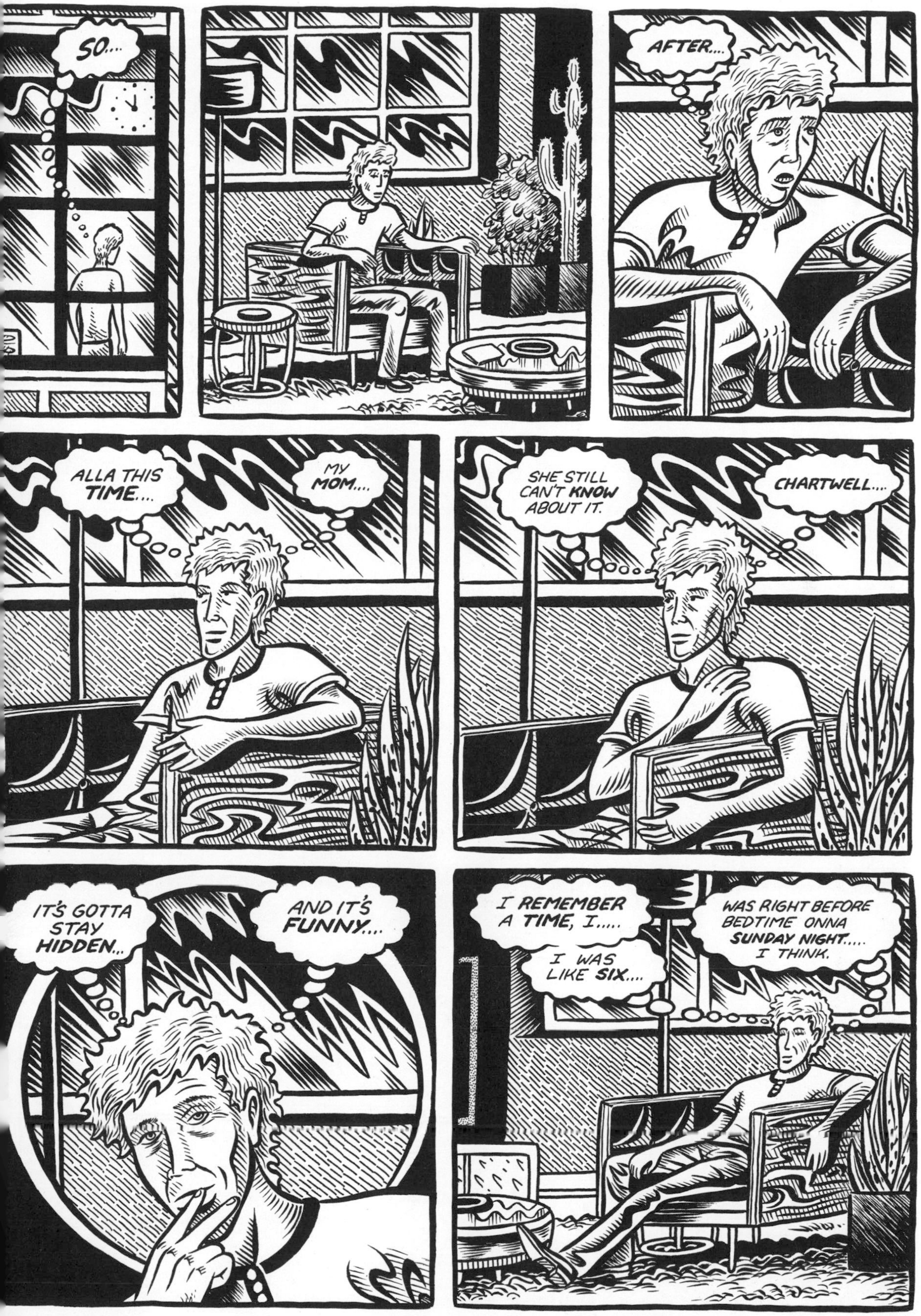
SO....
AFTER....
ALLA THIS TIME....
MY MOM....
SHE STILL CAN'T KNOW ABOUT IT.
CHARTWELL....
IT'S GOTTA STAY HIDDEN...
AND IT'S FUNNY....
I REMEMBER A TIME, I.....
I WAS LIKE SIX....
WAS RIGHT BEFORE BEDTIME ONNA SUNDAY NIGHT..... I THINK.

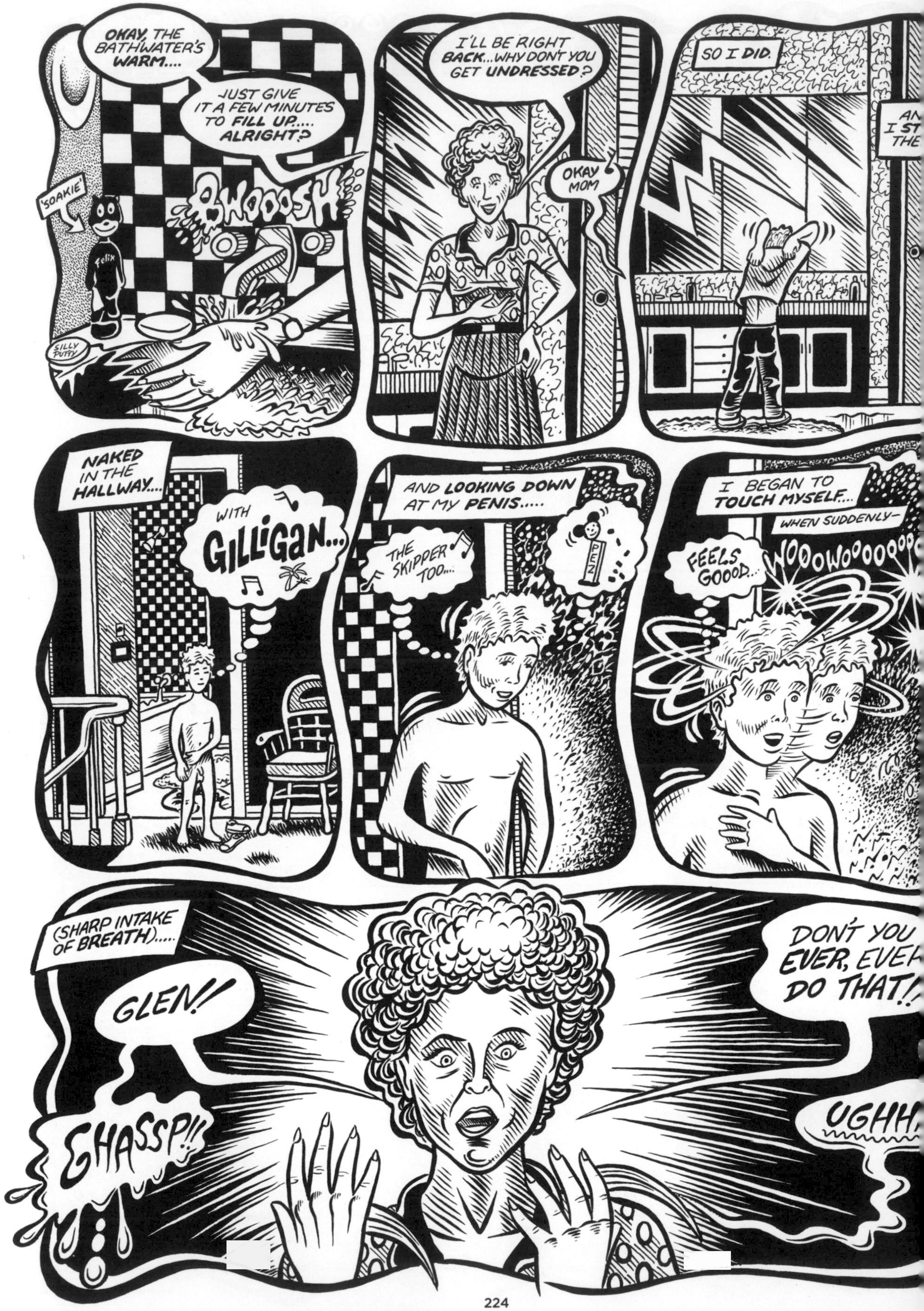
OKAY, THE BATHWATER'S WARM....
JUST GIVE IT A FEW MINUTES TO FILL UP.... ALRIGHT?
'SOAKIE'
Felix
SILLY PUTTY
BWOOOSH
I'LL BE RIGHT BACK...WHY DON'T YOU GET UNDRESSED?
OKAY MOM
SO I DID.
NAKED IN THE HALLWAY....
WITH GILLIGAN...
AND LOOKING DOWN AT MY PENIS.....
THE SKIPPER TOO...
PEZ
I BEGAN TO TOUCH MYSELF...
WHEN SUDDENLY—
FEELS GOOOD...
(SHARP INTAKE OF BREATH).....
GLEN!!
GHASSP!!
DON'T YOU
DO THAT!

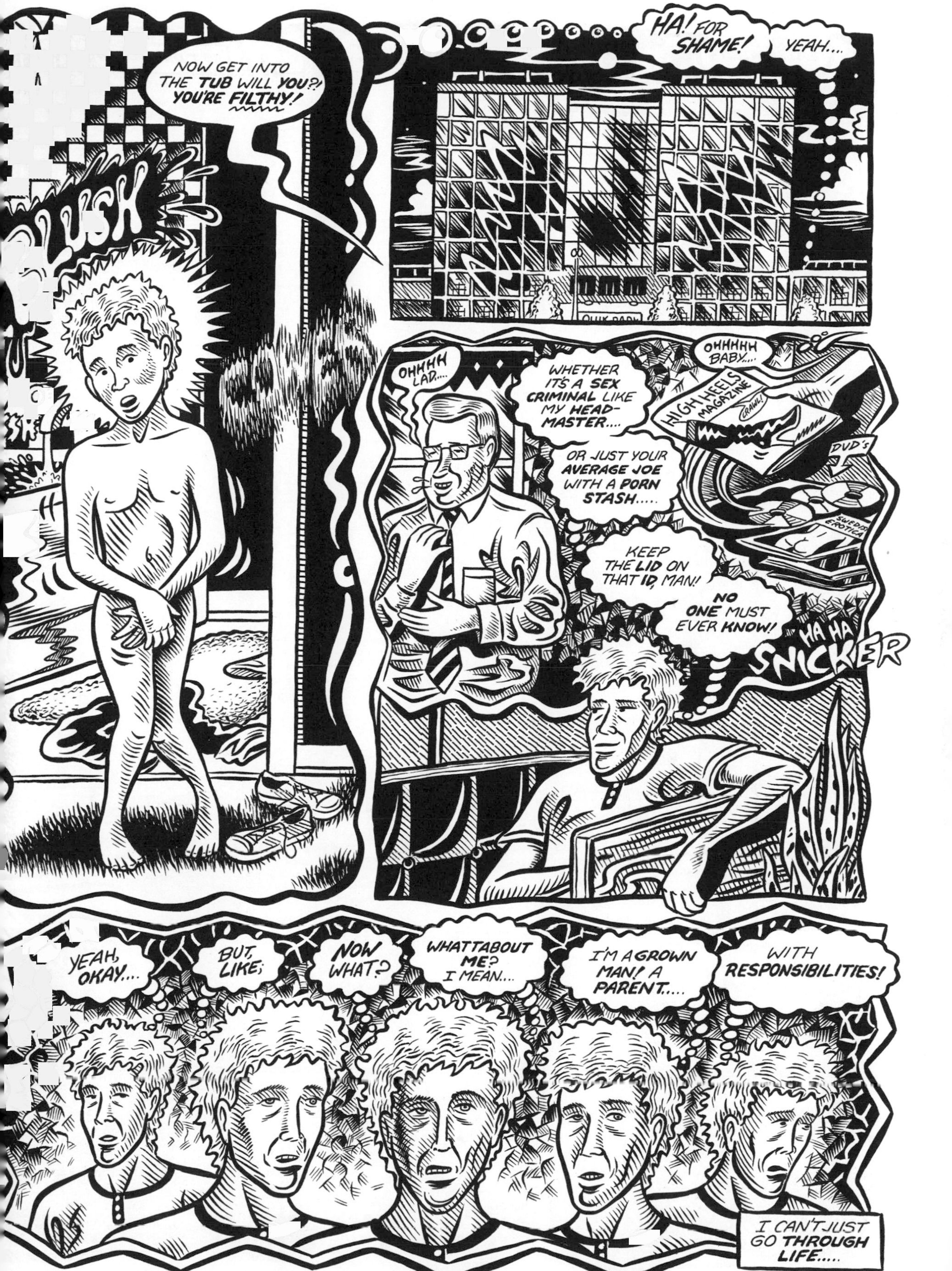

LUSH
NOW GET INTO THE TUB WILL YOU?! YOU'RE FILTHY!
HA! FOR SHAME!
YEAH....
OHHHH LAD....
WHETHER IT'S A SEX CRIMINAL LIKE MY HEAD-MASTER....
OR JUST YOUR AVERAGE JOE WITH A PORN STASH.....
OHHHHH BABY....
HIGH HEELS MAGAZINE
CRAWL!
DVD'S
SWEDISH EROTICA
KEEP THE LID ON THAT ID, MAN!
NO ONE MUST EVER KNOW!
HA HA SNICKER
YEAH, OKAY....
BUT, LIKE;
NOW WHAT?
WHATTABOUT ME? I MEAN....
I'M A GROWN MAN! A PARENT.....
WITH RESPONSIBILITIES!
I CAN'T JUST GO THROUGH LIFE.....

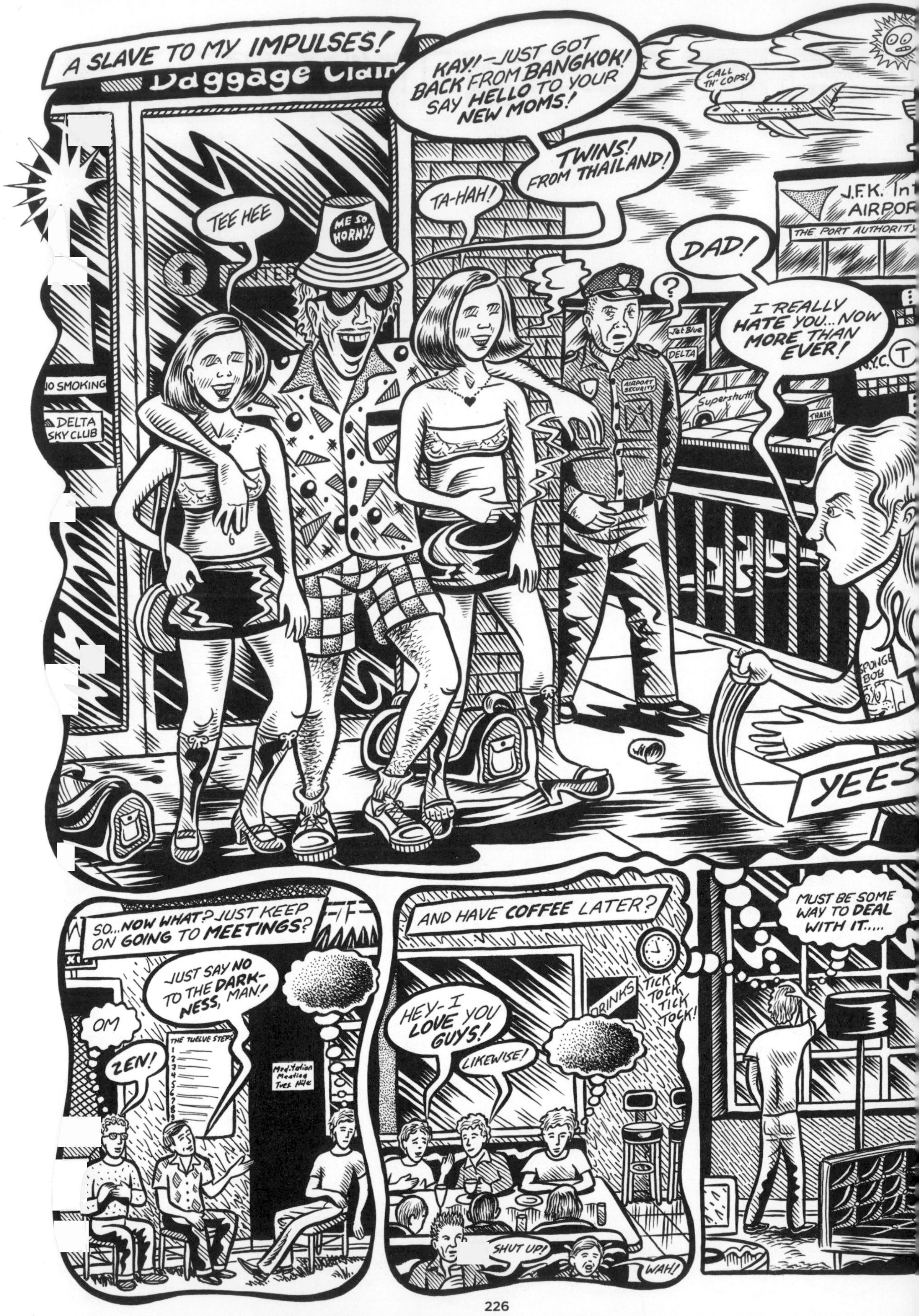
A SLAVE TO MY IMPULSES!
Baggage Claim
KAY!—JUST GOT BACK FROM BANGKOK! SAY HELLO TO YOUR NEW MOMS!
TWINS! FROM THAILAND!
CALL TH' COPS!
TEE HEE
ME SO HORNY!
TA-HAH!
DAD!
?
I REALLY HATE YOU... NOW MORE THAN EVER!
J.F.K. Int AIRPOR
THE PORT AUTHORITY
NO SMOKING
DELTA SKY CLUB
Jet Blue
DELTA
AIRPORT SECURITY
Supershuttle
TRASH
N.Y.C.
SPONGE BOB
YEES
SO...NOW WHAT? JUST KEEP ON GOING TO MEETINGS?
JUST SAY NO TO THE DARKNESS, MAN!
OM
ZEN!
THE TWELVE STEPS
Meditation Meeting Tues. Nite
AND HAVE COFFEE LATER?
DRINKS
TICK TOCK TICK TOCK!
HEY- I LOVE YOU GUYS!
LIKEWISE!
SHUT UP!
WAH!
MUST BE SOME WAY TO DEAL WITH IT.....

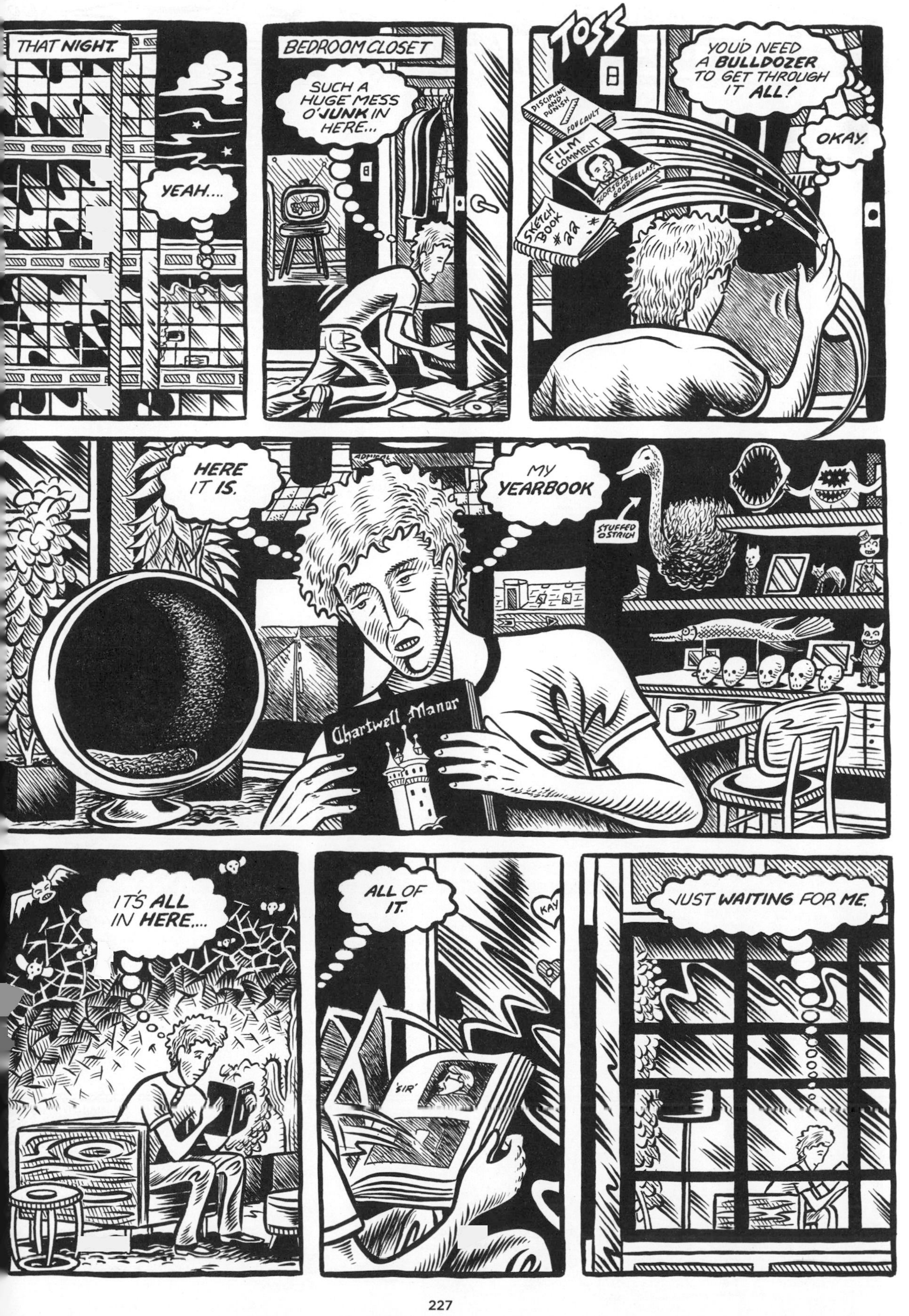

THAT NIGHT.
YEAH....
BEDROOM CLOSET
SUCH A HUGE MESS O'JUNK IN HERE...
TOSS
DISCIPLINE AND PUNISH
FOUCAULT
FILM COMMENT
SCORSESE: GOODFELLAS!
SKETCH BOOK #22
YOU'D NEED A BULLDOZER TO GET THROUGH IT ALL!
OKAY.
HERE IT IS.
MY YEARBOOK
STUFFED OSTRICH
Chartwell Manor
IT'S ALL IN HERE....
ALL OF IT.
KAY
'SIR'
JUST WAITING FOR ME.

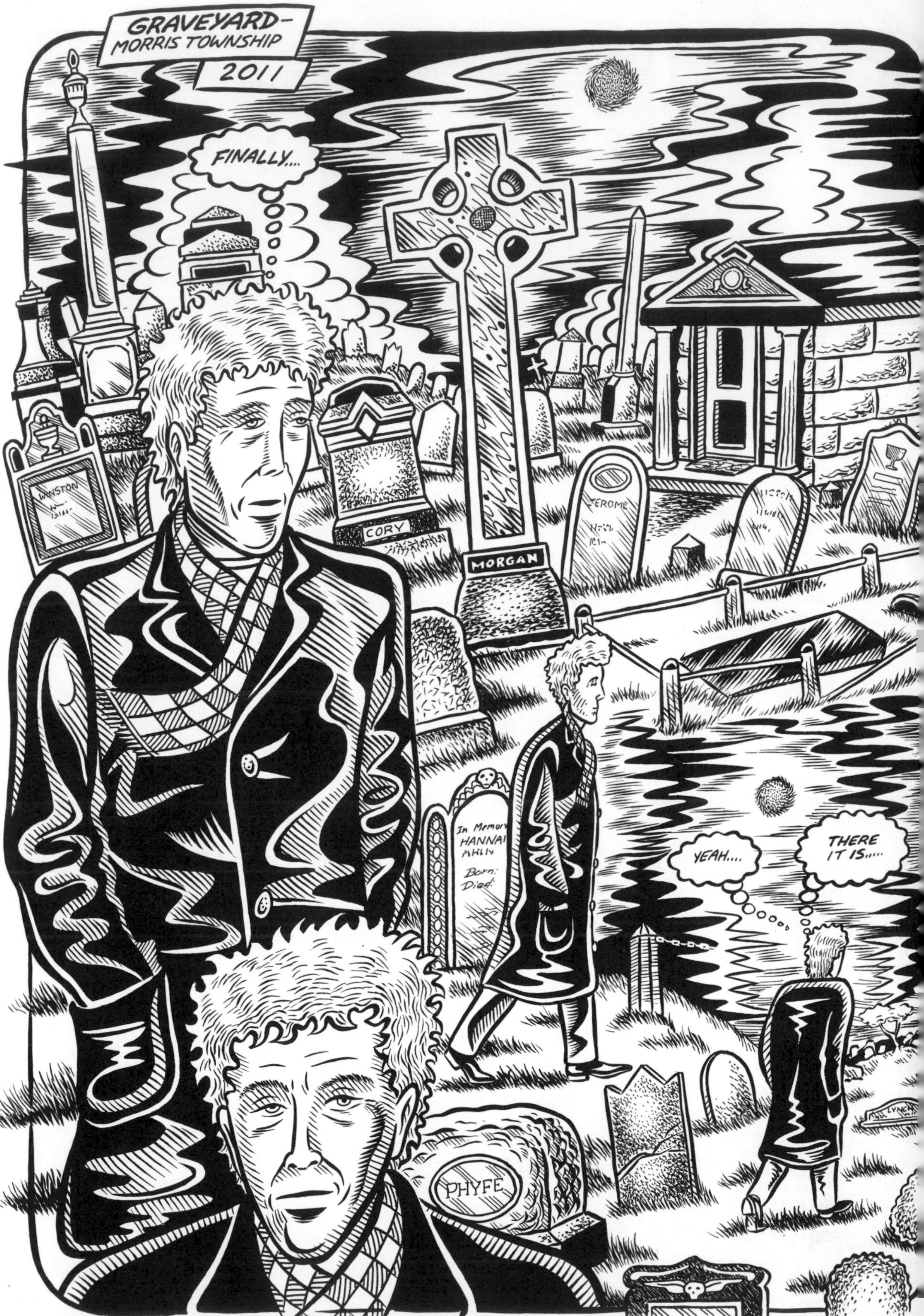
GRAVEYARD-
MORRIS TOWNSHIP
2011
FINALLY....
WINSTON
CORY
MORGAN
JEROME
In Memory
HANNAH
Born:
Died:
YEAH....
THERE IT IS.....
PHYFE
LYNCH

LYNCH
TERENCE MICHAEL   JUDITH ANN
1933-2011   R.I.P.   1939-2010

CONKLIN
1932
1972

UNZIP!

'BOUT TIME.

CONKLIN
1932
1972

LYNCH
TERENCE MICHAEL   JUDITH ANN
1939-2011   R.I.P.   1939-2010

DOGSHIT

THE BOGEYMAN

WELL, IT'S A NICE IDEA....

BUT NOT REALLY WORTH A **TRIP** OUT TO A NEW JERSEY **GRAVESITE**....

GOOGLED   LYNCH

JUST TO TAKE A PISS.

LYNCH
TERENCE MICHAEL   JUDITH ANN
1933 2011   R.I.P.   1939-2010

CALL FRESH DIRECT!

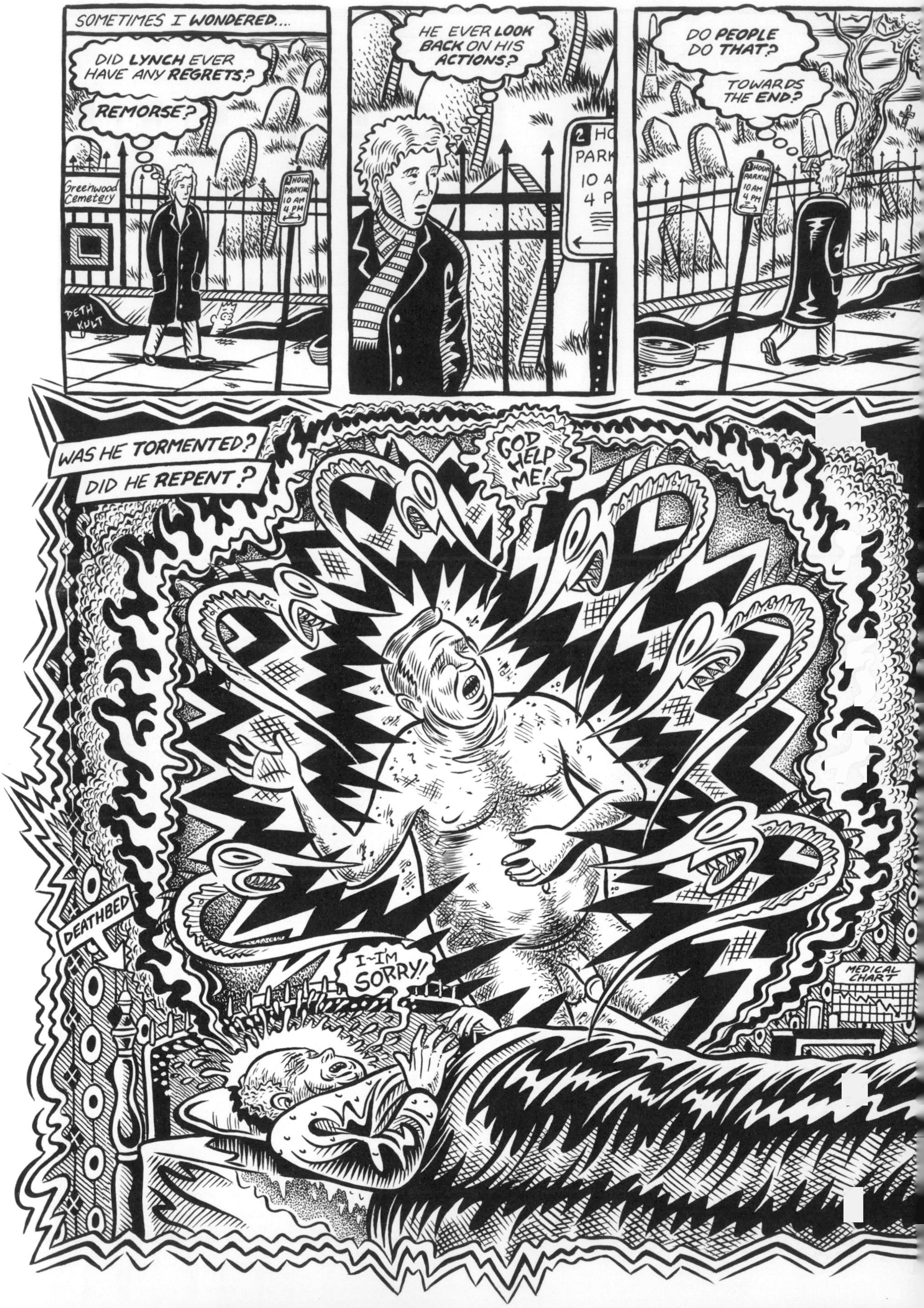
SOMETIMES I WONDERED....
DID LYNCH EVER HAVE ANY REGRETS?
REMORSE?
Greenwood Cemetery
2 HOUR PARKING 10 AM 4 PM
DETH KULT
HE EVER LOOK BACK ON HIS ACTIONS?
DO PEOPLE DO THAT?
TOWARDS THE END?
WAS HE TORMENTED?
DID HE REPENT?
GOD HELP ME!
DEATHBED
I-I'M SORRY!
MEDICAL CHART

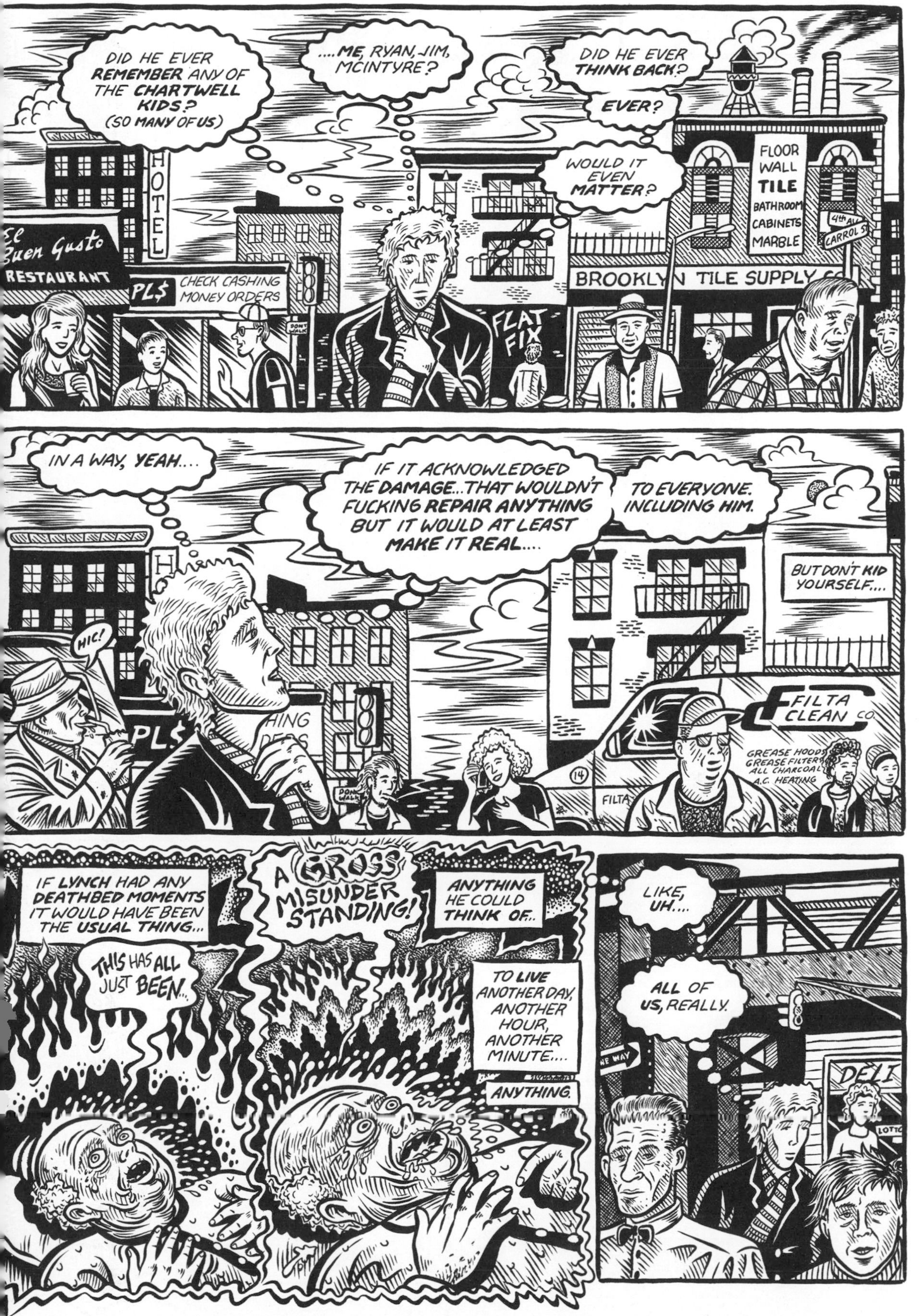
DID HE EVER REMEMBER ANY OF THE CHARTWELL KIDS?
(SO MANY OF US)
....ME, RYAN, JIM, MCINTYRE?
DID HE EVER THINK BACK?
EVER?
WOULD IT EVEN MATTER?
HOTEL
El Buen Gusto
RESTAURANT
PL$
CHECK CASHING MONEY ORDERS
DONT WALK
FLAT FIX
FLOOR WALL TILE BATHROOM CABINETS MARBLE
4th AV
CARROL ST
BROOKLYN TILE SUPPLY C
IN A WAY, YEAH....
IF IT ACKNOWLEDGED THE DAMAGE...THAT WOULDN'T FUCKING REPAIR ANYTHING BUT IT WOULD AT LEAST MAKE IT REAL....
TO EVERYONE. INCLUDING HIM.
BUT DON'T KID YOURSELF....
HIC!
PL$
FILTA CLEAN CO.
GREASE HOODS GREASE FILTERS ALL CHARCOAL A.C. HEATING
14
FILTA
IF LYNCH HAD ANY DEATHBED MOMENTS IT WOULD HAVE BEEN THE USUAL THING...
THIS HAS ALL JUST BEEN...
A GROSS MISUNDERSTANDING!
ANYTHING HE COULD THINK OF..
TO LIVE ANOTHER DAY, ANOTHER HOUR, ANOTHER MINUTE....
ANYTHING.
LIKE, UH....
ALL OF US, REALLY.
DELI
LOTTO

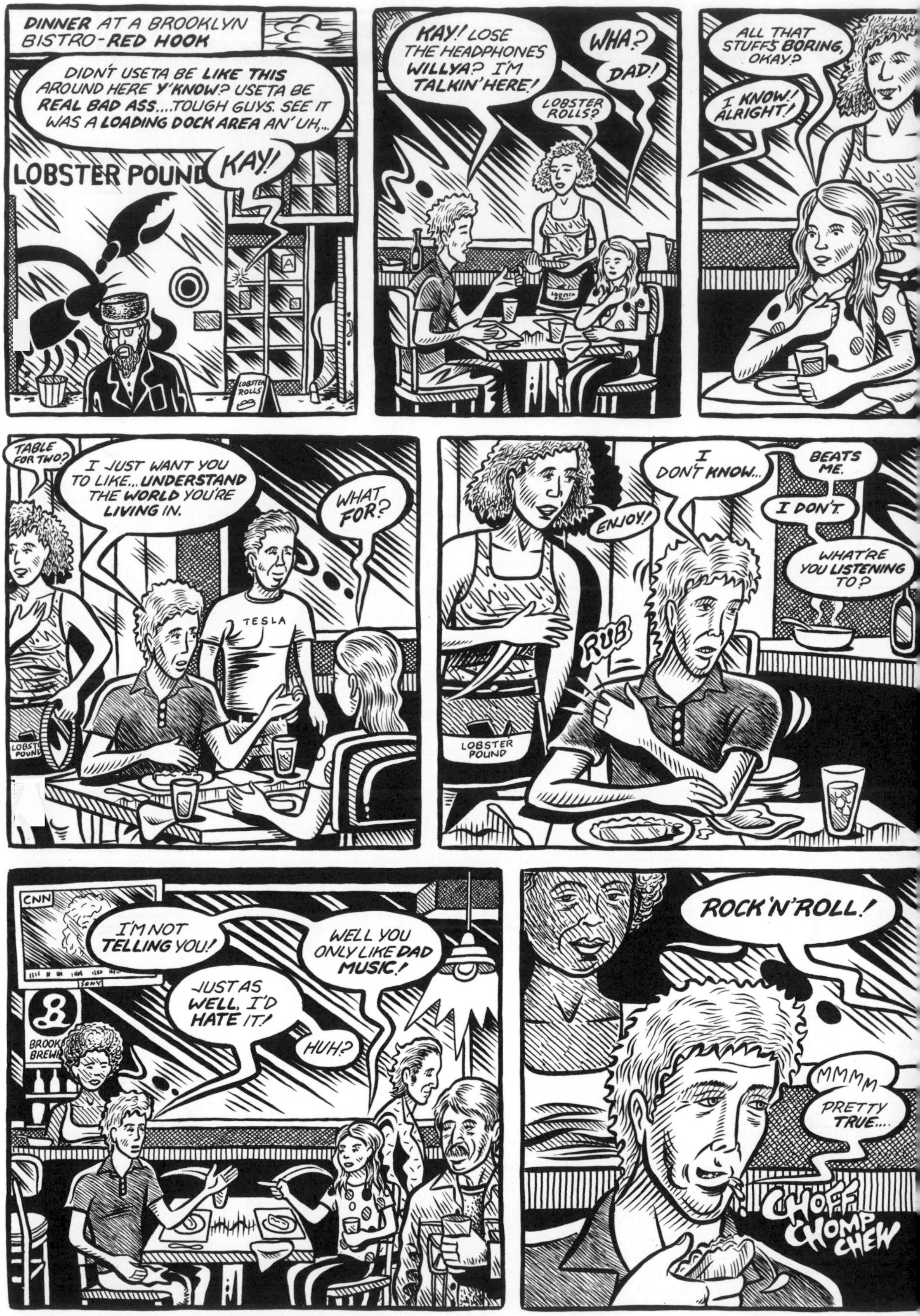
DINNER AT A BROOKLYN BISTRO-RED HOOK
DIDN'T USETA BE LIKE THIS AROUND HERE Y'KNOW? USETA BE REAL BAD ASS....TOUGH GUYS. SEE IT WAS A LOADING DOCK AREA AN' UH,...
LOBSTER POUND
KAY!
LOBSTER ROLLS
KAY! LOSE THE HEADPHONES WILLYA? I'M TALKIN' HERE!
WHA?
DAD!
LOBSTER ROLLS?
ALL THAT STUFF'S BORING, OKAY?
I KNOW! ALRIGHT!
TABLE FOR TWO?
I JUST WANT YOU TO LIKE...UNDERSTAND THE WORLD YOU'RE LIVING IN.
WHAT FOR?
TESLA
ENJOY!
I DON'T KNOW...
BEATS ME.
I DON'T.
WHAT'RE YOU LISTENING TO?
RUB
LOBSTER POUND
CNN
I'M NOT TELLING YOU!
WELL YOU ONLY LIKE DAD MUSIC!
JUST AS WELL, I'D HATE IT!
HUH?
ROCK'N'ROLL!
MMMM
PRETTY TRUE....
CHOFF
CHOMP
CHEW

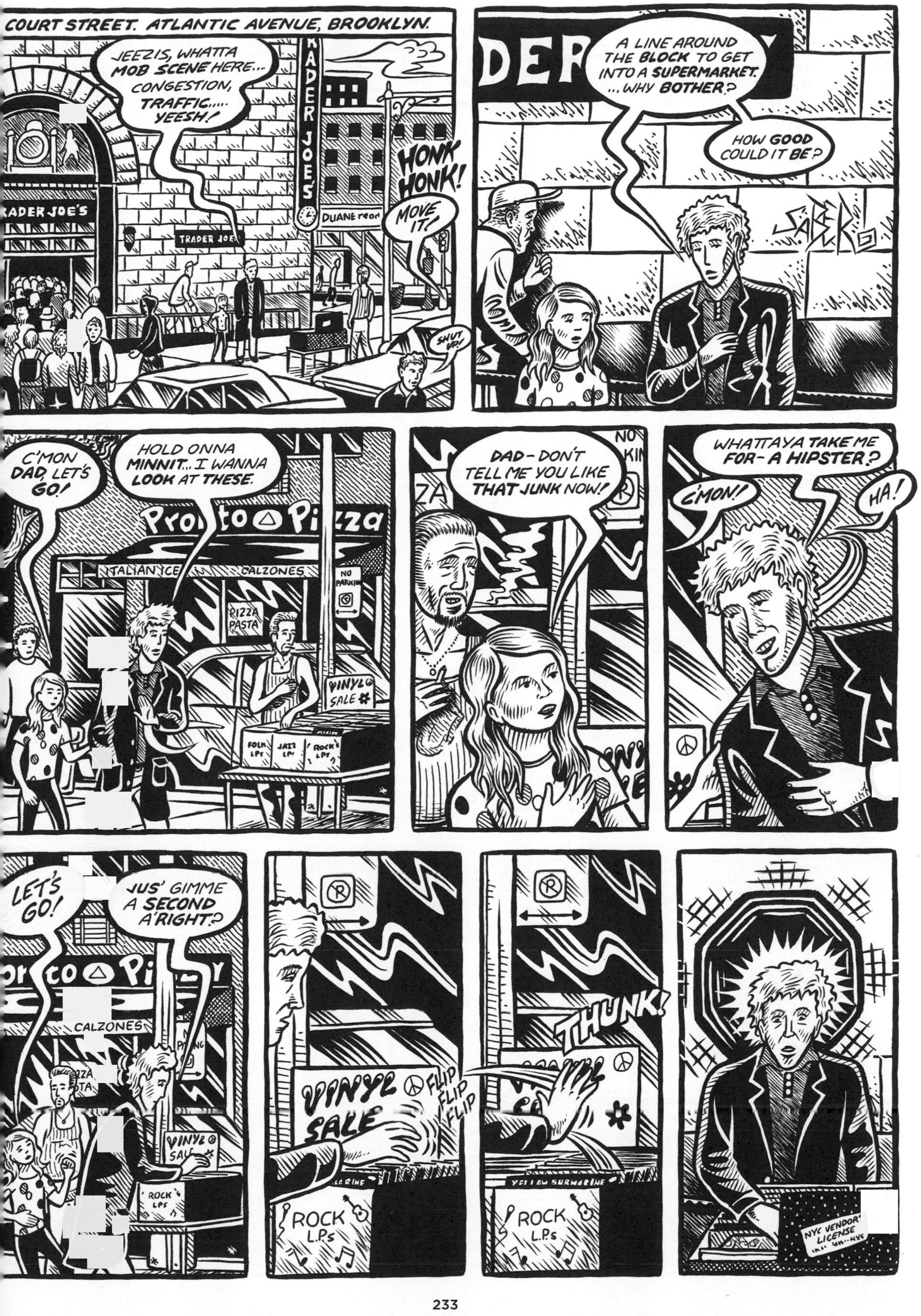
COURT STREET. ATLANTIC AVENUE, BROOKLYN.
JEEZIS, WHATTA MOB SCENE HERE... CONGESTION, TRAFFIC..... YEESH!
TRADER JOE'S
TRADER JOE'S
TRADER JOE'S
DUANE reade
HONK HONK!
MOVE IT!
SHUT UP!
A LINE AROUND THE BLOCK TO GET INTO A SUPERMARKET. ...WHY BOTHER?
HOW GOOD COULD IT BE?
C'MON DAD, LET'S GO!
HOLD ONNA MINNIT... I WANNA LOOK AT THESE.
Pronto Pizza
ITALIAN ICE
CALZONES
NO PARKING
PIZZA PASTA
VINYL SALE
FOLK LPs
JAZZ LPs
ROCK'S LPs
DAD- DON'T TELL ME YOU LIKE THAT JUNK NOW!
WHATTAYA TAKE ME FOR- A HIPSTER?
C'MON!
HA!
LET'S GO!
JUS' GIMME A SECOND A'RIGHT?
CALZONES
VINYL SALE
ROCK LPs
VINYL SALE
FLIP FLIP FLIP
ROCK L.P.s
THUNK!
YELLOW SUBMARINE
ROCK L.P.s
NYC VENDOR LICENSE

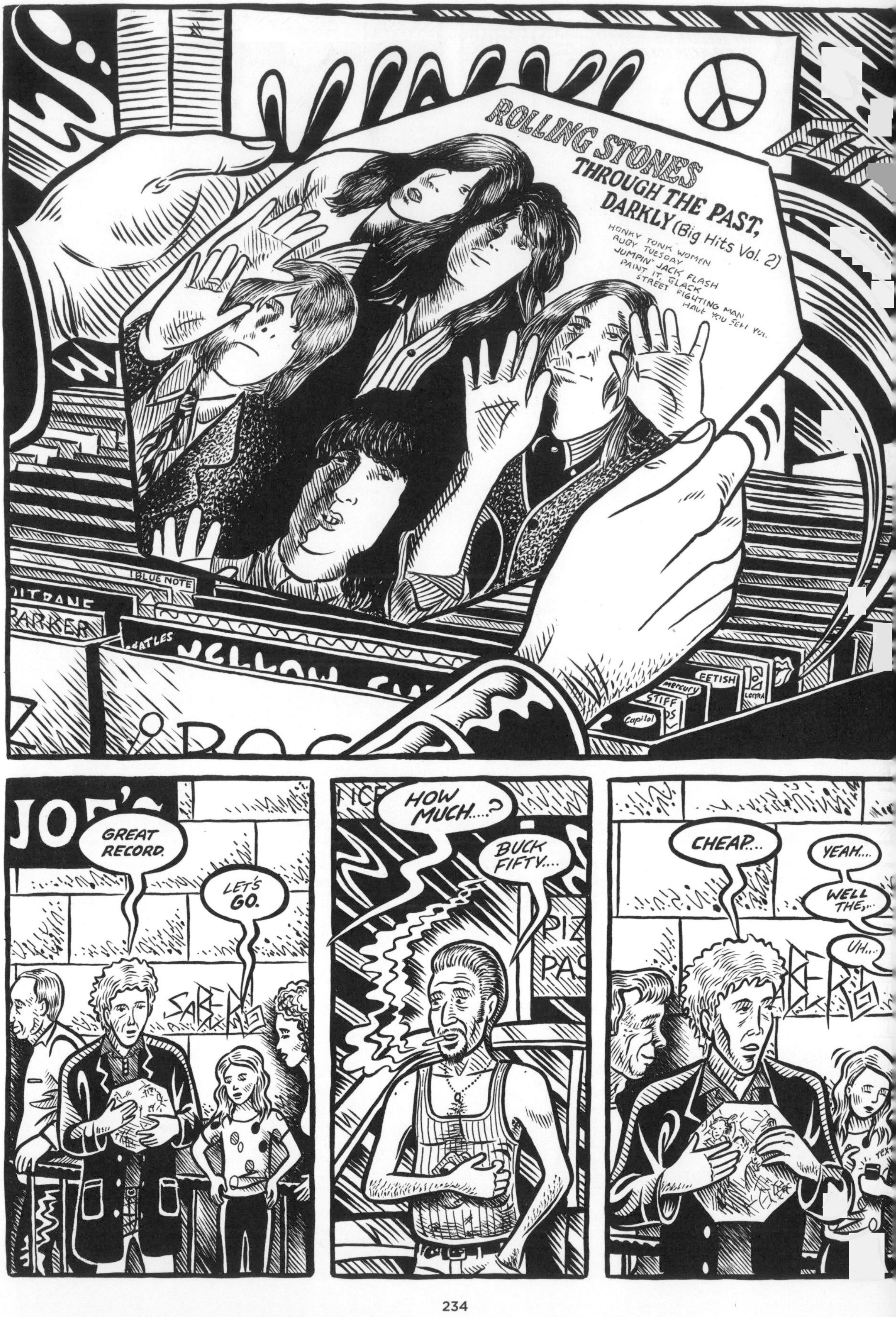
ROLLING STONES
THROUGH THE PAST, DARKLY (Big Hits Vol. 2)
HONKY TONK WOMEN
RUBY TUESDAY
JUMPIN' JACK FLASH
PAINT IT, BLACK
STREET FIGHTING MAN
BLUE NOTE
PARKER
BEATLES
FETISH
mercury
STIFF
Capitol
JOE'S
GREAT RECORD.
LET'S GO.
HOW MUCH....?
BUCK FIFTY....
CHEAP...
YEAH...
WELL THE,...
UH...

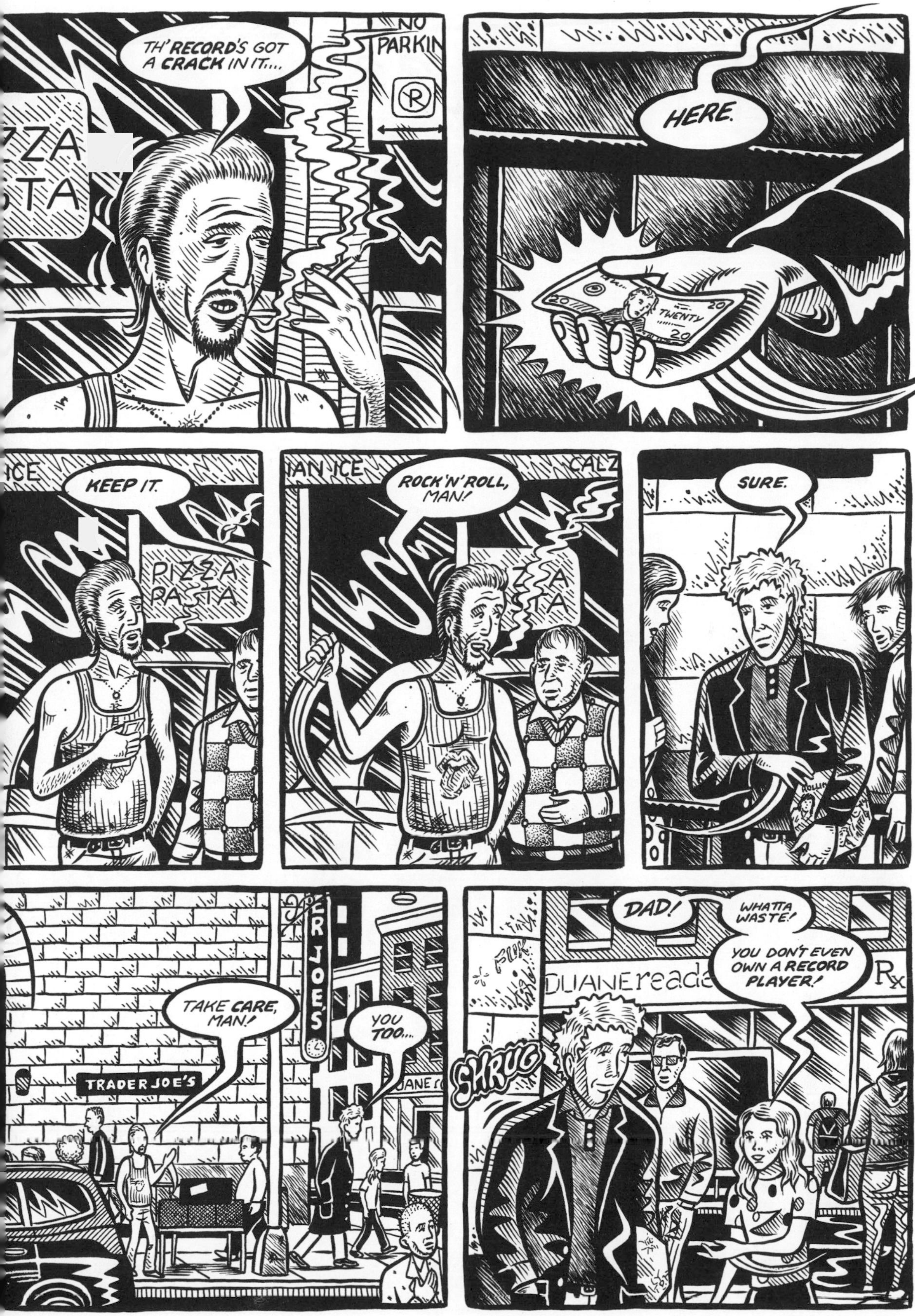
NO PARKIN
ZZA
TA
TH' RECORD'S GOT A CRACK IN IT....
HERE.
TWENTY
20
KEEP IT.
PIZZA PASTA
ROCK 'N' ROLL, MAN!
CALZ
SURE.
TAKE CARE, MAN!
YOU TOO...
TRADER JOE'S
SHRUG
DUANEreade
Rx
DAD!
WHATTA WASTE!
YOU DON'T EVEN OWN A RECORD PLAYER!

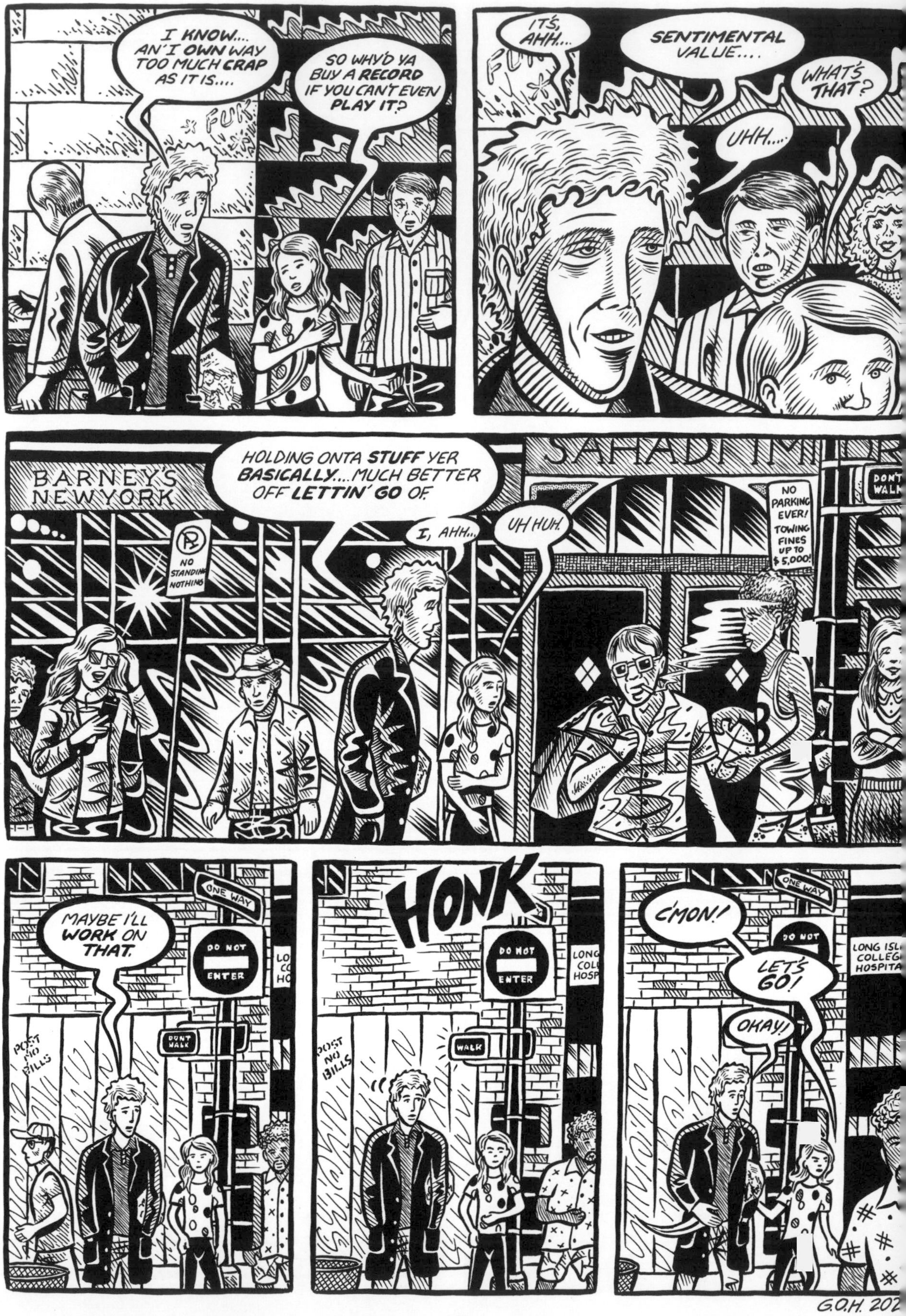
I KNOW.... AN' I OWN WAY TOO MUCH CRAP AS IT IS....
FUK
SO WHY'D YA BUY A RECORD IF YOU CAN'T EVEN PLAY IT?
IT'S, AHH...
SENTIMENTAL VALUE....
WHAT'S THAT?
UHH....
SAHADI IMPORTS
BARNEY'S NEWYORK
HOLDING ONTA STUFF YER BASICALLY....MUCH BETTER OFF LETTIN' GO OF.
NO STANDING NOTHING
I, AHH...
UH HUH.
NO PARKING EVER! TOWING FINES UP TO $5,000!
ONE WAY
MAYBE I'LL WORK ON THAT.
DO NOT ENTER
DON'T WALK
POST NO BILLS
HONK
DO NOT ENTER
LONG COLL HOSP
WALK
POST NO BILLS
C'MON!
ONE WAY
DO NOT
LONG ISL COLLEG HOSPITA
LET'S GO!
OKAY!
G.O.H. 202

ABOUT THE AUTHOR

Born and raised in Madison, NJ, Glenn Head fell in love with underground comics while attending boarding school and has been involved with them ever since. He is a Harvey and Eisner-nominated editor of two comix anthologies, *Snake Eyes* (co-edited with Kaz) and *Hotwire*. His solo work includes *Avenue D* (1986) and his graphic memoir, *Chicago* (2015), both published by Fantagraphics.

ACKNOWLEDGMENTS

There are a lot of people I'd like to thank here, so I'll just begin with the obvious: Eric Reynolds and Gary Groth for publishing and believing in *Chartwell Manor*. And everyone else at Fantagraphics for all their stellar work.

Thanks to my assistant, Jansiel Polanco, for the endless scanning and rescanning required to nail the details of my work.

Thanks to photoshop wizard Virginia Wilkerson for her brilliant color assistance on the covers and design work within.

Thanks to Mary Karr and Mary Gaitskill, for inspiring me to write about myself as ruthlessly as possible.

And special thanks to Robert Crumb, Justin Green, and Phoebe Gloeckner, who all showed me that anything can be grist for the comics mill if you have the guts to face it. I might never have drawn this book if it weren't for them.

And most of all thanks to my wife, Xeni, the best reader I've ever had. No one has ever been better for my comics than you, my love!

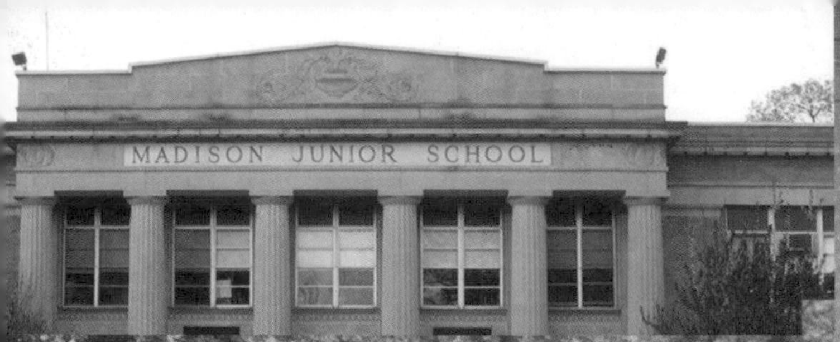
MADISON JUNIOR SCHOOL

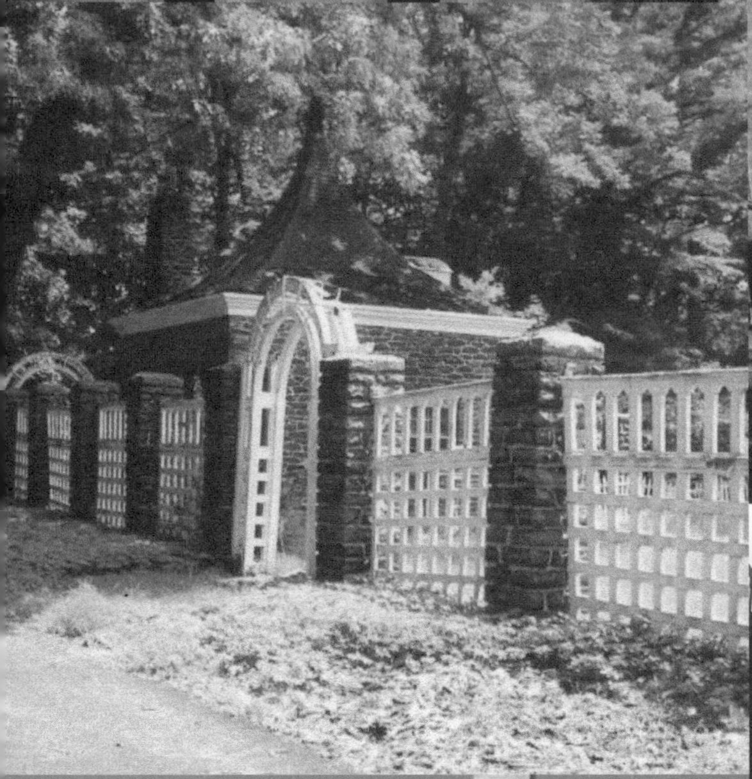

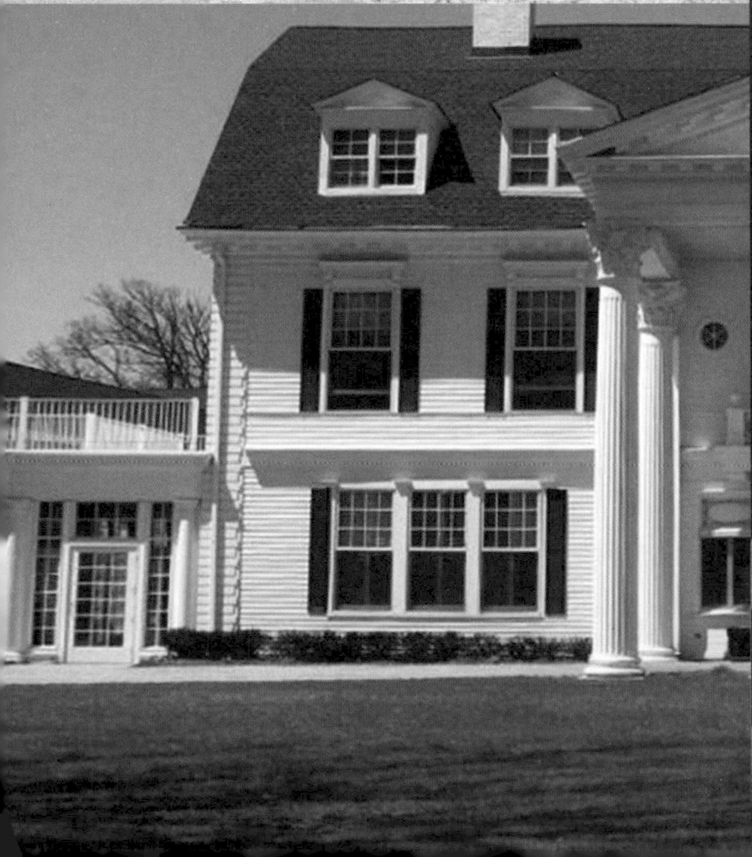

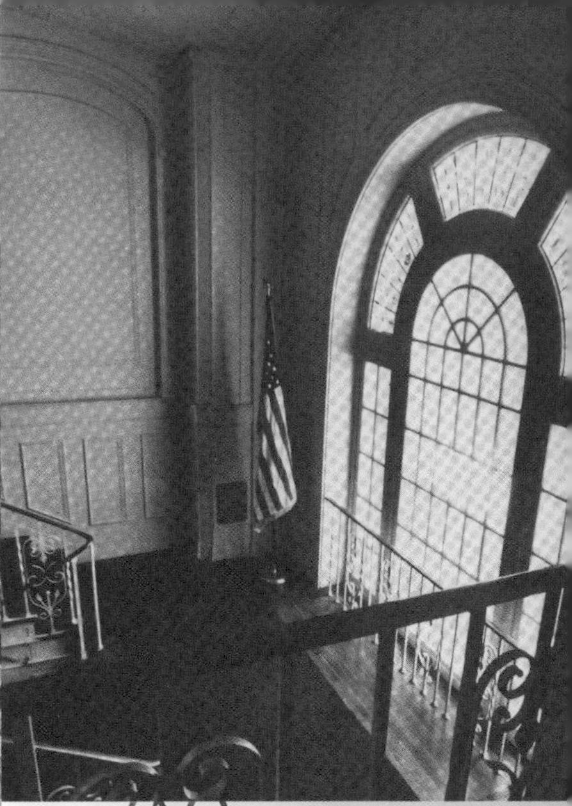

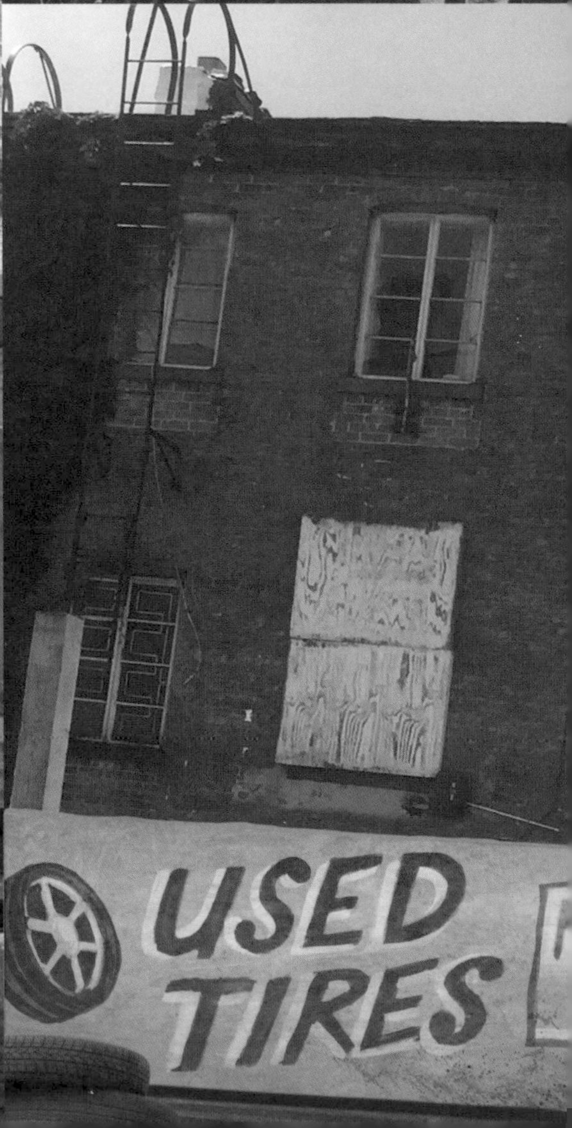
USED
TIRES